BLACK THEOLOGY

A Documentary History
Volume II
1980-1992

BLACK THEOLOGY

A Documentary History

Volume II
1980–1992

Edited by
James H. Cone and Gayraud S. Wilmore

ORBIS BOOKS

Maryknoll, New York 10545

The Catholic Foreign Mission Society of America (Maryknoll) recruits and trains people for overseas missionary service. Through Orbis Books, Maryknoll aims to foster the international dialogue that is essential to mission. The books published, however, reflect the opinions of their authors and are not meant to represent the official position of the society.

Copyright © 1993 by Orbis Books, Maryknoll, NY 10545
All rights reserved
Manufactured in the United States of America

Grateful acknowledgment is made to the following for permission to reprint from previously published material:

Augsburg Fortress Publishers: Excerpts from *We Have Been Believers* by James H. Evans, copyright © 1992 Augsburg Fortress. Reprinted by permission of the publisher. Excerpts from *Pastoral Theology* by James H. Harris, copyright © 1991 Augsburg Fortress. Reprinted by permission of the publisher.

Westminster/John Knox Press: Excerpts from *Black Theology in Dialogue* by J. Deotis Roberts. © 1982 J. Deotis Roberts. Used by permission of the publisher.

Duke University Press: For use of "African American Catholics and Black Theology" by Shawn Copeland. From *African American Religious Studies*, edited by Gayroud Wilmore, pages 228-248. Copyright Duke University Press, 1989. Reprinted by permission of the publisher.

Georgetown University Press: For use of "Church and Culture: A Black Catholic Womanist Perspective" by Diana L. Hayes. From The *Labor of God: An Ignatian View of Church and Culture*, edited by William O'Brien, pages 67-87. Copyright Georgetown University Press, 1991. Reprinted by permission of the publisher.

Library of Congress Cataloging-in-Publication Data
(Revised for vol. 2)

Black theology.

    Includes bibliographical references and indexes.
    Contents: [1] 1966-1979 — v. 2. 1980-1992.
    1. Black theology.   2. Afro-Americans — Religion.
3. Black power.   I. Wilmore, Gayraud S.   II. Cone, James H.
BT82.7.B56   230'.089'96   79-12747
ISBN 0-88344-041-5 (v. 1)
ISBN 0-88344-042-3 (pbk. : v. 1)
ISBN 0-88344-773-8 (pbk. : v. 2)

To all my doctoral students
—past, present, and future.
James H. Cone

To my wife of forty-nine years,
Lee Wilson Wilmore,
and to our children and grandchildren
—for love and patience.
Gayraud S. Wilmore

CONTENTS

vii

GENERAL INTRODUCTION

Black Theology: A Documentary History, Volume I, 1966–1979 tells the story of the origin and development of Black liberation theology. The word "Black" in the phrase was defined by the life and teachings of Malcolm X—culturally and politically embodied in the Black Power movement. The term "theology" was influenced by the life and teachings of Martin Luther King, Jr.—religiously and politically embodied in the Black Church and the civil rights movement. The word "liberation" was derived from the past and contemporary struggles for political freedom and the biblical story of the Exodus, as defined by the Black religious experience in the United States. Black liberation theology, therefore, was created out of our struggle to make sense of our tripartite identity: *Black, Christian,* and *free.*

What does it mean to be Black in a world that defines Whites as human and Blacks as less than human? Is Blackness an unfortunate accident of birth that African Americans should be ashamed of?

> If you're White,
> You're all right.
> But if you're Black,
> Get back, get back.

Or is Blackness a gift of creation to be affirmed with joy and thankfulness?

> Say it loud!
> I'm Black and I'm Proud.

As Black theologians wrestled with these consciousness-raising questions in the 1960s, we knew that our identity as Black could not be transcended or ignored but rather had to be enthusiastically embraced as the starting point of everything we did and said.

What does it mean to be a Christian, a follower of Jesus, in a world that portrays Jesus as a White man and Christianity as a European religion? Is Christianity a religion of love and hope that empowers oppressed Blacks to fight against racism and segregation, as Martin Luther King, Jr., proclaims in his sermons? Or is Malcolm X right when he calls Christianity "a perfect slave religion," "skillfully designed to make us look down on black and up at white"? As we pondered these disturbing questions, we knew that we could not accept

1

any religion whose Savior was White and whose values opposed the Black people's struggle for freedom.

What does freedom mean—integration into or separation from the White community? How do we achieve it—through "nonviolent direct action" or "by any means necessary"? As we examined these challenging questions, we knew that there were no either/or answers, no simple choice between the philosophies of Martin King and Malcolm X. The truth as we experienced it was much more complex than that. Black theology came into being as we struggled with the truth of our experience in all of its complexity.

It is important to emphasize that our struggle to define what it meant to be Black, Christian, and free was not easy. We were marginalized by both White and Black churches. Many White ministers called Black theology "racism in reverse" and urged the clergy of all races to oppose it as unchristian. "Theology does not come in colors," they said. "It is universal—not Black or White." Many Black ministers repeated what Whites said, as they frequently do in regard to issues that involve critical theological reflection. Most White scholars ignored Black theology, since it was nearly impossible for them to even consider the possibility that Black clergy had something important to say about the discipline of theology. Black Power activists, however, welcomed Black theology as an intellectual articulation of the religious dimensions of the Black liberation struggle. They viewed it as a way of exposing the racism in White churches and of making conservative African-American churches more militant and Black. In our attempt to affirm our Blackness in the church and to be involved in the struggle for justice in the society, we discovered that the intellectual and political battles we were fighting would not be won quickly but would involve a long protracted struggle.

Before the end of the 1970s, it also became clear to us that much more was involved in the struggle for justice than the fight against racism. Classism and sexism were also systems of domination that had to be resisted. Third World theologians, especially in Latin America, were helpful in raising our consciousness in regard to the former. Women theologians, especially Black and other women of color in the United States and the Third World, opened our eyes in regard to the latter.

More recently lesbians and gays have identified heterosexism in the church and the society as an evil that must be eradicated. The late James Tinney, gay pentecostal minister and professor of journalism at Howard University, was one of the first to address the Black Church and Black theology on the issue. Creative spokespersons today in the Black theological community include Renee Hill, a self-identified lesbian doctoral student in theology at Union Seminary in New York, and Elias Farajaje-Jones, a self-identified bisexual professor of history of religions at Howard University School of Divinity. They challenge the Black community to become more holistic in the struggle for human liberation. No theological issue is more potentially controversial in the Black Church and community than sexuality. Preachers and theologians tend to ignore it, apparently hoping homosexuals will go away or will remain in the closet. Lesbians and gays are breaking their silence and are openly fighting in defense of their humanity, their right to live in a just society and church, free of the violence of homophobia. Black theology and the Black Church, therefore, must also come out of the closet and take a stand with human beings who are struggling for liberation.

No issue is more important for humanity than ecology. Unless human beings raise their ecological consciousness and recognize the need to save the earth from our wanton behavior, it will soon become uninhabitable. Mother Earth is dying slowly but surely before our eyes. The time to stop the destruction and rape of the environment is now and not tomorrow. We need to create a spirituality that induces love and respect for the earth. We should ask not only what does it mean to be a human being, but also, what does it mean to feel like a tree and think like a mountain?

Like sexuality, Black theologians, unfortunately, have not said much about creation-centered spirituality. The reason for the silence may partly be understandable, since the White-dominated ecology movement in the United States is often insensitive to racism which impinges so heavily upon Black people's daily existence. But we should not allow our concern for the health of the environment to become muted by the failures of Whites to incorporate race criticism into their ecological consciousness. The time has come for Black theologians to become ecologians because the issues of race and ecology are tied together. Not only should we identify environmental racism as a major theological issue, our practice and theology should center on holistic justice—a quality existence not just for Whites or for Blacks but for all, not just for human beings but for nonhuman creatures too. When the third volume of *Black Theology: A Documentary History* appears, hopefully essays on creation-centered spirituality will occupy a prominent place in it.

To deal with the emerging complexity of Black people's struggle for holistic liberation in a global context, some of us began to realize early on that we had to ensure Black theology's continuing presence in the seminaries, churches, and the world by encouraging young Black women and men to consider teaching and writing as a form of ministry that is just as challenging and important for communicating and living the gospel as preaching and singing. Becoming a self-identified theologian—a critical thinker about the meaning of the faith in the life of church and society—is a new form of ministry in the Black church and community. Before the rise of Black theology, Black churches uncritically accepted the written theologies of White churches. We now know or at least should know that White theology is not adequate for dealing with the complexity of Black life. The Black Church needs its own theology, carefully thought out reflections on the Christian faith that arise out of the past and current history of the African-American religious experience. How are we going to deal with the challenging question, "what does it mean to be Black, Christian, and free?," if we do not have disciplined interpreters of the practice and the faith of Black people? What theological position should the Black Church take on the problems of classism, sexism, heterosexism, and ecology? How should the church arrive at its views when most of its members disagree? Is the Black Church going to continue to ignore these controversial issues and pretend that these problems do not exist in our community?

Every church needs a clearly defined theological place upon which to stand so it can be clear what to preach as the gospel of Jesus Christ. The theological place where the church stands should not be the private opinion of one person but should emerge out of the practice and creative debates of committed Christians. Just as the Black Church knows that it cannot retain its Christian identity unless the gospel is faithfully and repeatedly preached and celebrated in worship, it should also know that teaching the gospel is as important for its identity as preaching it. If the gospel is not continually taught, its meaning will not always be clear to those who have been called to preach it. Preachers cannot preach what we do not know. Everything that preachers say in their sermons is not the gospel. How do preachers know when the gospel is the gospel? That is a theological question. The purpose of theology is to identify what the gospel is so that preachers can preach it with clarity, confidence, and power.

Most of the early interpreters of Black theology were self-taught theologians. We did theology only because the times in which we lived demanded it. We felt we had no choice but to say what the gospel was since nobody else was saying it. The few of us who held terminal degrees in theology or a related discipline received no education in seminary that prepared us to talk about God's presence in the Black freedom movement of the 1960s. To do theology in the context of the civil rights and Black Power movements was challenging, requiring a creative theological imagination that often meant rejecting what we had learned in seminary. The anger we felt was deep. To keep our religious sanity, we had to create a Black theology that was empowering for us and our people. We did not care whether Black theology met the intellectual criteria for doing theology as defined by the White theologians who had taught us. We were listening to the voice of Malcolm X:

> The time that we're living in now and that we are facing now is not an era where one who is oppressed is looking toward the oppressor to give him some system or form of logic or reason. What is logical to the oppressor isn't logical to the oppressed. The black people in this country are beginning to realize that what sounds reasonable to those who exploit us doesn't sound reasonable to us. There has to be a new system of reason and logic devised by us who are at the bottom, if we want to get some results in this struggle that is called "the Negro revolution."[1]

Black liberation theology was our attempt to create a new logic in theology, a way of thinking about God from a Black, Christian, and liberation perspective.

Most of the writers in *Black Theology: A Documentary History, Volume II, 1980–1992* represent the second generation of Black theologians. Although many were inspired by the writings of the early interpreters of Black theology, none are imitators, not even the ones who studied with first generation Black theologians. The time is different. They feel a different kind of intellectual energy and spiritual urgency. They are not trying to justify their right to do theology. They assume it, with no apology to Whites. Many are women; only a few are pastors; most are professors in predominantly White seminaries, universities, and colleges. They read papers about Black theology and other topics on the Black religious experience and the Bible at the annual meetings of the American Academy of Religion (AAR) and the Society of Biblical Literature (SBL) — something almost unheard of for liberation-oriented Black scholars in the late sixties and throughout the seventies. Their sessions are among the most well attended. White scholars no longer reject Black theology as unworthy of intellectual respect but even acknowledge that there is a place for it in the academy.

The anger so visibly present in the writers of the first volume of *Black Theology* is not present here. During the sixties, the Black experience was clearly defined outside of the public discourse of theology, biblical studies, and church history as taught in the seminaries and university departments of religion. Our anger, therefore, was motivated in part by that exclusion, and we were determined to place our experience at the center of our talk about God. We were partly successful, and the new generation of writers in this volume are evidence of it. But with success comes new problems, and they are reflected in the discourse of the scholars in this volume.

Black Theology: A Documentary History, Volume II, 1980–1992 is divided into five parts, each indicating the intellectual activities of Black scholars. Six young male theologians and ethicists are included in Part I: The Second Generation. They are introducing fresh ideas into Black liberation theology that will define its future. Of course, there are continuities between the first and second generation Black theologians. Although the second consciously builds on the foundation laid by the first, the importance of the newcomers to Black theology is their determination to break new theological ground. At present, they are moving in several directions, and it is unclear when their ideas will burst forth into a powerful, revolutionary theological movement for freedom.

For a teacher to be taught by his or her students is a very rewarding experience. As I read my former students' writings, some of whom are included in this volume, I am impressed by their intellectual creativity and their commitment to do theology for Black people. I look forward to learning more from the challenge I know that they will continue to address to my theological perspective. What the Black community needs is not scholars who repeat what their teachers said. We need committed scholars who are organically linked to the Black community, young men and women who are determined to live the faith and speak the truth of the liberating gospel as defined by Black people's struggle for justice.

Part II: Black Theology and Pastoral Ministry represents the current state of Black theology's engagement of issues arising out of the pastoral ministry. Although the Black clergy in the National Conference of Black Christians were the major players in the origin and development of Black theology, they were not the ones to write the books and essays that defined its public meaning. NCBC no longer exists. The Black Theology Project of the Theology in the Americas is hardly active. Black theology today is being defined by seminary and university professors in the context of the Society for the Study of Black Religion (SSBR) and the AAR. These are not places where pastors are likely to spend their time. As a result, Black theology and the Black Church have not had a happy time together. Both have suffered a kind of isolation from each other.

There are signs, however, that both pastors and theologians want to create a more wholesome relationship. Theologians are being invited to churches to preach, lecture, and lead seminars on Black theology. The Hampton Ministers' Conference, the largest annual gathering of Black pastors (more than 4000), has begun to invite self-identified Black male and Womanist scholars as theological lecturers. In June 1992, an afternoon was devoted to the discussion of the relationship of Black Theology and the Black Church, focusing on the question that a small group of pastors and theologians had been discussing for several months, "What Does It Mean To Be Black and Christian?"

The creation of Document 12, "What Does It Mean To Be Black and Christian?," is an example of theologians and pastors working together, reflecting on theological and pastoral issues in the life of the church. The Kelly Miller Smith Institute, under the creative leadership of Forrest Harris, is the main initiator of this dialogue. It is difficult for pastors and theologians to accept each other's criticisms. But no real progress can be made in the churches and seminaries toward the liberation of Black people if pastors and theologians are unwilling to join together in solidarity with the poor, learning from and risking critical dialogue with each other.

I remember clearly the initial difficulty Black pastors and theologians experienced in our dialogue at the Kelly Miller Smith Institute at Vanderbilt University Divinity School in Nashville, Tennessee. Each side was suspicious of the other and that suspicion often prevented both from hearing legitimate critiques of the other. But the creation of this working document about the meaning of our *Black Christian* identity is a small step forward toward bringing Black theology into critical dialogue with the Black Church.

If Black Protestant theologians and pastors are able to create a meaningful dialogue with each other, they will then be able to relate more creatively with Black Catholic lay people, priests, and theologians. Both Black Protestants and Catholics can learn from each other in many common areas of concern and can help each other to engage the potentially controversial issues like sexuality.

In contrast to their marginal role in the early development of Black theology, African-American Catholics are today making major contributions to the intellectual interpretation of Black religion and theology. More than their Protestant counterparts, Black Catholic theologians have shown a deep concern for pastoral issues and thus are not as alienated from Black life in the parish. Their examples can be useful to their brothers and sisters in Protestant seminaries and universities.

Cyprian Davis has written an important book on the *History of Black Catholics in the United States* (Crossroad, 1990). Protestants now have easy access to the major role Catholics played in Black culture and history. Jamie Phelps of the Catholic Theological Union (Chicago) has played a major role in bridging the gap between Catholics and Protestants. Her impact has been felt not only as a teacher of theology but also as one of the founders of Black Theology Project and presently as an active participant in the SSBR. Along with Bishop Moses Anderson of Detroit, she has reminded the Black Protestant scholars of the SSBR of the important role of Black Catholics in defining the meaning of Black religion and the Black Church.

When the first edition of *Black Theology: A Documentary History, 1966–1979* was published, there was no section dealing with Black biblical scholars' responses to Black theology. In the revised edition, we included a section on Black Theology and the Bible. The only Black biblical scholar who critically engaged Black theology from the point of view of the discipline was Robert Bennett, an Old Testament Professor at the Episcopal Divinity School in Cambridge, Massachusetts.

Much has changed since 1979. A Black biblical revolution is taking place in the seminaries and the churches. Part III: New Directions in Black Biblical Interpretation is a representative sample of the recent writings of Black biblical scholars and their engagement of Black theology.

Cain Hope Felder, Union Seminary graduate and professor of New Testament at Howard University School of Divinity, inaugurated the new era of Black biblical interpretation with the publication of his *Troubling Biblical Waters* (Orbis Books, 1989). It started a revolution in the consciousness of Black biblical scholars that is having its most far-reaching impact in the Black churches. More than 30,000 copies of Felder's book have been sold and most in the Black churches. Felder also edited the influential *Stony the Road We Trod: African American Biblical Interpretation* (Fortress Press, 1991), the most important collection of writings by Black biblical scholars. Both *Troubling* and *Stony* were critically reviewed at the Kansas City meeting of the AAR (1991), showing that even White scholars have begun to give a measure of attention to Black biblical scholarship.

No group has made a greater impact upon Black theology and Black religious scholarship in general than the rise of Womanist theologians. Part IV: Womanist Theology comprises the largest and the most important section in this volume. Black women are the fastest growing and the most creative group of scholars among Blacks in religion. The writers in Part IV are theologians and ethicists, the counterpart of the second generation males. Womanists are also found in the other sections of the volume. Even more than Black male scholars, their sessions are well attended at the AAR.

In contrast to the second generation of Black male scholars in Part I, womanists are clear about their point of departure and the goal of their theological work. Their break with first generation Black male theologians is more radical. The enemy is clearly identified: Supporters of sexism, racism, and classism in the churches and the society. These evils are so interconnected that one cannot be adequately understood and resisted without attention to the others. Black women believe that their experience of survival and liberation in the context of these interlocking evils can open theological insights about God and humanity that both Black male and White women theologians have ignored or devalued.

Self-identified womanists have not been able to make much impact in the Black churches. The churches are still firmly in control of male clerical leadership, and it appears that most clergy plan to keep it that way. Womanists challenge male patriarchal leadership and thus threaten the status quo in the churches even more than male liberation theologians. That is why womanists have been excluded from influential leadership positions in churches. Some women have been appointed and called to major churches as pastors but not many. Women ministers who have been offered the opportunity to serve in major leadership positions do not speak out openly in favor of womanist principles. Among the womanists in this volume, Jacquelyn Grant (Interdenominational Theological Center) and Renita Weems (Vanderbilt University Divinity School) have received some recognition in the A.M.E. Church. Grant spoke to the Connectional Conference of the A.M.E. Women in Ministry on womanist themes (Atlanta, January 1991). Her address was later published under the title "An Epistle to the Black Church: What a Womanist Would Want to Say to the Black Church."[2] Prathia Wynn gave a challenging presentation on womanist themes at the Hampton Ministers Conference, June 3, 1992. I believe that Black men and women in the churches and the community should realize that liberation is for all and not the exclusive privilege of one race, gender or class.

The global vision of Black theology has been primarily defined by its involvement in the Ecumenical Association of Third World Theologians (EATWOT). Part V: The Global Context focuses mainly on Black theology's dialogue with Asia and Latin America, building on its dialogue with Africa — the primary focus of the volume one of *Black Theology*. Both Asian and Latin American theologians have enlarged our vision and reinforced the need for Black theologians to do theology from the standpoint of the world and the struggles of the poor to be free.

Although first generation theologians were the main initiators of Black theology's dialogue with Third-World theologians, global awareness is also found in the perspectives of the younger theologians. Most Black theologians include Africa in their perspective since it is our heritage. Many are also aware of the Caribbean and Latin America since our heritage is found there too. But Asia is less present in our theological frame of reference. Since Asia comprises one-half of the human population, it is time for us to take Asia more seriously. In view of the Asian immigration into the United States and the conflicts between Koreans and Blacks that became public in the wake of the Los Angeles riot (1992), the time has come for theologians and pastors on both sides to begin a dialogue. Theology, whether Black, Korean, Hispanic, or White, must be good for everybody or it is not good for anybody.

I would like to conclude this general introduction with a comment to Black scholars of religion. We are living in troubled times, and our people are suffering very deeply from structures of domination so complicated that they hardly know where to strike a blow against the evil system that is strangling them. Twelve years of Ronald Reagan and George Bush are small symbols of a much deeper and longer period of exploitation. The Los Angeles riot is only a spark of the fire that has been burning deep in the hearts of our people for hundreds of years. We need a theology that's been through the fire, knows existentially the pain of the oppressed, and thus can articulate their rage, and empower them to take charge of their history so they can make a new future for themselves. Are Black theologians today expressing the rage of oppressed Blacks and speaking the word of hope that empowers them to claim their God-given freedom?

The anger of oppressed young Blacks is conspicuously absent from our theology. Rap artists—like Ice Cube, Ice-T, Yo-Yo, Chuck D from Public Enemy, and Sister Souljah—know and express the pain and hurts of the Black poor far better than theologians. Why is that? Is it because theologians have moved into a White academic suburb and thereby have lost touch with ordinary people? Is that why Black scholars are so popular at the AAR and SBL and almost unknown in their own community? My questions are not intended to suggest that Black scholars should stop going to the AAR and SBL. On the contrary, I realize that it is one place young scholars need to go to search for a job. I have another concern about creating a context for discussion and debate about the vocation of the Black scholar in religion. How do we create a theology from the underside of the Black community? What role do the Bible and history, economic, gender, and race analyses, and popular culture play in constructing a prophetic theology for the poor in the African-American community? Can we make a liberating theology for poor Black people in the context of the AAR and SBL? These are some of the crucial questions Blacks need to discuss without the benefit of White presence.

Even the best revolutions can go awry when we internalize the values we are fighting. The worst crime that Whites have committed against Blacks, Malcolm repeatedly said, was to teach us to hate ourselves. No group in the African-American community is more susceptible to self-hatred than Black scholars who spend so much of their time trying to be accepted in the White academy. Unless Black theologians identify the demon of self-hate and exorcise it from our way of thinking about our vocation, we will not advance the cause of Black freedom.

Too often the second generation of a revolutionary movement is less radical and more accepting of the society than the first because they enjoy the fruits won by the sacrifices of their elders. They are often smarter and more intelligent than their elders because the educational opportunities denied their parents are freely given to them. While most young Black theologians will acknowledge with appreciation their debt to first generation theologians, most do not know well enough the history that gave birth to them. They know the writings of

Roberts, Cone, Washington, Wilmore, Cleage, and other highly visible theologians. But they do not know much about Leon Watts, Will Herzfeld, Theressa Hoover, Metz Rollins, Edler Hawkins, Anna Hedgeman, Herbert B. Shaw, Archie Rich, Calvin Marshall, and many others who organized and sustained the NCBC movement that created Black theology. Until this oral history is collected and preserved, I do not think that the second generation will be able to understand the intellectual rage and spiritual energy that created Black theology. The desire to write essays and books did not create Black theology. We were not concerned about tenure at White seminaries, universities, and colleges. Black theology was created by the Black liberation movement that demanded theological interpretation.

Too often the creators of a revolutionary movement grow weary of the struggle. They get tired after many years of fighting against great odds, often feeling unappreciated by the people in whose name they struggled. Perhaps something like that happened to many first generation Black theologians. A few who were once strong advocates of Black theology are now professors in White seminaries and universities who refuse to be associated with it today. Others left the field of theology and are pursuing other interests. Some retired and are no longer writing or talking about Black theology.

It is difficult to overcome theological fatigue and self-hatred without a clearly defined community of support and resistance. For Black theologians, this means first and foremost that Black people who are struggling against White supremacy and other interlocking evils (such as classism, sexism, heterosexism) must be our primary audience. It means, second, that we should join in solidarity with others who are struggling against the same evils. Our theological audience, therefore, should be both race-specific and universal—the African-American community and the human community. The more we write about Black people the more we write about everybody. If what we say is not good for everybody, then it cannot be good for Black people.

As we approach the twenty-first century, I urge Black theologians to constructively and critically engage each other and the world in which we live. Of course, womanists are talking to each other and to Black male theologians. Biblical scholars also are talking to each other. The publication of *Stony*, a great event, is the result of years of dialogue. Black pastors and theologians have begun to meet together. The same is true of self-identified second generation theologians. All of this is good for theology, church, and community.

But, despite the creative scholarship emerging from our conversations, I still contend that there is not enough *constructive* and *critical* dialogue with each other about our vocation and how we should be working together for the liberation of our community. We can publish hundreds of articles and books about Black theology and religion, Blacks in the Bible and history, but if what we do and say are not organically linked with the empowerment of Black people, then what we write is not worth the paper it is written on. We need to engage each other and our people about what we are doing, why we do it, how it liberates the poor, and how we can do it better. Scholarship is not for scholarship's sake.

Everything has a function. What function does our theology have in the liberation of poor Black people? That is the major question that we should critically engage in the seminaries, churches, and our communities if our theologies are to be more than the mere intellectual activity of privileged scholars.

J.H.C.

NOTES

1. *The Speeches of Malcolm X at Harvard,* ed. Archie Epps (New York: Morrow, 1968), 133.
2. *A.M.E. Church Review* (April-June 1991), 49–58.

PART I

THE SECOND GENERATION

INTRODUCTION

Most theological observers did not expect Black liberation theology to still be around during the 1980s and 1990s, not to mention the year 2000. They assumed that it was a product of the Black rage of the 1960s that would soon disappear. The victims in most societies are not expected to be capable of serious thought, especially about God. Blacks are expected to preach, to sing and dance, and to play basketball, but not to do theology.

The second generation of self-identified Black theologians shows that Black liberation theology is not only alive but is vibrant. With the young theological talent and commitment that make up Part I, I think it is safe to say that Black liberation theology will be around for many years to come. While they acknowledge the important contributions of the first generation Black theologians, they are not content merely to repeat what their theological elders said. The second generation builds upon the insights of the first in order to cut a new theological path for the future.

A graduate of Union Theological Seminary (New York) and currently teaching theology at Wesley Theological Seminary (Washington, D.C.), Josiah U. Young (Document 1, "God's Path and Pan-Africa") argues that the new path that second generation Black theologians ought to take is found in Pan-African theology, a "transcontextual discourse" that focuses on the liberation of Black people throughout the world. Pan-African theology is based on the thinking of W. E. B. Du Bois, Henry McNeal Turner, the insights of early Black liberation theologians, and the "new guard" contemporary African theologians, like Englebert Mveng, Jean-Marc Éla, Mercy Oduyoye, Patrick Kalilombe, and Barthélemy Adoukonou. Young acknowledges that there were signs of this Pan-African emphasis in the writings of early Black liberation theologians, but the idea was not developed fully. Whether Black theologians of the earlier period were Pan-Africanists is a debatable question, and it would be helpful for Young to initiate the debate in a context where the first and second generation Black theologians could have give-and-take discussions about it.

However, it is clear that Josiah Young offers a fresh perspective on Black liberation theology that deserves the attention of serious students of religion. He began to develop his Pan-African theological views as a doctoral student, writing a dissertation on a critical comparison of African and Black theologies. His study was later published under the title, *Black and African Theology: Siblings or Distant Cousins?* (Orbis Books, 1986). His most recent discussion is called *Pan-African Theology: Providence and the Legacies of the Ancestors* (Third World Press, 1992).

James H. Evans, Jr., also a Union Theological Seminary graduate, is moving Black liberation theology in another direction. Former Martin Luther King, Jr., Memorial Professor of Theology and Black Church Studies at Colgate Rochester Divinity School (Rochester, New York) and now its president, Evans is both a theologian and a literary critic. He is the author of *Black Theology: A Critical Assessment and Annotated Bibliography* (Greenwood Press, 1987). Evans makes use of his training in literary criticism in his interpretation of the origin and present tasks of Black theology. He urges Black theologians to take seriously the need to clarify the various contexts (historical, sociopolitical, cultural, and intellectual) in order to articulate and assess its affirmation in the world. What are the moral implications of faith? Evans' essay (Document 2, "Toward an African-American Theology") is taken from the introduction of his most recent book, *We Have Been Believers: An African-American Systematic Theology* (Fortress Press, 1992).

A graduate of the University of Notre Dame in the Department of Theology and currently assistant professor of social ethics at Perkins School of Theology (Dallas, Texas), Theodore Walker, Jr., offers another theological and ethical vision for Black theologians. He is a student of both Black liberation theology and process theology and philosophy, writing a doctoral dissertation on "a metaphysical and an ethical analysis of James Cone's conception of God as being 'God of the Oppressed.' " In Walker's work, he seeks to use both Black and process theologies in the development of a Black neoclassical social ethics. In his essay, "Theological Resources for a Black Neoclassical Social Ethics" (Document 3), Walker urges Black theologians to use the metaphysical philosophy and theology of Charles Hartshorne who "provides us with a social conception of God, a social conception of human existence, indeed, a social conception of all reality." Walker's most recent book is entitled *Empower the People: Social Ethics for the African-American Church* (Orbis Books, 1991).

Riggins R. Earl, Jr., is a graduate of Vanderbilt University Divinity School and is currently teaching social ethics at the Interdenominational Theological Center in Atlanta, Georgia. While acknowledging the important contributions of earlier theologians, Earl's main concerns are the present and future development of Black theology. In his essay, "Black Theology and the Year 2000: Three Basic Ethical Challenges" (Document 4) he identifies important issues with which Black theologians must struggle if Black theology is to achieve its full maturity. Black theologians must first learn how to effectively communicate to both the academy and the Black Church so Black theology can move beyond a marginal status in both. Second, Black theology needs to become institutionalized in the Black academic and church communities, by creating a graduate center for the study of Black religion and theology. The third challenge is to create a methodology of analysis that deals with the Christian and non-Christian values in the Black community and that encourages collegiality among Black scholars, nurturing debate and support of each other. Earl's book on slave religion, *Dark Symbols, Obscure Signs,* is forthcoming from Orbis Books.

Dwight N. Hopkins and George C. L. Cummings are participants in a group of young theologians who use the phrase "second generation" to describe their work. Both are Union Theological Seminary graduates. Hopkins is the author of the highly regarded text, *Black Theology USA and South Africa: Politics, Culture, and Liberation* (Orbis Books, 1989), and teaches theology at Santa Clara University in California. Cummings is the author of *A Common Journey: Black Theology and Latin American Liberation Theology* (Orbis Books, 1993) and is currently teaching theology at the Graduate Theological Union in Berkeley, California. Along with Will E. Coleman of Columbia Theological Seminary (Atlanta) and James Noel of San Francisco Theological Seminary (San Anselmo, California), Hopkins and Cummings created the Black Theology Forum and have been meeting regularly with each other, evaluating the past achievements of Black liberation theology, and outlining its future directions. All agree (as Hopkins and Cummings point out in Documents 5 and 6, "Black Theology and a Second Generation" and "New Voices in Black Theology") that Black theology must take more seriously the indigenous sources of our slave grandparents — the narratives, spirituals, blues, sermons, prayers, and other stories of struggle and survival. They have begun to develop a genuine theology of the slave narratives and folklore of Black people. Hopkins' and Cummings' initial publication (with contributions from Coleman and Cheryl Sanders of Howard University School of Divinity) is called *Cut Loose Your Stammering Tongue: Black Theology in the Slave Narratives* (Orbis Books, 1991). Hopkins has deepened his analysis in his most recent book, *Shoes That Fit Our Feet: Sources for a Constructive Black Theology* (Orbis Books, 1993).

J.H.C.

1

GOD'S PATH AND PAN-AFRICA

Josiah U. Young

Before I explore the implications of *God's path and Pan-Africa*, I should explain, in part, what Pan-African theology is, and address its doctrinal implications within the limitations of this essay. A more substantial exploration of this theology is found elsewhere.[1]

Pan-African theology is a *transcontextual* discourse: it focuses, simultaneously, on diverse Black people—such as the Black American underclass, the Haitian refugees, and the Zairian peasants—and commends a single, but "nuanced," commitment to their liberation. This commitment is informed by methodological principles of liberation theology, especially, the hermeneutic circle, and the social and religio-cultural analyses intrinsic to it. Of major concern is the problem of White supremacy, which dogs the path of African people everywhere.

The Pan-African theologian does not cover up the cultural and historical particularities of Black people, but celebrates them. Rich advantage is to be gained in multivocal, that is, Pan-African, resistance to the oppression of human beings. I should add, however, this caveat: the Pan prefixing the words "African theology" does not mean all Black people everywhere have, now and for all time, achieved unanimity in everything. To say *"Pan-*African theology"—it bears reiteration—is to recognize the many variations of African people, not to collapse their variations into a reified monolith. Still, one uses the word "Pan-African" appropriately any time he or she seeks to make ethnic, cultural, and geopolitical particularities among Blacks no barrier to their attaining unity-in-diversity.

Pan-African theology, in addition, is a development from Black Theology and African Theology; and as such it emerges from a transcontextual study.[2] I

Josiah U. Young is author of *Black and African Theologies: Siblings or Distant Cousins?* and teaches theology at Wesley Theological Seminary, Washington, D.C.

will address the African side of this development first; the Black theology side, second.

African theology is best represented today by theologians such as Jean-Marc Éla, Engelbert Mveng, Mercy Oduyoye, Barthélemy Adoukonou and Patrick Kalilombe. I call them the new guard;[3] they are liberation theologians for whom the misery of the African poor is not dissimulated in theological *négritude*.[4] Their work signifies that the acculturative force of dynamic African values is dissolving Eurocentric, colonial "norms," which had dictated the meaning of Christianity in Africa. These African values are also energizing the struggle for liberation, and primarily because they are emergent from the poor, whom Jean-Marc Éla calls *l'Afrique d'en bas* — the underside of Africa.[5]

The new guard is committed to the liberation of this underside. To quote Engelbert Mveng, "the only theology and the only spirituality possible [in Africa] are those of liberation [my translation]."[6] The heartfelt acceptance of Africanity is essential here. And it is the Africans, primarily, who, in my mind, have achieved a powerful vision of Black liberation. They, having reached new vistas in the Christ versus culture problematic, know that determinations regarding what is "pagan" and what is not are arbitrary — a theopolitical battle of the highest order!

Black theology anchors itself in the Black Church, in certain interpretations of slave culture, and in the socioeconomic struggles of the African-American poor. In Black theology, liberation is the gospel and is not secondary to the gospel. What is more, Black theologians such as J. Deotis Roberts have noted well that Black theology should always probe its connection to Africa. The African connection can also be seen in terms of Black theology's black nationalist heritage, reflected in the militant voice of James Cone's early work.

Yet Black theology, for the most part, does not insist that the valorization of the "globality" of African identity is at the heart of Black liberation. (The new guard, however — especially the "Afro-Gallic" contingent, such as Mveng, Éla and Adoukonou — does.) The argument is that members of the Black Church know little about Africa and that a Black theology that pushes a Pan-Africanist agenda would be out of touch with its constituency.

Pan-African theology grants one the freedom to push such an agenda, and to probe the implications of the Africanist presence, despite its absence in Western, including Black, theology. Black theology is not negated; the contextuality of African theology is not subverted. The implications of both are extended. Let me explain what the doctrinal implications of this are, with a focus on African theology.

Barthélemy Adoukonou has brought forth a new method and a new hermeneutic, which is pertinent to African-Americans as well as Africans. He forges a hermeneutic circle with a two-fold center: Vodun and Jesus Christ. Here, explains Adoukonou, the (Pan) African theologian, edified by his suspicion, bypasses the text where one finds the relation between Paul-Onesime-Philemon and focuses on that pericope where the Crucified (*le Crucifié*) — clairvoyantly explaining the meaning of his death, — "giving in advance the exegesis of his death"—informs his disciples that he is Lord. According to Adoukonou, that exegesis is analogous to the ritual disassociation one finds in Vodun: the phenomenon of possession trance is not unlike the hypostatic union of the Second Person with Jesus. That is, God is like the figure of the Other riding the devotee in Vodun. And God—as "the other present in Christ crucified"—is the One who emptied himself until death on the Cross.[7] What edifies me all the more regarding Adoukonou's Christology is that he makes this point in relation to the enslaved Africans. They first discovered the analogy between Christian faith and the return to Africa (*une signification touchante jusqu'au sublime*).

Adoukonou helps one explore Christology in *North America*—especially given the presence of Vodun among the Blacks in New York City! (New York is one of the most African places in the world today, with many religious currents of Africa and Diaspora meeting in places like Brooklyn.) From a Pan-African perspective one draws on African thought because it is eminently satisfying, even as one is edified, positively or negatively, by other Christian idioms, such as *communicatio gratiarum*.

Yet Westerners, including African-Americans, have trouble with Adoukonou's Christology because of a notion of Providence that equates African spirituality, such as Vodun, with benightedness. In such a view, African spirituality is—to quote Chinua Achebe—"a carrier on to whom the master unloads his physical and moral deformities so that he may go forward, erect and immaculate."[8] I want to draw out the implications of Achebe's statement in terms of God's path and Pan-Africa.

God's Path and Pan-Africa

God's path signifies a doctrine of Providence, that is, "God's prior knowledge of and provision for the world"—the divine, graceful, and benevolent direction of nature and human history. Such direction overcomes evil with divine intention.

Pan-Africa, an idiom used by W. E. B. Du Bois, signifies the shared ideas and practices related to and derived from Africa and Diaspora.[9] While Pan-Africa signifies space—that is a transatlantic world—it also suggests "a certain spiritual housecleaning" (Du Bois), whereby African people equip themselves to struggle for liberation. I like to think of Pan-Africa metaphorically—as if the idiom were a coded banner that gave impetus to slave revolts in the United States.[10]

In Pan-African theology, then, the workings of Providence are found in Pan-Africa. That is, God's path is discovered in an African spirituality, which may be understood as popular culture. As a symbol of African spirituality, Pan-Africa demands that Pan-African theology be understood in terms of the ancestors, to whom I can hardly do justice within the confines of this essay, though I have examined their legacies in more detail elsewhere.[11] Suffice it to say, I use the word ancestors without making a case for the numinous.

The ancestors not only signify the African spirituality I have been discussing, but an orientation to history as well, which "requires"—to quote Ralph Ellison—"a constant plunging back into the shadow of the past where time hovers ghostlike."[12] Plunging back—that is, historical analysis—is critical for the Pan-African theologian, possessed as she or he is with roots. Through such analysis, a species of social analysis, one valorizes values that link African people "trans-contextually"—thus giving substance to a Pan-African hermeneutics of liberation.

So in the remainder of this essay I will—in order to separate alienating, Eurocentric values from redemptive Afrocentric ones—revisit "ghostlike" time and discuss God's path in terms of a seminal ancestor, who was committed to "Pan-Africa." This ancestor is Henry McNeal Turner, a bishop of the African Methodist Episcopal Church, a courageous and heroic African American. Equipped with a certain hindsight, I will examine Turner's relationship to the American Colonization Society (ACS) and the implications of his relationship to slave culture and the settler regime, Liberia.

Prior to the Civil War, Henry McNeal Turner advocated emigration to Africa.[13] During the war, however, Turner had hoped Blacks would be treated fairly if the North won, and thus accepted President Lincoln's commission to be chaplain of the First Regiment of Black soldiers. After the war Turner saw clearly that little would change; he turned again to Africa—the only place, he believed, Blacks could be free. This indicates his understanding of Providence as well as his desire to flee White hostility.

Before, as well as after the war, Turner thought God, despite slavery, had raised up a westernized and christianized "talented tenth"—a Black élite emergent from slavery as a result of manumission, escape or other providential events. Such African-Americans, equipped with "civilization" and "true religion," were to return to Africa for the sake of their "benighted" kin.[14] Marked by a transatlantic trail, God's path was such that slave ships were less significant than those that bore African Americans to the continent of their ancestors.

Despite his virtues, Turner's Eurocentric view of civilization here is dangerous. Taken to its extreme, such a view constitutes alienation and promotes self-hatred, for it suggests that civilization and Europeanization are identical.

The Africans brought many skills to the Americas: mining, husbandry, artisan abilities of the highest order.[15] They were ethical and did not need the Victorian mores integral to Western interpretations of Providence. In their alterity, the Africans were already civilized—already in possession of the cultural substance in which the gospel could send its roots deep.

Black scholars and activists whom I regard highly have convinced me of this. Zora Neale Hurston set about collecting the folk wisdom owed to the ethical Africans—she said it gave her something "to feel about." Sterling Stuckey refers to this wisdom as the folk memory.[16] And Paul Robeson defined this memory as a collectivity—"an African cultural heritage that understood the primary importance of spiritual values, in contrast to the desiccated rationalism and the worship of technology and material accumulation that characterized the West."[17]

The hub of this memory in North America is slave culture, which Turner, sadly, thought was to be overcome. I grant you that the appeal to slave culture is problematic. No one perspective represents the totality of slavery or exhausts the implications of its meaning. But my theology is Pan-African—a theology that dictates what, in the final analysis, becomes essential regarding the political decisions one makes and the scholarship one valorizes. I stand, then, with Stuckey, Robeson, and Hurston because of the African values they uphold.

Those values that intrigue me most may be characterized as the communication between the living and the dead—a spirituality reappropriated in Pan-African theology today. I suspect that within certain cultures, namely those inherited by today's Gullahs,[18] such communication was established through the liminality of ritual. Liminality has to do with the suspension of the prevailing ethos that precedes and follows the limbo-like state. Such a state is really a sacred space, where a people discover, in the kinetic fervor of religious feeling, genuine liberation.[19] Here social distinctions are eschewed in favor of a spiritual, transcendent state, in which devotees experience the intensification of community, and revel in their most heartfelt commitments.

Black life, comprised by the interplay between the living and the dead, is known to be precious. The metaphors and metonyms of this preciousness are the unborn—the expectation (exchange) and continuation (succession) of a people.[20] This African spirituality, reverence of the unborn, is surely a mode of divine intention in Pan-African theology; for without it, a people fall into the horror of fratricide—such as that common among the Black underclass today. I am convinced that such fratricide, such decadence, is the deformed issue of the necrophilic preoccupation of Whites with Blacks and that the valorization of the unborn is the antidote to such necrophilia.

As integral as the unborn to the celebration of life has been polyrhythm, the embellished heartbeat of the African people. As the African theologian, Engelbert Mveng explains, polyrhythm must be understood in terms of the archetype, *le tambour* (the drum). The drum, he writes, is

the Logos of [Pan-African] culture, and expresses the human condition. Simultaneously king, artisan, warrior, hunter, young initiate, the drum's polyvalent voice (*sa voix multiple*), conveys, in the rhythm of its soulful vitality, the human voice, and the turmoil of human destiny [my translation].[21]

In Pan-African theology, part of this turmoil and destiny must be appreciated in relation to the Diaspora.

Poetically, Zora Neale Hurston makes my point. She writes that the Whites (*buckra*) sought to strip Africans of all manner of resistance. But the African, whom she typifies as *Cuffy*, coveted the drum—"hid it in his skin under the skull bones."[22] Through the assertion of their cultures, typified here as the drum,

African people found the logos in their most native selves, "under the skull bones," and refused to be totally "thingified" in the misery Mveng defines as *pauvreté anthropologique* (anthropological poverty = acquiescence in self-hatred).[23]

To the extent that "saltwater" slaves, such as the Bantu ancestors of South Carolina, were able to cross the threshold, from the conventions of slavery to an ancestral mode of self-affirmation, they were able to fly home to Africa. That is, they were able to valorize a sacred way of being in the world—itself constituted by the tribute to Africa, a tribute that laid the foundation of African-American culture.[24]

In its Christian mode this foundation expressed itself through the ring shouts, the "centrifugal force" out of which the spirituals were spun. Here, a de-Europeanized, Pan-Africanized Christianity was itself a vehicle for the expression of continuity with Africa. This continuity—reappropriated in Pan-African theology today—makes for true resistance as it alone constitutes the otherness that celebrates the God of Providence.[25] Despite slavery and colonizations, Pan-African theologians refuse to forsake the memory of their ancestors, and drawing close to them, they draw close to the God incarnate in the underside.

Again, it is regrettable—but understandable—that Bishop Turner did not see this. Turner's view of Providence was derived from the American Colonization Society (ACS) founded by Whites and run by them. These Whites, deeply ambivalent about African Americans, sought to deport nonslaves and ex-slaves to Africa. The Society founded the colony of Liberia in 1822, which was a euphemism for deportation as well as Providence and was the primary place to which African Americans were repatriated. The proliferation of "free persons of color" threatened the designs of both the Northern bourgeoisie and the Southern plantocracy. Neither had much use for Blacks—Northerners for slave or "free"; Southerners for "free" blacks. The ACS was a vehicle, then, for those who wanted to get rid of free Blacks who posed a political threat to White establishments.

As honorary vice-president of the Society, Turner was at odds with the providential values at work in certain slave quarters. From the perspective of Pan-African theology, these slave shelters—the memory and valorization of the Africans with "saltwater" ways—purvey redemptive mores because they undermine White supremacy and its necrophilic fascination with Blacks. Turner is not to be blamed for his alienation; the acculturative weight of racist values held, and still holds, most North Americans captive. He remains a great ancestor, one as opposed to White supremacy as anyone of his time could be. The Pan-African theologian is edified by Turner's work—the intense identification with Africa—but recognizes too that he confused decadence with Providence.

The irony of that contradiction is deepened by an examination of (Americo) Liberia. Having visited Liberia, Turner was sure that Africa's redemption was under way. Nothing could be farther from the truth. Expatriate African-Americans (Americo-Liberians) violently took the land from the Africans—the Vai, Mende, Grebo, Mano, etc.—and denied them participation in government.

What is more, White supremacy reproduced itself in the peculiar bigotry that assigns social values to people based on their resemblance to Whites. The so-called mulatto caste tended to constitute the élite in Liberia, as exemplified by President Robert Jenkins. It seems fair to say, the Americo-Liberians foreshadowed, perhaps even initiated, the era of colonialism in Africa—because they operated with the assumption that colonization was tantamount to Providence.

In Pan-African theology today, the memory of the Americo-Liberians gives impetus to a certain demythologization, whereby the Absolute and the path of Western civilization are felt to be antithetical, not identical. And this demythologization facilitates "re-Africanization," to make an allusion to the work of Amilcar Cabral, the late African theorist and revolutionary. Cabral defines re-Africanization as a "spiritual re-conversion" that de-Europeanizes and thus arrests the alienation that creates—as it did in Liberia—the gap between the Eurocentric élite and "the mass of people."

Re-Africanization is an essential of Pan-African theology; I like to think of it as an initiation: one, in crossing the threshold between Eurocentricity and Afrocentricity, discovers in the latter an otherness—a *communitas*—in which African-Americans still, and despite themselves, "reincarnate" their ancestors. The Vodun-like liminality of the Sanctified church; blues and jazz; an alleged infelicitous vernacular; the hairdos of black youth, revelatory of an African aesthetic; the rap rhythms, replete with the memory of field chants and hollers, and reverberating in the Niger-Congo-like dancing of Black youth—all these things comprise the popular idioms in which polyrhythm, diffused throughout a Black poetics, communicates the reality of Pan-Africa. That is God's path.

As a Pan-African theologian, I, for one, am at home in Pan-Africa. Western triumphalism has no place here ("under the skull bones"). Freedom from alienation is satisfying indeed, for one looks to God (in one's self) for beatitude.

NOTES

1. See my *A Pan-African Theology: Providence and the Legacies of the Ancestors* (Trenton, N.J.: Africa World Press, 1992).

2. See my *Black and African Theology: Siblings or Distant Cousins?* (Maryknoll, N.Y.: Orbis Books, 1986).

3. See my essay, "African Theology: From Independence to Liberation," *Voices From the Third World*, 10, no. 4 (December 1987): 41-48.

4. For a powerful, and *dangerous*, exposé of the disingenuous of *négritude*, see Stanislas Adotévi, *Négritude et négrologues* (Paris: Union Générale d'éditions, 1972).

5. Jean-Marc Éla, "Le rôle des Eglises dans la libération du continent africain." *Bulletin de théologie africaine* 6, no. 12 (juillet-décembre 1984): 281-302.

6. Engelbert Mveng, "Récents développements de la théologie africaine." *Bulletin de théologie africaine* 5, no. 9 (janvier-juin 1983): 141.

7. Barthélemy Adoukonou, *Jalons pour une théologie africaine: Essai d'une herméneutique chrétienne du Vodun dahoméen. Tome I: Critique théologique* (Paris: Éditions Lethielleux, 1980), 59.

8. Chinua Achebe, *Hopes and Impediments* (Garden City, N.Y.: Anchor Books/Doubleday, 1989).

9. See W. E. B. Du Bois, "Pan-Africa and the New Racial Philosophy," in *The*

Seventh Son, vol. 2, ed. Julius Lester (New York: Random House, 1971), 208.

10. See Peter H. Woods, *Black Majority. Negroes in Colonial South Carolina from 1670 through the Stono Rebellion* (New York: W.-W. Norton & Co., 1975), 316.

11. See note 1, above.

12. Ralph Ellison, *Shadow and Act* (New York: Vintage Books, 1972), xix.

13. On Turner, see Edwin S. Redkey, ed., *Respect Black: The Writings and Speeches of Henry McNeal Turner* (New York: Arno Press and the *New York Times*, 1971).

14. Redkey, *Respect Black*, 55.

15. See Joseph Holloway, ed., *Africanism in American Culture* (Bloomington, Ind.: Indiana University Press, 1990).

16. Sterling Stuckey, *Slave Culture: Nationalist Theory and the Foundations of Black America* (New York: Oxford University Press, 1987).

17. See Martin B. Duberman, *Paul Robeson* (New York: Ballantine Books, 1989), 173.

18. See Margaret Creel Washington, "Gullah Attitudes Toward Life and Death," in *Africanism in American Culture*, ed. Holloway, 69-97.

19. On liminality, see Victor Turner, *The Ritual Process: Structure and Anti-Structure* (Ithaca, N.Y.: Cornell University Press, 1977).

20. Stuckey, *Slave Culture*, 41.

21. Engelbert Mveng, *L'art d' Afrique noire: Liturgie cosmique, langage religieux* (Yaounde: Éditions CLE, 1974), 80.

22. See Zora Neale Hurston, *Jonah's Gourd Vine* (New York: Harper & Row, 1990). More precisely, she writes: " 'He will serve us better if we bring him from Africa naked and thingless.' So the buckra reasoned. They tore away his clothes that Cuffy might bring nothing, but Cuffy seized his drum and hid it in his skin under the skull bones" (see p. 29).

23. Engelbert Mveng, "Récent développements de la théologie Africaine." *Bulletin de théologie africaine* 5, no. 9 (janvier-juin 1983): 141.

24. See Holloway, *Africanism in American Culture*, 9.

25. See Stuckey, *Slave Culture*.

2

TOWARD AN AFRICAN-AMERICAN THEOLOGY

James H. Evans, Jr.

Theological reflection is central to the ongoing life of the African-American Christian church. Theology is essentially the church's response to the autobiographical impulse, and it grows out of the need to proclaim with authority and commitment the identity and mission of the church in the world. That is, in theology, the church both asks and answers the questions, "Who are we, and where are we going?" It has unfortunately been the case that the work of black theologians and the work of African-American churches have often been construed as separate types of activities. It would not be an exaggeration to say that the leadership of many black congregations, large and small, and the ranks of professional black theologians have looked on one another with caution and, at times, suspicion. This has resulted in a chasm in the black religious community between the theology and practice of Christian faith, leaving the churches with a religion that appears to be no more than a cultural performance, and the theologians with a theology that seems to consist only of abstract concepts. The question, then, is "How can the dialogue between professional black theologians and other members of the African-American churches be strengthened so that it becomes clear that black theology is rooted in the faith of the church and that the faith of the church is given intellectual clarity and expression in black theology?"

This intellectual clarity is not a substitute for, but a complement to, genuine, personal, and communal expressions of faith. In other words, African-American church leaders should be reminded that leadership means more than habitually performing the liturgical functions necessary to the structural maintenance of

James H. Evans, Jr., is president of Colgate Rochester Divinity School/Berley Hall/Crozer Theological Seminary, Rochester, New York. This essay is from the introduction to the author's book, *We Have Been Believers: An African-American Systematic Theology* (Minneapolis, Minn.: Fortress Press, 1992) and is reprinted with permission.

the community. Genuine church leadership requires sound theological judgment. At the same time, professional black theologians need to be reminded that theology is more than the writing of scholarly articles and books. Genuine theological judgment requires a praxiological commitment to the community of faith. Theologians as theologians cannot tell other Christians what they should believe; rather their task is to help the community understand more clearly what they do believe and to assess those beliefs in light of the major sources of Christian revelation.

Black theology differs from traditional theology in much the same way that African-American Christianity differs from the Christianity of Europe and the North Atlantic. Since the first Africans set foot on this soil, people of African descent have had a singularly unique experience in the New World. They brought with them an inherent philosophical heritage, including a distinctive religious sensibility; they encountered the most brutal form of slavery in human history; and they were introduced to North Atlantic Christianity. Because there was no precedent for the experience of people of African descent, they created distinctive ways of conceptualizing and speaking about their ultimate concerns. Black theology is a continuation of that discursive tradition. Therefore, African-American theological development can be best understood as the convergence of an African-derived worldview, the complexities of the experience of slavery, oppression, survival, rebellion, and adjustment in the New World, and their encounter with the biblical text. These realities shaped the African-American intellect and spirit.

Black theology reflects the passion, feeling, and expressiveness of African-American Christianity. It must be in touch with the "guts" of black religion. It must have, as Karl Barth once put it, "heavenly fire." Without this quality it would forfeit its claim to authenticity. On the other hand, theological reflection is not synonymous with the sermon, the litany, or the testimony, although they all participate in the same ethos of religious expression. Black theology is also a formal, self-conscious, systematic attempt to interpret the faith of the church. The form need not always be linear, nor the system based on Western philosophy. Black theologians may employ explanatory and formal devices such as story or biblical commentary. Black theology is passionate and incisive, reflecting what Paul Tillich called "ecstatic reason." The important factor, however, is that the theology that results must coherently interpret the experience of black people and the Gospel.

The contemporary African-American church needs theological acumen as much as it ever has. Not only must attacks on the integrity of black religion be resisted, but the continual evolution of religion in America and the often surprising turns that it takes require a constant "testing of the waters" by theologians of the black church. However, the need for theological reflection goes beyond the issues of the survival or integrity of the black church as an institution. In a world where black people, people of color, and poor people, are continually frustrated in their attempt "to have life, and have it more abundantly," black theologians must speak to those systems, persons, and conditions that impede the worship and adoration of the God of the Gospel and the living of a just life.

In light of these factors, there are several tasks that black theologians have before them today. *The first task is to clarify the contacts—historical, sociopolitical, cultural, and intellectual—in which African-American Christian faith is affirmed.* The historical context of the faith of black Christians includes a shared legacy of slavery, the struggle to adapt to legal manumission, and the ongoing battle to be recognized as full human beings. The development of slave religion and its relation to the early freedom struggle among people of African descent is the historical source of contemporary black Christian faith. African slaves who embraced Christianity also modified and shaped it to meet their existential needs and saw, even in the contorted presentations of the Gospel by some white people, a continuity between what they knew of God in Africa and the God of the Bible. Gayraud Wilmore describes the essential relationship between faith and freedom in the development of black religion:

> An exceedingly elastic but tenacious thread binds together the contributive and developmental factors of black religion in the United States as one distinctive social phenomenon. It is the thread of what may be called, if properly defined, "black radicalism." Black religion has always concerned itself with the fascination of an incorrigibly religious people with the mystery of God, but it has been equally concerned with the yearning of a despised and subjugated people for freedom—freedom from the religious, economic, social, and political domination that whites have exercised over blacks since the beginning of the African slave trade.[1]

This thread can be traced through the public annals of professional historians, but is also present—perhaps in even more striking manifestations—in the autobiographies, personal narratives, and journals of African-American women and men who felt compelled to give testimony to the work of God in their lives.

The sociopolitical context for the re-radicalization of African-American Christianity in the twentieth century is the civil rights/black power movement. Scholars differ on which aspect of the substantively crucial period in American history is most directly responsible for the religious and theological revival in the black community. Warner R. Traynham argues that the civil rights movement and its most visible leader, Martin Luther King, Jr., were most responsible for the religious and theological reawakening.[2] Both James H. Cone and J. Deotis Roberts suggest that the radical critique of American racism inherent in the black power movement is the source of contemporary black theology and prophetic black Christianity.[3] Gayraud Wilmore argues that radical black Christianity and black theology in the twentieth century emerged after many of the leaders of the civil rights movement had been coopted by the white power structure and before the full measure of black power had been seized.[4]

It seems clear that while there are differences in interpretation, the civil rights movement and the black power movement are part of a continuous tradition of protest and struggle in African-American religious life. The civil rights movement was based on the notion that the equality of black people was a function of their legal status in American society. Equality had been denied by the Fugitive Slave Law of 1850, the Dred Scott decision (1857), and the Plessy vs. Ferguson decision of the Supreme Court (1896). These legal conscriptions were subsequently reversed or eliminated by the Brown vs. Board of Education of Topeka Supreme Court decision of 1954 and the voting rights laws passed in the 1960s. These advances were engineered by people and groups directly or indirectly related to the African-American church. They were visible evidence of the reawakening of the black church militant that had slumbered for decades.

Not since the end of slavery, however, had the attitudinal and psychological dimensions of racism come to the forefront of discussion. The black power movement was, in part, the result of the failures and limitations of the early civil rights movement; especially its dependence on enfranchisement as a tool for liberation. Black power advocates asserted that control of the institutions that regulated *intellectual commerce* and *social values,* not legal prescriptions, were the most effective means for achieving the liberation of black people. Racism was seen as an attitudinal, psychological, and structural aspect of American life. Therefore, it could not be eliminated simply through legislation because people tend to structure their behavior according to deep-seated values and not in strict accordance to extraneous norms. Thus civil rights laws were widely ignored. The psychological, attitudinal, and structural aspects of racism also meant that racism was supported by the pseudo-Christian values prevalent in American society.

The most profound contribution of the black power movement to the development of black theology was its challenge to black people to show how they could be black and Christian at the same time. This challenge was multidimensional. Black Muslims called Christianity a "white man's religion" that had nothing to do with the spiritual heritage of African-Americans. Black secular Marxists argued that Christianity was an unscientific, irrelevant, and counterrevolutionary illusion that only hindered the liberation of black people. Pan-Africanists eschewed Christianity to the extent that it obscured the reality that black people were part of the African Diaspora. Black nationalists rejected Christianity on the grounds that it prevented black people from seeing the necessity of separating themselves from white culture as a prerequisite for their liberation.[5]

Black theology was in part a response to these objections. Black theologians were not willing to concede Christianity to its white abusers and based their legitimacy on the fact that African-American Christianity was the result of the encounter of black people with the liberating essence of the Gospel. Black theologians viewed the history of black resistance to white oppression, and the fact that the leaders of that resistance were more often than not black Christians, as evidence that the black liberation struggle was rooted in black religion.

Black theologians stressed that the connection with Africa was more evident in black religious life than anywhere else. Further, they pointed to the identification of black Christians with the biblical people of Israel as an example of an appropriate nationalist sentiment in the religious setting.

In addition to the historical and socio-political contexts, the cultural and intellectual contexts in which African-American faith is affirmed are part of the focus of this first task of theology. Black religion was shaped in the midst of a profound cultural conflict between the inherited cosmology, value systems, and philosophical constructs that African slaves brought with them to the New World, and the protean culture of the colonies that were struggling to define themselves over against the dominant European paradigm, and in light of the ironic position of the colonies as an imperialist presence. (The colonists presumably came to the New World to escape tyranny, but found themselves in the position of tyrants in relation to Amerindians and Africans.)

The cultural matrix of the African tended to affirm the infinite worth of the African as a human being in relation to other human beings and under the auspices of a benevolent creator God. The community (the no longer living, the living, and the yet to be born) was affirmed as the basic social unit and as the social framework in which the individual was defined. All creation, including nature, was seen as infused with the spiritual presence of God.

The formative culture of the colonies demeaned the African as a human being, by associating blackness, and thus black people, with evil; by denying the existence of an indigenous African culture and civilization; and by rejecting the notion that Africans had any idea of a Supreme Being, thereby condemning them to the state of God-forsakenness and justifying their continued enslavement and exploitation. The culture of the colonies devalued community and idolized the individual, making the protection of private property and individual rights the basis for social and political organization. Further, nature and those living beings thought to be most closely related to it became, in the minds of the colonists, the "wilderness" and the "savages," both of which were to be tamed, subdued, and domesticated.

This cultural conflict has not been resolved in contemporary American life. As African-Americans struggle with the pull of a secular, materialistic, hedonistic, narcissistic, and pessimistic culture, they also experience, to varying degrees, the magnetic hold of a spiritual, integrated, communal, and hopeful, counter-culture. African-American Christian faith is in part a response to this cultural conflict, attempting to navigate, with varying degrees of success, a course between the old and the new, the familiar and the strange.

The intellectual context of black faith reflects a similar struggle on the ideational and practical level. In the eighteenth century Gustavus Vassa, Phyllis Wheatley, and Jupiter Hammon attempted to reconcile the African intellectual tradition with their crisis-ridden status as slaves in the New World. In the nineteenth century, Henry Highland Garnet, T. Thomas Fortune, Martin R. Delaney, and Maria Stewart attempted to resolve the tension between the problematic presence of African-Americans with their relationship to Africa and the emerging national identity of the United States.[6] In the first two-thirds of the twentieth century Booker T. Washington, W. E. B. Du Bois, Marcus Garvey, Mary McCloud Bethune, Martin Luther King, Jr., and Malcolm X attempted to relate the plight of African-Americans to that of the insurgent liberation movements in Africa and the so-called Third World. The ideas generated in these historical moments owe much of their power and pertinence to the influence of African-American Christianity. These attempts to orient people of African descent in an alien environment were shaped by the fundamental encounter of a sternly held faith and the fierce desire for freedom. Moreover, black theology is the ideological progeny of these moments. Therefore, black theologians must take seriously these intellectual contexts and sources.

The second task is to articulate, interpret, and assess the essential doctrinal affirmations of African-American faith for the contemporary African-American community of faith. In spite of the unique history of the evolution of African-American faith, this faith cannot be reduced to its contexts. That is, sociological reductionism, cultural reductionism, or ideological reductionism does not reach the spiritual essence of black faith. Empathic intimacy with the heart of African-American faith requires that we move beyond the *contexts* to the *content* of that faith.

Briefly stated, the content of African-American faith is the story of God's dealings with God's people and the world. There are, in fact, two stories involved here. On one hand the Bible presents what I call "canonical stories." The canonical story is what we construe to be the message of the Bible and tradition. For African-Americans that story has always been, in some paradigmatic form, the story of the liberation of the Hebrew slaves and Jesus' liberating mission in his time. The elements in that story are linked by the providential will of God. That is, clearly God has been in control of events from the beginning and stands as the guarantor that, in the end, "everything will be all right." It is this guarantee that is the basis of faith. Yet there is a danger of distortion present here. It is also possible that this story can become a safe haven for those Christians who yearn to return to the pristine past or to create a religious subculture in which they might escape the demands of postmodern life.

On the other hand, African-Americans bring their own stories to bear on the Bible and tradition. They bring what I call "folk stories." Because we are historical creatures, we suffer under the tragic limitations of human finitude, and folk stories are our way of expressing the fears, frustrations, and struggle as well as the determination for freedom from existential anxiety, political oppression, and cultural exploitation that constitute our experience. We live uncertain of whether our hopes will be vindicated or whether the struggle for freedom will end; therefore we can only infer that, given the faithfulness of God, one day "the wicked shall cease from troubling, and the weary shall be at rest." That is, African-American existence may be characterized by a rugged determination for freedom and not by any certainty that this freedom will be realized. There is a danger of distortion connected with this story as well. This existence may also portray a kind of pathos and despair in which anomie and disorientation in a mass culture and secular society have all but extinguished the fires of the will and determination.

The black theologian must relate the "canonical" story, in its prophetic mode, with the "folk" story of a people who hope against hope. To do this the theologian cannot be so immersed in the assurance, optimism, or myopia of the canonical story (the proclamation of the churches) that he or she is unable to see the challenge of the folk story. Conversely, the theologian cannot become so enchanted by the pathos of the folk story or so disillusioned by the tragic dimensions of African-American experience that the hope expressed in the canonical story is not seen. In sum, black theologians must tell a story that relates the hope of the biblical message with the realism of black experience. Through the arrangement and explication of the basic Christian doctrines, from creation to consummation, black theologians must fashion a story that brings together the twin commitment of African-American Christians to faith and freedom.

The third task is to examine the moral implications of that faith for Christian witness in the world. African-American Christian faith is shaped by a variety of *contexts,* has a distinctive and identifiable *content,* and matures only through the fulfillment of its *intent.* The intent, goal, or telos of African-American Christian faith is the moral ordering of personal and collective human existence through Christian witness in the world. Christian witness here is understood to involve three moral moments. First, Christians must engage in moral discernment. The challenge is to read the signs of the times, to look into the hearts of people, institutions, and social systems, to find the sources of impediments to justice and truth. Therefore, Christians can and must employ those modes of analytical discourse that can make plain the origins of human misery. Depth psychology, literary criticism, and other forms of analysis may be helpful in this regard. However, given the morphology of human existence in postmodern society, it is imperative that moral discernment today include a socio-economic and cultural analysis of our world and its inner workings. Human suffering in our time cannot be fully explained by looking at the cruelty that one individual inflicts upon another; it must also be seen as the result of conflicting economic interests and conflicting social values.

Second, this moral discernment must be guided by moral norms. That is, one must have a set of criteria by which one can determine whether the present social order is just. These criteria must themselves be drawn from the content of African-American Christian faith, rather than from any extraneous philosophical norms of good and evil, right and wrong. Therefore, one cannot introduce a notion of justice, for example, as central to ethical behavior if the notion itself is not central to the theological affirmations of African-American faith. In other words, one must be able to act and live in a way that is consistent with one's beliefs.

Third, the moral norm must render judgment on society, and the participation of African-American Christians in that society, in such a way that one is forced to decide and is moved to action. It is not enough to analyze society and to announce that injustice exists. The full meaning of Christian witness in the world includes deciding for the victims and acting in solidarity with them. It is interesting that Jesus rarely talked about the issue of poverty, but constantly communed with poor people. People are rarely moved to compassionate acts by abstract issues, but are often moved by the encounter with specific people. Christians must refuse to sacralize poverty or to abandon the poor. Christians must resist victimization and minister to the victims. This requires a praxis that embraces moral acts as well as moral existence. Christians must act morally, but moral acts are grounded in a basic lifestyle and mindset that itself is moral. Christians must exist as moral people, but moral existence is buttressed by moral acts.

In sum, authentic Christian witness is an engagement in moral discernment and making moral judgments, in light of moral norms, that results in moral acts and lifestyles. Black theologians must contribute in a substantive and comprehensive way to authentic Christian witness. As "organic intellectuals" (Antonio Gramsci) their work involves social analysis, normative claims regarding the demands of the faith in the postmodern world, and actual engagement in communities of resistance. In this way, theology as a vocation can become a form of authentic Christian witness.

These, then, are the primary dimensions of African-American Christian faith. The contexts show how the external and internal forces that shaped and continue to influence black religious expression have brought faith and freedom into sharp relief. The doctrinal affirmations must form the story, or gestalt, of black Christianity around the twin elliptical centers of faith and freedom, the dialectic of which recasts and reinterprets the major sources of Christian revelation. The moral implications of this faith must guide and direct African-American Christian witness in the world in a way that manifests the twin commitments of faithfulness to God and the struggle for freedom.

> The content of God's *revelation* is *liberation.* The primary record of that revelation is the *Bible,* which has historically carried a special significance for those who are *outside* the corridors of power in society. It is *the ungiven God* of the oppressed who is revealed in the Bible. The zenith of God's self-revelation *is Jesus Christ,* who is affirmed as both *liberator* and *mediator.* Jesus Christ embodies *being black* in such a way that the result is the emergence of a distinctive *community of faith.* This community, vivified by *the spirit of freedom,* provisionally manifests and anticipates the justification of the present social and human order, a justification so radical and complete that those who are now counted as *last shall be first.*

Theology as introspection and as proclamation is crucial for the African-American church, and for all Christian churches, because the relationship between faith and freedom is, perhaps, the most pressing theological problem of our time. Faith seeks understanding; but in the present context that understanding must be a critical one. The point is not simply to understand the basis on which faith is affirmed, but to understand it in a way that makes the faithful a redeeming and transforming presence in the world. Faith seeks critical understanding. Likewise, freedom seeks expression; but the freedom of which we speak must be discernible in visible acts and modes of being in the world. Christian freedom, then, is never simply a spiritual reality, or only a spiritual possession, but is realized in and among those who, even in our midst, struggle for liberation. Freedom seeks public expression.

NOTES

1. Gayraud S. Wilmore, *Black Religion and Black Radicalism: An Interpretation of the Religious History of Afro-American People*, 2d ed. (Maryknoll, N.Y.: Orbis Books, 1983), x.

2. Warner R. Traynham, "Theology under Re-Appraisal: Black Theology," in *Today's Church and Today's World*, ed. J. Howe (London: CIO Publishing Co., 1977), 154.

3. See James H. Cone, *Black Theology and Black Power* (New York: Seabury Press, 1969); J. Deotis Roberts, *Liberation and Reconciliation: A Black Theology* (Philadelphia: Westminster Press, 1971).

4. See Gayraud S. Wilmore, "Black Theology: Its Significance for Christian Mission Today," in *International Review of Mission* 63 (April 1974): 211–31.

5. These objections to Christianity were not new, but were, in fact, reformulations of the primary objections to Christianity among black people voiced in the nineteenth century.

6. The historic and even divisive debates around various colonization schemes that would send African slaves back to Africa or to some other tropical destination symbolized the extent to which the African population of the United States had become embroiled in the dilemma of whether or not they were, by now, irrevocably "American." Frederick Douglass, using himself as the prototype, argued that the slaves built the wealth of the United States and therefore were heirs to its anticipated glory. Martin R. Delaney countered that people of African descent would never be "at home" in this land and should find refuge in Africa or Central America. By this time, however, going back to Africa had already ceased to be a realistic historical option for the majority of black people. Thus the debate was, in essence, about "ideology" and not "geography."

3

THEOLOGICAL RESOURCES FOR A
BLACK NEOCLASSICAL SOCIAL ETHICS

Theodore Walker, Jr.

This essay seeks to affirm the possibility of a systematic social ethics[1] which has two main resources. The first is black theology, that is, the systematic theologies of African-Americans and of Africans elsewhere. The second resource is "neoclassical thought," that is, the metaphysical philosophy and theology of Charles Hartshorne and others, also called "process philosophy/theology."

This possibility is suggested in part by reference to Preston Williams's way of doing systematic social ethics. Williams's procedure is to do social ethics with two basic resources: the first is reflection upon social context, specifically a social analysis of African-American experience; the other resource consists of a systematic aggregation of basic (*a priori*) anthropological and theological presuppositions.[2] Given, then, reflection upon the social-historical context of Africans in the New World as our primary resource, and Hartshornean neoclassical metaphysics as our secondary resource, there is the possibility of developing what will be called in this essay a black neoclassical social ethics.

This possibility will be discussed in a critical reflection upon Hartshorne's neoclassical thought from the perspective of black theology. We shall discover that Hartshorne's neoclassical or process theology is an especially credible resource for black theology because it offers a vision of God that affirms and complements many of the essential insights of black theology, and also because it, like black theology, takes exception to many of the characteristic features of the prevailing Western theological tradition. Moreover, Hartshornean thought provides us with a social conception of God, a social conception of human existence, indeed, a social conception of all reality. Therefore, black theology

Theodore Walker, Jr., is author of *Empower the People: Social Ethics for the African-American Church* and is assistant professor of social ethics at Perkins School of Theology, Dallas, Texas. This essay is reprinted from the *Journal of Religious Thought* 45, no. 2 (Winter-Spring 1989).

can make uniquely excellent use of Hartshornean resources when it engages, as black theology must, in social analysis and systematic social ethics.

I. Process Theology and Classical Theism

Most students of contemporary theology have a somewhat vague awareness of process theology as a theological school informed by the metaphysical philosophy of Charles Hartshorne and/or Alfred North Whitehead. Others are aware of the work of Schubert Ogden, John Cobb, and other Christian theologians who are usually classified as process theologians. While relatively few of us have actually studied process theology, most of us are familiar with its popular caricature. According to this caricature, process theology is distinguished from traditional or classical theologies in that the former says God is relative and changing (in the process of becoming), while the latter says God is absolute and unchanging ("pure being"). The traditional theologians who caricature process theology in this way offer in its place a theology that is sometimes called "classical theism" because it is rooted in a Western understanding of ancient Greek philosophy. According to such understanding, that which is absolute and unchanging is superior to that which is relative and changing; therefore, it is reasoned, the God of traditional theology is superior to the God conceived in process theology.

Actually, the caricature is wrong. The real distinction between a process theology based on Hartshorne and traditional theologies is this: Where traditional theology says God is absolute and absolute only, process theology says God is both absolute and relative (unsurpassably absolute in some respects and unsurpassably relative in other respects), not just absolute. Where a traditional theology says God is unchanging and unchanging only, process theology says God is both unchanging and changing (unsurpassably unchanging in some respects and unsurpassably changing/responsive in others); that God is both being and becoming, not just being. Where a traditional theology says God is abstract, process theology says God is both abstract and concrete. Where a traditional theology says God is transcendent, process theology says God is both transcendent and immanent; both spiritual and physical, active and passive, independent and dependent, simple and complex, necessary and contingent, each in its respective and unsurpassable way. Thus, Hartshorne conceives of classical/traditional theology as monopolar in contrast to the dipolarity of his own neoclassical thought. The dipolar conception of God, which distinguishes process theology from all monopolar theologies, is clearly a more inclusive vision of God (and in this sense a greater and superior version of God) than that affirmed by classical theism.

II. Black Theology and Classical Theism

The term "black theology" is here used to refer primarily to those contemporary African-American and native African systematic theologies which understand that the Christian witness to the modern world is more than less in accord with the liberation agenda of "black power."[3] Accordingly, black theology understands that liberating answers to questions pertaining to the circumstance of oppression and the struggle for freedom are essential to the Christian witness.

This understanding of Christian witness yields a particular vision of God that has been summarily formulated by James Cone and others under the conception of God as "God of the oppressed."[4] When black theologians speak of God as God of the oppressed, we do not mean merely that God is present with, related to, worshiped by, or somehow involved with those who are oppressed. This would be to understate the matter. From the perspective of black theology, to speak of God as God of the oppressed is to affirm that God actually experiences the suffering of those who are oppressed. Moreover, black theology knows, from the data of human experience, that the experience of suffering from oppression entails a desire to be liberated from such suffering. Hence, it follows that the God who experiences the suffering of the oppressed also desires their liberation.

Black theology has its deepest rootage in the experience of enslaved and oppressed Africans, and in their appropriation of the witness of scripture, but not in the philosophical and theological traditions of the Western academy and its medieval and Greek forebears. The essentially non-Western rootage of black theology is often concealed by the fact that most African-American communities of worship wear the labels of European-American Protestant denominations. It must be remembered, however, that African-American denominations are not "Protestant" in the sense of having been born in protest to alleged Catholic abuses; instead, African-American denominations are protestant in the very different sense of having been born in protest against oppression by European-American Protestant denominations. For example: the African Methodist Episcopal Zion Church is called "Methodist Episcopal" largely on account of the fact that white members of the John Street Methodist Episcopal Church of New York City were so oppressive of their black members that in 1796 about thirty African-Americans, under the leadership of James Varick, separated themselves from that white congregation and formed an independent denomination.[5] Most other African-American denominations and racially separated churches were born of similar protest and, typically, African-Americans retained the name of whichever European-American denomination or church they happened to have stood in protest against. Therefore, when African-American congregations are referred to by European-American denominational titles, one must understand that, ironically, such titles signify differences more than similarities. Black theology's roots in the tradition of that other great protest, schism, and reformation, which produced the racially separate African-American congregations, determine that it is not at all committed to that predominantly white-Western theological tradition which Hartshorne calls "classical theism."

To be sure, black theology is defined in considerable measure by its protest against the prevailing Western theological tradition. History has taught us that classical Western theism is quite capable of abiding peaceably with, and even of being very supportive of, such oppressive activities as the enslavement of Africans and the genocide of Native Americans. It is characteristic of black theology to be unforgivingly critical of any theology that fails to affirm that God favors the struggle for liberation. If God is conceived so as not to favor this struggle, then God is thereby conceived so as not to experience fully our pain and suffering. Such a conception of God is contrary to the Christian witness to God's suffering as indicated by the cross, and it is contrary to the vision of God as that utterly unsurpassable *Friend* whose love is perfect and all-inclusive. The logic of black theology is this:

> *First:* The most basic existential datum of black theology is that the experience of suffering from oppression entails or produces a desire, and inevitably a struggle, for liberation.
>
> *Second:* The most basic religious datum of black theology is that human experience becomes divine experience, that our suffering becomes divine suffering, in that God actually experiences our experience of humiliation, pain, and suffering.
>
> *Third:* Therefore, the most basic theological affirmation of black theology is that God desires and strives to achieve the liberation of those who are oppressed.

American black theology is characterized by reflection upon the context and experience of African descendants of the great transatlantic impress. According to this social analysis, to experience suffering from oppression is to desire, and inevitably to struggle for, liberation. Because we know that God actually experiences our oppression, we know that God favors our struggle for liberation. This is removed as far as can be from such classical attributes of God as immutable, totally impassible, wholly other, and unmoved mover. From the perspective of black theology, the prevailing classical Western (white) theism is logically, existentially, and religiously anathema. Insofar as classical theology aids and abets the structures of oppression, James Cone would describe it as the theology of the Antichrist.

We may then begin this critical reflection upon Hartshorne's "neoclassical theism" or "process theology" with the observation that both black and neoclassical theologies are defined in large part by their opposition to or protest against certain features of classical Western theism. Furthermore, we shall come to see that the African-American conception of God as God of the oppressed is far more in accord with Hartshorne's vision of God than with those classical Western theologies which are affiliated with denominations and traditions from which African-American congregations have sought to liberate themselves.

III. The Ethical Challenge That Black Theology Presents to Process Theology

At a November 1985 conference on process theology and the black experience held at the University of Chicago (in partnership with the Center for

Process Studies and Meadville-Lombard Theological Seminary) William R. Jones presented a paper in which he observed that process theology emphasizes the unconditional, indiscriminate, and universal character of God's love in a way that typically fails to indicate that God favors the struggle of the oppressed for liberation from economic, social, and political oppression.[6] Rather than indicating that God sides with the oppressed in their struggle for liberation, process theology seems to place God on everyone's side; and if God sides with everyone, says Jones, then God effectively sides with no one. Thus, from Professor Jones's perspective, black theology cannot find process theology acceptable until it is able to indicate that God is the God of the oppressed rather than merely that God's love is unconditional and universal. If neoclassical theism, like classical theism, is unable to present its vision of God in a way that indicates that God favors the struggle of the oppressed, then the neoclassical alternative will be unacceptable to black theology. Furthermore, Jones stipulates that the "litmus test" for compatibility is process theology's ability to "accommodate counter-violence."[7]

In challenging process theology to state explicitly that God sides with the oppressed, and to do so in a way that does not rule out the possibility of righteous counter-violence, Jones appears to be challenging process theology to explicate the social-ethical consequences of accepting certain metaphysical truths in order that black theology might measure its ethical content against the needs of the struggle for liberation. Broadly conceived, black theology asks not only about the metaphysical status of process theology, but also, and more important, black theology asks if process theology can illuminate social-political ethics in a way that contributes favorably to the liberation struggle.

In the fourth chapter of *Man's Vision of God* — "God and Righteousness" — Hartshorne teaches us how neoclassical theology illuminates ethics in a way that is socially critical and intellectually honest, that is, in a way that is adequate to both ethical and metaphysical criteria. Hartshorne holds that, "In general, the possibility of a theology depends upon the possibility of making our basic conceptions adequate to a supreme instance."[8] Hence, theology can illuminate ethics when ethics stands in critical relationship to an adequate understanding of the supreme instance and "maximal degree" of divine goodness — "perfect love."

In developing a theism which conceives of the supreme instance of goodness in terms of perfect love, Hartshorne argues that this "religious ideal of love" is "not a mere emotional glow toward others," but rather, love is "action from social awareness."[9] Hartshorne says, "The divine love is social awareness and action from social awareness."[10] According to the Hartshornean understanding of perfect love, we might interpret the scriptural command — "Be ye perfect" — to mean that we are commanded to act from a social awareness that is perfectly responsive to the interests of all others, and for the purpose of promoting the greatest liberty for all. Insofar as we fail to sympathize fully with the interests of others and to act accordingly, our love is imperfect, and we are not fully ethical. Hartshorne says that if ethical means "being motivated by concern for the interest of others, then God alone is absolutely ethical."[11] Thus, in Hartshorne's view, ethical status is measured by love, that is, by action from social awareness which takes into account the interests of others. While God alone is absolutely ethical (perfectly loving), we are commanded to be as nearly ethical and as nearly perfect in action from social awareness as we can. Here, then, Hartshorne's theological understanding of the supreme instance of goodness gives us the ideal towards which human ethical behavior must aspire.

From the perspective of black theology, it is important to observe that Hartshorne's account of theological ethics displays a sensitivity characteristic of liberation theologies in general. Hartshorne notes that an important ethical objection to classical theism is that it tends toward a faith that disarms criticism of, and struggle against, predominant social arrangements. Hartshorne describes the propagation of such sentimental faith as "smoothing the path of the oppressor."[12] In contrast to a view of divine love which does not admit that God sides with the oppressed, Hartshorne holds that God favors the creaturely exercise of freedom up to the point where it becomes excessive and is a threat to the freedom of others to pursue their interests. Hartshorne emphasizes "the energy of his [God's] resistance to the excesses of creaturely will at the point where these excesses threaten the destruction of creaturely vitality."[13] Thus, the logic of Hartshorne's conception of divine love is such as to place God decisively on the side of the oppressed in their struggle for liberation.

In the same chapter, Hartshorne rejects dogmatic pacifism by arguing that the religious ideal of love as action from social awareness "seems clearly to include the refusal to provide the unsocial with a monopoly upon the use of coercion."[14]

> Coercion to prevent the use of coercion to destroy freedom generally is in no way action without social awareness but one of its crucial expressions. Freedom must not be free to destroy freedom.[15]

The kind of action from social awareness that is demanded by perfect love is such as must admit the tragic reality that there are people who are genuinely intent upon using their freedom to destroy the freedom of others, and that, under certain circumstances, love itself may dictate that "It is better that many should die prematurely than that nearly all men should live in a permanent state of hostility or slavery."[16] Difficult though it is for humans with imperfect love, the demands of perfect love may, nonetheless, require that we kill an oppressor with whom we have sympathy. Hartshorne says,

> To decide to shorten a man's life (we all die) is not ipso facto to lack sympathy with his life as it really is, that is, to lack love for him.[17]

> To veto a desire is not necessarily to fail literally to sympathize with it; for sympathy only makes the desire in a manner one's own, and even one's own desire one may veto, because of other more valuable desires.[18]

Violent coercion and sympathy are not mutually exclusive. Thus, Hartshorne concludes that "The logic of love is not the logic of pacifism or of the unheroic life."[19]

Hartshorne's theological ethics is consistent with such expressions of black theology which, drawing upon the philosophy of black power, maintain that, under certain circumstances, the oppressed may be compelled to engage in violent struggle against an oppressor. We see, then, that Hartshorne's theology can be acceptable to black theology insofar as it does not smooth the path of the oppressor by disarming the oppressed, and also in that Hartshorne's vision of God supports the basic affirmation of all black and liberation theologies — that God sides with the oppressed in their struggle for liberation.

IV. The Theological Challenge That Black Theology Presents to Process Theology: The God of the Oppressed Is Greater than the Universal God of All

The challenge that black theology presents to the neoclassical alternative is sometimes formulated in this way: How is it possible to reconcile the so-called "particular" vision of God as the God of the oppressed (G-of-O) with the so-called "universal" vision of God as the God of all-embracing love (G-of-A)? In more Hartshornean language, the question is this: How does one reconcile the apparently restrictive theological assertion that God favors the struggle of the oppressed with apparently nonrestrictive neoclassical assertions — for example, that God is "the subject of all change?"[20] It is commonly said by critics of black theology that the conceptions of God which stress the universality of divine love are incompatible with the conception of God as God of the oppressed, because the latter conception is insufficiently comprehensive. This writer is not aware that Hartshorne, or any other neoclassical/process theologian, has given explicit attention to this matter.

Dialogue between black and neoclassical theology will be helped somewhat if an African-American perception is offered indicating the way in which it is possible to conceive without contradiction or confusion that God is both the subject of all change (G-of-A), and the God of the oppressed (G-of-O). That one should care to reconcile G-of-A with G-of-O is typically African-American. Throughout history, from the secret beginnings of the "invisible institution," through the second great schism and reformation up to the present, African-American religion has affirmed simultaneously both conceptions of God.

Social Analysis Informing Theology: A Case History Approach

Frederick Douglass is an illuminating example. Douglass (1817–1895) was an African Methodist Episcopal Zion (AME Zion) clergyman[21] who was born into slavery. He escaped from slavery and joined the abolitionist struggle as an internationally known orator, fund raiser, newspaper publisher, and editor.

Douglass wrote a letter to the man who had once been his slave master in which he said that God is the God of all, the God of master and slave alike, that God is "our common Father and Creator."[22] In the same letter Douglass wrote that God is—in Douglass's own words—"the Most High, who is ever the God of the oppressed."[23] Here, and in other writings Douglass expresses a traditional African-American commitment to both G-of-A and G-of-O.

The question of how to reconcile indiscriminate and all-embracing love with siding with the oppressed is one that Douglass gave attention to in his May 12, 1846 speech at Finsbury Chapel in Moorfield, England. On this occasion, Douglass was asking "the people of Britain" to join the struggle against American slavery. In order for his appeal to be successful Douglass knew he would have to reconcile a certain pious regard for the well-being of slaveowners with supporting the slaves' struggle for liberation. The audience at Finsbury Chapel would want to know how it was possible to side with the oppressed without being against the oppressor. Douglass argued that they should support the abolition of slavery not only because slavery was not in the best interest of African slaves, but also because slavery was not really in the best interest of slave owners and Americans in general.

In his life as a slave who was passed from one owner to another in the manner of chattel property, Douglass saw firsthand how becoming a slaveholder could alter one's existence. Here are two examples that Douglass offers on this point:

> Mrs. Auld [was] . . . a most kind and tender-hearted woman . . . on enter-ing upon the career of a slaveholding mistress . . . When I went into their family, it was the abode of happiness and contentment. Slavery soon proved its ability to divest her of these excellent qualities, and her home of its early happiness. Conscience cannot stand much violence.[24]

> A change had taken place, both in Master Hugh, and in his pious and affectionate wife. The influence of brandy and bad company on him, and the influence of slavery and social isolation upon her, had wrought dis-astrously upon the characters of both.[25]

Douglass summarized the influence of slavery upon the slaveholders by say-ing that "slavery can change a saint into a sinner, and an angel into a demon."[26] Therefore, Douglass maintained that slavery had a corrosive influence upon the "character" and general well-being of the slaveowner and of the whole slaveholding community, and that therefore the British could be appealed to "as strongly by their regard for the slaveholder as for the slave, to labor in this cause."[27] There is here an implicit distinction between the apparent self-interest of the slaveholder and the real self-interest of the slaveholder which allowed Douglass to maintain that it was genuinely in the best interest of the slaveholder that slavery be abolished.

We might add also that another corrosive influence upon the character of the oppressor is the kind of self-deception into which an oppressor is driven in order to maintain his/her self-image. One has only to examine statements by slaveholders to the effect that their activity was for the purpose of Christianizing Africans who would otherwise spend eternity in hell to see the tortuous self-deceptions to which slaveholders were subject. To be held in similar regard are statements by white South Africans who seek to convince us that apartheid is in the best interest of colored and black peoples, as well as statements by American entrepreneurs who argue that they have invested in South Africa for the purpose of enhancing the standard of living for black workers. Douglass is correct. Insofar as the oppressor is driven to such colossal acts of self-deception, oppression does indeed corrode the character of the oppressor.

A similar testimony is provided by another African-American abolitionist — William Wells Brown (1814–1884). Brown's life parallels that of Douglass in that he too was born into slavery and escaped to become an abolitionist, writer, and orator, who gave nearly a thousand lectures favoring the abolitionist cause in England, Ireland, Scotland, Wales, and France. Like Douglass, during his career as a slave Brown was the chattel property of several families, and he also recorded that being a slaveholder had a corrosive influence upon the character and well-being of the slaveholders and their families. In particular, Brown noted the damaging influence of slavery upon the children of slaveowners. To this end, Brown quoted from a 1788 letter by Thomas Jefferson in which Jefferson said:

> The parent storms, the child looks on, catches the lineaments of wrath, puts on the same airs in the circle of smaller slaves, gives loose to his worst passions; and, thus nursed, educated and daily exercised in tyranny, cannot but be stamped by it with odious peculiarities.[28]

William Wells Brown, Frederick Douglass, Thomas Jefferson, and many others have observed that slavery was contrary to the genuine self-interest of slaveholders, their families, and the surrounding community. Thus, the abolitionists maintained that siding with the oppressed in their struggle for liberation is also being for, rather than against, the genuine well-being of the oppressors and the community of oppression.

Theological and Ethical Implications

That siding with the oppressed can also be siding for the oppressor has obvious theological implications. The God who is "our common Father and Creator" (G-of-A) can also be "the God of the oppressed" in that siding with the oppressed in their struggle for liberation is genuinely in the best interest of all.

We can represent these theological reflections in the form of two deductions which show that, given the reality of oppression, the G-of-A must be the G-of-O.

First Deduction:

1) God experiences all experience.[29] (G-of-A)
2) African-Americans have suffered from oppression.
3) To suffer from oppression entails a desire to be liberated from such suffering.
4) God experiences the suffering of the oppressed.
5) Therefore, God desires the liberation of the oppressed. (G-of-O)

Second Deduction:

1) God experiences all experience. (G-of-A)
2) Anglo-Americans have been oppressors.
3) Being an oppressor entails a corrosion of one's character and well-being as well as that of one's community.
4) God experiences the corrosion of the oppressor's well-being.
5) Therefore, God desires that the oppressor cease being an oppressor. (G-of-O)

It is only by inserting a contingent statement—given the reality of oppression—that a nonrestrictive theological statement—say, for example, that God is the subject of all change—can come to entail what this writer wishes to call a "restrictive yet necessary statement"—that God is the God of the oppressed. Strictly speaking, that God is the God of the oppressed is not "necessary" in the sense in which metaphysical necessity is opposed to contingency; however, given the reality of oppression, that God be G-of-O is not a factual contingency in the sense that God could fail to be the G-of-O. In that God is the subject of all change, if oppression is among the changes to which God is subject, then God cannot fail to desire the liberation of the oppressed. But, of course, oppression is a contingent reality. Thus, while strictly speaking, the conjunction of a contingent statement—that oppression is real—with a metaphysically necessary statement—that God is G-of-A—yields what is technically another contingent statement—that God is G-of-O; there is a certain undeniable ineluctability about the truth that if oppression is real, then God cannot fail to be G-of-O, which compels me to indicate its ineluctable character by saying that it is "restrictive yet necessary" (and here necessary does not mean metaphysical necessity). This is somewhat analogous to Hartshorne's language of "hypothetical necessity." In any event, without the insertion of a contingent statement affirming the reality of oppression, it would seem impossible to bridge the gap between a nonrestrictive theological assertion and the characteristic and partially restrictive assertion of black theology—that God favors the struggle of the oppressed for liberation.

The status of a strictly metaphysical assertion taken alone, or only in combination with other strictly metaphysical assertions, is a matter about which black theology and most other theologies of liberation have shown little interest, and this is so for the best of reasons. The obvious reason is that strictly metaphysical assertions are, in regard to ethics, singularly uninteresting. If, according to neoclassical metaphysics, a properly metaphysical assertion is one that is affirmed by every actual and every conceivable fact,[30] then it would follow that nothing actual or conceivably actual is contradicted by a metaphysical assertion so that, in the words of Ivan Karamazov, "all things are lawful." But if, on the other hand, the metaphysical assertion that God is the subject of all change is conjoined with an assertion of the reality of oppression, then we can deduce that God favors the struggle against oppression, and that there are theological reasons for holding that some things are lawful and some not lawful. It is at this point that neoclassical metaphysics becomes relevant to ethics generally, and to the liberation agenda of black and liberation theologies, in particular.

The principles of method outlined by Charles Hartshorne in *Creative Synthesis and Philosophic Method* are entirely consistent with our liberation agenda. For example, Hartshorne says, "Philosophy has two primary responsibilities: to clarify the nonempirical principles and to use them, together with relevant empirical facts, to illuminate value problems of personal and social life."[31] Thus, the central challenge posed by black theology is that neoclassical metaphysics consider the realities of oppression as among the most important, if not *the most important* of the relevant empirical facts to be used together with nonempirical principles for the illumination of value problems of personal and social life. The varied circumstances of oppression have been too seldom among the relevant empirical facts considered by neoclassical thought. From the perspective of most of the world's people, the reality of suffering from oppression is not one fact among a great many others; rather, it is *the fact* of social existence to which so many others are subordinate. The challenge is, then, not a contrary view but, rather, a stimulus to follow through with the neoclassical logic in ways that further illuminate the problems faced by the world's oppressed majority.

Perhaps the most important theological point in this essay is that neoclassical theism, according to its own principles of method, must—given the reality of oppression—join black theology in affirming a certain priority for the conception of God as God of the oppressed. While, on the one hand, many critics of black theology regard the vision of God as God of the oppressed as an insufficiently comprehensive vision of God, Hartshorne's theism, on the other hand, must insist that the partially restrictive and partly contingent vision of God as God of the oppressed is *more inclusive* than any abstract vision of God as merely the universal God of all. In *Creative Synthesis and Philosophic Method,* Chapter V, "Some Principles of Method," Hartshorne argues that, in accordance with the principles of formal logic, "the necessary cannot include the contingent, and that the total truth, assuming there are both contingent and necessary truths, must be contingent."[32] In the same way that "Becoming includes Being, as the contingent includes the necessary,"[33] black theology maintains that its vision of God as G-of-O includes the abstract vision of God as the G-of-A, while the converse cannot be true. Therefore, the vision of God as G-of-O is greater than and altogether inclusive of the vision of God as the G-of-A. Insofar as the logic of Hartshorne's neoclassical theism requires us to affirm the priority of G-of-O over any wholly abstract vision of God, neoclassical theism is to this considerable extent more in accord with black theology than are most Western orthodox and neo-orthodox theologies.

V. Hartshorne's Social Conception of the Self from the Perspective of Black Theology

Among the most important of the classical Western notions that is challenged by neoclassical thought is what may be called the Western conception of the atomic individual. In *Creative Synthesis and Philosophic Method* Hartshorne says, "Our whole Western tradition is warped and confused by the concept of individual taken as ultimate."[34] Hartshorne understands the philosophical conception of the individual taken as ultimate to be an unfortunate consequence of an erroneous "substance theory." According to neoclassical metaphysics, there are, strictly speaking, no enduring substances. Rather than speaking of individuals, things, and substances, metaphysical exactness demands that we speak of "event-sequences or Whiteheadean 'societies.' "[35] Hartshorne's philosophy of "event pluralism" allows that "highly-ordered sequences of events" which normal discourse abstractly calls a self or individual to be properly recognized as a society of events participating in a larger society of events. Thus, Hartshorne opposes the classical Western conception of the atomic individual as ultimate with a social conception of the self, and indeed, with a social conception of all reality.

Black theology, insofar as it draws upon traditional African resources, also stands opposed to the classical Western conception of the atomic individual. This is so because the traditional African conception of human existence is primarily social rather than individual. On this point, John Mbiti is our teacher. He says:

> In traditional life, the individual does not and cannot exist alone except corporately. He owes his existence to other people, including those of past generations and his contemporaries. He is simply part of the whole. The community must therefore make, create or produce the individual; for the individual depends on the corporate group. . . . Only in terms of other people does the individual become conscious of his own being, his own duties, his privilege and responsibilities toward himself and towards other people. When he suffers, he does not suffer alone but with the corporate group; when he rejoices, he rejoices not alone but with his kinsmen. . . . Whatever happens to the individual happens to the whole group, and whatever happens to the whole group happens to the individual. The individual can only say: "I am, because we are: and since we are, therefore I am."[36]

Mbiti describes this as "a cardinal point in the understanding of the African view of man."[37] Mbiti's point is buttressed by another native African theologian, Gwinyai H. Muzorewa, who says, "Most African scholars agree that in traditional religion humanity is to be conceived as 'being in relation.' "[38]

Black theology agrees with Hartshorne against classical Western thought also insofar as black theology appropriates a traditional African view of the cross-generational character of ethical responsibility. The cross-generational character of African ethical thought is a consequence of its social conception of human existence. John S. Pobee teaches us in the "African World View" that the basic unit of African society is the family, and that the family "consists of the living, the dead, and the yet-to-be-born."[39] Thus, according to the traditional African vision, a person is not defined as an atomic individual, but as a member of an extended social community that stretches across generations — past, present, and future. The ethical implication is that moral responsibility is not confined to consequences which obtain for only our contemporaries in the present generation. A member of African society has a moral responsibility in regard to past generations to venerate the ancestors; a moral responsibility in regard to the present generation to consider the well-being of his/her contemporaries throughout the community; and a moral responsibility in regard to future generations to create conditions which serve the well-being of those who are called "the beautiful ones" by Ayi Kwei Armah in his classic novel — *The Beautiful Ones Are Not Yet Born.*[40]

From the perspective of those who see ethics in such cross-generational terms as never to neglect the well-being of the not-yet-born, nothing is more strikingly characteristic of Western ethics than its failure to concern itself with the beautiful ones. Typically, Western ethics, on account of its atomic individualism, is governed by considerations which extend not much beyond the immediate difficulties of a single generation. This is, in fact, one of the reasons that Western ethics has been so unable to deal adequately with long-term ecological difficulties. In contrast to the classical Western neglect of the beautiful ones, there is the Hartshornean theory of "contributionism" which, like traditional African thought, maintains that, given a social conception of human existence, "the rational aim of the individual must in principle transcend any mere good of that individual."[41] Hartshornean contributionism emphasizes the need to contribute to future life, that is, to the well-being of the beautiful ones. Here we find that, unlike classical Western theology, neoclassical thought affirms the traditional African wisdom which informs the social thought of black theology.

VI. Black Power and Process Thought

It is a historical fact that the philosophy of black power is one of the resources which has shaped black theology.[42] Insofar as black theology remains consistent with the philosophy of black power, it cannot but welcome a metaphysics which conceives that freedom has a metaphysically necessary aspect. Hartshornean metaphysics conceives that freedom is inherent in all existence. For Hartshorne, to be actual at all is to be an instance of "creative synthesis," and this means to have power to be partially determinative of self and others, as well as to have the capacity to be partly determined by other selves. Thus, insofar as Hartshorne conceives that freedom, power, and creativity are necessary aspects of all existence, neoclassical thought can be received as a metaphysical account of the philosophy of black power.

The philosophy of black power insists that, given the reality of oppression, there will be struggle against oppression. One of the founders of the contemporary philosophy of black power is Kwame Turé (Stokely Carmichael). Turé says that no matter how overwhelming the might of the oppressor, it is in the very nature of the people that they will struggle and struggle and struggle for as long as they are oppressed until at last they achieve their liberation.[43] Similarly, Vincent Harding's history—*There is a River*—emphasizes the inevitability of the African-American struggle for liberation.[44] From Harding we learn that while the meaning of liberation and the character of the struggle are variable, the fact that there will be struggle against oppression is a constant. Thus, for the African newly chained to the deck of a ship anchored at a West African harbor, the meaning of liberation and the character of the struggle are very different from that of the African-American who, three generations later, like Frederick Douglass and William Wells Brown, must consider how best to conduct an abolitionist campaign. We might add that the meaning of liberation and the character of the struggle were yet and again different for young Huey Newton (founder of the Black Panther Party) as he lay handcuffed and under armed guard even while in surgery as the result of having been shot by two policemen in 1967. Thus, Vincent Harding, Kwame Turé, Winnie Mandela, and many others have spoken in accordance with the philosophy of black power in maintaining that when there is oppression, there will also be some form of protest and struggle for liberation.

The late Howard Thurman once described this necessary aspect of the struggle for liberation by using an analogy from nature.[45] Thurman recalled that on one occasion during his childhood in Daytona Beach, he happened upon a tiny green snake crawling along a dirt path. In the mischievous way that is typical of a boy child, he pressed his bare foot on top of the little snake. Immediately, the little snake began to struggle to free itself. Young Thurman felt the tremor of the snake's struggle as it vibrated up his leg and through his body. Thurman reasoned that it is divinely given to the nature of all creatures, even little green snakes, to struggle and protest against oppression.

The necessity of struggle against oppression can also be described through the use of neoclassical resources. Moreover, Hartshornean thought must grant the truthfulness of the philosophy of black power when it insists that, under certain conditions, those who support the struggle may rightfully engage in armed resistance to oppression. Black power philosophy, and therefore black theology, can find neoclassical metaphysics acceptable, also insofar as each perceives that powerlessness is contrary to the just demands of any people for fully human existence. The agreement between black power and neoclassical philosophies can, therefore, be symbolized by transforming the black power slogan—"Power to the People"—into a more neoclassical formulation—"Creative Synthesis to the People"; and, reciprocally, the neoclassical philosophy of creative synthesis can be understood as a metaphysical way of saying "Power to the People."

VII. Black Power, Liberation Theology, Black Theology, and Black Neoclassical Social Ethics

From African-American sources we have learned a most important lesson for all social anthropology and theology: that given the reality of oppression, there will be struggle against oppression by the oppressed, and by the God of the oppressed who is not less than the God of all creation.

The socioanthropological point — that there will be struggle against oppression — is the first principle of the philosophy of black power. The philosophy of black power as currently expressed by Africans of the front-line states in southern Africa and in Azania–South Africa has as its popular motto, "the struggle continues." The struggle, according to black power philosophy, necessarily continues because the oppressed cannot fail to struggle for their liberation. Moreover, black power philosophy's first principle is marked by a concurrent principle of faith which is the conviction that "the cause" of liberation will eventually triumph over the structures of oppression, that, in more familiar words, "we shall overcome."

The theological point — that there will be struggle against oppression by God — is the first principle of liberation theology. Latin American liberation theology holds that God strives to set the captives free, that God is "the liberator" of the poor and the oppressed. Clearly, African-American theology is also a liberation theology. Moreover, this first principle of liberation theology also has its concurrent principle of faith which is the conviction that God will be victorious in his struggle for the liberation of the oppressed; that, in more familiar words, "God never fails."

The union of the socioanthropological point with the theological point (inclusive of their respective first and concurrent principles) is characteristic of virtually all black theology. The struggle continues. We shall overcome. God seeks the liberation of the poor and oppressed. God never fails. The beautiful ones are not yet born. The systematic formulation of this cluster of convictions from the perspective of the African and African-American struggle is the essential stuff of black theology.

When black theology seeks to think prescriptively, that is, when black theology engages in systematic social ethics, in addition to the use of specifically African and religious resources, there is also the possibility of employing neoclassical resources. We have already seen that Hartshornean resources are particularly credible in that Hartshorne affirms much of the indigenous wisdom of traditional African[46] and black power philosophies, and also in that Hartshorne, like black theology, rejects much of the prevailing Western theological tradition. Furthermore, we have observed that social ethics generally can be characterized by the use of at least two main resources: first, reflection upon a particular social context, and second, reflection upon a more general system of anthropological and philosophical theological presuppositions. If social ethics were done from the perspective of black experience and religion, and if its primary resource— reflection upon the concrete, particular, and contingent features of African and African-American social reality—were used in combination with deliberate reflection upon the universal and necessary features of all social reality as formulated by Hartshornean metaphysics; then this would be "a black neoclassical social ethics."

Reflection upon the social context of black experience in combination with reflection upon the necessary features of all social existence should enable black theology to pursue even more realistic, righteous, and liberating behavioral prescriptions; that is to say, such a combination should enable black theology to do even better social ethics. And conversely, we have seen that a combination of this sort can enable neoclassical metaphysics to become what it could not otherwise be — ethically significant. Thus, our effort to bring black and process theologies into creative synthesis can further the social-ethical utility of both, and this is especially significant since, from the perspective of black theology, it is service to the struggle for liberation that best measures the value of any philosophy or theology.

NOTES

1. "Ethics" is the study of prescriptions and descriptions of human behavior. Sometimes ethics focuses mainly upon individual behavior, that is, upon the moral aspects, or do's and don'ts, that prescribe individual behavior. At other times ethics focuses mainly upon the behavior of human groups or collectives, such as families, tribes, churches, states, political parties, nations, races, and so on. And this we call "social ethics." When social ethics is done from a deliberately Christian perspective, it may be called "Christian social ethics," or "systematic social ethics." Systematic social ethics is "systematic" in approximately the same sense that specifically Christian theology is called "systematic theology." We recognize, of course, that some social analysts and theologians prefer not to speak of specifically Christian social ethics.

2. See "Ethics of Universal Wholeness: An Assessment of the Work of Preston N. Williams," by William M. Finnin, Jr., *The Iliff Review,* vol. 36, no. 2 (Spring, 1977). Here Finnin notes that for Preston Williams, the starting point of his social ethics is the black experience, and that Williams's social ethics has reference to certain anthropological and theological presuppositions. Finnin describes the anthropological presupposition operating in Williams's social ethical thought as the primacy of inclusive human community as a model for understanding human nature; and, Finnin describes Williams's theological presuppositions as the "non-exclusive God" of the Christian tradition.

3. James H. Cone, *Black Theology and Black Power* (New York: Seabury Press, 1969).

4. James H. Cone, *God of the Oppressed* (New York: Seabury Press, 1975).

5. Bishop William J. Walls, *The African Methodist Episcopal Zion Church: Reality of the Black Church* (Charlotte, N.C.: A.M.E. Zion Publishing House, 1974).

6. William R. Jones, "Process Theology: Guardian of the Oppressor or God to the Oppressed? Insights from Liberation Theology." A paper presented at a conference on process theology and the black experience at the University of Chicago (and in partnership with the Center for Process Studies and Meadville/Lombard Theological Seminary), November 9, 1985.

7. Jones, "Process Theology," 17.

8. Charles Hartshorne, "God and Righteousness," chapter 4 in *Man's Vision of God and the Logic of Theism* (Hamden, Conn.: Archon Books, 1964, [1941]), 144.

9. Ibid., 166.
10. Ibid., 173.
11. Ibid., 162.
12. Ibid., 165.
13. Ibid., 173.
14. Ibid.
15. Ibid.
16. Ibid.
17. Ibid., 168.
18. Ibid., 166-167.
19. Ibid, 173.
20. For Hartshorne, metaphysical statements are "nonrestrictive"; whereas ordinary factual statements are "partially restrictive" (see *Creative Synthesis and Philosophic Method)*. For example: if one says, "The black liberation flag is red, black, green, and gold," this is a partially restrictive statement in that its affirmation includes the denial of some other possible facts, that is, "the liberation flag is red, white, and blue." If, on the other hand, one says, "Something exists," this is a nonrestrictive statement in that its affirmation includes the denial of no actual or conceivable actual facts. To affirm that God sides with the oppressed is to deny that there are no oppressed, and also to deny that God fails to side with them.
21. Walls, 150.
22. Frederick Douglass, *My Bondage and My Freedom* (New York: Arno Press and the *New York Times,* 1969), 427.
23. Ibid., 422.
24. Ibid., 152-153.
25. Ibid., 183.
26. Ibid., 142.
27. Ibid., 417.
28. From Lucille Schulberg Warner's *From Slave to Abolitionist: The Life of William Wells Brown* (New York: Dial Press, 1976).
29. That "God experiences all experience" is another way of saying "God is the subject of a change."
30. Charles Hartshorne, *The Logic of Perfection and Other Essays in Neoclassical Metaphysics* (LaSalle Open Court, 1962). Metaphysical truths may be described as such that no experience can contradict them, but also that any experience must illustrate them (p. 296).
31. Charles Hartshorne, *Creative Synthesis and Philosophic Method* (New York: University Press of America, 1983; 1970), xiv.
32. Ibid., 84.
33. Ibid.
34. Ibid., 190.
35. Ibid., 204
36. John S. Mbiti, *African Religions and Philosophy* (Garden City, N.Y.: Anchor Books, 1979), 32.
37. Ibid., 141.
38. Gwinyai Muzorewa, *The Origins and Development of African Theology* (Maryknoll, N.Y.: Orbis Books, 1985), 17.
39. John S. Pobee, "African World View" (Chapter 3), *Toward an African Theology* (Nashville, Tenn.: Abingdon, 1979), 49.
40. Ayi Kwei Armah, *The Beautiful Ones Are Not Yet Born* (New York: Collier Books, 1969). Also, see Ngugi wa Thiong'o's *Petals of Blood* (New York: E. P. Dutton, 1978).
41. John B. Cobb and Franklin I. Gamwell, eds., *Existence and Actuality: Conversations with Charles Hartshorne* (Chicago: University of Chicago Press, 1984), 188.
42. See James Cone's *Black Theology and Black Power* (New York: Seabury Press, 1969).
43. Paraphrasing Kwame Turé's speech at Southern Methodist University in Dallas, Texas, 23 October 1986.

44. Vincent Harding, *There is a River: The Black Struggle For Freedom in America* (New York: Harcourt Brace Jovanovich, Inc., 1981).

45. Howard Thurman narrated this story from his youth on the occasion to his visit to Livingstone College in Salisbury, North Carolina, during the spring of 1978.

46. For a treatment of the indigenous African wisdom regarding existence after death as compared to classical and Hartshornean views on immortality, see my essay "Hartshorne's Neoclassical Theism from the Perspective of Black Theology," in Santiago Sia, ed. *Charles Hartshorne's Concept of God: Critical Responses.* (Birmingham, Ala.: Martinus Nijhoff).

4

BLACK THEOLOGY AND THE YEAR 2000: THREE BASIC ETHICAL CHALLENGES

Riggins R. Earl, Jr.

Black theology now has a marginal place in the White academy as a result of James Cone, Gayraud Wilmore, J. Deotis Roberts[1] and others daring to challenge the racist presuppositions of White theology. Lasting longer than any White seance of higher education could have foretold, Black theology now faces the most critical moment of its existence. That moment being that its advocates must work to make Black theology an integral part of academic discourse without compromising its prophetic side. Put in the form of a question, we must ask: Can Black theologians maintain creative tension between Black theology's prophetic duties and its pedagogical ones?

In the last two decades an intentional effort has been made to increase the number of Black Americans with Ph.D. degrees in religious studies and theology. This preparatory effort has proven indispensable to the formal perpetuation of Black theology. A noticeable increase of Black scholars in such a field as Bible has broadened the scope of Black theological and religious inquiry. This has enabled Black theologians to better challenge White architects and planners of educational curricula to be both ethically and politically sensitive to the God-talk of all ethnic others.

Black theology, as social protest, has dared challenge the White Western assumption that all academic theology must be construed as only a cerebral exercise of inquiry and reflection. This challenge might be characterized as Black theology's prophetic, as opposed to priestly, stage of development. Black social protest theologians have given little critical attention to the fact that the very nature of all social protest theology tends to defy institutionalization. A classical contemporary illustration of this fact might be seen in Coretta Scott

Riggins R. Earl, Jr., is Professor of ethics and society at the Interdenominational Theological Center, Atlanta, Georgia.

King's failure, following Martin Luther King, Jr.'s death, to institutionalize her husband's dream of freedom.[2] Institutionalization defiance begs the questions: To what extent can Black protest theology be curricularized in seminaries, colleges, and universities without compromising its prophetic edge? What social value can be expected from pedagogical theology?

Despite these questions, there is an inevitable need for the pedagogical side of Black theology to serve as a balancing corrective of its social protest side. This is necessary in the academy where the science of instruction takes pre-eminence over social protest. Black protest theology will always be needed as long as racism, classism, and militarism continue to devalue the sacred worth of any persons. Given this undeniable fact, Black theologians must remain critically conscious of the dual need for Black theology to function both pro-phetically and pedagogically. Black protest theologians must rely upon the crit-ical thought of pedagogues of the academy for assistance in the rational clarification of their social goals. Many of the followers of Martin L. King, Jr., often failed, following his death, to heed this fact—sacrificing the need for the rational clarification of their actions for fiery emotionalizing rhetoric. During his lifetime, on the other hand, King rightly used the work of academic peda-gogues to inform his social protest strategy.

The basic thesis here is that the pedagogical aspect of Black theology faces three inevitable ethical challenges in the future: a) the communication chal-lenge; b) the institutional challenge; and c) the methodological challenge. It will be helpful to examine these challenges in the order delineated.

The Communication Challenge

Black theology was initially heard as an unknown tongue in the halls of White higher education even by the professional translators of dead languages. Over-coming this communication barrier has been part of the history of premier Black theologians' interpretive attempts to communicate the religious experiences of Black people. Most White intellectuals dismissed Black protest theology as no more than another one of Blacks' emotional outbursts during the tumultuous decades of the sixties and seventies. They were satisfied that such unconven-tional rhetoric would soon dissipate with the shifting winds of ideological change that were blowing across America's social landscape. Despite their wishful thinking, Black protest theology has challenged the very epistemological pre-supposition of White theological education. It has done so by claiming that talk about God's liberating power in America must be construed in a Black genre since the God of biblical faith is the liberator of the oppressed. This God can only be known by the oppressed, especially the suffering Black people. Black protest theology dared challenge Whites' claim to know God apart from their ethnic others of the Black community.

Black church leadership was not without its critics of Black theology. Many leaders thought such rhetoric bordered on madness because it countered what they had understood to be the ideal language about God's actions and nature.

How was it possible to tell Black clerics, who had proudly proclaimed God as being without color, that Black God-talk was a reality? Or, that authentic God-talk must speak of God as identifying with the Blackness of Black people? This was the equivalent of saying that God, incarnate in Jesus, took on the ethnic identity of the victimized of history. Such rhetoric about God challenged their historical assumptions about the place of Blackness in the value system of divine aesthetics.

Born outside of the margins of academic acceptability, it stands to reason that Black theology would inherently have a communication problem. Professional students of such mainline theologians as Karl Barth and Paul Tillich assumed that God was beyond such conceptual sociological terms as either race, gender, or class. Their primary presupposition was that Eurocentric theology, being what they believed was the truest intellectual reflection about God, transcended all of our cultural "isms" of social alienation. Black Americans, studying in predominately White seminaries before the birth of Black theology, naturally found such language about God valuable for countering white racism. Eurocentric theological language about God understandably dominates the formal writings of social protest theologians such as Martin L. King, Jr.[3]

Black protest theology's abrupt entry into the halls of formal academic discourse forced the communication issue by challenging the ethical insensitivity of White liberal theologians' use of God-talk. It questioned what had been their uncontested assumption (viewed as a divine right) to name the topics, parameters, and logistical rules of theological and ethical debate. Prior to the emerging of Black protest theology, White theology had benignly neglected any positive contributions by Blacks to the anatomy of theological knowledge. Despite this fact, Black protest theology has made clear to White theology its fragility. Edward Farley has rightly reminded those of us of the modern world of what he terms "the fragility of theological knowledge"[4]

Communicating the prophetic ideals of Black theology to Black church leadership has proven to be more of a difficult task than that of its marginal curricularization in the White academy. Some Black religious leaders have denounced Black protest theology as racist and unchristian. At best, most Black influential church leaders have merely tolerated Black theology's prophetic condemnation of many among them who refuse to be held morally accountable for the community's resources. The bottom line is that most Black church leaders have been slow, and at times even sullen, in their willingness to hear the prophetic message of Black theology's internal critique of their conduct.[5]

An opening scene in Spike Lee's film *Do the Right Thing* profoundly illustrates the ethical nature of the communication problem that Black theology faces both in the White academy and the Black Church. It is a scene of a man, with ear plugs in his ears, standing in the front of a storefront church listening to a radio. The name on the church's marquee is THE JESUS IS THE ONLY WAY BAPTIST CHURCH. In the film the man is given the name Smiley by the kids because he never smiles. In this scene Smiley, who has a speech impediment, stands before the church's marquee holding up a card with the picture of both Malcolm X and Martin King on it. Above the blaring sounds of rock and roll music, Smiley is heard uttering broken utterances regarding the pictures of both Malcolm and Martin. This is the only scene in which THE JESUS IS THE ONLY WAY BAPTIST CHURCH appears. There are, of course, repeated scenes of Smiley standing outside of the window of Sal's Famous Pizzeria in Brooklyn holding up the card with the pictures of Malcolm and Martin on it. In several scenes, Smiley is pointing to the "Wall of Fame" in Sal's pizzeria that has no pictures of Black Americans on it. The fact of 100 percent Black patronage does not change Sal's opinion about placing the pictures of Black heroes or heroines on the "Wall of Fame." For him it must remain exclusively for famous Italian Americans, such as Mickey Mantle and Frank Sinatra. This is the case until the business is destroyed by angry Blacks. It was during this chaos and destruction that Smiley places the picture of Malcolm and Martin on the wall of Sal's pizzeria. Destruction was the price eventually paid for the lack of communications between Blacks and Whites; between Whites and Whites; between Blacks and Blacks; and between the young and the old.[6]

Smiley symbolizes an incoherent prophetic voice crying in the Black urban wilderness of America. His speech impediment is symbolic of the fact that every generation hears the voices of its prophets as being broken and incoherent.[7] Advocates of Black theology stand in this same tradition of rejection both in the Black church community and the White academic community. Black theology will not grow to maturity, if its identity is marginal in both the academy and the Black Church. This marginal identity crisis can only be overcome when Black scholars and church leaders intentionally make a home for Black theology in the Black academic and church communities. This is what I have chosen to call an institutional challenge.

The Institutional Challenge

Black theologians, since Black theology's inception, have preoccupied themselves with proving to White seminary professors and students the academic relevance of the Black religious experience. Such a task has been tantamount, at times, to a language translator with a speech impediment having to translate for a group of aliens who all have a hearing disability. Even in the face of such a communication handicap, none can deny that the energy spent by the pioneer apologists of Black theology for its inclusion in the curriculum of seminary education has been well spent.

Black scholars, however, have spent enough time and energy giving a raison d'être for why Black theology should be a part of White seminaries. It is imperative now that we make the transition to the self-development stage of Black theology that calls for the building of an institutional infrastructure for its graduate academic study in the Black community. Such an academic context would allow Black scholars of theology and religion, who must work in academic communities where White scholars generally have no intellectual interest in

Blacks' experience, a common home. Here junior scholars might enjoy the critical wisdom of senior scholars in the intellectual market of ideational and experiential exchanges. It would provide a formal setting for them to forge their own sophisticated methods of constructive theological reflection.

The above is not a new idea. In the past twenty-five years Black scholars have repeatedly voiced concern informally and formally for a graduate study program of Black religion and theology. Some years ago James Cheek, at the time president of Howard University, appointed a committee to do a feasibility study for such a program at Howard University. Unfortunately, the committee's report never went beyond the recommendation stage. The burden of the actualization of the institutionalization challenge of the academic study of Black theology and Black religion is on the shoulders of senior scholars and progressive church leaders.[8] Failure of this generation of Black scholars to create a graduate center might very well suggest that Black theology is no more than convenient political rhetoric that we have used to gain employment in White schools. That is to say that we see it as being only self-serving. If we understand Black theology to be for the liberation of the Black community, then ethically we must hear its challenging need to be institutionalized in the Black community. Self-serving Black theological rhetoric will be a great disservice to the Black community. It compromises ethnic self-development for the economic reward of White accommodationism. Trying to do Black theology without a strong academic base in the Black community might be tantamount to Moses purporting to do liberation theology of the Israelites from an Egyptian seminary in Egypt. Minus an academic home for doing Black theology in the Black community, it becomes very difficult for students of Black theology to concentrate constructively on its internal needs.

The other side of the problem is that the leadership of Black theological schools has often evaluated itself by what the White community has called "authentic academic theology." One wonders would Cone have been received by some Blacks had he been at a predominantly Black school when he published his first book. The more painful questions are: How committed are Black schools' leadership to the idea of fostering a competitive intellectual environment? How might they make adjustments in teaching expectations when trying to attract research/publishing oriented Black scholars? Will Black school leaders rely upon White schools to set the institutional agenda for Black theology? Nowhere in the country yet has a Black seminary named a professorial chair in honor of James Cone. Will we wait for a White school to do this?

The establishment of a graduate center for the study of Black religion and theology in the academic sector of the Black community will be fundamental for the survival of this movement. This challenge becomes the moral litmus test for Black academicians and religious leaders.

The Methodological Challenge

Black pedagogical theology's survival in the academy will depend on its advocates' willingness to struggle with the relation between methodology and ethics.

Short of informal discussion, Black scholars have made little, if any, commitment to the need for formal discourse on this matter. This has been due, perhaps, to the fact that Black theologians have been primarily concerned to prove Black theology's existence. Recently younger scholars of Black theology and religion, such as George Cummings and Dwight Hopkins, have been more intentional about the relationship between the theoretical method of interpretation and the primary sources of Black people's experiences being interpreted. Hopkins and Cummings, in their introductory remarks to a collection of different scholars' essays on what they subtitled "Black Theology in the Slave Narratives," have observed that Black theology has come to its fourth stage of development. In summary, they characterize the first three stages as: 1) the ad hoc National Committee of Negro Churchmen's Black Power Statement stage; 2) the Society for the Study of Black Religion stage; and 3) the academic stage of Black theology. The fourth and present stage of Black theology is characterized by what the writers have called "an exploration of theology from any and all aspects of Black life, and most strikingly, the cutting edge challenge of womanists (Black female religion scholars) who have pressed for a holistic Black theology that entails an integration of race, class, gender, and sexual orientation analyses."[9]

It is the hope of Cummings and Hopkins, in *Cut Loose Your Stammering Tongue*, "to develop further a method of African-American theology and Black religion where the main resource for Black action and talk about God arises out of the lives and words of poor Black people's faith."[10] They want to recognize as still true both James Cone's emphasis on Christian liberation and Gayraud Wilmore's accent on non-Christian liberation. Cummings and Hopkins raise a critical methodological issue with their readers when they observed: "The question is how to develop further that foundational framework—the unity and distinction between Christian and non-Christian, church and non-church, and theological and religious resources in African-American faith and life."[11] This question is even more critical when discussed in relation to Black liberation in Third-World African nations where Christianity is not the dominant religion. Two examples come to mind. First is that of Blacks of South Africa's liberation efforts from the White apartheid system of that country. In a class that I teach in political theology, I asked one of my students from South Africa why was it that, except for clergy leaders, rarely do Black leaders ever use the name of God in their liberation struggle? His answer was that the very word *God* tends to polarize the liberation struggle among Blacks of his country, rather than unify, because of the different tribal understandings and interpretations. The student's answer was beyond most of our abilities of the Western world to grasp. His answer suggested political unity, intertribal loyalty and trust against White apartheid, were of greater value than God-talk. This notion presents a new methodological challenge for a Black theology that was born out of social and political protest in the American society. Concluding from the South African student's answer, the God of the liberation of Blacks in South Africa is only an ideal observer of the liberation struggle.

The second example can be illustrated by what happened in the Biafran warfare of Nigeria. The presupposition of God as the liberator of Black people is given a new kind of ethical litmus test when applied to this crisis. Especially is this the case when the struggle for freedom is seen through the eyes of the novelist Wole Soyinka. The struggle here is not a case of the Black oppressed struggling against White oppressors; it is a matter of oppressed Black people struggling against their own bestiality. Such examples require Black theology to critically re-examine our theological assumption of what constitutes original sin for oppressed people. It demands that critically new questions be raised about the oppressed individual's role as free agent in the liberation struggle.

Cummings and Hopkins rightly corroborate the problem of hermeneutical method with that of class when Black theology is only an academic exercise. This is particularly the case when Black theology is done by Black professional theologians and religionists of the academy. Cummings and Hopkins raise some sobering questions of professional scholars that will not be wished away: a) What does it mean for a Black theology of liberation if the main authorities for theology are European-Americans? b) How can we move beyond a mode of research and writings that footnotes preponderantly African Americans who talk about the Black oppressed but who themselves are highly educated and middle class? These two scholars have no problem with the need of the professional Black scholar in the academy. They are rightly concerned, however, about professional Black scholars using the materials of their victimized ancestors to promote their privileged position.

Another ethical issue that is equally as great, if not greater, that grows out of the problem of hermeneutical method is that of the possibility for comradery among Black scholars. The question could be asked: Can Black scholars differ ideologically while working as brothers and sisters in the same scholarly community? Or, will we eventually find the need to exclude each other on the bases of academic triviality? An even more poignant question is: To what degree will highly influential Black professional scholars of mainline White schools use their influence to enhance the scholarly mission of predominantly Black schools?

The future viability of Black theology as an academic enterprise will rely extensively on our ability to meet the three basic ethical challenges addressed above. Communication is ethically fundamental to Black scholars' ways of being and relating to each other in the world. The institutionalization of Black theology is ethically basic to Black scholars' self-esteem as makers of the world. Finally, hermeneutical method is ethically crucial to the way in which scholars make value judgments about the experiences of oppressed people.

NOTES

1. James H. Cone became internationally known for his provocative work *Black Theology and Black Power* (New York: Seabury Press, 1969). J. Deotis Roberts became widely known for his book *Liberation and Reconciliation: A Black Theology* (Philadelphia: Westminster Press, 1971). Gayraud Wilmore became widely known for his book *Black*

Religion and Black Radicalism: An Interpretation of the Religious History of Afro-American People, 2d ed. (Maryknoll, N.Y.: Orbis Books, 1983).

2. Here I refer to the dissension Coretta King caused, when she planned and built the King Center.

3. James Cone made a very valuable contribution along the same line. See *Malcolm & Martin* (Maryknoll, N.Y.: Orbis Books, 1991).

4. See Edward Farley, *The Fragility of Knowledge* (Philadelphia: Fortress Press, 1988).

5. See James Cone, *For My People: Black Theology and the Black Church* (Maryknoll, N.Y.: Orbis Books, 1984).

6. Spike Lee with Lisa Jones, *Do the Right Thing* (New York: Fireside/Simon & Schuster, 1989).

7. Karl Barth, *Epistle to the Romans,* translated from the sixth edition by Edwyn C. Hoskyns (New York: Oxford University Press, 1965). Here Barth poetically observes that: "For the voice of the preacher, even though it is pitched in the key of absolute truth, wobbles from note to note, is raucous, croaking and utterly unimpressive. It is, in fact, the cry of a Titan. And whether the preacher himself be good or bad, he simply bears witness to the judgement which hangs over all Titanism. Human exhortation, therefore, is justified only when it is seen to be void of human justification; that is to say, when it is grounded upon the mercies of God" (p. 429).

8. Charles Shelby Rooks, *Revolution in Zion: Reshaping African-American Ministry, 1960–1974* (New York: Pilgrim Press, 1990).

9. Dwight N. Hopkins and George C. L. Cummings, *Cut Loose Your Stammering Tongue: Black Theology in the Slave Narratives* (Maryknoll, N.Y.: Orbis Books, 1991), 13–14.

10. Hopkins and Cummings, *Cut Loose Your Stammering Tongue,* xiv.

11. Hopkins and Cummings, *Cut Loose Your Stammering Tongue,* xv.

5

BLACK THEOLOGY AND A SECOND GENERATION: NEW SCHOLARSHIP AND NEW CHALLENGES

Dwight N. Hopkins

Almost thirty years have passed since the ad hoc National Committee of Negro Churchmen (NCNC) published their theological statement on the Black Power movement in *The New York Times*. Subsequently in 1969, James H. Cone wrote the first and classical text *Black Theology and Black Power*.[1] Both events marked a radical shift in theological studies. NCNC's declaration linked faith in God to urban rebellions and cries for African-American cultural freedom; in other words, American Christianity needed to address the imbalance between power and conscience. Furthermore, Cone's book grounded all of Christianity and talk about God on the liberation of the Black oppressed and the universal poor. Lacking the essential emphasis of Jesus' liberation mission, the White church, therefore, was the anti-Christ.

These pioneering foundations layed by the first generation of Black theologians have provided firm footing for further doing Black theology today. Specifically, the earlier emphases of Cone, Gayraud S. Wilmore, and Charles H. Long offer possibilities for systematically synthesizing the nature of the Black Church's faith in the contemporary period. The heart of Cone's work has centered on the political and structural manifestations of White racism as demonic. If Jesus Christ calls the oppressed African-American community to fight for its liberation, then this faith gathering must wage a battle to deconstruct white supremacist power relations. There can be no participation in God's liberation movement on earth if poor Black folk do not achieve their liberation from visible evil systems created and perpetuated by principalities and powers with White faces.

Dwight N. Hopkins is author of *Shoes That Fit Our Feet: Resources for a Constructive Black Theology* and teaches theology at Santa Clara University in California.

Historically, Wilmore has nuanced theologically more toward the noninstitutional Black church and nonChristian realities of God's justice revelations. God also offers God's self on urban street corners and in nontraditional Black religious faith groups. And with Long, we confront his challenge to recognize how White people have conquered Black religion intellectually. Therefore Long's project seeks God's manifestations in the process of creating new Black ways of thinking religiously. Language, the expression of thought, is reality. Intellectually, African-American religion scholars need to cast aside the theological thought constructs of the White oppressors. The Black religion scholar should dare to pursue the creativity of Black folk faith discourse without the lethal and suicidal baggage of preconceived White theological categories.[2] An ultimate power appears in Black people's own way of talking and thinking.

A systematic Black theology of liberation today requires both the inclusion of first generation faith concerns and more. Essentially it demands a radical interplay of a series of theological interconnections. To do Black theology in the contemporay era calls for at least three guidelines, four relationships, and the use of four types of disciplines.

Three Guidelines

A constructive systematic Black theology of liberation functions within the contours of three guidelines. First, God has called humanity to empower all the earth's poor as a gateway to a universal freedom and a universal theology. From the Bible we learn that the Old Testament story centers around God's involvement with a band of persecuted slaves. In the particularity of these slaves' relation with the holy lies the general oppressed condition. Thus to reconnect with the divine—to re-immerse ourselves in the former right relationship prior to humankind's Fall—we must journey through a God-slavery way. Likewise, the New Testament hinges on the ultimate Christian revelation of Yahweh. That is, Jesus Christ shows clear, conscious intent that God chose to become manifest among specific oppressed strata in the real world, to be born, on the margins of society, in a manger amid cow dung, dirt, and straw. In Jesus, God publicly proclaims a heavenly mission on earth geared to freeing the poor and those victimized by oppression. Jesus, also, posits criteria for entrance into heaven's halls by designating sheep and goats in connection to justice work with the poor. And God, through Jesus, opted to die as a persecuted outlaw, a perceived threat to ruling powers and dominating ecclesiastical and theological authorities. Jesus' crucifixion takes place with two thieves and, lacking any resources, the Anointed One had to be buried in someone else's tomb. Subsequently, the Holy Spirit resumes the work of the Liberator, blowing through old barriers and creating new opportunities for a full humanity out of the flesh and bone and talk and work of the oppressed. Hence, God calls us to empower the poor.

Second, a constructive Black theology has to rely on its own indigenous sources, as foundation, but not exclusively. Black theology has to be based on the faith and religious experiences of the African-American poor, thus accenting liberation and justice for today's least in society. Black theology has a wealth of resources and sources in Black history and life from Africa until today out of which to study and learn about religious practices and construct theology. I make this claim because God is not an abstract floating God in an ethereal land; the holy justice is always and absolutely incarnational. Thus, throughout Black life, historically and today, there existed and has always existed some form of striving for freedom. The most dominant example of such a liberation quest has appeared within the African-American church since slavery. However, the thirst for, belief in, and work of freedom have and continue to appear in noninstitutional church movements. God's brilliancy supersedes human restrictions and offers the presence of grace in diverse global ways. Therefore, because God's loving freedom always comes to us concretely, Black theology looks for signs of the times wherever and whenever the African-American poor are struggling for freedom. Out of this foundation based on "the least of these" (with the Black Church at the center), a sorely needed dialogue and coalition must be pursued with the rest of society.

Third, to begin a theological dialogue, a constructive Black theology should link to Africa, Asia and the Pacific Rim, the Caribbean, and Latin America. For example in Asia we find such Christian theologies as Minjung (in South Korea), Dalit theology (in India), Jesus Christ is a Coconut Tree (in Tonga), and God is Rice (in Japan). In Africa, we perceive instances throughout the continent of African traditional religions that are Christian; we also encounter liberation theology in Cameroon, Zimbabwe, and of course in South Africa. In the Caribbean and Latin America, there are emerging Black consciousness movements that are crafting Black theologies in places such as Cuba, Brazil, and Haiti. All of these global regions are posing similar questions: What does it mean to be a Christian in the specific context of the developing world? Does the future survival of worldwide Christianity and God's revelations in other forms depend on what is happening in Africa, Asia and the Pacific Rim, the Caribbean, and Latin America? A working coalition of people and nations of color can form the hub for a more universal discussion.

Four Relationships

In addition to the three guidelines, a constructive and systematic Black theology of liberation recognizes the importance of four relationships: politics and culture; women and men; Christian and non-Christian; and church and non-institutional church.

Regarding the politics-culture link, faith expressions among the Black poor occur within a contested terrain where systemic power institutions and individuals abound. To ignore this fact would make Black theology stick its head in the sand while structural political power reigns over the folk and persists unchallenged. Thus we need to engage a theology arising out of efforts that find the poor attempting to determine their own space. As we note this political right to self-determination, we also parallel a move toward cultural affirmation. Black culture concerns itself with both identity and lifestyle. Black folk's cultural creativity shines out as self-recognition of God's unique African-American creation, equal to all humanity. Likewise culture speaks to a way of life, ingrained as a unique force of habit (of survival and liberation techniques). And culture may arise from power institutions. But it can become relatively independent and, in turn, affect and determine political systems. Structural power and group identity go together and interpenetrate.

Similarly, Black theology deals with African-American male-female connections because both share equal original creation and both embody resources for liberation. Moreover, Black women comprise at least half of the African-American community and (possibly) close to two-thirds of the Black Church. Both from the perspective of divine justice and mutual interdependent humanity, the faith experiences of women and men must share in and act as sources for constructing theology; both must share in their God-given expressions of political and cultural life. The degree to which poor African-American women (those suffering economic hardship, racial stereotypes, and gender abuse) achieve justice will measure the success or failure of faith in and acceptance and realization of God's plan for poor humanity.

Christian and non-Christian along with church and noninstitutional church communities round out the four relationships. Essentially, because God manifests freedom in faith movements holistically, Christians and the church must evangelize non-Christian and noninstitutional church realities and be evangelized by them. Of course, cross-fertilization evangelization hinges on all the poor's colaboring with God toward realization of an ultimate free kingdom on earth. Here we touch on ecumenical and interfaith dialogue and partnership within the African-American community as well as without.

Four Types of Disciplines

Just as God incarnates within the poor's specificity (hence, three guidelines), and the poor find themselves connected in diverse manners (hence, four relationships), so too does systematic theology find itself involved with the particularity of related disciplines. While interacting with other disciplines, theology seeks to discover how best to get at divine vocation for concrete liberation. For instance, political economy surfaces the issue of power control of politics, culture, and economics. This discipline demands a social analysis of structural interrelations: who has ownership, control, and decision-making power. Political economy is an unmasking of surface rhetoric that obscures the bottom line powerbrokers. After all is said and done, in the real world of people, classes, strata, and so forth, someone or some bodies make decisions about other people's lives. What are these power systems and people? Furthermore, political economy paints the constructive contours of the new democratic society. The new democracy on earth will include communal ownership of all the major industries in a society, whether those industries are economic, cultural, political, or linguistic.

Along with political economy, the discipline of biblical criticism also helps in constructing a Black theology. Source, form, redaction, and textual methodologies should be applied to Scripture itself. Likewise these methodologies must be utilized with instances of how African-American folk understand, use, and appropriate the Bible in their own indigenous lifestyles. Biblical criticism is not an abstract phenomenon. Thus from the perspective of the Bible's poor and that of the Black poor's use of the Bible, we employ biblical criticism.

Literary criticism, a third discipline, aids a three dimensional dialogue engaged by Black theology. In viewing various African-American sources for constructive theology, we seek to interrogate them as texts. Thus one conversation partner is the oral or written text itself; specifically the form and structure of the text within its own cultural and political context. The text's implications are put in dialogue with the text's effects on the readers and listeners (e.g., the second interlocutor); who are also questioned in relation to their own cultural and political context. And finally noting his or her political and cultural context, the author's presuppositions and intentions enter the conversation. Here a method of interpretation (of author-text-reader/listener) primarily helps the unearthing of nuanced theological meanings in poor Black folk's literary and vernacular traditions. In addition to fostering a three way interchange, literary criticism will help to privilege a Black English of the poor.

Comparative religions, the fourth and final discipline, lends itself directly to any efforts at constructing a Black theology from the entire African-American religious experience. Because Christianity (though the dominant form) is not an exclusive faith reflection in Black life, we need methods of comparing other expressions of ultimate convictions. In other words, Christianity, nonChristian institutional religions, and noninstitutional religions pervade Black beliefs about survival and liberation. Within the entire African-American community, there exists a religion embedded in the cultural and political fabric — a religious faith and quest for final justice and freedom. And so to detect such multifaceted contours, we need an instrument that will sound comparative theological notes from different songs with the same liberation faith riff.[3]

Role of the Theologian

Our methodology of doing Black theology with three aspects (e.g., guidelines, relationships, and disciplines) exemplifies an approach to constructive work on indigenous sources. Still a word needs to be said about the path the systematic theologian walks while implementing such a methodology. The theologian, in a word, brings presuppositional intent and vocational obligations. First, the theologian is called to make the church and the community accountable to what God had called the church and community to do as coagents in the current divine kingdom inbreaking for the poor on earth. This calling derives from the Bible, Jesus Christ (e.g., birth, life, death, and resurrection), and God's spirit of a living justice presence today. Second, the theologian places herself or himself in a community of faith. A communal gathering with convictions enables the systematic theologian to discern good and evil. A Christian church or faith group, linked to the theologian, is guided by and serves the interests of the poor. Third, the theologian employs criticism and self-criticism. Criticism signifies a prophetic role vis-à-vis faith groups and the poor. Self-criticism suggests a servant role dimension. There exists a dynamic, loving, and straightforward examination and self-examination where both parties—faith community and theologian—submit to the norm of freedom for the African-American folk and the poor. Finally, the theologian has to work with other African Americans (as a group) and justice-oriented people (in coalition) who labor in other spheres of society and are trained in other professions and jobs. The entire calling of a systematic theologian, we must recall, is not to privilege the theologian's status, but to change the world for the better.

The doing of a systematic Black theology of liberation is in response to God's call to covenant with poor people in a divine-human movement for freedom and full humanity. The theologian responds with more conscious intent. The folk respond instinctively. All the folk have an ultimate concern and dream to which they dedicate their lives and in which they have faith (e.g., it is faith because that which is sought after is not yet totally realized, thus a faith dimension appears for fulfillment). The task of the theologian is to make systematic that which is instinctive. The theologian is called by God to raise critical and self-critical questions about what the church and the community are called by God to preach, say, and do. And the theologian's role is to see if the called church, community, and theologian are practicing their vocations.

Basically, a constructive Black theology of liberation is a mediation between what poor African Americans of faith believe and do by force of habit, on the one hand, and a systematic tradition where oppressed Black folk self-consciously struggle for full humanity in God's divine realm, on the other hand.

Challenges for the Second Generation

Unlike the founders of contemporary Black theology, second generation members face some different challenges. For instance, older scholars literally had to fight for the right of the African-American church and community to think theologically. Prior to the National Committee of Negro Churchmen and Cone's *Black Theology and Black Power*, the juxtaposition of Black religious experience with serious intellectual implications for all of society was considered comic relief if not ignored by the White mainstream. Likewise the mushrooming civil rights and Black Power movements of the 1960s had not made a decisive break with White theology. Thus the first generation employed a passionate intellect that layed the foundation for all African-American religious thought since the late 1960s. The overarching historic significance of the first generation is that it successfully fought for the right of Black theology to exist.

Moreover, in some cases, Black theologians had to literally disrupt White religious and academic institutions as well as remind Black churches of the liberation role of the gospel and the historic prophetic impulse in Black folk's theological and practical heritage. For the founders of Black theology, the main issue was the gospel of freedom for the poor and not concerns for tenure in the academy.

Now the second generation has greater access to tenure, administrative leadership positions, publishers, and funding. The work of the past has moved younger scholars closer to the mainstream. And, consequently, new challenges present themselves. In a word, unlike the pioneers who primarily fought from the outside of the mainstream and who were compelled by and related to the life and death resistance of a larger societal movement, the second generation finds itself somewhat accepted if not fashionable. In the academy the excuse has changed from "there is no such thing as African-American religious thought" to "we want more Black scholars, but there aren't enough."

The persistent and subtle seductions of the academy will remain. However, the second generation of Black theologians can pursue and fulfill our vocational responsibilities in several ways. A crucial thread that should continue to tie all diverse disciplines and perspectives together is clear focus on the poor. The overwhelming majority in the Black Church and community fall within this category. Furthermore, the Christian gospel's emphasis on the bottom of society likewise determines the vocational direction of Black theology. Similarly, such a pro-poor posture will also sharpen the distinctions between a "Black theology of liberation" and an amorphous "Black theology." The former signifies a gospel of good news for all of broken humanity; while the latter tends toward the maintenance of bourgeois privileges. The former fosters social change; the latter preserves the status quo. In the midst of all the writing, teaching, preaching, and organizing, we must ask the question whether we have been faithful in our attempts to empower poor and working class blacks both culturally and politically. A Black theology of liberation is fundamentally a prophetic service.

We also need to write so our families, communities, ancestors, and unborn can understand their roles as the power of the poor in history. In contrast, the academy would have us follow the standard practice that labels the most indirect, obscure writing as the most profound. Unfortunately, this style of communicating usually means only the most formally educated can talk to and among themselves. Our communities, on the other hand, are left wondering what happened to those nice young Black folk who went off into White folks' schools. But when these same promising African Americans from the community bring back books they've written, hardly anyone in their families can read them.

For the poor, language means more than a mere convenient form to convey substance. Language itself is also substance. People's language reveals their faith, backgrounds, hopes, desires, and connection to community. Language tells poor people whether or not the writer comes out of their world or at least takes their world seriously. Language, therefore, serves as a window into the lifestyles and beliefs of the writer, as well as the writer's relation to her or his audience. If the majority of Blacks in our communities and churches are to see themselves in our work, then we must see them when we write. Thus religious language is part of life and should help make unjust relationships just.

In addition to issues of focusing on the poor and liberating language, the second generation of Black theologians faces the challenge of preserving positive and critical ties to the Black Church and other intimate faith organizations. The church is one community that holds us accountable to the liberation faith mandate in the gospel and African-American tradition. The church also helps to nurture our growth. But most of the educational system in the United States, particularly for full-time professors, pulls us away from meaningful organized faith communities. The academy seeks to perpetuate itself. And like all groups, it has established methods to suck professors into its own world. In this world, advancement and staying power depend on how well we give all of our time to publishing, teaching, and serving the academy. Clearly part of the gap between Black professors and the pew results from a well-organized educational system that demands our time. Still, we must maintain creative and critical relationships to the Black Church—whether in the forms of teaching and preaching in the church, associate pastors, leading workshops and seminars, consultants, or regularly sharing our ongoing work with lay people. Faith organizations, especially the Black Church, can help us to both serve the poor and challenge the poor when they fall short of a liberating gospel practice.

Women, too, continue to challenge the vocational tasks of African-American theologians. However, we need to emphasize more the life and death issues of the majority of Black women. This group consists of, at least, poor, working class, unemployed, and/or single heads of households Black women. How can we make their survival and full humanity prominent in our scholarship? Their day to day triple experiences of class exploitation, gender oppression, and racial discrimination can enrich the entire theological focus of Black religious studies. The point of convergence of intense human pain usually provides the most fertile grounds for creative and sustaining theological work.

Furthermore, the historical foundation of African-American religious life in North America compels us to rethink our doing of Black theology today. Particularly, the period of slavery (where Black people were actually forged into "African Americans" and the Black Church began to define itself) and the 1950s and 1960s civil rights and Black Power movements offer a storehouse of traditions, lessons, cultural values, and political strategies for today's Black community. What is in the faith of enslaved Black folk that provided the groundwork for survival and liberation of Black Americans even until today? What happened in the 1950s and 1960s so that the African-American community felt a sense of collective self-worth, transformative values, and a liberation faith inspired movement? The purpose of religious history is to change the world today. Yet, the effort to address unjust relationships in the contemporary period grows out of a historical legacy of Black and White interactions. Since White Europeans carried Africans into the New World in 1619, millions of poor and illiterate Black folk have developed an enduring faith. And such a rock-like faith has looked upon the eyes of the White demonic and survived. Moreover that historical faith has ensured Black positive self-identity and self-determination.

Finally, a large part of Black theology's serving to empower the majority of the African-American community means recognizing the governance of the United States by a monopoly capitalist economic system. This elite profit-oriented order breeds deep governmental distrust and profound wealth disparity. For instance, though it calls itself a democracy, the U.S. government is a caricature. The majority of adults do not register to vote and of those who do, most still do not vote, at least at the national levels. Likewise, roughly 200 White males (and their families) control the majority of wealth. Economically and politically, a handful impacts the fate of tens of millions of Americans. Within this web of warped democratic appearances and real minority control stands 25 to 40 million African Americans, most of whom are at the bottom of America's bottom.

The Twenty-First Century Calls

The second generation of Black theologians continues to produce new scholarship to meet new challenges on the threshold of the twenty-first century. Through the door of the year 2000, we hear the painful but powerful voices of the state of Black America and the cries of our unborn demanding to know what preparations we have made for their births. Basically, the second generation has to integrate a gospel of full humanity, a critical acceptance of African-American religious history, and an understanding of theological, cultural, and political power in the United States today.

But there exist blatant and subtle forces that attempt to negate formally trained intellectuals, the church, and the community from drawing on the potentiality of a radical African-American spirituality and thinking. On the one hand, this occurs when persons in mainstream decision-making positions say no to us or try to coopt our strengths. On the other hand, we trip and fall when we fail to balance the basic prophetic and servant roles in Black theology's vocation. In fact, Black theology has a calling to organize itself at the service of silenced voices. We must listen to and help empower them (and thereby ourselves). Without a faith context and the interest of the majority, we can often seem like a new form of intellectual minstrels performing before White folk's voyeurism in the academy. However, at the same time in our servant role, we shoulder the prophetic and critical responsibility. Not all Black churches are preaching and practicing the Christian gospel of returning all of society's wealth to the poor; thus, to have a Black preacher and Black congregation possibly can mean the propagation of a demonic theology. Service to, love for, and affirmation of the poor and the entire church and the community mean keeping them accountable to what they have been called to say and do. Ultimately, moving toward the twenty-first century, the vocation of the second gen-

eration of Black theologians will help bring about God's justice kingdom on
earth when our faith and works risk a new way of thinking and living now.

NOTES

1. The most recent edition of Cone's book is published by Harper & Row, San
Francisco, 1989. The NCNC statement is found in *Black Theology: A Documentary History,
1966-1979*, ed. Gayraud S. Wilmore and James H. Cone (Maryknoll, N.Y.: Orbis Books,
1979), 23-30.

On the NCNC and the origin and development of Black theology, see James H. Cone,
For My People: Black Theology and the Black Church (Maryknoll, N.Y.: Orbis Books,
1984); Gayraud S. Wilmore, *Black Religion and Black Radicalism: An Interpretation of the
Religious History of Afro-American People* (Maryknoll, N.Y.: Orbis Books, 1983); Gayraud
S. Wilmore and James H. Cone, eds., *Black Theology;* and Dwight N. Hopkins, *Black
Theology USA and South Africa: Politics, Culture, and Liberation* (Maryknoll, N.Y., Orbis
Books, 1989).

2. For critical interpretations of theological debates among the first generation of
African-American theologians, see James H. Cone's "Epilogue: An Interpretation of the
Debate among Black Theologians," in Wilmore and Cone, *Black Theology*, and Dwight
N. Hopkins, *Black Theology USA and South Africa*.

3. On the various liberation faith motifs found in Black Christian and nonChristian
practices, and the interplay of faith expressed in political and cultural Black life and
belief, see Gayraud S. Wilmore, *Black Religion and Black Radicalism*, and Dwight N.
Hopkins, *Shoes That Fit Our Feet: Sources for a Constructive Black Theology* (Maryknoll,
N.Y.: Orbis Books, 1993).

6

NEW VOICES IN BLACK THEOLOGY: THE AFRICAN-AMERICAN STORY AS A SOURCE OF EMANCIPATORY RHETORIC

George C. L. Cummings

The challenge of the first generation of Black theologians in the United States in the 1960s was to confront the hegemony of a European-American White theological perspective that had for centuries equated European-American White privilege and power with the omnipotence of God, and to establish a theological basis for the development of a Black theological discourse that was derived from the history, culture, and religion of African-American people. From its inception, then, Black theology had as its central concern the identification of racism and racist values within theology and the church, as well as the establishment of a new paradigm for the evolution of Black theological discourse. Thus, while the first generation of Black theologians established a broad basis for a critique of White Christian institutions and religions, declared their independence from their White Christian counterparts, and made the establishment of a theology that was accountable to the Black experience their focal point, it became the task of the second generation of Black theologians to further elaborate on the specific character of a Black theology. In recent years new voices have emerged to continue the work begun by the earlier pioneers and to further elaborate the specific contours of a contemporary Black theology.[1]

While the first generation developed the broad outlines of a contemporary Black theology that probed the linkage between religio-cultural values and racial oppression, it has been those in the second generation who have sought to evolve an explicit analysis of the religio-cultural traditions, values, and sym-

George C. L. Cummings teaches theology at the Graduate Theological Union, Berkeley, California. He is co-author, with Dwight Hopkins, of *Cut Loose Your Stammering Tongue: Black Theology in the Slave Narratives*.

bols that define African-American life. At the same time these new voices seek
to develop specific modes of analysis for understanding the manner whereby
these traditions, values, and symbols have functioned, both as a means of sustaining racist domination, on the one hand, and on the other, as a context for
sustaining an oppositional worldview of resistance, hope, and struggle among
the victims of racism.

I have contended that, while the pioneers articulated a critique of White
theology and the racist practices of White Christians, and showed how Black
churches have been influenced by the dominant culture, it is now necessary to
develop a theoretical framework within which to evaluate the explicit functions
of religion, culture, and language as structures of domination, or as structures
that sustain discourses of hope and resistance. An example of the contributions
of those Black theologians who constitute the second generation is the volume
I co-edited with Dwight N. Hopkins, *Cut Loose Your Stammering Tongue: Black
Theology in the Slave Narratives* (Orbis Books, 1991). In that work, Will E.
Coleman, one of the contributors, issued a specific challenge to Black theologians when he suggested that "A major focus of a contemporary Black theology
of liberation should be on how the symbols and metaphors used by slaves can
enhance the praxis of liberation on the hermeneutical, linguistic-poetic front as
well as in the political, social and economic struggle for full humanity . . ."[2]
Coleman echoes my own three-fold challenge. First, I argue that contemporary
Black theologians should incorporate the thematic universe of the Black poor
into their discourse. Second, I affirm the necessity of a specific mode of analysis
that will provide a comprehensive analysis of the diverse structures of domination within U.S. society. Third, I suggest the development of specific criteria
for scrutinizing the emancipatory or oppressive intent of the values, symbols,
and metaphors in a context of racist oppression.[3]

The focal point of the efforts of this second generation, then, brings together
several divergent strands that have emerged in my own research, and that
inform the current work of these theologians. Three of these divergent strands
are worth mentioning in this essay. First, the texts of the African-American
story can provide contemporary Black theology with counterhegemonic images,
metaphors, symbols, and values that sustained an oppositional perspective of
resistance and hope in the past, and can provide the raw material for the
creation of emancipatory modalities in the present. This, however, depends on
the capacity of contemporary Black theologians to explicate a vehicle, through
which to discover those counterhegemonic traditions and images that actually
enable the oppressed to struggle for their emancipation. This has meant, in my
own work, the appropriation of Antonio Gramsci's useful notion of hegemony,
and Cornel West's helpful elaboration of Gramsci's concept, as an instrument
of analysis. Gramsci intended that his concept of hegemony refer to the thorough organization of society on behalf of a dominant sector, or class, in such a
manner as to gain the adherence of subordinate groups. Accordingly, hegemonic culture and religion are comprised of the traditions and current practices
that effectively encourage persons to identify themselves with the habits, sen-

sibilities, and worldviews supportive of the status quo and the class interests that dominate it. Cornel West deepens Gramsci's ideas by further distinguishing between hegemonic, prehegemonic, neohegemonic and counterhegemonic cultures and religions.[4] Specifically, counterhegemonic religion and culture represent genuine opposition to the sensibilities, habits, and worldviews of the dominant society and represent possibilities that cannot be realized within the perimeters of the established order.

My point in utilizing this theoretical framework is two-fold: First, it enables contemporary Black theologians to critically and self-consciously develop criteria for evaluating the religions and cultures of African Americans to determine whether specific practices, images, symbols, and values have actually been emancipatory. Second, it discourages Black theologians from romanticizing about the liberational content of the varieties of views within the African-American story, and can assist in the quest to discern those aspects of African-American cultures and religions that function as counterhegemonic expressions of resistance. This emphasis becomes especially significant in light of the current emphasis on Afrocentric ideas as an indispensable aspect of the work of the Black theologian.

The second strand that emerges in the work of the second generation, specifically in the work of Dwight N. Hopkins, Will E. Coleman, and myself, is our desire to shift the terrain of discussion from definitions of Black theology as a theological enterprise based on the African-American story to one that investigates African-American discourses as signifying processes that are inspected as political rhetoric of emancipation out of oppressive situations. By treating them as rhetorical, I construe theologies as discourses of persuasion. By treating them as political I indicate my conviction that all discourses are construed out of, and create postures toward, the social order, even when they include no specific references to such matters. With this approach, Black theologians can explore not only the ways in which African Americans, who are constrained by a racist society, employ the Christian tradition, but also the role of these discourses as both emancipatory and failed practices in transforming the social order.[5]

Poststructuralist theories expose the complex way language is a process of signifying, rather than a representational medium that organizes with subjects and for which the directly oppressive forces can be identified simply with semantic forms. Black theologians, like Hopkins, Coleman, and myself, are probing Black writers, slave narratives, Black folk culture, Black intellectual traditions, Black music, and other expressions of African-American religions and culture in order to examine each genre as a text, at one level as a discourse that is a construction of a particular social world, not of the author's intent. Such texts, I contend, hide as much as they reveal, and thus cannot be understood only by their obvious semantic intent. By extending such a reading to include its rhetorical construction — examination of the way the African American is a subject matter, the tropes of problem and resolution, the rhetoric of rationality and evidence, implied audience, posture toward reality invoked, the polyphonic

character of the text and other such questions about how the text persuades—
it is possible to treat each text as a set of complex effects. These must be
respected as strategies of a particular local social world, one that excludes and
creates meanings about what is emancipating and oppressive for African Americans.

An additional reading of each text, at a second level, is made possible by
the use of Marxist cultural theory, which allows analysis of religious and cultural
discourses as realities of the social formation of contemporary capitalism, and
its ideological partner, White supremacy. Marxist cultural theory is defined as
an ordering of economy, state, religion, and culture in which the capitalist mode
of production is so related to culture and state that discourses that order social
desire toward consumption, White dominance, and male dominance are the
dominant persuasive language of the society. Using Raymond Williams, Amil-
bar Cabral, Manning Marable, and other Marxist theoreticians of culture, it is
possible to analyze these discourses as more than locally constructed rhetorics;
they are also cultural practices shaped by a social formation that creates a
variety of positions of subordination, as well as options for resistance. From an
analysis of the posture toward the world created by each text, it is possible to
inquire about the reach of the strategies of emancipation in each text, with an
assessment of linkages to the larger social processes constructed for them by
their texts. The link between analytical work that engages a social analysis of
the social order, and an analysis of the language that is derived from social
orders, is obvious and constitutes an important portion of the challenge to the
second generation. This project is necessary due to the complex diversity of
views within the African-American community as a consequence of increasing
class stratification in that community, as well as the widespread growth of the
Black underclass following the civil rights movement.

Third, the major challenge of Black theologians, in the context of these
emerging analytical possibilities, is to show how theology is a source of an
explicit criterion of assessment that can be employed to determine what counts
as emancipatory in the texts of the African-American story. While first-gener-
ation Black theologians broadly described the possibilities of utilizing African-
American history, culture, and religion as a context for a contemporary Black
theological discourse, Black theologians in the second generation must build
upon the earlier work by elaborating and reconceptualizing traditional theological categories in light of the insights gained from social analysis and Marxist
theory of culture. For example, the traditional concept of the *pneumatos,* as in
pneumatological christology, has been one attempt to reconceive the criterion
of assessment in light of a commitment to history. Much work needs to be done
in all areas of theological discourse in order to enhance the contributions of
Black theology to the broader discourse of theology.

Another aspect of the work of Black theologians today is the need to evaluate
and reconceptualize the nature, identity, and mission of the Black Church.
What, for example, does it mean to be the church in light of the insights derived
from social analysis, as well as from an analysis of the images, practices, symbols,

values, and institutions that purport to embody a commitment to the gospel in the modern world? The political commitments of the Black Church, despite its immense contributions to the struggle for Black liberation, require considerable scrutiny in order to discern whether or not its institutional self-interests are hegemonic, neohegemonic, prehegemonic, or counterhegemonic. Black theologians can contribute to the Black Church by assisting this institution to engage in a critical self-evaluation of its *identity* and *mission*. Black theological discourse has been defined as a distinctively Christian and liberational, or emancipatory practice because its resistance to oppression is ordered by the rules of Christian grammar as being consistent with the liberating work of the Christ of God. Nevertheless, as the work of Will F. Coleman suggests, there is a continuing need to probe the nature of the intersection of Christian and so-called non-Christian images, values, and practices within the texts of the African-American story.

In sum, the task outlined here is for those scholars in all generations who continue to devote themselves to the African-American project of human liberation on all levels. The vocabulary, values, images, metaphors, sensibilities, and institutions in the African-American community must be challenged to fulfill the humanizing mission of the gospel.

NOTES

1. The concept of first generation and second generation is used to distinguish between the pioneers of Black theology and those that followed them. The first generation includes James H. Cone, J. Deotis Roberts, Gayraud S. Wilmore, Major J. Jones, and Albert Cleage, Jr. The second generation includes Dwight N. Hopkins, Josiah Young, Kelly D. Brown-Douglass, Will E. Coleman, and me.

2. Will E. Coleman, "Coming Through Legion": Metaphor in Non-Christian Experiences with the Spirit(s) in African-American Slave Narratives," in *Cut Loose Your Stammering Tongues: Black Theology in the Slave Narratives,* ed. Dwight N. Hopkins and George C. L. Cummings. (Maryknoll, N.Y.: Orbis Books, 1991), 102.

3. See George C. L. Cummings, *A Common Journey: Black Theology and Latin American Liberation Theology* (Maryknoll, N.Y.: Orbis Books, 1992), pp. 152–64.

4. Cornel West, *Prophesy Deliverance: An Afro-American Revolutionary Christianity* (Philadelphia: Westminster Press, 1982), 120.

5. In choosing to utilize this approach I am indebted to many womanist and feminist theologians who have begun to use poststructuralist discourse theories and Marxist theory of cultural discourse in the development of their own projects. See, for example, Rebecca S. Chopp, *The Power to Speak: Feminism, Language, and God* (New York: Crossroad, 1991). In addition I am indebted to the work of the Black literary scholar, Henry Louis Gates.

PART II

BLACK THEOLOGY
AND
PASTORAL MINISTRY

INTRODUCTION

The two major criticisms of the Black theologians of the 1960s were that they had developed (1) a theology keyed to the liberation and transformation of society, but not for the conversion and nurture of Christian individuals, and (2) a theology for Black males but not Black females. For this section on pastoral ministry I have selected and will suggest a context for essays that deal with the first criticism. In Part IV James H. Cone deals with the second criticism by presenting important new work by Black women theologians.

It is true that Black theology made its first appearance in what might be regarded as a street brawl between racist thugs, some of whom were in the uniform of officers of the law, and Black revolutionaries, some of whom had guns. Its early focus, in other words, was on confrontation, conflict, and power. Black Power. Black womanist theologians might add—Black macho power.

In regard to the question of power, many questions needed to be answered that seemed, at first, to have little to do with efficacious power of the Holy Spirit to bestow individual salvation. What kind of power were we talking about? In what did power consist? How does an oppressed group achieve it? How should it be used "to get the White man's foot off the Black man's neck?" Those were the kinds of questions the first generation of Black theologians were asking, although no theological analysis of power was made by any of us, with the exception of the attempt I made in my first book, *The Secular Relevance of the Church* (Westminster Press, 1962).

Of course, the ragged edges of these questions were smoothed and softened by the fact that they were raised within the walls of the Black Church. The traditional orientation of the church to the gifts and demands of the gospel of love, its inclination to bring everything that concerns it "under the feet of Christ," and its penchant for reconciliation rather than protracted enmity, provided Black theology with a certain attitude and language that qualified its secularity and differentiated it from the reckless and belligerent ideology and rhetoric of Black Power revolutionaries like H. Rap Brown, Eldridge Cleaver, and James Forman. The fact remained, however, that in the early writings of James H. Cone, J. Deotis Roberts, and others, the theological perspective on combating racism and breaking the bonds of economic and political oppression overshadowed the traditional emphasis of the Black Church on saving souls and ministering to the needs of individuals in the pews.

Many Black ministers reacted negatively to Black theology on this account. Some who had grudgingly accepted the movement in the South because it was led primarily by a notable group of young Baptist pastors and enjoyed the support of the masses of ordinary people who remained loyal to their churches, were less than sanguine about the National Committee of Black Churchmen (NCBC) and the small group of church executives, racial justice professionals, and academics whose names were not generally known and who were even suspected by some of not being born-again, down-home Christians. William L. Banks belonged to this group of detractors and probably spoke for the majority of Black clergy when he wrote at the height of the Black theology movement:

> Some Negro ministers have become so involved in the civil rights struggle that perhaps they could be better called politicians, sociologists, religious humanists, or religious philosophers rather than preachers of the gospel. They seem totally unaware that "No man that warreth entangleth himself with the affairs of this life; that he may please him who hath chosen him to be a soldier" (II Tim. 2:4).[1]

What Banks ignored was the fact that throughout the period of slavery and even after emancipation, Black clergy had fewer scruples than their White counterparts about entangling themselves with "the affairs of this life." If they thought about it at all, they assumed on practical grounds that the words of the apostle Paul to Timothy had to be understood differently from Banks' reactionary interpretation. Most African-American ministers mixed full- or part-time secular employment with their Sunday preaching jobs. Many, like Andrew Bryan in Savannah, Georgia and Richard Allen in Philadelphia, were known to be shrewd businessmen who owned property, managed businesses, and counseled their flocks to follow their example by saving their hard-earned money and investing it wisely whenever opportunity knocked. They were "secular men who had heard the gospel," to use a phrase that I created in *The Secular Relevance of the Church*, not saintly hermits who withdrew from the world. In their own communities they were pragmatic, hard-headed leaders to whom people turned for mundane, no-nonsense advice about family affairs, social welfare questions, problems with the police and the courts, problems concerning the disposition of land owned by parents, relations with bankers, government bureaucrats, and politicians, and all the other myriad, daily questions of survival and elevation in the beleagured Black world of segregation and discrimination.

Although many Black pastors may have agreed with Banks' negative assessment of the Black theology movement, the mainline tradition of the Black Church was much closer to the position of the Reverend Dr. Joseph H. Jackson, who also opposed Black theology, than to that of the Reverend Dr. William L. Banks and other Black preachers who were more impressed with the apolitical evangelicalism of the twentieth-century "White Awakenings" of Billy Sunday and later Billy Graham, than they were by the biblical realism of Black faith. Peter Paris finds a prophetic moralism in the writings and ministry of Jackson who believed in opposing wrong in society by protest and virtuous action on the side of what is good for the whole society. In analyzing this more characteristic posture of the old-fashioned Black preacher Paris writes:

And the prophet's task is undertaken without breaking the law. Rather, the prophet, as viewed by Jackson, is one who corrects social wrongs by injecting new spiritual and moral substance into the social order. This person is not a political reformer who tries to bring about justice through conflict and agitation but is a religious seer whose personality demonstrates a higher order to which the social order should be conformed. Hence, the source of good social action is extraordinary personal, spiritual, and moral refinement.[2]

This basic sense of the prophetic vocation of the Black preacher and the traditional role of the Black Church as an agency for bettering the life of its people, made it difficult for members of the clergy to dismiss Black theology out of hand. Contrary to what some observers have noted, Black theologians like James H. Cone, Joseph R. Washington, Jr., C. Eric Lincoln, and J. Deotis Roberts were in constant demand at ministers' conferences, workshops, and retreats during the 1970s and our popularity as speakers and lecturers to Black pastors has not appreciatively diminished in the 1990s. This in itself is no guarantee that our positions have been adopted by Black preachers, but it does mean that grassroots church leaders are curious about what we stand for and still willing to give us a respectful hearing.

During the 1980s a new and younger group of Black ministers, an increasing number of whom are women, mostly seminary-trained, but sensitive to the traditional religiosity of the Black masses, began to press us to clarify the relevance of liberation theology for the pastoral ministry. It was not enough for historians of the movement to point out how Black theology gave pastors in the ghetto something to preach and march about during the 1960s when their children were in the streets listening to Malcolm X, or during the height of the urban rebellions, when God and the church seemed as remote from the center of the struggle as the National Baptist Convention, Inc., seemed from the Black Panther Party.

"This is not the sixties," some thoughtful Black pastors said, "this is the eighties. The civil rights movement is over. Martin and Malcolm are dead. Conservative Republican administrations have nipped Black radicalism in the bud—Christian, Muslim, and otherwise. People want their personal problems solved now. They want to go back to 'Goin' Up Yonder' gospel music and arm-waving preaching that declares, 'Thank yuh, Jesus—everything's gonna be alright!' In this postrevolutionary climate, what does Black theology have to offer the bemused and harried Black pastor who has to minister to these masses?"

James H. Harris, the writer of Document 7, "Black Church and Black Theology: Theory and Practice," is one of the most persistent of these new critics of Black theology's seeming inability to include ordinary church people and pastors in the development of critical reflection and action that is "of the people" and to deal with the real-life experiences of "Aunt Jane," her unemployed and frustrated husband, and her preyed-upon and alienated children and grandchildren.

Harris has the benefit of being in the academy and the pastorate at the same time. Moving from a church in Norfolk, Virginia where he taught at Old Dominion University, he continues to teach and is senior minister at the Second Baptist Church of Richmond. Although I have challenged some of his more facile assumptions in a dialogue we had in the pages of *The Christian Century*,[3] I agree with much of what he is writing and enthusiastically welcome the leadership he is giving to what we hope will become a national discussion.

Document 8, written by M. Shawn Copeland, O.P., who teaches theology at Yale Divinity School, continues the discussion about Black theology at the local church level in the context of Black Roman Catholicism. The strong liturgical and pastoral emphasis of ministry in the Roman Catholic Church made it natural for Black theology to find its first expression in worship and parish life. The questions of spiritual formation, evangelism, and catechesis predominated in the early discussions of theological renewal among Black Roman Catholics. In her essay Shawn Copeland traces this development over the past few years. The strong pastoral emphasis of the Black Roman Catholic appropriation of Black theology stands in unavoidable contrast with the paucity of careful work in this area by Protestants. Copeland, unlike most Black Protestant women theologians, has had a double exposure to pastoral and administrative ministries on both sides of the Protestant-Catholic line. In addition to being a Roman Catholic nun, she was, with the late Mohammad Kenyatta, a national staff person for the mainly Protestant Black Theology Project, Inc. of Theology in the Americas, which has been mentioned often in this book.

In Document 9, "Pastoral Ministry in the Origin and Development of Black Theology," I try to make a case for Black theology as a theology of the people and for the local congregation. I consider this essay and another that appeared in the published Parker Memorial Lectures in Theology and Ministry[4] as two of my most important writings because they forthrightly state that Black theology is first and foremost a *pastoral* theology; that it could not be *Black* and be otherwise, and it could not be *theology* in our sense of the word without dealing with the practical problems of preaching, parish administration, Christian education, and pastoral ministry as a whole.

Dennis W. Wiley, in the next essay, "Black Theology, the Black Church, and the African-American Community" (Document 10), underscores this point when he recites the litany of the problems of the African-American community, the solution of which he says is more important than either the survival of Black theology or the Black Church. As one of the second generation of Black systematic theologians who has answered the call to serve in the trenches of the local congregation, Dennis Wiley recognizes that the assault on the Black community of the 1980s and 1990s is more from within than without. No one, therefore, has a more difficult task making Black theology functional than the

Black pastors, whose prophetic reinterpretation and practice of the work of the theologians of the 1960s will help theology become more relevant to the inner as well as the outer oppression of Black people. Black theology must return, says Wiley, to the Black Church where it can perform a grassroots, "internal propheticism" that engages the folk where they are and helps them become both liberated individuals and liberators of their still enslaved communities.

An area of pastoral ministry that has been studiously avoided by the older generation of Black theologians is our understanding of human sexuality and the liberation of Black Christians from their homophobic fears and prejudices. Because of the obvious presence of gay men in both the pulpits and pews of our congregations, I was one who naively assumed that we did not have the same problem with gay and lesbian people that has been tearing apart many White churches at national and local levels. I did not consider that the reason for what seemed to be the aplomb of the Black Church about sexual noncon-formity had more to do with the decision of many Black gays and lesbians to stay in the closet. When such people declared themselves for what they were and demanded that the church face up to the inhumanities and injustices heaped upon them by an intolerant society, the Black Church, no less than others and more than many White churches, turned tail and ran away from the problem.

Document 11, "Breaking Silence: Toward an In-the-Life Theology," written by an avowed gay-identified, bisexual Black theologian, Elias Farajaje-Jones, associate professor of the history of religions at Howard University School of Divinity, opens up these issues for the first time in an anthology on Black theology. In this essay he explores how homophobia remains behind a wall of silence as a potent form of oppression in the Black Church, greatly endangering the struggle against AIDS that presently afflicts our community. Farajaje-Jones argues that the Black Church will not be able to enter the fight against AIDS with its full resources, nor experience holistic liberation in pulpit and pew until it has squarely faced the issue of sexuality in all its variform manifestations. This young theologian who is an archpriest of the Orthodox Church, studied at St. Vladimir Theological Seminary in Crestwood, New York, and earned his Ph.D. (magna cum laude) at the University of Bern, Switzerland, brings unusual gifts of intellectual, intercultural, and ecumenical education and experience to the theological round table of the Black Church. We expect many important contributions in the area of the history of religions and theology and pastoral ministry from him in the future.

We have saved the working paper "What Does It Mean To Be Black and Christian?" (Document 12), prepared by the Kelly Miller Smith Institute on African-American Church Studies of Vanderbilt University Divinity School, until last in Part II. That is partly because it is perhaps the most current of our ecumenical statements in an area that bears directly on the problem of the hiatus between Black professional theologians and pastors, between academic theology and pastoral theology. This paper is actually a call to a national dia-logue that is now in process. A dialogue between "scholars of the academy and pastors of churches, denominational and congregational officials, professionals, students, artists, clergy, laity, women and men" on the nature of the unprecedented crisis of faith within the African-American community. Out of it may come the means by which Black theological reflection, discourse, and action can help us choose life and blessing rather than death and cursing for ourselves and future generations.

I doubt that anything Black theologians are doing today is more important than this. This particular document was designed for study, discussion, and action on the part of members of the Black Church across the nation. It raises many of the critical questions already alluded to in the documents in Part II and, in a sense, summarizes them for consideration by ordinary members of the church who, it is hoped, will come together across denominational lines to discuss them. It also underscores what I have come to believe is the area of Black theology most needing explication and demonstration today—the relationship between our sometimes grandiose theologizing about the nature and destiny of Blackness in the Christian faith and the daily, ordinary clerical and lay ministries of the local congregation.

G.S.W.

NOTES

1. William L. Banks, *The Black Church in the U.S.: Its Origin, Growth, Contribution, and Outlook* (Chicago: Moody Press, 1972), 95.
2. Peter J. Paris, *Black Religious Leaders: Conflict in Unity* (Louisville: Westminster/ John Knox Press, 1991). For a broader analysis of this moralistic this-worldliness of the Black Church, see his *The Social Teachings of the Black Churches* (Philadelphia: Fortress Press, 1985), 57–80.
3. "Black Church, Black Theology," in *The Christian Century* 107, no. 19 (June 13–20, 1990): 599–604.
4. "Black Theology and Pastoral Ministry: A Challenge to Ecumenical Renewal and Solidarity," in Earl E. Shelp and Ronald H. Sunderland, eds., *The Pastor As Theologian* (New York: Pilgrim Press, 1988).

7

BLACK CHURCH AND BLACK THEOLOGY: THEORY AND PRACTICE

James H. Harris

There needs to be a close relationship between theology and ministry. After some twenty years of the development of black theology, black denominations, pastors, and congregations are not greatly moved by the insights of black theology or black theologians. A way needs to be found to change this. There is no way fully to estimate the value of black theological reflection to the life of black Christians, to the ministry and witness of black churches. Theology has been not only a faith response but a thoughtful engagement with the souls of black people. It not only aids in assessing the signs of the time, it is deeply anchored in the roots of black culture, history and church tradition. It has much to offer to black people toward self-understanding and social transformation.

—J. Deotis Roberts,
Black Theology in Dialogue

Samuel Proctor, pastor emeritus of Abyssinian Baptist Church, says, and I agree, that black theology is a needed corrective to all bad theology, and that "all good theology should be liberating."[1] But the "correctness" and "goodness" of black theology need to be understood and practiced by the Christian community, especially the black church. Few ministers and laypersons who labor in black churches are aware that black theology is a discipline of study and reflection. Consequently, interest in and understanding of black liberation theology barely exists among the majority of persons that I have encountered in the black church. While my own contextual experience as pastor has been limited to a few thousand people, my colleagues in the practice of pastoral ministry corroborate this perception.

Furthermore, many black pastors still think that black academicians who

---

James H. Harris is senior minister at Second Baptist Church, Richmond, Virginia. This essay was published in his book *Pastoral Theology: A Black Church Perspective* (Fortress Press, 1991).

construct theology outside of the practices of the church are largely out of touch with the very people about whom they claim to write. Because of this perception, few black ministers read and teach the works of prominent black theologians such as James Cone, Gayraud Wilmore, J. Deotis Roberts, C. Eric Lincoln, or Major Jones. Even fewer laypersons are familiar with the tenets of black liberation theology. I believe that the social and political life of black people can be transformed by bridging the gap between black theology and the ministry of the black church.

Theology and the Black Church

Theology is both an academic discipline and a practical responsibility of the church. In its pure seminary form, it is generally foreign to the church. After completing theology school, young ministers have to struggle to make their newfound knowledge relevant to churchgoers. Ordinary churchgoers are not interested in the arguments or theories about the existence of God or the color of God. This does not mean that these questions, debated by philosophers and theologians, are unimportant. However, persons in the church, struggling to practice the Christian faith, *are* interested in what God has done and can do to help them with their particular concerns and problems. These problems are often related to sickness, hunger, death, family, housing, crime, and education. Black churchgoers expect the preacher to have the knowledge and faith to assure them of God's power, not to question or doubt it. What these laypersons need to understand is that the process of faith development may sometimes be enhanced by searching the depths of the soul for a more comprehensive understanding of the nature and power of God. The pastor can challenge the church to deal with the issues of injustice and oppression by using black theology as a method of teaching and preaching liberation.

Not only is it true that clergy and laity are, to a significant degree, out of touch with black theology, but some black theologians are also out of touch with the black church. Somehow, academic theology is thought to be more meaningful and profound than the practical theology that actually grows out of the black church experience. Black theologians, consciously or unconsciously following their white counterparts, often articulate the black experience in language that is meant to impress each other, not the persons about whom they speak. As long as this is so, Cone's assertion that "black theology is not academic theology" will be met with apathy and indifference.[2] So, instead of the existence of a necessary and unmistakable nexus between the black church and black theology, there seems to be a chasm between what black theology articulates and what the black church actually does. Theologians may postulate that black theology grows out of the black experience (including the black church), but the black church still feels isolated and distant. Somehow black theology has failed in its ability to reach the very people that it is designed to liberate. This is characteristic of the chasm that often exists between theory and practice, regardless of the discipline. However, if liberation methodologies have any chance of being institutionalized and implemented on a comprehensive level, the black church is the place to make this a reality.

James Cone's statement that black theology is not academic theology is more myth than reality because outside the halls of academia, black liberation theology seems to be more foreign to the black community than evangelical theology. How can it be anything other than academic if only the academicians are discussing it and writing about it? Black preachers tend to talk about evangelism, building programs, stewardship, and other practical theological and congregational issues. Unfortunately, black theology tends to be a concern only of academically oriented preachers. This certainly needs to change! As a method of analysis, a model of ministry or simply a way of understanding life, black theology will have meaning and power when the masses of blacks begin to accept and practice it. This is not going to happen unless there is a conscious and systematic approach developed to gradually infuse the church with the concepts of liberation.

Some in the black church object to Cone's list of sources for black theology, which seems to include everything except the black church.[3] However, under his category labeled "Black History," he argues that black theology

> came into being when black churchmen realized that killing slave masters was doing the work of God. It began when black churchmen refused to accept the racist white church as consistent with the gospel of God. . . . The participation of the black churches in the black liberation struggle from the eighteenth to the twentieth century is a tribute to the endurance of black theology.[4]

Nevertheless, Cone fails to list the black church as a separate source of black theology and in effect relegates it to a subcomponent of black history. However, the black church is more than history—it is present and future. It is an intricate part of all the sources of black theology, such as experience, culture, scripture, revelation, and tradition. It was formed out of protest and the quest to be liberated in the midst of a society that was legally, morally, socially, economically, and politically oppressive. The black church needs to return to its protest posture, armed and ready to do battle with the help of a new and creative ally— black theology.

Gayraud Wilmore, in his classic book *Black Religion and Black Radicalism*, lists three sources of black theology: the black community, the writings and addresses of black preachers and public men of the past, and the traditional religions of Africa. Although Wilmore mentions the black church, he does not expressly acknowledge in this particular context how important it has been to black theology. Wilmore states: "The theology of the black community is developed not in theological seminaries but on the streets, in the taverns and pool halls, as well as in the churches."[5] If there is any importance to the sequence of Wilmore's list, then we can only infer logically that the substance of black theology is developed more on the streets and in the taverns and pool halls than in seminaries, not to mention the black church. Wilmore, like Cone, seems to inadvertently relegate the church to a secondary status when discussing the development of theology. It is hard for me to believe that the theology of the black church is being developed on the streets of urban America where there is an abundance of disinterest in the value of life. Maybe this is not what Wilmore means; however, I have come to believe that there is little talk about God going on anywhere among black people except in churches and seminaries. Therefore, I beg to differ with these eminent theologians and submit that the church deserves a more prominent role in the shaping and perpetuation of black theology.[6] Although black theology has grown out of the experiences of black people, I would not place the church and other places such as the "streets and pool halls" on the same level in the development of a theological perspective.

Recently, Cone has focused more on the influence of the black church in his book, *For My People.* He asserts that black theology "is a theology of the black poor, reconstructing their hopes and God's coming liberated world."[7] I agree that black theology in any authentic form should grow out of the social, political, and spiritual experiences of the people in the churches and the community on a daily basis. It should be a theology developed in conjunction with those who actually live in poverty and experience disrespect and degradation. It should also be taught, preached, and advocated by those black pastors who labor with the masses. If every black preacher in cities, towns, and rural areas who pastors the poor and labors in the trenches where the stench of poverty and the despair of blacks are self-evident would begin to think of freedom in existential terms, then black liberation could be realized in a short time.

Black theology as liberation theology must be, according to Gustavo Gutiérrez, the "theology of the people" if it is to affect the lives of people. Clearly the theological discourses of Gayraud Wilmore, J. Deotis Roberts, and James Cone have done much more to correct and offend the oppressor than the black church has done. The church seldom offends anyone. What Jens Glebe-Möller says about the Danish church can also be said about the black church in the United States: "It continues to contribute its mite to the legitimation of the status quo."[8] While it is justifiably argued that black liberation theology is experiential and biblical, it also appears to be more esoteric than pragmatic because black preachers shy away from the radical views of liberation theologians and side with traditional, conservative, evangelical theologians, and black theologians have been unsuccessful in bringing their message to the church. This happens out of apathy and fear, or the inability to understand the concepts and ideas that will bring about liberation. While the actions of a few radical scholars and preachers have established the basis for liberation, a significant majority of black preachers and laypersons continue to be oblivious to the endemic nature of oppression and the need for a theology of liberation. Once this changes, freedom will have a chance to become reality.

What Is Black Theology?

Black theology is situational theology, as Allan Boesak asserts.[9] Like all theology, it is contextual. More importantly, it is indeed liberation theology, as some of its most articulate proponents—James Cone, Gayraud Wilmore, Albert Cleage, J. Deotis Roberts, and Major J. Jones—have eloquently argued.[10] It is also existential or contextual in that it is a theology of the black experience.

The most enduring and comprehensive definition of black theology was issued by the National Committee of Black Churchmen over two decades ago. Because of its importance, it is quoted here almost in its entirety.

> Black theology is a theology of black liberation. It seeks to plumb the black condition in the light of God's revelation in Jesus Christ, so that the black community can see that the gospel is commensurate with the achievement of black humanity. Black theology is a theology of "blackness." It is the affirmation of black humanity that emancipates black people from white racism, thus providing authentic freedom for both white and black people. It affirms the humanity of black people in that it says no to the encroachment of white oppression. The message of liberation is the revelation of God in the incarnation of Jesus Christ. Freedom is the gospel. Jesus is the liberator! The demand that Christ the Liberator imposes on all men requires all blacks to affirm their full dignity as persons and all whites to surrender their presumptions of superiority and abuses of power.[11]

Theological language and method are seldom in synchrony with the practices of the church. Clearly, the church is in need of a black practical theology whose function is to liberate it from the forces of social, political, and economic oppression. After understanding the nature of black theology, the critical question is, What does black theology do to bring about liberation and change in the lives of black and poor people? Certainly it purports that Jesus is the liberator and argues that God is on the side of the oppressed. How do these assertions, however hermeneutically sound and exegetically valid they may be, address the reality of poverty and suffering that is a direct result of the greed and selfishness our capitalist system perpetuates? How does black theology deal with the eradication of systemic oppression?

One of the problems confronting black theology is that it is not taught in black churches, state and national conventions, regional associations, ministers' conferences, or Christian education congresses. Ministers and pastors who are "doing theology" must begin to do liberation theology on a microcosmic scale, that is, within the local church. It is distressing that ministers and laypersons who participate in the church and other gatherings spend their time debating fruitless questions of internal authority and power, conforming to an evangelistic paradigm of the black church that is often patterned after Billy Graham, Robert Schuller, or other popular evangelists. The black church needs to free those within its ranks from the despair and powerlessness that grip their bodies and souls. Black theology provides the theoretical framework for this freedom.

Black Theology as Liberation Theology

James Cone is generally perceived as the leading systematic exponent of black theology.[12] Indeed, all of his major writings to date are variations on the liberation theme. Black theology believes that liberation is the essence of the gospel of Jesus Christ, and any authentic Christian theology affirms that God is on the side of the oppressed.

The theme of liberation is found throughout the Old Testament, but specifically in the book of Exodus and the prophets. The history of the Israelites' bondage in Egypt and their subsequent freedom, orchestrated by God, while Pharaoh's army drowned in the sea, is a critical corollary to the experience of blacks in America, except that pharaohs of modern history still oppress us. The Exodus event shows Yahweh taking sides with the oppressed and fostering their liberation. As Boesak asserts, "This liberation message was the center and sustenance of the life of Israel."[13] James Cone made the point much earlier when he wrote, "The history of Israel is a history of God's election of a special, oppressed people to share in his creative involvement in the world on behalf of man."[14] Cone makes it clear that the church, in order to be authentic, has to participate in the activity of humanity's liberation. He is essentially concerned with the liberation of blacks from systematic oppression, designed and orchestrated by whites, and the structure of the political and economic system.

Cone began to discuss the theme of liberation in his initial works, *Black Theology and Black Power* and *A Black Theology of Liberation*. However, he developed the concept of liberation more thoroughly in his later work, *God of the Oppressed*. He argues that "Jesus is the Ground of Liberation" and ties liberation to salvation.

> Because human liberation is God's work or salvation in Jesus Christ, its source and meaning cannot be separated from Christology's sources (scripture, tradition, and social existence) and content (Jesus in his past, present, and future). Jesus Christ, therefore in his humanity and divinity, is the point of departure for a black theologian's analysis of the meaning of liberation. . . . Liberation is not an object but a "project" of freedom wherein the oppressed realize their fight for freedom is a divine right of creation.[15]

In Cone's view, liberation is the essence of Christianity and Jesus Christ is the liberator. Liberation manifests itself in the struggle for justice and freedom, and the black experience in the United States is the model of the struggle.

Moreover, Gayraud Wilmore correctly points out that black theology affirms the freedom of black people and negates that which seeks to deny them that freedom. He writes: "Black theology expresses both affirmation and negation. It affirms the real possibility of freedom and manhood for black people, and it negates every power that seeks to demand and rob black people of the determination of their own destiny."[16]

Black theology is self-affirmation with the understanding that God wills blacks to be free, equal, and at peace with themselves. In addition, black theology enables blacks to be free "from their traditional fear of whites, so that they not only can articulate their feelings but also so that they will act upon them."[17] The theme of self-respect and respect for all blacks is critical in black theology. Major J. Jones states:

> Black theology holds that to be a person is to act like a person within any human context. This is the ultimate aim of Black theology. Black people must feel that they are completely capable and fit to live full lives under God and in relation to all God's children. . . . Black theology generates within black people the strength needed to resist the forces that threaten their humanity and that attempt to reduce them to an inhuman status less than that of a child of God.[18]

The critical point made by Jones is extremely significant because it suggests that black theology can enable blacks to stop victimizing each other — whether it be black-on-black crime or poor self-esteem. Black theology agrees with Jesse Jackson when he says, "I am somebody." This may seem small and obvious, but it is neither. It is very difficult for persons to believe in themselves if they have been historically downtrodden.

During the early years when black theology was in its embryonic stages, struggling to make itself known and felt in the hearts and minds of blacks and whites, Cone masterfully articulated the task and aim of black theology.

> The task of black theology then is to analyze the nature of the gospel of Jesus Christ in the light of oppressed black people so they will see the gospel as inseparable from their humiliated condition, bestowing on them the necessary power to break the chains of oppression. This means that it is a theology of and for the black community seeking to interpret the religious dimension of the forces of liberation in that community.[19]

If the gospel gives blacks the power to "break the chains" of oppression and black theology is the method of analyzing the gospel for that purpose, then we need to move forward toward doing liberation. Black theologians have articulated cogently a theology of liberation; however, these same theologians along with the black church have fallen short in carrying it out. The painful truth is that practicing liberation theology is much more difficult than formulating it. But the formulation of it is a necessary precondition to systematically effecting change through Christian practice.

Let me hasten to say that black theology is purported to have grown out of the black community. In other words, it is a theology of the people coming out of the experiences of common folk. Cone and Wilmore make this point quite eloquently in many of their writings.[20] The truth of the assertion is basically unquestioned, but the principles of black theology need to be applied seriously to the work of the ministry, that is, the function of the church in the world today, if it is to be an effective agent of liberation and change. Jones is adeptly correct when he states:

Black theology has been and continues to be primarily a theology of protest. . . . Black theology calls for a more radical and complete revolutionary change. . . . Most current black theologians insist that to change the plight of blacks within the context of American culture will take nothing short of radical revolution. Whether or not such a revolution is violent is not the primary concern of many black theologians. Change alone is the concern. The call is for an unconditional commitment to change.[21]

Again, the call for change is one thing, but forcing change to occur quite another. The church, armed with black theology as a part of the "armor of God," can begin to move beyond the rhetoric and semantics of prophetic protest and begin to practice a theology of liberation. This is where theory and practice converge and join hands to change the structure of oppression and injustice in the United States and the world.

Black Theology as Holistic Ministry

Black liberation theology is the best available model to inform ministry in the black church if the church is to be more than a clone of white evangelicalism. Black theology is concerned with the total person as well as with the social structure in which we find ourselves. Roberts, in discussing the relationship of black theology and ministry, says:

Our life in Christ, together with our worship and lifestyle, as individuals and as a people, should focus upon the improvement of our economic situation. Black theology is holistic—it does not see the well-being of the soul as unrelated to life in the body. Salvation includes the whole person and all of life. Sin and salvation are both personal and social. Evil and suffering are structural as well as personal. Against the background of such an understanding of the gospel, we must deal with the economic factor. Here is an essential contact point of black theology and ministry in the black church.[22]

Improving the economic situation will indeed hasten the day of our freedom. Too many blacks live from paycheck to paycheck while simultaneously trying to "keep up with the Joneses." The black church is, without question, an independent and generally financially solvent institution. But the individuals who constitute the church and community are often plagued by poverty on the one hand and inadequate financial planning and practice on the other. Those who are economically secure should translate their individual and personal success into the economic success of the black community without selling the community to the highest bidder or sacrificing the integrity of community unity and commitment to social progress.

Black theology can also inform our ministry with the poor, the sick, and the homeless. It teaches self-respect and self-esteem in spite of the social and political reality that condescends to and oppresses blacks. Pastors need to empathize with the poor and develop ways to transform their status. This can start early with children and youth in order that they may aspire to become self-supporting individuals, committed to the betterment of church, community, and family. Indeed, black people have worked together to build some of the most beautiful, expansive and gloriously awesome church buildings that one could ever envision. Now is the time to harness that same creativity and commitment to deliberately and thoroughly make black liberation theology an intricate part of the everyday practice of ministry.

Black theology and practical theology should be two sides of the same coin. The practice of liberation theology is difficult because it begins with a hermeneutic that asks, How do I practice ministry according to the biblical text? What is the historical, social, and political context of the message that Jesus spoke according to the spokesmen for the early church?[23] In addition, we must ask, What does the Word of God mean to us as black people who are trapped in the seemingly inescapable web of socioeconomic and political disenfranchisement? These questions have to be specific because the interpretation or answers depends on who is asking and for what reason. White Western theologians and exegetes have historically interpreted the Scripture from an arrogant and dominant perspective because they represent the majority.

Hermeneutics is influenced by politics, experience, and culture. Black theology interprets the Scripture from a sociocultural perspective. White people have seen God through their privileged position, and, for a long time, blacks tried to use this same perspective. However, the development of black theology has taught blacks that their own experiences and culture are also important. More specifically, the black experience is uniquely akin to the experience of God's people as seen in the Bible. Therefore, blacks have come to understand God as seen through their own experiences of slavery, suffering, discrimination, and injustice.

Christianity for blacks has entailed a level of reality seldom visible to the dominant culture. Practicing Christianity has meant turning the other cheek, walking in humility, and enduring cruel and debased treatment as a social norm. Blacks learned how to sublimate their anger, and instead of destroying their chances for survival they learned how to live with the oppressors. This is real faith in the promise of God. This is why even today when we sing "There Is a Bright Side Somewhere," or "Climbing Up the Rough Side of the Mountain," everyone in the church is able to understand and identify with the words of suffering and hope, jubilation and reflection. Black theology endeavors to put in plain words the feelings, hopes, dreams, experiences, and practices of the black masses. These words used by black theology are girded by "the Word" of Scripture and the message of Jesus Christ.

Regretfully, some black churches have modeled themselves after the white church. Their worship services are characterized by brevity, quietness, anthems, and a general degree of formality. These blacks see this worship style as a form of sophistication that reflects compatibility with their educational level. However, I believe that black theology would wake these Christians up to the reality of their heritage, and help them to be proud of the struggles that their parents and foreparents endured for the sake of liberation. This pride would manifest itself in being unashamed to say "Amen" sometimes or even speak publicly about their difficult experiences. In this connection, I believe that Jesse Jackson pricked the conscience of black America when he referred to the "slop jar" and the "slave ship" in his nationally broadcast speech before the 1988 Democratic National Convention.[24] His heritage has shaped his ideology and his commitment to equity, fairness, and justice. Likewise, many blacks could identify with Jackson's experience because his experience is their experience. They too have lived with poverty and oppression.

Black professionals, that is, lawyers, doctors, professors, and so on, in a local area tend to attend the same Episcopal, Methodist, or Baptist church, thereby making these churches socioeconomically homogeneous. I am sure that in every city and town in America, there is a church within each major denomination that represents this paradigm. These enlightened, sophisticated, intelligent, successful blacks practice a European version of black religion. While black theologians highlight the uniqueness of black folk religion and the contributions of "Aunt Jane," these bourgeois blacks act as if they are trying to forget the days that Jesse Jackson chronicled and black theologians deem critical to our future. Some of these churches have no appreciation for gospel music, young people's choirs, innovative worship structures, or the use of other instruments in the worship setting except the organ and piano. This effort to imitate the oppressor holds these churches in bondage because they are unable to rejoice and weep with their other black brothers and sisters. Black theology will help them graduate from practicing religion as an exclusive experience of the head to understanding that it is also an experience of the heart. Until this is recognized, they too are not free. Cone reminds us that "liberation then is not merely a thought in my head; it is the socio-historical movement of a people from oppression to freedom — Israelites from Egypt and black people from American slavery."[25] Some blacks would do well to remember that their ancestors were also on those slave ships Jesse Jackson discussed. Blacks need to remember that neither education nor financial success cancels out our blackness. Whether we have a Ph.D., a D.D., or "no D at all," we are still black, and we possess a common heritage. The miseducation of blacks is still very much a part of our experience.

Black Theology in the Black Church

Black theology has little or no practical value apart from the black church; the liberation of black people cannot be achieved without the church's engagement of black theology. "Therefore, black liberation is, in part, dependent upon the attitude and role that the church assumes in relation to it."[26] Although some black preachers and theologians disagree as to the relationship of black theology to the church, the time for antagonism between preachers and theologians has passed. The urgency of achieving freedom and justice supersedes distrust and misunderstanding.

Black theology has rightly criticized the black church for being too other-worldly and conservative, and the church has been even harder on black theology by refusing to acknowledge it. The needed criticism of the church is what Cone calls "self-criticism," which started with a handful of progressive black ministers who saw the need for change. Now theology and ministry need to work together in order to bring about the freedom of our people. Black theology's rightful home is in the black church, and the black church needs to welcome black theology into the structure of its ministry. When this happens, liberation will be closer at hand.

Doing Liberation Theology: From Theory to Practice

There are several prevailing issues that face the church and society that must be addressed by pastors and church leaders. For example, sexism against black women should be addressed by black theology and the black church. Women in black churches outnumber men by more than two to one, but in positions of authority and responsibility the ratio is reversed. Although women are gradually entering ministry as bishops, pastors, deacons, and elders, many men and women still resist and fear that development. When the church where I formerly served as a pastor licensed a woman to the preaching ministry over a decade ago, almost all the male deacons and many women members opposed the action by appealing to tradition and selected Scripture passages. Black theology and the black church need to deal with the double bondage of black women in church and society.

There are two ways they can do so. The first is to treat black women with the same respect as men. This means that women who are qualified for ministry must be given the same opportunities as men to become pastors and to serve in such leadership positions as deacons, stewards, and trustees. Second, theology and the church must eliminate exclusionist language, attitudes, or practices, however benign or unintended, in order to benefit fully from the talents of women.

There are other ways that liberation theology can be practiced in the parish. Every black churchgoer, especially the economically secure, should understand that tithing or some larger form of proportionate giving significantly affects the liberation of blacks. A tithing church will be able to influence public policy issues such as housing for the poor and equal employment opportunities. It would spend less time and energy raising money to meet the ordinary demands of ministry and mission, and actually do ministry by using its financial resources to develop ways to stem the tide of drug abuse, teenage pregnancy, divorce, and family violence.

Black churches can also adopt public schools, into which they can send volunteers to "testify" to young blacks about the value of a quality education. Churches could provide "education mentors" to work with teachers and counselors in order to help children increase educational achievement, develop self-esteem, and enhance moral and intellectual integrity. This would be the first step toward a decentralized educational structure that would enable communities and churches to take control of the future of our young people. In this scheme, churches would monitor the progress of their young parishioners from kindergarten through twelfth grade and find tutors or provide volunteers qualified to teach subjects in which children need help.

Black churches need to pool their financial resources by withdrawing funds from institutions that do not address the development needs of the black community. In our society, money talks. Black people should assume control of their hard-earned money and invest it in financial institutions that will challenge traditional models of risk management. Thus they will begin the process of nurturing our neglected communities back to health. The fiscal integrity of the black church and community depend on biblical and ethical principles such as working together, loving one another, and caring for the poor. In order for the black community to become a viable place for external investment, blacks will first have to invest in black youth and in the black community before society as a whole will invest in the black community.

Each black congregation should develop ways to assess the needs of its constituents and those who live within a certain radius of the church. This will enable the pastor and staff better to understand their ministry context and to address specific community needs. For example, some neighborhoods need to learn how to read, while others may need better access to medical care. Still others may simply need to know that there are people nearby who care about their families and are willing to offer a helping hand.

Black theology teaches self-respect and self-esteem in spite of social and political condescension to and oppression of blacks. Black pastors should put this into action by developing programs and policies to transform the status of the poor. They can do this by sharing historical and biographical stories of black accomplishments. Blacks have to regain the confidence that they can persevere despite modern manifestations of oppression and injustice. These lessons on determination, freedom, and faith can be correlated with biblical stories that express similar virtues.

As a pastor, I have historically invited young people to speak or read during the worship service. Moreover, I publicly acknowledge their educational accomplishments by recognizing the high achievers and encouraging others to strive toward excellence. This helps to develop their self-esteem, sense of achievement, and social skills. It also gives me an opportunity to work closely with those who may need to be motivated or encouraged. I have encouraged the church to provide opportunities for young people to develop leadership skills that can be transferred to other areas of life.

All of us are compelled to do more to bridge the gap between theory and practice. Black theology and the black church, working together, can potentially transform our communities. All of us have to hear anew the words of Scripture: "But be doers of the word, and not merely hearers who deceive themselves.

... Those who look into the law of liberty, and persevere, being not hearers that forget but doers who act—they will be blessed in their doing" (James 1:22–25).

NOTES

1. As a postdoctoral fellow at United Theological Seminary, Dayton, Ohio, I have discussed this topic with Samuel Proctor, who is my mentor. In these discussions, class lectures, and in reviewing this manuscript, Dr. Proctor has expressed this sentiment.

2. James H. Cone, *For My People: Black Theology and the Black Church* (Maryknoll, N.Y.: Orbis Books, 1984), 117.

3. Cone, in *A Black Theology of Liberation* (New York: Lippincott, 1970), lists six sources of black theology: black experience, black history, black culture, revelation, Scripture, and tradition (53-74).

4. Ibid., 59.

5. Gayraud S. Wilmore, *Black Religion and Black Radicalism* (New York: Doubleday & Co., 1973).

6. Most black theologians are committed to the church and its role in the development of black theology. Professor Wilmore has been a leader in this regard.

7. Cone, *For My People*, 117.

8. Jens Glebe-Möller, *A Political Dogmatic* (Philadelphia: Fortress Press, 1987), 67.

9. See Allan Aubrey Boesak, *Farewell to Innocence* (Maryknoll, N.Y.: Orbis Books, 1976), esp. chap. 1, "On Theology," which is basically an analysis of black theology.

10. These persons (along with others) have written systematically on this subject and have developed black theology as it is known today. For example, besides *For My People* and *A Black Theology of Liberation* see these books by James H. Cone: *Black Theology and Black Power* (San Francisco: Harper & Row, 1989); *The Spirituals and the Blues* (New York: Seabury Press, 1972); *God of the Oppressed* (New York: Seabury Press, 1975). In addition to his classic *Black Religion and Black Radicalism*, Gayraud Wilmore's *Black Theology: A Documentary History, 1966–1979* (Maryknoll, N.Y.: Orbis Books, 1979), edited with James H. Cone, provides an excellent foundation for understanding black liberation theology. Other notable works include J. Deotis Roberts, *Liberation and Reconciliation: A Black Theology* (Philadelphia: Westminster Press, 1971); and *Black Theology in Dialogue* (Philadelphia: Westminster Press, 1987); Major J. Jones, *Black Awareness: A Theology of Hope* (Nashville: Abingdon Press, 1971); *Christian Ethics for Black Theology* (Nashville: Abingdon, 1974); and *The Color of God: The Concept of God in Afro-American Thought* (Macon, Ga.: Mercer University Press, 1974). Albert Cleage was one of the early interpreters of black theology; his *Black Messiah* (New York: Sheed & Ward, 1968) is a vital part of the literature. Joseph Washington in *Black Religion: The Negro and Christianity in the United States* (Boston: Beacon Press, 1964); *The Politics of God* (Boston: Beacon Press, 1967); and *Black Sects and Cults: The Power Axis in the Ethnic Ethic* (Garden City, N.Y.: Anchor Doubleday Book, 1975) have contributed enormously to the understanding of black theology.

11. Wilmore & Cone, eds., *Black Theology: A Documentary History*, 101.

12. See Wilmore, *Black Religion and Black Radicalism*, 295, and John C. Bennett, "Black Theology of Liberation," in Wilmore & Cone, eds. *Black Theology: A Documentary History*, (1979).

13. Boesak, *Farewell to Innocence*, 18.

14. Cone, "The White Church and Black Power," in *Black Theology: A Documentary History*, ed. Wilmore and Cone, 113.

15. Cone, *God of the Oppressed*, 138.

16. Wilmore, *Black Religion and Black Radicalism*, 297.

17. Jones, *The Color of God*, 6.

18. Ibid., 6-7.

19. Cone, *A Black Theology of Liberation*, 23.

20. See Wilmore & Cone, eds., *Black Theology: A Documentary History.*

21. Jones, *The Color of God,* 6.

22. Roberts, *Black Theology in Dialogue,* 117.

23. See Leonardo Boff and Clodovis Boff, *Introducing Liberation Theology* (Maryknoll, N.Y.: Orbis Books, 1987). They discuss three meditations: socioanalytical meditation, hermeneutical meditation, and practical meditation. Each of these three meditations is related to the larger issue of doing liberation theology. The socioanalytical meditation tries to discover what God is saying to the poor and practical meditation makes an effort to determine what can be done according to God's Word to change the situation.

24. Jesse Jackson, "Common Ground and Common Sense," *Vital Speeches of the Day* 54 (15 August 1988): 649–53.

25. Cone, *God of the Oppressed,* 152.

26. Cone, *For My People,* 99.

8

AFRICAN AMERICAN CATHOLICS AND BLACK THEOLOGY: AN INTERPRETATION

M. Shawn Copeland, O.P.

This is a report on the pastoral and intellectual appropriation of Black theology among African American Catholics. First, it will look backward to that thirty-five year period between 1889 and 1924 that was the scene of two attempts by Catholics of African descent to enjoy the heritage of their faith; to win for themselves, their progeny, and their people, the attention, the respect, and the care of their church; and to help secure the rights of citizenship for their race. By the power and grace of the Holy Spirit, these men and women gave birth to an indigenous *African American Catholic church tradition of struggle for social justice.* The story of their dedication enriches the common memory of all African American Christians and provides the historical context for the current twenty-year-old movement of Black Catholics in the United States. Second, it will identify the chief catalysts that have promoted the resurgence of that tradition. Third, it will present some illustrations of African American Catholic pastoral and intellectual appropriation of the impulses and insights of Black theology. For the sake of our movement, I will cite names, achievements, and events, but because of the limitations of space, the efforts of many valiant and worthy women and men must be omitted. Finally, I will offer some suggestions for the future of that movement and its talented, diverse, and complex company of women and men who are striving, in the words of Pope Paul VI, to enrich their church with their "precious and original contribution of 'Negritude' [Blackness] which she (the church) needs particularly in this historic hour."[1]

Contextualization

From 1889 until 1894 African American Catholic laity conducted an increasingly vigorous movement to importune their church to "take an active interest

M. Shawn Copeland, O.P. is assistant professor of theology and Black studies at Yale Divinity School. This essay was published in *African-American Religious Studies: An Interdisciplinary Anthology,* ed. Gayraud Wilmore (Duke University Press, 1989), pp. 228-48.

in what concerns, not only the spiritual but also the temporal welfare of all the people entrusted to your [its] care." The call for a meeting of "Colored Catholics . . . for the purpose of taking the status of the race in their relation to the church"[2] was the inspiration of Daniel Rudd, the publisher and editor of the *American Catholic Tribune*, the only national newspaper published by Catholics of African descent in the United States in the nineteenth century. On Tuesday, January 1, 1889, nearly one hundred Black [male] delegates from thirteen states, the District of Columbia, and South America, along with invited and sympathetic members of the white clergy and the hierarchy, met in congress in Washington, D.C.

At the end of the nineteenth century, the general state of African American Catholics within their church mirrored their condition in the wider American society. Although unlike the Presbyterians, the Baptists, and the Methodists, the Catholic church did not split over the question of slavery, the church long had purchased the culture and custom of racism; and, but for rare exceptions, ignorance, benign neglect, and segregation obtained. Catholics numbered about two hundred thousand in an African American population of seven million. A survey taken by the first congress cited twenty churches most with its own primary school, sixty-five other schools providing instruction for approximately five thousand children, nine orphanages, approximately one hundred fifty sisters in the two religious congregations founded for and by women of color,[3] seven seminarians, and one priest, Augustus Tolton.[4]

Four congresses followed, convening in 1890, 1892, 1893, and 1894, each assembly of delegates growing in confidence and in militancy. Their concerns and discussions were political and economic, social and religious, national and international in scope: an end to all forms of civic, economic, and political discrimination at home; the abolition of slavery abroad; the Back to Africa movement; just and equal treatment in their church. From the first, delegates had been eager for some permanent scheme, and at the third congress they organized the St. Peter Claver Union. However, neither the Union nor the congress movement lasted. It is not precisely clear why, but there were increasing clashes and differences with the white hierarchy and clergy over the identity, the direction, the purposes, and the leadership of the congress movement and the Union. Still, if their concrete accomplishments were few, this courageous group "recorded for posterity the perduring hopes and aspirations of the people they represented and left an embarrassing reminder of a plea for simple justice that would not be heeded."[5]

A broad-based movement among African American Catholics did not surface again until the second decade of the twentieth century with the concern of Dr. Thomas Wyatt Turner to meet the social, personal, and religious needs of Black Catholic servicemen during the First World War. The Committee for the Advancement of Colored Catholics, formed for this end, led to the Federated Colored Catholics. Turner had sought an action-oriented group dedicated to ending discrimination against Blacks within American society and within the church. For nearly a decade he was assisted by the Reverend John

LaFarge, S.J., and the Reverend William Markow, S.J. But rather than turn the Federated Colored Catholics in a less activist and practical direction, Turner parted company with the two Jesuits.

Catalysts in the Resurgence of the African American Catholic Struggle for Social Justice

The resurgence of an African American Catholic church tradition of struggle for social justice was catalyzed by radical change: change in the social, political, economic condition of Blacks in the United States and change in the Roman Catholic church itself. The civil rights movement challenged the dominant ethos and pattern of accommodation to segregation; the Second Vatican Council challenged the historic intellectual, theological, and cultural insularity of the Catholic church. Change in the social mood without change in the ecclesial mood might have forced Black Catholics in the United States to abandon their centuries-old religious tradition; change in the ecclesial mood without change in the social mood might have compelled them to barter their racial-cultural heritage for silver. There was a propitiousness to these times. This was God's time; this was *kairos*.

The civil rights movement gave the U.S. Catholic church a singular opportunity to witness concretely at home to the meaning of unity in the faith and diversity in race, culture, and ethnicity. The nonviolent determination of Blacks for just and equal regard under law challenged the conscience. Catholic lay men and lay women, sisters and priests, marched at Selma. True, the Catholic hierarchy had denounced the sin of racism; and some, though not all, Catholic bishops had begun either to integrate those parochial schools under their direct control or to condemn publicly the worst examples of discrimination. But, as a whole, as an institution, the Catholic church in the United States made no significant contribution to the civil rights movement. Black Catholic scholar-priest Jerome LeDoux declared the failure of the church at this crucial moment as one of "the most shameful scandals of modern Christianity: the damning exposure of the Church as the tail-light in matters of justice where the civil courts did not hesitate to be a head-light."[6] And writing from Gethsemani, Trappist Thomas Merton uncovered the dominant Catholic attitude as a "fake Catholicism." It was, he wrote, a "parody of unity which is not unity at all but a one-sided and arbitrary attempt to reduce others to a condition of identity with ourselves . . . one of the most disastrous of misconceptions."[7]

If the silence and indifference of their church wounded Black Catholics, the cry "Black Power" galvanized them. At least one Black priest, Lawrence Lucas, joined the predominantly Protestant National Committee of Black Churchmen. Around the country Black priests, Black sisters, and Black laity began informal, nourishing conversations and study-groups. They retrieved and consumed the work of Black cultural theorists, historians, and artists. All over the United States, Black Catholics stood up.[8]

Fourteen days after the death of Martin Luther King, Jr., a group of Black priests stunned the white Catholic hierarchy by publicly and collectively naming their church as "primarily a white racist institution."[9] Women were not among delegates to that first congress in 1889 and Robert L. Ruiffin of Boston lamented their absence in his address to that body. But a woman was present at the priests' deliberations—Sister Martin de Porres Grey (now Dr. Patricia Grey Tyree). The priests urged her to organize Black sisters and she did. In August 1968, following a national gathering of 155 women from seventy-nine different religious congregations, forty-five cities, the Caribbean, and Africa, the National Black Sisters' Conference (NBSC) was born pledging "to work unceasingly for the liberation of Black people."[10] The National Office for Black Catholics (NOBC) along with national assemblies of seminarians and laity soon followed.

But contemporary movement among Black Catholics was not without dissension and conflict. Black Catholics were never in complete accord over the function and organizational structure of the NOBC. There were heated objections to its presumed role as an umbrella agency for the various national groups. The clergy, sisters, and brothers were well-schooled in ecclesiastical protocol; at times they used this to disadvantage the laity. The new emphasis on lay leadership was no less threatening to Black clerics and religious, than it was to their white colleagues. Long denied pastorates and other appropriate outlets for their talent, they were not always eager to share leadership with the laity. But still, always—then and now—our arguments focused on the best means to importune our church to address itself to racism, on the style and strategy of our self-determination, but never on the validity of these needs, on the legitimacy of our demands, or on their substance.

Pastoral and Intellectual Appropriation of Black Theology

The efforts at pastoral and intellectual appropriation of Black theology by African American Catholics are, first of all, the products of the resurgence of an African American Catholic church tradition of struggle for justice in their church and in the wider society. Clearly the various projects and programs developed by African American Catholics derive inspiration from the pioneering theological and ministerial studies of Black Protestant theologians, church scholars, and pastors. But African American Catholic projects and programs also take impetus from the Black Power movement and Black cultural nationalism, from the Black separatism of the early Malcolm X and the Black Christian nationalism of Albert Cleage; from contact with the leaders and developments of post-Conciliar African Catholicism and the renewal of theology and pastoral ministry taking place in the universal church. On the other hand, two movements with deep Catholic roots, namely, the Theology in the Americas program (TIA)[11] and feminist theology, to date have exerted little influence on African American Catholic pastoral work and theological thinking as a whole.

The Black Catholic Clergy Caucus always has formed a visible and vigorous vanguard confronting ecclesiastical racism at every turn, collectively offering Black Catholics and our activities an offensive and defensive pastorate, and initiating communication with our counterparts in Africa. The increasing number and participation of Black bishops in the National Conference of Catholic Bishops keep the agenda of Black communicants before the wider American Catholic church. It is through the bishops' vigilance that the hierarchy issued the pastoral letter on racism, *Brothers and Sisters to Us*.[12] But it was the establishment and staffing of the various national offices, especially those of the National Office for Black Catholics and the National Black Sisters' Conference, that put teeth and soul into the shaping of a distinctive African American Catholicism. These two organizations carved out space for the development of leadership, for study, for spiritual and psychological formation, for the creative intellectual and pastoral interpretation of the Black Catholic experience in the United States.

Pastoral Application of Black Theology

Liturgical Rites and Rituals. Catholics of African American descent will be forever indebted to the Reverend Clarence Joseph Rivers who singlehandedly revolutionized the hymnody, the ritual form, the symbols, the mood, and the atmosphere of their worship. Well before the Second Vatican Council, Father Rivers had begun to compose, perform, and lecture on Catholic church music in a Black cultural style. In his *American Mass Program, Mass Dedicated to the Brotherhood of Man*[13] and subsequent compositions and recordings, Rivers introduced the idiom of African American music into Catholic worship. In the late 1960s and early 1970s, in order to bring greater cultural coherence to the liturgy, he began to critically reexamine the relation of the various elements of the mass to the Black idiom. In his commitment to articulate an authentic African American Catholic liturgical aesthetic, Rivers challenged the diluted liturgical experimentation that attempted to pass for renewal in so many places in the wider U.S. Catholic church. To his achievements are joined the work of other Black Catholic composers including Rawn Harbour, Leon Roberts, Marjorie Gabriel-Burrows, Grayson Brown, Avon Gillespie, Eddie Bonnemere, and Ray East.

The earliest pastoral attempts of African American Catholics to incorporate the insights of Black Theology centered on the Sunday worship of the local parish. These individual and initially isolated efforts, usually by priests or sisters, to add Black cultural shadings to the Catholic liturgy distinguish a first phase of adaptation or acculturation. Under the directives of the Second Vatican Council, the process of acculturation opens the Roman liturgy to the inclusion, substitution, and symbolic representation of compatible elements from particular cultures.[14] Black Catholics dove into the treasure chest of African American sacred music lifting up the spirituals, plundering the Baptist hymnal, tracking down organists competent in the Black musical genre and idiom—often from the Baptist congregation across town! Ever so tentatively the laity began to sing these songs at the eucharist liturgy, at prayer services, at Advent or Lenten devotions. The nationalist colors — red, black, and green — along with traditional African styles, patterns, and weaves were employed in the design of vestments, stoles, and altar linens used in the various ceremonies of the Roman rite. Crucifixes and statues of the mother of Jesus sculpted in African features, and Black cultural products began to appear on the walls and altars of Catholic parishes. Priests began to listen to and to appropriate the rhetorical style of their Black Protestant counterparts. It was not long before hand-clapping, call and response, the shout, the tambourine, and the drum sounded in the Catholic church. This phase of adaption or acculturation began a process of psychic healing as Cyprian Rowe observed:

> Catholics of African descent have suffered intensely from the sterility of liturgical rites, because they have somewhere in their bones a tradition of worship in which the sung and spoken word have been fused into celebrations of joy. Afro-Americans are therefore among the first to realize that it is a certain cultural ignorance, and even cultural imperialism, that have resulted in their almost total exclusion from worship, except as spectators.[15]

During this period there were widespread attempts simply to make Black culture welcome in Catholic parishes and among Black Catholics; but some measure of evaluation was needed so that parishes did not become "inauthentically Catholic in their scope while becoming authentically Black."[16] Under the leadership of its executive director, Brother Joseph M. Davis, S.M., and his successor, Brother Cyprian Rowe, F.M.S., NOBC's Program for Culture and Worship furnished the means to evaluate and to share liturgical activities; hence leading to the phase of indigenization. Through conferences, workshops, and the publications of monographs, the NOBC constructed a platform from which Black Catholic composers and liturgists could mold and direct an African American renewal of Catholic worship. The NOBC inaugurated an annual workshop, staffed by cultural specialists, dramatists, liturgists, musicians, gospel artists, and singers, to school liturgists, priests, musicians, choirs, and lectors in African American modes of worship. These workshops were attended by Black Catholic laity, sisters, brothers, and clergy, as well as white priests, brothers, and sisters who ministered in the Black community. Intensive sessions brought participants into contact with the slave moans and chants, the spirituals, traditional and contemporary gospel music, and freedom songs. Finally, these workshops created a climate for mutual exchange and collaboration among Black composers and musicians, as well as a stimulus for their professional growth.

The recent appearance of *Lead Me, Guide Me: The African American Catholic Hymnal*[17] is a sign of some maturity in this long and ambiguous period of indigenization. Thoroughly Black and thoroughly Catholic, the hymnal preserves spirituals as well as Gregorian plain chant, Black arrangements of Dr. Watts-style hymns as well as Catholic standards, traditional as well as contemporary Gospel Songs, Freedom Songs as well as African American Catholics composition. The hymnal also recognizes and affirms both the commonality and plurality of the Black Catholic experience since ". . . a Louisiana Black Catholic is not a West Baltimore Black Catholic; neither is a New York Haitian Catholic a Los Angeles Black Catholic or a Chicago Black Catholic."[18]

The eucharistic liturgy is at the heart and center of Catholic worship. Given the nature of the doctrinal position held by the Vatican on the ordination of women, there resides at the core of Catholic liturgical life a putative theological bias favoring men over women. In the Roman Catholic church, only celibate males may preside at the eucharistic ritual. Inevitably, this taints Roman Catholic liturgical life with a patina of clerical-centricism. Black feminist theologians of other Christian traditions will find this situation not so different from their own: for even if their churches are logo-centric, preaching is dominated by the male voice. In the effort to nourish its own membership at retreats and to foster the gifts of women like Sister Teresita Weind, S.N.D., and Beverly Stanton, the NBSC encouraged the design of non-eucharistic rituals in a Black cultural style. Litanies and chants, African customs and symbols, stylized gesture and dance interplayed to express purification and dedication, to celebrate points of passage or commitment, to mark repentance or resolve.

Spiritual Formation. Christianity is, above all, a way of life. Catholicism marks that way of life with features which differentiate its expression from those of other Christians. And Black Catholics—lay women and men, sisters, brothers, priests—were not long in identifying the need and ways to ebonize features of a Catholic Christian way of life.

A retreat, the setting aside of sustained and uninterrupted time for prayer, for meditation, for examination or refreshment or renovation of one's relationship with God, was an opportunity to transform a common Catholic practice in the light of Black Theology. The NBSC sponsored retreats for its own members, but it was not unusual for married or single women, brothers, and priests to join them. (And in the last few years, retreats either have preceded or followed annual joint conferences of the permanent deacons and their wives, sisters, brothers, seminarians, and priests.) Retreats included a variety of spiritual disciplines—private and communal reflective reading and praying of the Scriptures, singing spirituals or other appropriate hymns, fasting, silence, quiet or guided meditation. Devotional conferences were the locus of nourishing formative reflection. From the perspective of Black Theology, these conferences examined such topics as prayer, spirituality, celibacy, suffering, loneliness, and the meaning of eucharist in the Black sociopolitical context. Often these conferences were prepared by nonordained women and men who had formal training in Catholic theology or spirituality or who were well read in Black theology and in Catholic spirituality. These conferences attempted to work out new understandings of the Christian life by which Black Catholics could take their bearings.

In September 1969, Al McNeeley of Detroit's St. Bernard Parish, along with a team of lay leaders and priests, developed a pastoral training program to give Black men theological, spiritual, and personal formation and support to func-

tioning in the Black community as lay or nonordained ministers within their
parishes. The program took scriptural impetus from the work of deacons (Acts
6:1–7); it took pastoral theological motivation from the pressing socio-economic
and cultural needs of the local Black community; and it took personal inspiration from the promotion and cultivation of Black self-concept and Black
leadership. "Ministers of Service" fanned out into various city parishes, assessed
needs, and generated innovative ways to meet them. They helped families cope
with crises of all sorts, befriended Black youth, criticized crime and drugs,
cheered bed-ridden and home-bound residents, comforted those confined to
hospitals and nursing homes. They assisted at the eucharist, conducted Bible
study classes, and prepared youth and adults for participation in the sacraments.
These men carried the compassion, love, and mercy of God to people and places
the institutional church neglected.

Education, Evangelization, and Catechesis. With the Gospel imperative, "Go
into the whole world and proclaim the good news to all creation," all baptized
Christians are summoned to the work of evangelization and catechesis. Evangelization and catechesis are concerned with "church-building," that is to say,
with preaching the message of the good news of salvation in Jesus Christ, with
building up that message in the lives of individuals, and with achieving a community of believers who support and challenge one another to live up to the
gospel. The commitment of contemporary African American Catholics to evangelization and catechesis can be linked with that of the earliest Afro-American
Catholic Congress. Proceedings of that first assembly record an eagerness "to
cooperate with the clergy in the conversion and education of our race." Concerted measures to address the tasks of evangelization and catechesis from the
starting point of Black Theology can be traced over the past fifteen years and
take at least three forms: 1) education to African American and African American Catholic heritages, 2) the development of a theology of catechesis and of
catechetical materials, and 3) the pastoral letter from the Black Catholic bishops on evangelization.[19]

I cannot recount here the dozens of educational task forces, ad-hoc com-
mittees, and study groups which made the contributions, achievements, and
biographies of Catholics of African descent available to Black and white Catholics in parish, school, and diocesan settings. These women and men plowed
and toiled alone, often with little encouragement or financial support. Their
work was a labor of love, inspiring so many of us who now walk more proudly
and less hesitantly in the field they cleared. An early educational effort to
inform Black Catholics about their Catholic heritage was a monograph edited
by Al McNeeley: *Afro-American and Catholic*[20] retrieved the African Catholic
community of Christian antiquity—"Church Fathers" (Tertullian, Origen, Cyprian, and Augustine), popes (Victor, Melchiades, and Gelasius), saints, martyrs,
and desert monks (Benedict the Black, Peter Claver, and Moses the Black). It
retold the story of Black Catholic life in the United States and particularly in
the archdiocese of Detroit. And while *Afro-American and Catholic* cannot be
considered a critical scholarly history, it did what professional Catholic church

historians and educators had not—made accessible to Black Catholics in the pew a record of their presence in their church. Such publications continue to make an important contribution to the work of professional historians. They preserve life stories, put face and flesh on events and trends vital to social history. But, more importantly, these works continue to fill gaps in the spiritual, psychic, and historical experience of Black Catholics.

Among the Black Catholic bishops who have spoken on catechesis and evangelization, the most notable is Bishop James Lyke,[21] while the most differentiated articulation of a Black Catholic theology of catechesis comes from the writings of Toinette Eugene.[22] Methodical mediation of just such a theology has been the work of Nathan Jones[23] and practical translation of that method for pedagogy has been assumed by Sister Eva Marie Loomis, S.S.S.[24] Taken collectively and complementarily, these thinkers advance a type of catechesis that offers a liberating experience of religion, faith, and religious education—an education for the whole person, rooted in, attentive and faithful to the common and plural Black Catholic experience.

In his publications, lectures, and presentations, Nathan Jones is unparalleled in outlining the methodical programming of catechetical education. Tapping into African and African American folklore, music, poetry, aphorisms, history, theology, religious traditions, and Catholic doctrine, Jones has produced a program of catechesis, corrective and remedial, faithful to both our heritages. The pedagogical translation of an African American Catholic catechetical program into learning aids and classroom tools for directors of religious education and catechists is Sister Loomis's contribution to this over-all enterprise. Her ability to identify and to adapt resources, to demonstrate ways to employ Black cultural learning styles in a catechetical motif has been indispensable.

Through the IMANI Program, Loomis and her associate, Sister Addie Walker, S.S.N.D., have begun the collateral task of catechist formation—preparing catechists to work in the Black community. Loomis and Walker have shaped the IMANI curriculum under the influence of Black scholarship in psychology, sociology, culture, history, and theology as well as Catholic spirituality. Bishop Lyke's early ministry as a pastor was an important resource for his doctoral studies and consequent analysis and critique of the National Catholic Catechetical Directory. Lyke's contribution to the formation of catechists has been in underscoring the social context of catechesis. Catechists ought to be alert to the systemic injustice threaded through the Black community and eager to cooperate in practical schemes of social change. Indeed failure to do so, he insists, will "make a mockery of Christ and his transformating power." But the catechist is never a "social worker who is pious." The catechist teaches a new power and a new wisdom who is "Christ self-emptying and self-transcending, powerful with the power of God."

The most conspicuous example of the African American Catholic response to the challenge of evangelization is the pastoral letter by the Black Catholic bishops, "What We Have Seen and Heard." In this letter, the bishops have adopted a familiar and traditional format through which Catholic bishops convey their thinking on important matters to their communities. The letter integrates Black spiritual, cultural tradition and Catholic heritage to challenge decisively the pervasive notion that "Blackness" and "Catholicism" are inimical. Moreover, the letter is a sign of the "coming of age" of a people in their church: participation in apostolic succession, membership in the clergy and religious congregations of women and men, an increasing body of communicants, discernible models of Christian practice, programs and structures of institutionalization and maintenance, trained church scholars and theologians. The pastoral letter presupposes a maturing African American Catholicism by writing of evangelization as a challenge to Black Catholics to make a gift of their genius to the whole church.

There are countless other women and men who shoulder the theoretical, practical, administrative responsibilities of catechesis, and of evangelization, of spiritual formation, social ministry, teaching, and worship. But I cannot fail to mention African American Catholic cultural-spiritual griot, Sister Thea Bowman, F.S.P.A., whose preaching, lecturing, writing, and experimentation in ritual have gained international acclaim; or the Reverend Clarence Williams, who has pioneered the work of evangelization in television and video production; or the Reverend Boniface Harding and the Reverend Albert McKnight, who for more than twenty years have sought to realize the corporal and spiritual works of mercy among the poor, the hungry, the homeless, the neglected, the battered, the disenfranchised, the illiterate; or the members of the National Association of Black Catholic Administrators, the dozens of women and men all across the United States who are directors of diocesan offices, local secretariats, and programs designed for Black Catholics, who hold the key to the doors of the wider field of evangelization. Through all these as well as so many of the women and men, through all these ways and in so many others, African American Catholics press forward the process of indigenization in every dimension of leadership, of collaboration, of liturgy, of education, of catechesis, and of service.

Theological Appropriation

The meeting of African American Catholic ministry and Black theology has had fruitful results. Already, as I have indicated, this encounter has made distinctive and significant contributions to pastoral and social ministry by and among Black Catholics to the way liturgy is understood and celebrated by and among us, as well as to the wider renewal of liturgy and the liturgical arts in the Catholic church in the United States. In theology, however, the situation is quite different.

In his reflection on the relation of African American Catholics to Black Theology, James Cone has this to say: "Although black Catholics challenged the racist character of the Catholic Church in the U.S.A., they have not made a significant academic contribution in the field of black theology, and the reasons are at least partly obvious. The white power structure in the Catholic

Church is so restrictive on what blacks can do or say that it is almost impossible to think creatively."[25] In the paragraph that follows, Cone notes that Black Catholics do not lack the "conflictive situation" that provokes new theological thought. But he bemoans the absence of "space" for the development of indigenous Black Catholic leadership so necessary for creating a theological perspective accountable to the Black struggle for freedom, rather than to oppressive white structures. Cone continues: "As a black Protestant who looks at the Catholic Church from the outside, the immensity of the task of trying to challenge the tradition of Catholic theology *and* also remain inside the church is so great that it overwhelms me."[26]

Insofar as theology has been a privileged meta-language to which African American Catholics only recently have had full access, Cone is correct. But his comments neither sufficiently appreciate the ways in which Black Catholic organizations have functioned over the past twenty years to provide occasions for leadership, fellowship, collaboration, and criticism; nor do they acknowledge the fidelity of Black Catholics to their own best interests. Moreover, we are not overwhelmed: this is precisely how we perceive our sacred task. His assessment also fails to situate Black Catholic thinkers within the larger international context of Catholic theologians, church scholars, and pastoral ministers who are women and men of color. Though perhaps this latter omission is also our own. Still: given the dearth of formal-academically trained African American Catholic theologians, our intellectual appropriation and particular contribution to the ongoing development of Black theology await maturity. But some beginnings have been made.

In the fall of 1978, under the auspices of the National Black Catholic Clergy Caucus, the Reverend Thaddeus Posey, O.F.M., Cap., organized and chaired the first Black Catholic Theological Symposium. Coming only months after an attack on U.S. (Protestant) Black Theologians in the pages of *L'Osservatore Romano*,[27] the Vatican news organ, the four-day meeting was neither an exercise in apologetics, nor in posturing rhetoric. In his preface to the published proceedings, Posey placed the symposium in the context of basic theological praxis—faith seeking understanding. "Black Theology," he wrote, "is . . . not only natural but a prerequisite to natural growth in Christ."[28] One of the more immediate outcomes of the symposium was the establishment of the Institute for Black Catholic Studies, a summer graduate program administered through Black Catholic Xavier University in New Orleans. Posey along with the Reverend Bede Abram, O.F.M. Conv., and the late Reverend Joseph E. Nearon, S.S.S., have guided this effort. The Institute is staffed by Black Catholic scholars and theologians, is open to all interested persons, and is another instance both of the theological creativity of Black Catholics and their commitment to controlling structures for Black intellectual development.

The papers from the Black Catholic theological symposium represent some good examples of pastoral and existential mediation of Black theology in the ecclesial and socio-cultural contexts. Many of the participants are university and seminary teachers who lecture, research, and publish in their fields of theological specialization. Some have gained national and international attention. They form a cadre of scholars whom Cone admits "are determined to develop a black theology that is accountable to their experience in both the black and Catholic communities."

The work of thematizing a theology of African American Catholic spirituality has been carried on, in large measure, by Benedictine monk, scholar, and church historian Cyprian Davis. For nearly fifteen years he has presented monographs and lectures that retrieve, contextualize, and interpret both Black and Catholic models of sanctity and African American Catholic spiritual traditions of communal Bible study and prayer. By unsealing the neglected, antique and modern, history of Catholics of African descent and situating Black women and men within the stream of Catholic piety, Davis breaks open a tradition faithful to both Black religious experience and to multi-cultural Catholic spirituality. He suggests four characteristics of Black Catholic spirituality: it is contemplative, holistic, joyful, and communitarian. It is contemplative because the African American apprehension of religion mystically surrenders to the dark numinous power of God to hallow a home in the heart and soul, to infuse the whole person with awe at God's transcendent presence and with ecstatic joy at the intimacy of God's immanence. It is holistic because the African American personality is di-unital, and retains the capacity to manage ambiguity. This personality is gifted with a fundamental regard for person, for the human over products or things. Black spirituality is joyful resting in the power of God to protect, to defend, and to save; and this joy animates works of love and compassion, of reconciliation and peace. Black spirituality is communal and expresses itself in social concern and social justice; and this communitarian dimension opens Black Christians to all, excludes none. Davis's work displays a harmony neither artificial nor forced. He is a careful, painstaking historian able to tell the African American Catholic story in a style that emboldens and edifies. Currently Father Davis is at work on an extended history of African American Catholics.[29]

A Black Catholic theology of catechesis is one of the projects which occupies the scholarship of Toinette Eugene. Taking as her point of departure the African American religious experience as well as Roman Catholic church tradition, she sets evangelization and religious education in the place where revelation begins for Black people—in our own specific culture and ethos. Eugene's overall project in this area has been to lay our moral, ethical, and religious directions for Black Catholic catechesis. Those directions advocate Black culture as the "framework for embracing and synthesizing Church and community," a Christian love engaged in "meaningful and grateful praxis within the struggle for liberation," and a prophetic "self-sacrificial love and concern for others."[30] Eugene has done additional studies that focus the moral and ethical imperatives of Black Catholic catechesis on specific questions—family, sexuality, love, images and roles of women. Her participation on the committee of women advising the U.S. Catholic Bishops' Committee on their pastoral letter on the status of women, brings a nuanced and critical voice to predominantly white, middle-class, liberal feminist concerns.

Catholic theology as a whole still wants for dialogue with the social and human sciences. In exploring the psychosocial theme of Black self-concept, Black Catholic theologians contribute to furthering conversation with psychology. Dominican Sister Jamie Phelps has begun to delineate a prolegomenon to a fully differentiated theology of person that explicitly adverts to and affirms Black self-concept.[31] Her doctoral studies were preceded by a graduate degree in psychiatric social work as well as extensive clinical experience; and her career has always included parish involvement. Hence, Phelps's writing and lecturing on Black self-concept are characterized by practical as well as theoretical relevance and a nuanced grasp of varieties of Black lived experience. Committed to interdisciplinary work, Sister Phelps has benefitted from the cultural studies of Cyprian Rowe and the psychiatric studies of Edwin Nichols. Recently she has begun to link work in psychosocial development with studies in ecclesiology in order to document and to interpret more comprehensively the concrete mystery of the diversity of the church.

Canadian Jesuit philosopher-theologian, Bernard Lonergan has influenced the theological work of the Reverend Edward K. Braxton and me. Both of us have devoted doctoral research to Lonergan's work — Braxton on its relation to symbol and myth, me on its relation to contemporary political and theological thought on the common good.[32] Both of us are critical interpreters of contemporary theological movements and draw freely on the heuristic categories that Lonergan's reformulation of method in theology affords.

Braxton has written several articles analyzing and commenting on Black (Protestant) theology, as well as a lucid, thoughtful interpretation of changes in the church initiated by the Second Vatican Council.[33] James Cone has praised the potential of Braxton's "theological imagination and discipline" to make a significant Catholic contribution to Black theology. However, Cone suggests that classical and European theological motifs compete for Braxton's talent, evoking in him an "unresolved inner tension"[34] that prevents the flowering of his acumen. But, it is also possible that Edward Braxton is ensnared in that dilemma faced by all Black intellectuals seeking legitimation through an academy that is so inimical to their innermost concerns and so existentially and intellectually stultifying for them.

I served as Program Director for the first national consultation on Black Theology sponsored by the TIA Black Theology Project in 1977 and was Lonergan's teaching assistant during his final year at Boston College, where I have been associated with that university's group of Lonergan scholars. From the foundational categories of Lonergan's structure of the human good, I propose to rethink political theology in the American context with specific attention to issues of race, gender, and class.

Albert Raboteau's *Slave Religion*[35] is essential reading for an understanding of the Black religious experience. Here he made a study of the Herkovits-Frazier debate on the tenacity of African cultural elements in the life of the slaves. Raboteau argues a continuum of African influence, one of less degree in the United States than in Cuba, Haiti, and Brazil. And according to Raboteau, Catholicism accounts for this difference. In the Caribbean and Latin America, Catholicism offered points of contact with traditional African ritual and customs. In the United States, this was not the case as a de-ritualized Protestantism prevailed. Raboteau's historical interest in Black religion and Black religious experience complements the more specifically Catholic explorations of Cyprian Davis.

Archbishop Jean Jadot, the Apostolic Delegate of the Vatican to the United States, in an address to the Black Catholic Clergy Caucus, called for a corps of Black Catholic "scholars in theology, canon law and church history who can bring the reflection process of the black experience to the total affairs of the Church."[36] European educated Black Catholic scholars Diana L. Hayes and British-born Sheila Briggs promise to make significant contributions. But currently only a handful of African American Catholics are enrolled in graduate theological programs, with few obvious attempts on the part of American Catholic institutions of higher learning to recruit and challenge others to doctoral work. The need to cultivate and to support Black Catholic women and men in theological studies is even more compelling today than it was thirteen years ago.

Some Tentative Recommendations

Peter Sarpong, the Catholic archbishop of Accra, Ghana, has spoken on several occasions of the need to Africanize Christianity. Such a statement implies the need for a thorough-going re-formation: the refounding of the gospel in every age, in and by every culture. We, African American Catholics, have been doing just this: laying a new foundation—a new intellectual, moral, and religious basis for our reception and promulgation of the revelation of God in Jesus of Nazareth.

This is an ongoing task. I conclude with a few recommendations:

1. The newly created permanent Secretariat for Black Catholics will require the support of every one of this nation's 1.3 million Black Catholics. The Secretariat is a sign of the respect from the hierarchy for the potential of Black Catholics, and is a particular mark of respect for the Black Catholic bishops who played a major role in obtaining the office. No doubt Beverly Carroll, the Director of the Secretariat, will take up the national pastoral plan ratified at the 1987 National Black Catholic Congress. This plan deserves national, international, and ecumenical distribution, collaboration, and criticism.

2. Sexism still plagues the relations of Black Catholic women and men. In a certain sense, it cannot be (though it ought to be) otherwise: both the wider culture that adds its blows to our formation and the church we love are persistently patriarchal. Serious, informed, and frank dialogue is needed. New disciplines and asceticisms of love are required. Black men must choose humility, repentance, self-sacrifice, firm purpose of amendment, and change. Black

women must embrace anger, self-respect, courage, forgiveness, and change.

3. We must not be afraid of internal critique of our movement. Such critique is needed if we are to be faithful to our Black Catholic tradition and experience, if we are to honor our African American heritage, if our movement and our church are to be nourished and grow. At the same time, critique must be offered intelligently, rationally, responsibly, and lovingly: questioning, comparing, and understanding our experience; scrutinizing our analyses, planning, and judgments; critically reflecting on our evaluation and deliberation; and subordinating our decisions and action to the message and values of the gospel, to the common human good of the people of God.

Like their nineteenth-century ancestors, contemporary African American Catholics (1) have argued for inclusion and participation in the full life, maintenance, and direction of the Roman church in the United States; (2) have reiterated with righteous indignation their disappointment at the failure of the institutional church to live boldly its universal message; and (3) have demanded self-determination and self-definition in pastoral, educational, and theological affairs. In their Black consciousness, in their militant commitment to civil rights, and in their love of their church, these women and men are the "lineal descendants" of that earliest group of African American Catholics who spoke of their struggle as "an entering wedge in the breaking of the mighty wall of difficulties." When contemporary Black Catholics assert that they are "Black *and* Catholic," they stand (even when they do not know it) within a tradition of African American Catholic discourse of racial self-consciousness and self-identification. The participants in the congress movement spoke consistently of themselves and their co-religionists as "Colored Catholics" or "Afro-American Catholics." And when contemporary Black Catholics collaborate with other groups and organizations for the freedom, development, and welfare of the peoples of Africa and of African descent around the world, they carry on the work of those earliest African American Catholics who advocated the universal abolition of slavery. In these and countless other ways, contemporary African American Catholics uphold an indigenous church tradition of struggle for social justice that is one hundred years old.

NOTES

1. Paul VI, "To the Heart of Africa," The Teachings of Pope Paul VI-1969 (Vatican: Liberia Editrice Vaticana): 205; Reprint, *Catholic Mind* 67 (September 1969): 62-65.

2. Three Catholic Afro-American Congresses (Cincinnati: The American Catholic Tribune, 1893; Reprint New York: Arno Press, 1978): 14, 13. See David Spalding, C.F.X., "The Negro-Catholic Congresses, 1889–1894," *The Catholic Historical Review* 55 (October 1969): 337-57, and Cyprian Davis, O.S.B. "Black Catholics in America: A Historical Note," *America* 142, no. 3 (May 1980): 378-80.

3. The first pre-emancipation attempt to found a religious congregation for Black women was in 1824 through the work of Father Charles Nerinck in Kentucky. But the insensitivity of clergy and diocesan officials forced the dismissal of the group. In 1829 the Oblate Sisters of Providence was founded in Baltimore; in 1842, the Holy Family Sisters was founded in New Orleans. There is also a third Black religious congregation,

the Franciscan Handmaids of the Most Pure Heart of Mary, founded in 1917 to work in Harlem, New York. True to the meaning of Catholicity, i.e., universality, each of these congregations opened their ranks to white women who have joined them over the years.

4. Father Augustus Tolton is generally recognized as the first Black American Catholic priest, but there were three others: the Healy brothers—James Augustine, Sherwood, and Patrick. Sons of a slave woman and an Irish Catholic planter, they had been isolated by their father's money and social associations from the brunt of racism, but this left them with little explicit race identification and consciousness. By the time of the congress movement, Sherwood, a canon lawyer and theologian, was dead; James Augustine was the Ordinary Bishop of the diocese of Portland, Maine; and Patrick, a Jesuit, had served Georgetown University as vice president and president.

5. Spalding, 357.

6. Jerome LeDoux, "Christian Pastoral Theology Looks at Black Experience," in *Theology: A Portrait in Black* (hereafter *TAPB*), ed. Thaddeus J. Posey, O.F.M., Cap. (Pittsburgh: Capuchin Press, 1980): 115.

7. Thomas Merton, "The Black Revolution" (The Southern Christian Leadership Conference in Atlanta 1963).

8. For some personal accounts see Saundra Willingham, "Why I Quit the Convent," *Ebony* (December 1968):64-74; Lawrence Lucas, *Black Priest/White Church, Catholics and Racism* (New York: Random House, 1970); Sister Louis Marie Bryan, S.C., "History of the National Black Sisters' Conference," *Celibate Black Commitment: Report of the Third Annual National Black Sisters' Conference* (NBSC in Pittsburgh, 1971): 3-9; Sister Mary Roger Thilbodeaux, S.B.S., *A Black Nun Looks at Black Power* (New York: Sheed & Ward, 1972).

9. "A Statement of the Black Catholic Clergy Caucus, April 18, 1968" was first printed in *Freeing the Spirit* 1, no. 3 (Summer 1972); Reprinted in Gayraud S. Wilmore and James H. Cone, eds., *Black Theology: A Documentary History 1966-1979* (Maryknoll, N.Y.: Orbis Books, 1979), 322-34.

10. "The National Black Sisters' Conference Position Paper," *Black Survival: Past, Present, Future, A Report of the Second National Black Sisters' Conference* (NBSC in Pittsburgh, 1970): 155.

11. The National Black Sisters' Conference was invited through me, its executive director, to participate in the 1975 Detroit meeting of Theology in the Americas. I was unable to attend because of conference business and Sister James Phelps, O.P., attended.

12. *Brothers and Sisters to Us* (Washington, D.C.: USCC, 1979).

13. World Library Publications, 1966. See also his *Soulfull Worship* (Washington, D.C.: NOBC, 1974). *Spirit in Worship* (Cincinnati, Ohio: Stimuli, Inc., 1978), "Thank God We Ain't What We Was: The State of Liturgy in the Black Catholic Community," *TAPB*: 66-74, and "The Oral Tradition Versus the Ocular Western Tradition," in *This Far by Faith: American Black Worship and Its African Roots* (NOBC/and the Liturgical Conference in Washington, D.C., 1977): 38-49.

14. Vatican II, *Sacrosanctum Concilium,* Constitution on the Sacred Liturgy, 4 (December 1963): no. 14 and 37.

15. Cyprian Lamar Rowe, F.M.S., "The Case for a Distinctive Black Culture," *This Far by Faith,* 27.

16. Rivers, "Thank God," 73.

17. *Lead Me, Guide Me: The African American Catholic Hymnal* (Chicago: G.I.A. Publications, Inc., 1987). The Hymnal was authorized in 1983 by the National Black Catholic Clergy Caucus; its compilation and editing were coordinated by Bishop James Lyke, O.F.M.

18. J. Glenn Murray, S.J., "The Liturgy of the Roman Rite and African American Worship," *Lead Me, Guide Me.*

19. "What We Have Seen and Heard," A Pastoral Letter on Evangelization from the Black Bishops of the United States (Cincinnati, Ohio: St. Anthony Messenger Press, 1984).

20. Al McNeeley, *Afro-American and Catholic* (Detroit: Institute for Continuing Education, 1975).

21. Bishop James P. Lyke, O.F.M., "The Catechist in the Black Community," *Origins* 13 (June 9, 1983):70-73; see also his pastoral letter *So Stood Those Who Have Come Down Through the Ages: A Pastoral Reflection on the Family in the Black Community* (November 3, 1986).

22. See Toinette Eugene, "Training Religious Leaders for a New Black Generation," *Catechist* 6, no. 2 (October 1972):8-10; "Developing Catholic Belief: Catechesis as a Black Articulation of the Faith," *TAPB*: 140-60; "The Black Family That Is Church," in Sister Thea Bowman, F.S.P.A., ed., *Families Black and Catholic, Catholic and Black* (Washington, D.C.: USCC, 1985).

23. Nathan Jones, *Sharing the Old, Old Story: Educational Ministry in the Black Community* (Winona, Minn.: St. Mary's Press, 1982), see p. 286.

24. In addition to her post as NBSC catechetical coordinator, Sister Loomis is the executive director of BLOODTIES, a resource center for Christian education in the Black community.

25. Cone, *For My People* (Maryknoll, N.Y.: Orbis Books, 1984), 50-51; see also his "A Theological Challenge to the American Catholic Church," in *Speaking the Truth: Ecumenism, Liberation, and Black Theology* (Grand Rapids, Mich.: William B. Eerdmans Publishing Company, 1986), 50-60.

26. Cone, *For My People*, 50-51.

27. Father Bianbattista Mondin, *L'Osservatore Romano*, July 18, 1979.

28. Thaddeus J. Posey, O.F.M. Cap., "Preface," *TAPB*:3.

29. See Cyprian Davis, O.S.B., "The Christian Interpretation of the Black Experience," *TAPB*:91-102; also his "Black Spirituality," paper presented at the meeting of the National Black Catholic Congress, Washington, D.C., May 1987; "The Holy See and American Blacks in the Files of the Apostolic Delegation, 1904," Paper delivered at the American Catholic Historical Association, Washington, D.C., December 30, 1987.

30. Toinette Eugene, "Developing Black Catholic Belief," *TAPB*:14; see also her "Moral Values and Black Womanists," *Journal of Religious Thought* 44 (Winter-Spring 1988):23-34, and "While Love Is Unfashionable: Ethical Implications of Black Spirituality and Sexuality," in *Women's Consciousness and Women's Conscience: A Reader in Feminist Ethics,* ed. Barbara Hikert-Andolsen, Christine Gudorf and Mary D. Pellauer (San Francisco: Harper & Row, 1985), 121-41.

31. Jamie Phelps, O.P., "Black Self-Concept," *TAPB*:52-65; "Doctrine: The Articulation of Soul," in *Tell It Like It Is: A Black Catholic Perspective on Christian Education* (Oakland, Calif: NBSC, 1983):108-23; "Women and Power in the Church: A Black Catholic Perspective," Proceedings *Catholic Theological Society of America* 37 (1982):119-23.

32. See Edward K. Braxton, "Images of Mystery: A Study of the Place of Myth and Symbol in the Theological Method of Bernard Lonergan" (Ph.D. diss. Catholic University of Louvain, 1975). See my dissertation which offers a more political interpretation of Lonergan's work: "A Genetic Study of the Idea of the Human Good in the Thought of Bernard Lonergan" (Ph.D. diss. Boston College, The Graduate School of Arts and Sciences, Department of Theology, 1991). See my review of *Prophesy Deliverance! An Afro-American Revolutionary Christianity* by Cornel West, *Cross Currents* 33 (Spring 1983):67-71. "Black Theology," in *The New Dictionary of Theology,* ed. Komonchak et al. (Wilmington, Del.: Michael Glazier, 1987):137-41; "The Interaction of Racism, Sexism and Classism in Women's Exploitation," in *Concilium: Women, Work and Poverty,* ed. Elisabeth Schüssler-Fiorenza (Nijmegen and Edinburgh: Stichting Concilium and T. & T. Clark, 1987):19-27.

33. See his essay on Black theology in *America* (March 29, 1980):274-77; "Reflections from a Theological Perspective," in *This Far by Faith,* 58-75; "Black Theology: Potentially Classic?" *Religious Studies Review* 4 (April 1978):85-90, "What Is Black Theology Anyway?" *The Critic* (Winter 1977):64-70, and *The Wisdom Community* (New York: Paulist Press, 1980).

34. Cone, *For My People*, 52.

35. Albert Raboteau, *Slave Religion, The Invisible Institution in the Antebellum South* (New York: Oxford University Press, 1978).

36. Jean Jadot, "An Address to the Black Catholic Clergy Caucus," *Catholic Mind* 4 (March 1976):8.

9

PASTORAL MINISTRY IN THE ORIGIN AND DEVELOPMENT OF BLACK THEOLOGY

Gayraud S. Wilmore

I

W. E. B. Du Bois made the famous statement that the problem of the twentieth century is the color line.[1] What did he mean? He was making the point that race and color have ontological significance in the ethos and world-view of white Western societies. He was saying that the mystique of race and color, particularly of Blackness and Whiteness, would present an inescapable problem to our thinking, feeling, politics and economics, culture and religion, for at least a hundred years.

If the great man was right, and I believe he was, it makes no sense to talk about folklore, literature, art, science, philosophy, or even Christian theology as if they were somehow unaffected by the problem of race and ethnicity. That is the point with which we must begin this discussion. At least from the fifteenth century Christian theology has been tainted by racist thinking. Certainly the race problem has been ubiquitous and quintessential in the Western hemisphere. We breathe it in the air. We take it in with our mother's milk.

Two weeks ago, at an international conference on negritude and Afro cultures in the Americas, I heard a Black Peruvian anthropologist, Dr. Victoria Santa Cruz, say that when she was a young girl, Black mothers told their children that there was a stream somewhere between heaven and earth that everyone had to cross over when they died. When Blacks who were going to heaven crossed that stream their ugly black color would disappear and they would all turn white. "Often as a young girl," she said, "I wanted to die so I could find that passage and become white."

Presented as the eighth in the Charles B. Copher Annual Faculty Lecture series (1987) at Interdenominational Theological Center, this essay was published in the *Journal of the Interdenominational Theological Center* 13 (Spring 1986) and is reprinted with permission.

Such a story does not shock me. When I was a young boy growing up in the streets of North Philadelphia, there was a saying that circulated among us boys. It was a folk aphorism that evidently was being passed down from one generation of street urchins to another. It went like this:

> Dark man born of a dark woman, sees dark
>   days.
> He rises up in the morning like a hopper-grass,
> He is cut down in the evening like aspara-gras.

Where did it come from? That is one of the mysteries of folklore. But notice in this little maxim the faint allusion to Psalm 90:5–6.

> ... they are like grass which groweth up.
> In the morning it flourisheth, and groweth up;
> In the evening it is cut down, and withereth.

It is a very Biblical saying and suggests how a folk theology is born among a common people steeped in the language of Scripture. But to find such bitter words related to skin color on the lips of young children also tells us something about the consciousness of color discrimination among Philadelphia youth, and how it helped to shape our self-identity in the ghetto of the City of Brotherly Love.

Of course, there were other more positive sayings and proverbs, "The blacker the berry, the sweeter the juice." And, as Charles Buchanan Copher taught generations of I.T.C. students, for five hundred years the Black world celebrated the Blackness of Eben-melech who rescued Jeremiah from the pit; the Ethiopian eunuch who was baptized by Philip, the Evangelist; Simon of Cyrene who carried our Lord's cross behind him up the heights of Calvary; and other Biblical characters and texts that illustrate the fact that God did not despise his Black children, as some white Christians taught, but through suffering and struggle, prepared them for a great destiny. A study of the sermons of Black preachers in the nineteenth century will show that one of their favorite texts was Psalm 68:31 — "Princes shall come forth from Egypt, and Ethiopia shall soon stretch forth her hands unto God." Such was the raw material of a Black theology in North America, the Caribbean and West Africa from the beginning of our second introduction to Christianity.

Two points are being made by these observations. First, that this way of doing theology is at least as old as the Atlantic slave trade, if not older. It did not begin during the civil rights movement of the 1960s. Secondly, that African American ethnicity is inseparable from the doing of theology in Western societies. The God-talk that evolves from reflection on ethnicity in a culture that is as saturated with the consciousness of color and racial prejudice as this one, is not some *other* theology which stands over against a "genuine" Christian theology that is the property of the white Church, but *is* Christian theology, without qualification. Jesus Christ authenticates our will to be — to survive as a Black people in a racist-controlled environment. Jesus Christ must have something to do with our affirmation of Black being, our "power to be," or he was not involved in our creation, does not know who we are, and therefore, cannot be our Savior.

When young Black people accuse Christianity of being "a white man's religion," they are telling us, perhaps without knowing it, that they have not been taught what I am saying. They are expressing doubt and distress at the failure of the Black Church to portray Jesus Christ as a Black Messiah who not only has the power to satisfy their deepest yearning for self-affirmation, but who also takes upon himself their Blackness and triumphs over their encumbrances and adversities in a world dominated by white people.

Dr. King began to appreciate the agony of our young people toward the end of his life. Although he did not outwardly affirm Black theology, as such, one can see in his last sermons and writings a turn toward Black ethnicity as providential and Black people as destined for a special role in the economy of God. In his last book he spoke of African American people being called "to imbue our nation with the ideals of a higher and nobler order." Black theologians before him made that same messianic claim for the faith of their people. King was speaking out of a tradition that began here in the eighteenth century.

> This is our challenge. If we will dare to meet it honestly, historians in future years will have to say there lived a great people — a black people — who bore their burdens of oppression in the heat of many days and who, through tenacity and creative commitment, injected a new meaning into the veins of American life.[2]

So Black theology is not some strange and illicit teaching that some Black thinkers get involved in as they try to make sense of the Christian faith. And Martin Luther King, Jr., did not repudiate the implications of Black theology. The longer he lived the more explicit he became about the depth of white racism in American culture and the more convinced that Black Christianity, at its best, represented a purer form of the faith for the vocation of redemptive suffering that, in the mystery of providence, somehow became the lot of an African people.

II

But the issue before us is not an apology for Black theology. Black theological reflection has been researched, explained, attacked and defended now for almost twenty-five years. It has stood the test of time and we need not constantly defend it, as if it will have no validity until white theologians give up their objections to it.

The question today is Black theology's relevance for the pastoral ministry, its utility as a way of doing theology in the local congregation and the counseling room, its practicality for dealing with the normal, everyday needs of our people as we move among them as pastors and priests. It is my opinion that it is precisely in such settings during the civil rights movement that we became aware of the necessity of a contemporary Black theological perspective developed on the foundation of an earlier tradition. If Black theology today is failing to reach our pastors and congregations it may well be because it has ceased to harmonize the radical message of Black liberation with the more conservative message of healing and self-fulfillment through a saving faith in Jesus Christ. To be sure, that is more easily said than done, but the religious history of African-American people in this hemisphere proves that the capability of bringing about such a coherence between liberation and sanctification is the genius of the Black religious consciousness in North America.

It is my contention that our encounter as pastors with the militant young people of the 1960s helped to bring about this most recent burst of Black theological activity. One personal incident must suffice to illustrate my point about the origin of contemporary Black theology. On the night before James Forman was scheduled to present his Black Manifesto for reparations to the United Presbyterian General Assembly, meeting in San Antonio in May 1969, I found myself engaged in a heated discussion with a group of young urban guerrillas whom I had permitted to occupy my hotel suite. The discussion centered on the idea of the Black Manifesto, reparations and the Bible, the relevance of belief in Jesus Christ and the Church. At the climax of the argument, as proof that they were not just not talking revolution, but prepared to start one, one of the young people pulled out from under my bed two long wooden boxes tightly packed with automatic weapons and ammunition. I learned afterward that this ordnance had been shipped by Greyhound bus from Miami, although I cannot say that Jim Forman knew anything about their intention to intimidate the Assembly the next day when he was to present the demands of the Black Economic Development Conference for reparations from the United Presbyterian Church, U.S.A.

To say that I was shocked by the discovery of those weapons in my room would be the understatement of my life. I had to assume that my young guests were dead serious. I tried to disguise the fact that I was on the verge of panic as we continued to discuss whether such a tactic as violent confrontation could be strategically or ethically justified. The image in my mind, as I argued, was the picture of a ludicrous stick-up on the stage of the San Antonio convention hall, with the consequence of a bloody skirmish with the police and the F.B.I. that would set our cause back a hundred years.

We talked all night. The discussion ranged over what it means to be Black and Christian. We ruminated about God's judgment in political and cultural struggle. We dialogued about the failure of religion and what kind of theology would do justice to the legitimate grievances of young Black people and, at the same time, remain faithful to the demands of the gospel. We discussed the Black Muslims, holy war, and Jesus Christ as the liberator of the outcast and downtrodden.

When the sun finally came up over San Antonio I emerged from that smoke-polluted hotel suite, unshaven and bone-weary. I was not really sure what they would do that day, but I knew that I had been their pastor that night — perhaps the only pastor some of them had ever had. I knew that what was troubling their souls had an external source in our racist society. I knew that during that long night, I as pastor and they as my young, critical congregation had, in fact, been creating a Black theology of liberation together.

One of those young men was Irving Davis, of Teaneck, N.J., who died tragically on April 22, 1981. Before his death Irving became my good friend and something of a lay theologian. I wrote a eulogy for him that was published in *Presbyterian Outlook* that I entitled "A Prophet Without Portfolio." It read in part:

> I will remember Irving Davis most for what he did for me and several other clergy who were drawn, sometimes kicking and screaming, into the magnetic field of his vision of what the churches should be about in Africa and the Caribbean. Some of us used to say that we evangelized this hard-nosed black revolutionary who came to throw a monkey wrench into the ecclesiastical machinery which he believed was grinding the faces of the oppressed and stayed to become a partner in mission and a brother. We now know that he evangelized us.[3]

The point of all this is not to glorify young Black revolutionaries I have known, or to present Black theology as a new situation ethics that justifies anything it wants to and calls it Christian, as long as it serves Black prerogatives. I simply want to make two points: first, that incidents such as this one in San Antonio were not isolated incidents. Many Black urban pastors were forced to face the problem of how to minister to disillusioned young people during the 1960s and 1970s, and it was out of the struggle to find religious meaning in the cause of Black dignity and freedom that a contemporary Black theology came into existence. Secondly, and this is my main point: the new Black theology some of us were trying to develop was partly a *pastoral* theology. Rooted in the historic experience of the Black Church, it sought to bring the gospel to bear upon the most exasperating problems of marginated and cynical young people during one of the most difficult periods in American history.

III

In a book entitled *Soul Theology: The Heart of American Black Culture,* by Henry H. Mitchell, a Black theologian, and Nicholas C. Lewter, a Black Baptist pastor and psychotherapist in private practice, the authors convincingly argue that authentic Black theology is embedded in the "life-giving affirmations of the Black oral tradition," and that it is primarily communicated in a pastoral or counseling context. By studying clinical cases in Lewter's psychological practice, Mitchell and Lewter uncover the core belief system of the Black Church with the purpose of reconstructing what they will call our "Soul theology." What they are able to demonstrate is the possibility of leading persons to greater emotional stability, physical well-being and spiritual wholeness by raising latent folk affirmations to consciousness and encouraging their clients to reappropriate the therapeutic power of Black belief. Accordingly, Mitchell and Lewter contend that Soul theology, "unlike the widespread classification of Black theology with the theologies of liberation," preserves the "nourishing spirituality" of the belief system of ordinary Black folk.[4]

This book contributes an important corrective to Black theological reflection that has sometimes over-emphasized rationalistic polemics and political activism. It rightly brings us back to the pastoral dimensions of theology which had been neglected during the movement days. But not withstanding this virtue, the authors fail to make unambiguously clear that Black or Soul theology cannot be either-or, but must be *both*-and. It is precisely the pragmatic spirituality of Black faith that requires the pastoral emphasis of Black theology to include both the personal and the social aspects of our common experience. And because the personal and social realms are insuperable in real life, Black theology must refuse to make pastoral ministry a spiritual function that is separable from Christian political action.

My friendly, but most serious criticism of the Mitchell-Lewter interpretation of Black theology is that it does not take enough account of the way that personal ills, as C. Wright Mills was fond of saying, inescapably bisect social problems. That conjunction of the personal and social dimensions of life is simply taken for granted by mental health professionals who work in the Black community.

During the 1960s two Black psychiatrists, William H. Grier and Price M. Cobbs, published a study based on their clinical work with Black patients. They examined scores of cases of psychological suffering requiring professional counseling among Black men, women and children. They found that in many instances mental illnesses were directly traceable to internalized frustration and rage induced by the effects of racism and oppression in the environment.

> One of the problems in understanding the discontent of black people in America is highlighted in this material. The relationship between intrapsychic functioning and the larger social environment is exceedingly complex. Among other things, Negroes want to change inside but find it difficult to do so unless things outside are changed as well.[5]

Grier and Cobbs present an even more sobering discovery. It was their conclusion that the role of the Christian religion, when shaped by white norms and values, had more often served to depreciate and debase Black people than to make them more self-affirming and psychologically healthy.[6] In other words, their data would seem to argue for the necessity of a Black Christian theology to counteract the negative, guilt-producing effects of the religion which was foisted upon Blacks during slavery and continues to regard Blackness as a symbol of that which is innately inferior and evil.

I think, however, that both Grier and Cobbs, and Mitchell and Lewter, have overstated their cases in opposite directions from one another. A more correct view is that authentic Black religion has refused to disengage the spiritual from the secular. The best of Black preaching down through the centuries has made it clear that piety and practical action go together. That neither personal counseling nor political activity is sufficient to ensure peace of mind and individual happiness. My childhood pastor, Dr. Arthur E. Rankin, always reminded us that, "You ought to pray about it, but soon you have to get off your knees and *do* something." It was a familiar saying among some Black preachers I have known that "If you don't do the devil, the devil will sure do you." These choice examples of folk wisdom tell us that active discipleship, continuous engagement in struggle, is one way of keeping the devil off balance, of defending oneself and one's congregation against the ever-present machinations of evil.

Black preachers have been convinced that only those who know the Lord and have been sanctified by the blood of Christ, are able to fight off the forces arrayed against them—both in the depths of the psyche and in the external world of tribulation and injustice. It is the power of the Holy Spirit in a situation of extreme adversity that refreshes the weary soldier of the cross and equips him or her to "stay in the field, children, ah, until the war is ended"; to fight with all your might both in the physical body and in the body politic.

I am saying that Mitchell and Lewter are to be commended for trying to make Black theology more of a pastoral theology. But becoming more pastoral should not divest it of its theory and praxis as a theology of liberation. Because it cannot speak of wholeness and healing without, at the same time, speaking of health delivery systems, government bureaucracies, social security, houses and jobs, Black theology refuses to offer the people a spiritual bromide. Instead, it seeks to motivate them to bring about the political changes that abolish misery and promote long-term health for millions of individuals. The emphasis on pastoral ministry is, therefore, a needed corrective, but it must delve more deeply into the historic Black response to our Lord's prophetic summons: "to set at liberty those who are oppressed."

IV

The celebrated historian, the late Sydney E. Ahlstrom, made a remark about Black religious history that might well be applied to the field of theology. Ahlstrom observed the desirability of a "thorough renovation" of American church history. He went on to suggest that the paradigm for such a renovation is the Black religious experience which has been excluded from all previous synoptic histories.[7] With the same purpose of recovering marginal traditions that question the norms of the majority, it can be shown that Black theology provides a paradigm for the renovation of American systematic theology. Its particular contribution is the revalorization of African American spirituality and an emphasis upon the historic themes of Black religion in the United States: survival, elevation and liberation.[8]

Nothing is more obvious or more urgent than such a renovation in this period when the Jimmy Swaggarts, Jerry Falwells and Pat Robertsons are making successful inroads everyday into the white middle class with pious appeals for American intervention in Central America and the rejection of liberation theology. We dare not surrender the young, Black middle class constituency of our churches to this white theology. Here in Atlanta we learned recently that Bishop Earl Paulk, who is attracting an increasing number of Blacks, offers what he calls "kingdom theology." Paulk told an *Atlanta Constitution* reporter, "It is a whole new theology . . . What we're doing is setting up a network by which we can spread propaganda . . . We will accomplish enough [so] that the systems of the world will collapse because of their inability to survive, and what will be left will be a system the church has built."[9]

The kingdom theology of conservative evangelicalism intends to institute a Christian politics, a Christian public education, a Christian economics, and a born-again Christian culture that "will take dominion over the world." It would snatch us all from the jaws of the secular humanists and a Godless communism. It need not be concerned with poverty and degradation because it teaches that the poor and oppressed are God-forsaken because of their sins. It has no use for the World Council or the National Council of Churches because both affirm contextual theologies and cultural pluralism, twin works of the devil.

It should come as no surprise that Black theologians belong to a group that has long experienced racism at the hands of religious people who characteristically make such claims. We suspect that the conservative evangelical revolution of today frequently masks white supremacy. Because the white Church has as much to fear from this right wing resurgence as we do, some of us have urged our white friends to discover Black theology. Black theology has to do with more than the Black Church because it contributes to the enlightenment of white Christians by unmasking the racism and cultural imperialism under the garments of this new evangelical phenomenon. In its best form, therefore, Black theology teaches a theological option for the poor and oppressed that can help all of us to discover a compassionate and holistic pastoral ministry which recognizes the essential coherence between genuine spirituality and liberal politics.

In a new book for which I had the privilege of writing the foreword, the Dutch theologian Theo Witvliet discusses Black theology as representative of the underside of history where Christ is and where the Church must be.

The confrontation with black theology here represents an enormous positive challenge. Its polemic has a positive side, "Polemic is love." In its unmasking of the contradiction of Christianity there is a plea for conversion, *metanoia* for a radical transformation or perspective, which leads to the domain of the hidden history, the history which, judged by the usual church norms, belongs rather in the history of heresy. Black theology wants to argue from this specific history extending from the invisible church of the time of slavery [than in this history] there is a glimpse of liberation, of the great light that shines over those who live in a land of deep darkness (Isaiah 9:1, John 1:5).[10]

Although grossly misunderstood when he first made the statement, I believe that James H. Cone was on sound ground when he wrote in 1969 that white Christians have to become Black. "To be black," he wrote, "means that your heart, your soul, your mind, and your body are where the dispossessed are."[11] Some whites are incensed that anyone would dare suggest that they had to become Black in order to be born again. But Cone was saying that insofar as Blackness in the color symbolism of all Western art stands for the "despised and rejected of men," God is Black, Jesus is the Black Messiah, and it is impossible to be reconciled to the least of Christ's brothers and sisters without taking upon oneself the reproach of Blackness, i.e., identification with the oppressed and participation in their struggle for liberation.

V

When one combines the emphasis of Witvliet and Cone with the emphasis of Mitchell and Lewter, a view of Black theology as pastoral emerges with a quite specific meaning. Black theology becomes pastoral theology not merely because it "deals with those consequences for God's self-disclosure in history, as they pertain to the roles, tasks, duties, and work of the pastor" (Thomas C. Oden's definition of pastoral theology[12]), but because it also draws from tradition, culture, and experience that theoretical knowledge and praxis of social change that enables the pastor to unite sanctification and liberation. It helps him or her to see the connection between the health-giving experience of counseling and spiritual exercises, on one hand, and the *shalom-making* experience of action in the world, on the other.

Black theology, as a pastoral theology,[13] seeks to read the signs of the times to discover what God is doing with individuals trapped in the misery of personal sins, and communities trapped in worldly structures that oppose ethnic self-determination and encourage cultural suicide. Black theologians seek to engender in the church, through worship, preaching, teaching and exemplary action in the world, a pragmatic spirituality which takes hold of broken lives and leads people intelligently and hopefully into a healing conflict with every false power and illegitimate authority over their lives.

Although James Cone does not define what he does explicitly as a pastoral theology, he has consistently recognized the coherence between spirituality in the sanctuary and the struggle in the streets. For Cone, any study of the history of our pilgrimage from slavery will confirm the inseparability of sanctification and liberation. Thus, he stresses the necessary role that worship, preaching and pastoral leadership have played, not only in nurturing the souls of Black folk, but in shaping their churches as agents of liberation in the world.

The contradiction between the experience of sanctification and human slavery has always been a dominant theme in black religion. It is found not only in the rise of independent black churches but also in our songs, stories and sermons. When the meaning of sanctification is formed in the social context of an oppressed community in struggle for liberation, it is difficult to separate the experience of holiness from the spiritual empowerment to change the existing societal arrangements. If "I'm a chile of God wid soul set free" because "Christ had brought my liberty," then I will find it impossible to tolerate slavery and oppression.[14]

To the extent that Black preachers are seriously calling for a Black theology that is more relevant to what they do in the counseling room, the church school and the sanctuary, they must appropriate the whole of Black religion and not just a part of it. They need to be constantly reminded that the "old time religion" among our people had a powerful, though sometimes covert, social action and cultural renewal component that was utilized by our predecessors in lyceums, literary societies, benevolent clubs and abolitionist groups within the congregations, and active involvement in Reconstruction politics and Pan-Africanism in the wider community.

All of these activities were evidence of being "saved" and members of a saving community. It was this life and work of the churches that contributed inestimably to the psychological health and stamina of Black Christians. The point needs to be made over and over again, in the face of many temptations of educated young Black people today to retreat into anti-intellectualism, privatism and other-worldliness, that for our ancestors true spirituality was considered neither unreflective nor devoid of political relevance. Being born again, sanctified and rendering prayer and praise of God in daily life was a prerequisite to the exercise of cultural and political responsibility.

Whether or not our Black churches will be able to build for the future upon this rich inheritance depends upon its current leadership. The relatively newer denominations, like the Church of God in Christ, or increasingly popular forms of Christianity among Blacks — such as Black Roman Catholicism — must assume a larger responsibility alongside the older denominations, for shaping the message of the faith to meet the continuing needs of Black people for personal sanctification and survival, social and cultural elevation, and political and economic liberation. At the same time, some of us from the older denominations need to be more sensitive to the present deficiencies of Black theology, including its excessive activism and its debilitating sexism which ignores or subordinates the contribution of Black women.

If Black theologians will recognize that radical opposition to all forms of social injustice is a legitimate, but not the exclusive, concern of the logical refection, they will give greater assistance to local congregations in the development of the educational and pastoral dimensions of ministry. As I look at what is going on at this seminary and a few of them where Black men and women are preparing for ministry, I am hopeful about the utilization of Black theology in our churches. God is not through with Black people. We may yet witness an unprecedented revival of Christian faith among Africans of the Diaspora in all parts of the world. Such a revival cannot help but have an invigorating influence upon the whole ecumenical movement.

NOTES

1. W. E. B. Du Bois, *The Souls of Black Folk* (Greenwich, Conn.: Fawcett Publications, 1961), 23.

2. Martin Luther King, Jr., *Where Do We Go From Here? Chaos or Community* (New York: Harper & Row, 1967), 134.

3. *The Presbyterian Outlook* (25, May 1981), 9.

4. Henry H. Mitchell and Nicholas C. Lewter, *Soul Theology: The Heart of American Black Culture* (San Francisco: Harper & Row, 1986), 11, and see the statement on the dust jacket.

5. William H. Grier and Price M. Cobbs, *Black Rage* (New York: Basic Books, 1968), 22.

6. Ibid., 196-197.

7. Sydney E. Ahlstrom, *A Religious History of the American People* (New Haven: Yale University Press, 1972), 12-13.

8. I cannot analyze these themes in this paper, but have dealt with them at length in other essays. I consider them the building blocks of Black religious thought in the 19th century.

9. *The Atlanta Constitution,* March 3, 1987, Sec. A, 4.

10. Theo Witvliet, *The Way of the Black Messiah: The Hermeneutical Challenge of Black Theology as a Theology of Liberation* (Maryknoll, N.Y.: Orbis Books, 1987), 88.

11. James H. Cone, *Black Theology and Black Power* (New York: Seabury Press, 1969), 151.

12. Thomas C. Oden, *Pastoral Theology: Essentials of Ministry* (San Francisco: Harper & Row, 1983), x.

13. I first heard the Rev. Raul Suarez, president of the Cuban Ecumenical Council, challenge Black theology to "become a pastoral theology" in Havana in 1986. Suarez is one of the leading Cuban theologians of liberation and teaches at the seminary in Mantanzas.

14. James H. Cone, *Speaking the Truth: Ecumenism, Liberation and Black Theology* (Grand Rapids: William B. Eerdmans Pub. Co., 1986), 31-32.

10

BLACK THEOLOGY, THE BLACK CHURCH, AND THE AFRICAN-AMERICAN COMMUNITY

Dennis W. Wiley

Introduction

As we move swiftly toward the twenty-first century, my primary concern is not so much the survival of Black theology, or even the survival of the Black Church, as it is the survival and liberation of Black people.[1] African Americans, in particular, are at a critical juncture. After the holocaust of the Middle Passage, the atrocity of slavery, the terror of Jim Crow, and the illusion of "civil rights"—and just when we thought we had seen every ugly thing that racism could invent to thwart the development and progress of African-American people—we now find ourselves, once again, fighting for our lives against the insidious, relentless, and ravenous cancer of racism. The contemporary manifestation of this deadly disease includes the inundation of drugs within the African-American community, Black-on-Black violence, gross unemployment, rampant homelessness, disproportionate incarceration, the increased incidence of AIDS and other health threats, the continued perception of the African-American male (and, hence, African-American people) as "an endangered species," educational inadequacy, moral decay, spiritual emptiness, cultural ignorance, and social, political, and economic impotence. Furthermore, as racism continues its unchecked ascendancy, the right-wing conservatism nurtured by Ronald Reagan in the decade of the 1980s has now erupted into the full-blown, overt, blatant, and unabashed racial injustices in the Bush years of the early 1990s.[2]

A Double Assault

While racism is certainly nothing new, the intensity of its double assault on the African-American community over the past twenty years is unprecedented.

Dennis W. Wiley received his Ph.D. degree in Systematic Theology from Union Theological Seminary (N.Y.) and is pastor of Covenant Baptist Church in Washington, D.C.

This double assault has involved not only the traditional, overt attack on Black people from outside the African-American community, but also a more subtle, but equally deadly, attack from within. In response to the apparent gains of African Americans due to the civil rights movement on the one hand, and in reaction to the increasing confidence, self-awareness, and racial pride engendered by the emergence of "Black Power" on the other, White America began a "backlash" in the late sixties which has intensified, without abatement, until this very day.

The outside attack was exemplified in the rise to power of Republican presidents Richard Nixon, Gerald Ford, Ronald Reagan, and George Bush, all of whom embodied the growing sentiment that Black people had been "given" enough. Only temporarily, as a by-product of Nixon's Watergate fiasco, was this reactionary trend retarded to allow the anomaly of Democrat Jimmy Carter's brief presidency. The Republican presidents played a pivotal role in creating a climate, quite different from that which characterized the period of the civil rights movement, in which racist attitudes became not only acceptable, but respectable. It is within this climate that groups like the "Moral Majority," individuals like David Duke, issues like anti-affirmative action, and incidents like the brutal beating of Rodney King (as well as the subsequent exoneration of the four White police officers who beat him) have surfaced. It is a climate not unlike the post-Reconstruction atmosphere some one hundred years ago when the initial advances of African Americans, immediately following the Civil War, were soon buried under a thick layer of Jim Crow racism.

While the outside attack of racism has been severely crippling to the African-American community over the past twenty years, even more devastating has been the deadly assault from within. Of course, there have always been individuals within the African-American community who could be enticed or "bought off" to betray the race, whether intentionally or unwittingly. In some cases, these persons have been referred to as "Uncle Tom's" or, worse still, as "sell-outs." Never before, however, have African Americans been threatened from within by as treacherous and as stealthy a product of racism as illicit drugs and their inevitable consequence — Black-on-Black violence. Heretofore, despite the barrage of racist actions and attitudes that bombarded us from without, we always knew that we could find a haven of safety, understanding, and empowerment within by tapping the resources of our own community. In other words, we always knew that, no matter what happened to us on the outside, we could always, for the most part, trust in and depend on one another. The events of the last twenty years, however, have demonstrated that the long arm of racism is not only effective in tormenting us from the outside, but can also reach into the very depths of our community and turn us against ourselves. Heretofore, racism has often broken our bodies, but never our spirits. Only now, with the double onslaught of racism from within as well as racism from without, do we appear to be on the brink of losing the one thing that has sustained us when all else has failed — our spirituality.

This brings us to an understanding of why Black theology and the Black

Church are so significant for the survival and liberation of the African-American community. Essentially, the Black Church is the key to the salvation and liberation of the African-American community, and Black theology is the key to the survival and power of the Black Church. Whereas the Black Church is "the spiritual face of the Black community,"[3] Black theology is that which seeks to guarantee both the integrity of the Black Church's vertical relationship with God as well as the integrity of its horizontal relationship with the African-American community. The premise here is that without Black theology, the Black Church will crumble, and without the Black Church, the African-American community will be destroyed, from within as well as from without.

If Black theology is to help save and empower the Black Church, the relation between these two entities must first be clearly understood. To assist our efforts in understanding this relation, we will address the provocative question, "Has Black theology returned to the Black Church?" Secondly, if the Black Church is to help save and liberate the African-American community, the relation between these two entities must also be clearly understood. In order to apprehend this relation, we will consider the equally provocative question, "Is the Black Church one with the African-American community?" Only through a careful consideration of these critical questions will we be able to determine whether or not the Black Church will play a critical role in the survival and liberation of African-American people in the twenty-first century.

Has Black Theology Returned to the Black Church?

James Cone credits Gayraud Wilmore with having divided the development of Black theology into three stages.[4] Whereas the first stage was marked by the emergence of Black theology as a response by radical Black clergy to the civil rights and Black Power movements, and whereas the second stage was characterized by the departure of Black theology from the Black Church and community into White seminaries, universities, and churches as an academic discipline, the third stage was distinguished by an emphasis on the Third World, by a new concentration on sexism and classism in addition to racism, and, according to Cone, by *the return of Black theology to the Black Church*.[5]

This alleged "return" raises a number of questions: What does Cone mean when he says that Black theology returned? In what sense did it return? Just how complete was its return, and where is the evidence? Upon its return, did it remain, or did it leave once again? In essence, was Black theology graciously welcomed home to the Black Church like the prodigal son, or was it left standing outside, knocking at the door?

Whereas Cone points to a number of factors demonstrating the realization among Black theologians that they needed to become more accountable to the Black Church, there is less of an indication that the Black Church realized the necessity to become more accountable to Black theology. In other words, despite some notable exceptions, the "return" appears to have been largely a one-sided and somewhat tentative affair in which Black theologians, in their

eagerness to receive a warm "welcome home," softened their criticism of the
Black Church. By the same token, the Black Church welcomed the affirmation
of Black theology, but resisted its critique.

This is precisely the point Cone makes when he explains that the self-critical
feature of the Black Church, which was powerfully embodied in the emergence
of Black theology during the 1960s, was considerably weakened upon its return:

> When black theology returned to the black church, its negative critique
> was deemphasized and its positive side came into greater prominence.
> Negative critique. . . . was not as sharp as in the 1960s, because we did
> not want to alienate black theology from its base in the black church and
> community.[6]

In fact, Black theology had already become alienated from the Black Church.
According to Cone,

> When black theology sought to return to the church of its origin in the
> late 1970s, it found that its absence had created an alienation and that
> black church leaders were not open to criticisms coming from professional
> theologians teaching in white institutions. In order to cement their
> renewed connection with the churches, theologians neglected the pro-
> phetic criticism of the 1960s.[7]

This unfortunate compromise by Black theologians has cost the Black
Church dearly and, in effect, has resulted in what may be called the "incomplete" or "unfinished" return of Black theology to the Black Church. Black
theology entails both affirmation and critique, both celebration and self-examination, both joy and pain. Black theology is not Black theology unless it not
only discloses what is right with the Black Church, but also exposes what is
wrong. By forfeiting the prophetic sharpness of Black theology—particularly as
it relates to the internal critique of the Black Church—Black theologians failed
to finish what they had started and, hence, may have abdicated that which could
have rendered the Black Church infinitely more effective in dealing with the
immense social, political, economic, and spiritual ills that have plagued the
African-American community for the past twenty-plus years.

Prophetic Spirituality

While several religious scholars have correctly pointed to the need for the
political and prophetic emphases of the early stages of Black theology to be
balanced with equally important spiritual and priestly considerations,[8] perhaps
not as much attention has been paid to the need to develop a kind of "prophetic
spirituality" or "internal propheticism" that would empower the Black Church
to challenge not only the *outer* but also the *inner* systems of domination and
oppression. When we think of racism, we often think of it as an overt attack

from the outside rather than as a subtle attack from the inside. And even when we understand the dialectical relationship between the priestly and the prophetic functions of the Black Church, we tend to relegate the former to the inner dynamics of the church and the latter to its engagement with the outside world.

Note, for instance, that while C. Eric Lincoln and Lawrence H. Mamiya acknowledge the fact that the Black Church is involved in both the priestly and the prophetic, they distinguish these two functions as follows:

> Priestly functions involve only those activities concerned with worship and maintaining the spiritual life of members; church maintenance activities are the major thrust. Prophetic functions refer to involvement in political concerns and activities in the wider community; classically, prophetic activity has meant pronouncing a radical word of God's judgment.[9]

Ironically, this "word of God's judgment" within the Black Church has usually been directed outward toward someone or something else, rather than inward toward ourselves. If we would be true to the biblical model, however, we would understand that prophetic activity must proceed in both directions: Jeremiah's word of judgment to his own people is just as critical as Moses' word of judgment to the people of Egypt.

Even though Martin Luther King, Jr.—whom Cornel West calls an "organic intellectual"[10]—was one of the finest examples of a religious leader who knew how to combine the spiritual and the prophetic, still his prophetic pronouncements were primarily directed outward, against the manifestations of White racism in the institutions of White society, rather than inward, against the manifestations of White racism within the Black Church and the African-American community in general. Usually, the critique of the Black Church's internal structure, politics, and theology has come from persons outside the Black Church, like Malcolm X or Elijah Muhammad, rather than from persons inside the Black Church.[11]

The current debate over whether or not African Americans should blame our present plight on racism or on our own internal deficiencies misses the point. It is not an either/or question. There is no way that racism can be isolated or exonerated from everything that affects African-American people. But to say that racism is at the root of the problem does not, in and of itself, solve the problem. African Americans are still the ones primarily responsible for overcoming our oppression—internally as well as externally—if we would assure our liberation.

This is why Black theology emerged, and this is why Black theology—in the fullest possible sense—must genuinely "return" to the Black Church. Black theology is a tool that can empower the Black Church, and the Black Church is a vehicle that can liberate the African-American community. The return of Black theology to the Black Church is essential for the salvation and liberation of the African-American community.

Did Black Theology Ever Exist within the Black Church?

Cone, in support of his assertion that Black theology returned to the Black Church in the late seventies, points to several factors, including the renewed commitment of Black theologians to serve the Black Church, "mostly through the training of future ministers, conducting seminars and leadership training programs, participating in retreats, and writing with the black church as the primary audience."[12] He also emphasizes the emergence of several Black ecumenical organizations, including the National Congress of Black Churches, Partners in Ecumenism, and the Black Theology Project of Theology in the Americas. But did these factors really signify a return of Black theology to the Black Church?

While some may continue to debate whether or not Black theology truly returned to the Black Church, and others may even question whether or not it ever really left in the first place,[13] perhaps the more fruitful area of debate is to consider whether or not Black theology has ever fully existed in the Black Church, particularly as an instrument of internal critique. By raising this issue, we consciously bring the Black theology movement full circle and intentionally, though apprehensively, resurrect the ghost of Joseph Washington's *Black Religion*.[14] The critical difference here, however, is that, unlike Washington, our question is not whether or not the Black Church has an authentic Christian theology—that has already been demonstrated by the Black theology movement.[15] Instead, today's question is whether or not the Black Church has embraced its own theological autonomy and internalized its critical, as well as its affirming, aspects.

For instance, according to Cone, the pivotal event denoting the return of Black theology to the Black Church was the Black Theology Project conference in Atlanta, Georgia in August 1977 when "Pastors, theologians, and grassroots persons were all present" in an atmosphere reminiscent of the 1960s and, consequently, reminiscent of a time when Black theology "had no existence apart from the black church."[16]

If this particular event did symbolize the potential of Black theology to emerge from the people as a prophetic instrument of internal as well as external critique, it appears to have been the exception rather than the rule. Generally speaking, Black theology, as a conscious, rational, and disciplined attempt to reinterpret the gospel of Jesus Christ in light of the inner, as well as the outer, oppression of African-American people has never been a widespread phenomenon within the Black Church. Whether referring to the historical Black Church or to the contemporary Black Church, we find that aside from a few individual examples here and there, Black theology within the Black Church has been largely intuitive, unreflective, and unself-critical.

It is possible to romanticize the sixties to the point that we forget that of the forty-eight clergy who signed the Black Power statement by the National Committee of Negro Churchmen (NCNC) on July 31, 1966—a landmark doc-

ument viewed as having kicked off the contemporary Black theology movement—less than half were from independent Black denominations.[17] It is easy
to forget that in the first stage of its development, "black theology is almost
completely defined by radical black NCBC ministers, *most of whom were in white
denominations.*"[18] It is easy to forget that, although most major Black denominations were initially supportive of Black theology[19] (at least on paper), one
notable exception was the Reverend Dr. Joseph H. Jackson, who at the time
was the president of the largest Black denomination in the country.[20] And it is
easy to forget that, even now, while it is suggested that Black theology has
returned to the Black Church, a recent survey of over 1500 urban African-
American clergypersons reveals that two-thirds of the respondents claimed that
they had not been influenced at all by Black theology.[21]

The Essence of Black Theology in the Black Church

Only a handful of Black congregations across the country appear to be experiencing any real success incorporating Black theology as a central ingredient
into their overall programs.[22] Though their numbers are small, the efforts of
these few congregations and their pastors are exemplary. Cone refers to this
promising few in lamenting the fact that he and other Black theologians did
not pay more attention to these congregations in the early stages of Black
theology. I quote him at length here because the issues he raises are critical to
our discussion:

> I still am not convinced that the major black denominational churches
> are ready for renewal, but I do believe that there were and still are many
> genuinely committed black pastors and lay persons who transcend the
> limitations of their denominational identity by becoming identified with
> Christ through a commitment to the poor. They are found in all denom-
> inations (black as well as white) and they seemed determined to build
> more humane church structures that serve the community. They are feed-
> ing the hungry, holding workshops on economics and politics as well as
> black church history and theology, building alternative schools for black
> children, and working at many other creative projects of freedom. These
> pastors and members refuse to withdraw from the world by engaging in
> internal church politics. They are concrete examples that the black church
> is not an opiate of the people, but rather a liberating force in behalf of
> the victims of the land.[23]

As we can see from the above statement, Cone names several features which,
for him, are significant in identifying congregations dedicated to the concepts
of Black theology. These features may be summarized as follows: (1) the ability
to transcend denominationalism; (2) a commitment to the poor; (3) service to
the community; (4) economic, political, cultural, and theological education; and,
(5) the capacity to avoid being consumed and/or paralyzed by internal church

politics. While these features may signify congregations sensitive to the need for Black theology, they do not, in and of themselves, prove the existence of Black theology. Conspicuously absent from the above list are two other features that are essential to establish Black theology's presence in, or return to, the Black Church.

The first missing feature above is the "prophetic spirituality" or "internal propheticism," mentioned earlier, that would insure that these congregations are engaged not only in the glorification of the Black Church, nor only in an attack on the White Church, but that they are also actively engaged in an on-going process of self-critique. Without this self-criticizing mechanism, it is too easy for the Black Church to delude itself into thinking it is doing Black theology when, in actuality, it may be simply covering traditional European theology with a thin veneer of Black history and social programs. This "feel good" approach may do wonders for the psyche of the Black Church, but in the final analysis, it will do little to challenge and push the Black Church to realize its full liberating potential.

The second missing feature above has to do with a different pedagogical method required by Black theology. Black theologians must be engaged not only in the traditional European process of *teaching* theology from the top down, but they must also be involved in empowering the people to *do* theology from the bottom up. This grassroots approach has the potential of releasing African Americans from a kind of theological bondage that chains our people to theological views, concepts, and "authorities" that may or may not have liberating implications for the African-American community. I have found, in my experience as a pastor in a Black Church, that, initially, African-American lay people are generally reluctant to do theology. It seems as though they feel that theology must be done for them, and that theological credibility derives from the fact that it is either written in a book or passed down from the pastor, or from some other theological "expert" on high. Their resistance stems from a form of biblical literalism, rooted in the King James Version, that pervades much of the Black Church. It is not a strict literalism, since African Americans have never accepted certain biblical directives (such as the exhortation to slaves to obey their masters),[24] but it is a perceived literalism, which has a comparable effect.

Critical issues facing the African-American community, such as sexism, classism, AIDS, single parenthood, sexual morality, blended families, homophobia, drugs and violence, teenage mothers who want their babies blessed, premarital couples who are already living together, infant mortality, organ donation, and Black males as "an endangered species," require that the members of this community not simply seek easy answers imposed on us by someone else, but wrestle to determine what the Word of God has to say specifically to us in this particular place and at this particular time.

While many of these issues may appear to be personal in nature, they are so intertwined with the social, political, and economic realities of being Black in America, that there is no way to make a clear-cut distinction between the personal and the social. Hence, Black theology must empower the people to do theology for themselves. Failure to do so perpetuates a theological oppression in which those who know—whether they are members of the White male power structure or members of the Black male clergy—control and manipulate those who do not. It also perpetuates a hypocritical double standard within the Black Church, where people's professed beliefs are often inconsistent with their actual behavior. This in turn burdens members of the Black Church with an omnipresent sense of guilt that must be added to all of the other burdens endured by members of the African-American community by virtue of our existence in a White racist society.

Is the Black Church One with the Black Community?

The answer to this question, plain and simple, is, "Not anymore." Consequently, not only must Black theology return to the Black Church, but also the Black Church must return to the African-American community. Black theology requires that the Black Church must do more than be committed *to* the poor or provide service *to* the community. The Black Church must once again become one *with* the poor and one *with* the community. Not long ago, one could claim with relative confidence that there was no gap between the Black Church and the African-American community and that, indeed, they were one.[25] Quiet as it is kept, this identity between the Black Church and the African-American community is now probably more myth than reality. The Black Church and the African-American community are not identical, and the gap between them is growing wider every day.

This escalating separation between the Black Church and the African-American community actually began with the urban migrations of the first half of the twentieth century and was one of the negative by-products of the civil rights gains of the second half of the twentieth century. Expanded opportunities for African Americans, beyond the bounds of the rural South and beyond the walls of the Black Church, resulted in the breakdown of what Lincoln and Mamiya call the "Black Sacred Cosmos," that is, the African and African-American worldview, in which there is no dichotomy between the sacred and the secular, and in which all life is one.[26] It also resulted in what Lincoln and Mamiya call "partial differentiation" within the African-American community, where although the Black Church remains the central institution within the community, its power and influence have been diminished by the creation of class distinctions, secular organizations, and competitive religious groups.[27]

The fallout of all of this is that today, as we move toward the twenty-first century, there is within the African-American community a severe crisis of spirituality. No longer can it be assumed that African Americans—particularly of the younger generations—have any affinity for the Black Church, or that they know anything about it. Indeed, we are living in a time when a generation of our young people has grown up knowing nothing about the Black Church, nothing about Jesus Christ, and nothing about God. The mass media's aiding and abetting of this crisis has led to an even greater dilemma in which on the one hand, the Black Church is constantly ridiculed and caricatured, and on the other hand, the spiritual void of our children is filled with erotic rock videos, sexually explicit lyrics, and gyrating popular "messiahs" like Prince, Michael Jackson, and even Madonna.[28]

The gap between the Black Church and the African-American community is also seen in the fact that more and more of the Black middle class are deserting the inner cities and relocating in the suburbs of America's metropolitan centers. Yet, because of longstanding ties with inner-city churches, many of these same individuals and families travel back into the city to attend church. This commuter membership further increases the distance between the Black Church and the African-American community, not only in a socioeconomic sense, but also in a geographic sense.

The ultimate challenge for Black theology is to complete its return to the Black Church without compromising its responsibility not only to affirm the Black Church, but to critique it. It must do this by fostering a "prophetic spirituality" or "internal propheticism" that will constantly challenge the Black Church to be self-critical and to empower the people it serves not only to learn theology, as it is passed down from above, but to do theology from the grassroots up. Similarly, the challenge for the Black Church is not only to provide a space for Black theologians to do their work in a free, uninhibiting, and nonthreatening environment, but also to work diligently to close the gap between the Black Church and the African-American community. Taking the church to the community, as well as bringing the community into the church, are just two ways in which this gap must be bridged. Only by taking these tasks seriously and performing them faithfully can Black theology and the Black Church realize their God-given potential as the twenty-first century saviors and liberators of the African-American community.

NOTES

1. James Cone makes a similar statement in *For My People: Black Theology and the Black Church* (Maryknoll, N.Y.: Orbis Books, 1984), 116. Says Cone: "We must ask not what is best for the survival of black churches or black theology, but rather what is best for the liberation of the black poor in particular and the poor of the whole world in general."

2. As I write, the nation, and particularly the African-American community, is still reeling from the shocking verdict in the Rodney King case. In this case, an all-White jury acquitted four White police officers of the charge of brutally beating King, an African-American man, even though the beating was captured on videotape and a portion of the tape was aired numerous times on television for the whole world to see.

3. See C. Eric Lincoln, *The Black Church Since Frazier* (New York: Schocken Books, 1974), 115.

4. Cone, *For My People*, pp. 24ff. See also Wilmore's General Introduction in Gayraud S. Wilmore and James H. Cone, eds., *Black Theology: A Documentary History, 1966–1979* (Maryknoll, N.Y.: Orbis Books, 1979), 4ff.

5. Wilmore and Cone, eds., *Black Theology* (1979). It should be noted that this emphasis on the "return of Black Theology to the Black Church" as an aspect of the third stage appears to originate with Cone. In addition to 24-28, see his further discussion of this phenomenon on 109-111.

6. Ibid., 110.

7. Ibid., 114f.

8. See, for instance, J. Deotis Roberts, *Roots of a Black Future: Family and Church* (Philadelphia: Westminster Press), chap. 7; Nicholas C. Cooper-Lewter and Henry H. Mitchell, *Soul Theology: The Heart of American Black Culture* (San Francisco: Harper & Row, 1986); and Gayraud S. Wilmore, "Pastoral Ministry in the Origin and Development of Black Theology," *Journal of the Interdenominational Theological Center* 13 (Spring 1986), 213ff.

9. C. Eric Lincoln and Lawrence H. Mamiya, *The Black Church in the African American Experience* (Durham, N.C.: Duke University Press, 1990), 10ff.

10. See Cornel West, "Martin Luther King, Jr.: Prophetic Christian as Organic Intellectual," in his *Prophetic Fragments* (Grand Rapids, Mich.: Eerdmans Pub. Co., 1988), 3ff.

11. See James H. Cone, *Martin & Malcolm & America: A Dream or a Nightmare* (Maryknoll, N.Y.: Orbis Books, 1991), especially, chaps. 5 and 6.

12. Cone, *For My People*, 110.

13. When asked in a telephone interview on May 6, 1992 whether or not he thought that Black theology had returned to the Black Church, Lawrence N. Jones, former dean of the Howard University School of Divinity, replied, "It never left." In making this response, however, Jones was not referring to the Black theology movement of the sixties, which he calls "the 'academizing' of the Black Church." Instead, he was referring to "the fundamental theology of the Black Church," which "emerges out of experience" and, according to Jones, hasn't changed one bit.

14. Joseph R. Washington, Jr., *Black Religion: The Negro and Christianity in the United States* (Lanham, Md.: University Press of America, 1984).

15. See Cone, *For My People*, 8ff. for a brief summary of Black theologians' response to Joseph Washington.

16. Cone, *For My People*, 102 and 110.

17. See "Black Power: Statement by the National Committee of Negro Churchmen, July 31, 1966" in Wilmore & Cone, *Black Theology* (1979), 23ff. and (rev. ed. 1993), 19ff. Note that the name of this organization was later changed to the National Committee of Black Churchmen (NCBC).

18. Cone, *For My People*, 25 (italics mine).

19. Wilmore establishes this clearly in Wilmore & Cone, *Black Theology* (1979), 6. He notes, "With one notable exception all the major Black churches that had anything at all to say about theology in the 1970s gave open or tacit approbation to the main concepts of Black Theology. This little-known fact, well demonstrated by the documents, disproves the frequent allegation that the movement has no credibility in the Black Church."

20. Jackson was the perennial president of the multimillion member National Baptist Convention, U.S.A., Inc. Because of Jackson's political conservatism, his feud with Martin Luther King, Jr., and his monopoly of the office of president, King and others withdrew from the convention in 1961 and formed the Progressive National Baptist Convention, Inc. For a deeper understanding of Jackson's ideas concerning Black theology, see Joseph H. Jackson, *Nairobi: A Joke, a Junket, or a Journey?* (Chicago: Townsend Press, 1976), especially, p. 69.

21. Lincoln and Mamiya, *The Black Church in the African American Experience*, 169. The authors posed the following question to 1,531 urban Black clergy: "Have you been influenced by any of the authors and thinkers of black liberation theology (e.g., James Cone, Gayraud Wilmore, Deotis Roberts, Major Jones, William Jones, etc.)?" Whereas 34.9 percent responded, "Yes," 65.1 percent responded, "No."

22. These include, but are not limited to, the Trinity United Church of Christ in Chicago, Bethel A.M.E. in Baltimore, Ward A.M.E. in Los Angeles, Allen Temple Baptist in Oakland, Hartford Memorial Baptist in Detroit, St. Paul Community Baptist in Brooklyn, Elmwood Presbyterian in New Jersey, Shorter A.M.E. in Denver, Faith Lutheran in Chicago, Zion Baptist in Philadelphia, the Union Temple Baptist in Washington, D.C. and the Covenant Baptist Church in Washington, D.C., just to name a few.

23. Cone, *For My People*, 114.

24. See, for instance, Eph. 6:5, Col. 3:22, and Titus 2:9.

25. This claim has been made in a number of places, but perhaps most notably in Lincoln, *The Black Church Since Frazier*, pp. 115f. Here, Lincoln asserts: "To understand the power of the Black Church it must first be understood that there is no disjunction between the Black Church and the Black community." Similarly, in *For My People*, p. 99, Cone observes that the importance of the Black Church "is so great that some scholars say that the black church *is* the black community, with each having no identity apart from the other." Finally, the official statement of the National Conference of the Black Theology Project, 1977, entitled, "Message to the Black Church and Community" in Wilmore & Cone, *Black Theology* (1979) contains a section entitled, "The Inseparability of the Black Church and Black Community." An excerpt reads: "Therefore, the black church and the community which it serves are one in the Spirit of God, Who does not differentiate between the secular and the sacred and Who binds us inseparably to one another" (p. 348).

26. Lincoln and Mamiya, *The Black Church in the African American Experience*, chap. 1.

27. Ibid., 7ff.

28. For an interesting and comprehensive discussion of this phenomenon, see Jon Michael Spencer, ed., "The Theology of American Popular Music: A Special Issue of Black Sacred Music," *A Journal of Musicology* 3, no. 2, (Fall 1989). See, also, "Sex and Suicide," 155f. "In Memory of Marvin Gaye," 174ff. and "On Afro-American Popular Music: From Bebop to Rap," 177ff. in West, *Prophetic Fragments*.

11

BREAKING SILENCE: TOWARD AN IN-THE-LIFE THEOLOGY

Elias Farajaje-Jones

In Leviticus, Chapter 20, the Lord tells us: "If a man also lie with man-kind as he lieth with a woman, both of them have committed an abom-ination: they shall surely be put to death, their blood shall be upon them." There's no cause to wonder why medical science could not find a cure for this man's illness. How could medicine cure temptation? What drug can exorcise Satan from a young man's soul? The only cure is to be found in the Lord. The only cure is repentance, for Leviticus clearly tells us, . . . "whoever shall commit any of these abominations, even the souls that commit them shall be cut off from among their people." Shall be cut off from among their people: The words echoed in Jeff's head. His mind flashed back to scenes in the hospital: dingy, hospital green walls of an isolated room. . . . He remembered sitting quietly during visiting hours, not knowing what words of support to offer . . . Shall be cut off from their people, indeed.
Craig G. J. Harris, "Cut Off From Among Their People"[1]

Introduction

In his piece, "Cut Off From Among Their People," the late Black gay the-orist, AIDS activist and writer, Craig G. J. Harris tells the story of Jeff, a young African-American gay man whose life-partner has just died of complications resulting from AIDS. Jeff is shut out by the biological family of his partner, even though he was the primary caregiver throughout the long illness. But perhaps the most poignant moment in the short story comes when the Reverend Mack uses Leviticus 20 to explain that the death of a young Black gay man of complications resulting from AIDS is the fulfillment of the Word of God. In

Elias Farajaje-Jones, an avowed gay-identified, bisexual Black theologian, is associate profes-sor of history of religions, Howard University Divinity School.

139

these few sentences, we are given a glimpse of how only too often the Black Church has responded to issues of both sexuality and AIDS which has made inevitable the confrontation with *homophobia* and *biphobia*.

Even though I do speak of Black lesbians and bisexual (used here in the sense of people who experience affectional or physical attraction for people of either gender) women, I am dealing specifically with Black gay and bisexual men, for that is my context. Renee Hill deals elsewhere in this collection with a Black lesbian critique of Black theology. I will use a variety of terms: lesbian/ gay/bisexual/transgender; queer; in-the-life, etc. In talking about our African-American community, I am constantly reminded that we have a much more fluid spectrum of sexualities than does the white community. Categories such as homosexual or bisexual may not necessarily have the same meaning for Blacks as for whites. For example, there are women and men who behave bisexually, but who do not identify themselves as such. There are men who would define themselves as "gay-identified bisexual men," women who call themselves "lesbian-identified bisexual women," women and men who are "queer-identified bisexuals" and those who would label themselves as "heterosexual-identified bisexuals."

There are really as many definitions of bisexuality as there are bisexuals. Whereas bisexuals were once considered to have no politics, there is now a growing multicultural feminist bisexual movement in the United States. That is why I will also sometimes speak of homosexualities and bisexualities, of homosocialities (the phenomenon of people in various cultures, institutions or situations spending a significant part of their time and life-experience exclusively in the presence of people of their own gender group) and homosensualities (physical contact, or the exchange of physical affection, such as holding hands or kissing, between people of the same gender, which is non-genitocentric and non-orgasmocentric). I do not seek to impose any one term, realizing, for example, that for many people the term queer (which I myself prefer) is highly controversial. (The term "queer" is being used by people who feel that by reclaiming a term that has been used in a derogatory way, they are participating in their own liberation. Some of us say that much as the term "Black" used to be an insult or had negative connotations, but now is a source of strength and pride, so the use of the term queer is empowering. It refers to a radical tendency in our community that seeks liberation and self-determination, rather than assimilation into the white male-dominated heterosexual culture. It is a term that is inclusive of lesbians, gay men, bisexual people and transgender people.)

I do feel strongly about the use of the term, "in-the-life," because it has been used in our African-American tradition for generations to connote a broad spectrum of identities and behaviors, and because of the rich spiritual connotations of the word "life," especially for a people continually confronted with suffering and death. "In-the-life" also shows inclusivity, shows that we are all included *in-the-life*. Therefore, an in-the-life theology of liberation would be one that grows out of the experiences, lives, and struggles against oppression and dehumanization of those *in-the-life*. It understands our struggle for liberation as being inextricably bound with those of oppressed peoples throughout the world, as we all struggle against racism, classism, imperialism, sexism, ableism, and all other forms of oppression. Such a theology also offers to other theologies a liberation from the strictures of homophobia/biphobia, as well as liberation from heterosexism which creates the climate for homophobia/biphobia with its assumption that the world is and must be heterosexual, and by its display of power and privilege. Heterosexism is the systemic display of homophobia/biphobia in the institutions of society: they work together to reinforce compulsory heterosexuality and the nuclear family.[2]

There are many people in the African-American community who do not believe that those of us who are in-the-life live under constant and violent oppression, often risking our lives simply by walking down the street. In the minds of most people, our lives do not exist apart from sexual acts. Most people are not aware of the fact that many queers are barred from access to housing and to certain forms of employment. We are often at risk of losing our jobs if it is discovered that we are queer. If we have children, they may be taken from us. Certain insurance companies will not insure us because we are perceived as more at risk for HIV than other people. As queers, we exist as criminals in most states where there are anti-sodomy laws, laws based on a heterosexist, homophobic/biphobic interpretation of Genesis 19:1-10.

Many Black people believe that it is acceptable to be openly homophobic/ biphobic. The Black Church definitely encourages this through words and actions. Indeed, expressing homophobia/biphobia to reaffirm their heterosexual privilege is often the only situation in which many Black Christians feel that they have any form of privilege at all.[3] Furthermore, as is the case with male justification of crimes of violence committed against women, it is considered that we queers are provoking this violence in supposedly heterosexual men by the mere fact of our existence. To many, queer-bashing is justified because our behavior is perceived as having provoked it. This is the same kind of reasoning that presumes that if women dress or walk in a certain way, they are provoking men to rape. In this way of thinking, it is right to beat up and/or kill gay/bisexual men for the simple reason that they may have dared to hold hands in public. This is all the more the case with violence against lesbians and bisexual women. Their very existence raises serious questions about the assumption that women can only have identity through their association with men. Lesbians and bisexual women are the ultimate threat to the heteropatriarchal fantasy.

This is yet another example of the power of heterosexual men over women and queers, a power inextricably bound up with the capitalist class structure and fed by racism, classism, sexism and homophobia/biphobia.

Heterosexism is profoundly rooted in a need to preserve present social structures and strictures. How could one not speak of the oppression of Black lesbian/gay/bisexual/transgender people and its intersections with racism? What about the fact that those of us Black men who are in-the-life live at the intersection of several different forms of oppression? In our experience of alterity, of Otherness, we are doubly or triply the ultimate Other, the Different One.

As a Black queer man, I am oppressed as a Black man, I am oppressed as a queer, and I am oppressed as a Black queer. My oppression comes not only from the dominating culture, but also from within my own communities. In the Black community I am oppressed for being queer. In the queer community I am oppressed because I am a man of color.

Most of our people do not know that during the Inquisition and down through the years, European Christians killed same-sex identified women and men, or those whom they perceived to be same-sex identified.[4] It is not necessary to be same-sex identified to be persecuted; it need only be in the eyes of the persecutor or levelled as an accusation. A link was established, as we shall see later, between heretic, sorcerer, witch, queer; in short, anyone who was perceived as going against the norm.

With the Spanish invasion of the Americas in the fifteenth and sixteenth centuries, intense persecution and execution began of those Native Americans who were perceived as being same-sex identified.[5] During the Holocaust, the Nazis used the black triangle to designate "anti-social women," a category which included commercial sex workers (prostitutes) and lesbians; the pink triangle was used for gay men.

> It is impossible to give any accurate figure for the total number of people killed by the Nazis solely for their homosexuality. . . . During the twelve years of Nazi rule, nearly 50,000 men were convicted for homosexuality; the majority of these certainly ended up in concentration camps and did not survive. Large numbers of gay people found their way into concentration camps without any legal proceedings, and on top of this we must add those shot in the armed forces for homosexual offences. The total number who died, therefore, must have been several tens of thousands.[6]

To silence this persecution of queers is to condemn us to die twice; it is parallel to the paper genocide by which indigenous peoples of Central and South America are simply no longer listed as Native Americans. Many people in the Black religious community try to argue even now that it is not necessary to cut through the homophobia/biphobia to deal with AIDS. They maintain that this emphasis on tearing down homophobia/biphobia and accepting homosexualities/bisexualities obscures the real issues and alienates all of those good, "normal," morally upright people who are willing to work with people living with AIDS. As Cheryl Clarke says in her essay, "The Failure to Transform: Homophobia in the Black Community,"

> Homosexuality is viewed as a threat to the continued existence of the heterosexual family, because homosexual unions do not, in and of themselves, produce offspring — as if one's only function within a family, within a relationship, or in sex, were to produce offspring. Black family lifestyles and homosexual lifestyles are not antithetical. Most black lesbians and gay men grew up in families and are still critically involved with their

families. Many black lesbians and gay men are raising children. Why must the black family be so strictly viewed as the result of a heterosexual dyad?[7]

What about the fact that this kind of homophobic/biphobic thinking alienates Black lesbian/gay/bisexual/transgender people, that it alienates people with AIDS, that it makes us invisible and silent once again, even as we struggle for our lives? That this heterocentrism kills us while we are yet alive? Is it not precisely the presence and power of homophobia/biphobia in our communities, the power of this deadly silence, that has held the African-American religious community back from doing what we could do to save our lives? Is this not part of the reason that at many Black funerals for young men who have died of complications resulting from AIDS there is never any mention of this, as though it were a shameful secret that would reveal things that should remain hidden? Are we not called to be critical in our thinking and prophetic in action?

Religion, especially African-American Judeo-Christian religion, is still being used to persecute and oppress people who are in-the-life. It forces people to remain closeted. Perhaps one of the worst things about it is that it is used to destroy people's self-esteem and to augment their self-hatred. Religiously-inspired homophobia and biphobia are actually killing people. It is one of the main reasons that the United States is not more aggressive in dealing with AIDS; it serves as an inspiration for violent crimes against lesbian/gay/bisexual/transgender people, in much the same way that inflammatory anti-Jewish preaching often leads to pogroms. The religious right is using its heterocentric assumptions and its ideology of "traditional family values" to strengthen its fight against the queer community. But *whose* traditional family values are they? The nuclear family has drastically changed, especially in an era when its role as an economic unit has been made obsolete by a world economy based on multinational conglomerates. What about the diversity of ways in which we, as people of African descent, define and experience family? The white religious right is trying to co-opt the Black Church into supporting its homophobia/biphobia. Some of us need to articulate theologies for the Black Church that teach that we are inclusive, not exclusive; that we are about life and not about death. This is my struggle.

Story/Context

I am a tenured associate professor of sociology of religion and history of religion at the Howard University School of Divinity. The courses I teach fall into the overarching area of ethics, culture, and society. In fact, one might more aptly describe me as one who uses the tools of sociologies of culture and knowledge in the task of articulating an African-centered, womanist, in-the-life theology of liberation. I have been involved in the struggle against heterosexism, HIV/AIDS, aparthAIDS and AIDSphobia for the past ten years, first in Switzerland and then in Washington, D.C. This has provided me with the opportunity of observing how different people in different places respond to this pandemic. I came out politically as a queer in Switzerland in 1981 when I wrote a proposal for a doctoral dissertation on the religio-theological roots of homophobia. This dissertation topic was, of course, refused; my dissertation director would not even sit on the same couch with me to review my text! I became very involved in the queer movement, which drew heavily on Marxism as a tool for critiquing our oppression in a broader context. I am now involved in lesbian/gay/bisexual studies, which we now also call queer theory. My biological family is extremely accepting and supportive of my struggle.

As I write this essay I am profoundly aware of the fact that, as Audre Lorde says, the transformation of silence into language and action is an act of self-revelation and fraught with danger. I am weary of watching my sisters and brothers in-the-life eat the bread of multiple forms of oppression daily. I am tired of observing so much silent suffering. If this essay can help others to break silence, then it is worth it. As part of this liberation struggle, I have developed a course on the sociology of HIV/AIDS, taught from an African-centered, womanist perspective, as well as one on the sociology of heteropatriarchy which examines the inter-relatedness of racism, sexism, classism, heterosexism, ableism, etc. I have produced, along with my students in the sociology of AIDS, the first gospel musical that deals with AIDS and the African-American church, *Conviction: A Healing Stream.* I have also provided the opportunity to many of our students at Howard University to be trained as HIV educators and test counselors.

I live in a loving, caring, nurturing family with my companion of many years, a lesbian-identified bisexual woman of color and (until the time of his death on January 10, 1992), with my partner, who was also a Black gay-identified bisexual activist and AIDS educator. My extended family includes many close friends who are living with AIDS. In 1988, one of my cousins died of complications resulting from HIV. I vowed on his grave that I would not permit his death to have been in vain, and that I would dedicate my life and energy to fighting against AIDS, to tearing down the walls of silence, ignorance, and fear that are the true agents of death in our community. My partner, my cousin, friends and countless others died at the hands of the U.S. government, whose deliberate and continued lack of action, along with our churches' silence and negativity, kills one person by an AIDS-related death every seven minutes.

In addition to being trained and working as an HIV educator and HIV test counselor, and the work that I do with people living with AIDS, I also consider myself an AIDS terrorist and a guerrilla theologian, living out my theory as a queer bisexual activist in queer and AIDS groups in which we use civil disobedience and direct action to end the AIDS crisis. As a technician of the sacred, my work has been especially with African Americans in-the-life, some of whom are people living with AIDS. They often feel judged, condemned, abandoned, and rejected by the Black Church. My actions seek to embody an in-the-life theology of liberation that is shaped and redefined constantly by my praxis. So, these reflections are not merely the result of speculation on my part. They grow out of years of listening to the pains and joys of my sisters and brothers, of living and working with people with AIDS, of losing companions, friends and relatives to the pandemic, of burying a cousin and twelve close friends in six months, of accompanying people as they struggle to liberate themselves from the bondage of internalized homophobia/biphobia. The things of which I speak in this essay are realities that I must face every day of my existence.

In 1978-79, I began an in-depth study of liberation and feminist theologies. I was most interested in learning how I could use these as hermeneutical tools for theologizing out of my experience as a queer-identified bisexual man. I felt the great urgency of this task, because I could find nothing that had any message of liberation for lesbian/gay/bisexual/transgender people of color in general, and those of African descent in particular. It was my deep belief that Black theology, as a theology growing out of and in response to a people's experience of oppression, would certainly include a word for Black lesbian/gay/bisexual/transgender people. I was somewhat surprised to find out that we were totally invisible to Black theologians. Either we were included along with everyone else, or there was nothing to be said for us, no end offered to our oppression. Furthermore, there were no Black openly lesbian, gay, bisexual, or transgender theologians who were doing this work. It was interesting for me to note at this time that there was still not much reflection on the situation of women of color from a Black theology perspective. There seemed to be only generic Blackness.

What were the particular issues of African-American women in their struggle against oppression, and how could one understand these issues without a class-analysis of the socio-economic factors contributing to sexism as compounded by racism? Without sexism, homophobia could not exist. We cannot understand our struggle for liberation without seeing the interconnectedness of various forms of oppression such as sexism, racism, heterosexism, classism and homophobia/biphobia. They not only have common sources, but also common elements. We queers cannot be free until all peoples are truly free. Our liberation is not separate from that of other oppressed groups. I acknowledge my indebtedness to the writings of women of color, especially to Audre Lorde, who encouraged me and allowed me to find my voice. It was, indeed, my sisters who are womanist theologians who began to raise the question of the roles that gender and sexuality play in our understanding of oppression and began to reshape the contours of the project of Black theology.[8] Nevertheless, even womanist theology has been reluctant to deal directly with heterosexism and homophobia/biphobia.

Not satisfied with this silence and invisibility, I set out to examine the lived reality of how the Black Church received Black lesbian/gay/bisexual/transgender people. Growing up in an affluent African-American religious community (my background was Roman Catholic, United Methodist, and Episcopalian), I had never heard anything negative about homosexualities or bisexualities preached from the pulpit. Nevertheless, what strikes me the most is that I never heard anything *at all*. Not only did I never hear anything negative, but I also never heard anything positive or inclusive.

The rise of the AIDS pandemic has made this silence and forced invisibility particularly problematic, for our community is in danger of losing its life. Those who have been forced to be invisible are now no longer so invisible. The Black Church has, in collusion with the U.S. government, put us at least eleven years behind where we need to be in terms of AIDS education, condom-distribution, and needle-exchange programs. Why is it that the Black Church has never given birth to a theology out of the experience of Black lesbian/gay/bisexual/transgender people? Why has it never even acknowledged our existence in a positive way? We are in these churches silently and mostly invisibly. Our silence makes us accomplices to our own oppression. We would never sit through racist tirades by a white preacher Sunday after Sunday, yet those in-the-life sit through weekly homophobic/biphobic, sexist tirades and never react. What is the price of taking in so much negativity on a constant basis? In the Black Church today, dishonesty about sexuality is rewarded (with ordination, positions, etc.). What kind of message does this send? That it is acceptable to lie about sexuality? How does this transfer into honesty between partners in relationships, particularly in a time of AIDS when such honesty is absolutely necessary if people are to communicate openly about their sexualities?

While proclaiming itself the major institution of the Black community, the constant champion of the people, the Black Church has systematically denied Black lesbian/gay/bisexual/transgender people their place in the community. This has led many African Americans who are in-the-life to choose between living their lives as who they are, and being in conflict with the Church, or remaining silently invisible in the Church. In *Brother to Brother*, a Black gay men's anthology, Black religious homophobia is a recurrent theme.[9] When I would read Black theology of liberation, the question that always came to my mind was if and how this applied to me as a queer-identified bisexual man. Unfortunately, I felt invisible and silenced within Black theology as well as within European academic theology in general. Did not the word of liberation belong to me and my community, to those in-the-life as well? Am I not also called to do theology out of my context, to analyze and deconstruct my oppression, to see it in relation to other forms of oppression?

There is a suffocating silence which surrounds any discussion of sexuality in the Black Church, but particularly of homosexualities/bisexualities. No one ever mentions it, not even in progressive Black theological circles. Ultimately this silence kills. When homosexualities/bisexualities are mentioned, they are mentioned in homophobic/biphobic, life-threatening terms. Many preachers use their pulpits to propagate homophobic/biphobic messages that become a source of inspiration for crimes of violence against lesbian/gay/bisexual/transgender people. The refusal to discuss sexualities and homosexuality/bisexuality has placed our community at least eleven years behind where we need to be in the battle against AIDS. Countless men and women die in the fear of hell because of hearing their lives condemned by the Church.

In the eyes of the Black Church, queers have a "lifestyle" and not a life. Religiously-inspired homophobia/biphobia are so great that we can find its effect even in the statistics on AIDS in our communities. Many men who are gay or bisexual (at least behaviorally, even though they do not identify as such) would rather say that they are injecting drug users than that they are men who have sex with other men. This comes from what people have heard from the pulpit all their lives. Many queers of African descent live in fear because they have always been told that the way in which they are living is not pleasing to God. Parents threaten their queer children, telling them that God will punish them by ruining their studies, their careers, and ultimately their lives. They are not able to enter fully into their same-sex relationships, because they feel that they are doing something against God. Therefore, all sorts of negativity creep into the relational space. Often people feel that they do not have to be honest to someone with whom they are involved in what at best is perceived by the Church and society as being a mockery of a "real," heterosexual relationship. Thus, the Church encourages straight identification; she rewards "passing."

Bisexuality is coming to be viewed as even more dangerous than homosexuality. It brings homosexualities much too close to home. It is frightening because the ultimate Other is no longer so *other*. If the person next door who seems so much like us can be involved with persons of either gender, what does that say about us? Is this not what we so fear, the desire that we seek to police so carefully? Bisexuality must define itself in relation to both the heterosexual world and the lesbian/gay world. The real challenge to bisexuality comes as it struggles to name itself, yet at the same time seeks to subvert the either/or, monosexual paradigm which would have us believe that people are *either* lesbian/gay *or* heterosexual.

In addition to homophobia, bisexuals are often exposed to biphobia (a subset of homophobia) which says that there are no such things as bisexuals; that bisexuals don't know what we want; that we are fence-sitters or whiners; that we have no politics or community; that we are confused; that this is just a phase; that we are promiscuous transmitters of HIV, etc. Biphobia can be felt very strongly, even among so-called progressive heterosexuals who feel that they can accept lesbians and gay men, but that bisexuals are too much. Bisexuals are perceived as being too transgressive. This is perhaps because we blur what people consider to be the very clear lines separating *them* from *us* (however one chooses to define the *we* and the *they*). This is where a new theology of gender will have a very important role to play.

Already, when we look at the role of Two Spirit people in certain Native American cultures, we become aware of the fact that they represent another gender category which transcends the female/male binary unit. These Two Spirit people, known by different names in different indigenous languages (such as *nadle* in Navajo, or *winkte* in Lakota), are often those who mediate between the visible and the invisible worlds and have gifts of healing, vision, and prophecy.[10] Part of the transgressivity of bisexuality is that it says that love knows no gender. Most bisexuals do not choose their partners on the basis of their biologically-assigned gender, but rather on the basis of those elements of their personality that make them attractive to the other. This, however, can mean that someone might be attracted by elements in a woman or man that are not part of how we are socialized to perceive members of the female or male gender. This sort of gender subversion, or better yet, the subversion of identity based on biological gender, is what is extremely problematic for many people.[11] Nevertheless, this is an area that we cannot afford to neglect.

Furthermore, as we are faced with the rising visibility of the transgender community (which is not negligible in the Black community), we are really being called to grapple with these theological questions. Instead of reacting in disgust, we could be in the forefront here instead of having to wait for leadership from other quarters. In African religious traditions such as *vodun* (Afro-Haitian religion) or those based in the Yoruba tradition, there is a theology of gender that is very different from what most people in the Black Church are accustomed. For example, in the Yoruba religion there are manifestations of the divine (*orisha*) that are bi-gendered. Furthermore, a female *orisha* can manifest through a man, just as a male *orisha* can manifest through a woman. Whatever the gender of the *orisha* or the initiate, the newborn initiate who is attached to a particular *orisha* is considered to be the *iyawo* or bride of that *orisha*.[12] The body is not only the temple, but is also the place where the Spirit manifests (as when we shout in church). If sexuality can be perceived as a gift, then the body is to be celebrated. Unfortunately, we place too much emphasis on what is *not* to be done. Is it not part of our being African-centered to go back and examine these roots and see how they apply today? This will become of vital importance as we deal with AIDS, because an understanding of bisexualities in the African-American community will be absolutely necessary.

We are witnessing now the beginning of the rise of a wave of very pronounced biphobia. Already, Black writers in the press are portraying Black bisexual men as the *other*, as the transmitter of AIDS. This combination of biphobia and AIDSphobia is being used to discredit and destroy our community. We are being constantly portrayed as knowing and intentional transmitters of AIDS. In the discourse of heteropatriarchal society, bisexuals are construed as being promiscuous, pathological killers: we knowingly "contaminate" both the lesbian/gay worlds and put the heterosexual world at risk. It is interesting to note that some people in these various groups believe that they were supposed to be ontologically "protected" from AIDS. Instead of turning their rage against the government which does not provide explicit AIDS education or give enough money for research, they now use bisexuals as their scapegoat. As this construction of the bisexual as the *evil other* continues and intensifies, it will become more and more difficult for Black men to come out as bisexual.

This is a particularly vicious form of oppression for us. We are just beginning to organize our communities, to address the issues that surround the diversity of bisexualities that exist in our worlds. We are perceived as being more dangerous, even more the incarnation of evil, than are lesbians and gay men. There is something too transgressive about us blurring boundaries between worlds that are never supposed to meet. However, this is all complicated by the fact that there are still very few visible "out" bisexual activists in our communities. So-called authorities on AIDS and human sexuality feel free to say that bisexuals are cowards, that there is no such thing as a Black bisexual activist, and that we are consciously spreading AIDS. In the communities of color, bisexuals are being portrayed as dishonest people who are so obsessed with remaining in the closet that we put other people at risk because we refuse to speak about our sexuality. Although I acknowledge that there is some truth to some of this, it shows immediately that we are working with differing definitions of bisexual. Who are these bisexuals about whom these "specialists" are speaking? Are they men who are behaviorally bisexual, but who do not identify as such? Are they "out" bisexual AIDS activists? This confusion is potentially lethal; its subtext is homophobia/biphobia.

Homophobia/Biphobia

What is the reason for the existence of virulent homophobia/biphobia throughout Judeo-Christian history? How have religious systems affirmed and systematized/institutionalized this fear? What in the religio-theological vision excludes the queer entirely from society, making of her/him the Other, the foreigner/stranger, par excellence? What was the evolution of the relationship queerness-heresy (idolatry)-witchcraft-madness? Is there a relationship between the interests of the dominant culture and the theological support provided for homophobia/biphobia? What are the social, political, economic, historical contexts which have contributed to the formation of these attitudes?

Homophobia, the fear of homosexuality and of people who engage in same-sex behavior, has always had recourse to a certain theological discourse in order to support its positions. A certain complicity was thus established. The religious discourse nourished homophobia/biphobia which in turn reinforced the religio-theological discourse. In traditional religious societies, all deviance is conceptualized in theological terms and the deviant represents those forces which threaten to destroy the established order. This concept of evil, understood as a rhetorical process which justifies the expulsion of the source of danger, absorbs many cognitive distinctions. Thus, in the European Middle Ages, heretic, sorcerer, "queer," and witch were often perceived as being inextricably bound up together. The persistence of Earth-wisdom was perceived by the Church as a sign of devil-worship. Therefore, those who practiced the old ways of healing, who had knowledge of herbs, midwifery, etc., who were primarily women, soon came to be seen as "witches" who were in league with the devil. This was obviously not considered very different from being one who was out of line with the teachings of the official Church. To be a heretic was already to show that one was under the sway of the devil, that one was no longer "right-thinking." Some so-called heretical groups, such as the Bogomils or the Cathars, were believed to engage in homosexuality and lesbianism. Unorthodox sexuality would seem then, in the thinking of that period, to be an additional expression of being a heretic.

Accusations of homosexuality, lesbianism, or generalized "perversion" often accompanied charges of heresy and witchcraft. Already in the world of the

Hebrew Bible, there was a link established between male same-sex behavior and "idolatry."[13] The phenomenon of homophobia/biphobia is characterized by a refusal and an exclusion of the *Other* and at the same time the attempt to control the *Other*. As Michel Foucault says, "The crazy person is *Other* in relation to other people: the Other in the sense of an exception—amongst others—in the sense of the universal. . . . Between the mad person, and the subject who says 'That person is a mad person,' an entire abyss is created."[14] The "crazy" person, considered to be the Other, was totally and systematically separated from the rest of society. This is the same way in which society reacts to the queer, who is perceived as being the foreigner/stranger, the ultimate Other. Through this phenomenon of homophobia/biphobia, we witness a double process: a heterosexist, homophobic/biphobic society validates itself as *good* ("normal") and invalidates the Other as *evil* ("sick").

Thomas Szasz, a psychiatrist and historian of psychiatry, has suggested that the fear of conceptual or religious otherness might even be seen as a homophobic/biphobic response. This points once again to the link established between heresy and homosexuality, as well as that which was ultimately established between madness and homosexuality.[15] This also indicates the existence of a political, as well as a religio-political motivation for the persecution of queers. This phenomenon was particularly clear during the McCarthy era in the 1950s in the United States: In McCarthy's ideology, communism was the ultimate heresy, the very incarnation of evil. It is not surprising that it would be often linked with homosexuality. A mere accusation of communism and homosexuality would be sufficient to destroy a person. It was not necessary that the accusation be substantiated. As with the witch-hunts of Europe's Middle Ages, once a woman or man had been pointed out as Other, she or he had to be eliminated.

Based on interpretations of Genesis, Leviticus, Romans, etc., the Church has summarily condemned all lesbian/gay/bisexual/transgender people, *but especially those who dare to openly identify themselves as such*. In the anthropology of the Hebrew Bible, the male who is not married and the father of a family is not a real man. Procreation plays a central role in this definition. Given that in this construction of reality it was through one's progeniture that one lived on, and considering that sterility was considered as a cruel curse, then a deliberate same-sex act, an act that would be willingly sterile, would be scandalous in the eyes of Hebrew culture. Biblical Israel was an essentially patriarchal society where the role and the status of the male—husband and father—were of prime importance. As G. Rattray Taylor has shown, societies where divinity is often conceived and portrayed through paternal, male images are often the most violently opposed to same-sex practices. These patriarchal societies are conservative, authoritarian, and marked by a clear subordination of women and a total rejection of any form of same-gender sexual activity. On the other hand, societies where women play a more prominent role are often more liberal, more innovative, more democratic, more egalitarian as regards the status of women and men, and more tolerant of same-gender sexual activity.[16] It is important to mention the fact that in the ancient world, male-on-male anal rape was often used on those defeated in a war to show conquest, derision, and disdain: they were to be "treated as women." An example of this can be found in the epic of Horus and Seth.[17]

Thus, in societies that place a supreme value on male status, queer sexuality throws into question the entire basis of patriarchal society, of heteropatriarchy (the enforced belief in heterosexual male power and dominance). The ultimate problem, as reflected in the texts of Leviticus, is not in the sexual acts themselves, but in the fact that they reflect treating a man like a woman. There is no mention of any condemnation of lesbianism (with the possible exception of Rom. 1:26); in a patriarchal society, women's sexuality is without meaning (only male sexuality is invested with *meaning*). Therefore, lesbianism is even more insignificant in the eyes of the dominant heteropatriarchal society because it does not involve a "degradation" of the male status as is the case in sexual relations between men.

It may be redundant to speak of the androcentricity of patriarchal narratives, but the link between homosexuality, homophobia/biphobia and patriarchy commands more serious reflection. Most religious homophobia bases itself on misinterpretation of Biblical texts. First and foremost, the term homosexual does not exist in any of the original languages of the Bible. That is simple enough to understand, given that the word was not coined until the end of the nineteenth century, at a time when the concept of sexual orientation began to be developed. Thus, a negative meaning could be imparted to a Hebrew or Greek word by translating it with an English term that had negative connotations. Translations reflect the bias of society. All of those sermons that use the Bible to refer to homosexuality, as we understand it today, are really missing the mark. The texts to which they refer are not referring to what we today would call homosexuality/bisexuality. There are very few Biblical texts which actually refer to same-sex behavior, and Jesus never refers to it in his teachings. The text of Leviticus 20:10-16 is part of the Holiness Code, whose intention is to distinguish Israel as a people set apart for God. Part of its main concern is to avoid duplicating any of the practices or beliefs of the surrounding cultures. The most misquoted text, Genesis 19:1-10, is actually not about same-sex activity but rather about inhospitality. For people living in the desert, to not receive strangers is to condemn them to death. Other places in the Bible, such as Ezekiel 16:49-50 and Luke 10:10-13, which mention the story of Sodom and Gomorrah, do so in the context of their lack of hospitality to strangers, their neglect of the needy, and so forth. This narrative is totally patriarchal in focus. The women of Sodom are presented as insignificant, nameless characters in the story. What moral precept is to be derived from Lot's offering of his two daughters to the crowd? Yet the idea of the fire and brimstone that destroyed Sodom and Gomorrah would later inspire Justinian, head of the Byzantine Empire (77th Novella/538 CE), to require the death penalty for same-sex behavior. It is rather ironic to think that those who hurl the term "sodomites" at queers are actually themselves "sodomites," inasmuch as they refuse to include those whom they consider to be ultimate Others. In Romans 1:26-27, one of the favorite homophobic proof-texts of the Black Church, Paul's major concern is not to attack particular vices, but to use them to support his overarching theological discourse on God's justice and mercy as revealed through Jesus.

In Black preaching on sin, the main focus is always on sin as sex or vice versa.[18] With all of the Biblical injunctions against amassing wealth, it is still rare to hear a sermon on economic injustice as sin. Even racism and apartheid as forms of sin do not rank as highly as sex in African-American popular preaching. Many preachers have said that heterosexual adultery and fornication (however the two might be defined) are wrong, but are still better than any form of same-sex activity. Queer sexuality remains in the domain of those things about which one never speaks. People do it, but there is no need to talk about it, or to assume a political activist identity around it. In this particular case, this silence is a particularly dangerous one, because it is now taking people's lives. When the Black Church does speak about those who are in-the-life, it is never in a positive way. As long as people keep quiet about what they are doing, then there is no issue as such. As long as people don't fight for their rights as lesbian/gay/bisexual/transgender people within the Church, then there is no struggle and the Church is not obliged to confront its reality.

In AIDS work, we often encounter Black gay/bisexual men who have heard all of their lives that they are evil and bad. Many internalize this and then figure that there is no point in their practicing safer sex since they are condemned to be punished anyway. This, coupled with their fear of self-identifying as being in-the-life for fear of the consequences of such an act, makes them feel that they can ignore the AIDS materials that target gay/bisexual men, since they do not see themselves as falling into either of these categories, even though they are men who have sexual relations with men. They feel that if they don't label themselves, what they are doing is not so bad as if they actually labelled themselves as such. This is a very clear example of how the Black Church participates in the silencing and killing of Black gay/bisexual men. The same situation pertains for many African-American lesbians and bisexual women.

The current African-American religious homophobic discourse is unfortunately bolstered by what some Afrocentric writers have to say on the matter. Their attitude is that homosexualities/bisexualities are the result of contact with corrupt European cultures; in our traditional societies, no such thing ever existed, they claim. Molefi K. Asante, in his book, *Afrocentricity*, says

> Homosexuality is a deviation from Afrocentric thought because it makes the person evaluate his own physical needs above the teachings of national consciousness. An outburst of homosexuality among black men, fed by the prison breeding system, threatens to distort the relationship between friends. ... The rise of homosexuality in the African-American male's psyche is real and complicated. An Afrocentric perspective recognizes its existence but homosexuality cannot be condoned or accepted as good for the national development of a strong people.[19]

For Dr. Frances Cress Welsing, an African-American psychiatrist noted for her theories on the origins and perpetuation of racism, bisexuality and homosexuality amongst white men are rooted in their "genetic weakness." Bisexuality and homosexuality are what she calls the sexual expressions of white men's weakness, passivity, and effeminization. Once again, Black men do not come to bisexuality or homosexuality on their own; homosexuality and bisexuality are imposed on Black men by white society. Any Black acceptance of male bisexuality and homosexuality would be acceptance of a strategy for destroying Black people. "Black male bisexuality and homosexuality has been used by the white collective in its effort to survive genetically in a world dominated by colored people, and Black acceptance of this imposition does not solve the major problem of our oppression but only further retards its ultimate solution."[20]

Neither one of these writers refers at all to women. It would seem that only male bisexuality and homosexuality are problematic, as though Black women were not even important enough to matter. We are faced with a situation that requires serious deconstruction. When these Afrocentrists speak, they refer to same-sex behavior as the white man's disease[21] or as the result of having been imprisoned. What they fail to see is that the need to present homosexualities and bisexualities as something white, ultimately stems directly from the Eurocentric rewriting of our history and the erasing of our art and oral traditions that might have shown our own history of same-sex relationships. They seem to ignore the fact that European colonists brought their homophobia with them to Africa and saw that it was taught. These writers accept the premise that homosexuality and bisexuality are negative values. They never question the origins of their bias. They accept a negative Eurocentric definition of homosexuality/bisexuality, without looking to see if, in African cultures, there might be something that corresponds to same-sex behaviors, without necessarily having a European concept of sexual orientation attached to it. The rapidity with which people respond to the contention that homosexuality/bisexuality never existed in Africa is an indication of how thoroughly European homophobia spread. Once our memory has been erased, even those who claim to have reappropriated our true history from white revisions and see themselves as being authentically Afrocentric still ultimately insist upon clinging to a Eurocentric understanding of homosexuality/bisexuality and to Euro-Protestant morality.

Although both of these writers purport to represent Afrocentric thinking which is supposed to transcend the Eurocentric either/or dichotomy, they both insist that bisexuality or homosexuality is antithetical to Blackness. They totally ignore the fact that for most of us in-the-life, there is no dichotomy. While we do not place our sexuality before our Blackness, we do live out our sexualities within the context of our Blackness. This way of thinking does not articulate or respond to the interconnectedness of racism, sexism, classism, and heterosexism. Although these Afrocentrist theorists might have many very important things to say, their expressions of homophobia are unacceptable and raise the question of how one can claim to be African-centered yet advocate the submission of one group to another or simply brush that group away as something to be altered by an Afrocentric perspective. As Cheryl Clarke says,

> If we cannot tolerate the homophobia of the culture in general, we cannot tolerate it from black people. . . . Homophobia is a measure of how far removed we are from the psychological transformation we so desperately need to engender. The expression of homophobic sentiments. . . . the seeming lack of any willingness to understand the politics of gay and lesbian liberation collude with the dominant white male culture to repress not only gay men and lesbians, but also to repress a natural part of all human beings, namely the bisexual potential in us all. Homophobia divides black people as allies, it cuts off political growth, stifles revolution, and perpetuates patriarchal domination.[22]

Homophobia and biphobia have already significantly damaged the life of the African-American community and they continue their destructive work by creating the atmosphere for AIDSphobia, the fear of AIDS and of people living with AIDS and aparthAIDS, the systematic discrimination against and separating out of people living with AIDS.

AIDS/AIDSphobia/AparthAIDS

When it met in 1991, the Congressional Black Caucus flatly refused to place AIDS as an issue on the agenda, stating that it had already been discussed. HIV/AIDS is the axis around which so many of the issues that are besieging us actually revolve. Almost any issue that concerns African Americans somehow points to AIDS:

A) *Lack of a universal health care plan*: How do we realistically talk about AIDS treatments when most of us people of color cannot afford them and do not have access to them?

B) *The prison system*: When 25% of the African-American male population is imprisoned and when most prisons allow neither AIDS education nor condom distribution, because the latter would imply that there is same-gender sexual activity taking place in the prisons, is it not reasonable to conclude that a high percentage of these men would have come into contact with HIV and gone on to become HIV+?

C) *Teen pregnancies*: If a teenaged woman becomes pregnant, that means very simply and clearly that she and her partner are not practicing safer sex, at least not on a regular basis.

D) *Black women's health issues*: This also raises one of the many issues facing women of color with AIDS who make up 73% of women with AIDS. Since the CDC definition of AIDS was developed from observations of men, women will often die of an opportunistic infection before they are even considered eligible for an actual AIDS diagnosis. Not only will they not be counted in the statistical picture, they will also not get treated, will not qualify for health benefits, child care, rent subsidies or other support services for PWAs. They will not be provided with information on how to take care of themselves and how to protect the people with whom they share needles or have sexual relations. Many women with HIV disease are only diagnosed after they have died. This brings us to the issue of forced sterilization of HIV+ women, who are predominantly women of color, to have abortions or to be sterilized. Not only does the virus destroy our community, but the government and the medical industry would like to use this as a pretext to keep us from reproducing, to effectively make sure that we have no future. This is *genocide*, no matter if you look at it as intentional, or merely the consequence of everything else. As Sunny Rumsey-Ahmed, an African Caribbean Muslim sister and AIDS terrorist says:

Why should these women be treated any differently from white women with a family history of cancer, genetically transferable disease, chronic fatigue, multiple sclerosis, or a variety of potentially deforming disabilities? Many diseases are transferred *in utero*, and the law strongly protects the rights of women with these diseases. To advocate for sterilization and abortion because of a disease that affects primarily women of color looks like racism.[23]

E) *Unemployment*: When people cannot work/do not have jobs, they don't have access to health-care or job-related health-plans.

F) *Social services*: In an era in which social services and social service institutions are having their funding drastically cut, and as the face of AIDS changes, and it becomes increasingly an issue of people of color, of women and children and of poor people in general, who will be there to take care of us?

G) *Substance abuse*: Here we are faced with the whole question of HIV transmission through the sharing of works for the use of heroin. But we must also consider the fact that the spread of crack use throughout all levels of our communities, and the fact that people do perform sexual acts in return for crack, has devastating consequences for the spread of HIV amongst people of color. Cocaine, which does not grow in the United States, has been placed in our communities to accelerate the process of extermination. Let us consider the fact that in the 1960s when the Black Power movement was at its zenith, heroin became widely available (as it is again now) and played a great role in dismantling any movement for self-determination.

H) *Media*: The treatment of people of color in the mass media has traditionally been a crucial issue for us, but it becomes even more critical in an era in which the press, reflecting the dominant mentality, is busily assigning responsibility to various groups for the transmission of HIV. We were all aware of how the media tried to pin HIV on Haiti and Africa while also setting up a dichotomy between *innocent* = white middle-class heterosexual women with HIV, and *guilty, deserving-to-be-punished* = queers and people of color with HIV. The so-called innocent can offer very wild hypotheses, but when we speak *conspiracy and genocide*, then we are being wildly paranoid and irrational. Yet history and our experience speak loudly for themselves. Is it not still genocide when one does things to remove the possibility of life from a people? Why is it so strange to imagine that this has not been carefully thought out? Is this not perhaps a plan that went awry, or is it going according to plan? Considering the policies of genocide enacted on people of color on this continent over the last 500 years, why consider what I say to be wild and careless? We have only to look at the Tuskegee Syphilis Experiment in which, from 1932 to 1972, more than 400 African-American sharecroppers and day laborers in Alabama were subjects in a government study designed to determine the effects of untreated syphilis.[24] Why do we continue to insist on the government's innocence, while we know that our government has blood on its hands, as every seven minutes there is an AIDS-related death? As helpful as testing might be, mandatory testing for people is not the answer, especially not when the results of this testing can be used against us and, therefore, have very dire results for us as people of color. This new wave of media hype is precisely that, a diversionary tactic to keep us from looking at the real issues of inequality in our society.

I) *Education*: We must be very aware of the fact that AIDS education is still grossly inadequate in communities of color. It is often not accessible in languages or terms that we understand; many of our people do not read. We are squeamish about sex-education in this country, and in particular in our communities, but it is now a matter of life and death. When we become locked into endless debates about whether we can distribute condoms to our young people and encourage them to use them, we must remember that *there are over one million HIV+ people in the United States* and that *every seven minutes there is an AIDS-related death.*

J) *Affordable housing*: Given the high percentage of people of color amongst the homeless in the U.S. and the percentage of HIV+ people within that group, the right to housing does become an AIDS-related issue for people of color. What good does it do to have AZT, DDI, homeopathic, or Chinese herbal treatments, if you don't have running water with which to take them, or a house in which to sleep and eat?

K) *International community of people of African descent/people of color*: AIDS is an issue for all peoples of African descent and all people of color. We have only to look at the devastation that HIV is visiting on certain countries in Africa to be made aware of the fact that this will have extremely severe consequences on Africa and her participation in the international economy. Another example would be Puerto Rico (population: 3.5 million) where almost 6,000 Puerto Ricans (who are U.S. citizens) who have AIDS and tens of thousands who are HIV+ cannot get AZT, DDI, pentamidine (used in treating pneumocystis carinii pneumonia [PCP], one of the most prevalent opportunistic infections and the leading cause of death for people with AIDS), or receive medicaid coverage. According to some studies, by the year 2000, one-third of the population (more than a million people) will be HIV+. Puerto Rico's status as a U.S. territory/colony means fewer dollars in federal entitlements, especially medicaid, than states receive. Puerto Ricans with HIV lack access to the same quality of health care given to other U.S. citizens through federal AIDS programs. The same is true for access to pentamidine, even though the major pharmaceutical firms that produce these drugs are located on the island.

L) *The African American*: AIDS challenges us to move towards (or return to) a more inclusive understanding of inter-generational family. We can no longer afford to exclude, to decide to include some and exclude others. We are all the children of someone; we are all family to someone and to each other. Whether we like it or not, we are the only family that we will have. This involves moving away from the "we" versus "they" (lepers) mentality; we must understand *now* that AIDS is affecting all of us. In what is perhaps one of the most painful areas for us as a community, we are called to move beyond the heritage of puritanical Euro-Protestantism. Our homophobia/biphobia and our heterosexism are quite literally killing us. Those of us who make the effort to be compassionate to people with AIDS are more than willing (sometimes, not always) to run to the bedside of PWAs when they are ill and incapacitated. If they will only ask for forgiveness, we will take care of them and assure them that all will be well with their souls. But what about showing that love and compassion while people are still living and healthy? Do we yet not realize that our homophobia and biphobia, our shutting sisters and brothers, mothers and fathers, grandmothers and grandfathers, aunts and uncles, nieces, nephews, cousins, godparents, godchildren out of our lives because of our judgment on their sexual orientation, often condemns them to lives of isolation, alienation, fear, lack of self-love, poor self-esteem, lack of self-acceptance (many of the ingredients for leading people into self-destructive behavior)? Do we yet not realize that we drive so many people away from a loving God who is nowhere near as vindictive and hard-hearted as we? Do we yet not realize that we are killing ourselves? Do we not yet realize that we have blood on our hands? When we most need to be a nurturing, healing family, do we yet not realize that if we exclude you or me, we are depriving ourselves of the rich gift of diverse humanity that we each possess.

We must invent new ways in which we relate to the other, to the one who is different, as a meeting in joy and love, in which the other is not someone to be feared and marginalized, but rather embraced as someone who helps us to be more fully who we are. There is no shame in AIDS, only in society's attitudes toward it and in the treatment of people with AIDS.

In 1992 we people of color on Turtle Island (Native American name for the land-mass on which we live) will commemorate our heritage of 500 years of racism, oppression, and genocide. We were exterminated by European invaders. Our land was and still is taken from us. We were sent smallpox in blankets, then more of us were brought here to build the land. Then there were the infamous Tuskegee syphilis experiments. Yet through the grace of God and the fortitude of our ancestors, we have survived. Survival is our key issue as we enter the twenty-first century. But we cannot fight for survival without our lives. We cannot survive without our lives, as Audre Lorde puts it. But if we are to survive, we as faith communities are called, in this situation that might well be like no other holocaust that we have ever faced, to move beyond where we are now. We cannot fight enough. We have to struggle with our homophobia and our biphobia and stop assigning guilt for the transmission of HIV. We need to stop displacing the responsibility from the shoulders of our government and stop blaming members of our own communities. We have to stop bickering over condom distribution or over the distribution of clean works for IV drug users. Even if it does not meet our ideal principles, we need to re-visit those principles, but we definitely must take the steps that will assure the future of our communities.

Because of the importance of the Black Church in the lives of our people, it is necessary for Black Churches to be safe spaces, for Black clergy who are in-the-life to feel that it is possible for them to be themselves without practicing to deceive. It is imperative that all who speak and teach in the Church be helped to understand that it is necessary to be inclusive of women and men in-the-life when they speak, preach, and teach. Heteropatriarchy must be dismantled in the Black Church's liberative praxis.

We are called to move beyond the heritage of Euro-Protestantism, which has created the very world-view that has been used to oppress and alienate us both as people of color and as lesbian/gay/bisexual/transgender people. This Eurocentric interpretation of Christianity, which is rooted in an either/or view of the world, has spawned the homophobia/biphobia/AIDSphobia/sexism/heterosexism that are quite literally killing us. If Black theology is to be truly prophetic, it must now join in the struggle against heteropatriarchy, the source of multitudinous forms of oppression, for liberation from homophobia/biphobia will also free heterosexuals.

Even though Howard Thurman is speaking of the evils of racial segregation, his words in this quote can be easily applied to the creation of a new community in which homophobia/biphobia are no more, in which women and men in-the-life have found their voice and have taken their places in the community of believers.

> It is necessary, therefore, for the privileged and the underprivileged to work on the common environment for the purpose of providing normal expressions of fellowship. This is one very important reason for the insistence that segregation is a complete ethical and moral evil. Whatever it may do for those who dwell on either side of the wall, one thing is certain: it poisons all normal contacts of those persons involved. The first step toward love is a common sharing of a sense of mutual worth and value. This cannot be discovered in a vacuum or in a series of artificial or hypothetical relationships. It has to be in a real situation, natural, free.[25]

NOTES

1. Craig G. J. Harris, "Cut Off From Among Their People," in *In The Life: A Black Gay Anthology*, ed. Joseph Beam (Boston: Alyson Publications, 1986), p. 66.

2. Adrienne Rich, *Compulsory Heterosexuality and Lesbian Existence* (Denver: Antelope Publications, 1980), pp. 10-15.

3. Patricia Hill Collins, *Black Feminist Thought* (New York: Routledge, 1991), pp. 192-96.

4. Arthur Evans, *Witchcraft and the Gay Counterculture* (Boston: Fag Rag Books, 1978), pp. 89-99.

5. Walter L. Williams, *The Spirit and the Flesh: Sexual Diversity in American Indian Culture* (Boston: Beacon Press, 1986), pp. 131-151.

6. Heinz Heger, *The Men with the Pink Triangle* (Boston: Alyson Publications, 1980), p. 14.

7. Cheryl Clarke, "The Failure to Transform: Homophobia in the Black Community," in *Homegirls*, ed. Barbara Smith (New York: Kitchen Table Women of Color Press, 1983), p. 200.

8. Pauli Murray, "Black Theology and Feminist Theology" and Jacquelyn Grant, "Black Theology and the Black Woman" in *Black Theology: A Documentary History, 1966-1979*, ed. Gayraud S. Wilmore and James H. Cone (Maryknoll, N.Y.: Orbis Books, 1979), pp. 398-417 and pp. 418-433.

9. See David Frechette, "Non, Je Ne Regrette Rien"; Charles I. Nero, "Toward a Black Gay Aesthetic"; Ron Simmons, "Some Thoughts on the Challenges Facing Black Gay Intellectuals," in *Brother to Brother: New Writings by Black Gay Men*, ed. Essex Hemphill (Boston: Alyson Publications, 1991), pp. 119-20, 229-52, 211-28.

10. Williams, *The Spirit and the Flesh*, pp. 41-43.

11. Judith Butler, *Gender Trouble* (New York: Routledge, 1990), pp. 35-78.

12. Joseph Murphy, *Santeria: An African Religion in America* (Boston: Beacon Press, 1988), pp. 89-91.

13. See V. L. Bullough, "Heresy, Witchcraft and Sexuality," *Journal of Homosexuality* vol. 1, no. 2 (Winter 74-75): 185-202. Also, Evans, *Witchcraft and the Gay Counterculture*, pp. 51-61.

14. Michel Foucault, *Histoire de la folie à l'age classique* (Paris: Gallimard, 1972), p. 195.

15. Thomas Szasz, *The Manufacture of Madness* (New York: Harper Torchbooks, 1970), pp. 3-27, 242-59.

16. G. Rattray Taylor, *Sex in History* (New York: Harper and Row, 1973), p. 83.

17. *The Contendings of Horus and Seth* (XI: 3-4), trans. A. H. Gardiner, The Chester-Beatty Papyri, I, Oxford, 1931.

18. Elaine Pagels, *Adam, Eve and the Serpent* (New York: Vintage Books, 1989), pp. 78-97.

19. Molefi K. Asante, *Afrocentricity* (Trenton: African World Press, 1991), p. 57.

20. Frances Cress Welsing, *The Isis Papers* (Chicago: Third World Press, 1991), p. 57.

21. Compare this with the theory of Fanon that the Black men of the Caribbean had never experienced the Oedipal complex and therefore there was no homosexuality amongst them, homosexuality belonging to European cultures. Frantz Fanon, *Black Skins, White Masks*, trans. Constance Farrington (New York: Grove Press, 1963), p. 84.

22. Clarke, "The Failure to Transform," p. 207.

23. Sunny Rumsey-Ahmed, "AIDS Issues for African-American and African-Caribbean Women," in *Women, AIDS, and Activism*, ed. ACT UP/NY Women and AIDS Book Group (Boston: South End Press, 1990), p. 104.

24. James H. Jones, *Bad Blood* (New York: Free Press, 1981).

25. Howard Thurman, *Jesus and the Disinherited* (Richmond, Ind.: Friends United Press, 1981), p. 98.

12

WHAT DOES IT MEAN TO BE BLACK AND CHRISTIAN?

Kelly Miller Smith Institute, Inc.

*I call heaven and earth to witness against you today, that I have set
before you life and death, blessings and curses. Choose life so that you
and your descendants may live.*

Deuteronomy 30:19, NRSV

I. A Critical Choice

The African-American Church is in crisis. A crisis that calls for a national
dialogue. At a time in history when we are about to enter a new millennium,
the African-American Church stands at the crossroads of decision. Its traditional role as the conserver of Black culture and the conscience of the Black
community is at stake. It must choose either life or death, blessings or curses.
Whatever choice it makes will determine whether or not we and our descendants will live as a redeemed and redeeming community in this land where God
has befriended us.

The signs of the crisis we face today are unmistakable:

Witness — the social and economic descent of more than a third of the Black
population into a burgeoning and permanent underclass.

Witness — the children of our impoverished, drug-infested neighborhoods
coming to the point of birth, and yet dying in the womb of human
possibility.

Witness — the rate of incarceration of young Black males that has twenty-three
percent of those aged twenty to twenty-nine — almost one of every
four — in prison, on bail, on probation or parole.[1]

This working paper, prepared by the Kelly Miller Smith Institute on African-American Church
Studies, Vanderbilt University Divinity School, is a call to a national dialogue now in progress.

Witness — the turning of thousands of our young people toward illegal drugs in a vain, hedonistic escape from reality, or an attempt to enter a degrading, criminal career.

Witness — the unprecedented assault on Black family life by urban violence, poverty, homelessness, and teenage pregnancy on one hand, and on the other, the demands of an upwardly mobile, materialistic lifestyle that is scornful of God and has no place for the church of Jesus Christ.

Witness — the reversals in the public arena of hard won policies ensuring affirmative action for minorities and women.

Witness — the rampant individualism, the loss of community, and the decline of the Black Church as an effective agent for justice and liberation among all poor and oppressed people. The list goes on.

II. A Spiritual Crisis

The crisis that we are faced with does not simply reflect a crisis of social, economic, and political proportions, but also and more profoundly, a crisis of Black faith. As a people, we are losing the ability to hear God speaking to us in self-affirming and liberating ways. Hopelessness and despair have taken the place of faith for millions. For this reason, it is clear that what we are facing is essentially a *religious* crisis — a crisis of the Black Church in its historic role as the custodian of our values, and the moral arbiter and mentor of the African-American community — both the churched and unchurched.

All institutions in which we predominate, particularly our schools, colleges, seminaries and churches, are touched by this religious and moral crisis — this crisis of the Black spirit. As our ancestors heard and responded to God's call to come and "let us argue it out" (Isa. 1:18 NRSV), we too need to come together today in order to clarify and articulate truths relative to this crisis. The word *crisis* not only points to the impending danger in which we stand, but also challenges us to reassess our situation as a people and a church and to seize the opportunity for a faithful response to God.

III. A Call to a National Dialogue

The purpose of this document is to summon our people to a national dialogue. A dialogue between pastors and theological professors, clergy and laity, brothers and sisters — to articulate the broad outlines of *What it means to be both Black and Christian and to maintain, at one and the same time, both the unifying integrity of liberated individuals, and the rich diversity of a reconciled community of faith.* We speak, in this working paper, of a Black theology — a Black perspective on the faith of Jesus Christ and the faith of our ancestors — that will help us to straighten out the confusion in our minds, and that will clarify our purposes and goals as Black Christians.

If the ominous trends of oppression are to be turned back and the collapse of churches as agents of Black solidarity and liberation is to be reversed, then scholars of the academy and pastors of churches, denominational and congregational officials, professionals, students, artists, clergy, laity, women, and men must seriously engage in a protracted dialogue on *the nature of our dilemma, the means by which we can be extricated from it, and the reason for the hope that is in us* (see 1 Peter 3:15).

IV. Life or Death?

We have come to a moment in the 373 years of our pilgrimage in North America when we must make a decisive choice for life or death. Death means turning our backs on our historic identity as an African people transplanted on this soil by sinful people, but by God's good purpose (see Gen. 50:19–20), to help the United States realize the full measure of its potential. Death means turning our backs on our perennial struggle for justice and equality. Death means turning our backs on the God who delivers the oppressed. Life, on the other hand, means affirming and celebrating the spiritual inheritance passed down to us from a kidnapped, tortured, and enslaved people who were determined *to be* and *to become* in spite of every attempt to dehumanize them. Life means choosing the God of our forebears who has brought us thus far to be witnesses to the divine purpose of the redemption of all creation through struggle and hope (see Rom. 8:19–25).

V. We Begin by Confessing Our Sin

As pastors and seminary professors, clergy and laity, women and men of the Christian faith, we confess our personal sins and the sins of the churches and educational institutions we serve.

We have not — loved God or our neighbors as we ought. We have been bloated with our own conceit, blind to the needs of the Samaritan lying by the side of the road, and corrupted by our desire for power, fame, and personal gain.

We have not — taken care of the household of God, like good stewards. Rather we have used it to prey on our people's emotions or their intellectual pride and gullibility. Instead of making the Black Church a missionary outpost and the Black school a beachhead in enemy territory, we have made them safe havens for the fearful, complacent, and snobbish.

We have not — spoken the truth in love or taken pains to study and prepare our own minds for teaching and leading in the complex world in which we live today.

We have not — accepted all people as children of God, whether good or bad, educated or uneducated, female or male, but we have been respecters of persons, preferring those who flatter and reward us.

We have not — stayed on the battlefield to fight until the war is over; instead, we have abandoned the struggle to secular institutions, and have made the Black Church subservient to conservative politicians and socially indifferent personalities who call themselves evangelists.

We confess that we are profoundly ashamed of all wherein we have displeased and dishonored God. All the ways in which we have trivialized the church and corrupted the academy. In this unprecedented crisis of our congregations, schools, and communities, we throw ourselves upon the mercy of God, pleading that through this act of public confession we may prove ourselves sincerely repentant and through this proposal for national dialogue, worthy of giving leadership to a new life together.

VI. We Receive the Assurance of Pardon

The Scripture tells us that, "If we confess our sins, God who is faithful and just will forgive us our sins and cleanse us from all unrighteousness" (1 John 1:9 NRSV). We accept this assurance of pardon with joy and declare it for ourselves and all our brothers and sisters, within and outside of the church.

We celebrate the fact that despite all our shortcomings we are forgiven people; that because of God's grace the Black Church, the Black family, and the Black school are still alive, vibrant, and girded, with strength for dealing with this portentous crisis. We who have the courage to admit the painful truth — that we have often been greater enemies to ourselves than our oppressors, call all African Americans to confession of our sins and to the assurance that the blood of Christ redeems us from the curse of the law, which is our just condemnation.

Crisis suggests both negative and positive possibilities. We do not assume that nothing good is happening in the Black Church. We believe that many are being blessed because of foundational Black institutions; that Black theology is already being practiced in many places by thousands of unacclaimed pastors, teachers, lay leaders; and that obedience and faithfulness are normative virtues in many of our communities today. We thank God that the Black Church has stood for social transformation with a profound belief that "everybody talkin' 'bout heaven ain't goin' there"; that the gospel must be *lived out* in the tension between sociology and theology, between the public arena and the sanctuary.

The sociology of the Black Church is expressed in theological terms and the theology of the Black Church is expressed in sociological terms. Because of this tradition of theological realism the Black Church has always understood with crystal clarity what Jesus meant when he said:

For I was hungry and you gave me food, I was thirsty and you gave me something to drink, I was a stranger and you welcomed me, I was naked and you gave me clothing, I was sick and you took care of me, I was in prison and you visited me.

(Matthew 25:35–36 NRSV)

In fact, the supreme paradox of our situation is that despite the tragic overtones of our crisis, we can come together for study and dialogue in praise and thanksgiving to the God who has been so good to us. Despite our weakness and failures, despite all that we have endured in the past or will be called upon to suffer in the future, we can still say with the psalmist:

Lord, you have been our dwelling place
in all generations. Before the mountains were brought forth,
or ever you had formed the earth and the world,
from everlasting to everlasting, you are God.

(Psalm 90:1–2 NRSV)

VII. What Is Theology and What Does It Have To Do with Us?

Theology is the process of reflecting upon God's involvement in human life. Although an academic discipline, it is also the way any person appropriates the faith. In a real sense, all of us are theologians, for theology is the only way that reason and faith embrace each other. Every Christian is a theologian! It is our duty, as faithful believers, to do theology!

To do theology means to make an effort to understand, declare, and live out who God is, what God demands, and what God has done and is doing now for our salvation. Then, in the light of that *theology*, that is, the knowledge of ourselves, God, and the world, we must respond in faith, love, and obedience. *Theology in this sense is the work of the whole church and the individual members of every congregation.* Without question, preaching is one of the mightiest tools the Black Church has for expressing our theology.

The preaching moment in the Black Church is an opportunity to present a knowledge of ourselves and of God. The Black Church has long recognized the central role of preaching in the faithful presentation and doing of a relevant theology. One Black theologian put it this way:

It is the unenviable task of preachers to wrestle honestly with the word of God, to experience its critical power, for themselves and for the people they preach to—but always within the situation and the experience of their people, so that the preachers will be understandable and relevant. It is preaching that addresses their deepest existential problems, preaching that speaks to the whole of their existence. For Blacks this means that the preacher must address not merely their being in the world, but their being Black in the world.[2]

No one can do theology in a cultural vacuum. No one can respond to God outside of his or her existential context. We do not meet God as disembodied spirits, but in our flesh and blood, and as *physical, historical creatures in concrete, living situations*. This means that there is no absolutely unconditioned universal theology. Even the New Testament was written in Greek and reflects the character, mind-set, and situation of Greek-speaking people in Asia Minor during the first two centuries of the Christian era. Theology is bound to time, to culture, and to experience. Although we know God as individuals *all* theology is influenced by and reflects—in one way or another—the historical and experiential circumstances of a people, a nation, or a neighborhood. God comes to us and we respond to God where we are placed in the world. We can do no more nor less than apprehend and respond to God out of the content of our social situation and experience.

VIII. What Is Black Theology?

Black theology is story. It is the story of our tedious pilgrimage as daughters and sons of Africa in North America. It is the story of how we have scaled mountains that seemed unclimbable and made our way through valleys that have been a veritable low ground of sorrow.

Black theology is the story of our faith in God. The God who hears bondage groans and comes to deliver the oppressed; who causes them to become agents of their own salvation. Black theology is the story of our journey with Jesus Christ, our Savior, and Liberator.

Black theology is the story of our faith-understanding and our freedom struggle. It is the story of how our faith functioned as the cornerstone of our movement toward freedom.

Our faith has inspired, fueled, and fired our freedom struggle and enabled us to overcome extraordinary hardship and hurdles from the early days of our captivity until now.

Black theology is biblical. It is the recital of the story of Joseph who reminds us of Frederick Douglass, Harriet Tubman and other great abolitionists who refused to abandon the enslaved in a strange land. It tells the story of Esther who did not glory in the fact that she had become royalty, but heard the cries of her people. It tells the story of the three Hebrew boys who would rather choose death than forsake the God of their weary years and silent tears.

Black theology is contextual. Black theology interprets the Bible in the context of Black life because our questions and answers have not been, and cannot be articulated by others as fully and accurately as by ourselves. Black theology, by necessity, comes out of the context of Black life. It makes no claims for absoluteness, nor pretends unanimity. Not all Black Christians affirm the same faith. But we begin the national dialogue believing that those Black Christians who affirm that liberation from every form of oppression is at the heart of the gospel; that Jesus Christ is the Liberator; and that there can be no true knowledge of the God of the Bible without resistance to injustice and oppression of every kind will also affirm the legitimacy of a Black theology. We may say, therefore, that Black theology is first a story that is primarily biblically based, and second, rigorously contextual.

At a time when others make predictions about the future of our community and paint a gloomy picture of the extinction of African-American people as a distinct entity, we need Black theology. We need it because we must claim not only the faith of our mothers and fathers, but understand what we are up against today and the work we must do to claim our future. We need Black theology because many Black adults and children are being swept up by conservative White evangelical congregations and television ministries that speak of a "colorless gospel" that overlooks the age-old problems of race, class, and gender oppression. We need Black theology because some brands of White theology are being used to effectively brainwash our people. We need Black theology because it tells *our* story, and no one, not even the most trustworthy, and paternalistic White televangelist, can tell our story for us.

We must tell our story in the church school, and in the classrooms and clubrooms of our communities. We must tell it in video and film. We must tell it in pamphlets, denominational literature, magazines, and scholarly books. We must tell our story in denominational gatherings, in ecumenical ministerial alliances, in local, regional, and national dialogue sessions. *We must tell the story of what it means to be Black and Christian in America today. That story will inspire us and our children. It will inform us, and illuminate what God requires of us for the living of these days as God's African-American people. Thus, we turn to the central question of our dialogue.*

IX. What Does It Mean To Be Black and Christian?

It is not possible to be a Black Christian, in the sense in which we are using those terms in this working paper, without recognizing the deep ambiguity and paradox that are at the conjunction of these two ways of being. Malcolm X described Christianity as the "perfect slave religion" because he saw how White people invented a religion calculated to keep Black people passive in slavery and subservient after emancipation. Therefore, the first requirement for understanding what it means to be Black and Christian is to admit that Christianity has been used to subjugate Africans and African Americans. Too many of us lack the spiritual and intellectual courage to make that admission. But only after we have made it can we begin to see how Blackness, as a state of mind, as a hermeneutical suspicion, and as a theological and cultural demystification of Anglo-Saxon religion and culture, can correct the distortions that modern racism induced into the message and mission of Jesus.

To be *Black* means many things. It means to accept Africa as the place of one's cultural and religious roots. It means to be identified with the rich heritage left by African men, women, and children who were forcibly brought to this land and whose history is replete with stories of great empires, powerful queens and kings, and a way of life that traditionally appreciated the whole of creation and recognized a profound spiritual reality within and behind the artifactual universe. Being Black is to be immersed in a humanistic and pragmatic culture transmitted through a strong oral tradition of storytelling, proverbs, songs, music, dance, and sculpture.

In racist societies Blackness has carried a negative connotation. White has been defined as good and Black as bad. *Webster's Third New International Dictionary* gives the following character definitions under the words White and Black.

White: "free from blemish, moral stain or impurity; outstandingly righteous; innocent; not marked by malignant influence; notably pleasing as auspicious; fortunate; notably ardent; decent; in a fair and uprightly manner; a sterling man."

Black: "outrageously wicked, a villain; dishonorable; expressing or indicating disgrace, discredit or guilt; connected with the devil; expressing menace; sullen; hostile; unqualified; committing a violation of public regulation; illicit, illegal; affected by some undesirable condition."

With these definitions is it surprising that, even though he was not European, Jesus in both White and Black churches is imaged as a blond, blue-eyed, White man? It should be obvious why it is necessary to incorporate a race critique into our understanding of the gospel. How can the Black Church proclaim a liberating gospel and ignore the cultural and theological bondage of African-American Christians to European-American myths and values? To be Black means to imagine, think, and create out of an Afrocentricity accepted by God as the vehicle of revelation and redemption (see Acts 2:7–11).

To be *Christian* also means many things. It means, first, to be a follower, a disciple of Jesus of Nazareth; a believer in his Lordship and Messianic vocation. Like being Black, being Christian is clouded in many complexities and ambiguities. Just as there are Blacks who are self-esteeming and self-denigrating, enthusiastic and apathetic, loyal and disloyal, there are Christians who exhibit the same strengths and weaknesses. In the final analysis, to be authentically Christian must mean that one strives to walk in the way of Jesus and, in some measure, accepts Jesus Christ as Lord and Savior.

When we put together these two ways of being—being Black and being Christian—we have a unique combination of histories, cultural images and perspectives, moral visions, and commitments which Black religious thinkers—from Robert Alexander Young and David Walker to James H. Cone and Prathia Hall Wynn—have labored to spell out in terms of specific choices and decisions in specific times and places. *What it means to be Black and Christian cannot be static or carved in stone, rather, out of necessity it must change over time. It is dynamic and responsive to the movement of God through history and open to the winds of the Holy Spirit.* Blackness and the Christian faith are so often misunderstood, as a result of being placed too strictly in opposition to each other, or trivialized by being too easily reconciled and reduced to a premature and conventional sameness. This is precisely why dialogue and debate are urgently necessary today.

If Black theology is story, then to be Black and Christian means to pantomime that story—to act it out on the stage of one's own life; to participate in the message and meaning of that story in proclamation and demonstration, alongside sisters and brothers who see themselves as actors in the same story. Across the United States today hundreds, perhaps thousands, of African-American congregations are demonstrating that it is possible to integrate their Blackness and their faith in a way that not only bestows wholeness and healing upon individuals and families, but also engages communities in corporate ministries of intervention and transformation of the structures of social, economic, and political life.

We propose for the national dialogue the thesis that: Being Black and Christian is an individual, family, and congregational lifestyle that reflects our acceptance of our African origins, our inseverable ties to our slave ancestors, and our identification with the millions of excluded Black people who continue to sink in the quagmire of racism, sexism, and poverty. To be Black and Christian gives the mission of the realm of God a special configuration and character, creating a unique religious symbolism and liturgical expression, and a distinctive spirituality and worship that are characteristics of our historic peoplehood.

X. God's Special Challenge to the Black Church Today: Becoming Sisters and Brothers in the Same Struggle

We cannot conclude this discussion without acknowledging that one of the most disturbing aspects of the crisis in the contemporary Black Church and community is the Black Church's historical ambivalence toward women in the church. African-American churches have, in large measure, adopted the patriarchal attitudes of White Christians regarding women. To the extent that our churches have accepted the patriarchal doctrines and practices of White Christianity we are faced today with a Black religious dilemma that has critical implications for our liberation struggle. The issue is larger than women in ministry. *The issue is the church and women.* We desperately need a Black theological and social analysis to help us clarify this aspect of the crisis, lest the Black Church become a stumbling block to its own mission of salvation and liberation.

Sexism in the church represents a theological scandal. It exalts the genital fixations and sexual distortions of the culture to the level of a false theology and dares to blame that bigotry on God. Everything we know about God tells us clearly that the living God is not a bigot. Sexism, like racism, is idolatry. The scandal is even more outrageous when we who have been victims of the idolatry of racism, and know its abuse, stoop to practice the kindred idolatry of sexism. Careful examination of every biblical text commonly used to deny the equality and the ministry of women in church and society will liberate Black Christians from misinterpretations that dishonor the character of the Creator and of humankind.

We are called to confront not only the theological scandal of sexism, but also the sociological crisis it precipitates in our communities. African Americans have historically understood our survival and freedom to be dependent upon our togetherness. Some of us are attempting today to deny that sexism is a problem in the Black community, to do so is to ignore the struggle of our sisters. Any authentic dialogue between Black women and men will reveal that sexism is a problem; real, pervasive, and destructive to our individual and collective existence.

Sexism not only limits the development and progress of Black women, it also undermines and retards the progress of African-American people as a whole. The struggle for liberation will not move forward without the full participation and contribution of African-American women. The incomes of African-American women have always been critical to the survival and well-being of our families. Whether or not we admit it, Black women have always been at the heart of our struggle. The continued active commitment, participation, and leadership of Black women are critical. The model of leadership and followership which we must leave for our children who must go into the twenty-first century must be one of full partnership among sisters and brothers united in one struggle in the name of Christ.

Unfortunately, many destructive myths are being circulated about us and believed by us. The notion that the "over-achievement" of Black women has retarded the progress of Black men has been one of the most devastating. This false allegation is promoting the break-up of families and turning us against ourselves by making Black women scapegoats and permitting the real culprit, a racist, sexist, White society, to remain unchallenged. We cannot afford to be immobilized by attacks on each other. Being Black and Christian means, among other things, that our collective memories of our mothers and grandmothers and our unbiased observation of the contribution contemporary Black women are making, will not permit us to acquiesce in the lie that our Black sisters are the enemy. Black theology with its emphasis upon social analysis and praxis can liberate us from the counterproductive and destructive nature of sexism.

XI. Black Theology as Praxis

The brief congregational profiles below are examples of what being Black and Christian looks like in various settings. They are neither comprehensive nor exhaustive of what God is doing in the Black Church. Nor are they presented as models that must be duplicated in all congregations and communities. We present them as highly selective, but noteworthy examples of being Black and Christian in the world and, therefore, pointers in the direction of how Black theology is actually formulated and practiced in the United States today. These are only a few congregations of various denominations and in various parts of the nation that are examples of Black theology as *praxis*. Many more need to be identified and studied in the course of the national dialogue on what it means to be Black and Christian. The churches are listed in alphabetical order according to the name of the church.

Allen Temple Baptist Church, Oakland, California
Dr. J. Alfred Smith, Sr., Pastor

Allen Temple is concerned about ministry to the whole person, and has implemented a wide range of outreach ministries. Ministries in the area of education include: Hi-Rise Tutorial Program for elementary and secondary school students, Interface Institute, which assists junior and senior high-school students in college preparatory math, science, and computer science. Highland Elementary School Network, which provides support services, and educational enrichment for children in the neighborhood, adult education and community college in conjunction with the Oakland Unified School District and the Peralta Community College District, and The Business and Professional Women's Society, which raises an average of $50,000 a year for scholarships. Social Services include; food programs, housing assistance, clothes pantry, and Job Services Committee, which provides job readiness seminars and employment services. Allen Temple works in partnership with Shiloh Christian Fellowship to support Star Shelter, a thirty-bed facility for the homeless. Allen Temple has an AIDS Ministry Task Force, Oakland Crack Task Force, Boy Scout and Cub Scout programs, One Church One Child Program, and The Allen Temple Arms I and II; apartment complexes that provide housing for senior citizens and handicapped persons. The prison ministry of Allen Temple provides visitations, worship services, counseling, Bible study, and a re-entry program that assists parolees with employment, housing, education, and other re-entry needs. The Allen Temple Credit Union has over one million dollars in assets and provides loans and a wide range of financial services. Other ministries include: Senior Citizens Brown Bag, Sierra Leone Mission Project, Black Women's Support Group, Grief Counseling, and Cancer Support Group. Currently the church is in the midst of a campaign to raise five to eight million dollars for a Family Life Center that will include thirty to forty classrooms, a gymnasium, recreational facilities, a nursery, and office space.

Mariners' Temple Baptist Church, New York, New York
Rev. Dr. Suzan D. Johnson-Cook, Pastor

This congregation's ministry is divided into three major areas: worship, fellowship, and community outreach. The worship experience is diverse and consist of two major services—Sunday morning and a Wednesday "Lunch Hour of Power" that attracts some 500 participants from the business and professional community. The fellowship ministry is diverse and features an emphasis on education. There are Wednesday services in Church and Teaching. A thematic approach to Bible study allows participants to choose specific areas of interest over a six to seven week period. Survival Kit helps people who are new to the faith make the transition to a new style of life particularly targeted to the young adult community. Sunday Afternoon Youth Alive provides young people, seven through twelve years of age, with recreational activities, workshops, Bible study, and creative ministries that build self-esteem, trust, and discipleship. The Thursday Noon Educational Service is a multiracial, multiethnic, and multiclass lunch hour Bible study that ministers to a variety of persons, including the unemployed, senior citizens, students, and professionals. The Afrocentric focus of ministry at Mariners' Temple is expressed in preaching, teaching, and Bible study. Thus, there is a study of the Black Presence in the Bible, a Multiethnic Learning Center with an after-school program designed to be inclusive of the Asian American, African American, Latin American and other ethnic groups in the community surrounding the church. Finally, there is a prison ministry, a home for developmentally disabled persons, and an elder-care program that reaches out to senior adults.

Payne Chapel African Methodist Episcopal Church, Nashville, Tennessee
Rev. Sidney Bryant, Pastor

The ministry of this congregation is based on a holistic approach and a determination to serve the physical as well as the spiritual needs of the church and community. The Living Breadbox is a service that provides emergency food and staple goods to individuals in need. Prison Outreach is a weekly worship service in the prison. On Target is a multimedia campaign that is designed to develop and broadcast messages promoting abstinence from alcohol and other drugs among African-American males, ages twelve to fourteen. Payne Chapel sponsors Chi Rho Alpha—a group mentoring program for young men; Sister to Sister—an individual and group mentoring experience fostering positive development among young women; Study Up—a tutorial program assisting young people in elementary through high school. The church has also established Project TEACH—Targeted Education for the African-American Community Concerning HIV/AIDS.

Trinity United Church of Christ, Chicago, Illinois
Rev. Dr. Jeremiah A. Wright, Pastor

A few of the social ministries of this congregation include an after-school Afrocentric training program for kindergarten and grades one through twelve that teaches reading, math, and computer science fifty-two weeks a year; a housing ministry focusing on both the homeless and rehabbing and purchasing HUD homes; senior citizens' Section 202 housing projects that provide housing for the unemployed, elderly, and the indigent; a ten-month Head Start program for unemployed and low-income families; a day-care program, a feeding program, Alcoholics Anonymous, Narcotics Anonymous, "Free 'N One" Alcoholic

Recovery Ministry; a prison ministry to men, women, and youth in the prisons in the Chicago metropolitan area. Trinity Church also has mentoring and "rites of passage" programs for African-American youth; an employment ministry providing jobs for the unemployed and "unemployable"; and a legal counseling ministry to address the problems of the community and members of the church.

Windsor Village United Methodist Church, Houston, Texas
Rev. Kirbyjon Caldwell, Pastor

A few of Windsor Village's programs are: The Food Pantry, which distributes nonperishable foods in conjunction with a program that offers vouchers for meals; a clothing resale shop that sells new and slightly used clothing for fifteen cents to fifteen dollars; an apartment ministry in which the congregation adopted a local apartment complex for outreach; and Operation Back to School that gives school supplies and two outfits to school aged children. In 1991 Operation Back to School served 1,200 children. WAM, Windsor AIDS Ministry, offers food and case management to persons who are HIV positive. The Patrice House is a newly-opened shelter for abused and neglected children that has a crisis nursery where persons may drop off children in times of crisis, spouse abuse, and so forth. The Imani School for Young Children is a private school for children beginning at three years of age through the fourth grade. Most of the programs of Windsor Village United Methodist Church are fully funded by its 6,000 members, and ninety-nine percent of the people served are not members of the congregation.

XII. Conclusion

In this document for dialogue across the Black Church and community, we have described the momentous crisis of our times—its dangers and opportunities. We have presented the position that what it means to be Black and Christian is one of the most critical questions we face as individuals and as an ethnic community and culture. We have acknowledged what some churches and communities are doing to concretize a Black theology of liberation today, and the present threat posed by the persistence of sexism, which is the result of the divide-and-conquer strategy of a racist and sexist society.

Throughout this discussion we have emphasized the pragmatic spirituality of the Black religious tradition that makes spirituality and social transformation inseparable. Black faith will not permit us to hide behind pious passivity and spiritualization of religion, which make it an inward, private experience that has small consequences in the real world of power structures, social and economic decision-making, and electoral politics. We have implied throughout this paper that Black faith is a *working* faith—a faith that drives us out from our inward person to an outward behavior, from our prayer closets to our voting booths, from our personal bank accounts to our congregation's tithers' table, from Holy Communion to holistic community, and from the sanctuary to the streets.

There are many other things that we would like to say here, but we must leave them to the process of dialogue for exploration and decision. We would not, for example, neglect a macroscopic view which sees what it means to be Black and Christian in the light of centuries, continents, billions of faces on the planet, and God's ultimate purposes for all humankind. Our experience matches dramatically the experience of Israel in Egypt, Babylon, and Persia; harassed by the Seleucids and the Romans, and made exiles all over the world in a rejected diaspora for centuries. History has shown that any society will be different that has breathed the aroma of the Judeo-Christian ethos, because it automatically contains within it the seeds of its own radical self-correction and revolution.

America has the natural resources, founding ideals, and the vague outlines of a genuine humane community that is compatible with the biblical vision of the realm of God on earth. Our experience as African-American people makes us uniquely sensitive to the requirements of such a community and to the distant rumblings of that realm coming in judgment and grace. To be Black and Christian in the United States is to work and pray for its consummation here in the land of our evolution as an African-American people. But we work and pray not as though we were God's only chosen people with exclusive responsibilities and rewards for faithfulness, but on behalf of, and in community with, all the people of the earth.

We began with a call to make a decision between life and death, blessings and curses. We conclude with the same challenge. In Joshua 24 we see the closing of an era and God's call to another chosen people to make a profound choice about their faith for the sake of their future in a new era. There is the utterance of a divine litany that reminds this pilgrim people of the guiding hand of God, leading them from point to point, through their controversies to the moment when Joshua is to pass from the scene. Joshua, in his closing remarks, presses God's issue of a new level of faithfulness that will be required in the new habitation of Canaan:

"Now therefore revere the LORD, and serve God in sincerity and in faithfulness; put away the gods that your ancestors served beyond the River, and in Egypt, and serve the LORD. Now if you are unwilling to serve the LORD, choose this day whom you will serve, whether the gods your ancestors served in the region beyond the River or the gods of the Amorites in whose land you are living; but as for me and my household, we will serve the LORD." Then the people answered, "Far be it from us that we should forsake the LORD to serve other gods; for it is the LORD our God who brought us and our ancestors up from the land of Egypt."

(Joshua 24:14–17a)

NOTES

1. See *The State of Black America,* ed. Janet Dewart (New York: National Urban League, 1991).
2. Allan Boesak, *The Finger of God* (Maryknoll, N.Y.: Orbis Books, 1982).

PART III

NEW DIRECTIONS IN BLACK BIBLICAL INTERPRETATION

INTRODUCTION

In the second half of the decade of the sixties, when we began to use the term Black theology to describe how we were beginning to think about the Christian faith in the ghetto, Black biblical scholars were few and far between. Between 1923 and 1945, when Leon Wright received his doctorate in New Testament from Howard University, there were no Blacks who earned doctorates in biblical studies. Two years later, in 1947, Charles B. Copher received his Ph.D. in Old Testament from Boston University. Then we have a gap of ten years before George A. Sewell, a professor at Morris Brown College, received his terminal degree in New Testament in 1957. Both Copher and Sewell were early teachers at the then fledgling Interdenominational Theological Center (I.T.C.) of which the former is now a distinguished emeritus professor.

By the mid-sixties when Black theology came on the scene there were four or five serious Black students of the Bible, most of them uncredentialed, at Black colleges and theological seminaries, but no predominantly White theological seminary or university department of religion in the United States or Canada employed a single Black person in the biblical field.[1] For many years doctoral studies in the fields of Old and New Testaments was virtually closed to African Americans. Blacks were admitted to graduate programs in Christian ethics, theology, and Christian education, but this was not merely because those areas were of special concern to us. Blacks applied for terminal degree programs in the Bible, but were either turned down, or dropped out in frustration after a year or two. Why? The answer is not thoroughly documented, but it seems true that a certain aura of elitism surrounded these programs at the most prestigious institutions. The necessity of having mastered the languages of antiquity, being offered and able to accept invitations to accompany one's teacher on archeological expeditions to the Holy Lands, and the assumption that biblical studies was somehow above the emotion-laden issues of politics and race, all contributed to the creation of a small circle of students and professors who seemed to luxuriate in their Anglo exclusivity. For many years it was difficult for a Black person, no matter how well prepared, to break into that charmed circle at the center of the theological academy.

At the four White seminaries at which I taught over a period of almost thirty years I can remember only three of my colleagues in the biblical departments who showed any interest in the Black freedom movement, and only one of them made a serious effort to revise his courses to deal with issues in his field that were of particular concern to African-American students. Nor was there for many years, as far as I am able to tell, any indication that questions relating to African and African-American Christians were taken seriously by the guilds of White biblical scholars.

These considerations make it all the more ironic that among North American Christians none has been more ardent about the Bible and its importance for their faith journey than Black Americans. Although there was powerful opposition to teaching them the Bible until sufficient justification for slavery could be marshaled by Southern exegetes, the "Good Book" held a special place in the hearts of Black people. Most of their spirituals were influenced by biblical texts and their illiterate preachers committed vast sections of the Bible to memory. E. Franklin Frazier writes concerning the place of the Bible in slave religion:

> Of course, the illiterate slaves could not gain a first-hand knowledge of the Bible. But for an illiterate people it possessed great influence as a source of supernatural knowledge because it was a sacred book. Perhaps it is safe to say that among no other people has the Bible provided a better illustration of Frazer's statement in the preface of the second edition of his *Passages of the Bible* than among the Negroes of the United States. Especially is this true when he speaks of "the pathetic associations with which the faith and piety of many generations have invested the familiar words" and that it strengthens man in "the blind conviction, or the trembling hope that somewhere, beyond these earthly shadows, there is a world of light eternal, where obstinate questionings of the mind will be answered and the heart find rest."[2]

If any of these "obstinate questionings" were amenable to biblical scholarship on this side of the Great Divide, it is certain that the guild of White Bible professors had no intention of training African-American students to investigate them. One hesitates to lay more responsibility for bias in theological education on biblical scholars than on others in the academy, yet the dearth of Black doctorates, and the studied disinterest of White biblical scholars in issues having to do with Black Christians, until recent years, suggests an avoidance syndrome if not rank discrimination.

In notable ways White members of the biblical profession have given us the impression that they somehow thought that Black theology had nothing to do with the Bible, and therefore, was outside the bounds of their discipline. There is no question but that some of this indifference rubbed off on most of the Black biblical scholars who were around in the late sixties. We need not go into how they arrived at this incredible conclusion, given the importance of both the Old and the New Testaments in the early writings of James H. Cone, but almost no Black academic in the biblical field came forward to undergird and improve upon Cone's exegetical and expository work. Charles B. Copher of I.T.C. made an effort to categorize Black theologians according to their use of the Bible in a paper he read at a conference in 1970, but he did not identify himself with any of them. Latta R. Thomas wrote a book entitled *Biblical Faith and the Black American* in 1976,[3] and did cast his lot with Black theology in the early days. But it was Robert A. Bennett, who was teaching Old Testament at the Episcopal Divinity School (E.D.S.) in Cambridge, Massachusetts, who as early as 1971 wrote a precedent-making article on Blacks and the Bible.[4]

I remember Bennett as a key member of the team of Black professors that Warner Traynham organized within the Boston Theological Institute to offer what must have been the first interdisciplinary course in Black theology to students of Harvard Divinity School, E.D.S., Boston University School of Theology, and Andover Newton Theological School. Bennett received his doctorate in Old Testament at Harvard in 1974 after teaching for several years at E.D.S. Those of us who were writing and teaching Black theology at the time were grateful for his interest and support.

Until recently one could say that whether still under the sway of their former White professors, or by their own considered judgment, Black biblical scholars kept their distance from Black theologians. Even today there are few of them who use the term Black theology, or who are found actively collaborating with theologians, ethicists, and Christian educators in the Society for the Study of Black Religion (SSBR) to help develop a biblically centered theology of Black liberation. I will not attempt in this brief essay to discuss the reasons for the change we are beginning to sense in the interest of Black students of the Scriptures in the development of African-American theological education and, more specifically, the justification of a Black theological perspective on biblical grounds. Some of the essays to follow will help in that regard. But it would be remiss not to mention the fact that just as secular Black Power theorists and activists of the sixties, struggling to present a rationale for a more aggressive and realistic form of struggle in the waning days of the civil rights movement, had an unmistakable influence upon Black theologians, a similar influence from outside the religious community made an impression upon Black biblical scholars.

I remember talking with Black professors from several of the New York colleges and universities at various chance meetings in Harlem during the early 1960s about the theories, some well-grounded and destined for longevity, others fantastic and doomed to rapid extinction, of ancient Nile Valley civilizations, on Egyptology and cultural anthropology, the rediscovery of the writings of early twentieth-century Afrocentric historians, such as Edward Wilmot Blyden, W. E. B. Du Bois, Willis N. Huggins, John G. Jackson, John W. Cromwell, Joel A. Rogers, and Arthur Schomburg. There was an air of excitement for me about those conversations at Frank's Restaurant on 125th Street and other places, that later brought me into contact with the writings of J. C. deGraft-Johnson, John Henrik Clarke, G. G. M. James, Yosef ben-Jochannan, and Maulana Karenga. Among my contemporaries, these men, who were outside the traditional Black Church, were the real pioneers of Black Studies and serious investigations into African origins that have led us today to the work of younger scholars such as Molefi Kete Asante.[5]

Neither James H. Cone nor J. Deotis Roberts, founders of the two major schools of Black theology, was greatly influenced by this work in the late 1960s, but in recent years the writings of both men have reflected their acknowledgment of the importance of the religions of Africa and the Caribbean for doing Black theology. But it was inevitable that younger Black biblical scholars such as Cain H. Felder and Randall Bailey, encouraged by the positive response of seasoned students of the Bible like Charles B. Copher and Henry Mitchell, would take note of the contributions secular scholars were making to the rediscovery of Africa in the Old and New Testaments. Today Felder, Bailey, and others are delving for themselves into neglected areas of biblical history and hermeneutics to dislodge old prejudices and assumptions about Blacks in antiquity and how African-American Christians have interpreted Scripture over the years.

This is why, in planning Volume II, we decided that this update of Black theology would be incomplete without a discussion of new directions in Black biblical interpretation. Not all of the authors whose contributions follow have expressed an extraordinary interest in Black theology per se, but all of them in some sense have broken away from the relative disinterest of the White guild of biblical scholars and are creating a literature with which Black theologians can make contact as they seek to promote a theology of liberation in the Black Church. Part III represents, therefore, the dawning of a new day in the evolution of Black theology. Not only have we seen an impressive increase in the number of Black women and men earning the terminal degree in biblical studies (albeit their numbers are so few that a critical situation continues to exist in American theological education), but we also find these writers wrestling with issues that we were unaware of in the 1960s and technically unequipped to deal with, issues that promise to occupy revisionists of the biblical studies curriculum well into the twenty-first century. Despite the good work that Cone, Roberts, and other Black theologians did on biblical foundations in an earlier day, I would venture the opinion that, more than we could twenty years ago, we can testify today that God has not left Black theology without a witness in the biblical field!

Document 13, "Cultural Ideology, Afrocentrism and Biblical Interpretation," by Cain Hope Felder, opens up some of the questions touched upon above. How has the ideology of the dominant culture been so influential in the study of the Scriptures that one can speak of an academic racism when it comes to the customary treatment of the place of Black people in the Bible? What are Black biblical scholars learning about Afrocentric understandings of the text? What are the implications of the new research for theological metaphors like the Black Jesus, or the Black Messiah? Felder is professor of New Testament language and literature at Howard University School of Divinity and one of the leaders of the movement to correct the biblical hermeneutics and historiographic assumptions of the White academy.

Among the second generation of Black biblical scholars, if we may use the term we have employed to designate younger Black theologians who received their degrees in the 1970s and 1980s, no one has been more engaged with the implications of biblical study for Black theology than Thomas Hoyt, Jr., who teaches New Testament at Hartford Theological Seminary and was the principal architect of the series of seminars that Black biblical scholars held for several years at the Ecumenical Study Center in Collegeville, Minnesota. Hoyt, a minister of the Christian Methodist Episcopal Church, has been an active representative of his denomination on the Plenary Commission on Faith and Order of the World Council of Churches and in meetings of the National Council of the Churches of Christ in the U.S.A. It was in the former setting that he was exposed to the indifference of European and American theologians to Black theology and thereby forced to revert to his own discipline in defense of what he knew were authentic concerns of African and African-American Christians.

In Document 14, "Biblical Interpreters and Black Theology," Hoyt analyzes the biblical basis of Cone's organizing principle for Black theology and examines the Black presence in the Bible that he feels must be thoroughly appreciated before a meaningful dialogue can take place between Black and White Christians. In the end he appeals to Black biblical scholars and theologians to freely use the new paradigm shift in the social sciences away from sterile empiricism to more imaginative and subjective modes of perception and interpretation found, for example, among some of the basic Christian communities of Latin America.[6]

Document 15 reminds us of a fact almost too commonplace to mention: that there is as much diversity in the opinions of Black scholars of the Bible as among Black theologians! In " 'Rescue the Perishing': The Importance of Biblical Scholarship in Black Christianity," Vincent L. Wimbush, professor of New Testament and Christian Origins at Union Theological Seminary in New York, takes a diametrically different tack from Thomas Hoyt and insists that only through the descent through several layers of objective biblical scholarship will Black Christians be able to arrive at an understanding of the text that will enable them to accurately and faithfully reconfigure the biblical message to their own best interests. In this regard, Wimbush refers to the work of the Dutch theologian Edward Schillebeeckx who calls for a mastery of Jewish and Greek interpretive concepts and theoretical models for ordering experience if exegetes in every generation are to understand the "world" of the Bible and their own existential world.

Wimbush begins this essay with a brief, but interesting survey of how Blacks have used the Bible since slavery. If, he says, Black Christians were ever free from the befuddlement and intimidation of doctrinal issues related to certain supposedly authoritative interpretations of the Bible, that time is no more. Today the same ideological and cultural corruptions that infect the White Church infect the Black Church as well. For example, subliminal indoctrination by the official chaplains of the status quo and the smiling, slick-haired televangelists. Authentic Black spirituality is perishing in this new climate of sophisticated fundamentalism and it can only be rescued if the Black Church is willing to take biblical scholarship seriously as a necessary propaedeutic to any reconstruction of the faith such as Black theology proposes.

Document 16, "Womanist Reflections on Biblical Hermeneutics," was written by Renita J. Weems, one of the most prominent representatives of the new biblical scholarship among Black women. Weems is an assistant professor of the Hebrew Bible at Vanderbilt University Divinity School. In this essay she writes candidly and personally about past and present contributions of Black women scholars. Moreover, she seeks to break with the conventions of White feminist scholars by going beyond their critique of sexual oppression and repression in the Bible to a "hermeneutical suspicion," grounded in the "different" experiences of Black women that will unmask all forms of oppression. For example, says Weems, a womanist perspective on neoorthodox biblical scholarship will want to begin with an analysis of the biblical-theological concept of Israel's election. To what extent has that concept led to patriarchalism, to sexual and ethnic discrimination, and economic and political exploitation? That all structures of domination are organically connected may be the vocational insight of womanist scholars who wish to do much more with the androcentric bias of the texts than do their White sisters who know Sarah but not Hagar, Miriam, Deborah, Esther, and Mary, but not Miriam's Cushite sister-in-law, Ruth, not the Syro-Phoenician woman, not the Canaanite woman at the well. A study of these "lesser women" of the Scriptures may more effectively disabuse us of any notion of divine election based upon ethnicity. For Renita Weems a womanist perspective is as much an act of faith as a feat of scholarship. She believes that it will force marginalized biblical scholars into a posture of hermeneutic insubordination. But more than that—will lead them to go beyond the texts and rely more upon a faith that calls people of color all over the world to rise up and fight for their humanity and liberation.

Clarice J. Martin, who teaches New Testament at Colgate Rochester Divinity School/Bexley Hall/Crozer Theological Seminary in Rochester, New York, is another womanist biblical scholar whose work is rapidly gaining attention in the guild. In Document 17, "Womanist Interpretations of the New Testament," Martin further explicates the concept of womanist religious scholarship, focusing particularly on a word study of *doulos* that helps Black people and others understand more clearly in what sense we can and cannot speak of Jesus as emptying himself and taking the form of a slave. Like Weems, Martin is interested in supplementary service rendered to feminist interpretations by womanist perspectives, but she also is concerned not to miss analyses that illuminate racial, class, and other anthropological referents. "Not all of the suppressed voices in androcentric texts," she writes, "can be intoned in a feminine key." Expertly weaving back and forth between her womanist interpretation of the *doulos* texts and other views of Scripture that enjoin male domination, Clarice Martin offers us a stunning picture of the possible breadth and depth of womanist biblical scholarship. It is important to note that in this work she is not interested only in its academic implications, but is asking to what extent it can yield new inspiration for repentance in the relations between the oppressed and the oppressors, new insights for personal and social transformation.

We come finally to the essay by Itumeleng J. Mosala, Document 18, "The Use of the Bible in Black Theology." This brings Part III on new directions in the work of Black biblical scholars to a close. Mosala teaches in the department of religious studies at the University of Cape Town, South Africa, and is the author of *Biblical Hermeneutics and Black Theology in South Africa* (Eerdmans Pub. Co., 1989). Mosala's contribution is particularly helpful to this discussion because it brings us full circle to the question of whether or not Black biblical scholarship, which has been cool in the past, has anything specific to offer Black theology in the present. He uses the Old Testament Book of Micah to make the point that Black theologians must embrace a materialist hermeneutic of liberation that sees the Bible as the product and record of class struggles in which the ideological pretensions of ancient peoples conceal the economic, political, and cultural self-interests by which they oppress others.

Mosala believes that Black theologians have fallen into the trap of drawing our hermeneutical assumptions from White European-American theology. As a professor of biblical studies in racist South Africa he wants to put his discipline at the service of a critical break with capitalist ideology and calls upon Black scholars to take our own critique of its theological handmaiden, or shall we say—its *manservant*—more seriously.

G.S.W.

NOTES

1. I am indebted to Charles B. Copher, professor emeritus of the Old Testament at the Interdenominational Theological Center for this information. Dr. Copher has recently completed research on Black scholars in biblical studies since the late nineteenth century.

2. E. Franklin Frazier, *The Negro Church in America* (New York: Schocken Books, 1974), 18.

3. Latta R. Thomas, *Biblical Faith and the Black American* (Valley Forge, Pa.: Judson Press, 1976). Professor Thomas, like many Black scholars in religion, held a pastorate while he taught at Benedict College in Columbia, South Carolina. In the early years he was active in the National Committee of Black Churchmen.

4. Robert A. Bennett, "The Black Experience and the Bible," *Theology Today* 27 (January 1971): 422–433.

5. Molefi Kete Asante, *The Afrocentric Idea* (Philadelphia: Temple University Press, 1987).

6. See Ernesto Cardenal, *The Gospel in Solentiname*, 4 vols. (Maryknoll, N.Y.: Orbis Books, 1976–82), and Philip Scharper and Sally Scharper, eds., *The Gospel in Art by the Peasants of Solentiname* (Maryknoll, N.Y.: Orbis Books, 1984).

13

CULTURAL IDEOLOGY, AFROCENTRISM AND BIBLICAL INTERPRETATION

Cain Hope Felder

Throughout Western history the authority of the Bible has been predicated upon the tacit assumption of the preeminence of European cultures. They have been generally regarded as somehow the most suitable and thus the most reliable "bearer of the tradition" — a tradition that has been passed on and otherwise shared with the Americas and the Orient. The attitude developed, especially in the modern period, that African Americans, Afro-Asiatics, Asians, and Hispanics were quite secondary to the ancient biblical narratives. The European and European-American church and academy historically and unevenly struggled to speak and sometimes write with a vision of universalism and inclusiveness, but actually the church and the academy both daily thought and practiced particularity and exclusiveness without reference to the authority of the biblical authors and what they thought and did in their ancient contexts. Recent studies, however, help us to appreciate the biblical world as being one "before color prejudice."[1]

Part of my interest in the ideology of culture was prompted by a little book entitled *The Liberation of the Bible*,[2] which appeared a few years ago as part of ongoing Bible study groups of the Student Christian Movement of Canada. David Lochhead opens this book with a chapter on "The Ideological Captivity of the Bible" in which he identifies three different types of biblical captivity: (1) "Right-wing Reading," which appeals to absolute external authority and patriotism; (2) "Liberal Reading," done through the lens of capitalism and democratic institutions already framed and established as the model; and (3) "Racial Reading," which is rooted in the continuing struggle for justice and the attainment of equality.[3]

Cain Hope Felder is the author of *Troubling Biblical Waters* and is professor of New Testament language and literature, Howard University School of Divinity.

Each mode of interpretation is characterized by an informing ideological commitment that shapes the manner in which the text is read and interpreted and to which biblical authority is ascribed. It is possible to see that in each of these modes of biblical interpretation, the ideology of modern cultures arises from a certain contextualization. The result is a tendency to displace or to marginalize even dogmatic criteria such as the Rule of Faith, or doctrinal criteria such as *Sola Scriptura* for some, or, for us of the Wesleyan tradition—the Methodist Quadrilateral, that is to say Scripture, Tradition, Reason, and Experience, or the Roman Catholic *Dei Verbum*. Culture becomes a source for ideology and in a subtle way yields criteria for reading the Bible. Historically, this ideological reading seems predicated upon the primacy of the dominant culture and the politico-cultural-economic identity of its "primary" constituents.

The ideology of modern culture becomes particularly problematic in an age of postmodernism, because values, structures, and institutions are rapidly becoming destabilized. Yet, this very postmodern period has become the era of the global village and multiculturalism. One aspect of postmodernism as it pertains to the authority of the Bible is that through the sudden collision of cultures in the contemporary awakenings of racial and ethnic self-consciousness, many of us are summarily taken "back to the future" of the biblical world! We see this perhaps most clearly in a sobering verse in the Old Testament, for example, Hosea 4:6a—"My people are destroyed for the lack of knowledge." This single verse of Scripture finds its New Testament parallel in the Gospel of John 8:32 that reads simply, "You shall know the truth and the truth shall set you free." (It is striking that, in John 8:33, the Pharisees respond with an outright falsehood!) On this text, the Archbishop of Recife, Brazil, Dom Helder Camara said:

> If we believe that the truth will make us free, we must see that much of what passes for education is not concerned with the truth because it has not succeeded in freeing us. It is vital that we should unite in support of a liberating education.[4]

Basic to a "liberating education" would seem to be a re-commitment to basic truths—such truths that can resolve part of the problem in identifying appropriate criteria for biblical authority. On this, we may also cite a single line from the hymnody of the Black Church. "Plenty good room, plenty good room, there's plenty good room in my God's [Father's] Kingdom." In a simple, direct, and yet significant way, this one line highlights a truth that most of higher education in American life firmly resists and otherwise denies each and every day of its institutional life!

In an age of multiculturalism, there may be plenty of "good room" in America and on its seminary and university campuses for Native Americans, Latinos/Hispanics, Asians, Whites, Jews, and African Americans. But the Eurocentricism that has always guided American and Western history has consistently made precious little room for anyone but the dominant racial group in the

United States of America. Eleven o'clock on Sunday mornings remains the most segregated time in America; it is a time when each racial and ethnic group brings God and the text down to its own racial and culturally predetermined biases as socialized by the prevailing culture.

We are living in a very scary time in which the truth that would set us free evidently remains too painful, especially to the White male elite that runs America, to set *anyone* free. This applies even to the masses of White people who allow themselves to be manipulated daily by scare, fear, and downright miseducation! The matter is all the more frightful when one recognizes that television and videos have become the real educators in our nation, for, after all, the average American watches forty hours of television per week (so-called minorities tend to watch more!).

Worse yet is the persistence of subtle forms of what I have called "academic racism" that is entrenched within the curricula of each stage of formal education in the United States. Such academic racism expresses itself on the seal of Harvard University where the motto *Veritas* appears, representing the Latin word for "the Truth," but whose truth are they talking about? None other than the truth of the Harvard Corporation with its Ivy League reputation and multibillion dollar stock portfolio. There is an ancient Greek saying that bears upon this: *En chronō panta krēpta krummata pros phōti* ("In time, all that is hidden will come to light"). In our time, the truth about the ideology of culture in America is "coming to light" as a problem for discerning the true basis of biblical authority.

Today, at a scary time when not-so-subtle forms of racism are on the rise within the many "noncommunities" that symbolize our nation's universities and colleges, we must consider the ideology of culture. The record of racial incidents on campuses is clear. In 1987, the Lutheran campus pastor at the University of Michigan, Galen Hora, offered a sobering commentary entitled "The Rise of Racism on Campus: A Challenge to Campus Ministry."[5] He spoke then of the prospect of "raging flames" from long-neglected burning embers at the University of Michigan, the University of Wisconsin at Madison, at Purdue, Columbia, UCLA, the University of Massachusetts, St. Cloud State University, and Duke University where African American, Asian, Jewish, and other so-called minority students have been publicly harassed by misguided and miseducated Whites (many of whom are employees of these universities and colleges) who scarcely know their own history much less the history and culture of others. Hora urges: "Colleges must take seriously their role as a civilizing influence . . . racism on campus is attributed to a 'failure in moral leadership.' "

Ernest Boyer, president of the Carnegie Foundation for the Advancement of Teaching, wrote an editorial that the *New York Times* published in 1987 entitled "Racism: From the Closet to the Quad." He stated that "Both socially and intellectually, everything tends towards narrowness, fragmentation, and exclusivity, instead of broadness."[6] Can we not say the same with reference to the cultural ideology widely evident in contemporary readings of the Bible? Certainly, we United Methodists have used the term *inclusiveness* for decades as we plodded along to eliminate racially-segregated church structures. We continue ad nauseum to use such language, despite the fact that most of our local churches remain quite segregated and nearly all aspects of the core curriculum in our colleges and seminaries remain manifestly Eurocentric! What happens when "the heathen" learn to study the Bible and become awed by its authoritative vision of *universalism, inclusiveness,* and *multiculturalism* with all the tolerance for racial/ethnic pluralism so denied in much of the West today.

When any *one* culture, race, or ethnic group is valorized above all others, there is a tendency to subvert the Bible's vision and authority. As the decade of the nineties moves the Bible from being merely "his-story" to "our-story" this, in turn, requires us to seriously look upon it as the decade of multiculturalism. We need to insist that the constructive curricular paradigm shifts from history as "History" to a renewed appreciation for the discipline of "our-stories!" In this, we must be educationally purposeful, the campus must indeed be just in honoring the sacredness of each person and her or his segment of "our-story" (heritage and culture), as well as genuinely caring for the well-being of others while being in service and solidarity with their highest ideals.

I spent fifteen years of my life, 1974–1989, researching and completing a book that I thought might well become my academic "Waterloo." As an African male in White America I have long harbored the view that my native land and its political-economic construct—the American political economy, including both the religious establishment and higher education—only made sense to me when I assessed it through the lenses of upper-class White people. Neither the Bible nor most of Western theology makes any sense to me as an African-American male. For, more often than not, my theological studies in North America and Europe were unabashedly Eurocentric—mainline and normative.

But even as I developed my "theologically correct" library, I ached deep within because in precious little biblical scholarship was anything ever written in a favorable way about Blacks in biblical antiquity. It began to occur to me that I myself might have to write the book on the racial and ethnic pluralism of the Bible, even though I suspected that such breaking of ranks with my White colleagues might mean the end of my career as a Bible scholar in the guild. So the writing of *Troubling Biblical Waters: Race, Class, and Family* (Orbis Books, 1989) was somewhat daring, a "devil take the hindmost" adventure.

The message of that book was simply that the Bible is the best handbook for multiculturalism, racial tolerance, and racial/ethnic pluralism. Despite the academic hegemony of Eurocentric theologians and Bible scholars since the European Enlightenment, the authors of the Bible lived in a world *before* any color prejudice—as the title of Snowden's book, *Before Color Prejudice*, suggests. There was no systematic policy of enslaving Blacks; invariably the slaves of the New Testament period were nonBlacks. Aristotle's treatise in antiquity, "Natural Slaves and Natural Masters," had nothing to do with the relatively modern pseudoscientific notions of Aryan superiority. In *Troubling Biblical Waters,* as well as in the volume *Stony the Road We Trod: African American Biblical Interpretation* (Fortress Press, 1991), which I edited for a group of African-American

Bible professors, we document fully the fact that the Bible makes "plenty good room" for African Americans, Asians, and Hispanics—no less than for Whites. But this is a message that many people in the United States have heretofore been unwilling to accept as "good news."

An examination of the term Afrocentricity will make clear what I and other Black biblical scholars have found helpful in correcting the effects of the cultural ideological conditioning to which we have all been subjected. Afrocentricity is the idea that the land mass that the ancient Romans routinely called Africa and persons of African descent must be understood as having made significant contributions to world civilization as proactive subjects within history, rather than being regarded as merely passive objects of historical distortions. Afrocentrism means reestablishing Africa as a center of value and source of pride, without in any way demeaning other people and their historic contributions to human achievement. The term was coined by Molefi Kete Asante of Temple University and as used here it refers to a methodology that reappraises ancient biblical traditions, their exegetical history in the West, and their allied hermeneutical implications. In the past few years an impressive number of scholarly volumes have appeared on this subject. In various ways such books have attempted to clarify the ancient biblical views of race and ancient Africa. Together they represent efforts in corrective historiography, which demonstrates clearly that we have arrived at a new stage in biblical interpretation.

No longer is it enough to limit the discussion to Black theology or even African theology; instead Africa, her people, nations, and cultures must be acknowledged as making direct, primary contributions to the development of many early biblical traditions. Rather than viewing ancient Africa in a negative way, or minimizing its presence and contributions to the biblical narratives, as has been all too often the case in Western scholarly guilds, the continent obtains a more favorable appropriation by those who wish more accurately to interpret the Bible and appreciate the inherent racial and ethnic diversity or multiculturalism of salvation history.

Throughout the world it has become standard for Christians to think of almost all biblical characters from Noah, Abraham, Miriam, Moses, the pharaohs, even the Queen of Sheba, to Mary and Joseph, and virtually all of the New Testament personalities as typical Europeans. For example, in diverse ecclesiastical circles Mary, the mother of Jesus, is the beneficiary of reverential addresses and titles, but pictorial representations of her today are invariably the image of a European. This centerpiece of much modern Christian art is perceived as an accurate image of the original Madonna. Consequently, most people believe that the mother of Jesus of Nazareth was a woman who resembled the ordinary European of today. Such presumptions are only now beginning to be substantively challenged by Afrocentric modes of biblical interpretation as studies devote more attention to ancient iconography and the importance of Egyptian and Ethiopian civilizations in the shaping of the biblical world. Thus, today, there is a critical need to examine not only how the fraudulent view emerged in Western history, but also how the Bible specifically treats Africa in general and Black people in particular.

Three basic factors must be placed at the forefront of any discussion of this kind. First, we must consider the maps of the ancient Bible lands, while remembering that England and Germany, for example, have always been geographically located exactly where they are today. In the Bible there is not one single mentioning of either England or Germany; by contrast, however, countries in Africa (Egypt, Cush, Put, Punt, etc.) are mentioned again and again. The Old Testament alone cites Ethiopia over forty times and Egypt over 100 times. Many ancient biblical and extrabiblical sources often mention Egypt and Ethiopia together, almost interchangeably. Scarcely are such ancient African locations portrayed fully in Bible maps of Europe and especially the United States. Usually Western cartographers show as little as possible of the African continent, while by contrast they highlight areas to the north in Europe and Eurasia that are seldom, if ever, referenced in the Bible.

Second, the Bible provides extensive evidence that the earliest of its people must be located in Africa. The Garden of Eden story, found in Genesis 2:8–14, indicates that the first two rivers of Eden are closely associated with ancient Cush, the Hebrew term that the Greeks would later transpose as "Aithiops" or Ethiopia, meaning literally "burnt face people." The Pishon and the Gihon rivers are mentioned in this story. Biblical scholars usually date this composite Jahwist (J) tradition in the tenth century B.C., suggesting that, at that time, these were early references to the African river system known today as the Blue and the White Nile rivers. The term "Nile" after all derives from the Latin "nilus," but here we refer to a story that predates the existence of the Latin language. In any case, Genesis 2:11–12 connect the Pishon River with "Havilah"; one only needs to turn to Genesis 10:7 to see that "Havilah" is the direct descendant of Cush. For its part, the Gihon River, as the second river in Eden is cited in Genesis 2:13 and described as surrounding the whole land of Cush/ Ethiopia. Clearly, wherever else "Eden" extended, its beginning was within the continent of Africa.

Third, the ancient land of Canaan was but an extension of the African land mass and in biblical times African peoples frequently migrated from the continent proper through Canaan/Palestine to the east toward what was then included as Asia, namely, the "fertile crescent" or the Tigris and Euphrates rivers of ancient Mesopotamia. This fact helps us to appreciate the term "Afro-Asiatic" as probably the most accurate way to identify the mixed stock of people who populated the so-called ancient Near East. Eventually, "Eurasians" and even Europeans (Greeks and Romans) begin to feature in the more recent biblical narratives, but the fact remains that the earliest biblical people, by modern Western standards of "racial types," would have to be classified as "Blacks" (meaning only that they definitely had African blood and some physical features that resemble many individuals within the full range of African Americans today).

The modern student of biblical history and interpretation will have to keep in mind that the authors of the Bible together with the Greeks and the Romans had no notion of color prejudice. As startling as it may seem to many scholars in racialist European, South African, and American modes of scriptural interpretation in our modern period, the Bible actually reflects a world before color prejudice or racial discrimination. The authors/redactors of the Bible had a rather favorable attitude about Black people and the Bible as a result often reflects the ancient greatness of African people and their civilizations. Genesis 10:8 illustrates this quite well, for there, Nimrod, son of Cush, is identified as "the mighty warrior." Once we tackle the problem of how one defines a person as "Black," then it becomes quite easy to see that most of the early characters of the Bible would have to be so classified, even though the biblical authors had no notion of race in the modern sense of the term.

For more than a century, despite their exclusion from centers of theological education, leaders in the Black Church have undertaken studies of the Bible. Many of these efforts show clearly that Blacks themselves long ago rejected the latter-day, postbiblical view that they were the progeny of the accursed Ham (there being no such curse in Gen. 9:18–27). Daniel P. Seaton, as a prominent leader in the African Methodist Episcopal Church, is representative of the tendency of Blacks who identified more wholesome modes of interpretation of their place in biblical history. Writing in 1895, Seaton displays considerable knowledge about the Bible, the location of ancient religious sites, and the significance of many biblical characters. In fact, he made several field trips to Palestine. In a major work, a volume of 443 pages of text, notes, maps, and illustrations, he provides extensive descriptions of tombs, villages, and other ancient sites where he visited. Regarding Ham and his descendants, Seaton offers the following:

> Because these Hamites were an important people, attempts have been made to rob them of their proper place in the catalogue of the races. The Bible tells us plainly that the Phoenicians were descendants of Canaan, the son of Ham, and anyone who will take the time to read the Bible account of their lineage must concede the fact.

What is noteworthy about Seaton's study is his profound awareness of racism among the bona fide biblical scholars of his day. Nevertheless, as much as we may applaud Seaton's constructive intent, clearly he could have benefitted greatly from systematic historical critical engagement with the biblical text in its original languages.

Much more recently, in America and in Africa, there has developed a proliferation of books and pamphlets that represent a resurgence of what may now be called Afrocentric approaches to the Bible. Caution, however, is advised, for all students of the Bible must avoid the tendency of taking the sons of Noah — Shem, Ham, and Japheth — as representing three different races (Whites, Blacks, and Asians). Although this is the traditional approach of European missionaries and others who seized the opportunity thereby to designate

Ham as the father of Blacks who were allegedly cursed in Genesis 9:18–29, Ham does not mean *black* in Hebrew (it means only *hot* or *heated*). Moreover, there is not a curse of Ham in this passage, for the text explicitly says "Let Canaan be cursed." It is an absurdity of no small order to claim that Noah and his wife could produce offspring that would constitute three distinct racial types! Any reference book appearing on the subject of "Blacks in the Bible" must be held suspect, if its author tries to argue that Blacks constitute the "Hamitic" line only.

As I point out in *Troubling Biblical Waters: Race, Class and Family* (Orbis Books, 1989) and more recently in *Stony the Road We Trod: African American Biblical Interpretation* (Fortress Press, 1991), many Black women and men are fully part of the salvation history within the Bible itself. Moses himself was an Afro-Asiatic and he married an Ethiopian woman according to Numbers 12:1–10. The Queen of Sheba was a Black African (1 Kings 10:1–10 and 2 Chron. 9:1–9) and is called "the Queen of the South" in Matthew 12:42. The New Testament mentions another Black Queen in the person of the Kandake, Queen of the Nubians in her ancient Ethiopian capital of Meroe (Acts 8:26–40). For years, persons of African descent have taken heart upon reading the celebrated passage in Psalm 68:31 – "Let princes come out of Egypt and let Ethiopia hasten to stretch forth her hand to God!" But today there is a much greater basis upon which Blacks may celebrate and otherwise take seriously that rich ancient heritage in the sacred Scriptures, for the real Black presence is by no means to be limited to an isolated verse here and there!

Despite all the evidence that indicates a manifest Black biblical presence, Eurocentric church officials and scholars have tended to deny or otherwise overlook or minimize the fact that Black people are in any significant way part of the Bible itself. The standard academic and popular Western tendency has had grave consequences for persons of African descent. Thus, modern biblical scholarship is just beginning to overcome centuries of tragic biases against Blacks and their biblical history. Others have diligently tried to reinforce the view that Blacks are to be thought of as mere "hewers of wood" and "drawers of water." As astonishing as it seems, most of the prestigious academies and universities of Europe and the United States have conspired together to ridicule the idea that Blacks have any substantive history.

In America, it is ironic that such a distortion has been most vigorously championed in that part of the nation called "the Bible Belt" where obviously "the belt" of biblical interpretation has been much too tight for years. In the intervening period between A.D. 357 (the date of Bishop Athanasius' canonical lists) and the Enlightenment, Europe and America have recast the entire Bible into a religious saga of so many European-type people. Indeed, what makes this racialist tendentiousness so difficult is that such reinterpretations of ancient ethnographic realities are really taken as fact by the so-called well educated in Western civilization. Worse yet, others throughout the world have thereby been influenced by this effective recasting of Western history in terms and images distinctly favorable to Whites, while literally displacing Blacks. The result has been the creation of another world in which Blacks themselves portray biblical characters within Black churches as totally unlike themselves. For biblical characters to be viewed in Black images is still seen as a terrible thing by too many Blacks around the world today.

We can now return to the question of Jesus of Nazareth and his mother, the original Madonna. One need not hesitate in stating that Jesus' mother looked like the other Palestinian women of Nazareth of her day. Her physiognomy is doubtlessly more historically accurate when presented as an ancient Afro-Asiatic who probably looked like a typical Yemenite, Trinidadian, or African American today. Consider a few inescapable factors that challenge the traditional Western perception of the Madonna and Child. In the Gospel of Matthew, we find the celebrated quotation from Hosea 11:1 wherein Matthew 2:15 reads "out of Egypt, I have called my son." The passage is part of the notorious "flight into Egypt," which describes the way in which Mary and Joseph fled to Egypt to hide the one that King Herod feared would displace him. If one lends any historical credence to this tradition, imagine the divine family as Europeans hiding in Africa! This is quite doubtful. After all, Egypt has always been part of Africa, despite centuries of European scholarship that have diligently sought to portray Egypt as an extension of southern Europe. As I said earlier, for millennia, Africans had migrated out of biblical Ethiopia and Egypt through Canaan to Mesopotamia in the Fertile Crescent. Such migrations have yielded the most accurate description of the earliest biblical peoples, namely, African-Asiatics. It is hardly likely that these African-Asiatics looked like someone from Great Britain or Scandinavia.

Literally hundreds of Shrines of the Black Madonna have existed in many parts of North Africa, Europe, and Russia. These are not weather-beaten misrepresentations of some original White Madonna, rather, they are uncanny reminders of the original ethnography of the people who inhabited ancient Palestine at the time of Jesus of Nazareth and earlier. The "sweet little Jesus boy" of the Negro spiritual was in point of fact quite Black and while that song entones "we didn't know it was you," it reminds most modern Christians that they still don't know what Jesus actually looked like.

In precritical biblical circles, the apostle Paul is frequently credited with the authorship of 1 Timothy. In that New Testament epistle, one finds the saying "great indeed is the mystery of our religion," and every time I read that verse I think of just how great the mystery of Jesus' color really has become in a modern world that quite literally denigrates persons of the darker hue.

Yet, we today need to pause as we assess the maps of biblical lands again and consider the more recent studies that show the true attitudes about race in the ancient Greco-Roman ethos. Only in this way will persons remember that in that time, all of Africa was called Ethiopia, while present-day Sudan was called Ethiopia proper in biblical times. The greatness of the people from these areas was proverbial. Recall Psalm 87:1–4 that asserts that not only were the Ethiopians among those who fully knew God of ancient Israel, but it indicates that the Ethiopians were indeed also born there! Similarly, Isaiah 11:11

includes Blacks among the righteous remnant, whereas Isaiah 18:1–4 celebrates those from "the land of whirring wings sending ambassadors by the Nile" who send messengers to a people tall and smooth, feared near and far!

We have no need to down play or otherwise minimize the presence of Greeks and Romans in the Bible. They are there to be sure, but Mary, Joseph, and Jesus were neither Greek nor Roman! So any inquiring mind that seeks the "truth" of the matter (Hosea 4:6 and John 8:32) naturally would want to know "how did the sweet little Jesus boy of Afro-Asiatic birth become whiter and whiter over the years?" The answer is neither complicated nor profound. It is found in the simple matter called paint. The medieval and Renaissance artists skillfully employed the painter's brush with marvelous oils or water colors and gradually the world witnessed the rebirth of Jesus quite suitable for the portrayal of Christianity as itself a European religion.

European Christian art became the new norm as Jesus was depicted in images more familiar and favorable to persons of European descent. Thus, there developed a brand new manger scene and an infant Jesus for all the world, not least, the Third World, to adore. Jesus' mother and father also were reimaged as ancient darker and clearly more African icons were discarded or destroyed in favor of the more modern ones. The artistic re-presentations still stand in many cathedrals of Europe, North and South America as well as in a great new $100 million air-conditioned Basilica in Africa's Ivory Coast! Clearly, Africa has for too long stretched out its hand to biblical characters who have been remolded as non-Black.

In Jeremiah 13:23a, the rhetorical question confronts us afresh today, "Can the Ethiopian change his skin?" In the sixth century B.C., Jeremiah knew that it was totally unnecessary for any Ethiopian to attempt to do so. Doubtless, centuries later, Jesus' "father," Joseph knew that his skin color needed no change. Joseph was probably a proud Galilean Afro-Asiatic whose last thought — indeed the furthest thought from his mind — was attempting to change his color into that of a Roman or a Greek. That kind of thinking seems peculiar to our own modern age of pseudoscientific theories of White supremacy and Negroid inferiority (a most "enlightened" by-product of that glorious modern phase of Western intellectual history known as the Enlightenment). Evidently, church artists felt that they had to keep Joseph in light colors as well! And so, he, too, re-emerges as a European. Such is the nature of Western religious art since the Renaissance and the so-called Enlightenment.

One must not make light of the utterly serious ways that nations have risen and fallen with untold numbers of people killed, subjugated, and denuded of their history and culture in the name of the "objective historical" Mother and Child as absolutely sacred and unscathed by things African. Should we not dream of the day when archbishops and other prelates of the church develop a sense of humor about the subtle and blatant distortions and their terrible consequences that remain unacknowledged in the name of truth? Many religious doctrines, creeds, and symbols have fallen prey to the cultural captivity of those who have tended to win the big wars. The Muslims and others have done the same, despite the fact that we wonder how Muhammad, himself, envisioned the racial image of Mary whose chastity he so valiantly defended in Surah 19 of the Holy Qur'an.

Many in the 1990s may think of a Black Jesus as an oddity or scandalous distortion of historical facts. Perhaps, the claim is acceptable when limited to the theological metaphors of Black theologians like James H. Cone or Allan Boesak, but hardly, the thinking seems to go, can this be taken as serious ancient ethnography. I know that many Europeans and European-Americans have a frightful time thinking of such a ghastly possibility. They usually insist that Jesus was Semitic and as such Middle Eastern. To this, let me offer a humble little rejoinder. First, to call Jesus Semitic does not take us very far inasmuch as the nineteenth-century term refers not to a racial type, but to a family of languages including both Hebrew and Ethiopic. Second, about the same time that the European academy coined the term Semitic, it also created the geographical designation called the Middle East, an expression that would have made absolutely no sense to Herodotus, Strabo, or even Thucydides much less to the personalities of the Bible. The whole ridiculous point of creating a so-called Middle East was an effort to avoid talking about Africa! It was a sign of academic racism that thoroughly sought to de-Africanize the sacred story of the Bible along with the whole sweep of Western civilization.

Palestine has always been exactly where it is today, namely, in Northeast Africa. It is a sad commentary on modern civilization that some human beings must vilify other cultures and people in order to create a mythology to feel good about themselves. Whether or not one considers the table of the nations that appears in Genesis 10 as a historical record, the fact remains that centuries before Jesus of Nazareth, those who compiled that list of primeval peoples insisted that Canaan was a direct descendant to Ham, in fact, his son — the very one who is conveniently cursed in Genesis 9 in order to discredit his right to his own land. When the Greeks rose up eventually to conquer the land of Canaan, they did everything to infuse Greek culture within the subjugated peoples of the Empire.

From Greek architecture to the Greek language itself, the standard of acceptance in the high culture of Hellenism and thence the Greco-Roman world became showing the new masters just how thoroughly Greek one could be. However, while this standard was certainly operative for Herod the Great, it had little bearing on the life of the common folks like Mary and Joseph who knew they were not Greeks or Romans and who continued to speak Aramaic as their native tongue. Their Scriptures (the Hebrew Bible) spoke of many earlier sojourns into the mainland of the African continent. If the Matthew 2:15 proof text of Hosea 11:1 has any independent historical reliability, then, when Jesus' parents felt the need to flee Herod's domain in order to protect the innocent "sweet lil' Jesus boy," they followed the established trail to Africa — not to Europe!

Subsequent Western civilization, however, took a different path — namely, one leading straight to Europe aided first by those Christian artists who were paid handsome sums by the church and universities that the church created. Such artists sought to please those in power as opposed to rendering biblical characters in an accurate ethnographic fashion. Then, in our time, everything was left up to the pundits of Hollywood to finish the revisionist imaging and the result is Cecil B. DeMille's *The Ten Commandments, The Robe, The Greatest Story* [read fraudulent portrayal] *Ever Told,* and *Ben Hur.* Somehow Europeans magically populated the entire region of ancient Palestine. They appeared at precisely the right time in Judea to convince Mary and Jesus that their true color was White not Black, and ancient Palestine has never been the same.

NOTES

1. See Frank M. Snowden, Jr., *Before Color Prejudice: The Ancient View of Blacks* (Cambridge, Mass.: Harvard University Press, 1983) and other works cited in Cain Hope Felder, ed., *Stony the Road We Trod: African American Biblical Interpretation* (Minneapolis, Minn.: Fortress Press, 1991), 127–144.

2. David Lochhead, *The Liberation of the Bible* (Ontario, Can.: Student Christian Movement of Canada, 1977).

3. Ibid., 8–17.

4. Excerpt from "Crossing Borders, Challenging Barriers," in *A Guide to the Pedagogy and Philosophy of the Center for Global Education* (Minneapolis, Minn.: Augsburg College, 1988), 1.

5. Galen Hora citation. See *Entree,* National Lutheran Campus Ministry Publication (October, 1987, C.M. Reprint), n.p.

6. *New York Times,* 1 April, 1987.

14

BIBLICAL INTERPRETERS AND BLACK THEOLOGY

Thomas Hoyt, Jr.

Introduction

Black theology has spawned discussion among ethicists, historians, phenomenologists, sociologists, theologians and students of the Bible. The purpose of this essay is to consider the presuppositions of Black theologians and their influence upon biblical scholars. This consideration should be helpful in determining the direction biblical scholars should go and the corrections which Black theologians should ponder in their use of Scripture.

Experience and Biblical Interpretation

In 1991, Black biblical scholars collaborated on a book entitled: *Stony the Road We Trod: An African-American Biblical Interpretation.*[1] This book attempted to take seriously the Black theological agenda and move into the arena of biblical scholarship that could address the African-American heritage. We could not proceed to an exegetical analysis without consideration of the Black experience. We had learned from Black theologians the importance of considering one's sociological grid before one could adequately address the text.

We were obliged to listen to James H. Cone, who told us that an authentic Black theology makes sense of the black experience; recognizes the religious character of the Black community; relates the biblical experience to the Black experience; reveals God in Black culture, and depicts God as actively involved in Black liberation.[2] He says of the liberation theologies in general:

Thomas Hoyt, Jr., is professor of New Testament at Hartford Theological Seminary, Hartford, Connecticut. Hoyt was the principal architect of the series of seminars that Black biblical scholars held for several years at the Ecumenical Study Center in Collegeville, Minnesota.

We do not begin our theology with a reflection on divine revelation as if the God of our faith is separate from the suffering of our people. We do not believe that revelation is a deposit of fixed doctrines or an objective word of God that is then applied to the human situation. On the contrary, we contend that there is no truth outside or beyond the concrete historical events in which persons are engaged as agents. Truth is found in the histories, cultures, and religions of our peoples. Our focus of social and religio-cultural analyses separates our theological enterprise from the progressive and abstract theologies of Europe and North America. It also illuminates the reason why orthopraxis in contrast to orthodoxy has become for many of us the criterion of theology.[3]

Consideration of the role of experience in the explication of reality led us to consideration of the role of experience in the development of biblical texts themselves. Even the unlettered Black person had an intuitive interpretation that verified the truth of Scripture via his or her own experience.

We highlighted the truth that there is within the biblical text itself the development of various emphases based on the socio-economic-political situation in which persons found themselves. While there were in Israel's history various bases of salvation, as Gerhard Von Rad had shown, James Cone suggested that these bases had a constant, namely liberation.

Long before White theology in the South had learned, with the help of higher criticism, that the Bible was basically a history book describing and announcing concrete historical events and that it was itself born of those genuine, historical realities, Blacks had so read and heard the Bible simply because they came to it in terms of the historical reality of their oppression. James Cone writes:

The theme of liberation expressed in story form is the essence of black religion. Because black people were oppressed but not destroyed by it, they intuitively knew that servitude was a denial of their essential worth. They, therefore, looked for religious and secular themes in their social existence that promised release from the pain of slavery and oppression. It was not simply through an exegetical study of the Bible that blacks decided to center their preaching on the Exodus and not on Paul's letter to Philemon ... In view of their social situation of oppression, black people needed liberating visions so that they would not let historical limitations determine their perception of black being. Therefore, when Christianity was taught to them, and they began to read the Bible, blacks simply appropriated those Biblical stories that met their historical need.[4]

James Cone's Interpretive Key

It has been suggested that the key to Cone's understanding of Scripture is the Mosaic tradition rather than the David-Zion tradition, the Old Testament rather than the New, the Prophetic tradition rather than the Wisdom tradition.

Cone himself states that his hermeneutical principle for understanding Scripture is the revelation of Christ as Liberator.[5]

James Cone's traditio-historical approach to Scripture with liberation as its base presented a hermeneutic that challenged biblical scholars and others to ask, what is the hermeneutical key that opens all of Scripture? Of course, Von Rad had suggested that it was the traditional bases of salvation, like the Exodus, the covenant, the Davidic-Zion motif, which were constantly rehearsed in worship and became ever new in contemporaneous expressions. W. Eichrodt had contended that the covenant opened the whole of the biblical text.

Regardless of those who argue for inerrancy of Scripture, for accepting the canon as one's authority, or for experience as one's chief criterion for biblical interpretation, the behavior of interpreters, whether of the liberal or conservative persuasion, has been to establish a key principle that unlocks the other points of the biblical text. While James Cone insisted that liberation served as an organizing principle that enabled him to open the Scripture with insight, other African-American scholars, using the same canon, have propagated other organizing principles. For examples, Martin Luther King, Jr. (love of God, Jesus Christ, and human beings); J. Deotis Roberts (reconciliation through liberation); Joseph Washington, Jr. (Blacks as God's Chosen People); Albert Cleage, Jr. (Jesus as the Black Messiah); Major J. Jones (freedom and salvation in the context of love); Cecil Cone (An Almighty Sovereign God); C. Shelby Rooks (The Diaspora) and Joseph Johnson, Jr. (Jesus, the Liberator) are all illustrative of this propensity to use the same canon with different organizing principles to open the truths of Scripture.

As previously stated, having an interpretive principle is no different from other scholars like Eichrodt who chose the covenant; Von Rad who chose the biblical bases and traditions of salvation; Jürgen Moltmann who chose the suffering God motif; and Reformation and post-Reformation scholars who have concentrated on the theme of justification by faith rather than the theme of liberation and redemption as their major interpretive principle. It can be contended that there has been among scholars a canon within the canon. This has functioned among scholars and the majority of people, and needs to be recognized and affirmed. After recognition of the same, one must stand to be corrected and have one's vision enlarged by the views of others. This point alone argues for an ecumenical theology that recognizes the pluralism among us while addressing the connectedness of our approaches to the Scripture.

Cone's Biblical Methodology as a Case Study

A brief look at Cone's organizing principle will show certain biblical methodological considerations. First, the Exodus is the decisive event in Israel's history because of what it revealed. It revealed two things: God is on the side of the weak and oppressed; and God is able to break the bonds of the oppressor through God's power. Realizing the presence of God, the Israelites were willing to enter into a compact with Yahweh in order to solidify a permanent relationship. This covenant was based on what Yahweh had done, was doing and would do in relationship with a people who had experienced oppression, but who now experienced relative freedom with a chance to spread that freedom to all nations (Exodus 19:4–5).

Cone does a good job of connecting the traditio-historical approach of Von Rad to the principle of selectivity approach of Eichrodt. He thinks that the Exodus-Sinai tradition coupled with the theme of God's power in liberation that evolves from this tradition unlocks the Old Testament in a thematic or systematic approach.

When Cone moves from the Exodus-Sinai tradition and the covenant to other traditions in the Old Testament, it is interesting the way he handles them. God's liberating presence was with Israel even during those periods of Israel's disobedience. In periods of apostasy, and unfaithfulness, from the wilderness to the Promised Land, God was liberating God's people.

In the prophetic tradition, the Exodus-Sinai tradition is remembered and invoked in relationship to a disobedient people. Amos, Hosea, and Isaiah all called upon Israel to treat the poor, weak, oppressed as if they were the covenant people in order to offset the coming judgment of the Almighty God. Jeremiah and Micah both joined in with the latter emphasis. Cone saw in the David-Zion tradition the same emphasis as found in the Exodus-Sinai tradition. The prophet Isaiah of Jerusalem appealed to David's reign as the significant act of deliverance. Even here "Yahweh is the God of justice who sides with the weak against the strong."[6] It is interesting that in this instance of the David-Zion tradition, Cone concedes that there are other acts of deliverance besides the Exodus-Sinai event which could just as well unlock the door of the Old Testament. Yet, other events emphasize Yahweh's concern for the oppressed.

In the Poetry tradition, Cone sees the Davidic tradition undergirding the Psalms. However, in the Wisdom literature in which his process of selectivity breaks down, he says: "Even in the Wisdom Literature, where the sages seem to be unaware of Israel's saving history, God's concern for the poor is nonetheless emphasized."[7] God still protects the weak, poor and orphans.[8]

It is clear that Cone makes of the fact that God sides with the poor and oppressed of society his major theological basis. This is an example of a Black theologian who has consistently seen this theme appear in the biblical text and without it, he would argue, no biblical interpreter can tell the truth.

Truth Telling and Biblical Interpretation

It may be that James Cone, J. Deotis Roberts and Gayraud Wilmore have challenged biblical exegetes to go beyond the traditional biblical scholars who believe that the task of the exegete is to tell what the text meant in its own context and leave it to theologians to say what the text means today. Truth telling may indeed be more important than fact gathering. Gayraud Wilmore writes, "facts often deal with the superficial surface of reality. Truth has a way of dealing with the subjective ground of reality. There is something profoundly

personal about truth, for in the final analysis it relates to everything significant
to our lives."[9] Cone contends that it is the struggle for survival and liberation
that grounds Black religion in the truth, and the absence of such a struggle
condemns White religion to superficiality. "Truth is not an intellectual datum
that is entrusted to academic guilds. Truth cannot be separated from the people's struggle and the hopes and dreams that arise from that struggle. Truth is
that transcendent reality, disclosed in the people's historical struggle for liberation, which enables them to know that their fight for freedom is not futile."[10]

The Text Then and Now

As Black biblical scholars, we are convinced that we must find what the text
meant as well as what it means. This means that the questions we bring to the
text must have relevance to our communities as well as our personal lives. In
the book, *Stony the Road We Trod,* biblical scholars addressed problems of
racism, sexism, classism, the presence of Blacks in the biblical text, with a view
toward truth telling and eradication of myths that have developed from biased
interpretations of Scripture in the past. Our aim was to be prophetic, empowering, critical of normative Eurocentric worldviews, and hopeful of transformation of the socio-cultural-political-economic systems that oppress. This
pattern in biblical discussion is to be in touch with theological truth telling in
the best sense of the word.

This theological truth telling among biblical scholars, receiving its impetus
from the program of Black theologians, may mean that traditional biblical scholarship must be stood on its head. When there is a true community of scholarship
and dialogue with others, not traditionally those with whom one dialogues, new
insights may be the order of the day. For example, what if Randall Bailey is
right when he contends that association with Africans in the Hebrew texts is a
way to establish the positive status of a biblical character? What if he can show
this through the text of Psalm 68:31 in which Egypt and Cush are to Israel in
the Hebrew Scriptures what Rome is to Israel in the New Testament? In other
words, true universalism will have been achieved when these two nations come
to accept Yahweh as their deity. Would this change the future interpretation
of African nations in conjunction with Israel?

What if the view that the mentioning of Hagar as a servant of Abraham and
Sarah was more an enhancement of Abraham and Sarah than a degrading of
Hagar? Given the setting of the story at a time when Egypt was highly regarded
economically and politically, the Israelites having an Egyptian as a servant was
most uncommon. Since Abraham and Sarah are depicted as nomads, their
having a servant at that time is also most unusual. "The premise of the story,
then, is that the forebears of the nation Israel were rich enough to afford an
Egyptian servant. Thus, the mention of Hagar functions as a mechanism to
raise the esteem of the forebears." If this is true, must not a considerable
amount of scholarship be thrown out regarding this story?

Black Presence in the Bible

If we accept the criteria of Blackness of ancient and modern ethnologists and cultural anthropological affirmations, Black presence is much more present than has been allowed by Western interpreters of the Bible and in historical studies. By America's criteria, anyone with a drop of Black blood would have at one time been classified as Black. Of course we cannot attribute America's criteria to those of ancient Greece, Egypt, or Rome. By ancient standards, historians and contemporary ancient writers described themselves as persons with Negroid features. Church forbears and etymological expressions all affirm the presence of Africans in the ancient biblical text. Charles Copher applies these criteria to the text in an attempt to show the multifarious presence of Africans in the text. Why hasn't this truth telling been a part of the biblical landscape?

Biblical scholarship among African-American scholars must continue to discover the role and treatment of Africa in the development of ancient Judaism and early Christianity; plus the historical analysis of the long tradition of biblical interpretation among African Americans in this country. For example, as already stated, Randall Bailey, Cain Felder, and Charles Copher argue cogently that not only are Africans present in biblical history, but they are esteemed in positive and imitative ways. Biblical scholars and theologians need to continue the constructive search for the African presence in the biblical text as well as seek to recover the biblical paradigms that have sustained us throughout history and help African Americans to appreciate their heritage for future empowerment.

As the book *Stony the Road* contends, Blacks have lived not only in the paradigm of the Exodus story, but the creation story, the Jesus suffering and overcoming motif, the prophetic and priestly motif, and the "after a while and by and by" motif, which has provided hope for struggle in this world.

I suspect that Blacks have lived in various paradigms because of their belief that these aid in the liberating process. As a rule, human beings speak out of their various levels of need. Abraham Maslow, an industrial psychologist of note, would say that there are hierarchies of needs that people have. A need is a motivator only until it is fulfilled, and then the next higher need becomes the motivator. The first need is survival; then food, clothing, and shelter; then security; belonging, unity, participation in decision making, and self-actualization. Because our needs are different, our understanding of what is relevant discussion and relevant paradigm will be different, even in biblical interpretation.

There can be no meaningful dialogue until various levels of need are clearly articulated and understood. Liberation of a political nature is directly correlated with the perceived location of power. For workers, it is the boss who wields power: a statutory minimum wage, the right to organize, the regulation of health and safety are liberating. For women, it is men who wield power: the regulation of spousal abuse, rape, sexual harassment, and economic discrimination are liberating. For racial minorities, it is Whites who wield power: affirmative action in education, jobs, and housing are liberating. Where one stands in the society in terms of the social, economic, political, racial, and sexual scales conditions one's outlook on what liberation really is and on what the Scriptures really say. Truth telling and biblical interpretation are critical because one person's truth may be freeing for the messenger but condemning for the recipient. Yet, the hope is that truth will ultimately free both the messenger and the recipient.

A Black Midrash and Talmud

Black theologians have stressed the importance of the oral and written culture of the Black community. An oral-oriented culture views biblical history differently from a written-oriented culture. A written culture tends to value the authenticity of the printed word more than the spoken word. If something is written, it must be more important than if it is spoken. That's why texts and their criticism have been adjudged more significant than oral history, which has been inculcated in the life of people and may not have been codified. On the other hand, African Americans have not been without their writers. Just because the literature of Blacks has not been in the mainstream of American culture, or has been ignored by the wider culture, does not mean that there is not an abundance of African-American literature. Today the extant literature and the codified oral history and socio-political theory of Blacks are being written, collected, and codified by historians and writers such as Henry L. Gates, Cheryl Gilkes, C. Eric Lincoln, Katie G. Cannon, Albert J. Raboteau, Jacquelyn Grant, John Blassingame, James Washington, Delores Williams, Gayraud Wilmore, Charles Long, Lawrence Jones, Cornel West, and others too numerous to mention. We are seeing a body of literature that offers the opportunity for biblical scholars to do what Fernando Sergovia suggested in a critique of the book *Stony the Road*: further engage ourselves with Black esthetics, Caribbean studies, and cultural theory. There is no doubt in my mind that rapprochement with these disciplines will help Black biblical studies grow to maturity.

There are traditions within the African-American traditions that have developed through interaction with the biblical story and life experience that must be recaptured, and rehearsed as authentic examples of canon expressions standing alongside the church's accepted canon. These near canonical texts may indeed resemble the Talmud and Midrash of the Jewish community. The sources for this material may be found in sermons, testimonies, call narratives, Negro spirituals, slave narratives, and findings of Black biblical scholars. The question to be raised is will this near canonical canon be one of the people or of the scholars? Since Black religion has never been one that's scholar-directed, as was the case with Pharisaic involvement in Judaism, the Black Talmud may well be a mixture of popular and scholarly-directed material.

Feminist and Womanist Biblical Interpretation

White feminist and Black womanist theologians in their responses to the male-dominated society have made strong points regarding the Bible. Since the Bible is not self-explanatory, it is easily misused, misinterpreted, and abused. It requires careful and critical exegesis. However, the feminist theologians insist that they must view the Scriptures through the eyes of women. These women theologians are correct in asserting that exegesis that is dominated by males is likely to reflect a male bias. Context affects and often determines content. Furthermore, since Anglo-Saxon men dominate the social, political, economic, and theological arenas, realism suggests that biblical hermeneutics is in danger of being in the service of reinforcing, undergirding, or sustaining the privileged position of White men. The same can be said concerning African-American men in certain seats of power, especially in the churches. We clearly see that White women are oppressed and suppressed by the manner in which the Bible has been interpreted by some biblical theologians. If this can be said of White women, with the addition of racism and classism, the consequences are even more devastating for Black women.

As Black biblical scholars, we have listened to the black women theologians who have declared that they have not been adequately engaged or considered by Black male-dominated hierarchial structures. This is true as evidenced in confessions by James Cone.

When Cone began his theological work, the Black struggle against White racism was, for him, the chief social context of the contemporary scene. He now feels that we have gone through two stages of Black theology and presently are in the third stage, which began with the Black Theology Project conference in Atlanta in August, 1977. The third stage is ". . . characterized by a return to the Black church and community as the primary workshop of Black theology, a focus on the Third World, and the identification of sexism and classism as evils along with racism."[11] While the situation in which theology is done has changed, for Cone the biblical theme remains the same: — Liberation.

Professors Renita Weems and Clarice Martin have reminded us only too well that Black or White male biblical scholars must be conscious of a different mindset that separates them from the Black womanists. Even when biblical interpretation takes into consideration the race issue, one must still consciously deal with the gender issue. Black women biblical scholars must of necessity still deal with the triple jeopardy of race, sex, and class issues.

Professor Martin in her exegetical work on Paul would have Black men advocate against sexism in churches with the same fervor as they do against racism. Professor Weems would also remind us that as we hold up the Exodus theme as our paradigm for liberation, we must at the same time acknowledge that the Egyptians as Black people were themselves oppressors of Jews. The fact that we propagate the Egyptians as Africans, that they were oppressors of the Jews, and that God delivered the Jews from the hands of the oppressive

Egyptians, does not show as much a blind spot as a revelation. It reveals that Black people were in the beginning of biblical history and thus had a history before Europeans developed a consciousness of Yahweh and a subsequent understanding of Jesus.

This is invaluable knowledge for those who were stripped of their heritage through slavery by the European community. To those who would contend that we must stress both the Exodus as a paradigm and the negativity of Black Egyptians as an oppressor nation, I would say the following: we don't worship Egypt, but God. Egyptians as people of color who oppressed others at some time in the past does not mean that the total culture of Egypt is therefore tarnished forever. We are concerned about structural transformation, but also about attitudinal changes. When Cain Felder, Charles Copher, Randall Bailey, and John Waters convincingly seek to establish the Black presence in the Bible, firmly grounding the Black experience in the Jewish and Christian tradition via an Egyptian heritage, it is no insignificant concern. They are saying that Blacks have been a part of biblical heritage from the beginning. Christianity is not just a Western phenomenon. Furthermore, Egypt is appealed to in the way that we have appealed to the Jewish community as ancestors in the faith who were not without their bad moments, at least as far as the Canaanites were concerned. We can talk about Egypt as our cultural heritage without sacrificing the truth about a people who had the propensity to misuse power quite as much as any other nation or people.

Historical: Reader Criticism

Black theologians have stressed that there is need for theological methodology in order to be intelligible and credible so that dialogue with others can be facilitated. Black biblical scholars have been in dialogue with Black theologians concerning their hermeneutical method. We believe that the Bible is one of the bases of the Christian religion, and theology must have affinity with that Book. Theology must keep returning to the Bible and continually reinterpret it.

Black biblical scholars have witnessed the views of the liberation theologian Juan Luis Segundo as applied to the methodology of James H. Cone. Segundo speaks of a hermeneutical circle that arises out of two preconditions: profound and enriching questions and suspicions about our real human situation; and a new interpretation of the Bible that is equally profound and enriching. As a result, there are four decisive factors in the circle: (1) our experience of reality that leads to ideological suspicion; (2) the application of this suspicion to the whole ideological superstructure in general and to theology in particular; (3) a new experience of theological reality leading to the exegetical suspicion that prevailing interpretations have not taken important pieces of data into account; and (4) a new hermeneutic, that is, a new way of interpreting Scripture. Each new experience of reality initiates the circular process again.[12] Western theological scholars had criticized liberation theologians by denying that they had a methodology that was defensible. In order to test his methodology, Segundo ran the thought of Harvey Cox, Karl Marx, Max Weber and James Cone through his hermeneutical circle. Even though Segundo expressed great respect for Cone and his theological agenda, and was merely doing a methodological test, J. Deotis Roberts thinks that a disservice was done to Cone and to Black theology in the process.[13] Only Cone's thought completed the hermeneutical circle of Segundo. The fact that Cone completed the circle does not disturb Deotis Roberts so much as how he completed it and the resulting consequences.

What is useful for our discussion is the fact that Black theologians are struggling today for a methodology just as are Black biblical scholars. Black biblical scholars' emphasis on the social location of African Americans, while at the same time appealing to the historical-critical method, which calls for the presence of an objective and universal reader, is difficult to reconcile.

We may need to go beyond the historical-critical method, which to many is bankrupt. Black theologian Cecil Cone thinks that the historical-critical method is not appropriate for the Black interpreter. In an attempt to be true to what he terms the Black experience and harboring a basic distrust of the historical-critical method, Cecil Cone has also engaged in the spiritualization of the scriptural text. In a critique of his brother, James Cone, he puts his finger on the fear that prompts this spiritualization. He says of James Cone:

> Cone's Christ is being pulled apart: on the one hand, drawn by the attraction of Black Power, and on the other hand, driven by the force of critical-historical research, with both foci inadequate as the point of departure for an understanding of the black religious tradition.[14]

One may ask how one is alienated from the Black experience by the historical-critical method? Cecil Cone's answer is that the alienation is in two aspects. First, an alien methodology leads the Black scholar to ask and seek answers to questions that his or her people are not asking. Chief among those questions is the existence of God, which is not a problem for Black folks as far as Cecil Cone is concerned. Critical reflection is important for Cecil Cone, but its proper antecedent is experience with God, which means that one responds properly to revelation out of faith, not through an "alien discipline" to revelation. Second, since critical research can never yield knowledge that has the character of revelation, the only consequences for the Black religious experiences are twofold and counterproductive:

> that experience is reduced to the secularity of the liberation movements or to the terms of a Western historic apologetic. Either way, the substance of black religion is ignored in favor of secular modernity.[15]

What Cecil Cone is calling for is an interpretive schema, a hermeneutic, which makes clear the relation between the historical explanation and spiritual or moral appropriation. That is a crucial task for Black theology and for modern biblical study. We need an approach to the Bible that builds on what historical study has disclosed about it. Even though Cone's critique is needed, one feels that he does not need to reject historical methodology in order to ascertain the needed correlation with Scripture and the Black religious experience.

Because of the manner in which Scripture originated, it has become axiological that Scripture is not merely subject to the church's interpretation, but the church is also subject to Scripture's interpretation of its life. The historical-critical method has exposed the fact that the New Testament has an internal interpretive propensity in which the church has been critiqued from the start. Since, therefore, we all have ideological biases, there is a constant need to interpret Scripture while at the same time allowing the Scriptures to interpret us.

We may need to look at a pluriformity of methods, literary criticism and social criticism, including the reader-response criticism. We may have traditionally focused on historical-critical analysis, but Black biblical scholars are also stressing how the biblical paradigms have functioned in the life of their people. The question that has proven instructive for methodological consideration is: What have been the functional biblical stories or paradigms in the life of the African-American community that have provided meaning in the context of suffering. As such, our affinity has been with reader-response criticism.

This method stresses the presence of differences among readers, the inevitability of multiple interpretations of any one text, and the legitimacy of such multiple readings. We have stressed the relative power of the text or the reader vis-à-vis each other. We have looked at the influence of gender, racial and ethnic background, socioeconomic class, sociopolitical status and allegiance, sociocultural conventions, educational levels, ideological stance, and religious affiliation. The danger of such a method is that left to itself alone, the plurality of meanings may lead one into exactly what the historical-critical method sought to avoid: prooftexting, whereby the text can be used as a pretext for one's own context without regard to the given biblical context.

The critical question we need to ask is: Do we wish to escape any attempt to get away from relative objectivity and universality as we focus on interpreters and their social location? What does such focus do to the text that was written before our day and was derived from persons in their own socio-cultural-economic context? The historical-critical method is important for interpreting Scripture, but must be handled by different managers who will add their own questions to the method, which might lift up previously hidden truths. There is, after all, a direct correlation between right questions and right methodologies.

A Word on Biblical Imagination

Black biblical scholars and Black theologians may be enriched methodologically by being attuned to what is happening in the social and behavioral sciences regarding the imagination. We know that this imaginative mode of biblical interpretation has long been an intricate part of African-American biblical interpretation. There is a current swell of interest in the imagination evident in the social sciences that overthrows the comfortable reign of empiricism that once held sway. In matters of social science we are told that a paradigm shift is underway; the emergence of a science no longer captive to the great surge of the Enlightenment with its stress on rationalism. It is said that we are on the verge of a major renaissance in the social and behavioral sciences, one that promises to place the imagination back on center stage.

Biblical scholarship is afraid of subjective experience and so tries to avoid it. This avoidance is rooted in a residual dialectic of Cartesian dualism that separates mind from body, inner from outer, rational from irrational, and so on. Black theologians have stressed that a true experience touches the total person. This kind of thinking often goes counter to the opinion of Western culture which tends to separate body/soul, mind/emotion, oral/ocular, and order/freedom. A few examples might help us understand the implication of this manner of thinking. The worship style of many Black churches is warm, compassionate, practical, artistic, and emotionally free. Those, however, whose style of life is structured, ordered, unfeeling, scientific and "objective," are not equipped with either the tools or the capacity to enter into the warm and vibrant world of the religious experience of the Black worshiper.

This once all-embracing dualism is fortunately breaking down. Today even strict behaviorists recognize the validity of subjective experience as a source of data. Nor are intuition and the imagination foreign to the physical sciences. Einstein's famous Gedanken experiment, where he imagined himself traveling along with a wave of light at 186,000 miles-per-second, resulted in a total restructuring of our concepts of time and space. Einstein said he rarely "thought in words." His ability did not lay so much in mathematical calculations, but in "visualizing effects, consequences, and possibilities." For him, "visualizing" consisted of images that could be reproduced and combined at will.

My feeling is that what is taking place in the social and behavioral sciences is taking place in biblical studies and since oppressed and marginalized persons have always been utilizers of the imagination for survival purposes, living out of the context of biblical paradigms of hope, these persons are crucial for an enriched post-Enlightenment biblical interpretation involving all the people. One of the reasons that I used the paradigm of the people of Solentiname[16] and their imaginative interpretation of the Bible was to illustrate the fact that imagination that does not arise from our struggle for transforming the reality of the world cannot be authentic imagination, but will end up with illusion.

Conclusion

Let me close with some advice for Black theologians that applies equally to Black biblical scholars. In a book written in 1980 entitled: *Roots of a Black Future: Family and Church* (Westminster Press, 1980), J. Deotis Roberts reiterates that his view of Black theology is universalistic, embedded in the partic-

ularity of the Black religious experience and complementary to the various
programs of other Black theologians. His advice is "read all the Black theologians":

> We need unity without conformity to enable each black scholar to do
> what he can do best. We need serious and creative scholarship. Some will
> be interested in a Biblical theology; others will major in the historical or
> philosophical approaches. Some will major in methodology, others in con-
> tent . . . The problem of black suffering will challenge some. The nature
> and mission of the church will urge others on, while still others will pursue
> the Black Messiah. Black theology is a theology in the making and only
> the Lord of the Church knows at this moment the ultimate direction it
> will take.[17]

More directly, Deotis Roberts sets forth a clear methodology for his theological agenda, partially in reference to Cecil Cone, but also in reference to
other critics who see him as a theologian who is too universalistic, but independent from other Black theologians in terms of his approach to liberation
and reconciliation; too bound to European-American, Western thought; not
cognizant enough of sexism, racism, and classism as chains of oppression; and
not appreciative enough of the Black religious experience. In his book *Roots of
a Black Future*, he stresses his methodological approach to theology that has
implications for biblical scholars. In closing, I shall quote the entire statement:

> In this book, we will not move in the shadow of any other black theologian.
> Our effort will be to think out our own encounter with life, out of our
> own spiritual and intellectual pilgrimage, and as a member of a family
> and a church within the black experience. We will not be limited by the
> black experience, but will move within and without where necessary. Our
> anchor, however, will be within this ethnic setting. Black sources will be
> used and we will interact critically with several black writers, past and
> present. We will take our African roots seriously. Euro-American and
> Third World materials will be used freely but not uncritically. All mate-
> rials and ideas will be used descriptively and we refuse to place a greater
> value on Western sources than on any others. We categorically reject the
> colonization of the mind as well as the political domination of the West
> in reference to the rest of humankind. We shall strive to be human in
> our concern for the rights of women and will attempt to avoid male-
> dominated language where this is possible. We are aware of a network
> of oppression based upon race, sex, and class, and we endorse the right
> of all humans to be free and equal. At the same time our special focus
> is upon race as a form of oppression. Our particular context is the spiritual
> and cultural heritage of Afro-Americans.[18]

In my opinion, this is one of the most important statements made by any
theologian, White or Black, in relation to a theological agenda that is both

particularistic and universalistic. The statement gives credence to the inclusivity of women, different ethnic groups, and classes; recognizes diversities but realizes that unity is not predicated on uniformity; refuses to extol the Western paradigm over that of the Third World or different ways of perceiving the world. Roberts declares himself free to think within a particular context, and opens himself to be critiqued and responded to by others. What more can one ask of a theologian or a biblical scholar?

NOTES

1. Cain Hope Felder, ed. (Minneapolis, MN: Fortress Press, 1991).

2. James H. Cone, *A Black Theology of Liberation* (Philadelphia: Lippincott, 1970), 53–81.

3. James H. Cone, *For My People: Black Theology and the Black Church* (Maryknoll, NY.: Orbis Books), 148.

4. James H. Cone, *God of the Oppressed* (New York: Seabury Press, 1975), 60.

5. Ibid., 81–82.

6. Ibid., 69.

7. Ibid., 70.

8. See my article "The Biblical Tradition of the Poor and Martin Luther King, Jr.," in *Journal of the Interdenominational Theological Center* 4 (Spring 1977), 12–32.

9. Gayraud S. Wilmore, *Last Things First* (Philadelphia: Westminster Press, 1982), 15.

10. Cone, *God of the Oppressed*, 17.

11. Cone, *For My People*, 110. We must note that Warner Traynham early on called for this recognition of other liberation movements in his book *Christian Faith in Black and White: A Primer in Theology from the Black Perspective* (Wakefield, Mass.: Parameter Press, 1973), 65.

12. Juan Luis Segundo, *The Liberation of Theology* (Maryknoll, N.Y.: Orbis Books, 1979), 7–34.

13. The following discussion is based on the critique given by J. Deotis Roberts, *Black Theology Today* (New York: Edwin Mellen Press, 1983), 5–7.

14. Cecil Cone, *The Identity Crises in Black Theology* (Nashville, Tenn.: African Methodist Episcopal Church, 1975), 113.

15. Ibid., 144.

16. See *Stony the Road We Trod*, 38.

17. J. Deotis Roberts, "Black Theology in the Making," *Review and Expositor* 70 (Summer 1973), 330, cited in Roberts, *Roots of a Black Future* (Philadelphia: Westminster Press, 1980).

18. Roberts, *Roots of a Black Future*, 14–15.

15

"RESCUE THE PERISHING":
THE IMPORTANCE OF BIBLICAL
SCHOLARSHIP IN BLACK CHRISTIANITY

Vincent L. Wimbush

In the sense that they have sought to interpret biblical texts with a view to discovering "the biblical position" on such ideas as the universal parenthood of God and the universal kinship of humankind, eschatology and ethics, ethics and redemption, God and black suffering,[1] all black Christian leaders and scholars have been biblical theologians. All have viewed the Bible as the sine qua non of any discussion about faith and existence, of any effort in the direction of liberation and progress for their people. But very few of these leaders have had as their major concern the academic study of the Bible apart from preparation for, actual participation in, and the acceptance of the presuppositions of, confessional affiliations.

But two clarifications are in order. First, although the academic study of the Bible is nearly as old as the Bible itself,[2] historical-critical methods, now the common possession of reputable biblical scholars,[3] came to be applied to biblical texts on a wide scale in this country in the late nineteenth and early twentieth centuries.[4] Obviously, black people as a whole—not just the religious leadership—were preoccupied with other matters at the time. At any rate, they had very limited access to educational institutions, especially those institutions in which the historical-critical methods were being introduced and in which debates about them were being waged.[5]

Second—and perhaps more importantly—black people had already begun, in the period of the rise of the use of historical-critical methods, to appropriate Christian tradition in their own unique way. This appropriation, I would argue,

Vincent L. Wimbush is professor of New Testament and Christian origins, Union Theological Seminary, New York City. He is also the editor of *Ascetic Behavior in Greco-Roman Antiquity* (1990). This essay was published in *Reflection,* Yale Divinity School, 80, no. 2 (1983).

made irrelevant the crisis that, to a great extent, led to the adoption of the historical-critical methods in this country.

White American Christianity in the late nineteenth century was largely evangelical Protestant. Its reading of the Bible was an admixture of doctrinalist, moralist and pietist patterns of thought.[6] The Bible was seen either as a source for correct doctrine, or a handbook for moral guidance, decision making and pious living, or combinations of both. Since the biblical text was given so central a place in the life of the faithful, even in society as a whole, difficulties soon emerged from differences and conflicts in interpretations of texts, from differences in translations, from perceived contradictions within accepted texts, and especially from attempts to square the literalist reading of certain texts with a post-Enlightenment world. Questioning and dissenting voices from either the lecture podium or the pulpit were rebuffed by "defenders of the faith" who held forth histrionically with the historically honored arguments regarding inerrancy, infallibility and verbal inspiration. But these arguments were not to halt the revolution in the making. What was emerging was a change in the understanding of history itself, specifically, the manner in which educated women and men were beginning to understand the relationship between revelation and history.[7] This "transformation of human consciousness" involved the new conviction that cultures and their ideas, ideals, values and institutions—including religious ideals and institutions—are the products of history. It was this new consciousness that gave birth to the conviction that divine things must be known *within* the realm of history or not at all. This conviction forced the acceptance of the historical-critical methods in the study of the Bible.

During this same period, black Christianity, both because of the nature of the times and because of blacks' appropriation of Christian tradition, faced in another direction. It did not fit neatly into either the doctrinalist, moralist or pietist pattern of thought with respect to interpretation of the Bible. Having been denied from the beginning of their existence in the Americas the opportunity to learn to read and write, the "letters" of the biblical texts were not critical in the appropriation and shaping of Christian tradition. What became important to black folks—first as slaves, then as disenfranchised people—was the telling and re-telling, the hearing and re-hearing of biblical stories—stories of faith under trial, of hope in hopeless situations, of strength in weakness and under oppressive burdens. To these stories black Christians related. The emulation of the heroine or hero of the stories constituted "faith." The slave songs, black preaching and orations and the spirituals remain eloquent testimony to this assertion. (I shall forego the temptation of quoting selections from the numerous examples that would support the argument here. I shall refer the reader to the works of Howard Thurman, Benjamin E. Mays, and James H. Cone for excellent theological treatments of slave songs.[8] Henry Mitchell's *Black Preaching* [Lippincott, 1970] remains useful.)

Black Christianity did not experience the problems which white Christianity in America faced in the late nineteenth and early twentieth centuries because the experience of slavery and disenfranchisement simply did not afford the luxury. Black Christianity could not wrestle with the problems of a literalist reading of the Bible in an ever-changing post-Enlightenment world because black folk were allowed to engage neither letters nor the changing world. Biblical interpretation in black Christianity presumed that the Bible was Word of God insofar as it spoke to the present. What did not speak to the present was ignored. What was presented by slave-master or white preacher in a nonaffirming manner (pro-slavery, for example), in a way that seemed contradictory to the character of the heroines and heroes of the Bible, or in a way which seemed out of step with the thrust of the message of the Bible, they ignored altogether. (Howard Thurman has related incidents, in the days of his youth in which his grandmother refused to permit him to read to her from the letters of Paul with the exception of I Corinthians 13. As a young slave girl she had been told by the white minister to the slaves, who quoted the letters of Paul, "Slaves, be obedient to your masters . . ."[9])

Their illiteracy was not deafness. Blacks knew when the Bible was conveying the Word of God, and when it was not. They knew that they must, according to Martin Luther, "not only observe if it is God's Word, or if God has spoken it, but also to whom it is spoken." Blacks sensed that the "Word of God" about which the slavers spoke was not their "Word of God." They said, as Martin Luther said of the "false prophets" of his day who could point to the texts as the Word of God: "That is true, we cannot deny it, but we are not that people to which he speaks."[10]

The Bible was not mined for doctrinal propositions; it was heard for experiences that could inspire, convince and enlighten. Insofar as it was thought of as the legacy of the experiences of other underdogs, there was no need to interpret the Bible as handbook. As though in answer to a form-critic's prayer, black Christianity's New Testament interpretation was based on a sense of the text as the record of a community's life and its attempts to make meaningful the encounter with Jesus.

But a strange and frightening thing has happened to black people — including black Christians — on their way to progress and liberation. As the larger society has eased a bit its oppressive grip on the black community, granting, for example, limited educational opportunities, a very unfortunate specter has appeared — the white specter of doctrinalist Christianity in the black community. With more opportunity to learn to read and write, with more access to the letters of the biblical text, less emphasis was placed on the telling and hearing of stories. (To be sure, storytelling has by no means disappeared, but it now serves as vehicle for indoctrination.) The founding of independent black denominations and churches, the black control of black colleges and seminaries notwithstanding, black Christianity began — ironically after emancipation — to take thought for what it should believe and not believe, about what it should eat and drink. The decline was gradual at first. This new Christianity among black folk existed alongside historic "culturist" black Christianity as a less powerful, certainly less pervasive force, until the last few decades of this century. Until recently no black denominational group ever split over doctrinal issues. But today it is common to hear of Pentecostal or charismatic groups splitting off from certain "unfaithful" bodies. And evangelicals now experience rifts not only over certain doctrines, but over the degree of flexibility that doctrine requires.[11]

This most significant change in black Christianity is evident not only in doctrinal rifts on the denominational level; it is now evident in every local black parish as parishioners plead for more guidance in their reading of their Bibles, as astute comments are made and questions asked in response to sermons preached, as great interest is shown in the teaching claims of the electronic preachers, as befuddlement and intimidation are expressed in the face of the rise in number and complexity of books on religious subjects.

Perhaps the change was inevitable. It is difficult for a sub-culture group to defend itself completely and eternally from the ways of the larger dominant group. It was so with blacks. Increased literacy, seminary and sub-seminary-trained clergy, integration, confusion about the meaning of black experience in America, especially black experience coupled with "Christian" experience in America—these were the contributing factors to the change. Even if there is much discussion about the identity of the relevant contributing factors, there is little argument about the fact of the change itself. That Joseph Washington could in 1964 bemoan the lack of theological sophistication on the part of black folk, speak of black religion as *mere* folk religion (as opposed to a legitimate part of historic Christianity), advise black Christians to close down their churches and move to the suburbs for worship and indoctrination is evidence enough of the change which had already begun to infect black Christianity.[12]

Washington's perception was by no means singular. Many black Christians have begun to express their discontent with their churches on the basis of the inability of their churches to mimic white churches. The almost universal complaint black Christians voice against their own churches has to do with the perceived shortcomings of the education program. The model, of course, is the white church. Behind the complaint is the understanding of the need for a more serious study of the Bible and Christian doctrine.

The irony of the situation is that what now comes when blacks have freedom to formulate and pursue their own agenda is more slavery: more control from without through the transmission of authoritative ideas. For the first time—slavery, disenfranchisement notwithstanding—whites are capturing the minds of black people through black acceptance of white views and interpretations of Christian tradition and existence. Certainly not before the last few decades, the decades of "progress" and "liberation," did blacks begin to take seriously white folks' claims to, or views of, Christian faith. Even during the days of slavery, when freedom was quite limited, blacks refused to accept the religious ways of white folks.[13] Presently, through doctrinalist student groups on college campuses, through "big business" evangelists and miracle workers, through electronic preachers and teachers, through the prolific writers of spiritual "how-to" books, even through the seminary-trained black clerics, black Christians are learning their Bible and their Christian doctrine from whites.

Again, the development may have been inevitable. But what is most troubling is the failure on the part of black scholars in religion and trained black clerics to respond to the development. They seem neither to have taken note nor grasped the gravity of the present situation in which Christianity is still embraced by black people in great numbers while "black experience" is more and more difficult to define and circumscribe and square with Christianity. In such a situation, when so many others are willing to proffer their views to the uninitiated and unenlightened, when black theologians remain content to offer constructions of black theologies based on their perceptions of "black experience," black Christians have begun to fall easy prey to the peddlers of doctrine.

Black scholars of religion cannot continue to forget that black Christians need to be addressed both as blacks and as Christians. To fail to address them as such is to risk the judgment of irrelevance and to aid in the perishing of a people. What is required is a move beyond apologies for "black experience,"[14] even beyond "black religious experience."[15] The former, even when defined in the most inclusive terms, always seems to lag decades behind black folks' present experiences and existential situation. The latter, setting and ethnic origin of participants notwithstanding, is no longer *of* black people. Black evangelical Christianity, for example, is more *evangelical* (read: doctrinalist, traditionally nonblack) than *black.* The times require the same creative and intellectual energies which gave birth to the black theology movement to address the present needs of the black communities of faith. We cannot go back to more innocent times when faith came by hearing alone. Nor can we assume that all is well if all is quiet. That we have the bodies of black Christians is no indication that we have their minds. They must be rescued from the clutches of dogmatic Christianity and led in other more constructive, more affirming directions. For this task biblical scholarship is indispensable.

Because the Bible is the record of the experiences and reflections of those who encountered God before us, biblical scholarship involves the effort to "give voice to" that record. Every effort must be made to understand the world in which those who had such encounters lived. But even after we have thoroughly investigated the world of the earliest Christians, for example, the task is not complete. We must come to understand what Dutch exegete and theologian Edward Schillebeeckx refers to as "interpretative elements" of the times: Jewish and Greek experimental concepts. The fact that the New Testament betrays a number of different ways of describing the experience of salvation gives us freedom also in describing our own.[16]

Interpretations of experiences, however, never stand on their own; they are always part of a greater context of thought. Behind "interpretative elements" are "theoretical models" that help to order and synthesize and articulate basic experiences.[17] On this level we would be seeking to come to know not merely the world in which the earliest Christians lived, but the earliest Christians' understanding of "world." It is the understanding of "world" that opens up the understanding of the way in which revelation has been interpreted. To this understanding all generations of Christians are indebted and must remain faithful.[18]

Black Christianity must take biblical scholarship seriously because only through biblical scholarship can it discover the degree to which it can express in terms of its understanding of world its experience of salvation in Christ. It must take biblical scholarship seriously because only through such scholarship can it begin first to *reconstruct* as much as possible the world of early Christianity, that it may separate the wheat from the chaff, or *cut through* the heaps of accumulated traditions and interpretations which are not in its best interest. Then it can rightly proceed to *reshape* that chunk of Christendom of which it is part, and perhaps, contribute to efforts to reshape the form and priorities of the whole.

NOTES

1. See Henry J. Young, *Major Black Religious Leaders: 1755–1940* (Nashville: Abingdon Press, 1977), for more detailed discussion.

2. Origen Dionysius of Alexandria in the third century. See E. Krentz, *The Historical-Critical Method* (Philadelphia: Fortress Press, 1975), 6. Also W.G. Kümmel, *The New Testament; The History of the Investigation of Its Problems,* tr. S.M. Gilmour and H.C. Kee (New York: Abingdon Press, 1972), 15ff.

3. See Joseph Cahill, *Mended Speech* (New York: Crossroad, 1982), for discussion on present state of religious studies, including biblical studies, in American higher education.

4. Grant Wacker, "The Demise of Biblical Civilization," in *The Bible in America: Essays in Cultural History,* ed. Nathan O. Hatch and Mark A. Noll (New York: Oxford University Press, 1982), 121ff.

5. Cf. Krentz, 29ff.

6. Richard J. Mouw, "The Bible in Twentieth-Century Protestantism: A Preliminary Taxonomy," in Hatch and Noll, 142ff.

7. Ibid., p. 146ff.

8. See Thurman's *Deep River* and *The Negro Spiritual Speaks of Life and Death,* single vol. (Richmond, Ind.: Friends United Press, 1975); Mays' classic *The Negro's God* (New York: Atheneum, 1968); and Cone's *The Spirituals and the Blues* (New York: Seabury Press, 1972).

9. See his *Deep River,* p. 22.

10. Taken from Krister Stendahl's *The Bible and the Role of Women,* tr. Emilie T. Sander (Philadelphia: Fortress Press, 1966), 39 (note 38).

11. Mouw, 152. See also W.H. Bentley, "Bible Believers in the Black Community," in *The Evangelicals,* ed. D.F. Wells and J.D. Woodbridge (New York: Abingdon Press, 1975).

12. See Joseph Washington's controversial *Black Religion: The Negro and Christianity in the United States* (Boston: Beacon Press, 1969).

13. Albert J . Raboteau, *Slave Religion* (New York: Oxford University Press, 1978), 211ff.

14. See Cecil Cone's *The Identity Crisis in Black Theology* (Nashville: African Methodist Episcopal Church, 1975).

15. Against Calvin Bruce's "Black Evangelical Christianity and Black Theology," in *Black Theology II,* ed. Bruce and William R. Jones (Cranbury, N.J.: Associated University Presses, Inc., 1978), 163ff.

16. See his *Interim Report on the Books* Jesus *and* Christ (New York: Crossroad, 1981), 15.

17. Ibid., 16.

18. Ibid.

16

WOMANIST REFLECTIONS
ON BIBLICAL HERMENEUTICS

Renita J. Weems

After centuries of dictating which questions are appropriate and inappropriate to the study of biblical texts, the inherent biases and limitations of the historical-critical method as an objective, scientific approach to the Bible are becoming widely asserted.[1] While *the* method continues to exert enormous influence in the field and will probably continue to do so in the foreseeable future, still the historical-critical method can no longer be considered the method to which all biblical interpretation must submit itself. There is today considerable discussion going on in the field about such things as the nature of language and literature, the relationship of texts to reality, the role and social identity of the interpreter, the politics of interpretation, and what it means to speak of texts as having "meaning." These discussions are the result of the drastic "paradigm shift" that has gripped a wide spectrum of disciplines, including the biblical field, and has changed the way biblical historians and exegetes understand the past. More importantly, they have tempered previous confidence in the historical-critical method, as a device of modern technology, to make the past readily transparent. At the center of the re-formation of the field of biblical studies is the recognition that biblical interpretation is not isolated from the social and cultural values and political interests of the interpreter. No interpretive method, whether historical-critical or socio-literary, can completely inoculate the text from the biases of the interpreter. Indeed, one of the earmarks of the current discussion in biblical interpretation is that what one reads out of the text depends in large part upon what one reads into it. Most notably, feminist and other liberation thinkers have been at the forefront of those who have insisted

Renita J. Weems is Assistant Professor of Hebrew Bible at Vanderbilt University. She is the author of *Just a Sister Away: A Womanist Vision of Women's Relationships in the Bible* (1988). This essay, © 1993 by the author.

that the personal is political; and, as such, all interpretive strategies are advocacy positions.

Chief among the criticisms of the historical-critical method by liberation scholars has been the fallacy and fraudulent nature of claims for an "objective" versus a "subjective" reading of biblical texts. To the extent that no interpreter is able to divest herself of her values and assumptions, then all interpretation of data and texts reflect to some degree the subjective predispositions of the interpreter. Thus, a historical-critical reconstruction of biblical events is itself interpreted history. And to the extent that all interpretive strategies are advocacy positions, then no rendering of biblical history is ever simply "history of" but "history for"; that is, "history is told with an ideological goal in mind, and is written for a certain group of people."[2] In the case of American and European scholarship, for the last century biblical history has been dominated by the ideological interests of Anglo-Saxon male interpreters whose principal concern has been to rationalize and defend their own bourgeois social, economic, political, and militaristic orientation. This explains at least in part why patriarchal scholarship has been preoccupied in the Old Testament with such issues as origins, ancestry, warfare, statehood, and territorialism in matters of history; distinctiveness, coherence, authority, and unity in matters of theology; and coherence, continuity, development, and authenticity in matters of literary criticism. This is not to say that these themes are neither germane to nor significantly a part of the ancient Israelite worldview. However, they are not necessarily an inherent part of that worldview, and they are certainly not as unanimous in their expressions as patriarchal scholarship has asserted. Other themes are also evoked, other questions also raised, that deserve equal attention. These different themes and questions have been (and will only be) consistently raised as different kinds of interpreters—whose relationship to and perspective on power differs from that of Anglo-Saxon men—become part of the scholarly discussion on biblical interpretation.

For example, considerable diversity exists among feminists in terms of paradigm and philosophy as to how the Bible should be interpreted.[3] It is probably safe to say that all feminists, to the extent that they identify with such a term to distinguish their perspective, share some basic presuppositions (e.g., the equality of women, all scholarship as advocacy on behalf of some group, and patriarchy as hierarchal, dualistic, and androcentric in character); however, the "success" of feminist scholarship thus far has been in its insistence upon remaining grounded in women's experience (praxis) and, as a result, its ability to tolerate diversity within itself. Despite this appearance of diversity, however, the circle of dialogue is actually quite monolithic. Feminist scholarship, both within the theological field and outside the field, is largely an Anglo-American, bourgeois, matriarchal enterprise. Stated another way, although it envisions itself as a critique of dominating and exploitative structures in light of the struggles of the oppressed, as of today, feminist scholarship, like patriarchal scholarship, is threatened with the charge of seeking its own perpetuation, and therefore, is itself doomed. For its own integrity, Anglo-American feminist scholarship in general and Anglo-American feminist theological scholarship in particular needs desperately to broaden the circle of those engaged in hermeneutical reflection in order to insure its own critical and prophetic edge.

Although our scholarship is still emerging, and our voices are heard much too infrequently, the one clear, persistent theme of the writings of African-American female theologians is that theological discourse, in general, and feminist theological discourse, in particular, have much breadth and integrity to gain by taking seriously the critiques of those outside the inner circle of dialogue.[4] A survey of our writings over the years, especially beyond the theological domain, will show that a recurring message has been that as human beings we are all mutually connected to each other and dependent upon one another for our emancipation and for our survival. Therefore, while Anglo-American feminists ground their analysis in the experiences of women in their struggles for liberation, African-American women have tended to ground theirs in the experiences of all oppressed people struggling for liberation.

Most recently, the distinctiveness of our message has been underscored by one of us in the field of literature. To clarify what for some must seem like the audacious posture of African-American women, the poet and novelist Alice Walker borrowed a term indigenous to African-American culture that captured the commitment of African-American women to the survival of all peoples.[5] A "womanist," according to Walker, is "committed to survival and wholeness of entire people, male and female. Not a separatist, except periodically, for health. . . ."[6] Almost one hundred years earlier, in a speech to the Congress of Representative Women on the status of black women, the educator, suffragette, and "race woman," Anna Julia Cooper, sought to broaden the vision of her predominantly white audience by appealing to the example of her constituency:

> Now, I think if I could crystallize the sentiment of my constituency, and
> deliver it as a message to this congress of women, it would be something
> like this: Let woman's claim be as broad in the concrete as in the abstract.
> We take our stand on the solidarity of humanity, the oneness of life, and
> the unnaturalness and injustice of all special favoritisms, whether of sex,
> race, country, or condition. If one link of the chain be broken, the chain
> is broken. A bridge is no stronger than its weakest part, and a cause is
> not worthier than its weakest element. Least of all can woman's cause
> afford to decry the weak. We want, then, as toilers for the universal
> triumph of justice and human rights, to go to our homes from this Con
> gress, demanding an entrance not through a gateway for ourselves, our
> race, our sex, or our sect, but a grand highway for humanity. *The colored*
> *woman feels that woman's cause is one and universal; and that not till the*
> *image of God, whether in parian or ebony, is sacred and inviolable; not till*
> *race, color, sex, and condition are seen as the accidents, and not the substance*
> *of life; not till the universal title of humanity to life, liberty, and the pursuit*
> *of happiness is conceded to be inalienable to all; not till then is woman's*
> *lesson taught and woman's cause won — not the white woman's, nor the black*

*woman's, nor the red woman's, but the cause of every man and of every
woman who writhed silently under a mighty wrong.* Woman's wrongs are
thus indissolubly linked with all undefended woe, and the acquirement
of her "rights" will mean the final triumph of all right over might, the
supremacy of the moral forces of reason, and justice, and love in the
government of the nations of the earth.[7]

I include this lengthy quote for two reasons. First, it illustrates the fact that
Anglo women like Margaret Fuller and Elizabeth Cady Stanton were not the
only women in the nineteenth century thinking, writing, and strategizing on
behalf of women. Anna Julia Cooper is one of a number of African-American
women to travel the breadth of this country sowing the vision of "a grand
highway for humanity." Secondly, and more important, this lengthy quote by a
nineteenth century "race woman" should dispel the widespread assumption by
many that African-American women scholars have no intellectual heritage.
That simply is not so. The thinking and scholarship of twentieth-century African-American women are not *de novo*, a new thing on the earth. Therefore,
while our numbers may be few, our participation in certain realms of discourse
is recent, our demands are ancient. The point here is that a womanist perspective that takes as its departure a critique of all rationalizations for domination and exploitation both within the Bible and in scholarship comes from a
long and venerable line of African-American womanist philosophical thought.

An African-American womanist perspective calls for broader scope to the
feminist hermeneutical critique. It is simply not enough to treat sexism in the
biblical canon as paradigmatic or deserving alone of critical examination and
challenge. All insinuations in the canon of oppression and repression deserve
our critique and attention. Wherever one segment of biblical society presumed
theological legitimation for silencing, supplanting, or destroying another segment should sound an alert to our research. The argument here is that all
structures of domination are organically related to one another, meaning that
the effectiveness of one type of domination (say, gender oppression) depends
upon the support and collaboration of other institutionalized forms of domination (e.g., ethnic, class oppression). What we discover in the canon, therefore,
is a complex skein of ideological domination that evolved over a long period of
time undergirded and rationalized by an equally complex theological structure
that evolved over an equally long period of time.[8] Moreover, the Bible is a
thoroughly political document, both because of its adjudicating status in our
social world and because it reflects a long history of political decisions made
about interpretation, transmission, re-interpretation, and canonization. Issues
about who speaks and who is silenced; whose voice is authoritative and whose
is not; who belongs to the community of faith and who does not; who is empowered and who is disenfranchised; whose manuscript or scroll is preserved and
whose destroyed — these issues constitute the historical background of much of
religious literature. Therefore, whose voice the scholar-interpreter "hears,"
recovers, probes, scrutinizes and interprets within the Bible is also a decision

about whose voices are not heard. An insistence upon critiquing the widespread ideology of domination embedded in the canon is perhaps owing to the very different understanding and experience of oppression on the part of African-American and Anglo-American women.[9] Victimized by multiple categories of oppression (e.g., race, gender, class) and having experienced these victimizations oftentimes simultaneously, women of color bring to biblical academic discourse a broader, and more subtle, understanding of systems of oppression.[10]

To move to the personal, I am a product of the historical-critical method. Having been raised in a very conservative religious background, when I entered seminary I found the historical-critical method immensely liberating. Though I had always questioned many of the Bible's absolutes, until then I had had no framework for pursuing the issues I intellectually resisted. Moreover, as a woman without a religious voice, feminist theology succeeded in providing me a framework for understanding and analyzing gender oppression. Feminist biblical hermeneutics, like all liberationist perspectives, and even the historical-critical method, may be said to approach the Bible from the perspective of a hermeneutics of suspicion. That is, both question the present formulations of biblical texts and the self-understanding of their authors. Both argue, foremost, that the biblical world, and, hence, the texts which arose out of it, are prejudiced in favor of a certain way of perceiving and articulating reality, and that that way of perceiving and articulating reality differs in very important ways from modern thinking. And to the extent that the Bible insists that the reader consents first to its mode of perceiving reality in order to grasp its claims, both approaches resist in different ways, in varying degrees, the biblical mindset. Nonetheless, as an emerging biblical scholar I remained unsatisfied with the results of both approaches. That is because I am also an African-American, and as such I have sought an approach that attempts to address the ideological complexity of social reality, one that attempts to critique all systems of domination and exploitation wherever they exist in light of each person's right to achieve her or his full humanity.

By seeking to challenge all oppressive structures of domination and exploitation manifested in the biblical canon, what womanist scholars are calling for strikes at the very foundation of the biblical message. It may very well pose the most serious threat to neoorthodox biblical scholarship. For what functions as the cornerstone of the Bible's authority is not only its claim to a divinely guided history (which historical criticism challenges), nor is it simply its claim to a patriarchal value-system which is sanctioned by a patriarchal deity (which feminist theology rightly criticizes). Rather, the Bible's renown is grounded in large part in the claim of Israel's (and later the church's) election. Hence, to identify the biblical world as patriarchal (or parochial, for that matter) is only to talk about symptoms. Feminists, womanists, and liberationists who have been excluded from Judeo-Christian theological discourse and structures must begin their work with an analysis of the biblical worldview, specifically its claim to be unique, different, and elect.

According to the biblical authors, Israel's election was very particular: it was conferred upon a particular person, in this case a man named Abraham; it encompassed a particular people, in this case his ethnic progeny who would be known as the Israelite people; and it included particular promises of a material sort, namely a homeland (the land of Israel), divine intervention on behalf of Israel, and prosperity (which were understood as confirmation of the blessing and favor of the deity). Thus, that the deity chose of all the peoples of the earth a particular people to express in a particular manner divine favor is axiomatic for the biblical message. Invariably, the way Israel understood the particularity of that election, that is its peculiar relationship to its god, would influence the way Israel viewed reality, constituted itself, ordered society, shaped social and political institutions, narrated history, and reacted to its environment. In other words, Israel's theological understanding of itself became the ideological incentive and justification for various social and religious decisions and assorted political and economic campaigns throughout biblical history.[11] Some of that conduct, defined in liberation circles as patriarchal and oppressive, took the form of sexual discrimination, ethnic discrimination, religious repression, territorial expansionism, and economic exploitation. Therefore, any critique that aims to challenge the theological and cultural assumptions and biases of the biblical mindset must begin with an analysis of what it means and meant for Israel to claim to be elected.[12] (It is a precept of ancient Israel which at first the early church challenged, only in turn to appropriate for itself.) The premise here is simple: until criticism takes seriously the biblical peoples' pervasive belief in their election and their understanding of what it meant to be elected ("the people of God"), then we have not begun to resist the ideological foundation of the patriarchal world order, its ordering of society and its view of a select few in society in relation to the cosmos and the rest of the world. If, indeed, patriarchy is described as a system of exploitation wherein "a few men have power over other men, women, children, slaves, and colonialized people," then we cannot afford to limit our examinations to, say, gender oppression alone.[13] As the victims of "a simultaneity of oppression," the question women of color must continuously pose of the dominant scholarship, and of our own scholarship, is whether any one analysis — gender, class, racial/ethnic — is sufficiently comprehensive to do justice to the complexity of patriarchy. I think not.

Fortunately the Bible has canonized within itself some of its own most ardent critics. For example, the book of Amos is a model dissenting voice to what appears to have been the prevailing way of thinking about Israel's divine election. The intense social justice emphases of the book of Amos are frequently noted.[14] More attention, however, should be given to the manner in which the prophet sternly criticizes Israel's election traditions, or more accurately, the manner in which the prophet criticizes the hegemonic interpretation of what it meant to be God's elect people.[15] To this rural prophet who was outside the dominant interpretative circle, Israel's election did not give it special priority over others.

"Are you not like the Ethiopians to me, O people of Israel?" says the
Lord. "Did I not bring up Israel from the land of Egypt and the Philistines
from Caphtor and the Syrians from Kir?" (9:7)

Nor, according to Amos, did God's covenant with Israel absolve Israel from the
responsibility to "establish justice in [her] own gates."[16] To Amos, election did
not mean preference. It certainly did not mean that Israel's every social, political or religious impulse and formulation automatically found favor with God.
Evidently, whatever it meant to be elected by God, argues Amos, brought with
it grave responsibility for the wholeness of society. The prophecy of Amos is
one of a number of voices in the canon that counters those cultural structures
in ancient Israel designed to legitimate and defend the systematic exploitation
of the powerless. These counter-cultural voices, however oblique they may be,
deserve our attention.

Finally, from a womanist point of view, scholarship that liberates is scholarship that helps to expose the dominating cultural structures and attitudes
embedded in literature—be that literature religious or secular. Scholarship that
liberates also exposes the cultural biases of our own modern analyses and formulation. This is redemptive work. Biblical scholarship, therefore, is as much
an act of faith as it is a feat of learning. It reminds us not to place our confidence
in texts which may or may not present a scientifically reliable picture of the
world, which may or may not speak on our behalf. Rather our faith should
remain grounded in the history of our faith as, in this case, women of color,
women (and men) who "writhe silently under a mighty wrong," and who in the
face of unimaginable obstacles, both within the Bible and outside of it, continue
to search for something available in this canon(s)—something hidden, something familiar, but something eternal—that will inspire us to fight on and sing
a new-*er* song. It is our stubborn faith that even our small, uncelebrated, but
persistent acts of hermeneutical insubordination will eventually topple kingdoms.

NOTES

1. This chapter represents a substantially edited version of a paper delivered at the
"Gender, Race, and Class: Implications for Reading Religious Texts" conference held
in May 1989 at Princeton Theological Seminary. For a fuller, more developed formulation
of the author's thinking on African-American women's hermeneutical strategies, see
"Reading *Her* Way Through The Struggle: African-American Women and the Bible," in
Stony The Road We Trod: African American Hermeneutics, ed. Cain H. Felder (Minneapolis: Fortress, 1991).

2. Elisabeth Schüssler Fiorenza, *Bread Not Stone: The Challenge of Feminist Biblical
Interpretation* (Boston: Beacon Press, 1984), p. 142.

3. For the different taxonomies of feminist biblical perspectives, see Mary Ann
Tolbert, "Defining the Problem: The Bible and Feminist Hermeneutics," *Semeia* 28
(1983), 113-26; Carolyn Osiek, "The Feminist and the Bible: Hermeneutical Alterna-
tives," in *Feminist Perspectives on Biblical Scholarship*, ed. Adela Yarbro Collins (Atlanta:
Scholars Press, 1985), pp. 93-105; Katharine Sakenfeld, "Feminist Perspectives on Bible
and Theology," *Interpretation* 42(1), 1988: 5-18.

4. For a sampling of the range of our scholarship in the theological field, see: Katie G. Cannon, "The Emergence of Black Feminist Consciousness," in Letty M. Dussell, ed., *Feminist Interpretation of the Bible* (Philadelphia: Westminster Press, 1985), pp. 30-40; "Hitting a Straight Lick with a Crooked Stick: The Womanist Dilemma in the Development of a Black Liberation Ethic," *The Annual of the Society of Christian Ethics* (1987), 165-177; Cheryl T. Gilkes, "Roundtable: On Feminist Methodology," *JFSR* 1 (Fall, 1985): 80-83; "The Roles of Church and Community Mothers: Ambivalent American Sexism or Fragmented African Familyhood?" *JFSR* 2 (Spring, 1986): 41-60; Jacquelyn Grant, *White Women's Christ and Black Women's Jesus* (Atlanta: Scholars Press, 1989); "Womanist Theology: Black Women's Experience as a Source for Doing Theology, with Special Reference to Christology," *The Journal of the Interdenominational Theological Center* (Spring, 1986), 195-212; Renita J. Weems, "Roundtable: A Vision of Feminist Religious Scholarship," *JFSR* 3 (Spring, 1987): 105-107; "Roundtable: Critical Response to *Daughters of Jefferson, Daughters of Bootblacks*," *JFSR* 4 (Spring, 1988); Delores Williams, "Women's Oppression and Life-Line Politics in Black Women's Religious Narratives," *JFSR* 1 (Fall, 1985): 59-72; "Womanist Theology: Black Women's Voices," *Christianity and Crisis* (March 2, 1987), 66-70; for an excellent opportunity to "listen in" on a dialogue by African-American, Latina, Asian, and Anglo-American women around theological education, praxis, and the memories that threaten to keep us separated, see the collaborative effort of The Mudflower Collective, *God's Fierce Whimsy: Christian Feminism and Theological Education* (New York: The Pilgrim Press, 1985).

5. The term is slowly beginning to find currency within African-American women's scholarship. This suggests that African-American women perceive, whether correctly or incorrectly, that what they are calling for and calling attention to is sufficiently different from what others are calling for and calling attention to the fact that a different name (say, from "feminists"), one of their own choosing, is warranted.

6. *In Search of Our Mothers' Gardens: Womanist Prose* (New York: Harcourt Brace Jovanovich, 1983), p. xi.

7. This is a portion of the speech which Anna Julia Cooper delivered in 1893 in Chicago and can be found in Ms. Cooper's collection of essays, *Anna Julia Cooper: A Voice From the South* (Washington: Smithsonian Institution Press, 1981 [reprint]). Emphasis added.

8. That is, the Bible is a compilation of materials that accrued over a thousand-year period; and while it is capable of providing important illumination as to how patriarchy spread and flourished within a certain geographic region, it does not provide any information about the origins of patriarchy. Therefore, from a phenomenological point of view the Bible becomes an important case study of the interrelationship between patriarchy as a cultural phenomenon and "election" as a theological justification. For a discussion of this problem, see Judith Plaskow, "Blaming the Jews for the Birth of Patriarchy," in *Nice Jewish Girls: A Lesbian Anthology*, ed. E.T. Beck (Watertown, MA: Persephone Press, 1982), pp. 250-54.

9. For a discussion of why Anglo- and African-American women identify with different female stories in the Bible, see "Do You See What I See? Diversity in Interpretation," *Church and Society* 81 (September/October, 1991).

10. Our collective insights into oppression are broadened as feminist scholars from other cultural vantage points critique both the Bible and modern scholarship. See the works, for example, of Ada Maria Isasi-Díaz who is the first to my knowledge to use the expression "mujerista theology" in "The Bible and Mujerista Theology," in Susan Brooks Thistlethwaite and Mary Potter Engel, eds., *Lift Every Voice: Constructing Christian Theologies from the Underside* (San Francisco: Harper & Row, 1990), pp. 261-69 and the discussion of mujerista theology in *Journal of Feminist Studies in Religion* 8(1): 1992; and Kwok Pui-Lan, "Racism and Ethnocentrism in Feminist Interpretation," in *Searching The Scriptures* (working title), ed. by Elisabeth Schüssler Fiorenza (forthcoming).

11. Of course, the line of influence could very well be the reverse: Israel's ideological ambitions gave rise to its theological rationalizations.

12. I am well aware that any discussion about and challenge of the ancient Israelite

understanding of election by an African-American woman can be a very sensitive task in light of the oftentimes precarious state of Jewish-Christian, Jewish-Black, and Jewish-Arab-African relations in the modern period. Nevertheless, to the extent that we can do so, I hope that we can distinguish between the two different, though admittedly not necessarily unrelated discourses, modern race and ethnic relations and biblical hermeneutics.

13. For example, how do we appropriate into a liberation approach to the Bible the wholesale annihilation—in the name of God—of a whole group of people, such as the Canaanites by the newly emancipated Israel? How do we appropriate the anti-Semitic overtones of the New Testament into our liberationist outlook? These are the kinds of questions that also and equally occupy women of color as they contemplate the aims of hermeneutics.

14. See, e.g., Amos 2:6-8; 4:1; 5:7, 10-15, 21-24; 6:4-7; 8:4-6.

15. The relationship of Israelite prophets to Israelite traditions is, of course, a major area of debate in Old Testament studies. For an insightful discussion of the relationship of the prophet Amos to Israel's election traditions (e.g., Mosaic-Exodus, David-Zion traditions), see John J. Collins, "History and Tradition in the Prophet Amos," *Irish Theological Quarterly* 41 (1974): 120-133.

16. Cf. Amos 5:15.

17

WOMANIST INTERPRETATIONS OF THE NEW TESTAMENT: THE QUEST FOR HOLISTIC AND INCLUSIVE TRANSLATION AND INTERPRETATION

Clarice J. Martin

The subject of "womanist biblical interpretation" has come to the fore in recent years in conjunction with the growing body of literature on "womanist theology" in general. The term *womanist* was coined by Alice Walker in her book *In Search of Our Mothers' Gardens.* Describing the courageous, audacious, and "in charge" behavior of the black woman, the term *womanist* affirms black women's connection with both feminism and with the history, culture, and religion of the African-American community. Womanist literature represents the ongoing academic work of womanist scholars: in a variety of disciplines, including theology, ethics, sociology, and biblical studies.[1]

One discipline where womanist theological reflection is especially welcome is biblical studies. What concerns do womanist biblical interpreters bring to the translation and interpretation of the Bible? How does their interrogation of the text differ from that of their white feminist colleagues? These questions will be explored in this essay in preliminary fashion. Not meant to be an *ultimum verbum* (the last word) for all womanist biblical scholars, but only a *primum verbum* (first word) by one, it highlights some of the critical and methodological concerns and overarching interests of womanist biblical interpreters.

If, as theologian Delores Williams notes, womanist theologians bring black women's social, religious, and cultural experience into the discourse of theology, ethics, and religious studies,[2] they also bring black women's social, religious,

Clarice J. Martin is associate professor of New Testament at Colgate Rochester Divinity School/Bexley Hall/Crozer Theological Seminary, Rochester, New York. She is also the author of *Tongues of Fire: Power for the Church Today* (1990). This essay was published in the *Journal of Feminist Studies in Religion* 6, no. 2 (1990) and is reprinted with permission.

and cultural experience and consciousness into the discourse of biblical studies. Thus, African-American women's historical struggles against racial and gender oppression, as well as against the variegated experiences of classism, all comprise constitutive elements in their conceptual and interpretive horizon and hermeneutics, for experiences of oppression, like all human experience, affect the way in which women and men code and decode sacred and secular reality.[3]

In addition to importing gender, race, and class concerns to the task of biblical interpretation, womanist theologians have addressed the issue of linguistic sexism with increasing urgency.[4] Womanist biblical interpretation, then, has a "quadruocentric" interest ("four-fold," from the Latin *quadru,* meaning "four") where gender, race, class, and language issues are all at the forefront of translation (the science of expressing the original meaning as accurately as possible) and interpretation (the process of bringing together the ancient canonical texts with new, changing situations) concerns,[5] and not just a threefold focus, where gender, class, and language concerns predominate almost exclusively, as is often the case in white feminist biblical interpretation and translation.

In this essay I will examine the ways in which womanist concerns about the translation and interpretation of biblical terminology are focused. I will also examine the ways in which presuppositions about the significance of class in biblical narrative have been operative in contemporary biblical interpretation.

Doulos, doulē: "Servant" or "Slave"?

The tremendous proliferation of literature on inclusive language in ecclesial and academic discourse in recent decades[6] has reawakened our interest in the complexities of the translation of biblical terminology. Assessing the appropriate meaning of a particular Hebrew or Greek term, and rendering it with some fidelity in English, remains a thorny problem for interpreters. For example, the King James Version of the Bible describes Jesus and his disciples as walking "through the corn" in Matt. 12:1. As they walked, they began to "pluck the ears of corn and to eat." The twentieth-century student of the Bible may be tempted to imagine the itinerant group "strolling through a cornfield, stripping off a ripening cob, pulling back the husk and silk, to nibble on the tender kernels."[7] But in fact, the Greek term for "corn," *stachys,* should probably be rendered "grain," as it is in the Revised Standard Version of the Bible (the RSV uses the phrases "grainfields" and "heads of grain" respectively in Matt. 12:1). "Grain" in biblical usage is a generic term used to indicate the seed of cultivated cereal grasses such as wheat, barley, millet and sorghum (these grains were ground into flour as a major component of bread products—compare Deut. 33:28 in the KJV and the RSV).[8]

One of the more debated translation issues is the translation of the Greek term *anthrōpos.* Translators have regularly rendered *anthrōpos* as "man," concealing women or rendering them invisible under a blanket of male linguistic hegemony. Like blacks who must constantly "imagine" themselves as represented in so-called generic representations of Americans by all white groupings (whether on television or in other media), women must constantly "imagine" themselves as represented in so-called generic representations of all humanity in biblical traditions that are punctured by the almost exclusive usage of male-gendered pronouns. The real point, of course, is that *anthrōpos* does not always mean "man" or "men." As has been amply demonstrated (and as some common sense would dictate), *anthrōpos* does have a more generic meaning. It can mean "human, person, people, or humanity."[9] The Oxford Annotated RSV does grant this sense in the translation of Rom. 2:9: "There will be tribulation and distress for every human being who does evil. ...." According to the *Greek-English Lexicon of the New Testament*, *anthrōpos* also has a generic meaning in Matt. 5:13, but the RSV translates the term as "man" when it records the familiar words:

> You are salt of the earth; but if the salt has lost its taste, how shall its saltiness be restored? It is no longer good for anything except to be thrown out and trodden under foot by *men*. (Italics mine)

Surely the more generic usage of *anthrōpos* is indicated and appropriate in the Oxford Annotated Bible for such texts as the Matt. 5:13 pericope, as well as for such texts as Titus 2: "the grace of God has appeared for the salvation of all *men*"; the text in 1 Tim. 2:4, which says: "God desires all then to be saved"; and 1 Tim. 4:10: "we have our hope set on the living God who is the Savior of all *men*, especially of those who believe." Nancy Hardesty hits the mark when she says of the androcentric rendering of *anthrōpos* in these and other verses in the RSV, that the God described in those passages "does not offer much hope for me as a woman!"[10] The problem with these texts is that the translation of *anthrōpos* in these examples does not render in English what the Greek texts intend.

The task of faithfully rendering biblical terminology in English and assessing its ideological import and sociopolitical impact on communities of women and men is a major concern to womanist biblical interpreters. This is particularly the case with the Greek term *doulos*, usually translated "slave." As I have pursued my own research and study of the New Testament over the years, I have been asked frequently if *doulos* should be rendered "slave" or "servant" in modern translations of the Bible. The post-sixties era, with the rise of liberation theologies, and the recognition of how one's social location affects the interpretive task, has sharpened the question of how people of color and women "hear" certain texts, and with this comes some concern about whether the term *slave* is in some sense "offensive" to the African-American reader, given our "involuntary" participation in our nation's legacy of slavery. Does it recall an image that is painfully reminiscent of that legacy? Is the use of the term *infra dignitatem* (beneath one's dignity)? Would it not be better, people ask, to translate *doulos* regularly as the more euphemistic "servant"? This writer personally responds with a resounding No! for at least two reasons.

First, *doulos* in Greco-Roman parlance *is* generally translated as "slave." Arndt and Gingrich note that the use of "servant" for "slave" is largely confined to biblical translation and early American times.[11] *Doulos* and its cognates describe the "status of a slave" or "an attitude corresponding to a slave."[12] For slaves, the rendering of service is not a matter of choice—they must perform whether they like it or not because they are subject to an alien will, the will of the owner. Human autonomy is set aside and an alien will takes complete precedence over one's own.[13] The word *servant* usually suggests an element of voluntary submission. The *American Heritage Dictionary* has a threefold definition of a servant:

1. Someone privately employed to perform domestic services. 2. Someone publicly employed to perform services, as for a government. 3. Someone expressing submission, recognizance, or debt to another: your obedient servant.[14]

That the condition of the slave was usually not "voluntary" is clear from the definition of *slave* in the same dictionary:

1. One bound in servitude to a person or household as an instrument of labor. 2. One who is submissive or subject to a specified person or influence. 3. One whose condition is likened to that of slavery. 4. A machine or component that is controlled by another machine or component.[15]

A widescale translation of *doulos* as "servant" would promote an unrealistic and naively "euphemistic" understanding of slavery. First of all, "servant" is a euphemism. In their book, *Kind Words: A Thesaurus of Euphemisms,* Judith S. Neaman and Carole G. Silver note that the word *euphemism* comes from the Greek *eu,* "good," and *pheme,* "speech" or "saying," and thus means literally "to speak with good words or in a pleasant manner." Thus, "euphemizing is generally defined as substituting an inoffensive or pleasant term for a more explicit, offensive one, thereby veneering the truth by using kind words."[16] According to Joseph M. Williams, euphemisms are formed when unpleasant elements of response attach themselves strongly to particular words. One then substitutes another word free of negative associations.[17] Euphemisms can be formed by borrowing words from other languages. For example, we may use the word *halitosis* for "bad breath." Euphemisms may also be formed by a process called "widening," where a more abstract word is substituted for a term that has become too painful or vivid—"we move up the ladder of abstraction." An example of "widening" is seen in the renaming of *cancer* as a "growth."[18]

In actuality, "servant" is a euphemism for "slave," a point confirmed by Hugh Rawson in his book, *A Dictionary of Euphemisms and Other Doubletalk.*[19] According to Rawson, "servant" was a euphemism in colonial America that went out of fashion in the early nineteenth century because white servants, who weren't actual slaves, refused to accept the same label as black "servants," who were in fact slaves. ("Servant" had been widely used for black slaves for some time — even though they were "slaves," and the terms "servant" and "black" had become fairly synonymous.) In an essay published in *The History Book Club News* in 1775, it was noted that William Penn (1644–1718) was a slaveholder, "but he used the less pejorative term 'servant' instead of slave."[20] Euphemistic translations of *doulos* should be eschewed, then, because they do not always convey fully the etymological sense of the term. *In the final analysis, every single occurrence of doulos in the New Testament must be examined within its particular literary and sociohistorical context to determine the author's intention in the use of the term, including any nuance which should be assigned to it.*

A second and related problem with "servant" is that it minimizes the full psychosocial weight of the institution of slavery itself. I have always been troubled by exegetical arguments and interpretations of slave existence in the Common Era that suggest that ancient slavery was only a sporadically stressful interruption in an otherwise "quite normal" existence.

In his book *The Social Context of the New Testament,* Derek Tidball says the following about Paul's posture toward slavery:

In the first place, the institution of slavery was such an integral part of the social fabric in Paul's day that it would have been difficult for Paul or others to conceive of social organization without it . . . by the time of Paul it was not a severe and cruel institution. Of course there were exceptions . . . but the experience of most slaves was different. *In Carcopino's memorable phrase, "with few exceptions slavery in Rome was neither eternal, nor, while it lasted, intolerable. . . ."* There was no widespread discontent about slavery. So, to the early church the question of the abolition of slavery was probably insignificant. . . . What Paul offers to Christian slaves is a totally new appreciation of their value as persons. They are no longer "things" but people who have a standing and status before God (1 Cor. 7:20). In Christ the slave is a free man. . . . If only, Paul argues, they grasp this greater fact, slavery becomes inconsequential. *A slave can remain happily a slave and still serve the Lord in spite of his social limitations.* (Italics mine)[21]

In order to adequately address Tidball's idyllic notion of the "happy slave" in the first century of the Common Era it is necessary and appropriate to document the fact that the institution of slavery was not, in fact, as innocuous as he wants to portray it. Such a task is easily undertaken, and there is no dearth of literature on the subject.[22] While a full-scale discussion of Greco-Roman slavery is not possible here, I would make a few brief observations about Greco-Roman slavery pertinent to the present discussion.

First, that slavery was an integral part of the social fabric of Paul's day is not in dispute, but the thesis that it was not a "severe and cruel institution" has been challenged in recent years. In *Slaves and Masters in the Roman Empire,* K. R. Bradley argues that while harmonious relationships may have existed between masters and slaves, one must be cautious in concluding that such intimacy was necessarily characteristic of the master-slave relationship. While "simple, constant animosity between slave and slave master is too naive a concept to have had universal applicability or meaning," the less human side of Roman slavery should not be romanticized:

> But although the harmonious relations attested between some slaves and their masters should not be lost sight of, they were not in all likelihood characteristic of the Roman slave system as a whole ... the essential brutality of the slave experience in the Roman world and especially the kind of harsh pressures to which slaves were constantly exposed as a normal part of their everyday lives ... must be understood ... it is vital to understand something of the less elevated, less humane side of Roman social relations, of which the depressed conditions under which most slaves lived provide abundant illustration.[23]

Roman slave owners may have treated their slaves generously, but generosity alone did not, in Bradley's words, "secure the elite ideal of servile *fides* and *obsequium* that is to guarantee social stability. ... Generosity had to be tempered with either force or the threat of force in order for control to be maintained, and a climate of fear over those of subordinate social position had to be created ... 'fear in the slaves produced greater loyalty,' so it was said." Slaves were subjected to a number of indignities: capricious sexual abuse (slaves could be used as or sold for prostitutes, and they could be sexually exploited for as long as the master wished); flogging was a "widespread" punishment for which little justification was required; agricultural and mining slaves, domestic slaves and children were all subject to the same violence: "servile distinctions of status, function, age or sex gave no protection against arbitrary punishment."[24]

Second, even if some slaves in Greco-Roman society were treated with less severity than others, and could, indeed, become freedmen or freedwomen, psychosocial aspects of the institution itself were less than salutary. In his book *Slavery and Social Death,* Orlando Patterson analyzes the structure and dynamics of slavery based on a study of tribal, ancient, premodern, and modern slavery in sixty-six societies (including Greece, Rome, medieval Europe, China, Korea, the Islamic kingdoms, Africa, the Caribbean islands, and the American South).[25] He describes three constituent elements of slavery that typify master-slave relationships in all of these societies. Patterson argues that in anatomies of power in human relationships of inequality or domination, slavery is distinctive as a relation of domination in three ways.

1. Slavery is unusual in the extremity of power involved. That the master exercised total domination over the slave was normative, and a constituent feature of the relationship was the use of some forms of coercion. Force, violence and might both maintained and perpetuated slavery. When slaves were manumitted or died, it became necessary to "repeat the original, violent act of

transforming the free man into slave. . . . Whipping was not only a method of punishment. It was a conscious device to impress upon the slaves that they were slaves; it was a crucial form of social control particularly if we remember that it was very difficult for slaves to run away successfully."[26]

2. The slave relation is characterized by what Patterson calls the slave's "natal alienation." The slave, however recruited, is a socially dead person. "Alienated from all 'rights' or claims of birth, he ceased to belong in his own right to any legitimate social order. All slaves experienced, at the very least, secular excommunication."[27]

Slaves were "genealogical isolates." They had a past, but

> they were not allowed freely to integrate the experience of their ancestors into their lives, to inform their understanding of social reality with the inherited meanings of their natural forebears, or to anchor the living present in any conscious community of memory. That they reached back for the past, as they reached out for the related living, there can be no doubt. Unlike other persons, doing so meant struggling with and penetrating the iron curtain of the master, his community, his laws, his policemen or patrollers, and his heritage.[28]

The slave may have necessarily reached out to the "related living," but even the slave's own community and social relations were not usually recognized as legitimate and binding (marriages, removal of children, etc.).[29]

3. Slaves were persons who had been dishonored in a general way—their status held no honor; indignity, indebtedness, and the absence of all independent social existence reinforced the sense of dishonor. The slave was without power except through another; she or he had become "imprintable" and "disposable," the "ultimate human tool."[30]

But after admitting that slavery in Greco-Roman antiquity was more often attended by physical brutality, sexual exploitation, and emotional dehumanization than some care to think, the next question is: What are the implications of these data for our understanding of the New Testament (particularly references to slaves in such texts as Paul's letter to Philemon and allusions to slaves in the sayings of Jesus and in the *Haustafeln* [household codes])? I would argue that it is only as we move beyond euphemistic understandings of slavery in the lives of women and men in the Common Era that we can grasp some of the power of the biblical traditions that allude to slaves.

If Patterson is correct in his analysis of these three constitutive elements of slavery, then it is interesting to reread such passages as the christological hymn in Phil. 2:7 and note the force of the comparison being made with the *doulos:*

> Have this in mind among yourselves which was also in Christ Jesus, who though he was in the form of God, did not count equality with God a thing to be grasped, but emptied himself, taking the form of a *doulou,* being born in the likeness of man.

The *morphēn doulon* acquires its significance from the contrast with *morphē theou,* and it denotes Jesus' entry into humanity. But it is the particular "class" of humanity that sharpens the comparison here. The power and glory with which Jesus was invested is compared to that of one who was utterly powerless, for "there is no term which stands in greater contrast to *kyrios* or *theos* than *doulos.*"[31]

It is also interesting to note that the "slave" becomes a paradigm for discipleship elsewhere. Jesus himself washes the feet of the disciples—a task that was the duty of slaves (Jn. 13:1ff.).[32] Christians are often called the *douloi* of God and Christ (James 1:1; Titus 1:1; Col. 4:12). The significance of the *doulos* symbol of powerlessness, bondage, and limitation on the one hand, and as paradigm for discipleship on the other, should not be trivialized.

The importance of the comparison of Jesus with the *doulos* in Phil. 2:7 has also been noted by womanist theologian Sheila Briggs. Observing correctly that Phil. 2:7b is neither *about* slavery, nor does it attribute cosmic or soteriological significance to the institution of slavery through its description of Christ taking on the condition of a slave, she avers, nonetheless, that the metaphor is significant. The significance of portraying Christ as a slave derives both from a loss of status and also from the degradation of being a slave.

> This sense of degradation is heightened by the assertion that it is a divine being who has become a slave, that the two opposites in the realm of being and worth have met in one person and one fate.... The Philippians hymn conveys the extremity of the self-abasement of Christ by placing it in the metaphor of the enslavement of God. Christ as divine was absolutely too worthy to be enslaved.[33]

Christ does not take on the so-called moral inferiority of the slave, nor does Phil. 2:7b suggest Christ has a "morally defective" nature; rather, "Christ's obedience in his earthly existence makes him the anthropological model of the 'slaves of righteousness' (Rom. 6:16–18) who are characterized through their obedience to God."[34]

A realistic understanding of the complexities of the conceptual universe of slavery in Greco-Roman antiquity, then, is of central importance in assessing the propriety of adopting a more euphemistic translation of *doulos* in biblical translation. An etymologically faithful reading of *doulos* is preferred to the more euphemistic reading, even if the motive for the euphemistic reading is purportedly conciliatory.

Amplifying Marginalized Voices

A survey of the aims and methodologies of feminist translation and interpretation in the last decade reveals their plurality and complexity. And yet, among the many overarching themes there is, as Elisabeth Schüssler Fiorenza has said, a commitment to a "search for the lost traditions and visions of liberation among its inheritance of androcentric texts and their interpretations."[35] To this end, a feminist critique and hermeneutic must engage in a multipronged investigative analysis:

> In order to unearth a "feminist coin" from the biblical tradition it [feminist critical interpretation] critically analyzes contemporary scholarly and popular interpretations, the tendencies of the biblical writers and traditioning processes themselves, and the theoretical models underlying contemporary biblical-historical and theological interpretations.[36]

Such critical analysis will help us achieve what Jane Schaberg considers a constitutive dimension of feminist translation: "Feminist translation . . . must amplify the whisper of women that can be heard in certain places in or under the biblical text, that 'steady undercurrent in the oral tradition' of anonymous voices."[37]

Womanist biblical interpreters share with their white feminist colleagues a concern for amplifying the voices of women in biblical narrative. A recent study of women's relationships in the Bible by womanist biblical scholar Renita Weems achieves precisely this aim.[38] But for the womanist biblical interpreter, fervid, if painstaking, searches for women's voices must proceed not only with reference to women in biblical narratives, but also with a concomitant concern for all of those who by virtue of *race, class,* or other *anthropological referents,* have been historically marginalized by the biblical traditions and/or writers themselves, and by interpreters of those traditions. *Not all of the suppressed voices in androcentric texts can be intoned in a feminine key.*

Definitions of *patriarchy* in white feminist literature usually emphasize the transactions of power between men and women. In her helpful discussion of strategies for "depatriarchalizing" biblical texts, Phyllis Trible's discussion of patriarchy is concerned chiefly with that aspect of patriarchal domination centered on male-female relationships.[39] Mary Daly alludes to patriarchal institutions as institutions that "serve the interests of men at the expense of women."[40] Rosemary Ruether's analysis of patriarchy in *Women-Church: Theology and Practice of Feminist Liturgical Communities* explores male control and restrictions of women in the Hebrew Bible and the New Testament.[41] In secular feminist discourse, this preeminent focus on women's experiences of domination under patriarchy is retained. Adrienne Rich conveys this sense in her discussion of patriarchy, where she describes it as

> the power of the fathers: a familial-social, ideological, political system in which men—by force, direct pressure, or through ritual, tradition, law and language, customs, etiquette, education, and division of labor, determine what part women shall or shall not play, and in which the female is everywhere subsumed under the male.[42]

The critical exploration of predicaments posed by patriarchy in all human societies, ancient and modern, vis-à-vis *women,* is essential in any responsible feminist critique. But in fact, patriarchal domination did not—and does not—represent male domination of the female and the "feminine" only. Patriarchal oppression and degradation includes and transcends the category of gender. While many white feminist biblical interpreters would affirm this fact, their critiques of patriarchy are concerned preeminently with the oppression and marginalization of women.

In the patriarchal hierarchies of biblical antiquity, the dominant male-master figure was supreme in rank, with wife, children, and slaves as subordinates.[43] Elisabeth Schüssler Fiorenza's definition of patriarchy incorporates all of these elements succinctly.

> While androcentrism characterized a mind-set, patriarchy represents a socio-cultural system in which *a few men have power over other men, women, children, slaves, and colonized people.* (Italics mine)[44]

For the womanist theologian and biblical interpreter whose experience of oppression include the intrinsically linked aspects of gender, race, and class, critical analyses of patriarchal assumptions and paradigms in both the ancient and modern worlds must include a focus on *all* historically marginalized persons, women and men, who have been victimized by patriarchal dominance.[45] Womanist ethicist Toinette Eugene has noted that for the womanist and other non-white interpreters, it is not the issue of sexism alone that informs a critical womanist hermeneutics.[46] Thus, all ideologies of dominance and subordination in the biblical writers, the traditioning processes, and in the theoretical models underlying contemporary biblical historical and theological interpretations are *at once* invoked as constitutive of any womanist liberation hermeneutic.

> Patriarchal oppression is not simply identical with androcentrism or sexism, and thus unconnected to other oppressive ideologies. Patriarchy defines not just women, but also subjugated peoples and races as "the others" to be dominated.[47]

Womanist concerns about translation and interpretation of the Bible necessarily include, then, a concomitant concern about the need to amplify the voices of *all* persons who are marginalized in the text. A more "holistic and inclusive" biblical translation requires such an emphasis.[48] A liberating anthropology is able to affirm that in Christ there is neither male nor female, but also that, "at the same time in Christ there is neither slave nor free, Jew nor Greek." Otherwise, as Justo Gonzalez notes, "The male will be quite content with concentration on the fact that there is neither slave nor free; the free—and particularly the master—will piously agree that there is neither Jew nor Greek; and the Jew—the one who has the ethnic advantage—will gladly agree that there is neither slave nor free."[49]

There are traditions about men in biblical narrative who have suffered not sexist marginality but classist or racist marginality in the traditioning processes and in the history of the interpretation of those traditions.[50] Because of the limits of this paper, I will examine only one instance of an individual in the Bible who, by virtue of his class, has suffered class bias in the history of biblical interpretation — Onesimus.[51]

I have always read with interest some biblical commentators' disparagement of Onesimus as the "n'er do well slave." This supposition is based on one interpretation of verse 18 in Paul's letter to Philemon, "If he has wronged you at all, or owes you anything, charge that to my account."

At least as early as the nineteenth century, commentators concluded that Onesimus must have been a "rascal" and a "thief." Two illustrations of this sentiment are represented in commentaries on Philemon.

J. B. Lightfoot, writing in 1875, observes the following of Onesimus:

> He had done what a chattel or an implement might be expected to do, if endued with life and intelligence. . . . He had declined to entertain any responsibilities. There was absolutely nothing to recommend him . . . *he had confirmed the popular estate of his class and nation by his own conduct.* (Italics mine)[52]

Similarly, G. B. Caird, writing in the mid-1970s, also assumes some culpability on the part of Onesimus, saying that

> he may have simply "packed up a thing or two" belonging to Philemon to provide for his journey. . . . *He certainly had not been a model servant,* but we have no reason to think that he had been a dishonest one before his flight. (Italics mine)[53]

These commentators (and others) assume that Onesimus was guilty of major and minor infractions because he was a slave. They assume that slaves are inherently morally bankrupt, though there could have been a number of reasons that Onesimus was "parted from" (v. 15) Philemon for a while. Philemon could have sent Onesimus to Paul for some particular reason, and Onesimus decided to remain with him; or, Onesimus could have run away from Philemon because of the conditions of slavery itself.[54] If the complexities of slavery in the American South should remind us of anything, it is that we should not assume *sine dubio* (without doubt) that a "Christian" slavemaster or slavemistress automatically treated slaves with "Christian" charity, kindness, and compassion.

For the womanist biblical interpreter, holistic and inclusive translations and interpretations of the Bible must avoid euphemistic renderings of biblical terminology; euphemistic translation risks "masking" socioeconomic or political verities that are of fundamental significance in assessing historical and symbolic meaning. The quest for holistic and inclusive translations and interpretations must also include strategies for "amplifying the whisper" of *all persons* who by virtue of race, class or other anthropological referents, are assumed to be "morally bankrupt" or of negligible theological consequence within the narrative structure of biblical traditions. Alice Walker's words are instructive here. A womanist is "committed to survival and wholeness of entire people, male and female."[55]

Womanist Hermeneutics and the Function of the *Doulos* Paradigm in the History of Interpretation

As noted in the introductory paragraphs of this essay, womanist biblical scholars bring *black women's* social, religious, and cultural experience and consciousness into the discourse of biblical studies, for all of these factors comprise constitutive elements in their conceptual and interpretive horizon and hermeneutics. Not surprisingly, then, womanist biblical interpreters are concerned with the critical assessment not only of the linguistic and sociohistorical nuancing and interpretation of the *doulos* texts in the Common Era, but also with the critical assessment of the function of these texts in the history of the African-American experience. The limits of this essay have made it necessary to focus primarily on some of the linguistic and sociohistorical issues at stake in the nuancing and interpretation of *doulos* in the New Testament. Questions remain, however, regarding the political implications of these data for post-biblical—and particularly contemporary—interpreters.

How have the *doulos* texts functioned in the history of biblical interpretation in both pre- and post-modern societies? Can, or should, biblical traditions that designate Christians as "slaves of God and Christ"[56] be appropriated complete as a whole? What concerns have been, and should be, registered in the face of attempts to appropriate and utilize the slave sayings in communities of faith?[57] While these questions deserve extensive comment and analysis, which is not possible here, the four following observations underscore the importance of assessing and critiquing the political impact of these texts in church and society in the Western world. These points should inform future formulations and investigations of the problem.

First, the question of how the *doulos* texts functioned to legitimate the enslavement of African Americans in North America remains an important subject of critical-historical study for biblical scholars and theologians, as well as historians, sociologists, and ethicists. That biblical traditions were so used is well attested. Describing slavery as "the most abominable institution ever to challenge Christian morality,"[58] sociologist and historian C. Eric Lincoln recounts the way in which the Bible was used to solicit the obedience of black slaves to slavemasters and slavemistresses. The quotation of Scripture to legitimate the slaves' subjugation—so it was believed—would provide the *coup de maître* (master stroke) in any apologetic for human bondage.

> Servants, be obedient to them that are your masters . . . with fear and trembling . . . as unto Christ. . . . Remember, God required this of you. . . . There is something so becoming and engaging in the modest, cheerful, good natured behavior that a little work done in that manner seems better

done. . . . It also gains the goodwill and love of those you belong to. . . . Besides . . . your murmuring and grumbling is against God who hath placed you in their service.[59]

Not only was the Bible an important tool in proslavery ideology and rhetoric in general, H. Shelton Smith has noted that in the eighteenth- and nineteenth-century South "the Southern churchman's major argument in defense of human bondage was biblical in nature."[60] Both the Hebrew Bible and the New Testament served as the *summum jus* (the highest law) in the pronouncements of apologists for slavery. Authors of proslavery tracts appealed particularly to six New Testament texts to buttress their arguments: 1 Corinthians 7:20–21; Ephesians 6:5–9; Colossians 3:33, 4:1; 1 Timothy 6:20–21; and Philemon 10–18. Stressing that since the biblical writers expected the dutiful obedience of slaves to masters, and that the slaveholders in the biblical texts were, after all, members of churches founded by Paul and other apostles, the defenders of human bondage contended that slaveholding was quite consistent with biblical teaching.[61] These six *doulos* texts were thus used in the service of a hermeneutics of domination and sociopolitical hegemony for proslavery apologists.

An eclectic use of Scripture, a tendentious biblical literalism, and a wide range of hermeneutical distortions provided a steady stream of "grist" for the slave apologists' mill. In her helpful analysis of the ways in which Christian slave apologists employed hermeneutical distortions to keep racial slavery viable in the late eighteenth and early nineteenth centuries (to preserve economic benefits and sociopolitical power), Katie G. Cannon observes that the hermeneutical distortions were designed to achieve three aims:

1. Slave apologists argued that black people were either not members of the human race, or that they were an "inferior species" of humanity at best. "The humanity of black people had to be denied, or the evil of the slave system would be evident."[62]

2. Sacred and secular history were reconstructed to perpetuate the view that Africans, "bestial savages" and "heathen," were by nature and providence destined for slavery.[63] Thus North American slavery became a divine and redemptive tool to expose Africans to Christianity.

Being enslaved in a Christian country was considered advantageous to Africans' physical, intellectual, and moral development. Slavery exposed Africans to Christianity which made them better servants of God and better servants of men.[64]

3. Most important for the present discussion, the law of God, with the law of the land, conferred upon Christian slave apologists the right to deprive black people of liberty,[65] with all of the attendant expressions of brutality and dehumanization which accompanied the sale and trafficking in the human lives of black women, men, and children. Christian theologians, biblical interpreters, and clergy regularly pressed the New Testament injunctions into service to

legitimate slavery, even as others espoused juridical, economic, and political rationales.[66] Christian slave apologists in particular argued that since "neither Jesus of Nazareth, the apostles, nor the early church objected to the ownership of slaves," slavery was not a violation of God's law: "Physical slavery was spiritually meaningless under the all-embracing spiritualized hopes of salvation. This line of reasoning was of central importance in reconciling the masses of white Christians to the existing social order."[67]

The second observation concerns the nature of the hermeneutics employed by black women and men in the face of the overwhelming oppression that they (and their families) experienced during enslavement. Analyses of how the *doulos* texts functioned to support a hermeneutics of domination and sociopolitical hegemony for proslavery apologists must be accompanied by research that will further explore and identify the particular character of the black slaves' hermeneutics in the face of their oppression.

Black slaves were always distrustful of their masters' interpretations of the Bible, and preached the Christian Gospel in terms of their own experience.[68] Understanding God to be a God of liberation who would make freedom a reality for all persons in Jesus Christ, they rejected a selectively enforced and enslaving biblical literalism[69] and brought a "hermeneutics of suspicion" to bear against prevailing arguments that the *doulos* verses should be a normative guide for their behavior. The slaves promulgated a gospel that averred that God is liberator of all oppressed peoples, and that God is opposed to all persons determined to maintain oppressive social systems. "Unlike any institutions in the larger white society, black churches have made a non-racist principle the center of their associational life."[70] Ongoing research on how a "hermeneutics of suspicion" was operative in the interpretation of the *doulos* texts will enlarge our understanding of the distinctive character, development, and contribution of African-American biblical hermeneutics.

The third observation concerns the subject of the manumission of Christian slaves. Womanist exegetes (and others) must probe the layers of biblical traditions (and noncanonical writings) to determine whether anything in those traditions suggests that there were impulses at work in the earliest Christian communities which either ameliorated slavery and (or) advocated its abolition altogether. This amelioration and (or) abolition is suggested by such Hebrew Bible texts as the Exodus motif (Exod. 1:1–16:36); and, by such New Testament texts as 1 Cor. 7:23, "You were bought with a price; do not become slaves of human persons"; Rom. 8:15, "For you did not receive the spirit of slavery to fall back into fear, but you received the spirit of sonship. . . ."; Philem. 15–17, where Paul says to Philemon regarding the slave Onesimus, "Perhaps this is why he was parted from you for a while, that you might have him back for ever, no longer as a slave but more than a slave, as a beloved brother, especially to me but how much more to you, *both in the flesh and in the Lord*" (italics mine).

There is evidence in both early Judaism and early Christianity that slaves may have been manumitted upon their conversion to the respective faiths.[71] The slave injunctions in the *Haustafeln* (household codes) which enjoin slaves and women to submission in the latter decades of the first century may suggest that the Christian vision of a more inclusive discipleship created tension and conflicts within the dominant cultural ethos of the patriarchal household.[72]

There is certainly evidence that black slaves discerned in the Bible those traditions that protect them to intensify their efforts to secure their freedom. Slavemasters often sought to prevent slaves from learning to read the Bible, for it was said that religious instruction made slaves "more intractable" and "rebellious," leading some to "entertain too high an opinion of themselves."[73] Slave narratives and spirituals betray the strong conviction and recurrent theme that Jesus Christ came to "lift the meek, the weak and the oppressed."[74]

The fourth and final observation concerns the need to engage in critical reflection about the biblical traditions and traditioning process. It is important to remember that simply creating taxonomic tables of biblical traditions that are either "proslavery" or "antislavery" will still not achieve all of the aims of a constructive womanist critical biblical hermeneutics. As noted above in the discussion of the need to amplify marginalized voices, womanist biblical interpreters also must engage in a multipronged investigative analysis and critique of the tendencies of the biblical writers and traditioning process. We should recognize, for example, that the biblical texts convey little information about the agency of slaves and manumission of slaves in the early Christian movement because these stories, like the stories of women, were considered to be either insignificant or a threat to the gradual patriarchalization of the Christian movement.[75] A womanist critical biblical hermeneutics, then, must not only critique the tendencies of the biblical writers and traditioning processes themselves, but must also analyze contemporary scholarly and popular interpretations and appropriations of those traditions, and the underlying theoretical models. But that is not the end of the story. A womanist biblical hermeneutic must clarify whether the *doulos* texts, potential "texts of terror" for black people, can in any way portend new possibilities for our understanding of what actually constitutes the radicality of the good news of the gospel:

> If art imitates life, scripture likewise reflects it in both holiness and horror. Reflections themselves neither mandate nor manufacture change; yet by enabling insight, they may inspire repentance. In other words, sad stories may yield new beginnings.[76]

In his discussion of the injunctions about women's subordination in the *Haustafeln* (the household codes, cf. Col. 3:18–4:1; Eph. 5:21–9; 1 Pet. 2:18–37), Frank Stagg makes the following observation about the need to recognize that the historically conditioned regulations enjoining male domination of women should no longer be binding:

> The preoccupation for male authority over women is pagan, anti-Gospel. It cannot be redeemed; it can only be aborted. It is a negation of the Gospel of Jesus Christ.[77]

Stagg's statement has correspondent implications for the *doulos* texts, particularly since some of these texts are located in the household codes, where slaves as well as women are enjoined to be submissive to the patriarchal head of the household. Can these *doulos* texts in the household codes and elsewhere be "redeemed" in any of their occurrences in the Pauline and non-Pauline writings? Should some of them be "aborted"? Can any of them enable new insight? Should they inspire repentance and personal and social transformation in some sense? These questions invite further critical analysis and investigation.[78]

Chipping away at oppressive structures, and identifying those texts that help black women to celebrate and rename incidents involving human unpredictability in empowering ways, is at the heart of a womanist interpretive principle.[79] Similarly, the development, nurturance and critical employment of the hermeneutics of suspicion, resistance, liberation and hope in the interpretive process remain essential components of womanist biblical interpretation. This principle, and methodological tools from this hermeneutical cache, will make the possibility of holistic, inclusive, and kerygmatically empowering biblical translation and interpretation more real for all communities of faith.

NOTES

1. Alice Walker, *In Search of Our Mothers' Gardens* (New York: Harcourt Brace Jovanovich, 1983), xi. See the works of Katie G. Cannon, *Womanist Ethics* (Ithaca: Scholars Press, 1988); Toinette M. Eugene, "Moral Values and Black Womanists," *Journal of Religious Thought* 49 (Winter-Spring 1988): 23-34; Jacquelyn Grant, "Womanist Theology: Black Women's Experience as a Source for Doing Theology, with Special Reference to Christology," *Journal of the Interdenominational Theological Center* 13, no. 2 (Spring 1986): 195-212; Renita J. Weems, *Just a Sister Away: A Womanist Vision of Women's Relationships in the Bible* (San Diego: LuraMedia, 1988); Delores S. Williams, "Womanist Theology: Black Women's Voices," *Christianity and Crisis* 47 (March 2, 1987): 66-70. For a fuller listing of womanist scholarship see the helpful essay by womanist theologian Kelly D. Brown, "God Is as Christ Does: Toward a Womanist Theology," *Journal of Religious Thought* 46, no. 1 (Summer-Fall 1989): 7-16.

2. Williams, "Womanist Theology," 67.

3. Theo Witvliet, *The Way of the Black Messiah: The Hermeneutical Challenge of Black Theology as a Theology of Liberation* (Oak Park, Ill.: Meyer Stone, 1985), 61.

4. While there is not a plethora of literature on the subject by black women, black female and male academics and clergy are adopting and promoting inclusive language usage. See Yvonne Delk, "A Call to Wholeness," in *The Word and Words Beyond Gender* in *Theological and Liturgical Language,* ed. William D. Watley (Princeton, N.J.: Consultation on Church Union, 1983), 1-5; Angelique Walker-Smith, "Exclusive Language Reflects Inner Beliefs," *Christianity and Crisis* 45, no. 7 (April 29, 1985): 164-65. For examples of inclusive language usage in sermons, see sermons by ethicist Katie G. Cannon, "The Patience to Wait" and "On Remembering Who We Are," in *Those Preachin' Women: Sermons by Black Women Preachers,* ed. Ella Pearson Mitchell (Valley Forge, Pa.: Judson Press, 1986), 43-50, 84-90. Sociologist Cheryl Townsend Gilkes has documented the use of female imagery for God in African-American homiletical discourse in "Some Mother's Son, Some Father's Daughter: Gender and Biblical Language in Afro-Christian Worship Tradition," in *Shaping New Visions: Gender and Values in American Culture,* ed. Clarissa W. Atkinson, Constance H. Buchanan, and Margaret Miles (Ann Arbor: UMI Research Press, 1987), see especially p. 86. I have explored some

dimensions of the issue in "Inclusive Language and the Brief Statement of Faith: Widening the Margins of Our Common Confession," in *To Confess the Faith Today,* ed. Jack L. Stotts and Jane Dempsey Douglass (Louisville, Ky.: Westminster John Knox, 1990), 107-29; in my work, *Communicating a Liberating Word: Inclusive Language and African-American Religious Discourse* (Westminster John Knox, 1991) I explore inclusive-language usage in African-American social and religious history.

5. These abbreviated definitions of the terms translation and interpretation are based on discussions by Letty M. Russell and Sharon H. Ringe. See Russell's introduction in *The Liberating Word: A Guide to Nonsexist Interpretation of the Bible* (Philadelphia: Westminster Press, 1976), 20, and Ringe, "Bible Authority and Interpretation," in *The Liberating Word,* 29.

6. These are not the only arenas where inclusive language concerns have begun to alter the way we conceptualize and use gendered language. Casey Miller and Kate Swift *(The Handbook of Non-Sexist Writing for Writers, Editors and Speakers,* 2d ed. New York: Harper & Row, 1988) note that when the first edition of their work appeared in 1980, efforts to eliminate linguistic sexism had already gained support from a wide assortment of national and local organizations (pp. 1-2).

7. Nancy A. Hardesty, *Inclusive Language in the Church* (Atlanta: John Knox Press, 1987), 75.

8. See "Stachys," William F. Arndt and F. Wilbur Gingrich, *A Greek-English Lexicon of the New Testament and Other Early Christian Literature* (Chicago: University of Chicago Press, 1973), 773; Robert M. Good, "Corn," in *Harper's Dictionary of the Bible* (New York: Harper & Row, 1985), 189; Robert A. Coughenour, "Grain," in *Harper's Dictionary of the Bible,* 358.

9. Arndt and Gingrich, 67-68. All Scripture citations in this essay are taken from the *New Oxford Annotated Bible with the Apocrypha. Expanded Edition Revised Standard Version,* ed. Herbert G. May and Bruce M. Metzger (New York: Oxford University Press, 1977), unless otherwise indicated.

10. Hardesty, 80.

11. Arndt and Gingrich, 20.

12. Karl Heinrich Rengstorf, *"doulos, sundoulos, doule, douleuo, douleia, douloo, kaiadouloo, doulagogeo, ophthomodoulia."* *Theological Dictionary of the New Testament,* vol. 2, ed. Gernard Kittel, trans. Geoffrey W. Bromiley (Grand Rapids, Mich.: Eerdmans, 1974), 261.

13. Ibid.

14. *The American Heritage Dictionary of the English Language,* s.v. "servant."

15. *American Heritage Dictionary,* s.v. "slave."

16. Judith S. Neaman and Carole G. Silver, *Kind Words: A Thesaurus of Euphemisms* (New York: Facts on File Publications, 1983), 1.

17. Joseph M. Williams, *Origins of the English Language* (New York: Free Press, 1957), 202-3.

18. Neaman and Silver, 10.

19. Hugh Rawson, *A Dictionary of Euphemisms and Other Doubletalk Being a Compilation of Linguistic Fig Leaves and Verbal Flourishes for Artful Users of the English Language* (New York: Crown Publishers, 1981), 13, 61.

20. Ibid., 251.

21. Derek Tidball, *The Social Context of the New Testament: A Sociological Analysis* (Grand Rapids, Mich.: Academic Books, 1984), 114-16.

22. H. Bellen, *Studien zur Slavenflucht im römischen Kaiserreich* (Wiesbaden, 1971); M. I. Finley, *Ancient Slavery and Modern Theology* (New York: Penguin, 1983); Orlando Patterson, *Slavery and Social Death* (Cambridge: Harvard University Press, 1982); Alan Watson, *Roman Slave Law* (Baltimore: Johns Hopkins University Press, 1987).

23. K. R. Bradley, *Slaves and Masters in the Roman Empire: A Study in Social Control* (New York: Oxford University Press, 1987), 13-14.

24. Ibid., 116-19, 123.

25. Orlando Patterson, *Slavery and Social Death: A Comparative Study* (Cambridge, Mass.: Harvard University Press, 1982).

26. Ibid., 2-3.
27. Ibid., 5.
28. Ibid.
29. Ibid., 6.
30. Ibid., 7.
31. Rengstorf, 278.
32. Ibid., 277.
33. Sheila Briggs, "Can an Enslaved God Liberate? Hermeneutical Reflections on Philippians 2:6-11," *Semeia* 47 (1989): 143.
34. Ibid., 148.
35. Elisabeth Schüssler Fiorenza, *Bread Not Stone: The Challenge of Feminist Biblical Interpretation* (Boston: Beacon Press, 1984), 16.
36. Ibid.
37. Schaberg made this remark at the SBL section on Women in the Biblical World. The phrase "steady undercurrent in the oral tradition" is quoted from Gerda Lerner, *The Creation of Patriarchy* (New York: Oxford University Press, 1986), 226.
38. See Weems, *Just A Sister Away*.
39. Phyllis Trible, "Depatriarchalizing in Biblical Interpretation," *Journal of the American Academy of Religion* 41 (1973): 30-48.
40. Mary Daly, *Beyond God the Father: Toward A Philosophy of Women's Liberation* (Boston: Beacon Press, 1985), 3. Cf. pp. 13, 72, 162-63.
41. Rosemary Ruether, *Women-Church: Theology and Practice of Feminist Liturgical Communities* (New York: Harper & Row, 1985), 41-56.
42. Adrienne Rich, *Of Woman Born: Motherhood as Experience and Institution* (New York: Norton, 1976), 40.
43. William R. Herzog, II, "The Household Duties' Passages," *Foundations* 24, no. 3 (1981): 204-15.
44. Elisabeth Schüssler Fiorenza, *In Memory of Her: A Feminist Theological Reconstruction of Christian Origins* (New York: Crossroad, 1985), 29.
45. Delores Williams is correct in her assessment, however, that a redefinition of patriarchy must be advanced by African-American women. Patriarchy "loses its identity" for black women, because white women join with white men in oppressing black women. Williams observes that "patriarchy . . . is no longer just the power of fathers, or men, to oppress women. It is also the power of a certain group of females to oppress other groups of females. This inclusion of a group of women as oppressors—an assessment that speaks the truth of the Afro-American woman's history in North America—renders the feminist patriarchal critique of society less valid as a tool for assessing black women's oppression resulting from their relation to white-controlled American institutions. Therefore, one cannot claim that patriarchy, as it is understood by feminists, is the major source of all women's oppression." See Williams, "The Color of Feminism: Or Speaking the Black Woman's Tongue," *Journal of Religious Thought* 43, no. 1 (Spring-Summer, 1986): 48.
46. Toinette M. Eugene, "A Hermeneutical Challenge for Womanists: The Interrelation Between the Text and Our Experience," in *Perspectives on Feminist Hermeneutics,* ed. Gayle Gerber Koontz and Williard Swartley, Occasional Papers no. 10 (Elkhart, Ind.: Institute of Mennonite Studies, 1987), 21ff.
47. Ibid., 24.
48. Russell, *The Liberating Word,* 19.
49. Justo L. Gonzalez, "Searching for a Liberating Anthropology," *Theology Today* 34 (1978): 387-88.
50. For a discussion of the racialist marginalization of a biblical character, consult my essay "A Chamberlain's Journey and the Challenge of Interpretation for Liberation," *Semeia* 47 (1989): 105-35. The essay explores the history of the interpretation of Acts 8:26-40, the story of the Ethiopian eunuch.
51. We cannot speak with certainty about Onesimus's race, as that datum is not provided for the reader; however, since there is negligible evidence that slavery in Greco-Roman antiquity was ever based on race, we conclude that race is irrelevant here. For

a discussion of the black presence in the Greco-Roman world and in biblical narrative, see Cain H. Felder, *Troubling Biblical Waters: Race, Class, and Family* (Maryknoll, N.Y.: Orbis Books, 1989); and Frank M. Snowden, *Blacks in Antiquity: Ethiopians in the Greco-Roman Experience* (Cambridge, Mass.: Harvard University Press, 1979).

52. J. B. Lightfoot, *St. Paul's Epistles to the Colossians, and to Philemon: A Revised Text with Introduction and Notes* (Macmillan, 1875), 377-378.

53. G. B. Caird, *Paul's Letters From Prison: Ephesians, Philippians, Colossians, Philemon, in the Revised Standard Version, Introduction and Commentary* (Oxford: Oxford University Press, 1976), 214.

54. See M. I. Finley, *Ancient Slavery and Modern Ideology*, 95-97. Finley notes that awareness of the slave's unrestricted availability in sexual relations to their masters was a commonplace in Greco-Roman literature from the time of Homer.

55. Walker, *In Search of Our Mothers' Gardens*, xi.

56. Rom. 6:16-22; Eph. 6:6. The recurrence of such terms as *slave, freedman,* and *redemption* in the New Testament all echo the sociopolitical reality and pervasiveness of slavery in the Common Era; the terms predominate in the New Testament Epistles. For a helpful introduction to the usage and function of these terms in the New Testament, see Francis Lyall, *Slaves, Citizens, Sons: Legal Metaphors in the New Testament* (Grand Rapids, Mich.: Academie, 1984), and A. N. Sherwin-White, *Roman Society and Roman Law in the New Testament* (Oxford: Clarendon, 1963).

57. I am indebted to my womanist colleague Katie G. Cannon for sharing her reflections on this subject from the perspective of an ethicist-theologian.

58. C. Eric Lincoln, *Race, Religion, and the Continuing American Dilemma* (New York: Hill & Wang, 1984), 34. Lincoln is quoting Gilbert Osofsky, *The Burden of Race* (New York: Harper & Row, 1967), 40.

59. Lincoln, 35. Echoes of Eph. 5-6 and Col. 3:22 are discernible in Lincoln's paraphrase.

60. H. Shelton Smith, *In His Image, But. . .: Racism in Southern Religion, 1780-1910* (Durham, N.C.: Duke University Press, 1972), 129.

61. Ibid., 135.

62. Katie G. Cannon, "Slave Ideology and Biblical Interpretation," *Semeia* 47 (1989), 11.

63. Ibid., 13.

64. Ibid.

65. Ibid.

66. See, for example, the discussion of how legislative statutes and judicial decisions functioned to legitimate the subjugation of African Americans in A. Leon Higginbotham, Jr., *In the Matter of Color, Race and the American Legal Process: The Colonial Period* (New York: Oxford University Press, 1978).

67. Cannon, "Slave Ideology," 16.

68. Albert J. Raboteau, *Slave Religion: The "Invisible Institution" in the Antebellum South* (New York: Oxford University Press, 1978), 242-43.

69. James H. Cone, "The Sources and Norm of Black Theology," in *A Black Theology of Liberation* (Philadelphia and New York: Lippincott, 1970), 50-81, esp. 66-67.

70. Peter J. Paris, "The Christian Way Through the Black Experience," *Word and World* 6, no. 2 (1986): 129.

71. Schüssler Fiorenza, *In Memory of Her*, 140-54; 214-36 (esp. 214-18).

72. Ibid., 251-79.

73. Raboteau, *Slave Religion*, 122-23.

74. Lewis V. Baldwin, " 'Deliverance to the Captives': Images of Jesus Christ in the Minds of Afro-American Slaves," *Journal of Religious Studies* 12, no. 2 (1986): 35; cf. James H. Cone, *The Spirituals and the Blues: An Interpretation* (New York: Seabury Press, 1972); Clifton Johnson, ed., *God Struck Me Dead: Religious Conversion Experiences and Autobiographies of Ex-Slaves* (Philadelphia: United Church Press, 1969); Felder, *Troubling Biblical Waters*, 53-117.

75. Schüssler Fiorenza, *In Memory of Her*, 52.

76. The phrase "texts of terror" is adopted from Phyllis Trible's penetrating book on the subject, *Texts of Terror: Literary-Feminist Readings of Biblical Narratives, Overtures to Biblical Theology* (Philadelphia: Fortress Press, 1984). Quoted passage from p. 2.

77. Frank Stagg, "The Gospel, Haustafeln, and Women. Mark 1:1; Colossians 3:18-4:1," *Faith and Mission* 2, no. 2 (1985): 63.

78. See my essay, "The *Haustafeln* in African-American Biblical Translation: 'Free Slaves' and 'Subordinate Women,' " *American Biblical Interpretation,* ed. Cain H. Felder (Philadelphia: Fortress Press, 1991).

79. Katie G. Cannon, "The Emergence of Black Feminist Consciousness," in *Feminist Interpretation of the Bible,* ed. Letty Russell (Philadelphia: Westminster Press, 1985), 40.

18

THE USE OF THE BIBLE
IN BLACK THEOLOGY

Itumeleng J. Mosala

Introduction

This essay presupposes the contribution of Black Theology to human knowledge in general and to the black struggle for liberation in particular. No attempt will, therefore, be made to catalogue the virtues of this theology. Suffice it to recall that among its key contributions is its insistence on the necessary ideological rootedness of all theology. This, black theologians may not have pointed to in an explicit way. The fact, however, that they exposed the cultural assumptions of white theology and showed their link with white society and white values exploded the myth of rational objectivity in theology.

The paper will, however, take issue with Black Theology for not taking its own criticism of white theology seriously enough. It will be shown that this is particularly the case with regard to the use of the Bible. The first part of the paper will, therefore, extrapolate features of Black Theology which, it will be argued, represent an ideological captivity to the hermeneutical principles of a theology of oppression. It will further be maintained that it is precisely this slavery to the hermeneutics of white theology which is responsible for the inability of Black Theology to become a theoretical weapon of struggle in the hands of the exploited masses themselves. In this respect we will take our cue from the words of Marx when he writes:

> The weapon of criticism cannot, of course, replace criticism of the weapon; material force must be overthrown by material force, but theory

Itumeleng J. Mosala is the author of *Biblical Hermeneutics and Black Theology in South Africa.* He teaches in the department of religious studies, University of Cape Town, South Africa. This essay was first published in the United States in *The Unquestionable Right to be Free: Black Theology from South Africa,* ed. Itumeleng J. Mosala and Buti Tlhagale (Maryknoll, N.Y.: Orbis Books, 1986).

also becomes a material force as soon as it has gripped the masses. Theory is capable of gripping the masses as soon as it demonstrates *ad hominem,* and it demonstrates *ad hominem* as soon as it becomes radical. To be radical is to grasp the root of the matter. But for man the root is man himself.[1]

It cannot be contested that although Black Theology has developed and is well and alive,[2] it has not yet, as a weapon of theory, become the property of the struggling black masses. To this extent it is a theory that has not yet become a *material force* because it has not gripped the masses. It has served its purpose well as a weapon of criticism against white theology and the white society. That activity, however, does not replace criticism of the weapon itself. Elsewhere I have argued that part of the reason why Black Theology has not become the property of the toiling masses may lie in the class positions and class commitments of its proponents.[3]

The second part of the essay will attempt to set out a program for biblical hermeneutics of liberation using the book of Micah as a case study.

Black Theology's Exegetical Starting Point

All major black theological studies in South Africa draw, in some way, from the work of James Cone. While Cone cannot be faulted for the omissions of South African Black Theology, it is nevertheless necessary to trace the trajectory of the biblical hermeneutics of Black Theology back to its first and most outstanding exponent in order to see how it has been uncritically reproduced in this country.

Black Theology's exegetical starting point expresses itself in the notion that the Bible is the revealed "Word of God". The task of a black theologian is to recognize "God's Word" and help illuminate it to those who are oppressed and humiliated in this world. For Cone the "Word of God", therefore, represents one structuring pole of the biblical hermeneutics of Black Theology while the black experience stands for the other.[4] He summarizes Black Theology's hermeneutical position when he asserts that:

> The Bible is the witness to God's self-disclosure in Jesus Christ. Thus the black experience requires that Scripture be a source of Black Theology. For it was Scripture that enabled slaves to affirm a view of God that differed radically from that of the slave masters. The slave masters' intention was to present a "Jesus" who would make the slave obedient and docile. Jesus was supposed to make black people better slaves, that is, faithful servants of white masters. But many blacks rejected that view of Jesus, not only because it contradicted their African heritage but because it contradicted the witness of Scripture.[5]

Thus the black experience of oppression and exploitation provides the epistemological lenses for perceiving the God of the Bible as the God of liberation.

This process, however, does not alter Cone's perception of the nature and function of the Bible as the "Word of God". Rather, "scripture", in its status as the "Word of God", "established limits to white people's use of Jesus Christ as a confirmation of black oppression".[6]

Paradoxically, Black Theology's notion of the Bible as the Word of God carries the implication that there is such a thing as a nonideological appropriation of scripture. Black theologians condemn white people's view of God and Jesus Christ as apolitical and above ideologies on the one hand, but maintain a view of scripture as an absolute, nonideological Word of God that can be made ideological by being applied to the situation of oppression. This position is taken by even the most theoretically astute of black theologians, Cornel West. He argues:

> An interpretation of the black historical experience and the readings of the biblical texts that emerge out of this experience constitute the raw ingredients for the second step of black theological reflection. By trying to understand the plight of black people in the light of the Bible, black theologians claim to preserve the biblical truth that God sides with the oppressed and acts on their behalf.[7]

To be fair to West it must be added that he goes a step further than Cone and other black theologians by not resting the case at interpreting the black experience in the light of the Bible, but also advocates interpreting the Bible in the light of the black experience. Nevertheless West, like Cone, insists on there being a biblical truth according to which God sides with the oppressed in their struggle for liberation. This is true as far as it goes. But as any hermeneutics that derives from the crucible of class struggle will attest to, the biblical truth that God sides with the oppressed is only one of the biblical truths. The other truth is that the struggle between Yahweh and Baal is not simply an ideological warfare taking place in the minds and hearts of believers, but a struggle between the God of the Israelite landless peasants and subdued slaves and the God of the Israelite royal, noble, landlord and priestly classes. The Bible is as rent apart by the antagonistic struggles of the warring classes of Israelite society as our life is torn asunder by the class divisions of our society.

What then is meant by the Bible as the "Word of God"? The ideological import of such a theological statement is immense. For the "Word of God" cannot be the object of criticism. Least of all can the "Word of God" be critiqued in the light of the black experience. The only appropriate response is *obedience*. At best the black experience can be seen in the light of the "Word of God", but not vice versa. If the Bible is the "Word of God", therefore, the implication is that even the "law and order" God of David and Solomon cannot be the object of criticism in the light of the black experience. The black struggle cannot be hermeneutically connected with the struggles of the oppressed and exploited Israelites against the economic and political domination of the Israelite monarchic state which was undergirded by the ideology of the Davidic-

Zionist covenant (2 Samuel 7). Neither can any hermeneutic affinity be established with the landless peasants, exploited workers and destitute underclasses that made up the followers of Jesus. One cannot select one part of the "Word of God" and neglect the other.

South African black theologians are not free from enslavement to this neo-orthodox theological problematic that regards the notion of the "Word of God" as a hermeneutical starting point. S. Dwane displays this exegetical bondage when he writes:

> Liberation theology as an aspect of Christian theology cannot play to the gallery of secular expectations. It seeks to understand and to articulate what in the light of his revelation in the past, God is doing now for the redemption of his people. Liberation theology is theocentric and soundly biblical insofar as it points out that God does not luxuriate in his eternal bliss, but reaches out to man and to the world ... To say that liberation theology is not a Gospel of liberation is to state the obvious. *The Gospel, it is true, is good news for all men.* And no theology, Western or African, has the right to equate itself with the Gospel. The entire theological enterprise is concerned with the interpretation of *the one Gospel for all sorts of conditions.*[8]

The attempt to claim *the whole* of the Bible in support of Black Theology is misdirected because it ignores the results of biblical scholarship over the last century and has its roots in ruling-class ideology. By ruling-class ideology we refer to that activity on the part of dominant classes of society by which they seek to establish hegemonic control over other classes through a rationalizing universalization of what are in effect sectional class interests. James Joll makes this point succinctly:

> The hegemony of a political class meant for Gramsci that that class had succeeded in persuading the other classes of society to accept its own moral, political and cultural values. If the ruling class is successful, then this will involve the minimum use of force, as was the case with the successful liberal regimes of the nineteenth century.[9]

Thus the insistence on the Bible as the "Word of God" must be seen for what it is: an ideological maneuver whereby ruling-class interests in the Bible as in our society today are converted into a faith that transcends social, political, racial, sexual and economic divisions. In this way the Bible becomes an ahistorical interclassist document. Sergio Rostagno has exposed the ideological roots of this line of thinking when he asserts, concerning the church, that:

> Historically speaking, the church has always been a church of the bourgeoisie, even when it claimed to transcend class barriers or labored under the illusion that it pervaded all classes in the same way. Indeed, it has

been a truly bourgeois church, if the notion of interclassism is taken as part of bourgeois ideology ... The church has been the church of the class which has identified itself with the history of the West, in which Christianity may be considered to have been a major force. Only those members of the working class who accepted this view of history attended church. But most of the working people never accepted this view and only gave the church the kind of formal allegiance subjects give to the claims of their rulers. They could not really belong to the church of another class.[10]

Just as the church has always been the church of the bourgeoisie, theology and biblical exegesis have always been bourgeois theology and exegesis. It is, therefore, a tragedy that rebel theologies like Black Theology and Liberation Theology should adopt uncritically the biblical hermeneutics of bourgeois theology. According to Rostagno bourgeois exegesis shows the sterility of its ahistoricism in that:

It claims to consider humanity in certain typical existential situations which provide analogies for all historical situations resulting from the human condition. It deals, therefore, with *humanity,* rather than with *workers* as they try to wrest from the dominant class its hold on the means of production and its hold over the vital spheres of human life. In this sense, it could be said that exegesis was an interclass affair ... This was an indication that biblical exegesis had been effectively estranged from the labor movement.[11]

The belief in the Bible as the "Word of God" has had similar effects, that is, *prohumanity* but antiblack working class and black women. It has, to all intents and purposes, been bourgeois exegesis applied to the working-class situation. The theoretical tragedy of such a state of affairs is that claims in that direction have been made with confidence and pride. Boesak, for instance, states unashamedly that:

In its focus on the poor and the oppressed, the theology of liberation is not a new theology; it is simply the proclamation of the age-old gospel, but now liberated from the deadly hold of the mighty and the powerful and made relevant to the situation of the oppressed and the poor.[12]

Black Theology needs a new exegetical starting point if it is to become a material force capable of gripping the black working-class and peasant masses. Such a starting point needs to be rooted in the kind of epistemology that underlies the words of Marx and Engels when they declared: "The task of history, therefore, once the world beyond the truth has disappeared, is to establish the truth of this world."[13] The social, cultural, political and economic world of the black working class and peasantry constitutes the only valid hermeneutical starting point for a Black Theology of Liberation.

The Problem of Universality and Particularity in Black Theology

The abstract exegetical starting point of Black Theology leads inevitably to problems about the validity of the particularistic character of this theology. If the "Word of God" transcends boundaries of culture, class, race, sex, etc., how can there be a theology that is concerned primarily with the issues of a particular race? Conversely, if black people are right when they claim that in their struggle for liberation Jesus is on their side, how can the same Jesus remain the supreme *universal* disclosure of the "Word of God"?

This simultaneous concern for a cultureless and culture-bound, classless and class-based, raceless and race-oriented Jesus manifested itself fairly early in the development of Black Theology. Thus Gqubule states:

> Black Theology is not an attempt to localize Christ in the black situation but make him so universal that the Red Indian, the Pigmy, the Maori, the Russian, the Hungarian, the Venda and the American may each say: "This man Jesus is bone of my bone; he speaks in my own accent of things that are true to me!" Viewed in this way Christianity can never be a white man's religion although it was brought to us by a white missionary. It is natural that any white artist would portray Jesus as a white man.[14]

This line of thinking is corroborated by Mgojo who sees Black Theology as contextual. By this he seems to understand that it is the application of universal theological principles to a particular situation. Consequently he traces the development of universal theology from the Age of Apology through to the period starting in 1720 which he characterizes as the era of evolving theological responses to the technological society. He then concludes:

> In looking at the history of doctrine we can see in every period theology developed in response to challenges from the larger society. This being the case there is nothing strange in a particular segment of the Christian community reflecting on the nature of God in relation to its experience of suffering and oppression. Hence today there is Black Theology.[15]

Thus Mgojo's understanding of the origins and function of Black Theology is rooted in a belief in the fundamental universality of the gospel. This understanding stems from a hermeneutical commitment to the Bible as the "Word of God". As a result, he sees the emergence of Black Theology as a logical historical development of Christian theology, not a rebellion against traditional western theology. Indeed Black Theology is simply *contextual* theology, that is, white theology in black clothes. It is little wonder that he applies the following strictures against James Cone:

Cone's understanding of the theological task in his early work is in conflict with our definition of theology, in fact it is in direct opposition. This focus is on the analysis of the black man's condition, ours is on God as revealed in Jesus Christ and his relationship to the world and man. Cone's approach here could be classified as Christian sociology rather than Christian theology.[16]

This apologetic attitude on the part of black theologians is related to their enslavement to traditional biblical hermeneutics which we discussed above.[17] There are also forms of colonization that are connected to this hermeneutical bondage. In South African Black Theology the debate between African and black theologians exemplifies this crisis of cultural identity. Gqubule, for instance, in addressing one of the points of conflict between Christianity and African religion, locates himself unproblematically in a framework that reflects at once a cultural desertion and a biblical hermeneutical position based in the dominant western culture. He argues:

> There is a widespread belief about the role of the ancestors. One view is that they are an object of worship. Another view is that they are intermediaries who because they know our lot on earth, are better able to mediate to God on our behalf. However, for the Christian only the Triune God can be the object of worship; moreover the Christian Scriptures say: "There is *one God*, and also *one mediator* between God and men, Christ Jesus" (1 Tim. 2:5).[18]

The most explicit and often quoted criticism of African Theology and religion, which feeds on this cultural self-hate, is the one made by Manas Buthelezi. Buthelezi's strictures are rightly directed against tendencies to reify the African past, especially African culture. However, the terms of his strictures display an uneasiness about culture which characterizes the conflict between the universal and the particular in Black Theology. He writes:

> There is a danger that the "African past" may be romanticized and conceived in isolation from the realities of the present. Yet this past seen as a world view is nothing more than a historical abstraction of "what once was." Rightly or wrongly, one cannot help but sense something panicky about the mood which has set the tenor and tempo of the current concerns about "indigenous theology."[19]

Notwithstanding this rigorously antiabstractionist stance, Buthelezi proceeds to suggest equally abstractionist solutions to the problem of indigenous theology in South Africa:

> The shift from the "ideological" to the "human" expressions of ecclesiastical kinship solidarity will serve as a freeing factor for indigenous the-

ology. Considerations of *esprit de corps* will no longer be a haunting specter for theological freedom in Africa since there will be another way of expressing this kinship solidarity.[20]

The abstract universalizing category of the "human" as opposed to the concrete particularizing concept of the "African" helps Buthelezi to maintain ties with what is "universal" and, for him, non-ideological, while at the same time his theology is intended to address the indigenous and, therefore, ideological situation. It may even be argued that for Buthelezi the "human" or "anthropological" is finally given in the "Word of God" which he asserts addresses him within the reality of his blackness.[21] That is why in his view Black Theology is no more than a methodological technique of theologizing.[22]

Bereft of a theoretical perspective that can locate both the Bible and the black experience within appropriate historical contexts, Buthelezi and other black theologians are unable to explode the myth of the inherent universality of the "Word of God." They have been surpassed by the largely illiterate black working class and poor peasantry who have defied the canon of scripture, with its ruling-class ideological basis, by appropriating the Bible in their own way by using the cultural tools emerging out of their struggle for survival.[23] To be able to reopen the canon of scripture in the interests of black liberation, black theologians will need to take the materialist hermeneutical significance of the black experience much more seriously.

The problem of the lack of a black biblical hermeneutics of liberation, however, has its roots in the inherent crisis of the petit bourgeoisie of all shades but especially those of the colonized countries. Amilcar Cabral diagnoses the inherent malaise of this class when he declares:

> As I said, regarding culture there are usually no important modifications at the summit of the indigenous social pyramid or pyramids (groups with a hierarchical structure). Each stratum or class retains its identity, integrated within the larger group, but distinct from the identities of other social categories. By contrast in urban centers and in urban zones of the interior where the colonial power's cultural influence is felt, the problem of identity is more complex. Whereas those at the base of the social pyramid—that is, the majority of the masses of working people from different ethnic groups—and those at the top (the foreign ruling class) keep their identities, *those in the middle range of this pyramid (the native lower middle class)—culturally rootless, alienated or more or less assimilated— flounder* in a social and cultural conflict in quest of their identity.[24]

Cornel West has raised the same question of the cultural crisis of the petit bourgeois class in relation to Latin American Liberation Theology. In the case of this theology the problem expresses itself in terms of the conspicuous absence of blacks and Indians, or the issues related to them, in Liberation Theology. He suggests that when Marxists are preoccupied with an analysis that denigrates the liberating aspects of the culture of oppressed people, the implication is that such Marxists share the ethos — not of the degraded and oppressed minorities — but of the dominant European culture. Seen from the point of view of concern with the hermeneutics of liberation this means that the dominant European culture would constitute their material hermeneutical starting point. West makes the point succinctly when he asserts that:

> Historically, a central feature of this dominant European culture has been its inability to take seriously the culture of colored people and its tendency to degrade and oppress the culture of these people. For oppressed colored people, the central problem is not only repressive capitalist regimes, but also oppressive European civilizing attitudes. And even Marxists who reject oppressive capitalist regimes often display oppressive European civilizing attitudes toward colored peoples. In this sense, such Marxists, though rightly critical of capitalism, remain captives of the worst of European culture.[25]

Thus universal abstract starting points derived presumably from the biblical message will not do for a biblical hermeneutics of liberation. Black Theology for its part will have to rediscover black working-class and poor peasant culture in order to find for itself a materialist hermeneutical starting point. The particularity of the black struggle in its different forms and phases must provide the epistemological lenses with which the Bible can be read. Only such a position seems to us to represent a theoretical break with dominant biblical hermeneutics. Anything else is a tinkering with what in fact must be destroyed.

NOTES

1. Marx and Engels, *On Religion* (Schocken Books, 1964), p. 50.
2. See J. Noko, "The Concept of God in Black Theology," Ph.D. thesis, McGill University, 1977; Ntschebe, "A Voice of Protest," M.A. thesis, Rhodes University; S. Mogoba, "The Faith of Urban Blacks," M.A. thesis, Bristol, 1978; T.A. Mofokeng, "The Crucified among the Crossbearers," doctoral thesis, Kampen, 1983; and numerous articles in the various issues of the *Journal of Theology for Southern Africa*.
3. Itumeleng J. Mosala, "Black and African Theologies", unpublished paper read at the University of Cape Town (1982). See also the "Final Statement of the Black Theology Seminar", *Institute for Contextual Theology News* 1, no. 2 (Sept. 1983), pp. 9ff. S. Nolutshungu, writing on the political interpretation of the so-called "Black Middle Class", corroborates this contention. He writes: "As things stand, it is not surprising that attempts to define a modern cultural sensibility for Blacks in the late 1960s and early 1970s were so derivative in idiom and style — deep and authentic though the anguish which they expressed. 'Middle class' Blacks remained, even so, firmly attached to the common culture and even in the area of religion where much was written about the need for a black theology, radical dissent was still expressed by separatist churches that were predominantly non-middle-class in following", *Changing South Africa* (Cape Town: David Philip, 1983), p. 125.
4. See J. H. Cone, *God of the Oppressed* (New York: Seabury Press, 1975), p. 8.
5. Ibid., p. 31.
6. Ibid.

7. Cornel West, *Prophesy Deliverance: An Afro-American Revolutionary Christianity* (Philadelphia: Westminster Press, 1982), p. 109.

8. "Christology and Liberation", *Journal of Theology for Southern Africa* 35 (1981), p. 30. Italics mine.

9. James Joll, *Gramsci* (New York: Fontana Paperbacks, 1977), p. 99.

10. "The Bible: Is Interclass Reading Legitimate?", in *The Bible and Liberation*, ed. N.K. Gottwald (Maryknoll, N.Y.: Orbis Books, 1983), p. 62.

11. Ibid.

12. A. Boesak, *Farewell to Innocence* (Maryknoll, N.Y.: Orbis Books, 1977), p. 10.

13. Marx and Engels, *On Religion*, p. 42.

14. S. Gqubule, "What Is Black Theology", *Journal of Theology for Southern Africa* 8 (1974), p. 18.

15. E.K.M. Mgojo, "Prolegomenon to the Study of Black Theology", *Journal of Theology for Southern Africa* 21 (1977), pp. 26f.

16. Ibid.

17. See also E.K. Mosothoane, "The Use of Scripture in Black Theology," *Scripture and the Use of Scripture* (Pretoria: Unisa, 1979), p. 32.

18. S. Gqubule, *Black Theology*, p. 17.

19. Manas Buthelezi, "Toward Indigenous Theology in South Africa", in *The Emergent Gospel* (Maryknoll, N.Y: Orbis Books, 1978), p. 62.

20. Ibid., p. 73.

21. Ibid., p. 74.

22. Ibid.

23. For a helpful study of this process see J .M. Schoffeleer's "African Christology", unpublished paper, Free University, Amsterdam (1981), passim.

24. Amilcar Cabral, "The Role of Culture in the Liberation Struggle," *Latin American Research Unit Studies,* Toronto, 1, no. 3 (1977), p. 93.

25. "The North American Blacks", in *The Challenge of Base Christian Communities,* ed. Sergio Torres and John Eagleson (Maryknoll, N.Y.: Orbis Books, 1981), p. 256.

Part IV

WOMANIST THEOLOGY

INTRODUCTION

Womanist theology is the most creative development to emerge out of the Black theology movement during the 1980s and 1990s. It is both an affirmation and a critique of the liberation theology of Black male theologians. Like their brothers, womanists offer a powerful race critique of White supremacy. They separate themselves from the White feminist theologians who ignore racism and join with Black men in the struggle against white supremacy in the church, the academy, and the society. The Blackness of their experience means that White women do not know what Black women know even though their gender is the same.

Although womanists express solidarity with Black male theologians in the fight against White supremacy, they are feminists and therefore join with White feminists in the struggle against patriarchy, an evil as destructive to the freedom of the human community as racism. Womanists' identity as women means that Black men do not know what Black women know even though their race is the same.

Womanists are not defined by blending the insights of Black male liberationists and White feminists. Womanists insist that they have the right to name their own experience and to develop a way of doing theology accountable to the survival and liberation of Black women. Their theological analysis is *multidimensional*, because Black women's experience cannot be reduced to either gender or racial oppression. Both must be included simultaneously, along with classism and heterosexism.

Womanists often speak of not being able to separate gender, race, and class in defining the experience of the majority of African-American women. "Many Black men ask us whether we are 'Black first' or 'women first,' " a student said in my Black Theology class at Union. "We Black women get very angry about that question because it presupposes that we women can be compartmentalized like a machine. We are *Black women*. We cannot be Black from Monday to Thursday, then women from Friday to Sunday. We are Black women seven days a week."

The writings of Alice Walker have had a powerful influence on self-identified womanist theologians, especially her book, *In Search of Our Mothers' Gardens: Womanist Prose* (1983) and her widely acclaimed novel, *The Color Purple* (1982). Black women theologians derived the name "womanist" from *In Search of Our Mothers' Gardens* where Walker defined the term. Walker's definition is frequently quoted, interpreted, and debated as Black women scholars of religion

257

distinguish their feminist consciousness from White women and their Black consciousness from African-American men as will be seen in the following essays.

Delores S. Williams, Union Theological Seminary graduate and now associate professor there, is a Presbyterian called to be a theologian "from the stance of a laywoman and from the marketplace." A leading womanist who is deeply rooted in the faith and practice of the church, she has written several theological reflections on *The Color Purple*, showing its influence on womanist theologians and responding to the negative reactions of Black males to the novel and the movie.[1] Williams is both a poet and a systematic theologian. As her essay, "Womanist Theology: Black Women's Voices" (Document 19), shows, Alice Walker's definition of womanist in *Search* stimulates both her theological and artistic imagination as she speaks about "a theology of the Spirit informed by Black women's history, culture, and religious experience." Although survival is a recurring theme in the writings of all womanist scholars, it is *the* dominant emphasis in Williams' theology. She often contrasts it with the liberation theme of Black male theologians. The Exodus story, with Moses as the main character and liberation as the primary theme, was interpreted by Black male theologians in ways that made survival nearly invisible in the African-American religious experience. Williams showed the limitations of the Exodus-liberation focus—first in her M.A. thesis ("The Black Woman Portrayed in Selected Black Imaginative Literature and Some Questions for Black Theology," Union Theological Seminary, 1975) and explored it further in her Ph.D. dissertation ("A Study of the Analogous Relation Between African-American Women's Experience and Hagar's Experience: A Challenge Posed to Black Theology," 1990). In her re-reading of the Bible and the Black experience in the United States, Williams focused on Hagar's story as "most illustrative and relevant to Afro-American women's experience of bondage, of African heritage, of encounter with God/emissary in the midst of fierce survival struggles."

In another important essay, "Black Women's Surrogacy Experience and the Christian Notion of Redemption,"[2] Williams challenges the way images of redemption have been taught in Christian churches which focus on Jesus' death on the cross. Using Black women's surrogacy experience before and after slavery as the starting point of her powerful critique, she claims that a "surrogate-God" who "died on the cross in the place of humans" has no "salvific power for black women." In fact, "this image of redemption supports and reinforces the exploitation that has accompanied their experience with surrogacy."[3]

According to Williams, the time has come "to liberate redemption from the cross and to liberate the cross from the 'sacred aura' put around it by existing patriarchal responses to the question of what Jesus' death represents." For an alternative way of looking at redemption, Williams turns to the synoptic Gospels rather than Paul's letters and concludes that Jesus came not to die on the cross in our place but "to show human *life*—to show redemption through a perfect *ministerial* vision of righting relationships."[4]

While Williams' view challenges what Christian churches have said about the cross, she affirms God's revelation in Jesus as Christ, defined by the resurrection. She explores the themes of survival, surrogacy, and redemption further in her landmark work, *Sisters in the Wilderness: The Challenge of Womanist God-Talk* (Orbis Books, 1993). Williams has served as a visiting theologian in the Presbyterian churches in up-state New York, read papers at the AAR, and is in demand as a lecturer at many churches, seminaries, and universities.

Like Delores Williams' perspective, Jacquelyn Grant's theology is deeply rooted in the faith and practice of the Black Church. Along with her father, brother, and two sisters, Grant is an ordained minister in the African Methodist Episcopal (A.M.E.) Church and a consultant for its Commission on Women in Ministry. She is also a Union Theological Seminary graduate and an associate professor of systematic theology at the Interdenominational Theological Center. Like Williams, Grant has made a major contribution to womanist theology, especially in the area of Christology. Written first as a Ph.D. dissertation ("The Development and Limitation of Feminist Christology: Toward an Engagement of White Women's and Black Women's Religious Experiences," 1985), her highly regarded book, *White Women's Christ and Black Women's Jesus: Feminist Christology and Womanist Response* (Scholars Press, 1989), is a powerful critique of the Christologies of White feminists. She also outlines the beginnings of a Womanist Christology based on the faith experiences of Black women in the churches. Although Grant, in her essay, "Womanist Theology" (Document 20), rejects the traditional "male image of the divine," emphasizing "that the significance of Christ is not his maleness, but his humanity," she does not question the heart of the faith of the Black church—that Jesus died on the cross in our place to save us from our sin.

Grant's perspective on womanist theology has been influenced by the nineteenth-century Black feminist Anna Julia Cooper who emphasized the need to be "broad in the concrete." Grant interprets that principle to mean taking seriously Black women's "tri-dimensional experience of racism/sexism/classism." While her womanist perspective embraces a wide scope of specific issues, Grant's Christology has been shaped by the Black Church experience, especially as defined by women like Jarena Lee and Sojourner Truth. Sojourner preached from one text: "When I found Jesus." Jarena Lee based her right to preach on the christological claim that "the Savior died for the woman as well as for the man." "For me," Grant writes, "it means today, this Christ, found in the experience of Black women, is a Black woman."

Although Grant's christological claim is radical, it is a radicalism from within the faith of the Black Church and not from outside of it. Grant has presented her views on Jesus in the contexts of the World Council of Churches (preaching at the Seventh Assembly in Canberra, 1991), the Ecumenical Association of Third World Theologians conferences (she is Regional Co-ordinator of the Minorities), and the American Academy of Religion.

Kelly Delaine Brown-Douglass is also making an important contribution to womanist theology in the area of Christology. She is an Episcopal priest, a Union Theological Seminary graduate, and an assistant professor of theology at Howard University School of Divinity. As Jackie Grant focused her doctoral study on the strengths and weaknesses of White feminist Christologies, Kelly Brown-Douglass focused her research on the strengths and weaknesses of Black male theologians' perspectives on the Black Messiah ("Who Do They Say That I Am: A Critical Examination of the Black Christ," 1988). In her essay, "Womanist Theology: What Is Its Relationship to Black Theology" (Document 21), she shows the impact of Black Theology on the emergence of womanist theology, highlighting their similarities and differences.

Kelly Brown-Douglass's Christology is similar to that of Grant. Like Grant, Brown-Douglass does not question the images of redemption in Christian churches. "God is as Christ does," she writes in an essay with that title. She is critical of Black women's acceptance of "Jesus as God," which suggests that, "given Jesus' maleness," "God is also male." But she clearly affirms the salvific significance of the cross and the Nicea-Chalcedon faith that emphasizes that "Jesus is Christ, that is, God incarnate, Resurrected Savior."[5]

Nineteenth-century Black feminists Maria Stewart and Sojourner Truth receive special attention in Kelly Brown-Douglass' interpretation of Black women's experience. She emphasizes the need for an analysis that is both multidimensional (including racism, sexism, classism, and heterosexism) and bifocal (identifying oppression without and within the Black community). Brown-Douglass identifies survival and liberation as key themes in womanist theology. God is not only a liberator, as Black male theologians have claimed, but also a sustainer. Like Grant, she has presented her views at the meetings of the EATWOT and the AAR.

Katie Geneva Cannon, another Union Theological Seminary graduate, Presbyterian minister, and associate professor of African-American studies at Temple University, Philadelphia, is a leading voice among womanist scholars. She was the first African-American woman to receive a Ph.D. from Union Theological Seminary ("Resources for a Constructive Ethic for Black Women with Special Attention to the Life and Work of Zora Neale Hurston," 1983). Her dissertation was later published under the title, *Black Womanist Ethics* (Scholars Press, 1988). One of the contributors to the well-known book, *God's Fierce Whimsy* (Pilgrim Press, 1985), Cannon is an influential teacher and a widely sought-after lecturer for colleges, universities, churches, and community groups. She has also made major presentations at the AAR and the Society of Christian Ethics.

Although Cannon has done important study of the history and culture of Black women in the United States, she is best known for her investigation of the ethical resources in the life and work of Zora Neale Hurston. "Invisible dignity," "quiet grace," and "unshouted courage" are phrases Cannon uses to describe Hurston and the women in her fiction.[6] She shows how Hurston's life and writings "reveal a fundamental truth—self-fulfillment in a situation of oppression requires hitting a straight lick with a crooked stick."[7]

Cannon uses Hurston's truth to describe "the womanist dilemma in the development of a liberation ethic" (Document 22). Here she offers not only a powerful critique of White male scholars in ethics and theology but also of White feminists and Black male theologians and preachers. She is especially critical of the Black church and community for its "objectification, degradation, and subjection of the female in Black preaching." Her critique of the Black church, however, is internal, not external, thereby making her womanist perspective similar to that of Delores Williams, Jackie Grant, and Kelly Brown-Douglass.

Alice Walker defines a womanist as one who "*loves* the folk" and "committed to survival and wholeness of entire people." Love is a major theme among womanists, especially in writings of Toinette M. Eugene. Eugene is a prominent Catholic womanist who teaches social ethics at Chicago Theological Seminary. Before accepting her current position, she served several years as the Provost of Colgate Rochester/Bexley Hall/Crozer Theological Seminary. An author of many important essays,[8] Eugene, like other womanist scholars, has presented her views at the AAR and before a variety of academic and church audiences.

In her essay entitled, "While Love Is Unfashionable," Eugene makes "black liberating love" the starting point of her exploration of the "relationships between black spirituality and sexuality in the quest for mutuality among black women and black men." She rejects both sexist and spiritualistic dualisms that subordinate women in the churches and the society and urges the Black church to uphold "the beauty of black love in its most profound meaning. Wherever black love is discouraged or disparaged as an unfashionable or unattainable expression between black women and black men," writes Eugene, "the black church has an unparalleled option to model these gospel values of love and unconditional acceptance."[9]

In the essay, "Moral Values and Black Womanists" (Document 23), Eugene provides an excellent overview of the role of women in Black religious history. She shows the marked differences between Black and White women's experiences. Racism is deeply embedded in the history and culture of the United States, and Eugene believes that few White feminists have faced head-on its destructive consequences for human community. She is concerned about the development of an inclusive womanist theology, an analysis that is accountable to the "victims of the aggravated inequities of the tridimensional phenomenon of race/class/gender oppression."

Cheryl Townsend Gilkes shares many of the concerns of Toinette Eugene and other womanists. Gilkes received her doctorate in sociology at Northeastern University (Boston) and her Master of Divinity degree at Boston University School of Theology. She is currently an associate professor of sociology at Colby College (Maine) and the associate minister at the Union Baptist Church of Cambridge, Massachusetts. Gilkes is widely known for her original research on Sanctified churches, demonstrating the major roles that women have played in them. Like the Sanctified churches in relation to mainline Black denominations, the women in them are often overlooked by sociologists and other scholars. But Gilkes believes that this is a mistake, for the women of Sanctified churches embody a "holy boldness" that converges with Walker's definition of womanist.

They love the Spirit because they are prophets of the Black religious tradition. They "call to our remembrance traditions that are important for coping with crisis."[10]

In her essay, "Womanist Ways of Seeing" (Document 24), Gilkes explores further the meaning and the impact of Walker's definition of womanist in the writings of scholars and in the lives of Black women. "Walker's term 'womanist,' " according to Gilkes, "names differences and distinctiveness by constructing a way of seeing the world that embraces core themes from the African-American cultural experience. In doing that," Gilkes continues, "Walker has provided a most powerful ethical challenge to an oppressive society while calling a broad range of women to activism who can assert themselves as womanists and value their experiences of suffering and survival as gifts for human liberation."

A Catholic perspective on womanist ways of doing theology is presented by Diana L. Hayes. A convert to Catholicism from the A.M.E. Zion Church, she is a graduate of the Catholic University (Washington, D.C.). She received her doctorate in sacred theology from the Pontifical Faculty of the Catholic University of Louvain in Belgium, writing a dissertation on "Tracings of an American Theology of Liberation: From Political Theology to a Theology of the Two-Thirds World." Hayes is currently teaching theology at Georgetown University in Washington, D.C. In her essay, "Feminist Theology, Womanist Theology: A Black Catholic Perspective" (Document 25), she contends that Black Catholic women will make their most important contribution in "their reinterpretation of the role and presence of Mary, the Mother of God." Mary was not docile or submissive but strong, righteous, and womanish. Hayes sees Mary as a role model for Black women. "At a time when women were supposed to be silent," Mary, "a young, pregnant, unwed woman," "in her song (Luke 1:46-55) proclaims her allegiance with God."

Not all African-American women scholars in religion are enthusiastic about the womanist perspective. A Harvard Divinity School graduate and an ordained minister of the Church of God, Cheryl Sanders is currently an associate professor of Christian ethics at the Howard University School of Divinity. Her critique of the womanist perspective has received much attention. Her essay "Christian Ethics and Theology in Womanist Perspective" (Document 26), was first published in a roundtable discussion in the *Journal of Feminist Studies in Religion*. After acknowledging womanist ethics and theology as "one of the most exciting developments in the theological scholarship of the 1980s," Sanders asks: "Does the term *womanist* provide an appropriate frame of reference for the ethical and theological statements now being generated by Black women?" She believes that the womanist perspective conflicts with the claims of Christianity and with the survival and health of the Black community. "In my view," she writes, "there is a fundamental discrepancy between the womanist criteria that would affirm and/or advocate homosexual practice, and the ethical norms the Black church might employ to promote the survival and wholeness of Black families." Five Black women responded to Sanders (Emilie Townes of St. Paul

Theological Seminary in Kansas City, Shawn Copeland of Yale, Katie Cannon, well-known feminist theorist and cultural critic bell hooks, and Cheryl Gilkes). The reader is encouraged to read them and Sanders's reply.

While Cheryl Sanders criticizes Christian women theologians and ethicists for depending too much on Walker's idea of womanist, Renee L. Hill criticizes them for not taking seriously enough Walker's womanist principles. A doctoral student at Union Theological Seminary and a self-identified lesbian, Hill wrote her essay, "Who Are We for Each Other?: Sexism, Sexuality and Womanist Theology" (Document 27), in my Black Theology class. She chides womanist theologians for their silence on lesbianism. While Christian womanists speak of a multidimensional analysis of oppression, they, "like their male counterparts, focus for the most part on the impact of racism in the Black community" and much less on sexism. There is almost no discussion of sexuality and the need to fight against destructive consequences of heterosexism and homophobia. Hill's essay raises sexuality issues that need to be discussed not only among womanists but in the entire African-American church community.

When people reflect about matters that touch the essence of their identity as human beings, creative theology is born. Theological ideas are not created in heaven but on earth where people are trying to understand their relationship to each other and ultimate reality. Good theology is created out of the struggle to live authentically, refusing to compromise one's right to name one's experience of God. Womanists are creating theologies that will have not only profound consequences for African-American women but for men too. Black liberation theology cannot be the same after its creative encounter with womanist theology.

J.H.C.

NOTES

1. In addition to Document 19, see also Williams's "The Color Purple," *Christianity and Crisis* (July 14, 1986): 230–232; "Black Women's Literature and the Task of Feminist Theology," in *Immaculate and Powerful: The Female in Sacred Image and Social Reality*, ed. by C. W. Atkinson, C. H. Buchanan, and M. R. Miles (Beacon Press, 1985).

2. Delores S. Williams, "Black Women's Surrogacy Experience and the Christian Notion of Redemption" in Paula M. Cooey, William R. Eakin, and Jay B. McDaniel, eds., *After Patriarchy: Feminist Reconstructions of World Religions* (Maryknoll, N.Y.: Orbis Books, 1991).

3. *Ibid.*, 9.

4. *Ibid.*, 10, 11.

5. Kelly Delaine Brown, "God is as Christ Does: Toward a Womanist Theology," *Journal of Religious Thought* 46, no. 1 (Summer-Fall 1989): 14, 16.

6. See especially Katie G. Cannon, *Black Womanist Ethics* (Atlanta: Scholars Press, 1988).

7. Katie Geneva Cannon, "Resources for a Constructive Ethic in the Life and Work of Zora Neale Hurston," *Journal of Feminist Studies in Religion* (Spring 1985): 50.

8. See especially her "While Love is Unfashionable: An Exploration of Black Spirituality and Sexuality," in *Women's Consciousness, Women's Conscience*, ed. by B. H. Andolsen, C. E. Gudorf, and M. D. Pellauer (Harper & Row, 1987), 121–141; with Susan B. Thistlethwaite, "A Survey of Contemporary Global Feminist, Womanist, and Mujer-

ista Theologies," in *Critical Review of Books in Religion* (Atlanta: Scholars Press, 1991), 1-20.

   9. *Ibid.*, 122, 132.

   10. Cheryl Townsend Gilkes, "The Role of Women in the Sanctified Church," *Journal of Religious Thought* (Spring/Summer 1986): 24, 41.

19

WOMANIST THEOLOGY: BLACK WOMEN'S VOICES

Delores S. Williams

DAUGHTER: *Mama, why are we brown, pink, and yellow, and our cousins are white, beige, and black?*
MOTHER: *Well, you know the colored race is just like a flower garden, with every color flower represented.*
DAUGHTER: *Mama, I'm walking to Canada and I'm taking you and a bunch of slaves with me.*
MOTHER: *It wouldn't be the first time.*

In these two conversational exchanges, Pulitzer Prize-winning novelist Alice Walker begins to show us what she means by the concept "womanist." The concept is presented in Walker's *In Search of Our Mothers' Gardens* (Harcourt Brace Jovanovich, 1983) and many women in church and society have appropriated it as a way of affirming themselves as *black* while simultaneously owning their connection with feminism; and with the African-American community, male and female. The concept of womanist allows women to claim their roots in black history, religion, and culture.

What then is a womanist? Her origins are in the black folk expression "You acting womanish," meaning, according to Walker, "wanting to know more and in greater depth than is good for one . . . outrageous, audacious, courageous and willful behavior." A womanist is also "responsible, in charge, serious." She can walk to Canada and take others with her. She loves, she is committed, she is a universalist by temperament.

Her universality includes loving men and women, sexually or non-sexually. She loves music, dance, the spirit, food and roundness, struggle, and she loves herself. "Regardless."

Delores S. Williams is associate professor of theology, Union Theological Seminary, New York City. She is the author of *Sisters in the Wilderness: The Challenge of Womanist God-Talk*. This essay originally appeared in *Christianity and Crisis* 47 (March 2, 1987) and is reprinted with permission.

Walker insists that a womanist is also "committed to survival and wholeness of entire people, male and female." She is no separatist, "except for health." A womanist is a black feminist or feminist of color. Or as Walker says, "Womanist is to feminist as purple to lavender."

Womanist theology, a vision in its infancy, is emerging among African-American Christian women. Ultimately many sources—biblical, theological, ecclesiastical, social, anthropological, economic, and material from other religious radiations—will inform the development of this theology. As a contribution to this process, I will demonstrate how Walker's concept of womanist provides some significant clues for the work of womanist theologians. I will then focus on method and God-content in womanist theology. This contribution belongs to the work of prolegomena—prefatory remarks, introductory observations intended to be suggestive and not conclusive.

Codes and Contents

In her definition, Walker provides significant clues for the development of womanist theology. Her concept contains what black feminist scholar Bell Hooks in *From Margin of Center* (South End Press, 1984) identifies as cultural codes. These are words, beliefs, and behavioral patterns of a people that must be deciphered before meaningful communication can happen cross-culturally. Walker's codes are female-centered and they point beyond themselves to conditions, events, meanings, and values that have crystalized in the African-American community *around women's activity* and formed traditions.

A paramount example is mother-daughter advice. Black mothers have passed on wisdom for survival—in the white world, in the black community, and with men—for as long as anyone can remember. Female slave narratives, folk tales, and some contemporary black poetry and prose reflect this tradition. Some of it is collected in "Old Sister's Advice to her Daughters," in *The Book of Negro Folklore* edited by Langston Hughes and Arna Bontemps (Dodd Mead, 1958).

Walker's allusion to skin color points to an historic tradition of tension between black women over the matter of some black men's preference for light-skinned women. Her reference to black women's love of food and roundness points to customs of female care in the black community (including the church) associated with hospitality and nurture.

These cultural codes and their corresponding traditions are valuable resources for indicating and validating the kind of data upon which womanist theologians can reflect as they bring black women's social, religious, and cultural experience into the discourse of theology, ethics, biblical and religious studies. Female slave narratives, imaginative literature by black women, autobiographies, the work by black women in academic disciplines, and the testimonies of black church women will be authoritative sources for womanist theologians.

Walker situates her understanding of a womanist in the context of non-bourgeois black folk culture. The literature of this culture has traditionally reflected more egalitarian relations between men and women, much less rigidity in male-female roles, and more respect for female intelligence and ingenuity than is found in bourgeois culture.

The black folk are poor. Less individualistic than those who are better off, they have, for generations, practiced various forms of economic sharing. For example, immediately after Emancipation mutual aid societies pooled the resources of black folk to help pay for funerals and other daily expenses. *The Book of Negro Folklore* describes the practice of rent parties which flourished during the Depression. The black folk stressed togetherness and a closer connection with nature. They respect knowledge gained through lived experience monitored by elders who differ profoundly in social class and world view from the teachers and education encountered in American academic institutions. Walker's choice of context suggests that womanist theology can establish its lines of continuity in the black community with nonbourgeois traditions less sexist than the black power and black nationalist traditions.

In this folk context, some of the black female-centered cultural codes in Walker's definition (e.g., "Mama, I'm walking to Canada and I'm taking you and a bunch of slaves with me") point to folk heroines like Harriet Tubman, whose liberation activity earned her the name "Moses" of her people. This allusion to Tubman directs womanist memory to a liberation tradition in black history in which women took the lead, acting as catalysts for the community's revolutionary action and for social change. Retrieving this often hidden or diminished female tradition of catalytic action is an important task for womanist theologians and ethicists. Their research may well reveal that female models of authority have been absolutely essential for every struggle in the black community and for building and maintaining the community's institutions.

Freedom Fighters

The womanist theologian must search for the voices, actions, opinions, experience, and faith of women whose names sometimes slip into the male-centered rendering of black history, but whose actual stories remain remote. This search can lead to such little-known freedom fighters as Milla Granson and her courageous work on a Mississippi plantation. Her liberation method broadens our knowledge of the variety of strategies black people have used to obtain freedom. According to scholar Sylvia Dannett, in *Profiles in Negro Womanhood:*

Milla Granson, a slave, conducted a midnight school for several years. She had been taught to read and write by her former master in Kentucky . . . and in her little school hundreds of slaves benefited from her learning. . . . After laboring all day for their master, the slaves would creep stealthily to Milla's "schoolroom" (a little cabin in a back alley). . . . The doors and windows . . . had to be kept tightly sealed to avoid discovery. Each class was composed of twelve pupils and when Milla had brought them up to the extent of her ability, she "graduated" them and took in a dozen more. Through this means she graduated hundreds of slaves. Many of whom she taught to write a legible hand [forged] their own passes and set out for Canada.

Women like Tubman and Granson used subtle and silent strategies to liberate themselves and large numbers of black people. By uncovering as much as possible about such female liberation, the womanist begins to understand the relation of black history to the contemporary folk expression: "If Rosa Parks had not sat down, Martin King would not have stood up."

While she celebrates and *emphasizes* black women's culture and way of being in the world, Walker simultaneously affirms black women's historic connection with men through love and through a shared struggle for survival and for productive quality of life (e.g., "wholeness"). This suggests that two of the principal concerns of womanist theology should be survival and community building and maintenance. The goal of this community building is, of course, to establish a positive quality of life—economic, spiritual, educational—for black women, men, and children. Walker's understanding of a womanist as "not a separatist" ("except for health"), however, reminds the Christian womanist theologian that her concern for community building and maintenance must *ultimately* extend to the entire Christian community and beyond that to the larger human community.

Yet womanist consciousness is also informed by women's determination to love themselves. "Regardless." This translates into an admonition to black women to avoid the self-destruction of bearing a disproportionately large burden in the work of community building and maintenance. Walker suggests that women can avoid this trap by connecting with women's communities concerned about women's rights and well-being. Her identification of a womanist as also a feminist joins black women with their feminist heritage extending back into the nineteenth century in the work of black feminists like Sojourner Truth, Frances W. Harper, and Mary Church Terrell.

In making the feminist-womanist connection, however, Walker proceeds with great caution. While affirming an organic relationship between womanists and feminists, she also declares a deep shade of difference between them. ("Womanist is to feminist as purple to lavender.") This gives womanist scholars the freedom to explore the particularities of black women's history and culture without being guided by what white feminists have already identified as women's issues.

But womanist consciousness directs black women away from the negative divisions prohibiting community building among women. The womanist loves other women sexually and non-sexually. Therefore, respect for sexual preferences is one of the marks of womanist community. According to Walker, homophobia has no place. Nor does "Colorism" (i.e., "yella" and half-white black people valued more in the black world than black-skinned people), which often separates black women from each other. Rather, Walker's womanist claim is that color variety is the substance of universality. Color, like birth and death, is common to all people. Like the navel, it is a badge of humanity connecting people with people. Two other distinctions are prohibited in Walker's womanist thinking. Class hierarchy does not dwell among women who "love struggle, love the Folks . . . are committed to the survival and wholeness of an entire people." Nor do women compete for male attention when they "appreciate and prefer female culture . . . value . . . women's emotional flexibility . . . and women's strength."

The intimations about community provided by Walker's definition suggest no genuine community building is possible when men are excluded (except when women's health is at stake). Neither can it occur when black women's self-love, culture, and love for each other are not affirmed and are not considered vital for the community's self-understanding. And it is thwarted if black women are expected to bear "the lion's share" of the work and to sacrifice their well-being for the good of the group.

Yet, for the womanist, mothering and nurturing are vitally important. Walker's womanist reality begins with mothers relating to their children and is characterized by black women (not necessarily bearers of children) nurturing great numbers of black people in the liberation struggle (e.g., Harriet Tubman). Womanist emphasis upon the value of mothering and nurturing is consistent with the testimony of many black women. The poet Carolyn Rogers speaks of her mother as the great black bridge that brought her over. Walker dedicates her novel *The Third Life of Grange Copeland* to her mother "who made a way out of no way." As a child in the black church, I heard women (and men) give thanks to God for their mothers "who stayed behind and pulled the wagon over the long haul."

It seems, then, that the clues about community from Walker's definition of a womanist suggest that the mothering and nurturing dimension of Afro-American history can provide resources for shaping criteria to measure the quality of justice in the community. These criteria could be used to assure female-male equity in the presentation of the community's models of authority. They could also gauge the community's division of labor with regard to the survival tasks necessary for building and maintaining community.

Womanist Theology and Method

Womanist theology is already beginning to define the categories and methods needed to develop along lines consistent with the sources of that theology. Christian womanist theological methodology needs to be informed by at least four elements: (1) a multidialogical intent, (2) a liturgical intent, (3) a didactic intent, and (4) a commitment both to reason *and* to the validity of female imagery and metaphorical language in the construction of theological statements.

A multidialogical intent will allow Christian womanist theologians to advocate and participate in dialogue and action with *many* diverse social, political, and religious communities concerned about human survival and productive quality of life for the oppressed. The genocide of cultures and peoples (which has often been instigated and accomplished by Western white Christian groups or governments) and the nuclear threat of omnicide mandate womanist participation in such dialogue/action. But in this dialogue/action the womanist also should keep her speech and action focused upon the slow genocide of poor black women, children, and men by exploitative systems denying them productive jobs, education, health care, and living space. Multidialogical activity may, like a jazz symphony, communicate some of its most important messages in what the harmony-driven conventional ear hears as discord, as disruption of the harmony in both the black American and white American social, political, and religious status quo.

If womanist theological method is informed by a liturgical intent, then womanist theology will be relevant to (and will reflect) the thought, worship, and action of the black church. But a liturgical intent will also allow womanist theology to challenge the thought/worship/action of the black church with the discordant and prophetic messages emerging from womanist participation in multidialogics. This means that womanist theology will consciously impact *critically* upon the foundations of liturgy, challenging the church to use justice principles to select the sources that will shape the content of liturgy. The question must be asked: "How does this source portray blackness/darkness, women and economic justice for nonruling-class people?" A negative portrayal will demand omission of the source or its radical reformation by the black church. The Bible, a major source in black church liturgy, must also be subjected to the scrutiny of justice principles.

A didactic intent in womanist theological method assigns a teaching function to theology. Womanist theology should teach Christians new insights about moral life based on ethics supporting justice for women, survival, and a productive quality of life for poor women, children, and men. This means that the womanist theologian must give authoritative status to black folk wisdom (e.g., Brer Rabbit literature) and to black women's moral wisdom (expressed in their literature) when she responds to the question, "How ought the Christian to live in the world?" Certainly tensions may exist between the moral teachings derived from these sources and the moral teachings about obedience, love, and humility that have usually buttressed presuppositions about living the Christian life. Nevertheless, womanist theology, in its didactic intent, must teach the church the different ways God reveals prophetic word and action for Christian living.

These intents, informing theological method, can yield a theological language whose foundation depends as much upon its imagistic content as upon reason. The language can be rich in female imagery, metaphor, and story. For the black church, this kind of theological language may be quite useful, since the language of the black religious experience abounds in images and metaphors. Clifton H. Johnson's collection of black conversion experiences, *God Struck Me Dead* (United Church Press, 1969), illustrates this point.

The appropriateness of womanist theological language will ultimately reside in its ability to bring black women's history, culture, and religious experience into the interpretive circle of Christian theology and into the liturgical life of the church. Womanist theological language must, in this sense, be an instrument for social and theological change in church and society.

Who Do You Say God Is?

Regardless of one's hopes about intentionality and womanist theological method, questions must be raised about the God-content of the theology. Walker's mention of the black womanist's love of the spirit is a true reflection of the great respect Afro-American women have always shown for the presence and work of the spirit. In the black church, women (and men) often judge the effectiveness of the worship service not on the scholarly content of the sermon nor on the ritual nor on orderly process. Rather, worship has been effective if "the spirit was high," i.e., if the spirit was actively and obviously present in a balanced blend of prayer, of cadenced word (the sermon), and of syncopated music ministering to the pain of the people.

The importance of this emphasis upon the spirit is that it allows Christian womanist theologians, in their use of the Bible, to identify and reflect upon those biblical stories in which poor oppressed women had a special encounter with divine emissaries of God, like the spirit. In the Hebrew Testament, Hagar's story is most illustrative and relevant to Afro-American women's experience of bondage, of African heritage, of encounter with God/emissary in the midst of fierce survival struggles. Kate Cannon among a number of black female preachers and ethicists urges black Christian women to regard themselves as Hagar's sisters.

In relation to the Christian or New Testament, the Christian womanist theologian can refocus the salvation story so that it emphasizes the beginning of revelation with the spirit mounting Mary, a woman of the poor (". . . the Holy Spirit shall come upon thee, and the power of the Highest shall overshadow thee . . ." Luke 1:35). Such an interpretation of revelation has roots in nineteenth century black abolitionist and feminist Sojourner Truth. Posing an important question and response, she refuted a white preacher's claim that women could not have rights equal to men's because Christ was not a woman. Truth asked, "Whar did your Christ come from?. . . From God and a woman! Man had nothin' to do wid Him!" This suggests that womanist theology could eventually speak of God in a well-developed theology of the spirit. The sources for this theology are many. Harriet Tubman often "went into the spirit" before her liberation missions and claimed her strength for liberation activity came from this way of meeting God. Womanist theology has grounds for shaping a theology of the spirit informed by black women's political action.

Christian womanist responses to the question "Who do you say God is?" will be influenced by these many sources. Walker's way of connecting womanists with the spirit is only one clue. The integrity of black church women's faith, their love of Jesus, their commitment to life, love, family, and politics will also yield vital clues. And other theological voices (black liberation, feminist, Islamic, Asian, Hispanic, African, Jewish, and Western white male traditional) will provide insights relevant for the construction of the God-content of womanist theology.

Each womanist theologian will add her own special accent to the understandings of God emerging from womanist theology. But if one needs a final image to describe women coming together to shape the enterprise, Bess B. Johnson in *God's Fierce Whimsy* (Pilgrim Press, 1985) offers an appropriate one. Describing the difference between the play of male and female children in the black community where she developed, Johnson says:

> the boys in the neighborhood had this game with rope . . . tug-o'-war . . . till finally some side would jerk the rope away from the others, who'd fall down. . . . Girls . . . weren't allowed to play with them in this tug-o'-war: so we figured out how to make our own rope — out of . . . little dandelions. You just keep adding them, one to another, and you can go on and on. . . . Anybody, even the boys, could join us. . . . The whole purpose of our game was to create this dandelion chain — that was it. And we'd keep going, creating till our mamas called us home.

Like Johnson's dandelion chain, womanist theological vision will grow as black women come together and connect piece with piece. Between the process of creating and the sense of calling, womanist theology will one day present itself in full array, reflecting the divine spirit that connects us all.

20

WOMANIST THEOLOGY: BLACK WOMEN'S EXPERIENCE AS A SOURCE FOR DOING THEOLOGY, WITH SPECIAL REFERENCE TO CHRISTOLOGY

Jacquelyn Grant

Introduction

This essay is an exploration into the experiences of Black women for the purpose of providing alternative sources for doing theology.

Black theology and other third world theologies of liberation have shown through their challenge of the methodologies of classical theologies that experience of the dominant culture has been the invisible crucible for theologizing. They have demonstrated that theology is not unrelated to socio-political realities of existence; and that historically it has been used to maintain the social and political advantages of the status quo. The portrayal of the universal God was such that an affirmation of this God meant a simultaneous negation of all others' cultural perceptions of the divinity, as well as a negation of those very cultures. Nowhere was this more clear than in the area of Christian foreign missions where conversion to Christianity implicitly meant deculturalization and acceptance of the western value system on the part of Asians, Africans, and Latin Americans. Upon conversion, one had to withdraw from indigenous ways of imaging the divine reality, and embrace foreign, western ways which often served to undergird oppressive religious, social and political structures.

This is true not only in the foreign missions field but also in the western

Jacquelyn Grant, author of *White Women's Christ and Black Women's Jesus*, is associate professor of systematic theology at the Interdenominational Theological Center. Presented as the Charles B. Copher Annual Faculty Lecture at Interdenominational Theological Center, Atlanta, Georgia in 1986, this essay was published in the *Journal of the Interdenominational Theological Center* 13 (Spring 1986) and is reprinted with permission.

world; it is reflected in the ways in which oppressors deal with oppressed people within their own territory. We see this with respect to third world people in the first world context as well as with respect to women.

An illustration emerging out of Black theology and Feminist theology will make the point. Theologians in both these theological camps propose an alternative understanding, for example, of Christian love.

James Cone in an early work makes a distinction between a non-threatening love of many Christians and the radical love of Jesus which demands justice.

> There is no place in Christian theology for sentimental love — love without risk or cost. Love demands all, the whole of one's being. Thus, for the black [person] to believe the Word of God about [God's] love revealed in Christ, he/she must be prepared to meet head-on the sentimental "Christian" love of whites, which would make him/her a nonperson.[1]

Cone insists that one cannot practice Christian love and at the same time practice racism. He argues:

> It seems that whites forget about the necessary interrelatedness of love, justice, and power when they encounter Black people. Love becomes emotional and sentimental. This sentimental, condescending love accounts for their desire to "help" by relieving the physical pains of the suffering blacks so they can satisfy their own religious piety and keep the poor powerless. But the new blacks, redeemed in Christ, must refuse their "help" and demand that blacks be confronted as persons. They must say to whites that authentic love is not "help," not giving Christmas baskets, but working for political, social, and economic justice, which always means a redistribution of power. It is a kind of power which enables the blacks to fight their own battles and thus keep their dignity. "Powerlessness breeds a race of beggars."[2]

Black people do not need a love which functions contrary to the establishment of Black personhood. This understanding of love was just recently affirmed by Black theologians (lay and clergy, professional and non-professional) in Southern Africa in their challenge to the church through *The Kairos Document.* They cautioned, "we must also remember that the most loving thing we can do for both the oppressed and for our enemies who are oppressors is to eliminate the oppression, remove the tyrants from power and establish a just government for the common good of all the people."[3] Here, love is not defined in the interest of those who wish to maintain the present status quo. But it is defined from the point of view of those on the underside of history — the victims of the oppressors' power.

In a similar vein, feminists challenge traditional understandings of love. Valerie Saiving Goldstein expresses her suspicions of traditional theological works in the following way:

I am no longer certain as I once was that, when theologians speak of "man," they are using the word in its generic sense. It is, after all, a well-known fact that theology has been written almost exclusively by men. This alone should put us on guard, especially since contemporary theologians constantly remind us that one of man's strongest temptations is to identify his own limited perspective with universal truth.[4]

Lifting up the Christian notion of sin and love, Goldstein suggests that it would be equally unsatisfactory to impose universal understanding on those concepts. The identification of these notions with self-assertion and selflessness respectively, functions differently in masculine experience and feminine experience. She explains further:

Contemporary theological doctrines of love have, I believe, been constructed primarily upon the basis of masculine experience and thus view the human condition from the male standpoint. Consequently, these doctrines do not provide an adequate interpretation of the situation of women—nor, for that matter, of men, especially in light of certain fundamental changes now taking place in our own society.[5]

Because of their feminine character, for women love takes the form of nurturing, supporting and servicing their families. Consequently, if a woman believes

the theologians, she will try to strangle other impulses in herself. She will believe that, having chosen marriage and children and thus being face to face with the needs of her family for love, refreshment, and forgiveness, she has no right to ask anything for herself but must submit without qualification to the strictly feminine role.[6]

For women, too, the issue is one of personhood—are women to deny who they are in order to be saved?

Goldstein then argues that when experience in theology is scrutinized, we will discover that because it has been synonymous with masculine experience, it is inadequate to deal with the situation of women.

In other words, Black theologians and feminist theologians have argued that the universalism which classical theologians attempt to uphold represents merely the particular experiences of the dominant culture. Blacks identify that experience as White experience; and women identify it as male experience. The question then is, if universalism is the criterion for valid theology, how is such a universalism achieved?

[margin note: it is not universali...]

What I will be exploring here is how Black women's experiences can provide some insights into this question. In doing so, Black women not only join Blacks and feminists in their challenge of theology but they also provide an internal critique for Black men as well as for White women. In this paper, I will focus primarily upon Black women's experience as related to the development of feminist theology. (In a rather limited way, I have addressed the issue of Black women's experiences and Black theology in an article entitled "Black Theology and the Black Woman."[7] That subject certainly has not been exhausted, and shall be treated in more substantive ways in the future.)

But here I am interested in engaging feminist theology with reference to its constructive efficacy for Black women given the peculiarities of their experiences. The results will be the beginnings of a theology from a Black woman's perspective with special reference to Christology.

In order to create a common starting point, let's begin with a synopsis of the basic tenets of Feminist theology. First, Feminist theology seeks to develop a *wholistic theology*. Feminist theology rejects the traditional forms of oppressive and one-sided, male-dominated theologies which arise out of patriarchal religion(s).[8] Women have begun to see that their continuous oppression in the church and society has its basis in these patriarchal religion(s). Historically, the theologies of religions have emerged out of the experiences of men, making the theologies representative thereof. Because humanity is comprised of both men and women Feminist theologians seek to develop a more wholistic perspective in theology.

Second, in seeking to produce a wholistic perspective in theology Feminist theologians call for the *eradication of social/sexual dualisms* in human existence which are inherent in patriarchy. A patriarchy is characterized by male-domination and female submission and subordination. In such a society, men are considered strong, intelligent, rational and aggressive; women are considered weak, irrational, and docile.

A third function of Feminist theology is to *conceptualize new and positive images of women*. Throughout history, including the history of theology, women have been portrayed in negative ways. They have been sources of evil (snakes), authors of trickery (witches), and stimulants (therefore causes) for the sexual perversions of men (temptresses and prostitutes). These negative images must be changed to reflect reality.

Finally, Feminist theology must *evaluate male articulated understandings of the Christian faith*. Doctrines developed in a system of patriarchy merely perpetuate patriarchal structures. As the patriarchal theological system is challenged, so are the doctrines, e.g., God, Jesus Christ, the Fall and the Church.

Emerging Black Feminist Perspective

It has been argued by many Blacks that the women's liberation movement is a White middle-class movement. Therefore, it is believed to be totally irrelevant to the situation of Black women since the majority of them are not middle-class.

Brenda Eichelberger gives several reasons for Black women's non-involvement in feminist causes. Among them are such things as class differences, the lack of Black women's knowledge about the real issues involved and the suspicion that the middle-class White women's movement is divisive to the Black community which claims prior allegiance.[9] In spite of these and other negative responses to the White women's liberation movement, there has been a growing feminist consciousness among many Black women and some Black men. This consciousness is coupled by the increased willingness of Black women to undertake an independent analysis of sexism, thereby creating an emerging Black perspective on feminism. Black feminism grows out of Black women's tri-dimensional reality of race/sex/class. It holds that full human liberation cannot be achieved simply by the elimination of any one form of oppression. Consequently, real liberation must be "broad in the concrete";[10] it must be based upon a multi-dimensional analysis.

Recent writings by secular Black feminists have challenged White feminist analysis and Black race analysis, particularly by introducing data from Black women's experience that has been historically ignored by White feminists and Black male liberationists.

In only a few of them do Black women employ only a gender analysis to treat Black women's reality. Whereas Ntozake Shange focuses chiefly upon sexism, Michelle Wallace, like Alice Walker, presumes that White racism has had an adverse effect upon the Black community in a way that confuses and reinforces the already existing sexism. Sharon Harley, Rosalyn Terborg-Penn, Paula Giddings and Gloria Wade-Gayles all recognize the inclusiveness of the oppressive reality of Black women as they endure racism, sexism and economic oppression. Barbara Smith, Gloria Hull, Bell Hooks and Angela Davis particularly explore the implications of this tri-dimensional oppression of Black women. In so doing, Black women have either articulated Black feminist perspectives or developed grounds for doing so.[11] These perspectives, however, have not led to the resolution of tensions between Black women and White women, and they even have brought to the forefront some tensions between Black women and Black men.

On the contrary, the possibly irreparable nature of these tensions is implied in Walker's suggestion that the experience of being a Black woman or a White woman is so different that another word is required to describe the liberative efforts of Black women. Her suggestion that the word "womanist" is more appropriate for Black women is derived from the sense of the word as it is used in Black communities:

Womanist, from womanish. (Opp. of "girlish," i.e., frivolous, irresponsible, not serious.) A Black feminist or feminist of color. From the Black folk expression of mothers to female children, "You acting womanish," i.e., like a woman. Usually referring to outrageous, audacious, courageous or willful behavior. Wanting to know more and in greater depth than is considered "good" for one. Interest in grown-up doings. Acting grown up. Being grown up. Interchangeable with another black folk expression: "You trying to be grown." Responsible. In charge. Serious.[12]

Womanists were Sojourner Truth, Jarena Lee, Amanda Berry Smith, Ida B. Wells, Mary Church Terrell, Mary McCloud Bethune and countless others not remembered in any historical study. A womanist then is a strong Black woman who has sometimes been mislabeled as domineering castrating matriarch. A womanist is one who has developed survival strategies in spite of the oppression of her race and sex in order to save her family and her people. Walker's womanist notation suggests not "the feminist," but the active struggle of Black women that makes them who they are. For some Black women that may involve being feminine as traditionally defined, and for others it involves being masculine as stereotypically defined. In any case, womanist means being and acting out who you are and interpreting the reality for yourself. In other words, Black women speak out for themselves. As a Black feminist critic Barbara Christian explains, referring to Audre Lorde's poem about the deadly consequence of silence, Black women must speak up and answer in order to validate their own experience. This is important even if only to ourselves. It is to the womanist tradition that Black women must appeal for the doing of theology.

The Beginnings of a Womanist Theology with Special Reference to Christology

Womanist theology begins with the experiences of Black women as its point of departure. This experience includes not only Black women's activities in the larger society but also in the churches, and reveals that Black women have often rejected the oppressive structure in the church as well.

These experiences provide a context which is significant for doing theology. Those experiences had been and continue to be defined by racism, sexism and classism and therefore offer a unique opportunity and a new challenge for developing a relevant perspective in the theological enterprise. This perspective in theology which I am calling womanist theology draws upon the life and experiences of some Black women who have created meaningful interpretations of the Christian faith.

Black women must do theology out of their tri-dimensional experience of racism/sexism/classism. To ignore any aspect of this experience is to deny the wholistic and integrated reality of Black womanhood. When Black women say that God is on the side of the oppressed, we mean that God is in solidarity with the struggles of those on the underside of humanity, those whose lives are bent and broken from the many levels of assault perpetrated against them.

In a chapter entitled "Black Women: Shaping Feminist Theory," Hooks elaborates on the interrelationship of the threefold oppressive reality of Black women and shows some of the weaknesses of White feminist theory. Challenging the racist and classist assumptions of White feminism, Hooks writes:

Racism abounds in the writings of white feminists, reinforcing white supremacy and negating the possibility that women will bond politically across ethnic and racial boundaries. Past feminist refusal to draw attention to and attack racial hierarchy suppressed the link between race and class. Yet class structure in American society has been shaped by the racial politics of white supremacy.[13]

This means that Black women, because of oppression determined by race and their subjugation as women, make up a disproportionately high percentage of the poor and working classes. However, the fact that Black women are a subjugated group even within the Black community and the White women's community does not mean that they are alone in their oppression within those communities. In the women's community poor White women are discriminated against, and in the Black community, poor Black men are marginalized. This suggests that classism, as well as racism and sexism, has a life of its own. Consequently, simply addressing racism and sexism is inadequate to bring about total liberation. Even though there are dimensions of class which are not directly related to race or sex, classism impacts Black women in a peculiar way which results in the fact that they are most often on the bottom of the social and economic ladder. For Black women doing theology, to ignore classism would mean that their theology is no different from any other bourgeois theology. It would be meaningless to the majority of Black women, who are themselves poor. This means that addressing only issues relevant to middle-class women or Blacks will simply not do. The daily struggles of poor Black women must serve as the gauge for the verification of the claims of womanist theology. Anna Julia Cooper makes a relevant point:

have to look at. Classism

> Women's wrongs are thus indissolubly linked with all undefended woes, and the acquirement of her "rights" will mean the supremacy of triumph of all right over might, the supremacy of the moral forces of reason, and justice, and love in the government of the nations of earth.[14]

Black women's experience must be affirmed as the crucible for doing womanist theology. It is the context in which we must decide theological questions. More specifically, it is within the context of this experience that Black women read the Bible. A (brief) look at Black women's use of the Bible indicates how it is their experiences which determine relevant questions for them.

The Bible in the Womanist Tradition

Theological investigation into the experiences of Christian Black women reveals that Black women considered the Bible to be a major source of religious validation in their lives. Though Black women's relationship with God preceded their introduction to the Bible, this Bible gave some content to their God-consciousness.[15] The source for Black women's understanding of God has been twofold: first, God's revelation directly to them, and secondly, God's revelation as witnessed in the Bible and as read and heard in the context of their experience. The understanding of God as creator, sustainer, comforter, and liberator took on life as they agonized over their pain, and celebrated the hope that as God delivered the Israelites, they would be delivered as well. The God of the Old and New Testament became real in the consciousness of oppressed Black women. Of the use of the Bible, Fannie Barrier Williams quite aptly said:

> Though the Bible was not an open book to the Negro before emancipa-
> tion, thousands of the enslaved men and women of the negro race learned
> more than was taught to them. Thousands of them realized the deeper
> meanings, the sweeter consolations and the spiritual awakenings that are
> part of the religious experiences of all Christians.[16]

In other words, though Black people in general and Black women in particular were politically impotent, religiously controlled, they were able to appropriate certain themes of the Bible which spoke to their reality. For example, Jarena Lee, a nineteenth-century Black woman preacher in the African Methodist Episcopal Church, constantly emphasized the theme "Life and Liberty" in her sermons which were always biblically based. This interplay of scripture and experience was exercised even more expressly by many other Black women. An ex-slave woman revealed that when her experience negated certain oppressive interpretations of the Bible given by White preachers, she, through engaging the biblical message for herself, rejected them. Consequently, she also dismissed white preachers who distorted the message in order to maintain slavery. Her grandson, Howard Thurman, speaks of her use of the Bible in this way:

> "During the days of slavery," she said, "the master's minister would occa-
> sionally hold services for the slaves. Alas the white minister used as his
> text something from Paul. 'Slaves be obedient to them that are your mas-
> ters . . . as unto Christ.' Then he would go on to show how, if we were
> good and happy slaves, God would bless us. I promised my Maker that if
> I ever learned to read and if freedom ever came, I would not read that
> part of the Bible."[17]

What we see here is perhaps more than a mere rejection of a White preacher's interpretation of the Bible: it is an exercise in internal critique of the Bible. The liberating message of the gospel is seen as over against the oppressive elements in the Bible.

The truth which the Bible brought was undeniable, though perception of it was often distorted in order to support the monstrous system of oppression. Sarcastically responding to this tendency, Fannie Barrier Williams admonished, "do not open the Bible too wide." Biblical interpretation, realized Williams, a non-theologically trained person, had at its basis the prior agenda of White America. She therefore argued:

> Religion, like every other force in America, was first used as in instrument
> and servant of slavery. All attempts to Christianize the negro were limited

by the important fact that he was property of valuable and peculiar sort and that the property value must not be disturbed, even if his soul were lost. If Christianity could make the negro docile, domestic and less an independent and fighting savage, let it be preached to that extent and no further.[18]

Such false, pernicious, demoralizing gospel could only be preached if the Bible was not opened wide enough, lest one sees the liberating message of Jesus as summarized in Luke 4:18. The Bible must be read and interpreted in the light of Black women's own oppression and God's revelation within that context. Womanist must, like Sojourner, "compare the teachings of the Bible with the witness" in them.[19]

To do Womanist theology, then, we must read and hear the Bible and engage it within the context of our own experience. This is the only way that it can make sense to people who are oppressed. Black women of the past did not hesitate in doing this and we must do no less.

Jesus in the Womanist Tradition

Having opened the Bible wider than many White people, Black people, in general, and Black women in particular, found a Jesus who they could claim, and whose claim for them was one of affirmation of dignity and self-respect.

In the experience of Black people, Jesus was "all things."[20] Chief among these however was the belief in Jesus as the divine co-sufferer, who empowers them in situations of oppression. For Christian Black women in the past, Jesus was their central frame of reference. They identified with Jesus because they believed that Jesus identified with them. As Jesus was persecuted and made to suffer undeservedly, so were they. His suffering culminated in the crucifixion. Their crucifixion included rapes, and husbands being castrated (literally and metaphorically), babies being sold, and other cruel and often murderous treatments. But Jesus' suffering was not the suffering of a mere human, for Jesus was understood to be God incarnate. As Harold Carter observed of Black prayers in general, there was no difference made between the persons of the trinity, Jesus, God, or the Holy Spirit. All of these proper names for God were used interchangeably in prayer language. Thus, Jesus was the one who speaks the world into creation. He was the power behind the Church.[21] Black women's affirmation of Jesus as God meant that White people were not God. One old slave woman clearly demonstrates this as she prayed:

"Dear Massa Jesus, we all uns beg Ooner [you] come make us a call dis yere day. We is nutting but poor Etiopian women and people ain't tink much 'bout we. We ain't trust any of dem great high people for come to we church, but do' you is de one great Massa, great too much dan Massa Linkum, you ain't shame to care for we African people."[22]

Implicit in the description "nothing but poor Black women" and what follows is the awareness of the public devaluation of Black women. But in spite of that Jesus is presented as a confidant who could be trusted while White people could not be trusted. This woman affirmed the contribution of Abraham Lincoln to the emancipation of Blacks, but rejected Mr. Lincoln as her real or ultimate master. Quite a contrast to the master's (slave owner's) perception of his/herself.

This slave woman did not hesitate to identify her struggle and pain with those of Jesus. In fact, the common struggle made her know that Jesus would respond to her beck and call.

> Come to we, dear Massa Jesus. De sun, he hot too much, de road am dat long and boggy (sandy) and we ain't got no buggy for send and fetch Ooner. But Massa, you 'member how you walked dat hard walk up Calvary and ain't weary but tink about we all dat way. We know you ain't weary for to come to we. We pick out de torns, de prickles, de brier, de backslidin' and de quarrel and de sin out of you path so dey shan't hurt Ooner pierce feet no more.[23]

The reference to "no buggy" to send for Jesus, brings to mind the limited material possessions of pre- and post-Civil War Blacks. In her speech, "Ain't I a Woman," Sojourner Truth distinguished between White women's and Black women's experiences by emphasizing that Black women were not helped into carriages as were White women.[24] In the prayer, this woman speaks of that reality wherein most Blacks didn't even have carriages or buggys. For had she owned one, certainly she'd send it to fetch Jesus. Here we see the concern for the comfort and the suffering of Jesus. Jesus suffers when we sin—when we backslide or when we quarrel. But still Jesus is identified with her plight. Note that Jesus went to the cross with this Black woman on his mind. He was thinking about her and all others like her. So totally dedicated to the poor, the weak, the downtrodden, the outcast that in this Black woman's faith, Jesus would never be too tired to come. As she is truly among the people at the bottom of humanity, she can make things comfortable for Jesus even though she may have nothing to give him—no water, no food—but she can give tears and love. She continues:

> Come to me, dear Massa Jesus. We all uns ain't got no good cool water for give when you thirsty. You know Massa, de drought so long, and the well so low, ain't nutting but mud to drink. But we gwine to take de munion cup and fill it wid de tear of repentance, and love clean out of we heart. Dat all we hab to gib you good Massa.[25]

The material or physical deprivation experienced by this woman did not reduce her desire to give Jesus the best. Being a Black woman in the American society meant essentially being poor, with no buggy, and no good cool water.

Life for Black women was indeed bad, hot and at best muddy. Note that there is no hint that their condition results from some divine intention. Now, whereas I am not prepared to say that this same woman or any others in that church the next day would have been engaged in political praxis by joining such movements as Nat Turner's rebellion or Denmark Vesey's revolt, it is clear that her perspective was such that the social, political and economic orders were believed to be sinful and against the will of the real master, Jesus.

For Black women, the role of Jesus unraveled as they encountered him in their experience as one who empowers the weak. In this vein, Jesus was such a central part of Sojourner Truth's life that all of her sermons made him the starting point. When asked by a preacher if the source of her preaching was the Bible, she responded, "No honey, can't preach from de Bible—can't read a letter."[26] Then she explained, "When I preaches, I has jest one text to preach from, an' I always preaches from this one. My text is, 'When I found Jesus!' "[27] In this sermon Sojourner Truth recounts the events and struggles of life from the time her parents were brought from Africa and sold "up an' down, an' hither an' yon . . ."[28] to the time that she met Jesus within the context of her struggles for dignity of Black people and women. Her encounter with Jesus brought such joy that she became overwhelmed with love and praise:

> Praise, praise, praise to the Lord! An I begun to feel such a love in my soul as I never felt before—love to all creatures. An then, all of a sudden, it stopped, an I said, Dar's de white folks that have abused you, an beat you, an abused your people—think o them! But then there came another rush of love through my soul, an cried out loud—Lord, I can love even de white folks![29]

This love was not a sentimental, passive love. It was a tough, active love that empowered her to fight more fiercely for the freedom of her people. For the rest of her life she continued speaking at abolition and women's rights gatherings, and condemned the horrors of oppression.

The Womanist Traditions and Christological Reflections

More than anyone, Black theologians have captured the essence of the significance of Jesus in the lives of Black people which to an extent includes Black women. They all hold that the Jesus of history is important for understanding who he was and his significance for us today. By and large they have affirmed that this Jesus is the Christ, that is, God incarnate. They have argued that in the light of our experience, Jesus meant freedom.[30] They have maintained that Jesus means freedom from the sociopsychological, psychocultural, economic and political oppression of Black people. In other words, Jesus is a political messiah.[31] "To free [humans] from bondage was Jesus' own definition of his ministry."[32] This meant that as Jesus identified with the lowly of his day, he now identifies with the lowly of this day, who in the American context are Black people. The identification is so real that Jesus Christ in fact becomes Black. It is important to note that Jesus' blackness is not a result of ideological distortion of a few Black thinkers, but a result of careful christological investigation. Cone examines the sources of Christology and concludes that Jesus is Black because "Jesus was a Jew." He explains:

> It is on the basis of the soteriological meaning of the particularity of his Jewishness that theology must affirm the christological significance of Jesus' present blackness. He *is* black because he was a Jew. The affirmation of the black Christ can be understood when the significance of his past Jewishness is related dialetically to the significance of his present blackness. On the other hand, the Jewishness of Jesus located him in the context of the Exodus, thereby connecting his appearance in Palestine with God's liberation of oppressed Israelites from Egypt. Unless Jesus were truly from Jewish ancestry, it would make little theological sense to say that he is the fulfillment of God's covenant with Israel. But on the other hand, the blackness of Jesus brings out the soteriological meaning of his Jewishness for our contemporary situation when Jesus' person is understood in the context of the cross and resurrection. Without negating the divine election of Israel, the cross and resurrection are Yahweh's fulfillment of his original intention for Israel. . . .[33]

The condition of Black people today reflects the cross of Jesus. Yet the resurrection brings the hope that liberation from oppression is immanent. The resurrected Black Christ signifies this hope.

Cone further argues that this christological title, "The Black Christ," is not validated by its universality, but, in fact, by its particularity. Its significance lies in whether or not the christological title "points to God's universal will to liberate particular oppressed people from inhumanity."[34] These particular oppressed peoples to which Cone refers are characterized in Jesus' parable on the Last Judgment as "the least." "The least in America are literally and symbolically present in Black people."[35] This notion of "the least" is attractive because it descriptively locates the condition of Black women. "The least" are those people who have no water to give, but offer what they have, as the old slave woman cited above says in her prayer. Black women's experience in general is such a reality. Their tri-dimensional reality renders their particular situation a complex one. One could say that not only are they the oppressed of the oppressed, but their situation represents "the particular within the particular."

But is this just another situation that takes us deeper into the abyss of theological relativity? I would argue that it is not, because it is in the context of Black women's experience where the particular connects up with the universal. By this I mean that in each of the three dynamics of oppression, Black women share in the reality of a broader community. They share race suffering with Black men; with White women and other Third World women, they are victims of sexism; and with poor Blacks and Whites, and other Third World peoples, especially women, they are disproportionately poor. To speak of Black women's tri-dimensional reality, therefore, is not to speak of Black women exclusively, for there is an implied universality which connects them with others.

Likewise, with Jesus Christ, there was an implied universality which made him identify with others — the poor, the woman, the stranger. To affirm Jesus' solidarity with the "least of the people" is not an exercise in romanticized contentment with one's oppressed status in life. For as the resurrection signified that there is more to life than the cross of Jesus Christ, for Black women it signifies that their tri-dimensional oppressive existence is not the end, but it merely represents the context in which a particular people struggle to experience hope and liberation. Jesus Christ thus represents a three-fold significance; first he identifies with the "little people," Black women, where they are; secondly, he affirms the basic humanity for these, "the least"; and thirdly, he inspires active hope in the struggle for resurrected, liberated existence.

To locate the Christ in Black people is a radical and necessary step, but understanding of Black women's reality challenges us to go further. Christ among the least must also mean Christ in the community of Black women. William Eichelberger was able to recognize this as he further particularized the significance of the Blackness of Jesus by locating Christ in Black women's community. He was able to see Christ not only as Black male but also Black female.

> God in revealing Himself and His attributes from time to time in His creaturely existence has exercised His freedom to formalize His appearance in a variety of ways. . . . God revealed Himself at a point in the past as Jesus the Christ a Black male. My reasons for affirming the Blackness of Jesus of Nazareth are much different from that of the white apologist. . . . God wanted to identify with that segment of mankind which had suffered most, and is still suffering. . . . I am constrained to believe that God in our times has updated His form of revelation to western society. It is my feeling that God is now manifesting Himself, and has been for over 450 years, in the form of the Black American Woman as mother, as wife, as nourisher, sustainer and preserver of life, the Suffering Servant who is despised and rejected by men, a personality of sorrow who is acquainted with grief. The Black Woman has borne our griefs and carried our sorrows. She has been wounded because of American white society's transgressions and bruised by white iniquities. It appears that she may be the instrumentality through whom God will make us whole.[36]

Granted, Eichelberger's categories for God and woman are very traditional. Nevertheless, the significance of his thought is that he is able to conceive of the Divine reality as other than a Black male messianic figure.

Even though Black women have been able to transcend some of the oppressive tendencies of White male (and Black male) articulated theologies, careful study reveals that some traditional symbols are inadequate for us today. The

Christ understood as the stranger, the outcast, the hungry, the weak, the poor, makes the traditional male Christ (Black and White) less significant. Even our sisters of the past had some suspicions about the effects of a male image of the divine, for they did challenge the oppressive use of it in the church's theology. In so doing, they were able to move from a traditional oppressive Christology, with respect to women, to an egalitarian Christology. This kind of egalitarian Christology was operative in Jarena Lee's argument for the right of women to preach. She argued "... the Saviour died for the woman as well as for the man."[37] The crucifixion was for universal salvation, not just for male salvation or, as we may extend the argument to include, not just for white salvation. Because of this, Christ came and died, no less for the woman as for the man, no less for Blacks as for Whites. For Lee, this was not an academic issue, but one with practical ramifications.

> If the man may preach, because the Saviour died for him, why not the woman? Seeing he died for her also. Is he not a whole Saviour instead of half one? as those who hold it wrong for a woman to preach, would seem to make It appear.[38]

Lee correctly perceives that there is an ontological issue at stake. If Jesus Christ were a Saviour of men then it is true the maleness of Christ would be paramount.[39] But if Christ is a Savior of all, then it is the humanity—the wholeness—of Christ which is significant.

Sojourner was aware of the same tendency of some scholars and church leaders to link the maleness of Jesus and the sin of Eve with the status of women and she challenged this notion in her famed speech "Ain't I A Woman?"

> Then that little man in black there, he says women can't have as much rights as men, 'cause Christ wasn't a woman! Where did your Christ come from? Where did your Christ come from? From God and a woman. Man had nothing to do with Him.
>
> If the first woman God ever made was strong enough to turn the world upside down alone, these women together ought to be able to turn it back, and get it right side up again! And now they is asking to do it, the men better let them.[40]

I would argue, as suggested by both Lee and Sojourner, that the significance of Christ is not his maleness, but his humanity. The most significant events of Jesus Christ were the life and ministry, the crucifixion, and the resurrection. The significance of these events, in one sense, is that in them the absolute becomes concrete. God becomes concrete not only in the man Jesus, for he was crucified, but in the lives of those who will accept the challenge of the risen Saviour—the Christ. For Lee, this meant that women could preach; for

Sojourner, it meant that women could possibly save the world; for me, it means today, this Christ, found in the experience of Black women, is a Black woman.

Conclusion

I have argued that Black women's tri-dimensional reality provides a fertile context for articulating a theological perspective which is wholistic in scope and liberating in nature. The theology is potentially wholistic because the experience out of which it emerges is totally interconnected with other experiences. It is potentially liberating because it rests not on one single issue which could be considered only a middle-class issue relevant to one group of people, but it is multi-faceted. Thus, the possibility for wholistic theology is more likely. Feminist theology as presently developed is limited by virtue of the experience base for feminist theology. That is, when feminists say that experience is the crucible for doing [feminist] theology, they usually mean White women's experience. With few exceptions, feminist thinkers do their analysis primarily, and in some circles exclusively, based on the notion that because sexism is the longest and most universal form of oppression, it should claim priority.[41]

Black women, by and large, have not held this assumption. Many have claimed that because of the pervasiveness of racism, and because of its defining character for Black life in general, racism is most important. Though Sojourner Truth never did develop a sophisticated social analysis she was aware of the fact that she (and her people) were poor because she was Black, and perhaps poorer because she was woman. I say "perhaps" simply because in the slave economy one could argue that there was relatively little distinction between the property status of slaves by virtue of gender; women were no less property than men. As property, they were a part of the material distributed, rather than participants in the inequitable (system of) material distribution. Thus as indicated above in the Black woman's prayer, material possessions of Blacks were limited. In a sense one could say that by virtue of one's race, one was slave and by virtue of that status one was poor.

Still as we see the issues today, class distinctions which have emerged even in the Black community, and sex differences, which have taken on new forms of institutionalization, must be addressed. For liberation to become a reality, race, sex and class must be deliberately confronted. Interconnected as they are, they all impinge greatly on the lives of Black women. Overwhelming as are these realities, black women do not feel defeated. For Jarena Lee observed the hope of the struggle is based on the faith that Jesus died (and was raised) for the woman as well as the man. This realization gave inspiration for the struggle. Black women today inside and outside of the church still bring an optimistic spirit as reflected in the conclusion of Maya Angelou's poem, "Still I Rise":

> Out of the hut of history's shame
> I rise
> Up from a past that's rooted in pain

I rise
I'm a Black ocean, leaping and wide,
Welling and swelling, I bear in the tide
Leaving behind nights of terror and fear
I rise
Into a daybreak that's wondrously clear
I rise
Bringing the gifts that my ancestors gave
I am the dream and the hope of the slave.
I rise.
I rise.
I rise.[42]

NOTES

1. James H. Cone, *Black Theology and Black Power* (New York: Seabury Press, 1969), 53-54.

2. Ibid., 54-54.

3. The Kairos Theologians, *The Kairos Document: Challenge to the Church,* 2d ed. (Braarufontein, South Africa: Skotaville Publishers, 1985; Grand Rapids, Mich.: Eerdmans, 1986), 24-25.

4. Valerie Saiving Goldstein, "The Human Situation of a Feminine," *Journal of Religion* 40 (April 1960): 100.

5. Ibid.

6. Ibid.

7. Jacquelyn Grant, "Black Theology and the Black Woman" in *Black Theology: A Documentary History 1966-1979,* ed. Gayraud S. Wilmore and James H. Cone (Maryknoll, N.Y.: Orbis Books, 1979; and rev. ed. vol. 1, 1993).

8. See Sheila D. Collins, *A Different Heaven and Earth: A Feminist Perspective on Religion* (Valley Forge, Pa.: Judson Press, 1974); Mary Daly, *Beyond God the Father: Toward a Philosophy of Women's Liberation* (Boston: Beacon Press, 1973); Mary Daly, *The Church and the Second Sex: With a New Feminist Post Christian Introduction by the Author* (New York: Colophon Books/Harper & Row, 1975).

9. Brenda Eichelberger, "Voice of Black Feminism," *Quest: A Feminist Quarterly* III (Spring, 1977): 16-23.

10. This phrase is used by Anna Julia Cooper, *A Voice From the South* (1852; reprint, Westport Conn.: Negro Universities Press, 1969), cited by Bell Hooks, *Ain't I A Woman: Black Women and Feminism* (Boston: South End Press, 1981), 193-194. I use it here to characterize Black women's experience. To be concerned about Black Women's issues is to be *concrete.* Yet because of their interconnectedness with Black men (racism), White women (sexism) and the poor (classism), it is also to be, at the same time, concerned with broad issues.

11. See Ntozake Shange, *For Colored Girls Who Have Considered Suicide When the Rainbow is Enuf* (New York: MacMillan, 1975); Michelle Wallace, *Black Macho and the Myth of the Superwoman* (New York: Dial Press, 1978); Alice Walker, *The Color Purple* (New York: Harcourt Brace Jovanovich, 1982); and *In Search of Our Mothers' Gardens* (San Diego, Calif.: Harcourt Brace Jovanovich, 1983); Sharon Harley and Rosalyn Terborg-Penn, eds., *Afro-American Women* (New York: Kennikat Press, 1978); Paula Giddings, *When and Where I Enter* (New York: William Morrow & Co., 1984); Gloria Wade-Gayles, *No Crystal Stair: Visions of Race and Sex in Black Women's Fiction* (New York: Pilgrim Press, 1984); Bell Hooks, *Feminist Theory: From Margin to Center* (Boston: South

End Press, 1984); Barbara Smith, Gloria Hull, and Patricia Scott, *All the Women are White, and All the Blacks are Men, But Some of Us are Brave* (Old Westbury, N.Y.: Feminist Press, 1982); Angela Y. Davis, *Women, Race and Class* (New York: Vintage Books, 1981).

12. Walker, *In Search of Our Mothers' Gardens*, xi.

13. Hooks, *Feminist Theory*, 3.

14. Cooper, *A Voice From The South*, 91

15. Cecil Wayne Cone, *Identity Crisis In Black Theology* (Nashville: African Methodist Episcopal Church Press, 1975), passim, especially chapter III.

16. Ben James Loewenberg and Ruth Bogin, eds., *Black Women in Nineteenth-Century American Life: Their Words, Their Thoughts, Their Feelings* (University Park, Pa.: Pennsylvania State University Press, 1976), 267.

17. Howard Thurman, *Jesus and the Disinherited* (Nashville: Abingdon Press, 1949), 30-31.

18. Loewenberg and Bogin, *Black Women in Nineteenth-Century*, 265.

19. Olive Gilbert, *Sojourner Truth: Narrative and Book of Life* (1850 and 1875; reprint Chicago: Johnson Publishing Co. 1970), 83.

20. Harold A. Carter, *The Prayer Tradition of Black People* (Valley Forge: Judson Press, 1976), 50. Carter, in referring to traditional Black prayer in general, states that Jesus was revealed as one who "was all one needs!"

21. Ibid.

22. Ibid., 49.

23. Ibid.

24. Sojourner Truth, "Ain't I A Woman?" in *Feminism: The Essential Historical Writings*, ed. Miriam Schneir (New York: Vintage Books, 1972).

25. Carter, *The Prayer Tradition*, 49.

26. Gilbert, *Book of Life*, 118.

27. Ibid., 119.

28. Ibid.

29. Ibid.

30. James Deotis Roberts, *A Black Political Theology* (Philadelphia: Westminster Press, 1974), 138. See especially chapter 5. See also Noel Leo Erskine, *Decolonizing Theology: A Caribbean Perspective* (Maryknoll, N.Y.: Orbis, 1980), 125.

31. Roberts, *A Black Political Theology*, 133.

32. Albert B. Cleage, Jr., *The Black Messiah* (New York: Sheed & Ward, 1969), 92.

33. James H. Cone, *God of the Oppressed* (New York: Seabury Press, 1975), 134.

34. Ibid., 135.

35. Ibid., 136.

36. William Eichelberger, "Reflections on the Person and Personality of the Black Messiah," *The Black Church II* (n.d.): 54.

37. Jarena Lee, *The Life and Religious Experiences and Journal of Mrs. Jerema Lee: A Colored Lady Giving an Account of Her Call to Preach* (Philadelphia, Pa.: n.p., 1836), 15-16.

38. Ibid., 16.

39. There is no evidence to suggest that Black women debated the significance of the maleness of Jesus. The fact is that Jesus Christ was a real, crucial figure in their lives. However, recent feminist scholarship has been important in showing the relation between the maleness of Christ and the oppression of women.

40. Truth, "Ain't I A Woman," in Schneir, ed., *Feminism*, 94.

41. This question is explored further in Jacquelyn Grant, "The Development and Limitation of Feminist Theology: Toward an engagement of black women's religious experience and white women's religious experience" (Ph.D. diss., Union Theological Seminary, New York, 1985).

42. Maya Angelou, *And Still I Rise* (New York: Random House, 1978), 42.

21

WOMANIST THEOLOGY: WHAT IS ITS RELATIONSHIP TO BLACK THEOLOGY?

Kelly Delaine Brown-Douglass

Black women in the United States have given voice to a new theological perspective: womanist.[1] Although the meaning of the term "womanist" originated with Alice Walker's interpretation of the Black cultural expression, "You acting womanish," it goes beyond her words.[2] It points to the richness and complexity of being Black and female in a society that tends to devalue both Blackness and womanhood. Womanist symbolizes Black women's resistance to their multidimensional oppression as well as their self-affirmation and will to survive with dignity under dehumanizing social-historical conditions.[3] The use of the term womanist in religious and theological scholarship signals understandings of the Bible, various church communities, and God that have emerged from the social-historical contexts of Black women struggling to survive and be free.[4]

As Black female theologians work to bring womanist theology to fruition, they have encountered many questions. One such question is: What does womanist theology have to do with Black theology? This concern to clarify the relationship between the two theologies often stems from the recognition that various womanist theologians began their theological reflection through the crucible of Black theology.[5] Any attempt, therefore, to discern what womanist and Black theology have to do with each other must engage at least two issues: (1) the role Black theology played in the emergence of womanist theology and (2) the similarities and differences between the two theologies. This article represents one womanist theologian's attempt to address these two concerns.

The Role of Black Theology

My own journey from Black to womanist theology is suggestive of Black theology's role in the emergence of womanist theology. James Cone's book, *A*

Kelly Delaine Brown-Douglass, an Episcopal priest, is assistant professor of theology at Howard University of Divinity, Washington, D.C.

Black Theology of Liberation was my introduction to systematic theological reflection.[6] This book entered my life as I was struggling to understand the connection between my Blackness and my Christian faith. I wanted to know if the God of Jesus Christ was for or against Black liberation. Cone's book answered this question for me. It related God and Christ to the Black freedom struggle in a way I have never considered. It argued that the Christian God was on the side of the oppressed as they fought for justice. This meant that in a White racist society, that is, the United States, God and Christ were Black.

Reading Cone's book plucked a chord within me that changed my life. Empowered by the God of the oppressed I was able to fight against White racism with a firm and determined resolve. The image of a Black God gave me a new sense of pride in my own Blackness. After reading *A Black Theology of Liberation* I was compelled to pursue further theological study.

Black theological reflection sustained me for some time as I attempted to engage in a liberating praxis for the Black community. But as I developed an awareness of what it meant to be a woman in a sexist society I saw the limitations of the Black God and Christ.

The emergence of feminist theology, with its penetrating critique of patriarchy within the religious and secular realm, helped me to name the discriminatory treatment I encountered from many of my Black male colleagues. It was sexism. I became painfully aware that sexism was not just a "White woman's thing." It also pervaded the Black church and community. This meant that if the entire Black community was to be free, both racism *and* sexism, at the very least, had to be eradicated.

Shaped by the Black Power/civil rights movement out of which it emerged, Black theology focused only on one dimension of Black oppression — White racism. Its failure to utilize Black women's experience further prevented it from developing an adequate analysis of Black oppression. It did not address the multiple social burdens, that is, racism, sexism, classism, and heterosexism, which beset Black men and women. Consequently, it presented an image of God and Christ that was impotent in the fight for Black freedom. A Black God, one concerned only with the battle against racism, could not sustain and liberate the entire Black community. This God could not affirm or empower Black women as they confronted sexism. My recognition of Black theology's limitations set me on a quest for a theology more reflective of Black women's as well as men's efforts to "make do and do better."

What does my particular journey suggest about Black theology's role in the emergence of womanist theology? It points first to the significant role that Black theology has played in giving Black women and men access to systematic theological reflection. Black theology let it be known that God did speak through the Black community. The strident articulation of a Black God and Christ made clear that the Black story of suffering and struggle was God's story, and this was a story necessary to tell. Black theology opened the door for Black people to further explore the richness of their own experience in their efforts to understand the meaning of God's presence in human history. Essentially, Black theology laid the groundwork for the emergence of various theological voices from the Black community, including womanist voices.

My journey further points out how Black theology's failure to address sexism has contributed to the emergence of womanist theology. Affected both by the feminist movement in church and society, and their own experience of sexism, various Black women began to note the exclusion of Black women's experience in Black theology. In one of the earliest critiques of Black theology by a Black woman, Jacquelyn Grant observed that Black theologians had not seriously addressed the issue of sexism. She pointed out that although Black theologians claimed to write from the vantage point of the total Black experience, Black women were "invisible" in Black theology.[7] As Black female theologians began to recognize the inadequateness of Black theology in relation to their struggles, they endeavored to develop a more inclusive theological perspective. They soon gave voice to the womanist perspective. Womanist theology has emerged partly because of Black theology's failure to address the concerns of Black women.

Essentially, the role of Black theology in the emergence of womanist theology is twofold. First, by linking God to the Black experience Black theology gave Black women access to systematic theological reflection. Second, by ignoring Black women's experience Black theology forced Black women to develop their own theological perspective.

Let us now turn to what a womanist theology involves. Special attention will be given to its distinctiveness in relation to Black theology.

The Distinctiveness of Womanist Theology

The most obvious distinction between Black and womanist theology is their respective points of departure. While Black theology's starting point—the Black experience—does not include Black women's experience, womanist theology begins with Black women's story of struggle. Womanist theology reflects at least two aspects of that story: first, the complexity of Black women's oppression and second, Black women's resolute efforts to survive and be free from that oppression. Specifically, it confronts Black women's struggles within the wider society as well as within the Black community. It also affirms Black women's faith that God supports them in their fight for survival and liberation. This means that a womanist theology engages a social-political analysis of wholeness and a religio-cultural analysis.

A Social-Political Analysis of Wholeness

Black women's status in the feminist and Black freedom movements illustrates the peculiar social-historical reality associated with being Black and female in the United States, and hence, reveals the need for womanist theology to include a social-political analysis of wholeness. Let us first look at Black women in relation to the feminist struggles, that is, the women's movements.

Black women have consistently recognized that their freedom was not a priority of the two women's movements—traditionally dominated by White women—that have emerged in the United States. Both movements have been limited by a racial bias. Bell Hooks emphatically states, "Every women's movement in America from its earliest origin to the present day has been built on a racist foundation."[8]

The first distinctive women's liberation movement in America evolved out of abolitionism. These early feminists were struggling against what has become known as the Victorian idea of womanhood that undergirds patriarchy. This idea not only relegated White middle-class women to the domestic realm, but it also considered them fragile "dolls" who had to be placed upon a protective pedestal. Eventually the nineteenth-century fight against Victorian ideology centered on a concern for women's suffrage.

As White women fought for the right to vote, their concern for "women's rights" did not cross the barriers of race. They did not seem interested in the plight of their Black sisters. The White suffragettes did not acknowledge that most Black women's lives were not representative of the Victorian ideal of womanhood. Cheryl Townsend Gilkes aptly points out, "The realities of slavery guaranteed . . . that Black women were never treated as white women were. Black women were overworked, flogged and otherwise exploited, just like men."[9] The suffragettes' almost total disregard for the peculiar plight of Black women was evidenced during the 1848 Seneca Falls women's rights convention. The convention documents did not make "even a passing reference to Black women."[10]

In addition, the White suffragettes were disinterested in eliminating racial identification as a requirement for voting. They appeared unconcerned that racial bias, even without gender bias, would still keep their sisters of color disenfranchised.

Some antebellum Black women were very aware of their peculiar status. They realized that because they were "women," they too needed to affirm and claim the women's suffrage movement. But they also recognized that because they were Black, they could not ignore the issue of race. Black women such as Sojourner Truth and Maria Stewart involved themselves in both the women's movement and the abolitionist movement, though they knew that their status as Black and female meant they would have to defend their right to participate in either movement. Anna Julia Cooper put it best when she said, "The colored woman of to-day occupies, one may say, a unique position in this country. . . . She is confronted by both a woman question and a race problem, and is as yet an unknown or acknowledged factor in both."[11]

Unfortunately the contemporary women's movement was no less characterized by a lack of concern for Black women than the nineteenth-century suffrage movement. Similar to the earlier suffrage movement this movement also emerged out of the struggles for racial justice. As White women, especially middle-class college women, "gained experience in collective organizing" through their involvement in the Black protests, and confronted gender discrimination within the civil rights movement, they were radicalized to fight for their rights within American society. This fight was characterized by the struggle against the same patriarchal order that had earlier deprived women of voting privileges. They demanded freedom from their exile in the domestic realm and access to the male-dominated social-political realm.

White women's narrow focus on patriarchy continued to reflect their disinterest in Black women's freedom. Their focus led some Black women to claim, "feminism is a white female thing that has nothing to do with black women."[12] There were, in fact, few indications that the contemporary women's movement was other than a "white female thing." With particular reference to the book by Betty Friedan that for some symbolized the contemporary women's movement, *The Feminine Mystique* (1963), Bell Hooks said that White women's fight for freedom from the private sector ignored "who [poor Black women] would be called in to take care of the children and maintain the home if they [white women] were. . . . given access with White women to the professions."[13] Hooks further observed that the focus on patriarchy,

> deflected attention away from [white women's] classism . . . racism and sexist attitudes towards the masses of American women . . . concerned about economic survival, ethnic and racial discrimination.[14]

The contemporary women's movement's tendency to ignore issues of race only heightened Black women's suspicion that this movement was designed to distract from the fight against racism. One Black woman put it this way, "[the women's movement] is just a bunch of bored white women with nothing to do — they're just trying to attract attention away from the black liberation movement."[15] In addition to their suspicion of White women's motives, Black women rejected the women's movement because they did not want to participate in any movement that had the potential of pitting them against Black men. The well-known poet Gwendolyn Brooks said this:

> Black women, like all women, certainly want, and are entitled to, equal pay and privileges. But black women have a second "twoness." Today's black men, at last flamingly assertive and proud, need their black women beside them, not organizing against them.[16]

Given their apprehensions, many Black women refused involvement in the women's movement. They opted to put most of their energy and talents into the Black freedom struggle. For these women it was important that the Black community be one in its quest for freedom.

What was Black women's status in the Black freedom struggle? Many of the African-American women involved in this struggle soon discovered that the civil rights/Black Power movement was as sexist as the women's movement was racist. Although Black women helped found some of the freedom fighting organizations, spearheaded local protest activities, and risked their lives for the Black community's freedom, they were rarely afforded the opportunity to hold national leadership roles or have decision-making responsibilities within various organizations.

Moreover, the Black freedom struggle began to equate freedom from racism with Black men securing their men's rights to be "men." But these women soon reevaluated their position when their men's treatment of them made it evident that "manhood" was being defined "within paradigms constructed by white patriarchy."[17] Just as they realized that their freedom was not a priority of the White-dominated women's movement, Black women discovered that they could not obtain their freedom through the male-dominated civil rights/Black Power movement.

Black women's relationship to the women's and Black freedom movements points to what Alice Walker describes as a womanist's commitment "to the survival and wholeness of the entire people."[18] Black women apparently evaluated and related to these movements according to whether or not they promoted freedom for both them and their men. They were also reluctant to be a part of any movement that created hostilities and divisions between them and Black men. Black women were searching for a politics of "wholeness." They needed a political strategy that would insure Black people, men and women, rights to live as whole, that is, free, human beings and that would keep the Black community whole, that is, unified, struggling together to survive and be free in relationships of mutuality. What does this aspect of Black women's experience mean for a womanist theology?

Unlike Black theology, a womanist theology will not focus on only one aspect of Black oppression. Instead, it will engage a social-political analysis of "wholeness." This analysis is one which is not only multidimensional, but also bifocal. It will confront racism, sexism, classism, and heterosexism as they impinge the Black community, and also as they are manifested within that community. A social-political analysis of wholeness will not seek to give priority to different forms of oppression, or to pit women against men or the poor against the rich. It will seek to eliminate anything that prevents Black people from being whole, liberated people, and from living as a whole, unified community. For instance, while affirming Walker's observation in her womanist definition that "the colored race is just like a flower garden, with every color flower represented," womanist theology recognizes that one of the vestiges of racism in the Black community is "colorism."[19] Black people have oftentimes discriminated against one another based on each other's light or dark-skinned complexion. A social-political analysis of wholeness will confront this vestige of racism within the Black community just as it will confront the presence of gender, sexual or economic oppression within the community. Essentially, a social-political analysis of wholeness will help womanist theology to make clear that the Black community is not free if any of its members are "unfree" because of their color, gender, sexual preference or economic condition.

What does Black women's quest for wholeness imply about the meaning of God's presence for the Black community? Black women have been resolute in their belief that God is on their side in their struggle. Maria Stewart, for instance, revealed this faith when she proclaimed (alluding to Scripture as she frequently did), "the God in whom I trust is able to deliver me from the rage and malice of my enemies, and from them that rise up against me."[20]

A God on the side of Black women is one who not only liberates the Black community from the multidimensional oppression that besets it, but also brings judgment against the Black community for harboring within it any kind of oppression. Womanist theology, therefore, must go beyond the God of Black theology. It must emphasize God's role not just as liberator but also as judge. It must highlight the God of the Old Testament prophets. This God not only liberated Israel from Egyptian bondage, but also demanded that Israel eradicate from its community anything that kept it a divided community, and hence, caused one member of the community to be oppressed by another member of the community.

In sum, if womanist theology is to reflect Black women's struggle for liberation, it must engage a social-political analysis of wholeness and emphasize God's role in the movement toward wholeness.

A Religio-Cultural Analysis for a Spirituality of Survival

Not only has Black women's experience been characterized by their complex and determined struggle for freedom, but most significantly by their ability to survive with dignity in spite of demeaning social-historical circumstances, and their extraordinary commitment to the survival of their families. Historically, they did not acquiesce to an ideology that negated their womanhood. They also did not stand by and allow their children to be destroyed by a system that used them as chattel. Instead, they stridently affirmed their womanhood and consistently sought ways to help their families make it from one sunup to another sunup. The most poignant example of a Black woman's refusal to consider herself less than a "whole" woman is Sojourner Truth's much quoted speech, "Ain't I A Woman":

> That man over there says that women need to be helped into carriages, and lifted over ditches, and to have the best place everywhere. Nobody ever helps me into carriages, or over mudpuddles, or gives me any best place! And ain't I a woman! Look at me! Look at my arm! I have ploughed and planted, and gathered into barns, and no man could head me! And ain't I a woman? I could work as much and eat as much as a man — when I could get it — and bear the lash as well! And ain't I a woman? I have borne thirteen children, and seen them most all sold off into slavery, and when I cried out with my mother's grief, none but Jesus heard me! And ain't I a woman?[21]

Slave narratives provide numerous examples of the ingenious means African-American women utilized to help their children survive. One such narrative relates the following:

As we went out in the morning, I observed several women who carried their young children in their arms to the field. These mothers laid their children at the side of the fence, or under the shade of cotton plants, whilst they were at work; and when the rest of us went to get water, they would go to give suck to their children, requesting someone to bring them water in gourds, which they were careful to carry to the field with them. One young woman did not, like the others, leave her child at the end of the row, but had contrived a sort of rude knapsack, made of a piece of coarse linen cloth, in which she fastened her child, which was very young, upon her back, and in this way carried it all day, and performed her task at the hoe with the other people.[22]

What is it that has allowed Black women to transcend the negative, dehumanizing images that society has maintained of them? What has undergirded their fight, against numerous odds, to save their children. What has fostered Black women's relentless struggle to survive and to sustain their families?

The lives and words of Black women point to a "spirituality of survival" that they have nurtured and by which they have been strengthened. There are at least two aspects to this spirituality of survival: it fosters self-esteem and it affirms the presence of God in the day-to-day struggle for survival. Maria Stewart illustrates the characteristic features of a spirituality of survival when she exhorts various Black audiences to take responsibility for their survival and liberation. During her exhortations she often told her audience about their rich African heritage. She said:

History informs us that we sprung from one of the most learned nations of the whole earth, from the seat, if not the parent of science. Yes, poor despised Africa was once the resort of sages and legislators of other nations, was esteemed the school of learning, and the most illustrious men in Greece flocked thither for instruction.[23]

In addition, she frequently reminded her audiences that though the world considered them inferior, God did not. She told them that they were children of God, made in God's own image. She put it this way:

Many think, because your skins are tinged with a sable hue, that you are an inferior race of beings, but God does not consider you as such. He [sic] hath formed and fashioned you in his [sic] own glorious image, and hath bestowed upon you reason and strong powers of intellect.[24]

Stewart apparently understood that if an oppressed people have a pride in their own culture and historical heritage, as well as a knowledge that they are children of God, then they will not be as vulnerable to the oppressive structures, systems, and ideologies that attempt to convince them that they are nobody, and that their lives are not worth living.

Not only did Stewart attempt to foster self-esteem when she spoke to Black people but she consistently reminded them that they were not alone in their daily struggle. Using herself as an example she told one audience:

The frowns of the world shall never discourage me, nor its smiles flatter me; for with the help of God, I am resolved to withstand the fiery darts of the devil, and the assaults of wicked men.[25]

Stewart illustrates how Black women have believed that God, especially God's presence as the Holy Spirit, has been with them to shield them and their community from death and destruction. These women frequently testified that the Holy Spirit upheld them in their daily efforts to keep going. Their belief in the sustaining presence of God's spirit is perhaps indicative of what Alice Walker means when she says that a womanist "loves the spirit."[26]

What does the significance of spirituality of survival for Black women mean for the doing of a womanist theology? It means that womanist theology, again unlike Black theology, will engage in a religio-cultural analysis. This analysis will highlight those aspects of Black culture and religion that foster self-esteem for Black women as well as men, and that help them to transcend the negative images of themselves that a racist, sexist, classist and heterosexist society projects. This analysis will also confront those aspects of Black culture and religion that mitigate self-esteem and transcendence. Essentially, a religio-cultural analysis will point to the necessity of a spirituality of survival for the Black community.

Given Black women's ability to survive and their active commitment to their families' survival, womanist theology will be more than a liberation theology. It will highlight God's role as a sustainer of the oppressed. It will examine the sustaining presences of the Holy Spirit in Black women's lives. Womanist theology will emphasize God's role in the Old Testament Exodus event, not just as liberator but as sustainer. It will focus, for instance, on God's presence in the lives of the two midwives, Pharaoh's daughter, Moses' sister and mother as they worked to insure baby Moses' survival.

Such utilization of Black women's experience in doing theology, graphically illustrates the ways in which womanist theology is distinct from Black theology. Both theologies are concerned with the Black community's freedom and God's role in their freedom struggle. Womanist theology, however, goes beyond Black theology. It highlights the community's daily struggle to survive. It also utilizes more comprehensive analyses for understanding the Black community's struggle. The current challenge is for Black female theologians to move forward with the task of bringing womanist theology to fruition.

NOTES

1. From here on any reference to Black people will mean those in the United States unless otherwise designated.

2. Alice Walker, *In Search of Our Mothers' Gardens* (San Diego, Calif.: Harcourt Brace Jovanovich, 1983), pp. xi-xii.

3. I have expanded on this understanding of the womanist symbol in "God Is As Christ Does: Toward a Womanist Theology," *Journal of Religious Thought* 46, no. 1 (Summer-Fall, 1989), 7-16. Some of the history in this paper concerning Black women's involvement in the women's movement is also adapted from that article.

4. See for instance Katie Geneva Cannon, "The Emergence of Black Feminist Consciousness," in *Feminist Interpretation of the Bible,* ed. Letty Russell (Philadelphia: Westminster Press, 1985), and *Womanist Ethics* (Ithaca N.Y.: Scholars Press, 1988); Toinette M. Eugene, "Moral Values and Black Womanists," *Journal of Religious Thought* 44 (Winter-Spring, 1988), 23-34 (reprinted in this volume as Document 23); Cheryl Townsend Gilkes, "The Role of Women in the Sanctified Church," *Journal of Religious Thought* 43 (Spring-Summer, 1986), 24-41; Jacquelyn Grant, "Womanist Theology: Black Women's Experience as a Source For Doing Theology, with Special Reference To Christology," *Journal of the Interdenominational Theological Center* 13 (Spring 1986), 195-212 (reprinted in this volume as Document 20); Renita Weems, *Just A Sister Away: A Womanist Vision of Women's Relationships in the Bible* (San Diego: Lura Media, 1988); Delores S. Williams, "Womanist Theology: Black Women's Voices," *Christianity and Crisis* (March 2, 1987), 66-70 (reprinted in this volume as Document 19).

5. For instance Jacquelyn Grant and I both completed our doctoral work under the guidance of Black theologian, James H. Cone. I will say more about this in relation to my particular journey to womanist theology.

6. James H. Cone, *A Black Theology of Liberation,* 2nd ed. (Maryknoll, N.Y.: Orbis Books, 1986).

7. Jacquelyn Grant, "Black Theology and the Black Woman," in Gayraud Wilmore and James H. Cone, eds., *Black Theology: A Documentary History, 1966-1979* (Maryknoll, N.Y.: Orbis Books, 1979), 418-433.

8. Bell Hooks, *Ain't I A Woman: Black Women and Feminism* (Boston: South End Press, 1981), 124.

9. Cheryl Townsend Gilkes, "The Role of Church and Community Mothers: Ambivalent American Sexism or Fragmented African Familyhood," *Journal of Feminist Studies in Religion* (Spring 1986).

10. Angela Davis, *Women, Race, and Class* (New York: Random House, 1981), 57.

11. Anna Julia Cooper, *A Voice From the South: By A Black Woman of The South* (1892; reprint, New York: Oxford University Press, 1988), 134.

12. Cited in Helen King, "The Black Woman and Women's Lib," *Ebony* (March 1971).

13. Bell Hooks, *Feminist Theory: From Margin to Center* (Boston: South End Press, 1984), 1.

14. Ibid., 2.

15. King, 70.

16. Ibid., 71.

17. Bell Hooks, *Talking Back: thinking feminists, thinking black* (Boston: South End Press, 1989), 178.

18. Walker, xi.

19. Ibid., xi.

20. *Maria W. Stewart, America's First Black Woman Political Writer: Essays and Speeches,* ed. Marilyn Richardson (Bloomington, Ind.: Indiana University Press, 1987), 50.

21. Cited in *Feminism: The Essential Historical Writings,* ed. Miriam Schneir (New York: Vintage Books, 1972), 93.

22. Charles Ball, *Slavery in the United States: A Narrative of the Life and Adventures of Charles Ball, A Black Man* (Lewiston, Pa.: J. W. Shugert, 1836), 150-151, quoted in *Black Women in White America: A Documentary History,* ed. Gerda Lerner (New York: Pantheon Books, 1972), 48.

23. Richardson, 58.

24. Ibid., 29.

25. Ibid., 50.

26. Walker, xii.

22

HITTING A STRAIGHT LICK WITH A CROOKED STICK: THE WOMANIST DILEMMA IN THE DEVELOPMENT OF A BLACK LIBERATION ETHIC

Katie G. Cannon

As a Black womanist ethicist I have been invited to be the first speaker in a three-part concurrent session entitled "Towards a Black Liberation Ethic." This invitation places me in a most precarious predicament. On the one hand, my task as a *Christian social ethicist* is to transcend my blackness and femaleness, and draft a blueprint of liberation ethics that somehow speaks to, or responds to, the universality of the human condition. On the other hand, my assignment as a *womanist liberation ethicist* is to debunk, unmask, and disentangle the historically conditioned value judgments and power relations that undergird the particularities of race, sex, and class oppression. Zora Neale Hurston described this dilemma as trying to hit a straight lick with a crooked stick. In essence, I have been invited to speak as "one of the canonical boys" and as "the noncanonical other" at one and the same time. These two tasks stand in opposition to each other.[1] Thus, the question which has evolved from wrestling with this dilemma is the following: what importance do race and gender have as meaningful categories in the development of a Black liberation ethic?

Black Woman Ethicist as One of the Canonical Boys

Even though there is no clearly written statement among Christian social ethicists regarding the nature of scholarship, enough areas of agreement do

Katie Geneva Cannon, a Presbyterian minister, is associate professor of religion and African-American studies at Temple University, Philadelphia, Pennsylvania. She is the author of *Black Womanist Ethics*. This essay was originally published in the *Annual of the Society of Christian Ethics* (1987) and is reprinted with permission.

exist within the guild to make reasonable generalizations regarding the ethicist as scholar. Most of these have nothing to do with the realities of Black women. For instance, membership in this highly complex fraternity means investigation of abstract metatheory, traditional philosophical thought, and the established canon of ethical inquiry with supposedly calm and detached objectivity.[2]

To prove that she is sufficiently intelligent, the Black woman as Christian ethicist must discount the particularities of her lived experiences and instead focus on the validity of generalizable external analytical data. The dilemma she faces in joining the canonical boys is that of succumbing to the temptation of only mastering the historically specified perspective of the Euro-American masculine preserve.[3] In order to be a respected scholar in the discipline, the Black woman is placed under a double injunction. She has to face a critical jury, primarily white and male, that makes claims for gender-neutral and value-free inquiry as a model for knowledge.[4] The Black female scholar will have little opportunity to expand her creative energy in the direction of liberation ethics if she concentrates on searching for universal truths unhampered by so-called incidental matters such as race, sex, and class differences. In other words, there is an unspoken informal code within the guild that the Black woman academician must engage in this type of abstract moral discourse or else she runs the risk of being misunderstood, misinterpreted, and frequently devalued as a second-class scholar specializing in Jim Crow subject matter.[5]

What is important to grasp here is that both the inclusion of Black women and the inclusion of Black women's moral reasoning within the structure of traditional ethics are pioneering endeavors.[6] Black women's experience has been overlooked, neglected, or distorted in most of the existing ethical scholarship. For instance, Black women as subjects for scholarly research have been given little attention. Little writing in ethics focuses on the moral agency of Black females. Unfortunately, this situation is not peculiar to ethics; Black women as worthy subjects of study are ignored in most areas of scholarship.

From behind the veil of race and sex neutrality, the Black female scholar understands that the metaphysical and ethical issues are mutually connected. The accepted canonical methods of moral reasoning contain deeply hidden biases that make it exceedingly difficult to turn them to the service of the best interest of Black women.[7] Universality does not include the Black female experience.

Why does the discipline of ethics have so little to say about Black women's role in church and society? What value does the academy place on the history, culture, and traditions that Black women have created? Do we see Black women's moral wisdom as making a poor virtue of survival?

In scanning the canon in ethical studies, one finds that this omission of Black women provides continuing ideological support for conditions and public policies oppressive to Black women. The white masculine orientation that characterizes the field of study leaves Black women out. This type of academic invisibility reinforces racist/sexist stereotypes and justifies misapprehensions that lock Black women into marginal status. In other words, the concepts used by the majority of white male ethicists to discuss moral agency implicitly de-value Black women's contribution. Chanzo Tallamu in her review of *Slipping Through the Cracks: The Status of Black Women* argues that as long as current research methods do not reflect or pay enough attention to the needs of Black women, the policies and programs that result may benefit white women or Black men but not Black women.[8]

When ethical discourse provides truncated and distorted pictures of Black women, the society at large uses these oppressive stereotypes to define what it is to be Black and female in America. An even more basic manifestation of this trivialization of Black women has been the traditional practice of gener-alizing about Black women on the information gathered from white women or Black men.[9] The emphasis has to be placed on information derived from Black women talking about their own lives and religious experiences.

Until the advent of the civil rights movement in the 1960s and the women's movement in the 1970s, Black women were virtually ignored and their questions reduced to marginal absurdity as a result of sexist/racist assumptions. Black women's contributions to the academy have been considered incidental to the substance of theology and ethics—mere asides, insignificant to the conceptual framework that defines the body of thought as a whole.[10] Black women's moral agency must be understood on their own terms rather than being judged by essentially abstract external ideological norms and squeezed into categories and systems which consider white men the measure of significance. Lives of Black women cannot be fully comprehended using analytical categories derived from white/male experience. Oftentimes such concepts covertly sustain a hierarchy of white supremacy, patriarchy, and exploitative power.[11]

Black Woman Ethicist as Noncanonical Other

The dilemma of the Black woman ethicist as the noncanonical other is defined as working in opposition to the academic establishment, yet building upon it. The liberation ethicist works both within and outside the guild. The Black womanist scholar receives the preestablished disciplinary structures of intellectual inquiry in the field of ethics and tries to balance the paradigms and assumptions of this intellectual tradition with a new set of questions arising from the context of Black women's lives.[12] The tension is found in the balancing act of simultaneously trying to raise the questions appropriate to the discipline while also trying to understand what emphasis ought properly to be placed on the various determinants influencing the situation of Black women. In order to work towards an inclusive ethic, the womanist struggles to restructure the cat-egories so that the presuppositions more readily include the ethical realities of Black women.

The womanist scholar identifies the pervasive white and male biases deeply embedded in the field of study. As a liberationist, she challenges and reshapes the traditional inquiry and raises candid questions between the two locales of whiteness and maleness. She insists that new questions guide the research so that Black women's moral wisdom can provide the answers. In essence, she seeks to determine why and how Black women actively negotiate their lives in a web of oppression.[13]

The Black woman's ethical analysis distinguishes between "possibilities in principle" and "possibilities in fact." She extends Black women's existential reality above the threshold of that frustrating and illusory social mobility which forms the core of the American dream. That is, she strips away false, objectified conceptualities and images that undergird the apparatuses of systemic oppression.

The intersection of race, sex, and class give womanist scholars a different ethical orientation with a different ideological perspective. The experience of being both the participant from within and the interpreter from without results in an inescapable duality to the character of womanist ethics. Beginning with her own historical, socio-ethical situation, the Black woman scholar cuts off what is untrue and adds what is most urgent. In other words, she refutes what is inimical and coopts the positive. This task is difficult since Black women in general are dealing with vague, amorphous social ideals, on the one hand, and with the long-standing effects of American racism, sexism, and class elitism on the other.[14]

For example, Black female ethicists endure with a certain grace the social restrictions that limit their own mobility, and at the same time they demand that the relationships between their own condition and the condition of those who have a wide range of freedom be recognized. They bring into clear focus the direct correlation of economic, political, and racial alienation. As participant-interpreters, their direct contact with the high and the lowly, the known and the unrecognized, the comic and the tragic, makes them conscious of the myriad value systems which are antithetical to Black survival. To demystify large and obscure ideological relations, social theories, and, indeed, the heinous sociopolitical reality of tridimensional oppression, is a moral act. To do ethics inside out and back again is the womanist norm.

In other words, as the noncanonical other, these women rightly recognize how family life, cultural expression, political organization, social and economic roles shape the Black community. Furthermore, they identify the way Black women as moral agents persistently attempt to strip away the shrouding of massive dislocation and violence exacerbated in recent years by the nation's fiscal crisis.[15] Under extremely harsh conditions, Black women buttress themselves against the dominant coercive apparatuses of society. Using a series of resistance modes, they weave together many disparate strands of survival skills, styles, and traditions in order to create a new synthesis which, in turn, serves as a catalyst for deepening the wisdom-source which is genuinely their own.[16]

Black women ethicists use this framework of wisdom to compare and contrast Black female moral agency with the agency of those in society who have the freedom to maximize choice and personal autonomy. The womanist scholar focuses on describing, documenting, and analyzing the ideologies, theologies, and systems of values that perpetuate the subjugation of Black women. At the same time, she emphasizes how Black women are shaping their own destinies within restricted possibilities, resisting and overthrowing those restrictions, and sometimes, in the interest of survival, acting in complicity with the forces that keep them oppressed.[17]

To make this point clearer: Black women ethicists constantly question why Black women are considered merely necessary, no more than throwaway superfluous appendages in a society that claims "life, liberty, and the pursuit of happiness" as "inalienable rights." What theological systems relegate Black women to the margins of the decision-making mainstream of American religious, political, and economic life? And, what qualitative judgments and social properties establish a chasm between the proposition that Black women, first and foremost, are human beings and the machinations that allow glaring inequities and unfulfilled promises to proceed morally unchecked?

The womanist scholar stresses the role of emotional, intuitive knowledge in the collective life of the people. Such intuition enables moral agents in situations of oppression to follow the rule within, and not be dictated to from without. Untrammeled by external authority, Black female moral agents' intuitive faculties lead them toward a dynamic sense of moral reasoning. They designate the processes, the manners, and subtleties of their own experiences with the least amount of distortion from the outside. They go below the level of racial, sexual structuring and into those areas where Black people are simply human beings struggling to reduce to consciousness all of their complex experiences. Communion with one's own truths makes one better able to seize and delineate with unerring discrimination the subtle connections among people, institutions, and systems that serve as silent accessories to the perpetuation of flagrant forms of injustice.[18]

Intrigued by the largely unexamined questions that have fallen through the cracks between feminist ethics and Black male theology, the womanist scholar insists on studying the distinctive consciousness of Black women within Black women's institutions, clubs, organizations, magazines, and literature.[19] Appropriating the human condition in their own contexts, Black women collectively engage in revealing the hidden power relations inherent in the present social structures. A central conviction is that theo-ethical structures are not universal, color blind, apolitical, or otherwise neutral. Thus, the womanist ethicist tries to comprehend how Black women create their own lives, influence others, and understand themselves as a force in their own right. The womanist voice is one of deliverance from the deafening discursive silence which the society at large has used to deny the basis of shared humanity.

Conclusion

In order to move towards a Black liberation ethic, attention must be paid to an ethical vision that includes Black women. The substantial omission of Black women from theological discourse flows quite naturally from male theologians using analytical concepts and frameworks that take the male experience as the norm.[20] An inclusive liberation ethic must focus on the particular questions of women in order to reveal the subtle and deep effects of male bias on recording religious history.[21] As scholars, we must demonstrate the hidden assumptions and premises that lie behind our ethical speculation and inferences. Our task is to change the imbalance caused by an androcentric view, wherein it is presumed that only men's activities have theological value. If we are willing to unmask the male assumptions that dominate religious thought we will discover whole new areas of ethical inquiry.

Secondly, in moving towards a Black liberation ethic we must examine Black women's contributions in all the major fields of theological studies — Bible, history, ethics, mission, worship, theology, preaching, and pastoral care. The Black male biases operate not so much to omit Black women totally as to relegate Black church women to the position of direct object instead of active subject.[22] Too often Black women are presented in a curiously impersonal, dehumanizing way as the fused backbone in the body of the church.

A womanist liberation ethic requires us to gather information and to assess accurately the factual evidence regarding Black women's contribution to the Black church community.[23] Black women organized voluntary missionary societies, superintended church schools, led prayer meetings, took an active part in visiting and ministering to the sick and needy, and raised large amounts of money to defray the expenses of the Black church. Black women are conscious actors who have altered the theological picture in significant ways. Furthermore, this second area of research does more than increase our understanding of Black women in the church community; it also elicits reinterpretation of old conclusions about the church universal.

Finally, the development of an inclusive ethic requires us to recognize and condemn the extent to which sex differences prevail in the institutional church, in our theological writings, and in the Black church's practices.[24] A womanist liberation ethic directs critical attention not only to scholarship in the fields of study but also to its concrete effects on women in the pews. The work has to be done both from the basis of church practices and from the basis of continuing academic investigation. For instance, we need to do an analysis of sexist content of sermons in terms of reference to patriarchal values and practices. Particular attention needs to be given to the objectification, degradation, and subjection of the female in Black preaching.[25] At the same time, we need to analyze the social organization of the Black Church[26] — curricula, music, leadership expectation, pastor-member interactions — as well as outright sex discrimination. Far too often, the organization of the church mirrors male dominance in the society and normalizes it in the eyes of both female and male parishioners.

Whether the discipline of ethics has almost completely neglected Black women (as in white male scholarship) or treated them as incidental to central issues (as in Black male scholarship) or considered gender as the important factor for research (as in white feminist scholarship), the cumulative effect of womanist scholarship is that it moves us toward a fundamental reconceptualization of all ethics with the experience of Black women at center stage.

NOTES

1. For a provocative critique of this dilemma, see Vincent Harding, "Responsibilities of the Black Scholar to the Community," in *The State of Afro-American History: Past, Present and Future,* ed. Darlene Clark Hine (Baton Rouge, La.: Louisiana State University Press, 1986), 277-84; Oliver C. Cox, "The New Crisis in Leadership Among Negroes," *Journal of Negro Education* 19, no. 4 (Fall 1950), 459-65; also Cox, "Leadership Among Negroes in the United States," in Alvin W. Gouldner, ed., *Studies in Leadership* (New York: Russell & Russell, 1950), 228-71.

2. Robert K. Merton, "Insiders and Outsiders: A Chapter in the Sociology of Knowledge," *American Journal of Sociology* 78 (July 1972).

3. For example, read the essays in *Norm and Context in Christian Ethics,* edited by Gene H. Outka and Paul Ramsey (New York: Charles Scribner's Sons, 1968), and critique them in relation to this concern. Use the same process with Paul Ramsey, *Basic Christian Ethics* (New York: Charles Scribner's Sons, 1950); and Alasdair MacIntyre, *After Virtue* (Notre Dame, Ind.: University of Notre Dame Press, 1981).

4. For a selection of early works on this topic from the perspective of the Black male scholar, see John Hope Franklin, "The Dilemma of the American Negro Scholar," in Herbert Hill, ed., *Soon One Morning: New Writing by American Negroes 1940-1962* (1963), 64-69 passim and 73-74; Carter G Woodson, *The Mis-Education of the Negro* (Washington, D.C.: The Associated Publishers, Inc., 1933); W. E. B. Du Bois, *The Education of Black People: Ten Critiques 1906-1960,* ed. Herbert Aptheker (Amherst, Mass.: University of Massachusetts Press, 1973); and Harry Washington Greene, *Holders of Doctorates Among American Negroes* (1946).

5. For a comprehensive critique, see Mary Frances Berry, "Blacks in Predominantly White Institutions of Higher Learning," in National Urban League, *The State of Black America 1983* (New York: National Urban League, 1983); Robert Staples, "Racial Ideology and Intellectual Racism: Blacks in Academia," *The Black Scholar* 15, no. 2 (March-April 1984), 2-17; and John Wideman, "Publish and Still Perish: The Dilemma of Black Educators on White Campuses," *Black Enterprise* 10 (September 1978), 44-49.

6. This sort of observation has been made in numerous contexts. See for example, Harold Cruse, *The Crisis of the Negro Intellectual* (New York: William Morrow & Co., 1967); Betty D. Maxwell, *Employment of Minority Ph.D.s: Changes Over Time* (Washington, D.C.: Commission on Human Resources of the National Research Council, 1981); Jeanne Noble, *The Negro College Woman Graduate* (New York: Columbia University Press, 1954); and Oliver C. Cox, "Provisions for Graduate Education Among Negroes," *Journal of Negro Education* 11, no. 1 (January 1940): 222-27.

7. Sheila Ruth, "Methodocracy, Misogyny, and Bad Faith: Sexism in the Philosophical Establishment," *Metaphilosophy* 10 (1979): 48-61; Delores Williams, "Women's Oppression and Life-Line Politics in Black Women's Religious Narratives," *Journal of Feminist Studies in Religion* 1, no. 2 (Fall 1985): 59-71.

8. Chanzo Tallamu, "Review of *Slipping Through the Cracks: The Status of Black Women,*" *Black Scholar* (July/August 1986), 59.

9. Chandra Talpade Mohantz, "On Difference: The Politics of Black Women's Studies," *Women's Studies International Forum* 6 (1983): 243-47; Margaret A. Simons, "Racism and Feminism: A Schism in the Sisterhood," *Feminist Studies* 5 (1979), 384-401; and The Mudflower Collective, *God's Fierce Whimsy: The Implications of Christian Feminism for Theological Education* (New York: Pilgrim Press, 1985).

10. See John E. Fleming, *The Lengthening Shadow of Slavery: A Historical Justification for Affirmative Action for Blacks in Higher Education* (Washington, D.C.: Howard University Press, 1976).

11. Theodore Caplow and R. McGee, *The Academic Marketplace* (New York: Basic Books, 1958); Pierre Van den Berghe, *Academic Gamesmanship: How to Make a Ph.D. Pay* (New York: Abelard-Schuman, 1970); and Alvin W. Gouldner, *The Future of Intellectuals and the Rise of the New Class* (New York: Seabury Press, 1979).

12. Without doubt the most influential womanists who take this approach are: Angela Davis, *Women, Race and Class* (New York: Random House, 1981); June Jordan, *On Call: Political Essays* (Boston: South End Press, 1985); Alice Walker, *In Search of Our Mothers' Gardens: Womanist Prose* (San Diego, Calif.: Harcourt Brace Jovanovich, 1983); Audre Lorde, *Sister Outsider: Essays and Speeches* (Trumansburg, N.Y.: Crossing Press, 1984).

13. For examples see Bernice Johnson Reagon, "The Borning Struggle: The Civil Rights Movement," in *They Should Have Served That Cup of Coffee,* ed. Dick Cluster (Boston: South End Press, 1979); Barbara Smith, ed., *Home Girls: A Black Feminist Anthology* (Watertown, Mass.: Persephone Press, 1983); Bell Hooks, *Ain't I a Woman: Black Women and Feminism* (Boston: South End Press, 1981).

14. This kind of moral reasoning is delineated in Filomina C. Steady, ed., *The Black Woman Cross-Culturally* (Cambridge, Mass.: Schenkman Pub. Co., 1981); Toni Cade, ed., *The Black Woman: An Anthology* (New York: New American Library, 1970); and Gloria T. Hull, Patricia Bell Scott, and Barbara Smith, eds., *All the Women Are White, All the Blacks Are Men, But Some of Us Are Brave* (Old Westbury, N.Y.: Feminist Press, 1982).

15. Coalition on Women and the Budget, *Inequality of Sacrifice: The Impact of the Reagan Budget on Women* (Washington, D.C.: 1983).

16. All these works are either implicit or explicit analyses of this position: Dorothy Sterling, *We Are Your Sisters: Black Women in the Nineteenth Century* (New York: Norton, 1984); Jacqueline Jones, *Labor of Love, Labor of Sorrow: Black Women, Work and the Family from Slavery to the Present* (New York: Basic Books, 1985); Bert Loewenberg and Ruth Bogin, eds., *Black Women in Nineteenth-Century American Life: Their Words, Their Thoughts, Their Feelings* (University Park, Pa.: Pennsylvania State University Press, 1976); and Rosalyn Terborg-Penn and Sharon Harley, eds., *The Afro-American Woman: Struggle and Images* (New York: Kennikat, 1978).

17. See, in particular, Ellen N. Lawson, "Sarah Woodson Early: Nineteenth-Century Black Nationalist 'Sister,' " *Umoja: A Scholarly Journal of Black Studies* 5 (Summer 1981); Gerda Lerner, ed., *Black Women in Elite America: A Documentary History* (New York: Random House, 1972); and Dorothy Sterling, *Black Foremothers: Three Lives* (Old Westbury, N.Y.: Feminist Press, 1979).

18. Rennie Simson, "The Afro-American Female: The Historical Context of the Construction of Sexual Identity," in Ann Snitow, Sharon Thompson, and Christine Stausa II, eds., *The Powers of Desire: The Politics of Sexuality* (New York: Monthly Review Press, 1983), 229–35.

19. Darlene Clark Hine, "Lifting the Veil, Shattering the Silence: Black Women's History in Slavery and Freedom," in Darlene Clark Hine, ed., *The State of Afro-American History: Past, Present and Future* (Baton Rouge, La.: Louisiana State University Press, 1986), 223–49.

20. For example, see Gayraud S. Wilmore and James H. Cone, eds., *Black Theology: A Documentary History 1966–1979* (Maryknoll, N.Y.: Orbis Books, 1979); and Preston N. Williams, "Impartiality, Racism, and Sexism," *Annual of the Society of Christian Ethics* (1983): 147-59.

21. Ellen Carol DuBois, et al., *Feminist Scholarship: Kindling in the Groves of Academe* (Urbana, Ill.: University of Illinois Press, 1985); Beverly W. Harrison, *Making the Connections,* ed. Carol Robb (Boston: Beacon Press, 1985); Barbara H. Andolsen, Christine E. Gudorf, and Mary D. Pellauer, eds., *Women's Consciousness, Women's Conscience* (New York: Seabury Press, 1985).

22. For historical works, see W. E. B. Du Bois, *The Negro Church* (Atlanta: Atlanta University Press, 1903); Benjamin E. Mays, *The Negro's God as Respected in His Literature* (Boston: Chapman and Grimes, Inc., 1958); Benjamin E. Mays and Joseph W. Nicholson, *The Negro's Church* (New York: Institute of Social and Religious Research, 1933); and Carter G. Woodson, *The History of the Negro Church* (Washington, D.C.: Associated Pub., 1921).

23. Katie G. Cannon, "The Sign of Hope in Three Centuries of Despair: Women in the Black Church Community," in *Human Rights and the Global Mission of the Church,* Boston Theological Institute Annual Series, vol. 1 (Cambridge, Mass., 1985), 44–50.

24. For examples, see Edward M. Brawley, ed., *The Negro Baptist Pulpit* (Philadelphia: American Baptist Publication Society, 1890); Charles V. Hamilton, *The Black Preacher in America* (New York: Morrow, 1972); Henry Beecher Hicks, *Images of the Black Preacher* (Valley Forge, Pa.: Judson Press, 1977).

25. Henry H. Mitchell, *Black Preaching* (Philadelphia: Lippincott, 1970); William M. Philpot, ed., *Best Black Sermons* (Valley Forge, Pa.: Judson Press, 1972); Henry J. Young, ed., *Preaching the Gospel* (Philadelphia: Fortress Press, 1976); and Samuel Proctor and William D. Watley, *Sermons from the Black Pulpit* (Valley Forge, Pa.: Judson Press, 1984).

26. Harry V. Richardson, *Dark Glory: A Picture of the Church Among Negroes in the Rural South* (New York: Friendship Press, 1947); William L. Banks, *The Black Church in the United States: Its Origin, Growth, Contribution and Outlook* (Chicago: Moody Press, 1972); C. Eric Lincoln, *The Black Experience in Religion* (Garden City, N.Y.: Anchor Books/Doubleday, 1974); Albert J. Raboteau, *Slave Religion: The Invisible Institution in Antebellum South* (New York: Oxford University Press, 1978).

23

MORAL VALUES AND BLACK WOMANISTS

Toinette M. Eugene

> *I come out of a tradition where those things are valued; where you ask*
> *about a woman with big legs and big hips and black skin. I come out*
> *of a black community where it was all right to have hips and be heavy.*
> *You didn't feel that people didn't like you. The values that [imply] you*
> *must be skinny come from another culture. . . . Those are not the values*
> *that I was given by the women who served as my models. I refuse to be*
> *judged by the values of another culture. I am a Black woman, and I will*
> *stand as best as I can in that imagery.*
> Bernice Reagon, *Black Women and Liberation Movements*

The values black women have derived for themselves and have offered as options to the black community as well as to the members of a broader, dominant society cannot be understood or adequately explained apart from the historical context in which black women have found themselves as moral agents. Moreover, the moral values that black women have provided as a legacy to the black community as well as to the feminist movement in American society suggest a distinctive religious consciousness and documentable religious traditions which have been irrepressible in redeeming and transforming an entire human environment.

The central theses of this essay, which traces specific moral values and black feminism to their root causality within black religious traditions, are also theses derived in part from the highest expressions of moral and faith development as described particularly in the theoretical research and publications of Carol Gilligan and James Fowler.[1]

By drawing upon this psychological research and by reviewing black religious history, this essay asserts that public activism and private endurance are para-

Toinette M. Eugene, a Roman Catholic womanist, teaches social ethics at Chicago Theological Seminary. This essay appeared in the *Journal of Religious Thought* 44 (Winter-Spring 1988) and is reprinted with permission.

digmatic of black women's value indicators in both the black religious traditions and in feminist communities. Social activism, self-sacrifice, and other similar value indicators may be verified in the lives of Mary McLeod Bethune and Nannie Helen Burroughs, to name but two exemplary models. Nevertheless, these value measures and these valuable models represent more than unusual courage and strength; they also represent realistic responses to economic deprivation and political and social inequality. Black women have been forced to perform labor and to take risks that few white women have been called upon to do, either in the name of religious traditions or in behalf of the survival of their race.

Black women, however, are not special specimens of womanhood; rather, they are women who have been given less protected and more burdensome positions in society. As Michelle Wallace has so poignantly pointed out, this has resulted in the "myth of the superwoman," which is not a description of black women but, rather, a measure of the difference between what is regularly expected of white women and what is essentially required of black women.[2]

It is obvious that black women have experienced oppressive structures of racism, class bias, and male supremacy in both religion and society in this country. What is not always so obvious to a dominant white worldview, and even to feminist theological understandings, is that Afro-American culture and religion have generated alternative interrelated notions of womanhood contradictory to those of mainstream American economics, society, and theology.[3] These alternative experiences, visions, and images of womanhood have been forged out of the furnace of a moral value system endemic to the black church.

This essay will explore aspects of the moral consciousness and value system that guides black women in their ongoing struggle for survival through a commentary on black religious traditions in which black women share. Within this commentary some reflections will also be offered regarding black women's perspectives on feminism as a white women's movement and on feminist theologies.

Black Women and Moral Values during Slavery

Historically, the black church has been the fiery furnace through which systematic faith affirmations and liberating principles for biblical interpretation have been developed by black people. Within this "invisible institution," hidden from the observation of slave masters, black women, along with black men, developed an extensive moral value system and religious life of their own. In the language of moral-development theorist Carol Gilligan, they established and operated out of a web or network of relationships and intimacy with others in community.[4] The moral values of care, compassion, and cooperation with other black and oppressed persons served as criteria for decisions and actions intended to lay hold of the good, the true, and the beautiful.

The biblical interpretations of the antebellum black church which provided black people with webs of relationships centering on the God of justice and of liberation made slaves incontestably discontented with their servile condition.

In the case of black women whose bodies and spirits were wantonly violated by the immoral sexual advances of white masters, the moral value system of black people in this period encouraged slave women to eliminate the sources of their oppression in order to maintain and sustain their fragile nexus with God, community, and self as valued and trusted friends. Paula Giddings, in her text, *When and Where I Enter: The Impact of Black Women on Race and Sex in America,* reports on the moral resistance black slave women offered:

So, by the early eighteenth century an incredible social, legal, racial structure was put in place. Women were firmly stratified in the roles that Plato envisioned. Blacks were chattel, White men could impregnate a Black woman with impunity, and she alone could give birth to a slave. Blacks constituted a permanent labor force and metaphor that were perpetuated through the Black woman's womb. And all of this was done within the context of the Church, the operating laws of capitalism, and the psychological needs of White males. Subsequent history would be a variation on the same theme.

In its infancy slavery was particularly harsh. Physical abuse, dismemberment, and torture were common. . . . Partly as a result, in the eighteenth century, slave masters did not underestimate the will of their slaves to rebel, even their female slaves. Black women proved especially adept at poisoning their masters, a skill undoubtedly imported from Africa. Incendiarism was another favorite method; it required neither brute physical strength nor direct confrontation. But Black women used every means available to resist slavery—as men did—and if caught, they were punished just as harshly.[5]

In the midst of this dehumanizing slave environment, black families survived. They overcame the slaveholders' attempts to reduce them to so many subhuman labor units, managing to create an ongoing system of family arrangements and kin networks. Domestic life became critically important, for it was the only place where slaves had any equality and autonomy as human beings in relation to one another.[6]

Regarding domestic life and labor, Angela Davis, in *Women, Race, and Class,* has observed a paradox of great significance for black women and men:

The salient theme emerging from domestic life in the slave quarters is one of sexual equality. The labor that slaves performed for their own sake and not for the aggrandizement of their masters was carried out on terms of equality. Within the confines of their family and community life, therefore, Black people managed to accomplish a magnificent feat. They transformed that negative equality which emanated from the equal oppression they suffered as slaves into a positive quality: the egalitarianism characterizing their social relations.[7]

Harriet Tubman and countless others provided egalitarian images of slave women as strong, self-reliant, proud of their roots and of their ability to survive, convinced of their right to a place in society through the liberation of all black people. Equally oppressed as laborers, equal to their men in the domestic sphere, they were also equal in their moral resistance to slavery, participating in work stoppages and revolts, fleeing north and helping others to flee.

The ability of black people to cope in a hostile society has endured into the twentieth century; studies of black women in urban situations show that the means by which black families survived slavery still enable black women and their families to survive today.

Within this historical framework of past and present hostility black women have always perceived networks of relationality in the liberation struggle differently from white women. Domesticity has never been seen as entirely oppressive but rather as a vehicle for building family life under slavery; male/female relationships have always been more egalitarian; there has been less emphasis on women's work as different from and inferior to men's; slaves and freed persons, male and female, have consistently tended to rebel against the sexual oppression of black women as well as the emasculation of black men. It is easy to understand why many black people today see the white feminist movement as an attempt to divide black people. Contemporary black feminists caution against espousing the more "radical" white feminist stances because they leave out, as irrelevant, black men, black children, black families. Consequently, a primary moral value for black people is articulated in this overarching and enduring black feminist position: solidarity among black people is essential for survival.

A dramatic statement of black women's unique attitude toward solidarity with black men is found in the 1977 statement of the Combahee River Collective, a black lesbian feminist group from Boston.

> Although we are feminists and lesbians we feel solidarity with progressive Black men and do not advocate the fractionalization that white women who are separatists demand. Our situation as Black people necessitates that we have solidarity around the fact of race. . . . We struggle together with Black men against racism, while we also struggle with Black men about sexism.[8]

These black lesbian feminists explicitly rejected a feminist separatism that equates all oppression with sexual oppression and fails fully to comprehend the reality that black women *and men* are victims of shared racial oppression. Feminist separatism is not a viable political philosophy for most black women. Ethicist Barbara Hilkert Andolsen, in her remarkable assessment of racism and American feminism, *Daughters of Jefferson, Daughters of Bootblacks,* issues a strong caveat to white women who are desirous of understanding the black feminist experience:

Those of us who are white feminists need to be careful that we do not articulate limited strategies for dealing with sexism as if they were the only legitimate feminist strategies. White feminist separatist theories or strategies that ignore the strong bond forged between many black women and men in a shared struggle against racism do not speak to all women's experience.[9]

White feminists have a responsibility to learn about black women's perspectives on women's issues, to analyze how racist social structures may distort the impact of white feminist proposals, and to support black women in their self-defined struggle for liberation. Black feminists are creating their own analyses of sexism and of the interconnections between racism and sexism. White feminist theologians who are seeking to contribute to an inclusive feminist theology that respects and reflects the diversity of women's experience need to learn from the experiences, moral values, and feminist theology articulated by black women.

There is ample material to draw upon from the insights of the distinctive theological consciousness of black women during slavery. For example, the biblical exegetical abilities of Maria Stewart coupled with her assumptions (what would later be known as modernist thinking) gave black women in 1832 a freer rein to express and act upon ideas that liberated them from the oppression of both sexism and racism.[10] For Stewart, simple logic demanded that in light of the role of women in the past, "God at this eventful period should raise up your females to strive ... both in public and private, to assist those who are endeavoring to stop the strong current of prejudice that flows so profusely against us at present."[11] Maria Stewart was sure enough of her moral values to admonish others not to doubt the mission of her gender. "No longer ridicule their efforts," she counseled. "It will be counted as sin."[12]

At a women's rights convention in Akron, Ohio, in 1851, several of the most celebrated examples of early black feminist theological perspectives were rendered by the legendary abolitionist and mystic, Sojourner Truth, in her famous "Ain't I a Woman?" speech. From the very beginning of the conference, the white women were overwhelmed by the jeering ridicule of men who had come to disrupt the meeting. Their most effective antagonist was a clergyman who used both the gender of Jesus and the helplessness of the women to counter their feminist arguments. Sojourner squelched the heckler by correcting his theology first, noting that Jesus came from "God and a woman—man had nothing to do with Him."[13] Second, Truth asserted that women were not inherently weak and helpless.

Raising herself to her full height of six feet, flexing a muscled arm, and bellowing with a voice one observer likened to the apocalyptic thunders, Truth informed the audience that she could outwork, outeat, and outlast any man. Then she challenged, "Ain't I a Woman?"[14] She spoke of women's strength and moral abilities to set things aright: "If the first woman God ever made was strong enough to turn the world upside down all alone, these women together ought to be able to turn it back, and get it right side up again. And now they are asking to do it, the men better let them."[15] Moral values asserted by black women who give credence to the black Judeo-Christian tradition honor reconciliation as highly as liberation.

The accumulated experiences and expressions of black women during slavery were greatly influenced and nurtured by their webs of relationship with the black church and its biblical interpretations of the salvific power of God. These women who toiled under the lash for their masters, worked for and protected their families, fought against slavery and who were beaten, raped, but never subdued passed on to their nominally free female descendants a rich legacy of their own moral value system. It was a legacy of hard work so decidedly different from a White Anglo-Saxon Protestant (WASP) work ethic; it was a legacy of perseverance and self-reliance, a legacy of tenacity, resistance, and insistence on sexual equality—in short, a legacy of love spelling out standards for a new womanhood.[16]

Feminist Moral Values and Black Religious Traditions

The institution of chattel slavery in America was destroyed by the most momentous national event of the nineteenth century, the Civil War. Emancipation removed the legal and political slave status from approximately four million black people in the United States, which meant that, in principle, these blacks owned their persons and their labor for the first time. Unfortunately for the vast majority of Afro-Americans, the traditional practices of racial and gender subordination subjected them to incredible suffering after that war.

The black woman began her life of freedom with no vote, no protection, and no equity of any sort. Black women, young and old, were basically on their own. The patterns of exploitation of the black woman as laborer and breeder were only shaken by the Civil War; by no means were they destroyed. Throughout the late nineteenth and early twentieth centuries, black women were severely restricted to the most unskilled, poorly paid, menial work. Virtually no black woman held a job beyond that of a domestic servant or field hand. Keeping house, farming, and bearing and rearing children continued to dominate all aspects of the black woman's life. The systematic oppression and routinized exclusion of black females from other areas of employment served as confirmations for the continuation of the servile status of black women. As Jeanne Noble describes it, "While freedom brought new opportunities for black men, for most women it augmented old problems."[17] After emancipation, racism and male supremacy continued to intersect patriarchal and capitalist structures in definitive ways.

The religious consciousness of the black freedwoman in the latter nineteenth century focused on "uplifting the black community." The black female was taught that her education was meant not only to uplift her but also to prepare her for a life of service in the overall community. There was a general attitude, says Noble, that "Negro women should be trained to teach in order to uplift the masses."[18] This attitude provided an additional impetus for black women, such as Nannie Helen Burroughs, Charlotte Hawkins Brown, and Mary McLeod Bethune, to found schools. Although the curricula of these schools included academic subjects, there were large doses of industrial arts courses, particularly homemaking, and an environment that enforced codes of morality and thrift. It was biblical faith grounded in the prophetic tradition that helped black women devise strategies and tactics to make black people less susceptible to the indignities and proscriptions of an oppressive white social order.

Understanding the prophetic tradition of the Bible and of the black church has empowered black women to fashion a set of moral values on their own terms, as well as mastering, radicalizing, and sometimes destroying the pervasive negative orientations imposed by the values of the larger society. Also, they articulate possibilities for decisions and action which address forthrightly the circumstances that inescapably shape black life.

Flowing from black women's biblical faith grounded in the prophetic tradition, many black women have been inspired by the Bethune and Burroughs models to hold in high regard a diaconal model of black feminist theology which is extremely consistent with their experience and identity. Without necessarily rejecting white feminist models of theology that focus principally or only on mutuality and equality as essential components of liberation, the preferential choice made by many black feminists is for a theology of servant leadership that was espoused by Christ. This biblical model of feminist liberation theology is principally focused on solidarity with those who suffer or who are marginalized in any way. A much greater examination, integration, and expression of this black feminist perspective and alternative to "mainstream" models of feminist liberation theology are needed.[19]

Rosemary Ruether has been in the forefront among feminist theologians who have insisted that the eradication of racism must be a major priority. She has produced particularly illuminating analyses of the interconnections between racism and sexism.[20] When discussing the future of feminist theory in the academic world, Ruether acknowledges that she speaks from a "white western Christian context," and she calls for an inclusive feminist theology that must emerge out of "a network of solidarity" existing among many feminist communities "engaged in the critique of patriarchalism in distinct cultural and religious contexts," rather than "one dominant form of feminism that claims to speak for the whole of womankind."[21]

In contrast, black theologian Delores Williams has observed that although Ruether rightly emphasizes the increasing numbers of women students in theological schools and lauds the "enormous amount of solid work in all fields of feminist theology that has been accomplished in these past fifteen years," Ruether does not remind her audience that the work has been done by and on behalf of white women.[22] Black women are a tiny percentage among the graduate students in religion; they are an even smaller percentage of the faculties in departments of religion and seminaries. As of yet, there is no "enormous amount" of published work on black feminist theology to offset, or to dialogue with, the claims Ruether cavalierly makes about feminist theology as if black perspectives on feminist theologies were abundantly or equally included.

During the mass migration of southern blacks to the North (1910-1925), tens of thousands of black women and men left home, seeking social democracy and economic opportunity. During this colossal movement of black people, the black church continued to serve as the focal point and center for maintaining the moral value system and the network of relationships which sustained community life.

Not surprisingly, this accelerated movement of blacks out of the South impinged on the black woman's reality in very definite ways. Black women migrated north in greater numbers than black men. Economic necessity dictated that most black women who immigrated to the urban centers find work immediately. In order to survive themselves and to provide for their families, black women once again found only drudge work available to them.

The interaction of race and sex in the labor market exacted a heavy toll on the black woman, making all aspects of migration a problem of paramount religious significance. Her experience as a wife and a mother, responsible for transmitting the moral values, culture, and customs of the black community to her children, served as a decisive factor in determining how the Bible was read and understood. Simultaneously while the black woman was trying to organize family life according to black traditional roles, the white male-dominated industrial society required that she serve as a catalyst in their labor transition process. Her own unfamiliarities and adaptation difficulties had to be repressed because she was responsible for making a home in crowded substandard housing, finding inner-city schools that propagated literacy for her children, and earning enough income for her family to cover the most elementary needs.

The moral and religious value system of the black church served as a sustaining force and as an interpretive principle that guided migrant black women in facing life squarely, in acknowledging its raw coarseness. The white elitist attributes of passive gentleness and an enervative delicacy, considered particularly appropriate to womanhood, proved nonfunctional in the pragmatic survival of black women. Cultivating conventional amenities was not a luxury afforded them. Instead, black women were aware that their very lives depended upon their being able to decipher the various sounds in the larger world, to hold in check the nightmare figures of terror, to fight for basic freedoms against the sadistic law enforcement agencies in their communities, to resist the temptation to capitulate to the demands of the status quo, to find meaning in the most despotic circumstances, and to create something where nothing existed before. The expression of a moral value system for black women meant and required a "sheroic" self-sacrifice and self-giving that could not ever afford shyness, silence, softness, or diffidence as a response indicating subservience.

From the period of black urban migration through World Wars I and II, black women who were rooted in the strong moral values and prophetic traditions of the black church became religious crusaders for justice. Mary McLeod Bethune and her associates recorded and talked about the grimness of struggle among the least visible people in the society. Bethune was adamant about the unheralded achievements of black women, always encouraging them to "go to the front and take our rightful place; fight our battles and claim our victories."[23] She believed in black women's "possibilities," moral values, and their place on this earth. "Next to God," she once said, "we are indebted to women, first for life itself, and then for making it worth having."[24]

In response to the hostile environment, deteriorating conditions, and the enduring humiliation of the social ostracism experienced by black people especially during these war years, Bethune and company exposed the most serious and unyielding problem of the twentieth century—the single most determining factor of black existence in America—the question of color. In their strategic attacks against the ideological supremacy of racist practices and values, they appealed to the religious traditions of black people that began in their invisible church during slavery.

From the period of urbanization of World War II to the present, black women still find that their situation is a struggle to survive collectively and individually against the harsh historical realities and pervasive adversities of today's world. Federal government programs, civil rights movements, and voter-education programs have all had a positive impact on the black woman's situation, but they have not been able to offset the negative effects of inherent inequities that are inextricably tied to the history and ideological hegemony of racism, sexism, and class privilege.[25]

Precisely because of this reality and overwhelmingly oppressive national ideology, Rosemary Ruether warns white feminists to give explicit attention to the ways in which they are involved in race and class privilege. If they do not, she says, they risk social encapsulation.

> Any woman's movement which is only concerned about sexism and not other forms of oppression, must remain a woman's movement of the white upper class, for it is only this group of women whose only problem is the problem of being women, since in every other way, they belong to the ruling class.[26]

Moreover, both black and white feminist groups that do not give explicit attention to the realities yoking racism and sexism will find that they can be easily manipulated by dominant males who appeal to unexamined class and race interests to achieve economic exploitation of all women. Work and dialogue between feminists of color and white feminists in this essential area are, in some sense, just beginning. Meanwhile, black women and their families continue to be enslaved to hunger, disease, and the highest rate of unemployment since the Depression years. Advances in education, housing, health care, and other necessities are deteriorating faster now than ever before.[27]

Both in informal day-to-day life and in the formal organizations and institutions of society, black women are still the victims of the aggravated inequities of the tridimensional phenomenon of race/class/gender oppression. It is in this context that the moral values of black women and the emergence of black feminist consciousness shaped by black biblical and religious traditions must continue to make a decisive difference for a debilitated and nearly dysfunctional human environment.

Womanist Relationships, Moral Values and Biblical Traditions

Because of a social reality, which is so totally demoralizing, and because of the religious traditions from which most black women have come, the Bible has been the highest source of authority in developing and delivering a black moral praxis and a moral theology that is usable in all circumstances. By selectively utilizing the pages of revered Old Testament books, black women have learned how to refute the stereotypes that have depicted black people as ignorant minstrels or vindictive militants. Remembering and retelling the Jesus stories of the New Testament has helped black women to deal with the overwhelming difficulties of overworked and widowed mothers, or underworked and anxious fathers, of sexually exploited and anguished daughters, or prodigal sons, and of dead or dying brothers whose networks of relationality are rooted deeply in the black community. Black feminist consciousness and moral values grow out of and expand upon black, biblical experience and hermeneutics.

Black feminist consciousness may be more accurately identified as black womanist consciousness, to use Alice Walker's concept and definition. In the introduction to *In Search of Our Mothers' Gardens,* Walker proposes several descriptions of the term "womanist," indicating that the word refers primarily to a black feminist and is derived from "womanish," that is, outrageous, audacious, courageous, or willful behavior.[28] To be a faithful womanist, then, or to operate out of this system of black moral value indicators which flow from biblical understandings based on justice and love, is to express in word and deed an alternative ontology or way of living in the world that is endemic to many black women. It is precisely in womanist religious responses of endurance, resistance, and resiliency offered in the face of all attempts at personal and institutional domination that may provide a renewed theological legacy of liberation for everyone concerned.

In exploring the implications contained in Walker's richly descriptive prose, it is possible to make some concluding reflections on black moral values and on the contribution of black women's life experiences as they interface with white feminist liberation theologies.

Womanist responses and black moral values are meant to be alternative standards of womanhood contradictory and paradoxical to those of mainstream American society. Womanist images and black moral values are meant to be paradigmatic of an authentic Christian community of the oppressed that embraces not only the story of the resurrection, but is moreover a referent for the redemptive tribulations through which Jesus as Suffering Servant has come. Womanist moral values are expressed through radical healing and empowering actions with those who are considered as the very least in the reign of God.

Walker adds that a womanist is "committed to the survival and wholeness of entire people, male *and* female. Not a separatist . . . [she] is traditionally capable."[29] The practical implications of such meanings for interaction and dialogue between black women's moral values and the diverse tenets of white feminist ethics are obvious and challenging. Black womanist moral values can redeem us from naivete regarding the nature and function of liberation as well as deliver us from a simplistic, black pseudo expression of providence, that "de Lawd will provide." Nonetheless, a womanist religious tradition does subscribe to the black folk wisdom that God can make a way out of no way for those, like Zora Neale Hurston and others, who just refuse to resign from the human race.

Womanist moral values of "appreciation for the struggle, a love of the folk, and a love of self—*regardless*"[30] offer to all black people and to all others a continual and open means of interaction between those who claim diverse womanist and feminist identities and experiences, and among all those who have a significant agenda for more authentic theologies of liberation.

NOTES

1. Carol Gilligan, *In a Different Voice: Psychological Theory and Women's Development* (Cambridge Mass.: Harvard University Press, 1982) and James W. Fowler, *Stages of Faith: The Psychology of Human Development and the Quest for Meaning* (San Francisco: Harper & Row, 1981).

2. Michelle Wallace, *Black Macho and the Myth of the Superwoman* (New York: Dial Press, 1979).

3. Toinette M. Eugene, "Black Women Contribute Strong Alternate Images," *National Catholic Reporter* (April 13, 1984), 4.

4. Carol Gilligan as described in James W. Fowler, *Becoming Adult, Becoming Christian* (San Francisco: Harper & Row, 1984), 39-40.

5. Paula Giddings, *When and Where I Enter: The Impact of Black Women on Race and Sex in America.* (Toronto: Bantam Books, 1984), 39.

6. Herbert Gutman, *The Black Family in Slavery and Freedom, 1750–1925* (New York: Pantheon Books, 1976), 356-357.

7. Angela Y. Davis, *Women, Race, and Class* (New York: Random House, 1981), 18.

8. Combahee River Collective, "A Black Feminist Statement," in *This Bridge Called My Back: Writings by Radical Women of Color*, eds. Cherrie Moraga and Gloria Anzaldúa (Watertown, Mass.: Persephone Press, 1981), 213.

9. Barbara Hilkert Andolsen, *Daughters of Jefferson, Daughters of Bootblacks: Racism and American Feminism* (Macon, Ga.: Mercer University Press, 1986), 98.

10. Giddings, *When and Where I Enter*, 52.

11. Bert James Lowenberg and Ruth Bogin, eds., *Black Women in Nineteenth-Century American Life: Their Words, Their Thoughts, Their Feelings* (University Park, Pa.: Pennsylvania State University Press, 1976), 149.

12. Ibid.

13. Ibid., p. 236.

14. Ibid., p. 235.

15. Ibid., p. 236.

16. Davis, *Women, Race, and Class*, 29.

17. Jeanne L. Noble, *Beautiful Also Are the Souls of My Black Sisters: A History of the Black Woman in America* (New York: Prentice Hall Press, 1978), 63.

18. Jeanne L. Noble, as discussed in Giddings, *When and Where I Enter*, 101.

19. Eugene, "Black Women Contribute . . ."

20. Rosemary Ruether has written about racism many times. Two of her more detailed treatments of the topic are "Between the Sons of Whites and the Sons of Blackness: Racism and Sexism in America," in *New Women/New Earth: Sexist Ideologies and Human Liberation* (New York: Seabury Press, 1975), 115–33, and "Crisis in Sex and Race: Black Theology vs. Feminist Theology," *Christianity and Crisis* 34 (15 April 1985): 67–73.

21. Rosemary Ruether, "Feminist Theology: On Becoming the Tradition," *Christianity and Crisis* 45 (4 March 1985): 58.

22. Delores Williams, "The Color of Feminism," *Christianity and Crisis* 45 (29 April 1985): 164–165.

23. Elaine M. Smith, "Mary McLeod Bethune and the National Youth Administration," *Clio Was a Woman: Studies in the History of American Women,* Mabel F. Deutrich and Virginia C. Purdy, eds. (Washington, D.C.: Howard University Press, 1980), 152.

24. Ibid.

25. Davis, *Women, Race, and Class,* 231–232.

26. Ruether, *New Women/New Earth,* 116.

27. *Facts on U.S. Working Women,* U.S. Department of Labor Women's Bureau, Fact Sheet No. 85–6, July 1985.

28. Alice Walker, *In Search of Our Mothers' Gardens: Womanist Prose* (San Diego: Harcourt Brace Jovanovich, 1983), xi–xii.

29. Ibid., xi.

30. Ibid.

24

WOMANIST WAYS OF SEEING

Cheryl Townsend Gilkes

On a sunny day in 1983, I grabbed Alice Walker's latest book from a Harvard Square book store and rushed back to my office to read it. *In Search of Our Mothers' Gardens: Womanist Prose* (Harcourt Brace Jovanovich, 1983) immediately seized my attention as the dictionary definition of "womanist" enveloped and enthralled me. Walker's definition connected with my own experience at so many levels and it provided, for me and for many of my sisters whose professional lives were lived both in the pulpit and in the academy, a new way of seeing ourselves and the historical and cultural experience that had shaped us.

Walker's definition sparked an enthusiastic conversation among African-American women ethicists, theologians, critics, and social scientists. It also was a vehicle through which these women engaged others in dialogue. The idea caught fire among those who were particularly concerned, either theoretically, practically, or both, with spiritual and religious concerns. At least three African-American women, Katie Geneva Cannon, author of *Black Womanist Ethics* (Scholars Press, 1988), Jacqueline Grant, author of *White Women's Christ and Black Women's Jesus: Feminist Christology and Womanist Response* (Scholars Press, 1989), and Renita Weems, author of *Just A Sister Away: A Womanist Vision of Women's Relationships in the Bible* (LuraMedia, 1988), utilize Walker's perspective directly or indirectly to explore the relationship of African-American women's experiences to the construction of ethics, to theological and christological ideas, and to the meaning and importance of biblical stories about women. The popularity of their books among African-American churchwomen testifies both to their gifts as preaching women and to the very real desire among

Cheryl Townsend Gilkes is an associate minister at the Union Baptist Church, Cambridge, Massachusetts, and MacArthur Associate Professor of Sociology and African-American Studies at Colby College in Waterville, Maine. This essay appeared in *Peacework* (July-August 1991), a peace and social justice newsletter published by the New England Regional Office of the American Friends Service Committee.

African-American women to be nurtured by ideas and analyses that connect with their experiences.

Like Alice Walker, they embrace and reclaim African-American women's literature to expand horizons and to offer alternative ways of seeing religion and society. Cannon digs deeply into the insights of Zora Neale Hurston to construct new ethical categories and connect those categories with the work of Martin Luther King, Jr., and Howard Thurman. Weems, using a text so often embraced by African-American women and so often rejected by white feminist women, underscores the importance of biblical women's relationships with other women as critiques and models for the contemporary problem of sisterhood. Grant discusses two alternative ways of viewing the problem of Christology and articulates the deep distance between black and white women's experiences and the ways in which those experiences inform their religious worldviews.

This explosion of ideas has not been without its points and counterpoints. In a roundtable discussion in the *Journal of Feminist Studies in Religion* (Vol. 5, No. 2, Fall 1989), three ethicists (Emilie Townes, Shawn Copeland and Katie Cannon), a sociologist (Cheryl Townsend Gilkes), and a feminist theorist and critic (bell hooks/Gloria Watkins) all respond to Cheryl J. Sanders's question: "Does the term womanist provide an appropriate frame of reference for the ethical and theological statements now being generated by black women?" [See chap. 26 in this volume.] Several aims and mandates were made clearer in the discussion. Katie Cannon argued, "A Black womanist liberation Christian ethic is a critique of all human domination in light of Black women's experience, a faith praxis that unmasks whatever threatens the well-being of the poorest woman of color." Emilie Townes, utilizing insights from her study of Ida B. Wells Barnett, concluded: "The agenda of womanist Christian ethics and theology must articulate an understanding of liberation concerned with human equality and the ever-present, ever-sustaining, judging, and redeeming nature of God. Our additional task is to promote the full partnership of women and men in creation with God—to model and embody inclusivity enveloped by justice." Hooks points out that "Walker's term is enabling for women who are fearful that explicitly identifying themselves as feminists would alienate them from black communities. Evoking the term womanist, they are able to affirm their ties to black traditions while simultaneously rethinking and revisioning black experience from a feminist standpoint." What comes through clearly in all of the discussion is the way in which the term "womanist" names a critical perspective grounded in the African-American experience. "Womanist" is a way of seeing that affirms the validity of the black experience in spite of centuries of white supremacist negation.

Many African-American women activists have been deeply immersed in the institutions and settings of African-American communities. Their sense of discomfort with certain dimensions of the "feminist" or "women's liberation" movement was difficult to name. Indeed, Johnella Butler, in an article typical of the early 1970s, warned black women to "beware" of "Miss Anne's warmed over throne." For many African-American women there was a bitter irony in watching women "escape" from houses their grandmothers could only enter through back doors. Although black women participated in particular feminist programs and issues, there were other agenda items and commitments that many white women never seemed to understand and would unwittingly trample in their more radical and separatist positions and rhetoric. Thus it became difficult to reach out to women whose white skin privileges had placed them within a prison Betty Friedan had labeled "the feminine mystique," undermining their sense of competence and self-esteem. Although aware of the need for gender justice as well as racial-ethnic justice, I found it difficult to name the cultural, psychological, historical, and political differences I observed and felt in my encounters with white women activists, especially those from privileged backgrounds. Finally there was the recognition that the African-American tradition was busy fashioning a sexism out of racial self-hatred that was perhaps unique in the annals of human patriarchies: African Americans were learning to denigrate women's strength, competence, self-reliance, occupational participation, and political leadership largely in response to embarrassment caused by the Moynihan Report that had insisted that the foundations of black inferiority lay in the strength and dominance of black women matriarchs.

Alice Walker's term "womanist" and the dictionary-style definition she provides open a conceptual and emotional doorway for "black feminists[s] or feminist[s] of color." Rather than dwelling in negativities, she drew from the traditional discourses among African-American women, particularly mothers and daughters, to affirm certain cultural experiences and images and to emphasize certain aspects of being and struggle. Her term is rooted in "the black folk expression of mothers of female children, 'You acting womanish'. . . ." She identifies a tension that had long been a part of our experience: the demand that black girls grow too quickly and their corresponding desire to hurry up and grow—"usually referring to outrageous, audacious, and courageous or *willful* behavior." Walker goes on to point out the importance of women's love for other women and for a women's culture that includes laughter, tears, and strength.

Perhaps the most important aspect, the part of her definition that named many African-American women's orientation to justice overall, is her insistence that a womanist was "committed to survival and wholeness of entire people, male *and* female. Not a separatist, except periodically, for health." Walker goes on to use the term "universalist" as part of the definition and conclude her definition with a list of loves that resonate loudly with the sacred and secular traditions of African-American cultural life: justice, dance, the Spirit, love, food, roundness, struggle, and the Folk. She emphatically states, "Loves herself. *Regardless.*"

Walker's definition spoke to and named one of the central discomforts many black women activists experienced when listening to some feminists and the implications of their perspective for black women's commitments to the men and boys with whom they suffered. The need for the kind of male-female solidarity within the African-American community that leads toward personal growth, healing, and empowerment is still a significant need. By combining the issues of commitment to wholeness, love of women and of men, and love of self with this urgency for community, Walker in her own way gave African-American women permission to love themselves while loving and nurturing others—something that popular stereotypes and community mythology did not allow.

The womanist idea is also an ideal. It is not realized. Black girls and adolescents still grow too fast and they do not always grow into a womanhood in which they are in control of their bodies or their destinies. They may be outrageous and willful but they are not always responsible, in charge, and serious. The impediments of poverty, urban deterioration, joblessness, miseducation, and educational underdevelopment all combine to blunt the development of wholeness and self-love that will make them effective activists in the traditions of Harriet Tubman, Fannie Lou Hamer, Mary McLeod Bethune or Mary Church Terrell. The ideal that Walker proposes assumes a culture that does not induce pathological self-hatreds and an equitable society that does not destroy people's capacities to love. Although bell hooks/Gloria Watkins in her recent volume, *Talking Back: Thinking Feminist, Thinking Black* (South End Press, 1989), suggests that some women use the term "womanist" to avoid asserting they are "feminist," I think that the issue is more complex. Walker's term "womanist" names differences and distinctiveness by constructing a way of seeing the world that embraces core themes from the African-American cultural experience. In doing that, Walker has provided a most powerful ethical challenge to an oppressive society while calling a broad range of women to activism who can assert themselves as womanists and value their experiences of suffering and survival as gifts for human liberation.

25

FEMINIST THEOLOGY, WOMANIST THEOLOGY: A BLACK CATHOLIC PERSPECTIVE

Diana L. Hayes

In an age of liberation movements, women have, historically, been the unheard voices calling for recognition and the freedom to speak of their lives in words of their own choosing. Women of color have especially suffered from the oppression of others, including women, speaking for and about them. The "coming to voice" of women of color has been a slow and painful but steady progress towards articulating the truths of their lives in ways that are meaningful for them.

Black women's voices have been missing from the dialogue of both the feminist and the Black liberation movements in the United States despite the fact that they were present and active in both movements since their earliest beginnings.

In this paper, I will attempt to address the historical reasons behind the failure to address the issues of women of color, especially Black women, in the feminist movement and present the tracings of an emerging womanist movement, with particular attention to the development of a Black Catholic womanist theology of liberation.

The "Mule" of the World

Writing with a poignancy that betrayed the pain of her own existence, Zora Neale Hurston depicted the condition of African-American women with a stark-

Diana L. Hayes, a Roman Catholic lay woman, is assistant professor of theology at Georgetown University, Washington, D.C. This article is a substantially revised and edited version of a talk given as part of the Ignatian Lecture Series at Georgetown University in 1990–1991 and was published in *The Labor of Love: An Ignatian View of Church and Culture*, ed. William O'Brien (Washington, D.C.: Georgetown University Press, 1991).

ness that, sadly, is still relevant today. She addresses us in the voice of Nanny, the former slave woman in *Their Eyes Were Watching God,*[1] who is speaking to her granddaughter Janie:

> Honey, de white man is de rule of everything as fur as Ah been able tuh find out. Maybe it's some place way off in de ocean where de black man is in power, but we don't know nothin' but what we see. So de white man throw down de load and tell de nigger man tuh pick it up because he have to, but he don't take it. He hand it to his womenfolks. De nigger woman is de mule uh de world so far as Ah can see. Ah been praying fuh it to be different wid you. Lawd, Lawd, Lawd.[2]

And so our mothers, and our foremothers, have been praying since Blacks were first forcibly introduced to the United States as an enslaved and dehumanized people.

That slavery was not one which encouraged the development of a people but rather thrived upon their degradation. The newly arrived slaves were separated from motherland, family, language, friends—all that was meaningful to them and defined them as a people. Yet, paradoxically, they survived, although not completely whole because the devastation was overwhelming. As a people, however, they managed to retain many aspects of their culture, whose fragmented memories they nurtured and expressed in their music, their prayers, and in their coming together in what community they were allowed to share.

There has been much discussion and debate about the impact of slavery on the African-American people and whether or not that impact continues to the present day. I will not enter that debate here other than to note that a significant result was the development of a mythology that continues to serve to alienate Black and White women as well as Black women and Black men to the present day. That is the myth of White womanhood. An integral part of this myth was the polarized depictions of Black and White women in which the latter retained all of the stereotypical positive characteristics—gentle, nurturing, sensitive, intuitive, helpless, dependent—that served to place White women on a pedestal while the former, given the negative feminine attributes—temptress, promiscuous, independent, unnatural mother—were seen as the lowest depths of humanity or, usually, outside of humanity entirely. A Black woman was all that a White woman should not be. She was, indeed, the "mule" of American society, forced to bear burdens the lowest animal was not required to bear and denounced for the very degradation forced upon her. The dichotomy was plain to see. They were women in both groups yet, as Sojourner Truth pointed out:

> nobody ever helps me into carriages, or over mud-puddles, or gibs me de best places. And ain't I a woman? Look at me! Look at my arm! I have ploughed, and planted, and gathered into barns, and no man could head me! And ain't I a woman? I could work as much and eat as much as any man when I could get it, and bear de lash as well. And ain't I a woman?

I have borne thirteen children, and seen 'em mos' all sold off to slavery, and when I cried out with a mother's grief, none but Jesus heard me! And ain't I a woman?[3]

From this distorted mythology came the often asserted belief that White women were equally victims of the oppression of slavery. It was often argued, especially by women active in the abolitionist movement, that the "physical assaults against black women in slavery; as well as the psychological deprivation resulting from their lack of control of their own persons," could be equated "with the white slave mistresses' psychological pain at their husbands' behavior"[4] in engaging in sexual activity with their female slaves. Yet, as Linda Brent, herself a slave, wrote of her White mistress and the issue of slavery:

I was soon convinced that her emotions arose more from anger and wounded pride. She felt that her marriage vows were desecrated, her dignity insulted; but she had no compassion for the poor victims of her husband's perfidy. She pitied herself as a martyr; but she was incapable of feeling for the condition of shame and misery in which her unfortunate helpless slaves were placed.[5]

The raped slave woman was all too often treated, not with compassion and understanding, but harshly, beaten often to the point of death, at the order of, and sometimes by, her enraged and "violated" mistress.

This same blindness towards the existence of racism still serves as a barrier to concerted action on the part of feminists of different races today. The feminist movement, both in society and within the Christian churches, has been one of White women—usually educated, middle-class women—with the freedom and privilege to become militant without fearing consequences as harsh as a woman of color or lower-class White woman would be subjected to. In the Roman Catholic Church, especially, the greater number of women advocating equality have been women religious with similar education, freedoms, and privileges. The result has been that the experience of White women has been presented as universal, incorporating and speaking for the experience of all women. It is not that women of color are assumed to be incapable of speaking for themselves; rather, their silence or absence is, simply, not even noted.

This failure to include or acknowledge the existence of other women's voices leads to the masking of specific differences among women in this country in an effort, albeit unconscious perhaps, to present a united face to the oppressor. It is condemned to failure for "the master's tools will never dismantle the masters' house."[6] It is vital that we, as women, uncover and vanquish, as best we can, the sins of racism and classism that persist in the feminist movement so that we can then work against these evils, as well as the evil of sexism, in our society and the church. We must first remove the beam from our own eye before we can attempt to remove the splinter from the eyes of others. Many women, of all races, have serious problems with the feminist movement and, therefore, with feminist theology. The image they have received from the media, from Rome and from other sources, is an extremely distorted one but they are unaware of the distortions. They fear the labels of radical or lesbian, which they wrongly believe are synonymous with the movement. They assert that they are unable to identify with either the movement or its theological expression because the agendas are too different from their own. Finally, they also dismiss both because of their failure to fully address issues of class and race.[7]

For these distortions to be removed, other voices must be enabled to emerge. We must recognize that women's voices, and the experiences that feed them, *are* different. The language used may be the same but the understandings can be quite different. This can and usually does lead to confusion at times but accepting and learning how to work with these differences can and will also lead to the emergence of a creative diversity in coalition.

This diversity must be recognized for the challenge it brings, a challenge that leads us to a fuller understanding of what it means to be Catholic and Christian. Thus, when we speak in terms of Black Catholicism; of a Black Catholic spirituality, a Black Catholic theology, a Black Catholic presence in the church, we are living up to the fullness of what it means to actually be catholic, to be a universal church. Those who insist on only one understanding of what it means to be Catholic find their claim to Catholicity in their own self-definition — an ethnocentric definition — which places them at the center and all others on the margin, a definition that fails to truly reflect the diversity of God's creation.

We are all the people of God; we are all part of God's creation. From the earliest beginnings of the Christian church, diversity has been upheld as being a reflection of the *imago Dei*. All of us, in our various races and ethnicities, reflect God in God's oneness for God created us as diverse peoples speaking diverse tongues and having diverse cultures. This is all part of God's salvific plan. That oneness in God should, therefore, be seen not as a monolithic oneness but as varied as the sands of the seashore. The constant insistence by one race or ethnic group that there can be only one vision, one expression of church is sinful because it denies the diversity of creation and of the *imago Dei* and, instead, restricts that image to one race or group.

Susan Brooks Thistlethwaite, in her insightful book, *Sex, Race and God*,[8] applies this understanding directly to the feminist movement. She asks whether the insistent desire on the part of White women to bond with Black women and other women of color "under an undifferentiated label of 'sisterhood' " should be labeled as sin, seen as an "inability to respect the boundaries of privacy"[9] of others. The answer to her question must be a firm and unequivocal yes. Room must be made for boundaries of cultural and racial differences so that all may have the freedom to explore and develop their own definitions of themselves and thereby grow into adulthood. Sisterhood is powerful, yes, but only when it is freely offered and freely received, not when it is imposed, in a too-often patronizing way, by one race of "sisters" upon another while the imposer continues to live the lie of that "sisterhood" in her own life and praxis in the world.

Womanist Theology

Black women, in their triple oppression of race, class, and gender, must have the freedom and the space to empower themselves, to engage in their own efforts at consciousness-raising as well as to share those efforts with others, both male and female. This is now beginning to happen with the evolution of the womanist movement whose strongest voice is that of womanist theologians.

A womanist, as Alice Walker defines the term, is a black feminist or feminist of color. She is one "wanting to know more and in greater depth than is good for one . . . [she is] outrageous, audacious, courageous and [engages in] wilful behavior."[10] A womanist is too grown and doesn't mind letting everyone around her know it. A womanist is universal in the sense that her loving includes men and women, sexually and nonsexually, as well as music, dance, food, roundness, the struggle, the Spirit, and herself, "regardless." She is "committed to survival and wholeness of an entire people, male and female" and is opposed to separation, "except for health."[11]

Thus, a womanist sees herself both individually and in community. Her goal of liberation is not simply for herself but for all of her people and, beyond that, for all who are also oppressed by reason of race, sex, and/or class. Sexism is not the only issue for her; rarely is it the most important issue. Rather, it is the intertwined evils that act to restrict her and her community that are the cause for her concern. Thus, womanism in many ways can be seen as encompassing feminism as it opens itself up to all who are oppressed.

Womanist theologians, therefore, have difficulty with some of the issues raised in both White feminist theology and in Black male liberation theology. Both can be seen as engaging in "God-talk" from a too narrowly particular and exclusive context. Both err in seeing their own particular experiences as the norm for all theologizing. Womanist theology, however, insists that full human liberation can only be achieved by the elimination, not of one form of oppression only, but of all forms.

White women, as seen herein, can be both oppressor and oppressed, oppressor in their behavior towards women of color or lower-class women while at the same time being oppressed by a male-dominated patriarchal society. Black men, also, have the dubious distinction of occupying similar dual roles of oppressor of women, especially their own, for it must be acknowledged that sexism exists in the Black world as it does elsewhere in others, and oppressed as Black men. This leaves the Black women on the bottom, stigmatized and condemned both for her strengths and her weaknesses and too often denied a space of her own in which to grow, explore, and develop into full womanhood. It also leaves her, paradoxically, with a challenging freedom.

Black women with no institutionalized "other" that we may discriminate against, exploit or oppress often have a lived experience that directly challenges the prevailing classist, sexist, racist social structure and its concomitant ideology.[12]

This experience provides Black women with a consciousness that enables them to critique the persistent evils still prevalent both in our society and in our church, as well as to provide a voice that can enrich the debate on liberation and a praxis that models it.

Black Catholic Womanist Context

When we speak of oppression in the Roman Catholic Church, we cannot look simply, as already noted, at the experiences of our White sisters nor can we look only at the experiences of our Black men. Neither is nor can be truly reflective of what it means to be Black, Catholic, and female in the Catholic church today.

Despite the changing demographics that reveal a Catholic church increasingly made up of people of color, the church's public image is not Black or multihued, it is White, an image that denies the history of the church's origins in the Middle East and Africa.

We do not know our history as Catholics. Unfortunately, what we do know has, all too often, been bleached beyond recognition. When told of the African fathers of the church, of the three African popes (Militiades, Victor, and Gelasius) and of the many African martyrs and saints, the usual response of most Catholics, regardless of race or ethnicity, is surprise, disbelief, and too often, denial. The true history of the Black presence in the church is only today beginning to emerge.[13]

The importance of consciousness-raising for a people is well known, but what is often not acknowledged is how that reflection on self, to be truly valid, must incorporate insights from others who are distinctly "different" so that we can be privileged to see ourselves as we are mirrored in the eyes of others who are, indeed, "other."

A quiet revolution is brewing within the Catholic church, one that has gone unnoticed until very recently. The prophet Isaiah proclaimed that "the people who walked in darkness have seen a great light" (Isa. 9:2 NRSV). Those people today are African-American Catholics and, I would argue, most particularly African-American Catholic women. As an almost invisible and voiceless people within the Roman Catholic Church, Black Catholics have had the freedom, in some ways, to "do our own thing." Thus, they have been coming to consciousness of themselves as a people with something of value to offer, not just to themselves and other African Americans, not just to the Roman Catholic Church but to the Christian churches and the world at large. African-American Catholic women and men have been hard at work in the vineyards of the Lord for a long time and the harvest is now coming due.

African-American Catholics are in the process of "naming and claiming" themselves, of going back into their history, including their history within the church, and are affirming that which they find there. They are excavating the memories of their sojourn in this country, memories often painful but necessary to recall. For they recognize that they are a people of struggle and "our struggle is also a struggle of memory against forgetting" (South African Freedom Charter). Black Catholics also understand that they are a people of survival and, as part of that survival, they are not ashamed nor afraid to name themselves Catholic.

Over the centuries of the Black presence in this country and in the Catholic church, Black Catholics have, in many ways, been co-opted and corrupted into supporting the status quo, in forsaking their own unique identities in their quest to be seen as truly Catholic. This is not unique to only Catholics, however. Today, however, African-American Catholics are speaking out on what it means to them to be "truly Black and authentically Catholic" in a holistic, life-affirming and community-building way. They are articulating that meaning for themselves and others in the development of a spirituality and a theology that arises out of the context of their own lived experience in the United States.

Black Catholic Womanist Theology

The late Sister Thea Bowman is the example, par excellence, of Black Catholic women today. Whether Sr. Thea ever involved herself in a discussion of feminist, womanist, or any other form of liberating theology as such is irrelevant for she lived out their meaning in her own life. She was, just as Alice Walker defined, a bold, daring, audacious, courageous woman, overwhelming to some but loving and caring to all. She was a Black Catholic woman and in all that she said and did, she lived out the meaning of Black Catholic womanhood. She challenged the status quo, redefined the meaning of church, and called all within the Catholic Church to live up to the gospel message. She theologized in song, in story, in praise of God, in the witness of her life. Sr. Thea was a shooting star who flamed through our lives for a brief moment in time and then went home to God. But in that brief time she shared with us, she, in her own way, shook the foundations of our world and caused them to tremble.

Other bold and daring Black Catholic women are taking up Sr. Thea's flung banner and holding it aloft for all the world to see. There are only seven Black Catholic theologians in the United States today,[14] sad testimony to the lingering legacy of racism in the core of our church. Yet, interestingly enough, five of them are women. They are joined by catechists, liturgists, and administrators of both sexes in proclaiming the voice and spirituality of African American Catholics.

Our spirituality is biblically-centered. We do not reject sacred Scripture but neither do we swallow all of it blindly. Our experience in slavery taught us to read the Bible with Black eyes and to proclaim the Word of God with Black voices and understanding. We were not moved by the efforts of our masters to implant a biased and distorted Christianity within us, rather we re-Christianized Christianity, opening it up to its fullest understanding, as a religion of liberation proclaiming a God who created free men and women in God's own image and who gave them a Liberator in Christ Jesus, the Son of God.

Our understanding of God and Christ is therefore "colored," if you will, by that liberationist understanding. God and Jesus are not problematical; they are both immanent and transcendent in our lives. The immanent God loves us and nurtures us like a parent bending low over a child yet, as transcendent, God is free to judge those who oppress us and to call us forth into freedom. Jesus as immanent is brother and sister, he is in many ways one of us, walking and talking with us, sharing our journey and carrying our burdens, and suffering the pain of our oppression and rejection yet, as transcendent Son of God, he will come forth in glory to lead us to the Promised Land. And we rejoice in the Holy Spirit, that balm of Gilead sent to heal our sin-sick souls, to abide within us and to strengthen us on our journey while giving us the courage to fight back against our oppressors and to "keep on keepin' on."

This theology is still in embryo as Black Catholics gather in their parishes, revivals, diocesan meetings and, most importantly, nationwide events such as the National Black Congresses,[15] to engage in God-talk from their own context and perspective. As Protestant Blacks did, they are raising questions of crucial significance for themselves as a people who are both Black and Catholic: Who is God for us? What does it mean to witness to Christ as a Catholic who is Black? Is there a Black understanding of the church, of Scripture, of Mary, the mother of Jesus and, if so, how do we articulate that understanding?

They are aware of the pitfalls, of relying on a Eurocentric interpretation of their Catholicism rather than developing a true Afrocentric understanding; of accepting a dualistic understanding that pits male against female rather than seeing them as a unified whole. They recognize the importance of freeing themselves to both express their love for the church and to critique it for its failures towards them.

They seek what is distinctive about Black Catholicism, a sharing of African roots with their Black Protestant brothers and sisters[16] as expressed in their celebration of Christ in song and word but also an appreciation of the importance of both Scripture and tradition intertwined with an emphasis on a sacramentality centered on the sacrifice of the Eucharist that is Catholic in its foundation but Black in its expression.[17] Black Catholics in the United States share the tradition of the church from its earliest beginnings but they also bring a critique of that tradition, serving as a "subversive memory" within the church itself and calling it to live up to its proclamation of Scriptures that reveal God's consistent option for the poor and the oppressed but which have been, too often, submerged by a praxis which ignored the plight of those same poor and oppressed.

It is, perhaps, in their reinterpretation of the role and presence of Mary, the mother of God, that Black Catholic women can make a significant contribution. Too often seen as a docile, submissive woman, Black Catholic womanists, instead, see a young woman sure of her God and of her role in God's salvific plan. She is a woman who, in her song (Luke 1:46–55) proclaims her allegiance with God and with her brothers and sisters with whom she lived, as a Jew under Roman oppression, a poor and marginalized existence similar to the existence of Blacks in the church for so long a time. We relate to her by sharing in her experiences as women who are also oppressed but who continue to bear the burden of faith and to pass on that faith to generations to come. At a time when women were supposed to be silent and invisible, when women were considered of little importance, Mary accepted a singular call from God to stand out as "blessed among all women" as a young, pregnant, unwed woman who would have a lot of difficult questions to answer but who had the courage to say a "yes" to God that shattered all of time. She is a role model, not for passivity, but for strong, righteous, "womanish" women who spend their lives giving birth to the future.

It is African-American Catholic women who have been the bearers and the preservers of our culture, of our heritage, of our faith, and who have passed these treasures on to the next generations. It is they, our foremothers, our sheroes, who have, through their abiding faith in a God who provides, a God who makes a way out of no way, given us the courage and the strength to persevere.

Finally, Black Catholic womanists call upon the universal aspect of the church and the holistic understanding of it that they share. As they look at the world today, they realize that as a people of color, they are not in the minority, nor are they a minority as a people of faith. Nor are they, collectively, as women of all races, in the minority. That is the knowledge and the foundation upon which a womanist theology, inclusive of a Black Catholic womanist theology, must be built today. It is a theology that is based in community and draws upon the experiences of all in that community, both male and female, in seeking change.

All women must look at themselves, black, white, yellow, red, and brown, and at each other, with new eyes reflective of the interconnectedness of our worlds today. Yet, we must also look with eyes respective of the colorful diversity which makes of us, especially, a catholic people.

Conclusion

Theology begins from within a context. It is from the particular context of a particular people that all theology develops, whether that is recognized or not. We cannot be objective, yet we must be aware of and be able to articulate our subjectiveness. Today, we must allow the myriad voices of women to ring out in joyous celebration of our diversity and in the faith-filled hope of our coming together in a universality that is truly reflective of who and whose we are.

True universalism must be able to embrace existing pluralism, rather than trying to fit every people into the mould of religion and culture generated from one historical experience. Only God is one and universal. Humanity

is finally one because the one God created us all. But the historical mediators of the experience of God remains plural.[18]

The situation in the Roman Catholic Church is fraught with problems that
pose a challenge to those of us within its embrace. We are challenged to be
more than we are for we are called, as Mary was called, to recognize our own
vocation in Christ Jesus, the Liberator of all humanity. We can, as women, react
to the oppression, whether of race, class, or sex, simply by leaving the church
in frustrated anger and pain or we can remain and continue to serve as a thorn
in its side remembering that the institutional structure is well and truly "man-
made" but that we make up the people of God who are the church. We can
also make the sad and futile mistake of those who seek not to change the
structures themselves but only their outward manifestation, resulting in empowerment for only a few, a few more Black priests and bishops, a few, in time,
women priests, but leaving the hierarchical, authoritarian entity intact or we
can work to restructure, from within, our church and make it truly ours. We
can do this as individuals, Blacks working for Black liberation, Hispanics for
Hispanic liberation, Native Americans, Asians, White women, Black men, or
we can choose to work together as Catholics and as Christians, recognizing and
rejoicing in our differences while finding solidarity in our mutual struggle and
shared faith. We must, in all reality, learn to survive together or surely we will
be destroyed one by one. It is this challenge that womanist theology with its
holistic, communitarian, worldview seeks to meet. Black Catholic women who
have fought, against all odds, oppressors both within and without their community of race and faith to be able to retain that faith and to pass it on serve
as able models of that effort in their ongoing struggle to bring forth new life
within the Roman Catholic Church.

We are presented, as women, with the challenge not "to ignore our differences, or to view them as causes for separation and suspicion" but to see them
"as forces for change."[19] It is the challenge that lies before us all, regardless of
race, class, or gender—to see with newly opened eyes who we are, as Black
women and men, and to accept our differences as cause for celebration not
fear. We must learn from each other, share with each other, grow with each
other and, thereby, "mother" a new world into creation.

Black Catholic womanist theology is an embryo still in the birthing process.
It must be nurtured and sustained with the truths of our lives and the lives of
those who have gone on before us as well as with the traditions of our faith
heritage, as we have experienced and shared it, so that we can come to terms
with the fullness of new life that will, in time, sustain and nurture us all.

NOTES

1. Zora Neale Hurston, *Their Eyes Were Watching God* (1937; reprint, New York:
Harper & Row, 1990).
2. Hurston, 29.

3. See Bell Hooks, *Ain't I a Woman? Black Women and Feminism* (Boston: South End Press, 1981), 160.

4. Susan Brooks Thistlethwaite, *Sex, Race, and God: Christian Feminism in Black and White* (New York: Crossroad, 1989), 33.

5. See Hooks, *Ain't I a Woman*, 28.

6. Audre Lorde, *Sister Outsider: Essays and Speeches* (Freedom, Calif.: Crossing Press, 1984), 112.

7. See Gloria I. Joseph and Jill Lewis, *Common Differences: Conflicts in Black and White Feminist Perspectives* (Boston: South End Press, 1981) for a fuller discussion on this point as well as the many writings of Bell Hooks on feminism.

8. Thistlethwaite, *Sex, Race, and God*, 33.

9. *Ibid.*, 86.

10. Alice Walker, *In Search of Our Mothers' Gardens: Womanist Prose* (San Diego, Calif.: Harcourt Brace Jovanovich, 1983), xi.

11. *Ibid.*

12. Hooks, *Feminist Theory*, 15.

13. See Cyprian Davis, O.P., *A History of Black Catholics in the United States* (New York: Crossroad, 1990).

14. They are myself, at Georgetown University; Sr. Shawn Copeland, O.P., at Yale University; Sr. Jamie Phelps, O.P., at the Catholic Theological Union, Chicago; Sheila Briggs, an African British, at the University of Southern California; Toinette Eugene, at Chicago Theological Seminary; Fr. Edward Braxton of the Archdiocese of Chicago and Fr. Brian Massengale at St. Francis Seminary in Milwaukee, Wisc.; an eighth, Fr. Philip Linden, is completing his doctoral dissertation at the Catholic University of Leuven (Louvain) in Belgium and is at Xavier University of Louisiana, the only Black Catholic university in the United States.

15. The first such congress was held in Washington, D.C. in 1889. After five successful meetings, it was suppressed yet has re-emerged in this century as a vehicle for Black Catholics to engage in God-talk. See the *U.S. Catholic Historian*, 5 (1986) and 7 (1988) as well as Davis, *A History of Black Catholics in the United States.*

16. See my "Black Catholic Revivalism: The Emergence of a New Form of Worship," *Journal of the Interdenominational Theological Center*, 14 (Fall 1986-Spring 1987), 87–107.

17. See Bishop's Committee on the Liturgy, National Conference of Catholic Bishops, *In Spirit and In Truth: Black Catholic Reflections on the Order of Mass* (Washington, D.C.: USCC Office for Publishing and Promotion Services, 1987) and Secretariat for the Liturgy and Secretariat for Black Catholics, National Conference of Catholic Bishops, *Plenty Good Room: The Spirit and Truth of African American Catholic Worship* (Washington, D.C.: USCC Office for Publishing and Promotion Services, 1991).

18. Rosemary Radford Ruether, *To Change the World: Christology and Cultural Pluralism* (New York: Crossroad, 1981), 39.

19. Lorde, *Sister Outsider*, 112.

26

CHRISTIAN ETHICS AND THEOLOGY
IN WOMANIST PERSPECTIVE

Cheryl J. Sanders

One of the most exciting developments in the theological scholarship of the 1980s has been the emergence of womanist ethics and theology. *Womanist* refers to a particular dimension of the culture of black women that is being brought to bear upon theological, ethical, biblical and other religious studies. These new interpretations of black women's religious experience and ideas have been sparked by the creative genius of Alice Walker. She defines the term womanist in her 1983 collection of prose writings *In Search of Our Mothers' Gardens.*[1] In essence, womanist means black feminist.

As early as 1985, black women scholars in religion began publishing works that used the womanist perspective as a point of reference. The major sources for this work are the narratives, novels, prayers and other materials that convey black women's traditions, values and struggles, especially during the slavery period. Methodologically, womanist scholars tend to process and interpret these sources in three ways: (1) the celebration of black women's historical struggles and strengths; (2) the critique of various manifestations of black women's oppression; and (3) the construction of black women's theological and ethical claims. The content of womanist ethics and theology bears the distinctive mark of black women's assertiveness and resourcefulness in the face of oppression. The womanist ideal impels the scholars who embrace it to be outrageous, audacious and courageous enough to move beyond celebration and critique to undertake the difficult task of practical constructive work, toward the end of black women's liberation and wholeness.

Does the term *womanist* provide an appropriate frame of reference for the ethical and theological statements now being generated by black women? To

Cheryl J. Sanders, a Church of God minister, is associate professor of Christian ethics, Howard University School of Divinity. This essay was published in a roundtable discussion in the *Journal of Feminist Studies in Religion* 5 (Fall 1989) and is reprinted with permission.

answer this question it is necessary first to examine critically Walker's own understanding and use of the term, and then to construct some basis for assessing its adequacy as a rubric for Christian ethical and theological discourse.

In 1981 Alice Walker wrote a review of *Gifts of Power: The Writings of Rebecca Jackson* for the *Black Scholar*.[2] The review lifts up the spiritual legacy of the nineteenth-century black Shaker, Rebecca Jackson, who had an unusual conversion experience, left her husband for a life of celibacy, and lived thereafter in close relationship with a Shaker sister, Rebecca Perot. Walker gives high praise to editor Jean McMahon Humez, but takes exception to Humez's suggestion that Jackson was a lesbian. Walker identifies at least three errors in judgment by Humez with respect to Jackson's sexual orientation: (1) her disregard of Jackson's avowed celibacy; (2) her questionable interpretation of Jackson's dreams about Perot as erotic; and (3) her attempt to "label something lesbian that the black woman in question has not." Walker's own position regarding Jackson's sexual orientation is that it would be "wonderful" either way. Having thus disclaimed the moral significance of Jackson's alleged lesbianism, she then goes on to suggest that lesbian would be an inappropriate word in any case, not only for Jackson, but for all black women who choose to love other women sexually. Walker offers her own word *womanist* as a preferred alternative to *lesbian* in the context of black culture. Her concern is to find a word that affirms connectedness rather than separation, in view of the fact that Lesbos was an island whose symbolism for blacks "is far from positive." Furthermore, Walker concludes that "the least we can do," and what may well be for black women in this society our only tangible sign of personal freedom, is to name our own experience after our own fashion, selecting our own words and rejecting those words that do not seem to suit.

Walker gives a more complete definition of womanist as a preface to *In Search of Our Mothers' Gardens*, her 1983 collection of womanist prose that includes the *Gifts of Power* review. This definition has four parts, the first showing the word's derivation from *womanish* (opposite of *girlish*) and its primary meaning "black feminist" or "feminist of color." The second part conveys the sense of the word as explained in the book review; as a woman who loves other women but is committed to the survival and wholeness of entire people; who is not separatist, but is "traditionally" universalist and capable (these traits being illustrated with excerpts of dialogue between mother and daughter). The third part celebrates what the womanist loves—music, dance, the moon, the Spirit, love, food, roundness, struggle, the Folk—herself ending with the word "regardless," presumably an allusion to Walker's earlier call in the review for a word that affirms connectedness to the community and the world "*regardless* of who worked and slept with whom." The fourth and final part of the definition compares womanist to feminist as purple to lavender, expressing in vivid terms the conclusion that womanist has a deeper and fuller meaning than feminist.

Walker's definition of womanist represents a shift in emphasis from her earlier discussion of womanist in the book review. In the first instance womanist carries the connotation of black *lesbian*, and in the second it denotes black *feminist*, a designation that includes women who love women and those who love men. In both cases, however, her point is to name the experience of audacious black women with a word that acknowledges their sensibilities and traditions in ways that the words *lesbian* and *feminist* do not. Walker's womanist definition and writings send a clear and consistent signal to celebrate the black woman's freedom to choose her own labels and lovers.

It is apparent that a few black women have responded to this call for celebration by writing womanist theology and womanist ethics and by calling themselves womanist scholars.[3] Those who have made use of the term womanist in their writing have cited the definition that Walker gives in her preface to *In Search of Our Mothers' Gardens* generally without giving attention to Walker's explanation of womanist in her review of *Gifts of Power*. Walker's definition has been subjected each time to the writer's own editing and interpretation, partly because each writer seems compelled to construe its meaning in light of her own thought. This process of appropriation and adaptation merits close scrutiny. In our efforts to tailor Walker's definition to suit our own purposes, have we misconstrued the womanist concept and its meaning? Is the word womanist being co-opted because of its popular appeal and used as a mere title or postscript for whatever black women scholars want to celebrate, criticize or construct? Are we committing a gross conceptual error when we use Walker's descriptive cultural nomenclature as a foundation for the normative discourse of theology and ethics? On what grounds, if any, can womanist authority and authenticity be established in our work? In other words, what is the necessary condition for doing womanist scholarship? To be a black woman? A black feminist? A black lesbian?

One approach to resolving these concerns would be to devise some reasonable categories for evaluating the extension which womanist theological and ethical thought conforms to (or deviates from) Walker's basic concern for black women's freedom to name their own experience and to exercise prerogatives of sexual preference. If we assume, rather boldly, that Walker never intended to reserve exclusive authority to use the word as her own private vehicle of expression, it can be argued that the authority to label one's work as a womanist derives directly from one's ability to set forth an authentic representation of Walker's concept in that work. Three categories are suggested here as grounds for comparison and evaluation: context, criteria, and claims.

The context of the womanist perspective is set forth quite clearly in Walker's long definition of the word. While its general context is the folk culture of black women, its specific context is the intergenerational dialogue between black mothers and their daughters in an oppressive society. The origin of the word *womanist* is a traditional warning given by black mothers to their daughters, "You acting womanish," in response to their precocious behavior (i.e., "You trying to be grown"). The behavior in question is further described as outrageous, audacious, courageous, and willful, words suggesting rebellion against the mother's authority, as well as resistance to oppressive structures that would limit knowledge and self-realization. However, it is evident that Walker's concern is to include the mother in the womanist context by ascribing to her the role of teacher and interpreter, and by portraying her as resigned to the daughter's assertion of her womanhood. This can be seen in the mother-daughter dialogues cited to illustrate the meaning of "traditionally universalist," with reference to the diversity of skin tones among blacks, and "traditionally capable," i.e., the determination of slaves to persist in their pursuit of freedom.

The criteria of the womanist perspective are very clearly spelled out in Walker's definition. To summarize, the womanist is a black feminist who is audacious, willful and serious; loves and prefers women, but also may love men; is committed to the survival and wholeness of entire people, and is universalist, capable, all-loving, and deep. Perhaps it is unrealistic to expect complete compliance with all of these criteria as a prerequisite for employing womanist nomenclature. But it is intellectually dishonest to label a person, movement or idea as womanist on the basis of only one or two of these criteria to the exclusion of all the others. Two of these criteria tend to have the broadest appeal in theological-ethical statements: Commitment to the survival and wholeness of entire people and love of the Spirit. The reason for this should be obvious; these two criteria point directly to the self-understanding of the black church. However, they would seem to merit the prominence theologians and ethicists ascribe to them, especially in view of the fact that they are not given any particular priority within the definition itself: In other words, it may be a distortion of Walker's concept to lift up these two criteria because they resonate with black church norms, while quietly dismissing others that do not. The fact is that womanist is essentially a secular cultural category whose theological and ecclesial significations are rather tenuous. Theological content too easily gets "read into" the womanist concept, whose central emphasis remains the self-assertion and struggle of black women for freedom, with or without the aid of God or Jesus or anybody else. The womanist concept does lend itself more readily to ethical reflection, given that ethics is often done independently of theology, as philosophical discourse with greater appeal to reason than to religious dogma. Walker's definition comprises an implicit ethics of moral autonomy, liberation, sexuality and love that is not contingent upon the idea of God or revelation. In any case, to be authentically "womanist," a theological or ethical statement should embrace the full complement of womanist criteria without omissions or additions intended to sanctify, de-feminize or otherwise alter the perspective Walker intended the word *womanist* to convey.

Despite the proliferation of theological claims that have been issued under the authority of the womanist rubric, Walker's womanist nomenclature makes only one claim—that black women have the right to name their own experience. This claim is inclusive of the prerogative of sexual preference; to choose one's own labels and lovers is a sign of having fully come into one's own. It may be understood theologically as the right to name one's own deity and sources of revelation, but to do so is to move beyond interpretation to the more dubious task of interpolation. Moreover, neither Walker's definition nor her discussion of womanist addresses the nature and purpose of God in relation to the plight of the oppressed, as blacks and/or as women. So it appears that womanist theology, with its liberatory theological claims, has been built upon a cultural foundation that not only was not intended to sustain theological arguments, but actually was fashioned to supplant ideas and images, theological or otherwise, that might challenge the supremacy of self-definition. This is not to deny the possibility of a genuine congruence between womanist theological-ethical discourse and the claim of personal and collective self-definition. The real problem here is the appropriation of the womanist concept as the prime ground and source for theological claims that have been extracted from the testimony of black women whose theology and ethics rested upon other foundations and who, given the opportunity to choose labels, might have rejected womanist even as a name for their own experience.

It would seem that to do ethics in womanist perspective presents less of a problem, insofar as the construction of ethical claims can be pursued independently of theological considerations. Even so, one must take care not to force the ethical statements of one era into the ethical categories of another, nor to ascribe to our black foremothers womanist sensibilities shaped by a modernist impulse that they might not have endorsed or understood.

The necessary and sufficient condition for doing womanist scholarship has to be adherence to the context, criteria, and claims inherent in Walker's definition; it would be a mistake to recognize anything that any black woman writes with a womanist title or reference as womanist discourse simply because the author is black and female. Ultimately, the authority to determine what qualifies as womanist discourse rests with Alice Walker, who has defined and demonstrated the meaning of the word in her writing with great skill and consistency. However, given the fact that so many black female scholars have already taken the liberty of using her word in our work, we need to come to terms with the responsible exercise of the authority we have claimed.

I am fully convinced of the wisdom of Walker's advice to black women to name our own experience after our own fashion and to reject whatever does not suit. It is upon the authority of this advice that I want to explore further the suitability of the term womanist for theological-ethical discourse. The context, criteria, and claims of the womanist perspective provide an appropriate basis for raising critical questions concerning the suitability of this label for the work black women scholars are currently doing in theology and ethics.

First, there are contextual problems, beginning with tensions inherent in the dialogues presented in Walker's definition. There is an intergenerational exchange where the traditional piety of the acquiescent mother is in conflict with the brash precociousness of the womanish daughter. The definition conveys a spirit of celebration, evoking approval of the daughter's rebellion and the mother's resignation to it. This push to be "womanish" or "grown" also bears a hint of self-assertion in a sexual sense, where sexual freedom is a sign of moral autonomy. Thus, the context of womanist self-assertion includes two apparently inseparable dimensions: the personal struggle for sexual freedom and the collective struggle for freedom in the political-social sense. Yet, in the theological-ethical statements womanist is used to arm the faith of our mothers principally in the collective sense of struggle, that is, for freedom from racist and sexist oppression. Further, it should be noted that although the question of Rebecca Jackson's sexual orientation is Walker's point of departure for discussing the meaning of womanist, she refrains from applying the term to Jackson. Walker chides Humez for not taking seriously Jackson's description of herself as celibate, but Jackson's choice of celibacy (i.e., not to love either women or men sexually, not even her own husband) as an act of submission to a spiritual commitment to follow Jesus Christ evidently is not regarded by Walker as a womanist assertion of sexual freedom. Thus it would seem inappropriate to label as womanist those saintly rebels (e.g., Sojourner Truth) whose aim was not to assert their sexual freedom but rather to work sacrificially toward the liberation of their people as followers of Jesus Christ. To designate a historic figure as womanist solely on the basis of political-social engagement without addressing the personal-sexual dimension is a contextual error typical of womanist theological-ethical discourse. To be authentically grounded in the womanist context, these statements cannot be simply celebrations of black women's assertiveness, but must also give attention to the inherent dialogical and intergenerational tensions within the black woman's struggle for freedom, and to both dimensions of that struggle, the personal-sexual and the political-social.

A further contextual problem stems from the fact that Walker's definition gives scant attention to the sacred. Womanist is defined in secular terms centered on a worldly premise of self-assertion and self-sufficiency. The womanist's concern for the sacred is demonstrated in the definition by italicizing the verb in the statement that she "*loves* the Spirit," but otherwise finds no distinctiveness among her loves for other aspects of nature and culture (she also "*loves* the folk"). The term *womanist theology* is in my view a forced hybridization of two disparate concepts and may come to resemble another familiar hybrid, the mule, in being incapable of producing offspring. Novelist Zora Neale Hurston once declared in the voice of one of her characters that the black woman is "the mule of the world" but unlike the mule the black woman has often sought to cast upon the Lord those burdens too hard for her to bear, and has reproduced herself; body and spirit, through many generations. Not only does this scant attention to the sacred render the womanist perspective of dubious value as a context for theological discourse, but it ultimately subverts any effort to mine the spiritual traditions and resources of black women. The use of black women's experience as a basis for theology is futile if that experience is interpreted apart from a fully theistic context. One might argue here that it is inappropriate to make such an issue of the distinctiveness of the sacred in black theological discourse in view of our African heritage that allegedly draws no such distinctions, at least not the way they are drawn in the West. In the African tradition, however, the basis for denial of the distinction between sacred and secular is the notion that the sacred pervades everything. By contrast, Western modernity exalts the secular to the point of disregarding or circumscribing the sacred in unhealthy ways. African-American Christians, poised historically in a peculiar position between two incompatible world views, have tended to resolve this dilemma by fashioning for ourselves a world view that derives its power, character, and spirit from the sacred realm, from which we have drawn wisdom and hope to survive within the profane world of those who have oppressed us in the name of God and mammon. Thus it would appear incongruous to try to do black women's theology, or even just to articulate it in words, within a context that marginalizes the sacred within black women's existence. The search for our mothers' gardens, and our own, seems pointless if we remain oblivious to our mothers' gods.

The womanist concept sets forth a variety of criteria that convey specific moral values, character traits and behavior, especially with regard to sexuality. One important question to raise is whether or not the sexual ethics implied by the womanist concept can serve the best interests of the black family, church, and community. Part of Walker's original intent was to devise a spiritual, concrete, organic, characteristic word, consistent with black cultural values, that would describe black women who prefer women sexually, but are connected to the entire community. *Womanist* is a preferred alternative to *lesbian* because it connotes connectedness and not isolation, and a womanist is one who loves other women, sexually and/or non-sexually and who appreciates and prefers women's culture. Clearly, in Walker's view sexual preference is not a morally or ethically significant factor in determining whether or not one is "committed to the survival and wholeness of entire people, male *and* female." But the affirmation of the connectedness of all persons within the black community regardless of sexual preference is not the only issue at stake with respect to the well-being of black people. In my view there is a fundamental discrepancy between the womanist criteria that would affirm and/or advocate homosexual practice, and the ethical norms the black church might employ to promote the survival and wholeness of black families. It is problematic for those of us who claim connectedness to and concern for the black family and church to engage these criteria authoritatively and/or uncritically in the formation of theological-ethical discourse for those two institutions. If black women's ethics is to be pertinent to the needs of our community, then at least some of us must be in a position to offer intellectual guidance to the church as the principal (and perhaps only remaining) advocate for marriage and family in the black community. There is a great need for the black churches to promote a positive sexual ethics within the black community as one means of responding to the growing normalization of the single-parent family, and the attendant increases in poverty, welfare dependency, and a host of other problems. Moreover, it is indisputably in the best interests of black children for the church not only to strengthen and support existing families, but also to educate them ethically for marriage and parenthood. The womanist nomenclature, however, conveys a sexual ethics that is ambivalent at best with respect to the value of heterosexual monogamy within the black community.

Thirdly, it is problematic for black women who are doing womanist scholarship from the vantage point of Christian faith to weigh the claims of the womanist perspective over against the claims of Christianity. The womanist perspective ascribes ultimate importance to the right of black women to name our own experience; in the Christian perspective, Christ is the incarnation of claims God makes upon us as well as the claims we make upon God. While there may be no inherent disharmony between these two assertions, the fact remains that there are no references to God or Christ in the definition of womanist. For whatever reason, christology seems not to be directly relevant to the womanist concept. And if we insist upon incorporating without the womanist rubric the christological concessions of black women of faith, or discerning therein some hidden or implicit christology, then we risk entrapment in the dilemma of reconciling Christian virtues such as patience, humility and faith, with the willful, audacious abandon of the womanist. Walker only obscures the issue by making vague references to the spirit instead of naming Christian faith and practice. For example, she uses terms like *general power* and *inner spirit* to describe Rebecca Jackson's motive for leaving husband, home, family, friends and church to "live her own life." Yet it seems obvious that Jackson would name her own experience simply as a call to follow Christ. I suspect that it is Christianity, and not womanism, that forms the primary ground of theological and ethical identity with our audacious, serious foremothers.

In conclusion, the womanist perspective has great power, potential and limitations; it may be useful as a window to the past, but a truly womanist tradition has yet to be fully created and understood. I have raised some questions concerning the suitability of womanist as a rubric for black women's ethics and theology, yet I have no better word to offer, nor do I feel especially compelled to come up with one. I am aware that many of my colleagues in theological scholarship are wholly committed to the womanist perspective, and my principal aim has been to prod us all further in the direction of critique and construction. If we are going to be serious about the constructive task, then we must be celebrative and critical at the same time, neither letting ourselves become so enraptured in celebrating our heroines and ideals that we sweep aside the critical questions, nor allowing the critical process to dampen our zeal for the content of our work. I have great faith that black female theologians and ethicists are on target to give significant direction to both church and society by further exposing the roots of oppression in all its forms and manifestations, and by discovering more keys to our personal and collective survival, regardless of which labels we embrace.

NOTES

1. Alice Walker, *In Search of Our Mothers' Gardens* (San Francisco: Harcourt Brace Jovanovich, 1983).

2. Jean McMahon Humez, ed., *Gifts of Power: The Writings of Rebecca Jackson (1795–1871), Black Visionary, Shaker Eldress* (Amherst, Mass.: University of Massachusetts Press, 1981); Alice Walker, review of *Gifts of Power: The Writings of Rebecca Jackson (1795–1871), Black Visionary, Shaker Eldress,* edited with an introduction by Jean McMahon Humez, in *Black Scholar* (November-December 1981): 64–67. Reprinted in Alice Walker, *In Search of Our Mothers' Gardens,* 71–82.

3. See, for example, Katie Geneva Cannon, *Black Womanist Ethics* (Atlanta: Scholars Press, 1988); Toinette M. Eugene, "Moral Values and Black Womanists," *Journal of Religious Thought* 44 (Winter-Spring 1988): 23–34; Jacquelyn Grant, "Womanist Theology: Black Woman's Experience as a Source for Doing Theology, with Special Reference to Christology," *Journal of the Interdenominational Theological Center* 13 (Spring, 1986): 195–212; Renita J. Weems, *Just a Sister Away* (San Diego: LuraMedia, 1988); and Delores S. Williams, "Womanist Theology: Black Women's Voices," *Christianity and Crisis* (July 14, 1986): 230–232.

WHO ARE WE FOR EACH OTHER?: SEXISM, SEXUALITY AND WOMANIST THEOLOGY

Renee L. Hill

Womanism, Black women's way of acting and being first defined by Alice Walker,[1] is having a tremendous impact on the ways in which some African-American Christian women are defining and developing their theologies. Christian womanist theologians[2] seek to create theology in the gap between Black male liberation theology and White feminist theology. Yet Christian womanist theology is not simply a blending of the two. Christian womanist theology attempts to root itself in the lives and experiences of Black women. The sources for constructing Christian womanist theology are the records of the everyday (physical, emotional, spiritual) experiences of African-American women. "Female slave narratives, imaginative literature by black women, autobiographies, the work by black women in academic disciplines, and the testimonies of black church women"[3] are some examples of these sources. The text of the everyday lives of Black women in contemporary communities must be added to this list. The source for constructing any type of womanist thought is in the being and doing of Black women's lives.

Kelly Brown in her article, "God is as Christ Does: Toward a Womanist Theology," highlights the symbolic meaning of womanism. It "symbolizes black women's resistance to their multidimensional oppression."[4] The fact that womanism claims to speak from the perspective of resistance to multidimensional oppression is what gives it its power and potential.

Womanism recognizes the complexity of oppression in the United States society. Christian womanist theologians have recognized that both race and gender oppression must be confronted simultaneously. Some have named classism as a third aspect of the multidimensional oppression that Black women

---

Renee L. Hill, a self-identified lesbian, is a doctoral student at Union Theological Seminary. The essay was written for a Black theology class taught by James H. Cone.

face. However, Christian womanists have failed to recognize heterosexism and homophobia as points of oppression that need to be resisted if *all* Black women (straight, lesbian, and bisexual) are to have liberation and a sense of their own power. Some womanists have avoided the issues of sexuality and sexual orientation by being selective in appropriating parts of Walker's definition of womanism. This tendency to be selective implies that it is possible to be selective about who deserves liberation and visibility. If Black Christian theologians are going to appropriate Walker's definition of womanism, relationships between women, including lesbianism must be addressed.[5]

Danger in the Definition: Womanist Silences

Alice Walker's definition of womanism is about Black women shaping community. It is about Black women struggling and surviving. Walker's womanism is about Black women celebrating themselves and their communities. Her definition is also about relationships: relationships between Black women and the Black community; between Black mothers and daughters. Womanism as defined by Walker is also about relationships *between* Black women. Walker writes that a womanist is "a woman who loves other women, sexually and/or nonsexually. Appreciates and prefers women's culture, women's emotional flexibility (values tears as natural counterbalance of laughter), and women's strength."[6] The womanist is women-oriented. She *loves* women. Womanism includes the lesbian voice, the voice of Black women in relationship with each other.

The lesbian voice is silenced in Christian womanist theology. Heterosexism and homophobia are nonissues in the Christian womanist paradigm for liberation. There is no widespread discussion of sexuality in African-American Christian theology in general. Christian womanists, like their male counterparts, focus for the most part on the impact of racism on the Black community. The Christian womanist focus on gender is to a great degree a focus on the retrieval of Black women's stories, words, and perspectives. There is no great emphasis on the impact of sexism on the Black community. This may be a key to the lack of discourse on sexuality.

The hesitancy to discuss sexism in the Black community may be a result of a fear of being accused of imposing outside issues on the community ("sexism is a White women's issue"). It is a result of being warned against "airing the dirty laundry" of the Black community ("why give the White community any more fuel to add to the fire?"). It also comes out of a fear of being accused of being lesbian (man-hater, bull dagger, etc.).

The appropriation of the term "womanist" can be used to avoid addressing sexist oppression as defined by White feminists. Delores Williams writes of her interpretation of Walker's connection between womanism and feminism:

> In making the feminist-womanist connection, however, Walker proceeds with great caution. While affirming an organic relationship between womanists and feminists, she also declares a deep shade of difference between

them ("Womanist is to feminist as purple to lavender."). This gives womanist scholars the freedom to explore the particularities of black women's history and culture without being guided by what white feminists have already identified as women's issues.[7]

Williams is correct in her interpretation of Walker's "shade of difference" between womanism and White feminism. Womanism is concerned with Black women's particularity and how that particularity shapes or can shape Black women's thought and praxis. However, it is important to keep in mind that according to Walker's definition, a womanist is a "Black feminist." Walker never denies the political importance of feminism. Her feminism is rooted in the experiences of Black women. It comes from the perspective of Black women, but it is feminism nonetheless. The goal of womanists must be to define the issues of Black women without denying the important issues that the feminist movement (a movement that involves women of many different races and cultures) has raised. Many of these issues are issues that center on sexuality and male domination, including sexual violence, spousal abuse, and compulsory heterosexuality. The feminist movement has been vitally important in unmasking society's denial about sexuality as a social issue ("the personal is political"). It is not a White women's issue. Sexuality is not a sin and it should not be a "dirty little secret."

Sexuality *is* an issue for Christian womanist theologians. It is not any less or any more important than community or survival. It simply is a part of community and survival. Sexuality (and male dominance) must be discussed in the Black community. Only then will we be able to begin to address subjects like rape, the AIDS epidemic, as well as sexual orientation in the Black community.

Sexuality is also an issue for Christian womanists because it is a fundamental part of life, God-given life, the life that Christ as incarnate in Jesus, shared with humanity; it is a profound theological issue. Sexuality is a part of human nature, the human nature that God created and called good. It should not be defined simply in terms of a sex act (genital sexual contact), but it should be understood as a part of living, as an aspect of understanding one's self, and as a way of being in relationship with other people.

Spirituality enters sexuality because it is a part of human life, sexuality is part of God's creation. "Spirituality is no longer identified simply with asceticism, mysticism, the practice of virtue, and methods of prayer. Spirituality, i.e., the human capacity to be self-transcending, relational, and freely committed, encompasses all of life, including our human sexuality."[8] Christian womanists who are committed to the physical and spiritual health, wholeness, and well-being of Black people cannot afford to overlook the issue of sexuality.

In addressing sexuality, Christian womanists who use Walker's definition as the foundation of their work in theology and ethics must confront the realities of Black women's relationships with each other, including lesbian relationships. Christian womanist theology as a theology of liberation has to confront the oppression of lesbians and gay men in the Black community, including (if not

particularly) the Black church. It must also focus on strengthening and celebrating woman to woman relationships (sexual and nonsexual) in the Black
community without fear of lesbian or separatist baiting.

Who Are We for Each Other?: The Acts of Women in Relationship

• *Black women gather* in a kitchen, perhaps in someone's home or at the
church, preparing the food for a church supper. A group of them cutting,
chopping, stirring, kneading. These are the ritual acts of a women's community,
acts of women in relationship. Mothers, daughters, aunts, cousins—all of them
sisters, working in community, in relationship to create a space of welcome and
hospitality for the church community.

• *Black women gather* in a living room or on a porch, after a week of hard
work. Talking, listening, arguing, agreeing. These are the ritual acts of women
in relationship. They struggle to support each other's struggles, and to celebrate
each other's triumphs. Friends from childhood they are also sisters. They
embody the strength of female friendship.

• *Black women gather* one another up into one another's arms, the two of
them—holding, touching, kissing—the acts of women in relationship. Friends
in sisterhood, they are also lovers. They embody women's love for one another.

The acts of Black women in relationship, woman-loving between and among
Black women, are critical in the formation of any understanding of womanist
spirituality and in the creation of womanist theology, Christian or non-Christian.
In positive, nurturing relationships between Black women womanists can find
models for mutuality, self-determination, and self-love. All of which are important elements in liberation thought and praxis for Black women, and for the
Black community in general.

Intentional mutuality is important for womanists in redefining power relationships and challenging the hierarchy in the community and in the church.
Mutual, autonomous female friendship has the potential to challenge patriarchal domination in the Black community. Black women in relationship with one
another have always been able to live, work, love, and struggle together without
men, by choice or by necessity. Mutuality among women—sisterhood—is a bed-
rock of power for survival and transformation in the Black community. Perhaps
it is because of the potential power of mutuality that it is discouraged (or
perhaps destroyed) by forces in society including means such as lesbian-baiting
and the promotion of male-identified consciousness.

For Christian womanists mutuality serves as a guideline for re-creating relationships within patriarchal structures of Christian communities. For some it
might also influence the ways in which human relationships with God are understood and discussed. For example, is God Lord *over* humanity or is there any
sense of mutuality in that relationship (e.g., do we co-create community, life,
spiritual transformation *with* God?).

Self-determination and self-love are important for womanists in creating a
body of thought. Self-determination would mean taking the power to name

one's self and to accept or reject the roles and images that society tries to impose. For the Christian womanist, self-determination has meant creating theology out of Black women's experiences, putting Black women at the center. It could and should also mean answering the question: who are we for ourselves and each other?, first, before we are drawn into the role of nurturing and bolstering the entire Black community. Care for the community has to begin with care of and for the self. This is where self-love becomes important in the transformative work of womanist spirituality and theology.

The acts of Black women in relationship also provide keys to the ways in which justice can be linked to spirituality and sexuality. Mutuality, self-determination and self-love can give Christian womanists the power and the resources to claim sexuality as an important issue for theology, spirituality and justice-making in the Black community. This is especially important, for Christian womanists who, if they are going to be true to Walker's definition of womanism, must be willing to listen to the lesbian voice of womanism.

The Lesbian Voice of Womanism

We cannot settle for the pretenses of connection, or for parodies of self-love. We cannot continue to evade each other on the deepest levels because we fear each other's angers, nor continue to believe that respect means never looking directly nor with openness into another Black woman's eyes.[9]

In order to accept the challenge to resist multidimensional oppression, the resistance that "womanism" implies, Christian womanists need to confront the homophobia and heterosexism that exist in African-American communities. They also must be willing to listen to the Black lesbian voices that are helping to shape womanism. These lesbian voices are a powerful witness to woman-loving in the Black community.

Listening to lesbian voices is essential to womanists for several reasons. By acknowledging the existence of lesbians (and gay men) in the Black community, including the Black church, womanists will confront the denial and invisibility of homosexuality that is a symptom of heterosexist oppression. It would be a way of raising the issue of oppression within the Black community. African Americans need not only theories of resistance and liberation from oppressive forces in the dominant white society, but also those theories which will address oppression *within* the community.

Listening to the lesbian voice would also compel the Black community to challenge the different sexual stereotypes and images that have been assigned to Black women. The lesbian has been regarded by many as either inadequate or dangerous. Inadequate because, according to the stereotype, she does not produce children (in reality lesbians, like all other women, may or may not have children; may or may not want children). Dangerous because she challenges compulsory heterosexuality[10] and she may also challenge male supremacy depending on her politics. The lesbian is seen as "other." Her otherness has been such a powerful source of fear that she has had to be made invisible, her liberation and well-being made non-issues. But in looking directly into the eyes of the "other" and by listening to her voice, womanists may find the tools to re-examine and do away with not only lesbian stereotypes, but also other negative images of Black women (the "Mammy," the "whore," and the baby maker for example). In recognizing the oppressive images that lesbians have been given in the community (including the invisibility that has been maintained by womanist scholars thus far), womanists can begin to work toward liberating images for all Black women. In listening to the lesbian voice womanists, heterosexual and lesbian, can learn the importance of self-naming.

For Christian womanists the issue of listening to the lesbian voice of womanism is a justice issue. Lesbians and gay men have been excluded from the Christian community for many of the same reasons that Black women and men have been excluded from full participation in society. They have been excluded for being who they are or who they are perceived to be. The Bible has played a major role in the exclusion and oppression of lesbians and gay men. Womanist theology as a liberation theology in resistance to multidimensional oppression has a responsibility to challenge this. Brown writes:

> Womanist theology must articulate Jesus Christ's significance in such a way that black church women as well as men are compelled to criticize those claims concerning women's submissiveness found in the later New Testament epistles, for example, the same way that black church people have put forth critiques of similar New Testament claims regarding slavery.[11]

Along with refuting female submissiveness and slavery Christian womanist theology must be willing and able to articulate the love and liberation of Christ as a love and liberation that encompasses and embraces all, including lesbians and gay men.

Womanist theology is based on the experiences of Black women. It is a source for multidimensional resistance and celebration. Because of the sources and character of womanism, Christian womanists are greeted with the challenge of constructing theology that speaks to the richness and diversity of the entire Black community. In order to do so they must be willing to be the "outrageous, audacious, courageous and willful" women that Walker describes in her definition.

NOTES

1. Alice Walker, *In Search of Our Mothers' Gardens* (New York: Harcourt, Brace, Jovanovich, 1983), pp. xi–xii.

2. M. Shawn Copeland points out in the "Roundtable Discussion: Christian Ethics and Theology in Womanist Perspective" (*Journal of Feminist Studies in Religion*, 5, no. 2, [Fall 1989]) that "if it is possible to speak of secular feminists and Christian feminists,

surely it is possible to speak of secular womanists and Christian womanists" (p. 99).

3. Delores Williams, "Womanist Theology: Black Women's Voices," *Christianity and Crisis* 47, no. 3 (1987), p. 67. Reprinted in this volume as Document 19.

4. Kelly Delaine Brown, "God is as Christ Does: Toward a Womanist Theology," *Journal of Religious Thought* 46, no. 1 (Summer-Fall 1989), 8.

5. See especially Cheryl Sanders et al., "Roundtable Discussion: Christian Ethics and Theology in Womanist Perspective," *Journal of Feminist Studies in Religion,* 5, no. 2 (Fall 1989). See Document 26 in this volume for Sanders' remarks.

6. Walker, xi.

7. Williams, 68.

8. Toinette M. Eugene, "While Love is Unfashionable: Ethical Implications of Black Spirituality and Sexuality," in *Women's Consciousness, Women's Conscience*, ed. Barbara H. Andolsen, Christine E. Gudorf, and Mary D. Pellauer (San Francisco: Harper & Row, 1985), 124.

9. Audre Lorde, "Eye to Eye: Black Women, Hatred and Anger," in *Sister Outsider: Essays and Speeches* (Trumansburg, N.Y.: Crossing Press, 1984), 153.

10. See Adrienne Rich, "Compulsory Heterosexuality and the Lesbian Existence," in *Blood, Bread and Poetry: Selected Prose 1979–1985* (New York: Norton, 1986).

11. Brown, 15.

PART V

THE GLOBAL CONTEXT

INTRODUCTION

Black liberation theology has been steadily deepening its global perspective since the late 1960s. In *Black Theology: A Documentary History, 1966–79*, Part V: Black Theology and Third World Theologies focused mostly on the dialogue between Black theology and African theology. During the 1980s, Black theologians increased their involvement in the Ecumenical Association of Third World Theologians (EATWOT) especially their dialogue with Asian and Latin American liberation theologians.

My three essays, that are reprinted in this section, were written as reflections on my participation in the major meetings of EATWOT. "A Black American Perspective on the Asian Search for a Full Humanity" (Document 28) was written following the first Asian theological conference of EATWOT, held in Wennappuwa, Sri Lanka, January 1979. It was included in the published papers of the conference, entitled *Asia's Struggle for Full Humanity: Toward a Relevant Theology* (Orbis Books, 1980).

Both the live-in experience that preceded the conference and the dialogue with Asian theologians had a profound effect on my theological perspective. Born and reared in the context of the Black church where Jesus Christ was the beginning and the end of faith, the Asian experience transformed my christological perspective and thereby opened my religious sensibilities to other experiences of ultimate reality. No longer do I feel comfortable speaking of Jesus Christ as *the* absolute and final truth of God's revelation. Jesus Christ is God's presence in human experiences of liberation but not the only way God is present with human beings. God can choose to be present in the experiences of others in ways we do not understand. This discovery first made its decisive impact on me while living in a Buddhist home with a family of little means. They shared what they had with me and my friend, Sergio Torres. I felt the power of God's presence with no need to refer to Jesus as the only way to talk about the experience of transcendence.

Theology is a second word; the first word is our experience of God's liberating presence with the oppressed. Inherent in an act of theological reflection, therefore, is humility, a recognition that what one says in theological discourse is so much less than what people experience when they encounter God.

"From Geneva to São Paulo" (Document 29) was written as an interpretation of Black Theology's dialogue with Latin American liberation theology and as a reflection on the EATWOT conference on Latin American liberation theology, February 1980, São Paulo, Brazil. My essay first appeared in the published papers entitled, *The Challenge of Basic Christian Communities* (Orbis Books, 1981).

Unlike Black theology's relationship with Asian theology, its dialogue with Latin American liberation theology has been intense and often conflictive. My essay was written at the beginning of our mutual openness to learn from each other. Ten years have passed since it was published, and both Black and Latin American theologians have incorporated many aspects of the other's concern into their perspectives. As the reader might expect, the debate between us focused primarily on the role of class and race analyses in the doing of liberation theology. Many Blacks and Latins now acknowledge that the choice is not either/or, but both race and class analyses in relation to one another and in relation to other structures of domination as well, especially sexism.

"Black Theology and Third World Theologies" (Document 30) was written as a reflection on the fifth EATWOT International Conference, held in New Delhi, India, August 1981. It was included in the published papers of the meeting entitled, *Irruption of the Third World: Challenge to Theology* (Orbis Books, 1983).

No EATWOT members envisioned that our dialogue with each other would be as difficult as our nearly twenty years have been. My essay focused on the similarities and differences between Black theology and Third World theologies. Because we shared similarities did not mean that our dialogue was easy. We discovered soon that our differences often influenced our dialogue more. In my dialogues with Third World liberation theologians and in my writings about our debates, I have tried to speak and write in such a way as not to minimize our differences, and, at the same time, refuse to allow them to have the last word about our relationship to one another. The last word should be our commitment to each other and the struggles out of which our theologies are made. We should always remember that no theology has the final truth. Paul was right: "Now we see in a mirror, dimly" (1 Cor. 13:12 NRSV) and never perfectly. Therefore, whatever we say, no matter how deeply we feel about its importance, is limited by the particularity of our experience. Oppressors do not like to acknowledge that, or if they do, they act as if they have not internalized it. Oppressed people, especially theologians, frequently display intolerant behavior toward each other similar to the dominant theologians who taught them when their cherished views are called into question.

Kelly Brown-Douglass gives her "Reflections on the Second General Assembly of EATWOT" (Document 31) held in Oaxtepec, Mexico, December 1986. It was her first EATWOT conference, and EATWOT's most difficult dialogue. It was painful and a few persons left saying that they would not return again. Others became more committed to intercontinental dialogue. Through unselfish commitment and the influx of new members for all regions, EATWOT became a much stronger ecumenical association. Brown-Douglass' reflections describe the challenges of dialogue and how one is transformed by it. Her essay first appeared in the published papers of the conference, *Third World Theologies: Commonalities and Divergences* (Orbis Books, 1990).

J. Deotis Roberts has been in dialogue with Third World theologians for many years. He has lectured on Black theology in Asia, Africa, and Latin America and has responded to the liberation theologies on each continent. His essay, "Common Themes: Black Theology and Minjung Theology" (Document 32) is a useful comparison, showing that they perhaps have more in common than Black and Latin American theologies. It was first published in his book appropriately entitled, *Black Theology in Dialogue* (Westminster Press, 1987).

Cornel West, professor of religion and director of Afro-American studies at Princeton University, has made an important contribution to the dialogue between Black liberation theology and Latin American liberation theology. An honorary chair of the Democratic Socialists of America and a committed member of the Black Church, West has creatively shown the limitations of Black theology when it fails to incorporate class analysis in its perspective. He has made a similar point in relation to Latin American liberation theology in regard to race analysis. West has been a participant in the EATWOT meetings. He offered a powerful critique of Latin American liberation theology at the São Paulo meeting. While he was a professor at Union Theological Seminary (New York City), we regularly taught a course on "Black Theology and Marxist Thought." In our dialogue, I learned a lot about the importance of Marxian class analysis and have endeavored to incorporate insights from it into my theological perspective.

West's essay, "Black Theology of Liberation as Critique of Capitalist Civilization" (Document 33) was first presented to a Latin American audience at the Seminario Bíblico Latinamericano in San José, Costa Rica, August 1980. He identifies five stages in the "evolution of the prophetic stream in the Black Christian tradition." After pointing out the shortcomings of the earlier conceptions of Black liberation theology, he challenges Black theologians "to put forward an understanding of the Christian gospel in the light of present circumstances which takes into account the complex ways in which racism . . . and sexism . . . are integral to the class exploitative capitalist system of production as well as its repressive imperialist tentacles abroad." West's essay was later published in the *Journal of the Interdenominational Theological Center* 10 (Fall 1982-Spring 1983).

J.H.C.

28

A BLACK AMERICAN PERSPECTIVE ON THE ASIAN SEARCH FOR A FULL HUMANITY

James H. Cone

What has Asian theology to do with black theology? This is the question that defines the focus of this essay. To answer this question is not easy because there has been a limited dialogue between Asian and black theologians. In contrast to many conferences and workshops dealing with the relationship of black theology to African, Latin, and Caribbean theologies, no such conferences or workshops have been organized for the purpose of examining the relations of black and Asian theologies. When black theologians and church people have encountered persons born in Asia and who presently live and work on that continent, usually it has been in the context of the World Council of Churches with an ecumenical agenda not related to the unique concerns of Asians and black Americans. Because of our differences in cultural origin and the large geographical distance that separates us, the assumption has been that Asians and blacks do not have much in common with each other.

For comparison, it is important to note that a similar assumption has not been made in regard to black theology's relation to African, Caribbean, and Latin theologies. That black theologians have something to talk about with African theologians is obvious by our common racial origin. During the 1960s, it was not unusual to hear black nationalists say that "we are an African people," and the publication and television production of Alex Haley's *Roots* reinforced the significance of Africa for the masses of black people. But even prior to the rise of popular black nationalist groups in the 1960s and before Alex Haley's *Roots,* the significance of Africa for the identity of black Americans had been emphasized in the religious and secular contexts of black life in the United

Presented at the Asian Theological Conference, January 7-20, 1979, Wennappuwa, Sri Lanka, this paper was included in the published papers of the conference titled *Asia's Struggle for Full Humanity: Toward a Relevant Theology*, ed. Virginia Fabella (Maryknoll, N.Y.: Orbis Books, 1980).

States. Marcus Garvey's "back to Africa" movement and W. E. B. Du Bois' pan-Africanism are prominent examples of the importance of Africa in the political and intellectual life of black people.[1] Because many blacks believe that who we are and what we shall become cannot be separated from our African heritage, it was only natural for black theologians to seek to deepen their theological vision by turning to Africans for mutual dialogue on the common faith and struggles of our peoples.[2]

As we pursued our historical roots in Africa and began to investigate the African slave trade, there was no way we could ignore the significance of Latin America and the Caribbean for the African world. There are more black people of African descent on the continent of South America than in North America. This fact alone suggests that black, Caribbean, and Latin theologians have something of mutual interest to talk about. When the theme of *liberation* and its relation to race and class is introduced into our discussions the dialogue between black, Latin, and Caribbean theologians is deepened.[3]

Unfortunately when black theology is related to Asian theology, their common interest is not easily recognized. What has an essentially black, racial struggle for justice in North America to do with an Asian struggle for full humanity in the context of immense poverty and the perpetual dehumanizing effects of European colonialism? Because black and Asian peoples' knowledge of and personal contact with each other is limited, their respective cultures and life-experiences seem vastly different and far removed from each other. But is that assumption correct? I do not think so. In fact, I contend that Asians and black Americans have far more in common than what is immediately obvious, and that this commonality arises from a similar experience of ultimate reality in the historical context of our struggle against slavery and oppression. In this essay, I want to explicate my assumption about the common interests of Asian and black theologies by examining three experiences I have had on the continent of Asia.[4]

Japan and Korea: May 1975

The first occasion in which I had to deal with the relation of black and Asian theologies occurred in May 1975 when I was invited by the Korean Christian Church in Japan to lead workshops for church leaders on the theme: "The Church Struggling for the Liberation of the People." After my nearly three-week stay in Japan, I also visited South Korea at the invitation of struggling Christians in that country. Before these experiences in Japan and Korea, my knowledge of and personal contact with Asian people had been limited to the contexts of the World Council of Churches, the diaspora Asian communities in the United States, and the speeches and writings of white scholars and missionaries. None of these contexts adequately prepared me for the creative challenge that Asia would provide for the theological perspective through the Korean Christian Community in Japan and the Korean struggle for democracy and justice in South Korea.

In Japan, it was not difficult to perceive the similarities between the Korean experience in that country and the black experience in the United States. As blacks were stolen from Africa by Europeans and enslaved in the Americas, Koreans were taken against their will from their homeland and brought to Japan in order to serve Japanese people. Like blacks who expressed their struggle for justice by creating songs of liberation derived from the biblical account of the Exodus, Korean Christians in Japan expressed their determination to be free in a similar fashion. As blacks experience discrimination in employment and in every other aspect of American society, Koreans have an analogous experience in Japan.[5]

White racism against blacks and Japanese racism against Koreans are so similar that I was tempted to suggest that the latter was derived partly from the former. In fact, after only a short stay in Japan, I could easily determine the composition of my audience, even though there are no obvious physical differences between Korean and Japanese peoples. I could tell who was in my audience by the kinds of questions asked, the reactions to liberation struggle of poor people, and the respect for the openness to learn from another people's culture. Japanese people had an attitude of superiority and their questions about the attitude towards oppressed people were very similar to whites in the United States. Almost without exception, in churches as well as seminaries and universities, Japanese Christians were hostile towards the liberation focus of the Christian faith and were more interested in analyzing the dominant theologies of Europe and North America. I found it very strange that the theological systems of Barth, Brunner, Tillich, and Niebuhr still occupied important places in Japanese theology with almost no reference to liberation theologies in Asia, Africa, and South and North America.

In contrast to Japanese people, Korean Christians reminded me of black people in their openness to the liberation theme in the gospel. The four workshops, several worship services, and many private conversations provided excellent occasions on which to talk about the black experience in North America as well as to hear about the Korean experience in Japan from the people who have lived it. Initially, however, some Koreans were suspicious of my emphasis on liberation in the gospel, because the translation of that term into their language had many negative implications for their situation. But when they realized that my interpretation of liberation was derived from my people's struggle against slavery and injustice, they immediately identified with black people's fight for justice in a white racist society and expressed that identification by readily accepting me as one of their own. To be at home in such a totally different culture from my own was a very strange, but rewarding experience. The language and other cultural barriers were transcended through a mutual openness to each other's struggles, and through a common recognition that the universalism in the gospel is found in God's will to liberate all oppressed people from the shackles of human bondage.

I will never forget my experience with Korean people in the four workshops as we discussed the biblical meaning of salvation. Having such a "conservation" orientation towards the Bible (as is also true of blacks in the United States), Koreans first wanted to explore where I stood regarding the biblical view of salvation. I centered my interpretation of salvation in the Bible as it is defined by the Exodus, articulated by the prophets, and consummated in the life, death, and resurrection of Jesus. I contended that to be saved is to be liberated. And as evidence, I pointed to the liberation of Israelites from Egypt, the prophets' stand on justice, and Jesus' claim that he came "to preach good news to the poor," "to proclaim release to the captive" and "to set at liberty those who are oppressed" (Luke 4:18 RSV). I emphasized that my perspective on the scripture was not derived primarily from white scholars and missionaries, but rather from the history and culture of black people who have been struggling for justice and freedom for nearly four hundred years in North America. Black people in North America are an historical representation of the hermeneutical privilege that God gives to the poor in order that they may recognize that their struggle for freedom is also God's struggle.

In order for Koreans to hear the black folk expression of this view of salvation, I recited such spirituals as "Go Down Moses," "Oh, Freedom," and "Oh, Mary, Don't You Weep." When Koreans heard the lyrics of these songs, they realized that my view of salvation was not an abstract philosophical concept but rather a reality that has been derived from the lived-experiences of black people. We both also realized that the Korean experience in Japan is similar to the black experience in the United States, and we spent much time talking about our common interests. While we recognized our obvious differences, these did not separate us, but instead brought us closer together in our struggle against the racism of both Japanese and white peoples.[6]

When I left Japan for Seoul, Korea, I realized for the first time that blacks and Asians do have some things in common. But the Korean experience in Japan had not prepared me for my subsequent experience in Seoul. It is one thing to read and hear about a political dictatorship, but it is quite another thing to have a concrete, existential experience of one. When I arrived, the famous "Presidential Emergency Measure No. 9" had just been issued (May 13, 1975), which allowed the police to arrest and imprison any person who criticized the Park regime. The universities had been closed for several months but were allowed to re-open just before my arrival. It was thought best that the university context would not be the appropriate place for my lectures, since the government had threatened to close them again if I were allowed to speak. Many persons who had been associated with my visit had been arrested, and others anticipated arrest and imprisonment at any moment.

During the time between my arrival at the airport and my first lecture at the YMCA (about one hour), I was told about the political repression and the difficult struggle for democracy and justice now taking place in Korea. Because I did not understand clearly the complexities of the Korean political situation, I asked several persons about what should be the theme of my lecture, and what especially should I avoid. I did not want my particular perspective on the gospel to cause anyone any unnecessary pain and suffering. But their reply was:

"Speak the truth of the gospel, and do not worry about us." But what is the truth of the gospel in this Asian situation of extreme political repression? How could I speak about the gospel's empowerment of people in the struggle for justice, and also remain sensitive to the immediate political dangers of my Korean friends? I agonized over these and related questions in the presence of nearly fifty Korean CIA agents and about three hundred people who had taken the political risk to hear my lecture.

I decided to lecture on the theme of "God the Liberator as Found in the Black Slave Songs in North America." This theme enabled me to express my solidarity with the Korean struggle for justice and democracy, and to partly camouflage my utter distaste for the current Park regime. The impact of my lecture on the Korean situation far exceeded my expectations. Because of the conspicuous presence of so many Korean CIA agents, it was thought best not to take any unnecessary political risks by entertaining questions. The audience simply joined hands and sang: "We Shall Overcome." That was indeed a very moving and spiritual experience. To know that the black struggle for justice in the United States was a source of empowerment for Korean Christians engaged in a similar struggle enhanced the possibility for a creative dialogue between Koreans and blacks.

I have traveled extensively in many parts of the world, but no experience anywhere is comparable to this frightening experience in South Korea. The only analogous experience was work in the southern parts of the United States during the civil rights movement of the 1950s and 1960s, and especially in Mississippi and Alabama. The conspicuous presence of Korean CIA agents reminded me of southern policemen and other white supporters of the "white way of life." In both contexts, to create the fear of arrest, torture, and death in those who would challenge the "law" defined the character of the government. I was afraid in both situations, but much more in Korea than in Alabama or Mississippi. The reason was obvious. In the South, the place of my birth and early training, I had had enough experience with white folks there to be able to predict fairly accurately what responses they would give to anything I said or did. But not so in Korea. All I knew was the volatile situation in which I found myself, and that perhaps the lives of my friends depended upon how well I could speak the truth of the gospel without being stupid politically.

Initially I thought about the safety of my life, but soon realized that the most that was likely to happen to me personally would be my deportation from the country. But Korean Christians engaged in the struggle for democracy did not have the luxury of deportation as an option. And that fact alone made a radical distinction between them and me. Their only option was passivity or struggle, and the latter could easily lead to arrest and imprisonment. In this Korean context, I realized once more how relative our verbal pronouncements about justice are. The radical nature of any political challenge to injustice, whether in words or deeds, is dependent on the situation in which it is made.

Something happened to my theological perspective in Korea that is difficult to explain. What I encountered in that country was not so much "new" theological concepts that could be added to the current theological discussion. Rather than ideas, I met people whose commitment to the gospel in their struggle for justice and democracy was so clear (despite the risks) that I was simply awed by the humility and lack of self-righteousness which characterized their presence and speech. When I compare the modest attitude of Korean university students and professors with the self-righteous attitude of their North American counterparts, I feel compelled to say that the latter is possible because of a sense of privilege that characterizes their class position in the United States.

In this small community of Korean Christians, I knew that I had much to learn which would confirm my theological conviction about liberation and also compel me to relate liberation to a larger cultural and political context than my present focus on black Americans. For the Koreans who were engaged in the struggle for justice and democracy reminded me of my own people who have made similar commitments in order to fight against white racism. It was not a matter of being absolutely right and the government being absolutely wrong. It was a simple matter of taking a stand for human rights and the dignity which governmental policies did not seem to take seriously. They knew that their stand meant that it would possibly cause their arrest, torture, and imprisonment. In the context of living, talking, and being with these Korean Christians, Gustavo Gutiérrez's reference to theology as the "second step"[7] was reinforced in my theological consciousness. The first step is the political commitment on behalf of the poor and weak in society. The Korean Christians I met in May 1975 had taken the first step and they have paid a heavy price.

Sri Lanka: January 1979

The Korean experience (in both Japan and South Korea) did much to prepare me for the Asian Theological Conference held at Wennappuwa, Sri Lanka, January 7–20, 1979.[8] But there was much that I learned in that two-week conference that went beyond the Korean experience. For example, my experience among Koreans had been primarily limited to Christians, and thus the christological center of my theology had not been seriously challenged. Such was not the case in Sri Lanka. In the three-day live-in experience, I stayed with a very poor Buddhist family in Ratmalana. During the day, I met many Buddhist labor leaders engaged in the struggle for justice on behalf of industrial workers. This three-day live-in encounter radically challenged the christological perspective of my theological and political commitment. The challenge did not arise from the verbal questioning of Buddhists about the absoluteness of Jesus Christ. No Buddhist even indirectly questioned my commitment to Jesus, even though they knew that all of the members of our group were Christians. They simply wanted to know where we stood on justice and liberation in terms of the concreteness of our political commitments.

The raising of the christological issue in my theological consciousness was forced upon me by the Asian religio-cultural and socio-political context. I simply said to myself that if I had to do theology in an Asian context, the political and the cultural situation would require a reinterpretation of Jesus Christ so as to be effective in communicating precisely what the biblical Jesus represents. When I came to that conclusion, my theological perspective was deepened by its new-found openness to experiencing the heart and soul of Asia as lived by the people and expressed in their culture.

In questioning the Western formulation of the christological emphasis in theology, I had to ask, what is the source from which Christian theology arises? In classical Western theology, the Bible or revelation has often been given as the answer to that question. But my participation in a three-day live-in at Ratmalana and my subsequent involvement in the Conference itself at Wennappuwa prevented me from accepting a pre-fabricated Western answer to an Asian question. Therefore during my first days in the Conference, I did not say much, because I was trying hard to listen to Asians as they struggled to make sense out of the complexity of their situation.

By merely hearing Asians speak about and struggle with the plurality of issues in their various situations (they came from eleven countries), I realized once again that theology arises out of life and not from theological textbooks. Therefore, the critical question is: Whose life does your theology represent? Theology is not applied to the situation as if it exists apart from it. Rather theology arises out of concrete life-situations and derives its reasons for being from people who are seeking to make sense out of their lives. If Asian theology (or any theology for that matter) is to be accountable to poor people's struggle for justice, then it must arise from their situation of struggle, and not from some abstract European concept of revelation. Most persons participating in the Asian Theological Conference seemed to recognize this fact, even though they often disagreed on the practical theological consequences of this assumption.

Although Asian theologians and church officials criticized the Western church and its theology, some young workers felt that the Asian church establishment was too closely tied to the Western interpretation of Christianity. If the European missionaries who introduced Christianity to Asia also brought with them the culture of the West, and if Christianity was and still is in the hands of the Asian ruling classes, how is it possible to create an Asian theology that is accountable to the liberation of the poor? If the phrase "Asian theology" means more than "theology in Asia" and thus reflects an "Asian sense," how can this Asian sense be created in theology if theology in Asia is in the hands of rulers who are Western in sense? These are some of the questions that were hotly debated in small groups and plenary sessions.

At this point, it may be useful to point out one significant difference between black theology and Asian theology. The rise of black theology is inseparable from an independent black church movement that is nearly two hundred years old.[9] In fact, ninety percent of all black Christians belong to independent black churches. Even most blacks in white denominations have an independent black consciousness which means that they are much closer to other blacks in independent churches than they are to whites in the same denominations. In this sense, black theology is not and has never been in the hands of the white church establishment. Rather it represents an independent black church constituency whose religious consciousness is defined by black people's struggle for freedom. That is why black theology could say that the white church and its theology represents the anti-Christ. We black theologians knew that our accountability was and is located in the oppressed black community, even though we have not always reflected that accountability as clearly as we should have.

When one turns to the church establishment in Asia, whether Catholic or Protestant, the radical independence found in black Christianity is absent. That was why so many young workers at the Conference questioned even the possibility of an Asian theology. How can there be a true Asian theology when the church structures are accountable to Western theology? As I listened to this discussion between church officials and young workers, I began to perceive the creative possibilities in the black church and its theology. But these possibilities have not been realized, and it does not appear that their realization is near at hand. Because the black church is independent, it is only natural that one would expect some radical expressions of this independence in action and words. During the eighteenth, nineteenth, and most of the twentieth centuries, it was not difficult to find creative expressions of the black church's commitment to the righteousness of God as revealed in the human struggle for justice. Martin Luther King, Jr., was an international symbol of that commitment.

But when I examine more critically contemporary black church denominations, I am very disappointed with their inordinate concern with themselves and their own institutional politics. With more resources at their disposal than ever, black denominations do less in creating justice and liberation for their people than they did in the nineteenth century. Why is it that no black church denomination has created a distinct confession of faith, defined by the liberation struggle of its people? Why is it that there is no ecumenical structure that unites black denominations so that they can be more effective as creative agents of liberation?[10]

While Asian churches are not independent, there are ecumenical structures that transcend the Western identity of their ecclesiastical institution. An important example is the Christian Conference of Asia (CCA). This ecumenical body has resisted the importation of European theologies and church structures into Asia. It has convened conferences in order to examine the relation of the "Confessional Families and the Churches in Asia." The CCA has continued the discussion by asking what it means to confess the faith in Asia today.[11] Therefore, whatever may be said about the dependence of Asian theology and church structure on their European counterparts, the CCA consultations and the Asian Theological Conference clearly reveal an ecumenicity that is genuinely creative and could serve as a useful example for black Christians.

The Asian Conference delegates' stress on the particularity of their theological enterprise raised for me the question of the universality of the Christian gospel, a point that is applicable to any theological expression. I found myself asking, in what way does the Asian struggle for a full humanity embrace other human strivings for liberation? I realized that there is a serious danger inherent in the question, for it may serve as a distraction from the urgency of the present situation as found in Asia. Preman Niles has expressed a strong warning against this danger:

> Asian theology is suffering from a crisis of identity, for it is often domi-
> nated by theological thinking in the West and, more recently, by Latin
> American and Black American liberation theologies. Indeed it is difficult
> to perceive what is distinctive about Asian theology. If theology in Asia
> is to have its own identity, it must cease to be merely an extension of
> Western theologies, and instead speak meaningfully to all within the con-
> text of Asian suffering and hope. The true identity of Asian theology will
> emerge only when we begin to perceive and articulate the relevant word
> in our situation.[12]

It is within this context that we ought to understand the small number of non-Asians invited to the Sri Lanka Conference and their status as fraternal delegates.[13] Asians were rightly concerned about the distinctiveness of the theology. That is also why there is a sharp resistance among Asians to Latin American liberation theologians who are often perceived by them (and also by some Africans and black Americans) as being arrogant and dominant in their relations to other Third World peoples. While most participants were not resistant to Marxism and class analysis, they did resist what some perceived as the dogmatic approach of the Latin Americans. Unlike most Latin theologians, Asians could not avoid the religio-cultural situation of Asia as they spoke about socialism and class analysis. In fact one of the most heated debates was generated in the conference regarding the relation between the religio-cultural and the socio-political situations in Asia. This issue was sharply raised by Aloysious Pieris' paper, "Towards an Asian Theology of Liberation: Some Religio-Cultural Guidelines." He emphasized that, unlike Latin American liberation theology, an Asian theology of liberation cannot avoid the "multifaceted religiosity" of the Asian context. But the delegates from the Philippines gave an equally sharp reply in their emphasis on "socio-political liberation of the poor, the deprived, and the oppressed." Neither Pieris nor the Filipinos denied each other's emphasis, but each was concerned that their own emphasis did not receive the proper recognition.

I was fascinated by this debate between culture and politics among Asians, a discussion that was especially useful to me in my struggle with a similar issue in the black North American context.[14] But while every theology must wrestle with the particularity of its cultural and political context, we must be careful not to become imprisoned in our starting points. We must be careful that we do not allow our own historical reality to blind us to the universal dimension of humanity that transcends our particular locality. This radical universality is not to be confused with European intellectual abstractions. I believe that it is a universalism that embraces and illuminates the struggles of the oppressed throughout the world. Therefore, black theologians must ask: What is it in our particular analysis of the Christian faith that embraces the Asian search for a full humanity? Asian theologians should ask: What is it in the Asian search for a full humanity that expresses solidarity with the black struggle for justice in the United States? And both theologies must extend this question to other oppressed peoples.

By the time we reached the point of writing the "Final Statement," no one questioned that liberation will occupy a central focus in Asian theology. But it would not be a mere repetition of its meaning as found in black theology or Latin American liberation theology. The Asian emphasis on liberation would affirm some continuity with other Third World theologies, but it would also express its own uniqueness. Thus the "Final Statement" begins its first major section with the "Asian Context" and then moves to the "Issues." Both the context and the issues set the stage for the distinctive approach to Asian theology in the next section under the heading of "Towards a Relevant Theology." Liberation is made the chief focus of Asian theology, because the poor, in the struggle for freedom, are its subject. It is within the context of struggle that poor people's culture is emphasized as a source of empowerment, and social analysis is introduced as indispensable for accomplishing the goals of freedom.

The biblical perspective was introduced in the "Final Statement's" section on Asian theology not as an afterthought nor as an absolute, objective authority. The delegates at this conference were at least partly aware of the Western influence in what is often called the "biblical perspective." Therefore while there was not much discussion about the relation of Asian and biblical histories, there was an underlying assumption that the latter could not exercise an absolute authority over the former. Many delegates seemed to be aware of earlier discussions of this matter in the writings of Choan-Seng Song and Preman Niles.[15] Therefore they affirmed the authority of the Bible in the context of Asia's struggle and not separate from it.

I left the Asian Theological Conference with the realization that Asian theology represents one of the most distinctive and creative theologies on the world scene.

Japan and Korea: May 1979

During my visit to Japan in May 1975, I also had the privilege of speaking at the organizing meeting of the Citizen's Movement in Ichinomiya. This was not a Christian movement, but rather a small group of Japanese citizens concerned about justice and liberation for all human persons. I remember clearly the public testimonies of children and adults, the physically handicapped, and Koreans — all of whom were united in the struggle for freedom. In that meeting, I experienced a unity among people that transcended physical, mental, racial, and cultural differences, thereby giving sociological concreteness to the oneness of humanity. That small community of people symbolized for me the universal humanity that philosophers and other intellectuals often talk about, but they seldom take the political action necessary for its realization in society.

In May 1979, four years later, I was invited to return to Japan by this same citizen's group, which is now known as the National Association for the Protection of Children's Rights. At their May 5 national meeting in Tokyo, their concern was limited to the "Re-evaluation of Children's Day in the International Year of the Child," and they chose as their central theme: "Children Cry." May 5 is "Children's Day" in Japan, a national holiday that has always emphasized the ritual and festival dimensions of this event, thereby completely ignoring the suffering of the children of the poor. In order to express another perspective, the National Association for the Protection of Children's Rights invited people from all over Japan so that they could collectively register their solidarity with the victims, that is, the children of people who are ignored by the governmental officials in Japanese society. I was invited to make a presentation on the suffering of black children in the United States so as to give an international focus to their concern.

I was impressed by this gathering of nearly four hundred people, whose main commonality was not a particular confession of faith but rather a socio-political concern for the right of children to survive in a world free of suffering and inhumanity arising from the insensitivity of adults. Because only two Christians were present, the limitation of a rigid christological approach was clearly revealed. As to be expected, I also found out that not all Japanese people are insensitive to human suffering. The meeting lasted for nearly five hours, and I heard testimonies from the mothers and fathers of dead children, from parents whose children had been seriously injured, and from Japanese children themselves. I was struck by their mutual solidarity and determination to make structural changes that would recognize the right of the children to survive with dignity.

In this meeting was disclosed a dimension of Japanese humanity that I hardly saw at all in 1975. Most of the Japanese people I met in 1975 were university and seminary students and faculty, church people, and their pastors, very few of whom seemed particularly concerned about poor people's struggle for justice. But in the 1979 visit, I saw a different side of a Japanese society which represents an unusual concern for the liberation of oppressed people. This fact alone increased my openness to the Asian reality.

From Japan I went for the second time to South Korea, and I found very little change, except an increased determination by Korean Christians to resist the Park regime. In four years almost all of my friends were either in prison or had served their time there expecting to return at any moment. We had more time and an appropriate context to talk theology, because one of my books *(Black Theology and Black Power)* had already been published in Korean.[16] I was especially surprised and also pleased that Korean Christians struggling for justice have expressed so much interest in black theology.

Korean theologians spoke a great deal about the "theology of people" (*minjung*),[17] which they claim embraces both the socio-political struggles of Koreans and also the cultural foundation of that struggle. Black theology's emphasis on culture in the context of political struggle and our exploration of our culture through an examination of the songs, prayers, and sermons of our people appealed to many Korean theologians. I also found their analysis of a "theology of people" to be creative, even though there is much work still to be done. I was invited to return in order to share in their struggle to give some shape to their theological vision. I readily accepted this challenge, because I know that black theology has much to learn from Asians generally and Koreans in particular. I only hope that we blacks will have as much to give to them as they to us.

NOTES

1. For an excellent documentary history of the development of black nationalism, see *Black Nationalism in America,* ed. John H. Bracey, Jr., August Meier, and Ellion Rudwick (New York: Bobbs-Merrill, 1970). See also Gayraud S. Wilmore, *Black Religion and Black Radicalism* (New York: Doubleday, 1972).

2. For an account of the dialogue between African and black theologians, see my analysis of it in Gayraud S. Wilmore and James H. Cone, eds., *Black Theology: A Documentary History, 1966-1979* (Maryknoll, N.Y.: Orbis Books, 1979), 492-501.

3. For an account of the dialogue between Latin and black theologians, see ibid., 510-530.

4. For my early reflections on the relation of Asian and black theologies, see my analysis of it in ibid., and my "Asian Theology Today: Searching for Definitions," *Christian Century,* May 23, 1979.

5. My invitation by the Korean Christian Church in Japan was partly determined by their perceptions that blacks and Koreans have a similar experience. See the report of the "Consultation on Minority Issues in Japan and Mission Strategy," May 6-10, 1974, Kyoto, Japan, *IDOC,* No. 65, September 1974. See also Ha Lee, "Race and Minority Issues in Theological Perspective," in *Towards a Theology of People: I,* published by the Urban Rural Mission and the Christian Conference of Asia, 1977.

6. The fact that two of my books had already been translated into Japanese greatly aided my dialogue with both Korean and Japanese peoples. *Black Theology and Black Power* (New York: Seabury Press, 1969) was published in Japanese in 1971 by Shinkyo Shuppansha Publishing Co., Tokyo, Japan. *A Black Theology of Liberation* (Philadelphia: Lippincott, 1970) was published in 1973 by the same company. My *God of the Oppressed* (New York: Seabury Press, 1975) was published in Japanese by the same company in 1976, and *The Spirituals and the Blues* (New York: Seabury Press, 1975) was published in Japanese in 1983.

7. See his *A Theology of Liberation* (Maryknoll, N.Y.: Orbis Books, 1973), 11.

8. For an earlier account of this conference, see my essay "Asia's Struggle for a Full Humanity: Toward a Relevant Theology," in Gayraud S. Wilmore and James Cone, eds., *Black Theology: A Documentary History, 1966-1979;* also my "Asian Theology Today: Searching for Definitions," *Christian Century,* May 23, 1979.

9. The best historical account of the development of the black church is Gayraud S. Wilmore, *Black Religion and Black Radicalism* (Garden City, N.Y.: Anchor Books/ Doubleday, 1973). More recently, even white historians have begun to give prominent recognition to involvement of the black church and its preachers in the abolition of slavery. For an account of black slave religion and its independence from white religion, see especially Albert Raboteau, *Slave Religion* (New York: Oxford University Press, 1979); Olli Alho, *The Religion of the Slaves* (Helsinki: Soumalanen Tiedeakatemia, 1976), and Eugene D. Grenovese, *Roll, Jordan, Roll: The World the Slaves Made* (New York: Pantheon Books, 1972).

10. The National Conference of Black Churchmen represented such a structure during the 1960s and early 1970s. However it is not nearly as effective as it once was. For an account of NCBC, see Wilmore and Cone, eds., *Black Theology: A Documentary History, 1966-1979.* See also Gayraud S. Wilmore, *Black Religion and Black Radicalism* and Leon W. Watts, "The National Committee of Black Churchmen," *Christianity and Crisis* 30 (Nov. 2 and 16, 1970).

11. See especially *Confessional Families and the Churches in Asia*, a report from a consultation convened by the East Asia Christian Conference (now called the Christian Conference of Asia) and held at Kandy, Ceylon, December 6-8, 1965; and *Confessing the Faith in Asia Today*, a statement issued by the consultation convened by the East Asia Christian Conference and held in Hong Kong, Oct. 26-Nov. 3, 1966. The role which CCA has played in uniting Protestant churches in Asia is enormous. And it has served as a context for the development of Asian theology. See especially *Christian Action in the Asian Struggle* (Singapore: CCA, 1973); Yap Kim Hao, ed., "Asian Theological Reflections on Suffering and Hope," *Asia Focus*, no. 661, 1977; and *Towards a Theology of People: I.*

12. See his "Towards a Framework of Doing Theology in Asia," *Asia Focus*, no. 661, 1977.

13. There were only seven non-Asians invited to attend, two each from Africa, Latin America, and the United States and one from the Caribbean. There were some questions raised about both the number and the fraternal status of the non-Asian delegates, since this conference was being sponsored by the Ecumenical Association of Third World Theologians. When the fraternal delegates requested a meeting with the Organizing Committee, it was readily granted. And the members of this committee explained that their effort to make sure that the development of Asian theology would remain in the hands of Asians alone accounted for both the small number of non-Asian delegates and also their fraternal status. Our openness to respect their concern increased our participation in the Conference. To my surprise, I was even selected to serve on the writing committee for the "Final Statement."

14. For my discussion of the politics-culture debate among black theologians, see my essay, "An Interpretation of the Debate among Black Theologians," in Wilmore and Cone, eds., *Black Theology: A Documentary History, 1966-1979.*

15. See Choan-Seng Song, "From Israel to Asia: A Theological Leap," in Gerald H. Anderson and Thomas F. Stransky, eds., *Mission Trends No. 3: Third World Theologians* (New York: Paulist Press, 1976), 211-222. An enlargement of this discussion is found in his *Christian Mission in Reconstruction: An Asian Attempt* (Maryknoll, N.Y.: Orbis Books, 1977). For Preman Niles' critique of Song and Song's reply, see "Reviewing and Responding to the Thought of Choan-Seng Song," in *Occasional Bulletin of Missionary Research* 1, no. 3 (July 1977).

16. It was published by Cheong-Sa Press in Seoul in 1979.

17. See the important essay by Y. Kim, "Christian Koinonia in the Struggle and Aspirations of the People of Korea," in *Asian Theological Reflections on Suffering and Hope*, ed., Yap Kim Hao; and also *Toward a Theology of People: I.*

29

FROM GENEVA TO SÃO PAULO: A DIALOGUE BETWEEN BLACK THEOLOGY AND LATIN AMERICAN LIBERATION THEOLOGY

James H. Cone

What is the relation between class and race oppression? This is the primary question that has defined the focus of the dialogue between North American black theologians and Latin American liberation theologians. The dialogue has been characterized by the attitudes of indifference, hostility, and mutual support. Although these three attitudes have been present among some Latin and black theologians during the entire period of our dialogue, there have been occasions in which one of the three has dominated the consciousness of most of the participants. In this essay, my purpose is to evaluate the development of this dialogue (from Geneva, 1973, to São Paulo, 1980) in the light of my participation in it and also with the hope of deepening our understanding of each other.[1]

Before Geneva, May 1973, black and Latin theologians had had almost no contact with each other, and thus knew very little about each other's historical projects and the theologies arising from them. Since most black theologians do not speak or read Spanish, and since Latin American theologians are under European influence and consequently not trained to look for theological ideas among people of color, the theological works of both blacks and Latin Americans were virtually unknown to each other. Of course, black theologians had heard about Camilo Torres, Archbishop Dom Helder Camara, and the 1968 Latin American Episcopal Conference at Medellín. We had also read Paulo Freire's *Pedagogy of the Oppressed*[2] and Rubem Alves's *Theology of Human*

This paper from the International Ecumenical Congress of Theology, February 20-March 2, 1980, São Paulo, Brazil was published in *The Challenge of Basic Christian Communities*, ed. Sergio Torres and John Eagleson (Maryknoll, N.Y.: Orbis Books, 1981).

Hope.[3] But it was not until Gustavo Gutiérrez's *A Theology of Liberation* was published by Orbis Books in 1973 that black theologians began to take seriously Latin American liberation theology as a distinct perspective, completely different from the theologies of freedom from Europe and North America.

Latin American theologians, of course, had heard about the black civil rights movement and Martin Luther King, Jr. They also knew about Black Power and the black unrest in the urban cities during the 1960s. Some had heard also about a black theology emerging from the black struggle of the sixties. However, it was not until the publication of the Spanish translation of my book *A Black Theology of Liberation*[4] in 1973 that a significant number of Latin American theologians were presented with the opportunity of dialoguing with black theology.

Since the origin of black and Latin American theologies happened independently of each other,[5] it is revealing that both chose the term *liberation* to describe the major emphasis of their theological perspectives. One might expect that their mutual focus on liberation would also make them natural partners for dialogue in the struggles of freedom, but that has not always been the case. The Latin American theologians' emphasis upon the class struggle, with almost no mention of race oppression, made black theologians suspicious of their white, European identity. Black theologians' focus on race oppression, with almost no mention of class, made Latin American theologians suspicious of our capitalist, bourgeois identity. However, because both groups were speaking and writing about theology from the perspective of the poor, neither group said much about the theological enterprise of the other. Each acquired an attitude of indifference, speaking about the other's theological viewpoint only when questioned about it by their mutual enemy, namely, white European and North American theologians and church people.

Geneva 1973

The first major encounter between Latin and black theologians occurred in Geneva, May 1973, at the World Council of Churches.[6] The occasion was a symposium on black theology and Latin American liberation theology. The title of this symposium suggests that its major concern was to initiate a dialogue between these theologies, but that was not the case. The chief concern of this symposium was to introduce Latin and black theologies on the agenda of the WCC. That was why more than sixty Europeans and North American theologians were invited to participate in the discussions, along with a much smaller number of blacks and Latin Americans. However, during the course of our debate with Europeans about the nature and significance of black and Latin American theologies of liberation, each of the black and Latin American participants realized that we should be talking to each other and not to Europeans. Hugo Assmann, one of the Latin American presentors, expressed this concern sharply.

My biggest mistake in the first days of the symposium was that I was speaking to the participants [Europeans] and not to my friends who represent Black Theology. In my group . . . it was a dialogue between Latin American Theology of Liberation and European questions and problems. I would like to enter into dialogue with Black Theology. . . . It would be terrible to remain in "incommunication" with Black Theology.[7]

Assmann expressed a concern that was deeply felt by all Latin American and black participants. But we did not know what to do about it. For both blacks and Latin Americans knew that creative dialogue would not be easy to accomplish. No one at the symposium expressed the problems of dialogue between blacks and Latin Americans any clearer than Assmann. He referred to the western and European character of Latin American theology of liberation and the difficulty it has in being understood by the non-western part of Latin America, that is, "the Brazilian Africans, the people of the Caribbean Islands, the mysterious Mexicans. . . . Traveling in Latin America, I have had the experience of terrible 'incommunication' with these people."[8] Assmann rightly anticipated that a similar problem would emerge in his attempt to talk with black people in the United States.

Until now I have had very little communication with Black people in the United States because when as a Westernized Latin American I read books and articles about the problem of black people, . . . I am tempted to introduce Western Marxism. What must I do in order to have a better dialogue with you?

I don't know how this dialogue with you can be improved, but it is more important than European theology for us Latin Americans. I don't want to destroy the connection with you. But I do want to reach a state of tension with you — a third kind of tension which is found more and more in the Third World.[9]

Other black and Latin American participants in the symposium also expressed the need for dialogue with each other. But unfortunately the limitation of time and the European context prevented a deeper encounter with each other. Despite these difficulties, however, the fact that both Assmann and Freire spoke of North American blacks as Third World people meant that an openness was created from the Latin American side,[10] while several blacks made similar gestures from our side.

Blacks left the Geneva symposium feeling that the dialogue between Latin American theologians and us had already begun to move from indifference (created largely by a lack of knowledge) to mutual support. But the preparation for and the event of the 1975 Detroit conference proved us wrong.

Detroit 1975

The August 1975 Detroit conference of the Theology in the Americas was organized by Father Sergio Torres with the expressed purpose of initiating a dialogue between Latin American theologians of liberation and North American white theologians. An announced statement of the conference read:

> The intention of the planners of the "Theology in the Americas: 1975" conference is to invite a group of Latin American theologians, representing the theology of liberation, to dialogue with North American theologians concerning the context and methodology of this new theological current. It is hoped that such a dialogue would help both groups: the Latin Americans to understand the complex reality of the U.S.; the North American theologians to initiate a process of evaluation of the American reality from the viewpoint of the poor and the oppressed.

Black theologians were surprised and angry when they were confronted with the plan of the conference, and we protested vigorously. Several blacks had heated discussions about this matter with Sergio Torres, but he seemed incapable of understanding our concern. I reminded him of the Geneva symposium and Hugo Assmann's comment that Latin American theologians' dialogue with black theology was more important than their conversations with European theology. If Assmann is right, then why are Latin Americans being invited to the United States for dialogue primarily with white North American theologians and not with blacks and other racial minorities? Indeed the manner in which the conference was being organized seemed to disregard completely black theology's presence in North America as a theology from the perspective of the oppressed.

Despite the vehement protest from many black theologians, the preparations for the 1975 Detroit conference proceeded as planned. I was so upset about the failure of our protest to effect a change in the planning process that I decided initially not to attend. But the opportunity to meet personally for the first time many Latin American theologians of liberation helped to change my mind.

The structure of the conference was designed according to the stated intentions of the brochure. About fifteen Latin American theologians were given the opportunity to state their theological and political perspectives to about two hundred North American white theologians and church people. The small number of oppressed racial minorities of the United States were given a secondary role in the conference, and their minor status was based apparently on the assumption that they did not have much to contribute to the discussions. It was also assumed by most Latin Americans and white North Americans that race oppression can best be understood in the context of class analysis. These assumptions did not go over well with black and other minority participants from the United States. The reason for our resistance to the Latin American emphasis on class analysis was our deep distrust of the white religious left in North America whose past and present behavior in our communities contradicted the public affirmations of their solidarity with the struggles of poor people for freedom. For minority people at the Detroit 1975 conference, class analysis appeared to be used by whites as a camouflage for evading the fact of racial oppression in the world, the United States, and also in the conference itself. In protest to the white takeover of the conference, minorities formed a caucus and issued a joint statement expressing our concerns. To my knowledge, this was the first occasion for such strong expressions of unity among U.S. minorities in a theological and church context.[11]

In addition to our distrust of the white religious left, we were also concerned about the failure of most Latin Americans to be open to the suggestion that they might have something to learn from our struggles for justice in the United States and from the theologies emerging from those struggles. How can Latin Americans claim that Christian theology must come from poor people's struggles when they seemed more interested in dialoguing with dominant white theologies than with theologies arising from the poor in North America? Also, if Latin American theologians really wanted to talk with black theologians about class and race, why do they invite white Americans to be the dominant participants in the dialogue?

In an attempt to move beyond the hostility in the conference sessions, black and Latin American theologians called for a dialogue (in the late evening) between Latin Americans and other racial minorities in the United States. On the Latin American side, Hugo Assmann, Enrique Dussel, José Míguez Bonino, and others were present. On the black side, J. Deotis Roberts, Preston Williams, and I, along with others, were present. There were approximately twenty persons present. The discussion began on a hostile note, with blacks emphasizing the importance of race oppression and Latin Americans stressing class. I was very disappointed that we began by pointing to a weakness in the other's perspective rather than its strength. Apparently a negative atmosphere had already been set by our earlier conversations in the conference itself. Whatever the case, most blacks felt that Latin Americans suggested this late night discussion in order to set us straight regarding the primacy of the class struggle. Latin Americans probably had a similar feeling about blacks regarding the race struggle. It does not really matter who started our heated exchange. We were all responsible for the alienation, and most persons on both sides participated in it. Blacks came close to saying that the Latin Americans were white racists, and the Latin Americans accused blacks of being North American capitalists. I felt deeply frustrated as we hurled accusations at each other. It was as if the Geneva symposium had not taken place. What had happened to our concern to learn from each other, stated so clearly by Assmann in Geneva? This late night discussion did more to alienate blacks and Latin Americans than any other encounter during our eight years of dialogue.[12]

Fortunately, Hispanic Americans from Texas and California played an important role in minimizing our tensions; but the words between blacks and Latin Americans were too harsh for reconciliation to take place during the evening. Black theologians left the meeting thinking that Latin Americans were hopelessly European and racist. And it was natural for Latin Americans to leave thinking that we were too North American to see the global significance of the class struggle.

Mexico City 1977

Between the Detroit conference of August 1975 and the Encounter of Theologians in Mexico City in October 1977, the hostility between blacks and Latin American theologians was greatly reduced by Sergio Torres and Gustavo Gutiérrez. Sergio Torres eventually heard the concerns of the racial minorities at the Detroit conference. Through his influence Theology in the Americas was completely reorganized with an emphasis on the theology projects of black, native, Hispanic, and Asian Americans. Because minority projects did not have many resources for financial support, Torres spent some time generating help from other sources. At the second Detroit conference of Theology in the Americas (August 1980), racial minorities, with the help of some whites, continued their reorganization of TIA for the purpose of developing a unique North American theology of liberation as based on the struggles of racial minorities in this country. This reorganization of TIA by racial minorities could not have happened without the support and encouragement of Sergio Torres.

A similar role has been played by Gustavo Gutiérrez. He arrived late at the 1975 Detroit conference and was not a part of the hostile dialogue between Latin Americans and blacks. But even during his brief stay at the Detroit conference and in the midst of a hostile atmosphere, most blacks recognized that Gutiérrez had a more open attitude toward black theology. We blacks speculated as to whether his openness to black theology was due to his Indian origin.

In 1976, Gutiérrez was invited to Union Theological Seminary as the Henry Luce Visiting Professor. During his stay at Union, we spent much time together talking about the similarities and differences between black and Latin American liberation theologies. We also taught a course together, focusing primarily on black, Asian, Latin American, and African theologies. Black theologians' encounter with Gutiérrez has been entirely different from that with any other Latin American theologian. The chief reason for this is our feeling that he has really learned from us, and we have learned much from him in particular and Latin American liberation theology generally. Without exception, every black person that I know who has met Gutiérrez speaks of his openness to listen to black people and to be taught by our culture and history. I have heard similar comments from Africans, Asians, women, and other racial minorities in the United States.

An indication of the widespread appreciation among blacks for Gutiérrez's openness to learn from their culture and history was shown in the black response to his presentation at the recent Theology in the Americas conference in Detroit (August 1980). His analysis of the role of joy in poor people's struggle and his use of black music as an illustration of his point was so illuminating that even blacks were amazed by the profundity of his interpretation. Their response to Gutiérrez was similar to their response to one of their own. One could hear blacks saying "Amen," "Speak, sir," "Tell it like it is," and other responses of agreement. We could hardly believe what we heard. "How could a non-black be so accurate in his interpretation of our experience?" we asked ourselves. It was at this point that we reminded ourselves that such insight comes from not mere academic reflection but from the gift of the Spirit. God's Spirit transcends racial and national boundaries and joins poor people together in the one struggle of freedom.

Through the influences of Gutiérrez, Torres, and others, the impact of the Latin American liberation theology upon black theology began to happen in a visible manner at the Black Theology Project Conference in Atlanta, Georgia, August 1977.[13] Several black theologians had come to realize that, regardless of our personal feelings about the racism of some Latin Americans, we cannot continue to avoid saying something about the issue of socialism versus capitalism. Neither can we ignore the global context of our struggle for freedom. We must seek ways of expressing our solidarity with the poor throughout the world. Indeed we can no longer speak of racism as if it is the only problem in the United States and the world. For if the black poor in the United States are to achieve freedom, the achievement will take place only in solidarity with other poor people in the United States and the world context.

In recognizing that race analysis must be combined with class and sex oppression, we also realized that an analysis of imperialism reveals the importance of Marxism as one of the primary tools of social analysis. In my address "Black Theology and the Black Church: Where Do We Go From Here?" I raised the issue of Marxism and socialism, inviting black theologians, church people, and others to move beyond our exclusive preoccupation with race oppression to an inclusion of class and sex oppression.[14] The response was much more positive than I expected, and it is reflected in the "Message to the Black Church and Community" drafted and adopted by the conference. This message not only condemned racism but also capitalism, sexism, and imperialism. There was also a concern to find ways to support our brothers and sisters engaged in the struggle for freedom.

> The Black Church must be one with and inseparable from our brothers and sisters around the world who fight for liberation in a variety of ways, including armed struggle. We affirm whatever methods they decide best in their particular situations and make no pious and hypocritical judgments which condemn those efforts to bring an end to their oppression, recognizing we in this country have ourselves been compelled to make similar choices and may be so compelled again.[15]

The Atlanta conference was the first major public declaration by a group of black theologians and church people to express the intention to enter into dialogue with Marxism and the expectation to learn from it. Therefore when I was invited to Mexico City (October 1977) to participate in the Encounter of Theologians, I went prepared to communicate a black openness to dialogue with Latin Americans about class oppression and the global context of our struggle against it.[16] Even though the Encounter of Theologians appeared to be designed primarily to chastise Jürgen Moltmann for his "Open Letter to José Míguez Bonino,"[17] there was time for dialogue about the relation of Latin American and black theologies on the issue of race and class immediately following my presentation on "Christian Theology and Political Praxis."[18] In this dialogue, our differences in emphasis emerged but not with the hostile overtones found at the 1975 Detroit conference. There was unquestionably much more of an openness to each on both sides.

The presence of Sergio Arce Martinez of Cuba at the encounter helped our conversations. No one could question his commitment to Marxism, and unlike most Latin American liberation theologians, he was doing theology in the context of socio-political structures more conducive to the implementation of his theological project. His public display of his willingness to learn from black theology helped other Latin Americans to do the same. I would point to the Mexico City conference as the turning point in the attitude of many Latin American theologians toward black theology. At this meeting, the indifference and hostile attitudes began to be transformed into a creative openness to learn and share in a common struggle of freedom. For the first time since the 1973 Geneva symposium, most Latin Americans referred to black people in the United States as their oppressed brothers and sisters in the First World.

EATWOT: Dar es Salaam, Accra, Wennappuwa

The Ecumenical Association of Third World Theologians (EATWOT) has been the most creative force in removing the attitudes of indifference and hostility from our conversations. The first major meeting of EATWOT was held in Dar es Salaam, Tanzania, August 1976.[19] Only one black North American was present at that historic meeting. The reason for our absence was the ambiguity in some people's mind regarding the meaning of the term "Third World." Perhaps remembering our previous unpleasant encounters in the 1975 Detroit conference, and forgetting their earlier more inclusive definition of the Third World, Latin Americans were vehement in their rejection of North American blacks as members of an association of Third World theologians. They wanted to limit its meaning to geography, that is, to persons born and presently living in Asia, Africa, and Latin America. But Africans (and some Asians) were even more vehement in their insistence on the inclusion of North American blacks, because Africans said that the Black World is one. They contended that the Third World referred to the condition of dependence, a situation of exploitation and oppression.[20]

No final decision was made in Tanzania regarding the inclusion of North American blacks as members. But Africans and Asians were sensitive to the attempts of Latin Americans to dominate EATWOT by insisting on the dominance of Marxist analysis to the exclusion of other concerns. As one Asian reported:

The Latin Americans were the whole time harping on socio-economic-political dimensions as the major or only reality, and applied rigorously the Marxian tool analysis. All the other realities were so insignificant for them that they could be integrated into the economic-political domination or its consequences. This was questioned strongly by Asians and Africans though they agreed with the analysis and results of socio-economic-political reality.[21]

It was interesting to find out that the same issue that alienated blacks and Latin Americans also produced a similar relation between Latin Americans and other Third World peoples in Africa and Asia.

In an attempt to counter the Latin American endeavor to exclude North American blacks, Africans invited eight black theologians to the second EATWOT conference, which was held in Accra, Ghana, December 1977.[22] The major emphasis of the conference focused on African theology. Among the black theologians present were Gayraud S. Wilmore, Jacquelyn Grant, George Thomas, and I. Among the Latin Americans present were Sergio Torres, Gustavo Gutiérrez, Enrique Dussel, and José Míguez Bonino. To my surprise, Latin Americans, Asians, and North American blacks worked together with Africans for the purpose of developing an African theology for that continent. There were no obvious tensions among Latin Americans and blacks at Accra.

The absence of tensions at Accra does not mean that the issue of race and class had been solved to the satisfaction of both sides. The lack of tension between Latin Americans and blacks can be accounted for in several ways: (1) There was indeed a new openness on both sides, as indicated in our discussion of the Mexico City conference. (2) The focus of the Accra conference on African theology rather than the issue of race and class meant that the second EATWOT meeting did not provide an appropriate context for a discussion of problems relating primarily to Latin Americans and blacks. (3) Sergio Torres and Gustavo Gutiérrez were the most active Latin Americans at Accra, and blacks found both very open to their concerns. (4) The question of the meaning of the term "Third World" and black North Americans' eligibility for membership in EATWOT was postponed until a later time.

The third EATWOT conference was held in Wennappuwa, Sri Lanka, January 1979.[23] Although the focus was on Asian theology, some Latin American, black, and African theologians were invited as fraternal delegates. Our status as fraternal delegates proved to be very revealing. I found out that the Asians resented the dominant and seemingly dogmatic attitude of Latin Americans at least as much as blacks did. When the status of "fraternal" delegates was seriously questioned by some Latin Americans and others, Asians said in a gentle but firm way that they were not going to allow outsiders, who know so little about Asian reality, to come to their conference and tell them how to do theology. Although I was among the fraternal delegates, I found myself agreeing with the Asian position.

I found out later that there had been some discussion among Asians as to whether EATWOT was really a Third World association or merely Latin American. The Christian Conference of Asia (CCA) refused to sponsor the EATWOT meeting because of the dominance of the association by Latin Americans. Preman Niles, Secretary for Theological Concerns, expressed it sharply:

> Asian theologians have usually been co-opted into theological agendas and theological positions which originate elsewhere. This is a constant danger, and is in many ways why clear Asian theological positions are either slow to emerge or do not emerge at all. The danger of co-option is particularly evident when an organization [EATWOT] seeks to speak for the whole of the Third World while taking its basic theological impetus from one section of the Third World, namely, Latin America. This is not to say that insights from Latin American theologies have no significance for Asia. They do; and many Asian theologians owe much to the breakthroughs accomplished on that continent. Also, many of these themes were already being explored in Asia before the so-called Latin American Liberation Theology hit the theological market. Taking this whole rather complex situation into account the CTC Commission on Theological Concerns of the CCA felt that it should support [not sponsor] this consultation in a discriminating and critical way so that the motif of liberation is explored in relation to Asian contexts and situations.[24]

When Asians found out that many blacks had similar feelings about Latin Americans, we found ourselves supporting each other's concerns. Since Africans and blacks have always supported each other, and since only two Latin Americans were present at the Sri Lanka meeting, I was invited to become a member of EATWOT without controversy.

Matanzas 1979

Immediately following the EATWOT meeting in Sri Lanka, several blacks were invited to a conference on "Evangelization and Politics" in Matanzas, Cuba, February-March 1979.[25] This conference marked another significant movement in our dialogue, similar to the Mexico City meeting. Until this time, most Latin Americans had limited their openness to black theology to oral conversation. Very few references to black theology are found in their written works. Although Juan Luis Segundo's *The Liberation of Theology* is a significant exception,[26] this single exception is not enough to remove the suspicion that Latin Americans still regard black theology as being hopelessly limited by its concern with race oppression.

At the Cuba conference, I decided that I would be more direct in my challenge to Latin Americans in regard to their silence on racism. Is it because they are *white* Latin Americans and thus blind to their own racism? Why are there no black theologians among the large number of Latin American liberation theologians, especially since there are more blacks in Latin America than in

North America? Even if class analysis is primary, this fact does not give Latin Americans the right to remain silent on race. Furthermore, no white person, not even a Latin American, has the right to say to blacks that race is secondary, especially since white people are responsible for our racial oppression.

These comments and questions generated heated debates in the plenary sessions and small discussion groups. Because of the vigor with which I pressed my position, I was invited to serve on the writing committee for the "Final Document" so that race oppression could be made an integral part of it.[27] But I declined on the grounds that Latin Americans should struggle to come to terms with the inclusion of race analysis as we blacks are trying to do with class. I did not want Latin Americans to include race in their document merely because of pressure from me. I think the "Final Document" of the Cuba conference represents a significant step forward, and it shows that some Latin Americans have been trying to listen to black theologians.

One major reason for the Latin Americans' openness to black theology was the dominant presence of Cuban theologians. Since my first contact with Cuban theologians in Mexico City, 1977, I have been impressed by the willingness of Cubans to learn from black theology. And since the "Evangelization and Politics" conference was held on their soil and because they have a strong influence among Latin American liberation theologians, the Cubans' open attitude toward black theology caused others to be open as well.

São Paulo 1980

Because of black theologians' dialogue with Latin Americans, we have become much more aware of the importance of class analysis and the global context of theology. This awareness is found not only in my recent writings but also in the writings of Gayraud Wilmore[28] and Cornel West.[29] It is also found in the Black Theology Project (BTP) of Theology in the Americas. At the Ventnor, New Jersey, meeting of the BTP, December 1979, Cornel West made a provocative presentation on the relation of class and race analysis. At that meeting, the BTP affirmed the importance of class analysis and also of socialism. Recently BTP participated with the Democratic Socialist Organizing Committee (DSOC) in a joint publication of my essay "The Black Church and Marxism: What Do They Have to Say to Each Other?" This essay was written for the purpose of initiating a dialogue of black theologians and Marxist-socialist groups. With Cornel West as its director, BTP has made its dialogue with labor and Marxian socialism one of its major concerns for the future.

As black theologians have become more aware of class oppression, Latin American theologians have shown that they are aware of race oppression in their own context and in the world. An awareness of the importance of race and its conspicuous absence from their theology motivated the Latin Americans of EATWOT to hold a conference on "Race, Class, and Liberation Theology" in Mandeville, Jamaica, December 1979. The purpose of this dialogue was to prepare Latin Americans for a serious discussion of race at the then forthcoming fourth EATWOT conference in São Paulo, Brazil. Cornel West and I were invited to attend. Also present were several Caribbean theologians, including Robert Cuthbert and Ashley Smith. Among the Latin Americans were Sergio Torres and Pablo Richards, and a black priest from Costa Rica, Lloyd Stennette.

Enrique Dussel could not be present, but he sent a paper on "Black People in the History of Latin America Social Formation," which served as one focal point of our heated debates. Blacks from the Caribbean and the United States were vehement in their unanimous rejection of Dussel's analysis of racism. Black theologians contended that it was an analysis too much dependent on the conceptual tools derived from the European culture responsible for black people's oppression. Such an analysis is typical among white intellectuals who claim to be in solidarity with our struggle to eliminate racism but fail to turn to the history and culture of the victims for intellectual resources in order to understand the nature of the problem, and what must be done to combat it. It appeared to black theologians that Dussel assumed that black victims had nothing to contribute to our analysis of and the struggle against racial oppression. For the resources he used were exclusively European, with Sigmund Freud's *Civilization and its Discontents* occupying a central place in his analysis. I only regret that Dussel was not present to hear our critique because the issue at stake is very important for our future dialogue.

The central question for most blacks regarding Dussel's paper was this: Can we assume that the culture that enslaves people will also be the one that will provide the resources for their liberation? Almost without exception blacks said an emphatic no! Dussel's paper was strongly rejected because blacks said that it showed no knowledge of or concern for the genuine voices of the victims of racism. We blacks are accustomed to reading essays and books on racism by white university people who think that they know everything about black oppression without even having to consult what black people think regarding their victimization. Unfortunately Dussel's approach to the theme of racism reminded us very much of that white intellectual blindness. Our discussion of this matter with Pablo Richards, whom we blacks were meeting for the first time, did more to reinforce what we felt about Dussel's paper than to eliminate it.[30]

Most blacks left Jamaica having grave doubts about the possibility of Latin American liberation theologians taking racism seriously at the forthcoming São Paulo conference (February-March 1980). The fourth major meeting of EATWOT was called an International Ecumenical Congress of Theology with a major focus on the "Ecclesiology of Popular Christian Communities." Several blacks who attended the São Paulo conference said that the meeting merely confirmed their doubts experienced in Jamaica. While I had a similar feeling, I think that there is a broader context in which to evaluate the question of racism and Latin American theology. We must not minimize the major importance of the São Paulo conference for Latin American Christians struggling for freedom, and what their struggle symbolizes for Christians everywhere. Neither should we underplay the growth that Latin American theologians have made on the issues of racism and sexism. In addition to the Jamaica Conference, Latin American theologians of EATWOT also held conferences on "Women, Praxis and Liberation Theology" (Tepeyac, Mexico, October 1979) and "Indigenous Mobilization and the Theology of Liberation" (San Cristobal de las Casas, Mexico, September 1979). The fact that these three conferences were held shows an openness among Latin American liberation theologians not previously present among them. Unlike the conference on racism, the conferences on sexism and indigenous people were well organized with excellent reports being presented at São Paulo to the EATWOT assembly. In addition there was time spent in the plenary sessions that focused on blacks, women, and the indigenous population with excellent spokespersons for each group. I can therefore say with much confidence that Latin American liberation theologians have come a long way since Geneva 1973. This growth could be seen not only in the São Paulo conference itself but partly in the "Final Document" of the conference. It is within the wider context of our eight years of dialogue that I offer my appreciative comments regarding Latin Americans and the question of racism.

However I do not want my positive comments to lead to a misunderstanding. I am not saying that the São Paulo conference showed that Latin Americans are now dealing with the racism issue to my satisfaction or to the satisfaction of other blacks. For I must say that despite their advances on racism and sexism at São Paulo, there was little evidence that blacks, women, and the indigenous population made any significant impact on the nature of Latin American liberation theology. Indeed Miguel Concha's presentation, "Interpreting Situations of Domination: The Poor, Ethnic Groups, and Classes Made up of the Common People," had the same kinds of problems found in Enrique Dussel's essay discussed in Jamaica. There was no evidence of any investigation of the perspectives of the victims about whom they speak. It seemed that the concerns of blacks, women, and the indigenous people were peripheral for most Latin Americans, and their conspicuous absence from the plenary sessions during the discussion of these issues confirmed this suspicion for many non-Latin American participants.

It should be revealing to the Latin Americans that the nonparticipants at São Paulo offered a similar critique of the Latin Americans' failure to take seriously the culture of the poor. In our view, this failure conflicted sharply with the Latin Americans' claim to be in solidarity with the liberation of the poor. What *kind* of liberation are Latin American liberation theologians offering the poor blacks and Indians (both men and women), if the cultures of these people are not to be taken seriously in the liberation process? As early as the Geneva 1973 symposium, it appeared that Hugo Assmann recognized precisely this problem when he said:

Until now the Latin American Theology of Liberation has used mostly Western and European theories and this poses a great question. We are trying now in Christian revolutionary groups to find a new communicative language. The Christians for Socialism movement in Chile is attempting to reinterpret in Marxist popular language the history, the revolution, the struggles and the processes of the proletarian movement in Chile. This strikes a somewhat false note, I must say, in an effort to communicate with Black Theology. It is false, because *who* is making this effort of communication in a popular language, a popular translation? Western people — Latin Americans, but Western people. There is another language — a grassroots language. They have a language; we don't want to give them one. . . . It is necessary to have a dialectic relationship between our Western, colonized, dependent language and their language.[31]

Assmann's comment in 1973 summarizes well the concerns of non-Latin Americans at the São Paulo conference. I only wish he could have expressed similar remarks there as well. Of course, some Latin Americans did recognize the culture and history of the poor and spoke to it. Gustavo Gutiérrez's lecture on the "Irruption of the Poor" was a case in point. But such exceptions did not change the fact that most non-Latins felt that the culture of the non-European poor remained invisible in Latin American liberation theology. Preman Niles summarized the feelings of most non-Latin Americans. After expressing his appreciation for the presence of the poor "at the center of theological construction and ecclesial practice in Latin America," he said:

We detect a certain rigidity in the understanding of who the poor are, a rigidity that leads to exclusivism in spite of some attempts to be open and not albeit overly dogmatic. At this point we can learn a lesson, a negative one, from models of capitalistic development in Asia. When the people ask questions about their participation, they are often told: Wait; first the skilled people must do their job of developing the country; then you will be included. Our experience has been that the people are never included, and they continue to be simply the objects and not the subjects of history.

The basic question is this: Do the poor speak for themselves, or do others speak on behalf of the poor and incorporate them or accommodate them into a given schema? This question applies particularly to the participation of the blacks and the indigenous people in the process of liberation.[32]

Preman Niles's comments were reinforced by other non-Latin participants from Asia, Africa, the Caribbean, and the United States. I was disappointed that many Latin Americans seemed unable or unwilling to hear the critique of the non-Latin American panel. But some Latin Americans did hear it, and their hearing is already being implemented in their theological work.

In addition to the dialogue of black North American theologians with white Latin Americans, the São Paulo conference enabled black North Americans to meet a significant number of black Latin Americans, and we began the discussion of the possibility of organizing a theological conference for blacks in the United States, the Caribbean, and Latin America. Such a conference was expected to take place in July of 1980 in Costa Rica, but the shortness of time prevented it. I do hope that the Black Theology Project and the Caribbean Conference of Churches will be able to realize this event. There is little doubt that such a conference will be helpful in black theology's dialogue with Latin American liberation theology.

The Future

Where do we go from here in the dialogue with Latin American liberation theology and black theology? I would like to make some concluding comments about our future.

1. It is important to recognize that we have moved from indifference and hostility to serious dialogue on race and class with the expressed purpose of supporting each other's theological projects. I hope that we can keep sharply before us the history of our eight years of dialogue so that we will not be tempted to make the mistakes of the past and thereby create hostile and indifferent attitudes toward each other.

2. There is no need to decide which is primary, race or class, before dialogue begins. There will undoubtedly be persons on both sides of the issue in both groups. What is needed is an openness to reality on both sides. This openness can be created best by persons who come from the same contexts and are committed to the same struggle but who represent different perspectives on race and class. This means that it would be helpful, for black theology's dialogue with Latin American liberation theology, if the former included in its group black Marxists. The same is true for white Latin Americans in regard to the race issue. They need black-consciousness theologians in their group so that they can learn how to face squarely the issue of racism.

3. Both black North American and Latin American theologians need to plan a conference in which the issue of race and class is the central theme. In this conference, we need people who represent both sides of the issue in both of our contexts. I believe that such a conference is needed so that we can begin to work more creatively with each other.

4. If Latin Americans and black North Americans expect to deepen their dialogue, then our mutual encounter must move beyond the context of international conferences. Neither black theology nor Latin American liberation theology is made in international meetings. Rather the origin and meaning of both theologies are defined by the concrete struggles of the people that they seek to represent. To understand each other's focus on class and race, therefore, we need to live among the people for whom these contradictions are everyday realities. Black theologians need to spend some time with the poor people of Latin America so they can experience for themselves the class contradictions in that country. And Latin Americans need to spend some time in the ghettoes of the United States so they can experience what it means to be black in this

society. This mutual participation in each other's communities will unquestionably deepen our dialogue. For much of our disagreement on the issue of race and class arises from the lack of knowledge of each other's praxis.

5. Whatever our future together might be, we must now know that nothing is more important than the fact that we are committed to the one faith that also requires a political commitment in the same struggle of freedom. Our disagreements must not be allowed to blind us to the knowledge that we are fighting a common enemy and our victory is certain only to the degree that we struggle for it together.

NOTES

1. For an earlier report on the dialogue between Latin American liberation theologians and black theologians, see my "Black Theology and Third World Theologies," reprinted here as Document 30.

2. New York: Herder and Herder, 1970.

3. Washington: Corpus Books, 1969.

4. *A Black Theology of Liberation* was translated by Manuel Mercader and published by Carlos Lohle, Calle Tacuari 1516, Buenos Aires, Argentina.

5. For an account of the origin of both theologies, see Wilmore and Cone, *Black Theology*, and José Míguez Bonino, *Doing Theology in a Revolutionary Situation* (Philadelphia: Fortress Press, 1975).

6. An account of this dialogue is found in *Risk*, 9, no. 2 (1973). The major participants in the dialogue were Paulo Freire, Hugo Assmann, Eduardo Bodipo-Malumbia, and myself.

7. Ibid., 59.

8. Ibid.

9. Ibid., 59-62.

10. Paulo Freire said: "I look at my friend James Cone . . . as a Third World man—it does not matter that he was born in the United States—it's an accident. He is in a world of dependence—of exploitation—within the First World" (p. 58). Assmann also referred to a Third World in the First World: "In the United States and Europe, there are people of the Third World—the poor and oppressed world" (p. 62).

11. This statement can be found in a book on the conference by Sergio Torres and John Eagleson, eds., *Theology in the Americas* (Maryknoll, N.Y.: Orbis Books, 1976), 359-60. It is also found in Wilmore and Cone, *Black Theology* (1979), 529-30.

12. Enrique Dussel, who was present at the Detroit 1975 conference but absent from the Geneva symposium, has a different interpretation of both events. He says: "This meeting, held August 18-25, 1975, began to overcome the incommunication with black theology (as could be seen in Freire-Assmann-Bodipo-Cone . . .). At Detroit there was a fruitful dialogue between black and Latin American theologians. . . . " (see his "The Political and Ecclesial Context of Liberation Theology in Latin America" in Sergio Torres and Virginia Fabella, eds., *The Emergent Gospel* [Maryknoll, N.Y.: Orbis Books, 1978], 192, note 45). I think Dussel gives an unfavorable representation of the Geneva symposium because he was not present and thus misread the emphasis on "incommunication." The "incommunication" at Geneva was not primarily referring to the dialogue between black and Latin American theologies but rather between both theologies and the theologies of Europe. I just do not understand how he can say that we left Detroit with a deeper understanding of each other.

13. For Gayraud Wilmore's account of this impact, see his "The New Context of Black Theology in the United States" in Wilmore and Cone, *Black Theology* (1979), 602-8.

14. This essay is included in ibid., 350-59 and in rev. ed., vol. 1, as Document 23.

15. This document is found in ibid., 345-49. This quotation is found on page 349.

16. For an account of this conference, see Jorge V. Pixley and Jean-Pierre Bastian, *Praxis cristiana y producción teológica* (Salamanca: Ediciones Sígueme, 1979).

17. Jürgen Moltmann, "On Latin American Liberation Theology: An Open Letter to José Míguez Bonino," *Christianity and Crisis*, 36, no. 5 (29 March, 1976).

18. This essay is included in *Praxis cristiana y producción teológica* under the heading *"Fe cristiana y praxis política,"* 75-88.

19. An account of the meeting is found in *The Emergent Gospel*.

20. For two discussions of this matter, see my "Black Theology and Third World Theologies," in Wilmore and Cone, *Black Theology* vol. 1 (1993), 364, note 13; and Sergio Torres's "Introduction" in *The Emergent Gospel*, ix-x.

21. D.S. Amalorpavadass, "News and Comments: Ecumenical Dialogue of Third World Theologians," *Indian Theological Studies*, 14, no. 4 (December 1977).

22. An account of this meeting is found in Kofi Appiah-Kubi and Sergio Torres, eds., *African Theology en Route* (Maryknoll, N.Y.: Orbis Books,1979).

23. An account of this meeting is found in Virginia Fabella, ed., *Asia's Struggle for Full Humanity* (Maryknoll, N.Y.: Orbis Books, 1980).

24. See HAYYIM, vol. 1, no. 1 (January 1979), 5. For a fuller discussion of this matter, see my " 'Asia's Struggle for Full Humanity: Toward a Relevant Theology' (An Asian Theological Conference)" in Wilmore and Cone, *Black Theology* (1979), 593-601; see also my "A Black Perspective on the Asian Search for a Full Humanity" in Fabella, ed., *Asia's Struggle for Full Humanity*, 182ff.

25. For an account of this conference, see my "Black Theology and Third World Theologies" in Wilmore and Cone, *Black Theology* vol. 1 (1993), 349f. Although several blacks were invited, I was the only black from the U.S. who attended this meeting.

26. Maryknoll, N.Y.: Orbis Books, 1976. See also Paulo Freire's "Prólogo a la edición española" in the Spanish edition of *A Black Theology of Liberation*.

27. This document is found in Wilmore and Cone, *Black Theology*, 543-51.

28. See his "The New Context of Black Theology" in ibid., 602f.

29. See his "Black Theology and Marxist Thought" in ibid., 552-67 and in rev. ed. (1993), vol. 1, as Document 34; "Socialism and the Black Church," *New York Circus: A Center for Social Justice and International Awareness*, 3, no. 5, October-November 1979, 5-8; and "Black Theology and Socialist Thought," *The Witness*, 63, no. 4 (April 1980), 16-19.

30. Since the Jamaica meeting, Pablo Richards and blacks have overcome the tensions we experienced in Jamaica. We have come to realize that most of the difficulties we experienced in Jamaica had more to do with language than with the issue of race and class. Blacks spoke almost no Spanish (with the exception of Lloyd Stennette, a black priest from Costa Rica) and Richards could speak only a little English.

31. See *Risk*, 9, no. 2 (1973), 59.

32. See *The Challenge of Basic Christian Communities*, ed. Sergio Torres and John Eagleson (Maryknoll, N.Y.: 1981), 253.

30

BLACK THEOLOGY AND THIRD WORLD THEOLOGIES

James H. Cone

BEGINNINGS OF BLACK AND THIRD WORLD THEOLOGY

All Third World theologies began as a reaction to the dominant theologies of Europe and North America.[1] Whether one speaks of Latin American, African, Asian, or Caribbean theologies—all of these recent theological developments in the churches and seminaries of Third World nations signal the rejection of the missionary theologies of their former colonizers.

Instead of accepting the prefabricated theologies of Europe and North America, Third World peoples are developing their own theologies. Most of them show a special interest in liberation, understood as the attempt of a poor people to gain its freedom. The focus on liberation is partly a reaction to the missionary emphasis on spiritual salvation, as if the gospel of Jesus had no interest in the material conditions of life. Almost universally, awakened Third World peoples began to realize that the Bible is concerned about the salvation of the whole person, including his or her physical well-being. The neglect of the political and economic aspects of the gospel by European and North American missionaries came to be understood as a deliberate cover-up by oppressors so that Third World victims would not challenge the unjust international economic order.

As long as Third World peoples believed that the meaning of the gospel is defined by Europe and North America, they could not develop theological perspectives that would challenge their domination by the First World.

The rise of Third World theologies, with their almost universal interest in

This paper from the Fifth International Conference of the Ecumenical Association of Third World Theologians, August 17-29, 1981, New Delhi, India was published in *Irruption of the Third World: Challenge to Theology*, ed. Virginia Fabella and Sergio Torres (Maryknoll, N.Y.: Orbis Books, 1983).

liberation, is directly related to the emergence of national, political movements of liberation in the countries of their origin. When grassroots peoples of the Third World began to rebel against colonial rule by insisting, sometimes through armed revolution, upon self-rule, theological perspectives also began to develop with a similar focus.

It was no accident that Third World theologies of liberation began in the context of struggles for political liberation. The precise character of the liberation sought depended upon the political needs of the country as defined by a people struggling to liberate itself from foreign domination. Africans began to speak of a distinct African theology with a special interest in the africanization or indigenization of the gospel so that they would not have to become European in order to be Christian.[2] Latin Americans spoke of theology with an emphasis on liberation as defined by Marxist class analysis.[3] Asians also used the term "liberation" in defining Asian theology, but they included in its meaning a special focus on their culture as defined by their great religions. They spoke about contextualization instead of indigenization, and began to relate it to an Asian Principle.[4] Although Caribbean peoples have not developed a distinct theological perspective comparable to Asian, Latin, and African theologies, there are several indications that they also share many of the concerns for liberation as found among other Third World peoples. Perhaps Caribbean theology will be a theology of liberation that will address itself to the issues of imperialism, classism, and racism.[5]

It is clear that all Third World theologies began as a direct reaction to the theologies of the First World. A similar point can be made regarding theologies of liberation among the oppressed in North America. Black, Asian, Hispanic, and native North American minorities have begun to develop distinct theologies of liberation as defined against oppressive white North American theologies.[6] Like Third World peoples in Asia, Africa, Latin America, and the Caribbean, the oppressed peoples of North America do not believe that white oppressors can define for them what the gospel of Jesus is.

Included among our liberation theologies of North America is also a distinct feminist theology that seeks to address the evils of sexism.[7] Although feminist theology began among white North American women, some of the aspects of this theology have been adopted by minority women as well.[8] Although minority women have not, for the most part, adopted the extreme radical rhetoric of some white women, minority women do realize that their men are not exempted from sexism. Furthermore, minority men have internalized many of the sexist values of the white male culture that defines the woman's place as the home, thereby limiting her contribution in the liberation struggle.

Although the theologies of liberation have been in dialogue with the dominant theologies of North America and Europe, they have not been, until recently, in dialogue with each other. They have been so preoccupied with correcting and uncovering the hypocrisy of European-American theologies that they have tended to ignore their relationship to each other. Like their colonizers and oppressors, unfortunately, many Third World persons do not believe that they have anything intellectual to learn from another oppressed people. Although some Third World peoples may turn against their white colonizers and oppressors, as is true also of liberation theologians, they are not likely to turn to their Third World brothers and sisters on other continents for intellectual resources of liberation. What they know about each other is often determined by white missionaries and other European mediators. This is tragic because missionaries are just as prejudiced against one Third World people as they are against another. The information supplied by white missionaries becomes suspect, because they do not intend for Third World peoples to build a coalition among themselves.

If Third World people were to build a coalition among themselves in their common struggle, it would be more difficult for Europeans and North Americans to control the Third World. When Third World persons become Christians, they must be persuaded that Europeans and North American whites are the only ones who know what Christianity means. Whatever the oppressed attempt to do, their oppressor must convince them that they need their help. The control of a people's thinking is an essential element in socio-political oppression.

When I first began to write black theology, in 1968, the first thing white theologians and ecclesiastics told black and other Third World persons was that there is no such thing as black theology, because theology does not come in colors. What was so amazing is that many blacks rejected black theology, because white theologians, missionaries, and preachers said black theology was not "real" theology. It is unfortunate that many Third World persons even today ignore each other because they do not think that they could have anything of theological value to say. Even today there are still some Third World and North American black seminaries that offer courses in systematic theology but do not include their own theology or that of other oppressed peoples alongside North Atlantic theologies. Some North American black theologians are black in color only, not in their thinking, because they still contend that only Europeans and others who think as do they are "real" theologians.

It is very difficult for Third World persons to liberate themselves from a dependence on European thought, because we were trained by them and thus have a certain — inordinate — admiration of their thought processes. Even when we rebel against Europeans or North American whites, our rebellion is often limited to negative reactions.

My interpretation of black theology during the late 1960s and early 1970s is an example of this weakness. When one reads *Black Theology and Black Power* (1969) and *A Black Theology of Liberation* (1970), my dependence on white theological concepts is obvious. And my black colleagues were quick to point out this contradiction in my perspective. Since the publication of *The Spirituals and the Blues* (1972) and *God of the Oppressed* (1975), I have been struggling to incorporate the experience and culture of the oppressed into the conceptual raw material for articulating black theology. For I contend that our rebellion against a European mentality should lead to a second step, namely, to an affirmation of our own cultural resources as well as those found among other oppressed peoples who have had similar experiences of oppression.

As a North American black theologian, I have emphasized the need of oppressed Christians of the world to begin to develop structures of coalition among themselves so that we can pursue a common struggle for freedom. In an organization called Theology in the Americas, oppressed black, native American, Hispanic, and Asian Christians have begun to dialogue on their common plight of oppression.[9] In the Ecumenical Association of Third World Theologians, Asians, Africans, Latin Americans, and oppressed minorities of North America have begun to dialogue with each other. It has been within the EATWOT context that black theology has developed a dialogue with other Third World theologies. Other settings for dialogue include the World Council of Churches and the individual efforts of black and Third World theologians to be in conversation with each other.

In the next two sections of this paper, I want to focus my attention on the similarities and differences of black theology when compared with some literary expressions of Third World theologies in Asia, Africa, and Latin America. (I have not included Caribbean theology, because its distinctive features are still at an early stage of development.)

Black and Third World Theologies: Some Similarities

Black and Third World theologies are in agreement that the dominant theologies of Europe and North America must be rejected. In their rejection of the white theologies of North America and Europe, black and Third World theologians used the term "liberation" as a focus of their theological concern.

The earliest references to liberation, as the heart of the gospel and as a definition of Christian theology, were made by black and Latin American theologians and church persons. It is important to note that black and Latin theologians began to use the term "liberation" almost simultaneously but independently of each other. Liberation became the dominant emphasis of black theology from its beginning with the publication of my *Black Theology and Black Power* (1969) and *A Black Theology of Liberation* (1970). One year after the publication of the second book, the Spanish edition of Gustavo Gutiérrez's book, *A Theology of Liberation* (1971), was published. Other black and Latin theologians followed with an emphasis on the same theme.

The theme of liberation is not limited to Latin and black theologies. A similar concern is found among Asian and African theologies as well. The common concern of rejecting the dominant theologies of Europe and North America and the emphasis on liberation led Third World theologians to organize EATWOT. In the New Delhi meeting, efforts were begun for the development of a Third World theology within the context of the non-Christian world. When one analyzes the Final Statements of the five EATWOT conferences to date, the rejection of European theology and an affirmation of liberation are common characteristics.

In addition to the rejection of European theology and the affirmation of liberation, black and Third World theologies also stress the need to reread the Bible in the light of the struggles of the poor for freedom. They have begun to speak of the "hermeneutical privilege" of the poor, and of God's option for the poor—that is, God's decision to reveal Godself to all humankind preferably in and through the poor. Rereading of the Bible in the light of God's option for the poor has led to an emphasis on the Exodus, the prophets, and Jesus Christ as the liberator of the poor and the downtrodden.

It has been within the context of our attempt to reread the Bible in the light of the struggles of the oppressed that the theme of the "suffering God" has become important in our theological reflections. Jürgen Moltmann's writings on the "crucified God" have stimulated our theological imagination, as has also Luther's distinction between the "theology of glory" and the "theology of the cross." But it has been the actual suffering of the oppressed in Africa, Asia, Latin and North America that has been the most decisive influence in our reflections on the cross of Jesus Christ. As Gustavo Gutiérrez has said: "We cannot speak of the death of Jesus until we speak of the real death of the people." It is in the deaths of the poor of the world that is found the suffering and even death of God.

The political implications of Luther's insight on this point seem to have been completely distorted with his unfortunate emphasis on the two kingdoms. Contemporary Lutheran scholars are even worse, because they appear to turn the cross of Jesus into a theological idea, completely unrelated to the concrete historical struggles of the oppressed for freedom. For most Lutheran scholars, the theology of the cross is a theological concept to be contrasted with philosophical and metaphysical speculations. It is a way of making a distinction between faith and reason, justification by faith through grace and justification through the works of reason.

But when the poor of the Third World and of North America read the passion story, they do not view it as a theological idea but as God's anguished solidarity with the victimized of the world. Jesus' cross is God's election of the poor, taking their pain and suffering upon himself. This is what Third World theologians mean when they say that "God is black," "God is red," "God is rice," and other strange ways of speaking when compared with the metaphysical reflections of Europeans. This apparently crude anthropomorphic way of speaking of God is the Third World theologian's way of concretizing Paul's dictum: "To shame the wise, God has chosen what the world counts folly, and to shame what is strong, God has chosen what the world counts weakness. He has chosen things low and contemptible, mere nothings, to overthrow the existing order" (1 Cor. 1:27–28).

Another common emphasis among black and Third World theologians is their de-emphasis, though not complete rejection, of the Western theological tradition and an affirmation of their own cultural traditions. If the sufferings of God are revealed in the sufferings of the oppressed, then it follows that theology cannot achieve its Christian identity apart from a systematic and critical reflection upon the history and culture of the victims of oppression.

When this theological insight impressed itself upon our consciousness, we Third World theologians began to realize that we had been miseducated. In fact, European and North American theologians and missionaries stifled the indigenous development of theological perspectives of Third World peoples by teaching them that their own cultural traditions were not an appropriate source for an interpretation of the Christian gospel. Europeans and white North Americans taught us that the Western theological tradition, as defined by Augustine, Aquinas, Luther, Calvin, and Wesley, is the essential source for a knowledge of the Christian past. When black and Third World theologians began to concentrate on distinct black, African, Asian, and Latin theologies, they also realized that their own historical and cultural traditions are far more important for an analysis of the gospel for their struggle of freedom than are the Western traditions that participated in their enslavement.

African traditional religions and the African independent churches have played a vital role in the development of African theology. Black spiritual blues and folklore as well as radical nineteenth-century black freedom fighters played a special role in the rise of North American black theology. The major religions of Asia, including Hinduism and Buddhism, are being integrated into the current shape of Asian theology. In Latin America, the most Western of all liberation theologies, theologians have also turned to their own cultural history for guidance and inspiration.

All Third World theologians began to realize that those responsible for our enslavement are not likely to provide the resources for our liberation. If oppressed peoples are to be liberated, they must themselves create the means to make it happen.

The focus on our culture in the light of our liberation struggle has led to an emphasis on praxis as the context out of which Christian theology develops. To know the truth is to do the truth — that is, to make happen in history what is professed in church. All proponents of liberation theology contend that the masses are not poor by accident. They are *made* and *kept* poor by the rich and powerful few. This means that to do liberation theology, one must make a commitment, an option for the poor and against those who are responsible for their poverty.

Because liberation theology is not simply something to be learned and taught in colleges and seminaries but something to be created in the struggles of the poor, social analysis becomes a critical component of all forms of liberation theology. How can we participate in the liberation of the poor from oppression if we do not know who the poor are or why they live in poverty? Social analysis is a tool that helps us to know why the social, economic, and political orders are composed as they are. It enables us to know who benefits from the present status quo. Unlike European and North American theology, whose interlocutor is philosophy, liberation theologians dialogue with sociology. Agreeing with Karl Marx's eleventh thesis on Feuerbach, they say: "The philosophers have only interpreted the world in various ways; the point, however, is to change it."

Black and other Third World theologians have been searching for ways in which they can change the world together.

In our use of the tools of the social sciences for an analysis of the social, political, and economic structures that dehumanize the poor, Third World theologians almost universally endorse democratic socialism and condemn monopolistic capitalism. When we speak of democratic socialism, we do not have in mind Soviet Russia, Eastern Europe, or any other so-called socialist country under the influence of the Soviet Union. Socialism by definition means democracy, and the U.S.S.R. is not a political democracy. Many Third World thinkers refer to Russia as an example of state capitalism.

Although there are no perfect exemplifications of our socialist vision, its authentification is based upon the struggles of the poor in the Third World who believe that there is no invincible reason why the present unjust order must continue. And the struggles of the peoples of Tanzania, Zimbabwe, Nicaragua, and other Third World countries symbolize the partial realization of our socialist vision.

For what we do know is that monopolistic capitalism is evil and must be opposed. Latin American liberation theologians have taken the lead in condemning and exposing the international capitalism of the United States and Europe, and their voices have been joined by Asians, Africans, Caribbeans, and Third World theologians in the United States. Our discussions together have widened our vision and enabled us to analyze more clearly the complexity of the international machinations of monopolistic capitalism.

Although Africans, Asians, and black North Americans have emphasized the role of culture in the bestowal of identity in the struggle for freedom, we also see more clearly now the importance of Marxism and the role of class analysis in the doing of theology. Both race and class analyses are important, and their importance is reflected in our support of each other.

Black and Third World Theologies: Some Differences

Although black and Third World theologies share many common concerns, they are not identical. The differences between black theology and Third World theologies in Asia, Africa, and Latin America can be classified in two general areas. There are differences that alienate us, and there are others that complement and enlarge our liberation perspectives. Both kinds of differences are present in the relationship of black theology with African, Latin American, and Asian theologies.

The two main focuses around which our differences have shown up are sociopolitical liberation, on the one hand, and cultural liberation, on the other. In our dialogue with African theologians, North American black theologians have placed more emphasis on socio-political liberation, and Africans have stressed cultural liberation. Our dialogue began in 1971 and has continued to the present. In each of our meetings, Africans have shied away from the term "liberation," because they say that the gospel is not political. It is not an ideology of the oppressed. Some have even said that the gospel is concerned about all—the rich and the poor alike.

In lieu of liberation, Africans often prefer the terms "africanization" and "indigenization," because they locate the problem at the point of culture, not politics. But black theologians have been adamant in their insistence that the God of the Bible is a political God who has identified divine righteousness with the bodily liberation of the poor. The differences between African and black theologians on this point have led some African theologians, such as John Mbiti, to say that African and black theologies have nothing in common. But the presence of black theology in southern Africa has cast a shadow over Mbiti's statement. Desmond Tutu, the present director of the South African Council of Churches, says that black and African theologies are soulmates and not antagonists. A similar point has been made by black Lutheran Bishop Manas Buthelezi.[10]

The concern of North American black theologians has not been to reduce theology and the gospel to blackness or political liberation. Like our African brothers and sisters, we believe that there is a spiritual ingredient in the gospel that transcends the material conditions of human life. What we reject is the tendency, among some African theologians, to reduce the gospel and theology to a spirituality that has not been carved out of the real life sufferings of the poor who are engaged in political liberation. When the sufferings of the poor are individualized, privatized, it becomes possible to identify their sufferings with God without challenging the existing socio-political structures responsible for their suffering. A suffering God and Jesus' cross become mere intellectual, theological concepts totally unrelated to the daily life of the poor. This is precisely José Míguez Bonino's and other Latin theologians' critique of Jürgen Moltmann's writings on the "crucified God."[11] A much more severe critique can be made of contemporary Lutheran reflections on Martin Luther's theology of the cross. Some liberation theologians would even make the same critique of Martin Luther because of his failure to extend his theological analysis of the cross to society.

Whether it is Moltmann's crucified God, Luther's theology of the cross, or African theology's theme of indigenization, the question of the socio-political ingredient of the gospel must be faced head-on. This has been and still is black theologians' chief concern in our dialogue with African theologians.

In the dialogue between black theology and Latin American liberation theology the opposite pole has been stressed. The main question has been: What is the relationship between race and class oppression? Because the Latin Americans are Marxists, they emphasize class oppression, almost to the exclusion of race oppression. Inasmuch as black theologians live in the white racist society of North America, with a heritage of two hundred fifty years of slavery and over a hundred years of white capitalist oppression, it is not likely that they will ignore cultural oppression as imposed by white racism.

Unfortunately black theologians have not always been sensitive to class oppression or to the role of U.S. imperialism in the Third World. Sometimes we have given the impression that all we want is an equal piece of the North American capitalist pie. Therefore Latin Americans have rightly asked for a social analysis in our theology that criticizes capitalism. In this dialogue with Latin theologians, we have come to realize the importance of Marxism as a tool for social analysis.

As Latin Americans have pressured us on the issue of class analysis, we have pressured them on the importance of race analysis. Similar to black theologians in their approach to Marxism, Latin theologians have not taken up race analysis enthusiastically. Our dialogue began in 1973, and we have struggled with the issue of race versus class since that time. Although the tensions between us have been high, we have learned a lot from each other and intend to carry on the dialogue.

It is revealing to note the changing dynamics and emphases in black theology and its dialogues with African and Latin American theologies. With Africans, we black theologians often appear very "political" in our view of theology, and the Africans seem more "cultural" and "spiritual." In our conversations with the Latins, black theologians seem very "cultural" and "spiritual," and the Latins appear to reduce theology to politics. The reason for these differences in dynamics and emphasis is partly due to the way we read the Bible and analyze the gospel with our respective situations in view. Another reason is our limited knowledge of each others' situation and the role of our theologies in our liberation struggles. Sometimes we try to impose our particular theology upon another situation.

The crucial issue is whether our theological perspectives have achieved and still retain their identity out of the struggles of the poor. For I contend that any theological perspective that does not remain committed to the liberation of the oppressed cannot be Christian. It does not matter on what continent a theology may be found. What is crucial is *whom* it represents: the poor or the rich, the black or the white, the First or Third World?

There has been less dialogue, and almost no conflicts, between black and Asian theologians. Asians do not know much about North American blacks, and we do not know much about Asians. The differences in culture and geographical distance are so great that we seldom have much to say to each other. This situation began to change when I was invited in 1975 by the Korean Christian Church in Japan to lead a three-week workshop on the theme "The Church Struggling for the Liberation of the People." Since 1975 I have returned to Japan and South Korea several times. Black theologians have met with Asian theologians in the Ecumenical Association of Third World Theologians. We found that we have many differences and similarities that complement each other.

Important for my perspective on Asia have been my colleagues Kosuke Koyama and Preman Niles of the Christian Conference of Asia, both of whom have done much to teach me about Asian theology. In addition to Koyama and Niles, I must also mention Asian students who have been in my classes at Union Seminary. Their presentation of the Asian reality and their commitment to participate in the struggle to liberate the oppressed on that continent have done much to illuminate my perspective on Asian theology. Like black theology, Asian theology seeks to bring together in dialectical tension the commitment to cultural identity and socio-political liberation. As I have suggested in my discussion of African and Latin theologies, they seem to be in danger of minimizing one side: the Africans socio-political liberation and the Latins cultural liberation. In Asian theology, there is a recognition of the importance of both these elements. My perspective on black theology has endeavored to recognize both elements as well.

Because our differences and similarities seem to complement each other's perspective, black and Asian theologians have begun to discuss the possibility of a dialogue with each other outside the Ecumenical Association of Third World Theologians. Preman Niles has explored this possibility among Asian Christians, and I have done a similar exploration within the context of the Black Theology Project of Theology in the Americas. No dates or agenda for a dialogue have been decided, but we are both anxious to initiate it, because we believe that we will have much to learn from each other.

Because black and Asian theologians have had few conflicts in our dialogue, we have been able to transport this experience of mutual support to our respective dialogues with Africans and Latin Americans. Why should we fight each other when we have so much to lose in division and so much to gain in unity? Asians and blacks seem to recognize that point in our theological conversations, and this recognition has enabled us to move to a deeper understanding of each others' struggles.

On the basis of Third World theologians' dialogues together, it is clear to us all that the future of each of our theologies is found in our struggles together. I am firmly convinced that black theology must not limit itself to the race struggle in the United States but must find ways to join in solidarity with the struggles of the poor in the Third World. The universal dimensions of the gospel message require that we struggle not only for ourselves but for all. For there can be no freedom for any one of us until all of us are free. Any theology that falls short of this universal vision is not Christian and thus cannot be identified with the Jesus who died on the cross and was resurrected so that everyone might be liberated in God's emergent kingdom.

NOTES

1. The term "Third World" is the object of much discussion. When I use the term in this essay, I am referring primarily to Asia, Africa, and Latin America. For a discussion of this term in a theological context, see Sergio Torres and Virginia Fabella, eds., *The Emergent Gospel: Theology from the Underside of History* (Maryknoll, N.Y.: Orbis Books, 1978), vii-xxii.

2. For one of the earliest texts on African theology, see Kwesi Dickson and Paul Ellingsworth, eds., *Biblical Revolution and African Beliefs* (London: Lutterworth, 1969); see also Gwinyar Muzorewa, *African Theology: Its Origin and Development* (Maryknoll, N.Y.: Orbis Books, 1985).

3. One of the best introductions to Latin American liberation theology is that of

José Míguez Bonino, *Doing Theology in a Revolutionary Situation* (Philadelphia: Fortress Press, 1975).

4. A good introduction to Asian theology is that of Douglas J. Elwood, ed., *Asian Christian Theology: Emerging Themes* (Philadelphia: Westminster Press, 1980).

5. For the emerging themes in Caribbean theology, see Idris Hamid, ed., *Troubling of the Waters* (Trinidad: Ruhaman Printing, 1973).

6. For an introduction, see Gerald H. Anderson and Thomas F. Stranksy, eds., *Mission Trend No. 4: Liberation Theologies in North America and Europe* (New York: Paulist Press, 1979).

7. Writings on feminist theology among whites are well known. For a good introduction see Carol P. Christ and Judith Plaskow, eds., *Womanspirit Rising* (San Francisco: Harper & Row, 1979).

8. For an emerging black feminist theology, see "Black Theology and the Black Woman," in G. S. Wilmore and J. H. Cone, eds., *Black Theology: A Documentary History 1966-1979* (Maryknoll, N.Y.: Orbis Books, 1979 and rev. ed. 1993, vol. 1).

9. See Sergio Torres and John Eagleson, eds., *Theology in the Americas* (Maryknoll, N.Y.: Orbis Books, 1976), for information on the origin of this organization. For information on Detroit II and the Inter-Ethnic/Indigenous Theologies' Dialogue, see "Message from the Haudenosaunee Dialogue/Retreat" (New York: Native Self-Sufficiency Center); see also Gregory Baum, "Theology in the Americas: Detroit II," *The Ecumenist*, (Sept.-Oct. 1980); C. West, C. Guidiote, M. Coakley, eds., *Theology in the Americas: Detroit II* Probe Series (Maryknoll, N.Y.: Orbis Books, 1982).

10. See John Mbiti, "An African Views American Black Theology" in Wilmore and Cone, *Black Theology: A Documentary History* (1979 and rev. ed. 1993, vol. 1); Desmond Tutu, "Black Theology/African Theology," in Wilmore and Cone, *Black Theology* (1979) pp. 483ff.; Manas Buthelezi, "An African Theology or a Black Theology?" in *Black Theology: The South African Voice,* Basil Moore, ed. (Atlanta: John Knox, 1973), 29ff.

11. See especially Míguez Bonino's *Doing Theology in a Revolutionary Situation.*

31

REFLECTIONS ON THE SECOND GENERAL ASSEMBLY OF EATWOT

Kelly Delaine Brown-Douglass

As a black woman trying to understand the meaning of God's liberating activity for the poor, and as one who had read most of EATWOT's publications, I had high expectations for Oaxtepec.[1] I looked forward to being challenged by the different contexts of oppression represented by EATWOT's members. I knew that the socio-cultural situations of Africa, Asia, and Latin America might reveal some aspects of God's meaning that the socio-cultural situation of black women did not. Therefore, I eagerly anticipated an exchange that might broaden my knowledge concerning the significance of God's revelation in human history.

During my week at Oaxtepec my expectations were fulfilled. Therefore, in this paper I will share some of my experiences as a first-time participant in EATWOT's discussions and some of the issues which challenged my own theological perspective.

During the week I encountered passionate dialogue as each delegation expressed the nature of the oppression found within its own country. As I expected, the dialogue challenged all of us, as members of EATWOT to broaden our analysis of the oppressive systems within our own contexts. However, there were puzzling aspects of the dialogue.

The heated exchange which often occurred between black Americans and Latin Americans initially surprised me. It seemed strange that black Americans and Latin Americans would have so much tension and distance between them since we are so close to each other geographically and have more opportunity

Kelly Delaine Brown-Douglass, an Episcopal priest, is assistant professor of theology at Howard University School of Divinity, Washington, D.C. A reflection on the second General Assembly of the Ecumenical Association of Third World Theologians, December 1986, Oaxtepec, Mexico, this essay was published in *Third World Theologies: Commonalities and Divergences*, ed. K.C. Abraham (Maryknoll, N.Y.: Orbis Books, 1990).

to get to know each other. However, the history of differences provided clues to the hostility between the two groups.[2]

The Latin American theologians have been consistently accused of ignoring the problem of racism within their own context. Who other than their black American neighbors are a better reminder to them of this shortcoming? Not only have black American theologians verbally reminded Latin Americans of their silence about, and thus perpetuation of, racism, but black Americans' mere existence, which symbolizes a history of racist oppression in the United States, also acts as a constant reminder. Thus, it is no wonder that a nonblack delegation from a continent with a sizable black population and concomitant race problem would be uncomfortable with its black American neighbors.

On the other hand, black American theologians have been consistently accused of not having a socioeconomic analysis, and hence not having a critique of capitalism. There have been no better reminders of this shortcoming than the Latin American theologians. They have not only verbally reminded black American theologians that a lack of economic analysis serves to ignore class issues present within the black community and to perpetuate capitalist oppression across the Third World; but their mere presence, which symbolizes a history of capitalistic class oppression within Latin America, also acts as a constant reminder. So again, it is no wonder that black American theologians would be most uncomfortable with their Latin American neighbors.

In addition, I was also initially puzzled by the dialogue between black American women and the other women of EATWOT. A week prior to the second general assembly, women from Asia, Africa, and Latin America met in order to share experiences and to express their mutual concern for the elimination of gender oppression. Black American women were not invited to be a part of this week-long meeting. Black American women's exclusion from the meeting was an outgrowth of EATWOT's long struggle to understand the role of First World minorities in a Third World organization. Consequently, the EATWOT women of the Third World accepted an organizational procedure which resulted in the marginalization and oppression of some of their sisters in the struggle.

During the meeting of the general assembly, an overture was made to the U.S. black women. However, it was made as a step toward meeting with white feminist theologians of the First World. The women of Asia, Africa, and Latin America had already accepted an invitation to dialogue with white North American feminists. They reasoned, however, that it would be beneficial to meet with black American women first, since it was we who had the most experience of and interaction with the white feminists. At this point in the dialogue I began to wonder if the women from Asia, Africa, and Latin America were more interested in those who have contributed to their oppression than in getting to know their sisters in oppression.

If Third World women are going to move toward a world community where gender oppression is eliminated, we must first be careful not to adopt, for whatever reasons, the kinds of structures which might keep us separated from each other. Second, if God truly came to "the least of these," there can be no greater representative of the least of these today than the poor, Third World women whom we as EATWOT women claim to represent. Therefore, if we are truly committed to the struggles of our sisters, we must forge links with each other whether we are Third World women living in Third World countries or Third World women trapped in the First World. It is only together that we will be able to free our societies from the evils of race, class, and gender oppression that keep our sisters in bondage. Sojourner Truth put it best when she said:

> "If the first woman God ever made was strong enough to turn the world upside down all alone, these women together ought to be able to turn it back, and get it right side up again."[3]

It is *together* that Third World women will be able to turn the world right side up again. Fortunately, by week's end, EATWOT women from the Third and First Worlds were united in their desire to get to know more about each other.

In general, the dialogue at Oaxtepec made me realize that as members of EATWOT, male and female, we must recognize that the oppressive structures which we are forced to live under will thrive if they keep us divided. Their job is done when those of us who are oppressed are not about to come together and speak as one voice against systems of oppression. In essence, division is a demon of oppression. Therefore, following the lead of Jesus, we must name and call out all the demons that keep us in bondage. Jesus called forth the Gerasene demoniac so that the man inhabited by it could be set free from his "bonds and fetters" and become once again a part of his community (Luke 8:26ff.). In similar fashion, EATWOT must name and call forth its demons of divisiveness, so that we can be set free from the bondage that keeps us from talking to and learning from each other and becoming a part of a liberated community.

On the other hand, in spite of tense moments which occurred during the dialogue, there were still much fruitful exchange and theological challenge. The issues I found most compelling were raised by the Asian theologians: the religio-cultural issue, and the christological issue.

The Asian theologians reminded us that their continent is the home of all the great world religions. Moreover, confessed Christians are a very small percentage of the Asian population. In addition, each religion brings with it a particular culture. Consequently, the challenge for persons on the Asian continent is to maintain their particular religious belief while respecting the religion and culture of others. More specifically, the challenge for the Christian theologian is to do theology in such a way that it shows a deep and sincere respect for the other religions and cultures.

Related to being part of a religiously and culturally pluralistic society is the problem of Christology. An Asian theology of liberation must speak of Jesus' divinity in such a way that it does not preclude or impede other equally valid incarnations of God in human history.

To this point, Tissa Balasuriya of Sri Lanka suggested that instead of focusing on Jesus as the only example of the Christ, the only incarnation of divinity, Christians need to begin to concentrate on seeing the Christ present within all people. In this respect, Jesus should be viewed as only one example of the divine/human encounter.

After hearing the Asian Report I asked myself: What do the religio-cultural situation of Asia and the related christological problem mean for poor, black women and the development of a black feminist theology? First, given the fact that the Asian continent contains at least fifty-eight percent of the world's population, to do theology and ignore the situation of Asia is to show blatant disregard for the majority of the world's oppressed. Such a theology could not be a Christian theology; for, although it might have significance for a particular situation, there would be no universal significance. Therefore, even if our own particular context is one in which the majority of persons are Christians, as is the situation with black Americans, we must struggle to do theology in a way that speaks to and respects the other religions and cultures of the world.

Second, the representatives from the Asian continent reminded me that oppression has respect for neither persons, nor cultures, nor religions. The systems which oppress do not ask questions about a person's ethnic background or confession of faith. In this regard, neither should our theologies of liberation. Although they emerge from our own context of oppression, they must link us to other contexts. If it is true that one is not free until we are all free, then such a freedom can be achieved only if our liberation theologies become just as inclusive of people from various cultures as systems of oppression are. This means that a true liberation theology in the context of black women cannot be developed apart from a dialogue with others around the world who are oppressed. EATWOT has provided the opportunities for such a dialogue. It is my hope that it will continue to do so.

Finally, the christological concern raised by the Asian context caused me to reflect further upon the Christ's significance in black women's lives. For black Christians, male and female, there is rarely a distinction made between Jesus and God. Jesus is understood as God; that is why black church people sing:

> He's King of Kings, and Lord of Lords,
> Jesus Christ, the first and the last.
> No man works like him.

This understanding of Jesus as God, as the Christ, allowed black slaves to know that what their masters said about God was not true. God did not ordain and support their slavery. Instead, God's revelation in Jesus showed that God was there to sustain them in their sufferings and to free them from their bondage. Because black Christians have known Jesus, through scripture and in their own lives, they have known that God is for them and not against them.

Thus, people's confession of Jesus as the Christ is an affirmation of God's commitment to the poor and oppressed. It is a confession born, not out of the tradition of Nicea and Chalcedon, but out of the history of slavery. Therefore, such a confession is not an effort to show that because Jesus is the divine/human encounter he is unique; instead it is an affirmation that God is a liberator, not an enslaver.

On the other hand, this confession of Jesus as Christ has had an oppressive aspect within the black community. Specifically, it has contributed to black women's marginal status within the black church. For instance, black women are often told that the reason they cannot be ordained is because Jesus, the church's model for the ordained ministry, was male, not female. In addition, similar to Asians, when confessing Jesus as the Christ—that is, linking Christ so firmly to the historical Jesus—we must ask if such a confession will ever allow black women to see themselves in Christ and Christ in themselves. Can Christ or God be conceived of as anything but male? The urgency of this problem was made clear to me when a black woman asked me not to refer to God as she. "It just does not sound right," the black woman said.

While the confession of Jesus as the Christ has had liberating significance for black Christians, it has also contributed to the oppression of black women. So, like Asian theologians, black women must seek ways in which to speak of Jesus as the Christ (given the liberating history of that confession) which do not impede perceiving Christ in others, particularly in black women.

To this end, a black feminist theology of liberation must make at least a twofold affirmation. First, it must affirm that for black Christians Jesus is the Christ; it is he who is the ultimate witness to God's revelation in human history. Yet, given the oppression which can be the result of such a claim, a black feminist theology must also affirm that Jesus is not the only example of Christ or incarnation of God in the world. Instead, Jesus should act as a guide for allowing black Christians to see other manifestations and incarnations of God present within different contexts of oppression.

In summary, when looking back over my week at Oaxtepec, it is best characterized as a continual challenge from different social, political, and cultural situations of oppression. EATWOT members were challenged to find ways of listening to and sharing with each other, as well as ways of developing theologies which have liberating significance for the poor and oppressed outside of our own context. Moreover, as I look to EATWOT's future and my continued participation in it as a black American woman, it is my hope that EATWOT will offer a glimpse of God's reign, not just because it represents a community of people committed to the poor and powerless, but because it represents a community liberated from its own demons of oppression. Just as our theology should not fall short of its commitment to God's liberating reign, neither should the organization under which we come to dialogue fall short of such commitment.

NOTES

1. The publications that I am referring to are: Sergio Torres and Virginia Fabella, eds., *The Emergent Gospel* (Maryknoll, N.Y.: Orbis Books, 1977); K. Appiah-Kubi and

S. Torres, eds., *African Theology en Route* (Maryknoll, N.Y.: Orbis Books, 1979); V. Fabella, ed., *Asia's Struggle for Full Humanity* (Maryknoll, N.Y.: Orbis Books, 1980); Sergio Torres and John Eagleson, eds., *The Challenge of Basic Christian Communities* (Maryknoll, N.Y.: Orbis Books, 1981); Virginia Fabella and Sergio Torres, eds., *Irruption of the Third World* (Maryknoll, N.Y.: Orbis Books, 1983).

2. J. Cone provides a good history of U.S. minorities' relationship to EATWOT with special attention being paid to the relationship between North American blacks and Latin Americans in "From Geneva to São Paulo: A Dialogue between Black Theology and Latin American Liberation Theology," in Torres and Eagleson, *The Challenge of Basic Christian Communities*, 265–81; reprinted above as Document 29.

3. Sojourner Truth, "Ain't I A Woman" (1851), in Miriam Schneir, ed., *Feminism: The Essential Historical Writings* (New York: Vintage Books, 1972), 95.

32

COMMON THEMES: BLACK THEOLOGY
AND MINJUNG THEOLOGY

J. Deotis Roberts

We will explore some common themes in two theological traditions in what may generally be designated as "liberation theologies." To so identify them may be confusing, but Latin American liberation theology cannot be considered as normative for this worldwide movement, except in a representative sense. It would appear that black theology has more in common with Minjung theology than it has with some other options in liberation theology, such as the Latin American program.

Black theology itself is not monolithic. Black theology is based upon the black religious experience, culture, and church tradition. It is a unity in diversity. Black theologians differ in the manner in which they conceive a common tradition, and their intellectual and spiritual journeys are varied. For example, Howard Thurman and Martin Luther King, Jr., are both black theologians who did their work out of the heritage lifted up by the latest group of so-called black theologians. While much of the latter thought is based upon "a political model," some of the earlier work was *ethical* but *cultural* as well. Black theology should be broadly conceived, including a strong emphasis upon history and culture, without toning down the essential liberation thrust.

This more comprehensive view, which balances cultural and political interests, has the advantage of a strong outreach in reference to both African and Asian theological development. For example, the political model relates directly to the South African situation, but as John Mbiti reminds us, it does not have the same strong affinity with most of Africa which is postcolonial. A cultural affinity does exist with all of Africa, however, yet this does not get adequate

J. Deotis Roberts is Distinguished Professor of Philosophical Theology at Eastern Baptist Theological Seminary, Philadelphia, Pennsylvania. This essay was published in J. Deotis Roberts, *Black Theology in Dialogue* (Philadelphia: Westminster Press, 1987) and is reprinted with permission.

attention in all black theology programs. Here we will use this more comprehensive view which will provide a more serious response to Minjung theology.

Reflection on Roots

Let us consider the similarities in history and culture that inform black theology and Minjung theology.

The situation giving rise to black theology has been given serious attention in the United States by several religious and secular scholars for almost twenty years. It is not necessary to chronicle this history here. A brief review is all that we will attempt.

Black theology arose out of an upsurge of black consciousness and Black Power in the late 1960s. It was a combined search for cultural roots and the power or means of liberation from racist oppression. It continued "the stride toward freedom" of the Martin Luther King, Jr., project. The new movement had both continuity and discontinuity with the work of King. In fact, it was the culmination of more than three centuries of struggle.

A similar foundation can be laid for the emergence of Minjung theology in the Korean setting. Korea has been caught between the great Asian powers for many centuries. It has been in the crossfire of conflicts between such powers as Russia, China, and Japan. This has led to much suffering on the part of the Korean people. In more recent times, Korea was a colony of Japan; then, following World War II, it was divided into North Korea and South Korea. The invasion of South Korea by Communist North Korea led to a tragic war, involving the United States as well as other nations. In the period since that tragedy, South Korea has witnessed several oppressive governments. Even today it is in a real sense a security state, with frequent infringements upon human rights. The masses of Korean people have been victimized by these crucial historical realities. They have had to search for meaning and seek survival under these repressive circumstances.

This history of suffering has run parallel with the Christian missionary movement. First the Roman Catholic Church established itself in Korea. This was followed by the Protestant missionary effort which has been present in Korea for about a century. Because of the Korean experience of so much mass suffering from political oppression, the gospel took on a prophetic as well as a priestly interpretation from its introduction in Korea. This seems especially true of Protestant missions.

Christian efforts therefore, in both the Korean and the black theological developments, have non-Western foundations. Blacks are African-Americans. Black theology affirms African roots. Minjung theology is built upon pre-Christian religious, ethical, and cultural factors. Apart from traditional African cultural and religious traits, it is not possible to have an in-depth understanding of black theology or the black church, family, or cultural tradition. Confucianism, Buddhism, Shamanism, and other elements are likewise essential to the Korean context. These are related to the development of Minjung theology.

Finally, there is a holism in the African and Asian worldviews that may account for a real affinity between blacks and Koreans in their way of developing theological thought. For example, in both cases there is a ready acceptance of the exodus paradigm in doing theology.

Response to Oppression: People as Subjects of History

One of the most difficult actions for a people victimized by situations of oppression is to find a constructive nonviolent response and resistance. It is easier to resort to fatalism or violent revolution than it is to formulate a plan for massive resistance against structural evil through nonviolent means. This is why the work of Martin Luther King, Jr., has such worldwide significance. Even though the method was introduced by Gandhi, it was given its classic expression in the Christian love ethic by King.

The need for an active response to oppression has been underscored by David Shanon, a black biblical scholar and educator. He strongly emphasized the need for African-Americans to become "subjects" rather than "objects" of history. Persons who have been victimized and handicapped by a long history of oppression, whether blacks, Hispanics, native Americans, women, or the aged, will be defeated by circumstances unless they take their destinies into their own hands. While this expectation is difficult when one has suffered a depletion of material resources and psychological resources as well, it does seem to be an essential posture for the underclasses in American society.

Some blacks have resigned themselves to what they consider the fate of alienation and suffering. Rampant unemployment had led to alcohol and drug abuse and all types of personal and familial tragedies. Others have turned to the solace of religion. Emotional and otherworldly aspects of religion have provided compensation for those who are denied the fulfillment of life here and now. On the other hand, from the resources of religion there have emerged advocates of social justice who have given black people the courage to claim their dignity and struggle for freedom in spite of the hopelessness of the real world in which they live. Religious faith can provide "resources of grace" that enable people who are by circumstances "objects" of history the means to become "subjects" of history. This is in essence what the "exodus" theme in black religious history is all about.

This concern to become subjects rather than objects of history has been evident in many parts of the world. It was especially prevalent in countries moving from colonialism into periods of nationalism, development, and liberation. The writings of Frantz Fanon are noteworthy in this regard. Paulo Freire's writings on consciousness-raising have been celebrated not only in Latin America but worldwide. A people who internalize their desire to be free are not easily enslaved. A former GI who fought in Vietnam reflected upon his experience. He observed that from the first engagement with the Viet Cong, he knew they were likely to win the war because of their determination. They were programmed psychologically and ideologically not to be defeated. When a people change from being objects of history to subjects of their history, they become a force to reckon with. Then they are motivated from within and are prepared to confront whatever odds they must face in the quest for liberation.

Like black Americans, the Korean people compare their experience with that of the Israelites of the Bible. So much of their history seems to parallel that of the people of the Old Testament. Korea has been the battleground of the great nations of the Far East. Its people have suffered because of power struggles between the great nations. The theme of the Exodus and the message of the prophets of social justice help to define their reality. They see God as acting in their history as in the Old Testament period.

In this regard there is a similarity between the experience of African-Americans and Koreans in the manner in which they have appropriated the message of the Bible as they have understood their experience. In both cases the leadership style of Moses and the theme of the Exodus have been freighted with great meaning of freedom from oppression. The slave songs, especially the spirituals, and Korean music, dance, and drama have taken up this message in a powerful way.

The Meaning of the Cross

Because of the common experience of suffering, black theology and Minjung theology focus strongly upon the meaning of suffering. Theodicy is a controlling category. The problem of structural evil and the consequence of mass suffering are inescapable. This reality can be met with resignation as well as skepticism or it can be translated into a source of strength.

Recent black theologians as well as Minjung theologians, upon contextualizing the experience of suffering, have elected to engage it. They not only accept it as a given but they seek to transmute it into a source of moral and spiritual resistance to evil. They do not attempt this out of defiance as some existentialists such as Albert Camus have done. Neither do they accept the "humano-centric" approach of William Jones in *Is God a White Racist?* But they adopt a christocentric model, for the most part. In both cases the Jesus of history is also the Christ of faith.

In developing an approach to evil and suffering, they are moved to reexamine their Christology. Minjung theologians have examined the message of Jesus to the poor. They have sought a deep understanding of the Jesus of history and the secular meaning of the gospel. Bonhoeffer's writings have been very helpful as a backdrop to much reflection on the life of Jesus and the meaning of his cross.

Concurrently, black theologians have sought after the Jesus of the "disinherited." The adoption of the symbol of the "Black Messiah" has surfaced as a way of dealing with the self-identity crisis and the situation of racism and poverty. There has been an examination of traditional christological models, but with a view to how these may speak more forcefully to the reality of black suffering based on the experience of continuous oppression. Again this has led to a serious engagement with the cross of Christ.

In black and Minjung theological programs there is a reluctance to dwell upon the regal or kingly role of Jesus. The stress upon the resurrection does not overshadow the weight given to the cross of Christ. The lordship of Jesus so easily undergirds a situation of domination of the weak by the powerful. Emphasis upon the resurrection easily points to otherworldliness and triumphalism to the disadvantage of any oppressed group. In black and Minjung theologies the emphasis upon Jesus' cross leads to a balanced view of the resurrection. There is no resurrection without a cross. The regal role of Jesus is brought into a dynamic relationship with his priestly and prophetic ministry.

A christological model that is either otherworldly or only regal is generally acceptable to a repressive order. It does not challenge the established order which is in violation of human rights for the mass of humanity suffering from oppression such as poverty and racism. It does not speak redemptively to the underclass. The tendency, therefore, is for the privileged class to enthrone a regal Christ as the sanctifier of the status quo. Those who see Christ as the liberator are likely to be subject to denunciation and persecution by those in power. This is why black as well as Minjung theologians have chosen a different dimension of Christology in which the cross is central. But the cross is not a symbol of escape; rather, it is a symbol of engagement with evil and suffering. Christ's victorious resurrection is seen in relation to the cross as its sequel and ultimate vindication.

Conclusion

This brief excursion into comparative theology is highly suggestive of the rich possibilities toward human understanding that could result from vigorous activity on this theological frontier. In a comparison of black and Minjung theologies we note important differences, but there are significant similarities between them.

There are a cluster of factors in both backgrounds that are similar and that result in holistic ethicoreligious outlook. When we translate this into biblical terms, it leads to a view that blends social justice concerns with the healing dimensions of the gospel. In both instances the Exodus theme points to the message of the prophets of the Old Testament who denounced oppression and advocated justice as well as mercy. Again, both black and Minjung theologies seek to find the historical Jesus and the secular meaning of the gospel for human liberation. This in no way dilutes the meaning and power associated with the cross-resurrection event. The Christ of faith is Lord, but he is also liberator. In these and other ways black and Minjung theologies may open new doors to crosscultural understanding and the ecumenical dialogue and mission of the church of Jesus Christ.

33

BLACK THEOLOGY OF LIBERATION AS CRITIQUE OF CAPITALIST CIVILIZATION

Cornel West

In this essay my basic aim is to put forward a conception of black theology of liberation which is simultaneously anchored in the prophetic Christian tradition and the progressive Marxist tradition.

My strategy shall be as follows: First, I shall examine briefly the evolution of the black prophetic consciousness in the liberation. It is my argument that a black theology and theology of liberation as a critique of capitalist civilization, is the present expression of this prophetic consciousness in our troubled times. Second, I will attempt to explain what I mean by the vague phrase "critique of capitalist civilization." Third, I shall probe the theological dimension of my project and suggest that the adjective "black"—viewed symbolically and literally—describes a crucial aspect of this dimension owing to the unique role and particular plight of black people in the emergence, duration and decline of capitalist civilization.

In order to grasp more fully the evolution of the prophetic stream in the black Christian tradition (which I assume here to be linked to the prophetic Christian tradition), it is important to make a distinction between the activity of black theological reflection and the codification of this activity in highly visible and widely accessible books and articles. The activity of black theological reflection began the moment African slaves, laboring in sweltering heat on plantations owned and ruled by primarily white Christians, tried to make sense of their lives and understand their situation of servitude in light of biblical texts, Protestant hymns and Christian testimonies.[1] This activity of black theological

Cornel West is professor of religion and director of Afro-American studies at Princeton University. He is also author of the widely read *Prophesy Deliverance!* (1982). First delivered in lectures at the Seminario Bíblico Latinamericano, August 19, 21, and 26, 1980, San José, Costa Rica, this essay was published in the *Journal of the Interdenominational Theological Center* 10 (Fall 1982-Spring 1983) and is reprinted with permission.

reflection is inseparable from the African (or black) Christian Community of believers, the Black Church. The Black Church, a mere rubric which designates the set of black Christian communities of various denominations (primarily those of the left wing of the Reformation, e.g. Baptist, Methodist, Pentecostal) came into being when African slaves decided, often at the risk of life and limb, to make "Jesus their choice" and to share with each other their common Christian sense of purpose and similar Christian understanding of their circumstances. Similar to the traditions of other Christian communities, this sharing contained many streams, some more prophetic than others. The evolution of this multiplicity of streams constitutes the rich diversity within the history of the activity of black theological reflection. The recent highly visible and widely accessible codification of the activity of black theological reflection is part and parcel of the Christian tradition which ushers forth from the Black Church.[2] This holds for both the prophetic and priestly streams in black theological reflection and action.

In this essay I shall focus only on the prophetic stream in the black Christian tradition. I suggest that this prophetic stream has passed through four stages and is presently entering a fifth stage. These stages are characterized by particular theological responses to the perceived source of oppression most directly and immediately impinging upon black people.

The **first stage** can be viewed roughly as: **Black Theology of Liberation As Critique of Slavery**. This stage, lasting approximately from the midseventeenth century to 1863, consisted of black prophetic Christian viewpoints and actions grounded in the black slave experience and critical of the institution of slavery. Many petitions of black Christians during the first two centuries of slavery express this prophetic viewpoint. For example, black Christian slaves wrote in 1779 to the General Assembly of Connecticut:

> we perceive by our own reflection, that we are endowed with the same Faculties with our masters, and there is nothing that leads us to a Belief, or Suspicion, that we are any more obliged to serve them, than they us, and the more we Consider of this matter, the more we are Convinced of our right (by the laws of Nature and by the whole Tenor of the Christian Religion, so far as we have been taught) to be free. . . .[3]

The prophetic Christian view that the gospel stands unequivocally opposed to slavery led, in some cases, to unsuccessful slave revolts spearheaded by black Christians. In 1800 Gabriel Prosser, a young Christian, derived his self-understanding of being the divinely elected deliverer of black people from the Samson story of the Old Testament. Subsequently he engaged in the first thoroughly planned and overtly revolutionary attempt to liberate black people from slavery. This attempt involved, according to conservative estimates, over six thousand black Christians and non-Christians.[4] Like most other slave insurrectionists, young Gabriel was executed. The famous examples and executions of Denmark Vesey (leader of a slave insurrection in 1822) and Nat Turner (leader of a slave insurrection in 1831) also exemplify the cost black prophetic Christians were willing to pay in their Christian-inspired fight for liberation.

The major codified theological expression during this stage is found in David Walker's "appeal to the colored citizens of the world," which appeared in 1829. Walker's appeal, as it came to be known, is one of the most powerful theological critiques of slavery to emanate from the black Christian tradition. Gayraud Wilmore, a noted black Christian social ethicist and historian, goes as far as to state:

> Walker's appeal is steeped in Biblical language and prophecy. It is certainly one of the most remarkable religious documents of the Protestant era, rivaling in its righteous indignation and Christian radicalism Luther's "Open Letter to the Christian Nobility of the German Nation," published in Wittenberg in 1520.[5]

In his theological antislavery text, Walker proclaims that slavery,

> is ten thousand times more injurious to that country than all the other evils put together; and which will be the final overthrow of its government, unless something is very speedily done: for their cup is nearly full. — perhaps they will laugh at or make light of this; but I tell you Americans! that unless you speedily alter your course, you and your Country are gone! For God Almighty will tear up the very face of the earth![6]

The **second stage** can be viewed as: **Black Theology of Liberation As Critique of Institutional Racism.** This stage, which occupied a little over a century (1864-1969), found black prophetic Christians principally focussing attention on the racist institutional structures in the United States which rendered the vast majority of black people politically powerless (deprived of the right to vote or participate in governmental affairs), economically exploited (in dependent positions as sharecroppers or unskilled jobs) and socially degraded (separate, segregated, unequal eating and recreational facilities, housing, education, transportation and police protection). This period contains the vicious lynching of thousands of black people alongside the historic refusal of President Woodrow Wilson to sign an antilynching law in 1916; and the migration of millions of job-hunting black people into rat-infested dilapidated ghettoes in the urban North which triggered the historic race riots of 1919, 1943, 1964, 1967, and 1968.

It is no accident that many of the salient black prophetic Christian leaders — such as Bishop Henry McNeal Turner and Marcus Garvey — favored during this stage a return of black people to Africa. They were led to this viewpoint from their theological critiques of institutional racism in the United States. They held that this institutional racism so deeply pervaded and permeated U. S. society that only emigration to the black homeland could rid black people of their immediate oppression.

The most effective Christian during this stage was, of course, Martin Luther King, Jr. Upon the strength of the black prophetic church and liberal white allies, he mobilized and organized black and white people against blatant institutional racism and waged a successful struggle for black civil rights—integrated transportation, eating and recreational facilities, and most importantly, the right to vote. The tragic murder of King in 1968 triggered not only some of the worst race riots the United States has ever witnessed, including the National Guard protecting the White House for the first time since the Civil War. King's death, along with the Black Power movement led by Stokely Carmichael and H. Rap Brown, also precipitated a great wave of the academic expression of black theological reflection.

Besides pioneer works by Benjamin Mays, Howard Thurman, George Kelsey and a few others, black prophetic Christians had not systematically codified their viewpoints.[7] But with the publication of Albert Cleage's *The Black Messiah* (1968) and James Cone's *Black Theology and Black Power* (1969) a **third stage** commenced: **Black Theology of Liberation as Critique of White North American Theology.** In this stage, which lasted less than a decade (1969–1977), we witnessed the first full-fledged academic expression of liberation theology in general and black theology of liberation in particular in the United States. James Cone's second book, *A Black Theology of Liberation* (1970), deepened a theological discourse in which many black theologians played a crucial role, including figures such as Cecil Cone (James Cone's brother), Major Jones, William Jones, Charles Long, J. Deotis Roberts, Joseph Washington, Leon Watts, Preston Williams and Gayraud Wilmore.[8]

This particular stage was an intellectually creative one—partly in response to the spontaneous rebellion of black people in the streets, the more disciplined political praxis of Black Power groups and the paralysis of most white North American theologians. Yet the conception of black theology was, in retrospect, understandably narrow: It focused principally on the failings of white North American theology, especially its silence on racial justice and the white racism within mainstream establishment churches and religious agencies. In response to this criticism, echoed partially by Cecil Cone, Charles Long and Gayraud Wilmore, James Cone attempted in his next two books—*The Spirituals and the Blues* (1972) and *God of the Oppressed* (1975)—to broaden his focus by delving into black cultural sources for theological reflection, such as the spirituals, blues, folktales, sermons and stories. As Cone notes:

> . . . I have learned much from this discussion on Black religion and Black Theology, because there is a basic truth in the critiques of Long, Cone and Wilmore . . . If the struggle of the victims is the only conclusion for the development of a genuine Christian theology, then should not theology itself reflect in its speech the language of the people about whom it claims to speak? This is the critical issue. When this assumption is applied to Black Theology, I think that Black religion or the Black relig-

ious experience must become one of the important ingredients in the development of a Black Theology.[9]

The **fourth stage** — and the stage black prophetic theologians are presently transcending — can be viewed as: **Black Theology of Liberation as Critique of United States Capitalism.** With the appearance of the Black Theology Project's (which is part of a progressive interethnic, interracial, interdenominational Christian organization called, Theology in the Americas) "Message to the Black Church and Community" and James Cone's essay "Black Theology and the Black Church: Where Do We Go from Here" — both papers presented at a Black Theology Conference in Atlanta, Georgia, 1977 — black theological reflection focused on United States capitalism as a major enemy of black people. In the section entitled "The Roots of the Crisis," the Black Theology Project collectively stated:

> The issue for all of us is survival. The root problem is human sinfulness which nurtures monopolistic capitalism, aided by racism and abetted by sexism.
>
> Our crisis is spiritual, material and moral. Black people seem unable to effectively counter disruptive forces that undermine our quality of life. We seem unable to collectively define our situation, discover the nature of our problems, and develop sustained coalitions that can resolve our dilemmas.
>
> Exploitative, profit-oriented capitalism is a way of ordering life fundamentally alien to human value in general and to black humanity in particular. Racism and capitalism have set the stage for despoliation of natural and human resources all around the world. Yet those who seriously challenge these systems are often effectively silenced. We view racism as criminality and yet we are called freaks. The roots of our crisis are in social, economic, media and political power systems that prevent us from managing the reality of our everyday lives.
>
> It is this intolerable, alien order that has driven us to Atlanta seeking a word from the Lord out of the wellsprings of black theological tradition.[10]

And in his essay, Cone explicitly notes,

> There is little in our theological expressions and church practice that rejects American capitalism or recognizes its oppressive character in third world countries. The time has come for us to move beyond institutional survival in a capitalistic and racist society and begin to take more seriously our dreams about a new heaven and a new earth. Does this dream include capitalism or is it a radically new way of life more consistent with African socialism as expressed in the *Arusha Declaration* in Tanzania?[11]

This focus was deepened and sharpened by two of my own essays—"Black Theology and Marxist Thought" (1979) and "Black Theology and Socialist Thought" (1980)—which, in a sense, initiated a dialogue between black prophetic theologians and progressive Marxist thinkers, as well as practicing socialists and communists.[12] In these essays, black theologians are primarily criticized for their lack of a clear-cut social theory which impedes them from putting forward a precise idea of what constitutes socioeconomic and political liberation. I harshly suggest that without some version of a Marxist social theory their conception of socioeconomic and political liberation,

> ... roughly equates liberation with American middle-class status, leaving the unequal distribution of wealth relatively untouched and the capitalist system of production, along with its imperialist ventures, intact. Liberation would consist of including black people within the mainstream of liberal capitalist America. If this is the social vision of black theologians, they should drop the meretricious and flamboyant term "liberation" and adopt the more accurate and sober word "inclusion."[13]

I also praise black theologians (and subsequently criticize vulgar Marxists) for stressing the positive role culture and religion can play in the struggle for liberation and noting the complexity of racial oppression.

> ... Black theologians recognize that cultural and religious attitudes, values, and sensibilities have a life and logic of their own, not fully accountable in terms of class analysis. Subsequently, racist practices are not reducible to a mere clever and successful strategy of divide-and-conquer promoted by the ruling class to prevent proletarian unity. Rather, racism is an integral element within the very fabric of American culture and society. It is embedded in the country's first collective self-definition; enunciated in its subsequent laws; and imbued in its dominant way of life.[14]

Based on the works of two major Marxist theorists of culture, Antonio Gramsci and Raymond Williams, I try to show how the black prophetic, religious tradition can become a more counterhegemonic, anticapitalist force in the United States. This move toward a neo-Marxist theory and praxis of culture and religion is based on the fundamental claim that,

> a refusal to come to terms with class inequality results in a highly limited view of black enhancement.[15]

James Cone's essay, "The Black Church and Marxism: What Do They Have To Say To Each Other?" pursues this crucial dialogue.[16]

Yet it seems to me, the prevailing conception of black theology of liberation remains inadequate. I believe that a new conception of black theology of liberation is needed which preserves the positive content of its earlier historical stages, overcomes its earlier (and inevitable) blindness and makes explicit its present challenges. I view the positive content of the earlier conceptions of black theology of liberation as follows:

1) The theological claim (or faith-claim) that God sides with the oppressed and acts on their behalf.
2) The idea that religion of the oppressed can either be an opiate or a source of struggle for liberation.
3) The idea that white racism is a cancer at the core of an exploitative capitalist U.S. society.

I understand the limitations and shortcomings of earlier conceptions of black theology of liberation to be:

1) Its absence of a systemic social analysis, which has prevented black theologians from coming to terms with the relationships between racism, sexism, class exploitation and imperialist oppression.
2) Its lack of a social vision, political program and concrete praxis which defines and facilitates socioeconomic and political liberation.
3) Its tendency to downplay existential issues such as death, disease, dread, despair and disappointment which are related to yet not identical with suffering caused by oppressive structures.

I claim that the present challenge to black theologians is to put forward an understanding of the Christian gospel in light of present circumstances which takes into account the complex ways in which racism (especially, white racism) and sexism (especially, male sexism) are integral to the class exploitative capitalist system of production as well as its repressive imperialist tentacles abroad; and to keep in view the crucial existential issues of death, disease, despair, dread and disappointment that each and every individual must face within the context of these present circumstances. I believe this theological perspective requires a move into a **fifth stage: Black Theology of Liberation as Critique of Capitalist Civilization.** In short, I think that black theological reflection and action must simultaneously become more familiar with and rooted in the progressive Marxist tradition, with its staunch anticapitalist, antiimperialist, antiracist, antisexist stance and its creative socialist outlook; and more anchored in its own proto-Kierkegaardian viewpoint, namely, its proper concern with the existential issues facing individuals.

In this section I will try to explain what I mean by the vague phrase "critique of capitalist civilization." I shall begin by defining what I mean by "critique." First, I understand this term in a Marxian way; that is, critique is not simply moral criticism of a state of affairs. Rather, critique is a theoretical praxis which

1) presupposes a sophisticated understanding of the internal dynamics or power relations of a society or civilization. This understanding requires

a social theory whose aim is to demystify present ideological distortions or misreadings of society, to bring to light who possesses power and wealth, why they do, how they acquire, sustain and enlarge it and why the poor have so little.

2) is integrally linked with a praxis of faith or political movement which is capable in the near future of fundamentally transforming the present order.

3) is capable of ushering forth a new order, of organizing, administering and governing a more humane social order.

Therefore the crucial characteristics of an acceptable and appropriate critique are moral sensitivity to the plight of the exploited and oppressed; high-level social analysis of the sources of exploitation and oppression; objective possibility of weakening the present order; and praxis of faith or political movement with organization, power and social vision, with leaders of impeccable integrity.

Let us now look briefly at the capitalist system of production which undergirds what I call "capitalist civilization." Capitalism is an antidemocratic mode of socioeconomic organization in that it requires the removal of control of production from those engaged in production. Capitalism is a particular system of production in which capital accumulation for profit-maximization is achieved at the expense of excluding democratic participation (of those principally responsible for production) in investment decisions. Presently, capitalism is inseparable from imperialism in that the latter is an extension of capitalism across national borders and political boundaries. Imperialism is a system of capital accumulation for profit-maximization based on developed countries' acquisition of control over the land and means of production in less developed countries. This control is preserved and protected by the military and political resources of developed countries. Multinational corporations—the materialization of international capital—are the principal controllers of the land and means of production in less developed countries.

The antidemocratic character of capitalism is seen most clearly in its present imperialist manifestation. On the one hand, capital accumulation for profit-maximization requires that multinational corporations promote its products no matter how appropriate these products may be for the less developed countries; and the effect of the multinationals' stronghold on the local economy is to restrict local entrepreneurs to low-return routine kinds of production. On the other hand, the products promoted by multinationals (principally luxury consumer goods) find their market primarily among the elite groups in less developed countries.

This mode of capital accumulation contributes to antidemocratic conditions in two basic ways. First, it encourages the exclusion of producers—and casts the organizing efforts of workers in a negative light—since an increase in wages would threaten the attractiveness of a less developed country as a site for multinational corporate investment. Second, this mode of capital accumulation contributes to gross economic and class inequality since it ensures a market for multinational products geared principally to the affluent. This dialectic of capital accumulation and political exclusion often leads to military rule and abominable repression—under the guise of "development" or "democratic openings."[17]

Let us now look briefly at what I mean by "civilization." Civilization is often understood as an achieved condition or way of life characterized by refinement and order.[18] I understand "civilization" in my phrase "capitalist civilization" as those self-images and self-identities, values and sensibilities, institutions and associations, ways of life and ways of struggles which are shaped and molded by the four major kinds of oppression in our time: imperialist oppression, class exploitation, racial and sexual oppression. The concrete consequences of these forms of oppression are not only poverty, disease, lack of self-esteem and despair but also the suppression of individuality (or self-realization within community). Ironically, the ethos of rapacious individualism in capitalist civilization prohibits the flowering of individuality.[19]

Capitalist civilization is circumscribed primarily by the two major modern historical events and processes: the Industrial Revolution and bourgeois political revolutions. These two epoch-making historical processes reinforced the four major types of oppression—and these kinds of oppression persist in so-called "postindustrial" capitalist societies. Let us look briefly at both the Industrial Revolution and the American bourgeois political "revolution" to see why this is so.

The Industrial Revolution can be defined as "the triumph of capitalist industry which results in the creation of a mechanized production unit which yields such vast quantities of goods and products and at such rapidly diminishing cost as to be no longer dependent on existing demand, but to create its own market."[20] The Industrial Revolution, as is well known, emerged and escalated in the late eighteenth century in Britain. Britain was the fertile soil for this flowering, not because of its scientific advancement or technological superiority— France and Germany were far ahead in these areas—but rather owing to its rapid and propitious dissolution of the feudal British peasantry and the strong commitment of its government to economic development. Britain had, by various means (e.g. Enclosure Acts, etc.) transformed its old collective economy of the feudal village into a capitalist mode of agricultural production, that is, into a few profit-oriented landlords and a moderate number of tenant-farmers who employed a large number of landless hired laborers. This capitalist mode of agricultural production was geared primarily to feed a rising non-agricultural, urbanized population and to yield a surplus for the accumulation of capital to be used for further industrialized differentiation in the economy. Primarily due to overseas colonial trade and the cheapest labor available—namely, African slaves in the diaspora—the cotton industry was the first major industry to be revolutionized. The cotton industry, whose raw materials were literally picked by the hands of African slaves, was the first to secure a large export market and thereby insure rapid expansion. It also was the first major industry to establish mass production, as witnessed in the famous Lancashire mills, the very symbols of the first stages of the Industrial Revolution. In short, the cotton industry was the modus operandi of the early stages of the Industrial Revolution, the heart of Britain's economy. As Eric Hobsbawm has noted,

> Cotton manufacturers formed between 40 and 50 percent of the annual declared value of all British exports between 1816 and 1848. If cotton flourished, the economy flourished, if it slumped, so did the economy.[21]

This brief yet important illustration of the first major industry to be revolutionized displays the central presence of the four types of oppression mentioned earlier. Forms of class exploitation occurred in both the cotton plantations in the Americas and in the mines in Britain; imperialist oppression took place in Britain's control of territory, resources and people in the Americas; racism provided the chief ideological justification for the use of Africans as slaves in the Americas; and sexism was employed to defend the abuse of women on both the plantations in the Americas and within the mills in Britain.

This crude example can serve as a kind of microcosm of the kind and associations, ways of life and ways of struggle required and reinforced by the capitalist system of production. Already we can see the contours which partially shape and mold capitalist civilization: how the profit-maximizing activity of a few is integrally linked to the dehumanization of the many; the collapse of organic communities and the growth of impersonal bureaucratic control; the prohibition of individual norms of possessive individualism; the richness and plurality of cultures discouraged in lieu of a shoddy, homogenizing cosmopolitanism. And most importantly, the early stages of the Industrial Revolution embody and prefigure, promote and encourage the idea of white supremacy and male supremacy. In short, from its emergence through its duration to its decline, capitalist civilization remains racist and sexist at its core and based upon class exploitation and imperialist oppression.

The four major types of oppression also set the framework for our view of the American bourgeois political "revolution." This event, along with the crucial French Revolution, provided the emerging capitalist civilization with its liberal political language, its rhetorical self-understanding. The grand ideals of liberty and equality, the principles of procedural justice and the notion of participatory democracy were — and remain — restricted and restrained by the cancers of class exploitation, imperialistic oppression, racism and sexism. Even the most cherished idea of bourgeois political revolutions — namely, that of the nation-state or nationalism — is opposed by the profit-making activity of firms (and later corporations) of capitalist civilization which have more loyalty to self-aggrandizement than allegiance to their native territories. And, of course, at its inception, the United States government excluded African (or fifth generation black natives) from the human race, all women from participation in government (as well as propertyless men) and had its eyes on further territorial expansion and imperialist dominion over indigenous and Mexican people.

In this last section, I will present the theological dimension of my critique of capitalist civilization and suggest that the adjective "black" describes a crucial aspect of this dimension owing to the peculiar role and particular plight of black people in the emergence, duration and decline of capitalist civilization by putting forward three crucial theological commitments which inform my critique.

1) my commitment to a Christian notion of the self-realization of each and every individual within community.
2) my commitment to a Christian notion of original sin.
3) my commitment to an understanding of the Christian gospel as inescapable penultimate tragedy and the persistent hope for ultimate triumph.

I shall begin with my first commitment. I believe that the basic ideational contribution of Christianity to the world — and its fundamental moral message — is that each and every person, regardless of class, country, caste, race or sex should have the opportunity to fulfill his or her capacity or potentiality. I shall call this radical egalitarian idea: the Christian principle of the self-realization of human individuality within community.[22] The notion of a transcendent, Wholly Other god before whom all men and women are equal endows the well-being and salvation of each person with equal value and significance. Needless to say, the Christian principle of self-realization of human individuality within community has been, in many instances, narrowed and distorted, for example, the salvation of souls (individuality) in heaven (community). This narrowing and distorting has never been accepted by the prophetic elements in Christian communities down through the centuries. Instead, this prophetic tradition has insisted that socioeconomic well-being as well as existential salvation of persons has equal value and significance in the eyes of God. In fact, I suggest that a major reason Marxist analysis and praxis is attractive to many committed prophetic Christians is that the principle of self-realization within community is deeply embedded in Marx's own writings.[23] Similar to the history of Christianity, the history of Marxism exemplifies, in many instances, the narrowing and distorting of this principle in Marx, for example, the socioeconomic well-being of persons regimented by bureaucratic control.

It is crucial to point out that this narrowing and distorting has never been accepted by the progressive elements in Marxist communities and societies down through the decades. Instead, this progressive tradition has insisted that political liberties and cultural diversity as well as socioeconomic well-being are indispensable for any acceptable community or desirable society. In short, participatory democracy is imperative for a socialist regime.

My critique of capitalist civilization is based, theologically and morally, on the Christian principle of the self-realization of human individuality within community. My understanding of this principle rests upon the prophetic Christian tradition and the progressive Marxist tradition. This principle, in my judgment, unequivocally condemns class exploitation, imperialist oppression, political liberties, cultural diversity and existential salvation of persons.

My second theological commitment is to a Christian notion of original sin. In fact, my support for a socialist civilization, in which the socioeconomic well-being, political liberties, cultural diversity and existential salvation (if chosen) of persons is promoted, is grounded in my deep belief in a Christian notion of original sin. My understanding of this notion is that human beings in any society, culture or community have basic drives and impulses characterized by a will to survive and live which usually takes the form of human proclivities toward selfish, self-centered behavior. I believe human beings can change their conditions and change themselves, but neither perfect their conditions nor perfect themselves. Therefore my viewpoint precludes the possibility of human perfection and hence human utopias. Instead, it claims that conditions and circumstances can always be improved, that persons, communities, societies and civilizations can always be better than they are. Therefore, I hold that human selfishness and self-centeredness must be expected and entertained, hence discouraged and restrained, rather than naively believed to be eliminable and replaced, hence forgotten and disregarded.

My acceptance of this Christian notion of original sin leads me to give the notion of human accountability to other persons the high priority in my social vision. People and institutions must be accountable to the people they purport to serve. This accountability occurs primarily when people have a voice in and control over the people and institutions which serve them. This is why I believe that peoples' participation in the decision-making processes within institutions that regulate and govern their lives is essential for the actualization of the Christian principle of self-realization within community. This principle, along with my acceptance of a Christian notion of original sin, renders genuine democratic participation—in the spheres of the production and distribution of goods and services, governmental affairs and cultural activities—indispensable for socialist civilization.

It is worth noting that the formal idea of human accountability to other persons is found in capitalist civilization. This idea is articulated by the liberal vision within capitalist civilization. This vision was—and is—the grandest vision capitalist civilization has to offer. But it is limited to the sphere of governmental affairs (in an abstract way), corrupted by the institutionalization and legitimation of the ideas of white supremacy and male supremacy and rendered nearly obsolete by unaccountable economic power principally in the form of unaccountable multinational corporations.

My third theological commitment is to an understanding of the Christian gospel as inescapable penultimate tragedy and the persistent hope for ultimate triumph. I believe that any social vision, political praxis or existential concern must take seriously the tragic aspects of our fallen, finite conditions and circumstances. To take seriously the tragic aspects of being human means to acknowledge the inevitable gap between human aims and human accomplishments, between human aspirations and human achievements. The tragic aspects of being human should not be taken seriously in solely an intellectual way, for such a response leads to an ironic skepticism, cynicism and narcissistic detachment from the lives and plight of others. Instead, the encounter with the tragic aspects of human life must be not simply intellectual but existential — of putting one's whole self in the midst of struggle, responsibility, commitment and engagement.

The inescapable realities of human death, disease, despair, dread and disappointment must be faced with courage and hope. This also holds for the intense class struggles at the heart of capitalist civilization. The acceptance of a Christian notion of original sin means that these class struggles will more than likely continue to (or ultimately) take the forms of principled or unprincipled armed struggle. In this sense, human beings are condemned to life-and-death struggles between good and evil, forces of liberation and forces of oppression, with the hope for betterment of the present. And no matter how complex the world is or intricate the situation may be, one must choose sides. For Christians, this choice is grounded theologically in the understanding of the gospel and guided practically by our understanding of our circumstances. As a Christian, my choice is to side with the poor, oppressed, exploited and degraded, with the working classes and underclasses of capitalist civilization. This choice is grounded theologically in the Christian principle of the self-realization of human individuality within community. I understand this principle in light of the prophetic Christian tradition. I view the circumstances of the working classes and underclasses of capitalist civilization in light of the most sophisticated Marxist analysis available and work for the creation of a socialist civilization, which should reflect the best of the prophetic Christian tradition and the progressive Marxist tradition.

I believe this socialist civilization will neither perfect human beings nor eliminate many of the tragic aspects of being human. But it will be much better than our deplorable, abominable capitalist civilization. I also believe that it is a historical possibility, not historical necessity, that this socialist civilization will be established. And given the most probable means of establishing it — namely, ultimately by some form of armed struggle — it may be unlikely that a socialist civilization, which reflects the best of both traditions, will ever be established. But for the committed prophetic Christian or progressive Marxist, it is a cause worth dying for.

This hope, for committed Christians, is grounded in the ultimate triumph of Jesus Christ. For committed Marxists, this hope rests upon the workings of the historical process. The distinctive identity of the prophetic Christian is that his or her hope — in the face of the tragic aspects of human life and against overwhelming odds in capitalist civilization — is founded on the paradoxical revelation of a transcendent God in historical clothing, who best exemplifies our humanity and provides for our fullest self-realization within community.

I suggest that the adjective "black" describe a crucial aspect of the theological dimension of my critique of capitalist civilization because the role and plight of black people in the emergence, duration and decline of capitalist civilization symbolize the underside of capitalist civilization—the working classes and underclass of this civilization.

Without denying, overlooking or minimizing the atrocious poverty and abominable oppression of other peoples, I believe that the concrete plight of black people best signifies the inhumanity at the core of capitalist civilization for three basic reasons. First, African Americans (a particular set of black people) are the most proletarianized and urbanized people in capitalist civilization. Over ninety-eight percent of African Americans are working class (or underclass) people and over ninety percent of African Americans live in capitalist metropolises. Their working conditions of filth, danger, speed-ups, harassments; living conditions of dilapidated, rat-infested, twenty-story projects, inadequate health care, education and police protection—in the midst of the most prosperous country in the history of the world, in the heart of the monster of capitalist civilization—symbolize the inhumanity at the core of this civilization.

Second, black people represent an exploited yet believing people, an oppressed yet Christianized people. The Black Church is the central institution in the black community and this is especially so for the black lower working class and underclass. This Black Church principally stands for a gospel which identifies Jesus Christ as the one who liberates people from death, disease, despair, dread and disappointment out of a strong sense of dignity and self-worth. In this sense, the plight of black people and their Christian-inspired fight against oppression serve as an appropriate symbol for prophetic Christians regarding the inhumanity of capitalistic civilization and the Christians' struggle against it.

Third, and this holds for black people wherever and whenever capitalist civilization has impinged upon their lives. Black people, I suggest, are unique among oppressed peoples in capitalist civilization in that they have not only suffered imperialist and class exploitation (and black women sexual oppression), but, also have had to endure racial oppression which takes the form of denying the basic humanity of black people, a continual and systematic denial of membership in the human family. The "authority" of this denial is unprecedented in capitalist civilization. It has been supported and promoted for over two centuries in "scientific" textbooks, the halls of higher learning (from Oxford to Harvard, the Sorbonne to the University of Berlin), the Royal Academies of Science, popular folklore, national constitutions, legal documents, encyclopedias, film, television, radio, and, we must not forget, in the pulpits of Christian churches. No other oppressed people in capitalist civilization have had their humanity attacked and assaulted to this extent. In this regard, the plight of black people symbolizes the very worst and most inhumane aspects of capitalist civilization.

Is it providential that the first major industry to be revolutionized, the cotton industry, and hence to establish one of the early pillars of capitalist civilization, was built primarily upon the blood, sweat and tears of black people? And that two centuries later, the plight of black people would not only symbolize the underside of this civilization, but that the adjective "black" would describe a crucial aspect of the theological dimension of a critique that seeks to undermine and promote the demise of this civilization—with a black triumph in South Africa more than likely hastening this demise? In the words of my black Baptist tradition, "God indeed works in strange and mysterious ways."

NOTES

1. For a full-length treatment of this neglected phenomenon, see Albert J. Raboteau, *Slave Religion* (New York: Oxford University Press, 1978).

2. It is important to note that black churches in the United States evolved as independent churches, separate from white control. Therefore black religious leadership and black theological reflection could arise autonomous (or at least, relatively so) from white censorship, as is not the case for black people in Catholic and Anglican churches in Latin America and Africa. It is no accident that Pentecostalism—the denomination which vigorously promotes the development of indigenous religious leadership free from the control of church bureaucracies—was founded by black Baptists, principally Rev. W. J. Seymour in Los Angeles, California in 1906. Pentecostalism is the only denomination of the Christian faith founded by black people and is one of the fastest-growing denominations in the world, especially among oppressed people.

3. Cited in Gayraud S. Wilmore, *Black Religion and Black Radicalism* (Garden City, N.Y.: Anchor Books/Doubleday, 1973), 49.

4. Ibid., 76.

5. Ibid., 53-54.

6. Ibid., 57.

7. Benjamin E. Mays, *The Negro's God* (New York, 1938). Howard Thurman, *Deep River and The Negro Spiritual Speaks of Life and Death*, single vol. (Richmond, Ind.: Friends United Press, 1975)—the first book was originally published in 1945, the second in 1947. Howard Thurman, *Jesus and the Disinherited* (Nashville: Abingdon, 1949). George D. Kelsey, *Racism and the Christian Understanding of Man* (New York, 1965).

8. Albert Cleage, *The Black Messiah* (New York: Seabury Press, 1968). James H. Cone, *Black Theology and Black Power* (New York, 1969). James Cone, *A Black Theology of Liberation* (Philadelphia, 1970). Cecil Cone, *The Identity Crisis in Black Theology* (Nashville, 1975). Major Jones, *Black Awareness* (Nashville, 1971). Major Jones, *Christian Ethics for Black Theology* (Nashville, 1971). William Jones, *Is God a White Racist?* (Garden City, 1973). Charles Long, "The Black Reality: Toward a Theology of Freedom," *Criterion* (Spring-Summer 1969), 2-7 and "Perspectives for a Study of Afro-American Religion in the U. S." *History of Religion* 2 (August 1977), 54-66. J. Deotis Roberts, *Liberation and Reconciliation Theology* (Philadelphia, 1974). Joseph Washington, *The Politics of God* (Boston, 1967). Joseph Washington, *Black Sects and Cults* (Garden City, 1972). Leon Watts, "Transcendence and Mystery in Black Theology," *IDOC International Documentation*, 71 (March-April 1976), 60-75. Preston Williams, "The Black Experience and Black Religion," *Theology Today*, 26 (October 1969), 246-261 and "James Cone and the Problem of a Black Ethic," *Harvard Theological Review*, 65 (October 1972), 483-494. Gayraud Wilmore, *Black Religion and Black Radicalism* (Garden City, 1973).

9. *Black Theology: A Documentary History, 1966-1979*, ed. Gayraud S. Wilmore and James H. Cone (Maryknoll, N.Y.: Orbis Books, 1979), 618. James Cone's essay, which appears in this volume as "Epilogue: An Interpretation of the Debate among Black Theologians," is the best available treatment of the discussion and dialogue among black theologians of this stage.

10. Ibid., 348.

11. Ibid., 355-356.

12. My first piece is found in Wilmore and Cone, *Black Theology* (1979), 552-567 and rev. ed. (1993), vol. 1, as Document 34. The second article appeared in *The Witness*, 63, no. 4 (April 1980), 16-19.

13. West, "Black Theology and Marxist Thought," Wilmore and Cone, *Black Theology*, (1979), 556 and in rev. ed. vol. 1 (1993) as Document 34.

14. Ibid., 560.

15. West, "Black Theology and Socialist Thought," *Witness* 18.

16. This important essay was jointly published by the Black Theology Project of Theology in the Americas and the Democratic Socialist Organizing Committee. This joint effort signifies neither James Cone's nor the Black Theology Project's support of DSOC's social democratic political stance.

17. The best recent treatment of these issues I know are Peter Evans's *Dependent Development* (Princeton, 1979) and the superb collection of essays in *Contemporary Marxism*, No. 1 Synthesis Publications, special issue on Strategies for the Class Struggle in Latin America.

18. Raymond Williams, *Keywords* (New York: Oxford University Press, 1976), 48-50. Raymond Williams, *Marxism and Literature* (New York: Oxford University Press, 1977), 13-16.

19. This is a central theme in the noteworthy writings of C. B. Macpherson. See his *The Political Theory of Possessive Individualism: Hobbes to Locke* (Oxford, 1962); *The Real World of Democracy* (New York: Oxford University Press, 1966); *Democratic Theory: Essays in Retrieval* (New York: Oxford University Press, 1973).

20. My understanding of the Industrial Revolution follows closely the scenario painted by E. J. Hobsbawm in his classic work, *The Age of Revolution 1789-1848* (New York: 1962), 44-73.

21. Ibid., 57.

22. Hegel makes a similar claim (or at least related claim) regarding the Christian principle of self-consciousness or subjectivity in his *The Philosophy of History*, trans. J. Sibree (New York, 1956), 19, 319 334. For a treatment of the Christian principle of individuality within the history of African-American thought and praxis, see my conception of the African-American humanist tradition in "Philosophy and the Afro-American Experience," *The Philosophical Forum*, 9, nos. 2-3, 117-148.

23. I will quote from three major works from Marx to illustrate this theme in his thought: In bourgeois society, therefore, the past dominates the present; in communist society, the present dominates the past. In bourgeois society capital is independent and has individuality, while the living person is dependent and has no individuality. . . . In place of the old bourgeois society, with its classes and class antagonisms, we shall have an association, in which the free development of each is the condition for the free development of all ("Manifesto of the Communist Party," *The Marx-Engels Reader*, ed. Robert C. Tucker, New York, 1972, 347, 353). . . . the communal relationship, into which the individuals of a class entered and which was determined by their common interests over against a third party, was always a community to which these individuals belonged only as average individuals, only insofar as they lived within the conditions of existence of their class — a relationship in which they participated not as individuals but as members of a class. On the other hand, it is just the reverse with the community of revolutionary proletarians who take their conditions of existence and those of all members of society under their control (*The German Ideology*, excerpts therefrom in *Writings of the Young Marx on Philosophy and Society*, ed. and trans. Lloyd D. Easton and Kurt H. Guddat [Garden City, N.Y.: 1967], 460).

The barrier to capital is that this entire development proceeds in a contradictory way, and that the working-out of the productive forces, of general wealth, etc., knowledge etc., appears in such a way that the working individual alienates himself (sich entaussert); relates to the conditions brought out of him by his labor as those not of his own but of an alien wealth and or his own poverty. But this antithetical form is itself fleeting, and produces the real conditions of its own suspension. The result is: the tendentially and potentially general development of the forces of production — or wealth as such — as basis; likewise, the universal development of the individuals from this basis . . . (Grundrisse: *Foundations of the Critique of Political Economy*, trans. Martin Nicolaus [New York, 1973], 541-542.)

ANNOTATED BIBLIOGRAPHY
OF BLACK THEOLOGY
1980–1992

Mark L. Chapman

The article and books listed below reflect the range of issues that Black theologians have addressed over the past decade. The list below is highly selective because an exhaustive bibliography would be prohibitive for our purposes. This period in the development of Black theology saw the emergence of many younger African-American scholars who raised critical issues for Black theology such as its relationship to Marxism and the problem of sexism in the African-American church and community. Black theologians continued to address the problem of White racism, but they also paid more attention to: their dialogue with Third-World theologies; the need for social analysis that critiqued imperialism, classism and sexism; and the need to relate Black theology to the practice of ministry in the Black Church.

Perhaps the most important development in this period is the emergence of womanist theology. A number of the articles and books selected are representative of the work of the most prolific womanist theologians who launched a critique of Black male theology and began to reflect theologically on the religious experience of African-American women. It is hoped that readers will find this annotated bibliography useful in their study of the most recent developments in Black theology.

Articles Published

Brown, Kelly D. "God Is as Christ Does: Toward a Womanist Theology." *Journal of Religious Thought* 46 (Summer-Fall 1989): 7–16.

This article seeks to define the womanist concept and point to its significance for the development of a womanist Christology. The author believes that womanist theology must challenge interpretations of Jesus that are oppressive to Black women by making it clear that there is no relationship whatsoever between the maleness

Mark L. Chapman is instructor of Afro-American Studies at Fordham University in New York City.

of Jesus and his being as the Christ—God incarnate. The author concludes that womanist Christology must emphasize the liberating activity of Jesus' ministry.

Cone, James H. "The Gospel and the Liberation of the Poor: How My Mind Has Changed." *The Christian Century* 98 (February 18, 1981): 162–166.

This article is an autobiographical discussion of the author's theological career. The author identifies the problem of Black suffering in a racist society and its relation to the Christian gospel as the central issue that shaped his theological consciousness. The author reflects on his upbringing in Arkansas; his graduate education; and the impact of Black Power on his theology. This article provides an excellent introduction to the author's life and work.

Cone, James H. "Black Theology and Third World Theologies." *Chicago Theological Seminary Register* 73 (Winter 1983): 3–12.

In this article the author analyzes the relation between Black theology in the United States and Third-World theologies. The author examines the similarities between them, namely their common rejection of the methodology and content of the dominant White theologies of Europe and North America; their emphasis on liberation as the core of the Christian gospel; and their rereading of the Bible in the light of the struggles of the oppressed. The author also discusses Black theology's dialogue with Latin American, African, and Asian theologies within the context of the Ecumenical Association of Third World Theologians (EATWOT).

Cone, James H. "Martin Luther King, Jr., Black Theology, and the Black Church." *Theology Today* 40 (January 1984): 409–420.

In this important article the author examines the impact of the Black Church on the life and theology of Martin Luther King, Jr. Contrary to those White scholars who emphasize King's graduate training in liberal and neoorthodox theologies, the author believes that the Black Church was the most decisive source that shaped his theology. The author discusses Martin King's theology in the context of describing the themes of freedom and hope in African-American religious thought. The author concludes by demonstrating the connections between King's theology and his own work in Black theology.

Cone, James H. "Black Theology in American Religion." *Journal of the American Academy of Religion* 53 (December 1985): 755–771.

This article examines the roots of Black theology in the context of African-American religious thought. The author discusses the themes of justice, love, suffering, liberation, and hope in Black religious thought from slavery to the civil rights movement and the theology of Martin Luther King, Jr. The author concludes with a discussion of the impact of Malcolm X and the Black Power movement on the emergence of Black theology.

Eugene, Toinette M. "While Love Is Unfashionable: Ethical Implications of Black Spirituality and Sexuality." In *Women's Consciousness, Women's Conscience*, edited by B. H. Andolsen, C. E. Gudorf, and M. D. Pellauer. New York: Winston-Seabury Press, 1985: 121–141.

In this article the author examines the relationship between Black spirituality and Black sexuality in the context of Black male-female relationships. The author believes that the current crisis in Black male-female relationships can be overcome when Blacks reject the body-spirit dualism of Hellenistic Christianity and embrace the holistic nature of their African spirituality. The author concludes that healthy Black love expressed through the integration of spirituality and sexuality can be a source for liberating social transformation in the African-American community as well as in the world.

Eugene, Toinette M. "Moral Values and Black Womanist." *Journal of Religious Thought* 44 (Winter-Spring 1988): 23–34.

In this article the author examines aspects of the moral consciousness and value system that have served to guide Black women's struggle for survival from slavery to the present. The author demonstrates that historically, Black women have been committed to their own survival in a racist-sexist society as well as the survival and liberation of the entire Black community. The author concludes that the womanist moral values of endurance, resistance, and resiliency in the face of oppression provide a renewed theological legacy of liberation for all.

Evans, James H., Jr. "Black Theology and Black Feminism." *Journal of Religious Thought* 38 (Spring-Summer 1981): 43–53.

In this article the author examines the challenge posed by Black feminism to Black theology. The author argues that Black male theologians can no longer ignore the problem of sexism in the church and community and be true to their stated theological norm: Jesus Christ, the Liberator of the Oppressed. The author discusses the methodology of Black theology in relation to its sources in order to show its sexist character, and then urges Black theologians to reject both overt and covert sexism.

Evans, James H., Jr. "Deconstructing the Tradition: Narrative Strategies in Nascent Black Theology." *Union Seminary Quarterly Review* 44 (1990): 101–119.

This article examines the emergence of Black theology as a deconstructive critique of the Western theological tradition. The author shows how Black theologians demystified the theological tradition by exposing its European-American class bias and social conditioning. The author also discusses two important literary tasks of the Black theologian: the recording of the unwritten raw material of Black theology, and writing as a political act of liberation that is grounded in the will to be free. The author concludes that as writers, early Black theologians served the dual purpose of edifying and preserving the religious resources of the Black community and boldly confronting the structures of oppression.

Grant, Jacquelyn. "The Tasks of a Prophetic Church." In *Theology in the Americas*, edited by Cornel West et al. Maryknoll, N.Y.: Orbis Books, 1982: 136–142.

In this article the author discusses the need for the church to take a prophetic stand against racism, sexism, classism, and imperialism. The author locates the biblical basis for this mission in Luke 4:18, and concludes that the prophetic church will reject the status quo, be self-critical, and confront all forms of oppression and injustice.

Grant, Jacquelyn. "Subjectification as a Requirement for Christological Construction." In *Lift Every Voice: Constructing Christian Theologies from the Underside*, edited by Susan B. Thistlethwaite and Mary Potter Engel (New York: Harper & Row, 1990): 201–213.

In this article the author argues that the christological question, "Who do you say that I am?" requires the respondent to be the central subject in the dialogue. The author traces the objectification of Blacks as slaves and Black women as domestic workers and sexual commodities, and discusses the African-American struggle to gain status as subjects in history who determine their own destiny. The author concludes with an examination of the christological reflections of Black women that emphasize Jesus' identification with the suffering of the oppressed.

Harris, James Henry. "Practicing Liberation in the Black Church." *The Christian Century* (June 13–20, 1990): 599–602.

In this article the author argues that the Black Church must be an indispensable source for the development of an authentic Black theology that is relevant to the masses of African-American Christians. The author believes that academic Black theology serves no practical purpose for the Black Church, and must therefore become a practical theology that addresses the systemic poverty and suffering in the Black community. The author concludes by offering concrete recommendations for churches as they seek to address the social, political, and economic needs of the African-American community.

Harvey, Louis-Charles. "Black Theology and the Expanding Concept of Oppression." *Journal of Religious Thought* 38 (Fall-Winter 1981–82): 5–15.

This article discusses the shift in Black theology from an exclusive focus on the particularity of racial oppression in the United States to a more global understanding of class and gender oppression at home and in the Third World. The author believes that while this dialogue with other oppressed groups is important, there is a danger if Black theology loses its specific focus on racial oppression. The author calls for the further development of a Black theology that takes the particularity of Black oppression in the United States as its point of departure.

Jones, William R. "Religious Humanism: Its Problems and Prospects in Black Religion and Culture." *Journal of the Interdenominational Theological Center* 7 (Spring 1980): 169–186.

In this article the author analyzes the place of religious humanism in the African-American experience. The author argues that there are two religious traditions in Black culture: a mainstream of Christian and non-Christian theism and a minority tradition of humanism. The author argues against the simple equation of Black religion and theism, and seeks to resurrect the disvalued tradition of religious humanism that has been an ever-present reality in the African-American experience. The author concludes by discussing the challenge of Black religious humanism to Black theology and the Black Church.

Long, Charles H. "Assessment and New Departures for a Study of Black Religion in the United States of America." In *African-American Religious Studies: An Interdisciplinary Anthology.* Edited by Gayraud S. Wilmore (Durham: Duke University Press, 1989): 34–49.

This address was delivered at the tenth anniversary of the Society for the Study of Black Religion in 1981. The author assesses the work of black theologians in the context of 20th century African-American religious scholarship and suggests new areas of research for future work. The author concludes that African-American religious scholars must develop an interpretive framework that provides an evaluation of religion and culture that is distinctive from the Euro-American norm.

Williams, Delores S. "Black Theology's Contribution to Theological Methodology." *Reflection* 80 (January 1983): 12–16.

In this article the author examines the methodology of Black theology in light of the methodological debate between liberal (Adolph Harnak) and neoorthodox (Karl Barth) theologians. The author discusses the role of the Black experience in the theological methodology of James Cone, J. Deotis Roberts, William Jones, and Cecil Cone. The author concludes that Black theology's greatest contribution to Christian theology is that it maintains the unity between the sacred and the secular by holding together in dialectical tension the transcendence and immanence of God.

Williams, Delores S. "Women's Oppression and Lifeline Politics in Black Women's Religious Narratives." *Journal of Feminist Studies in Religion* (Fall 1985): 59–71.

In this article the author examines the theme of Black women's oppression as represented in Zora Neale Hurston's *Jonah's Gourd Vine* and *Their Eyes Were Watching God*; Margaret Walker's *Jubilee*; and Alice Walker's *The Color Purple*. Using these literary works, the author describes the multidimensional assault on Black women, and the political strategies (lifeline politics) they use to combat that oppression. The author concludes that these strategies are informed by the religious beliefs and practices of Black women, and thus make a contribution to feminist theology in general.

Williams, Delores S. "The Color of Feminism: Or Speaking the Black Woman's Tongue." *Journal of Religious Thought* 43 (Spring-Summer 1986): 42–58.

In this article the author explores the relationship between Black and White women in the feminist movement. After describing the legacy of racism from the nineteenth-century women's movement to the present, the author argues that the experience of racism at the hands of White women means that a broader framework for interpreting Black women's oppression is required. The author terms the racist-gender oppression of Black women "demonarchy." The author concludes that the mission of the Black Church is informed by the demonarchal critique of racist-gender, political, and economic oppression.

Williams, Delores S. "Black Women's Surrogacy Experience and the Christian Notion of Redemption." In *After Patriarchy: Feminist Reconstructions of the World Religions*, edited by Paula Cooey, William R. Eakin, and Jay B. McDaniel (Maryknoll, N.Y.: Orbis Books, 1991): 1–14.

This article examines Black women's historic experience with surrogacy roles before and after the Civil War. The author argues that the experience of surrogacy reveals the unique character of Black women's oppression, and raises challenging questions about the traditional concept of redemption where Jesus is imaged as the divine surrogate sent to die for the sins of humanity. The author concludes that the redemption of humanity is not accomplished by the death of Jesus on the cross, but rather by the ministerial vision of righting relationships that he implemented in his life.

Wilmore, Gayraud S. "Black Theology and Pastoral Ministry." In *The Pastor As Theologian,* edited by Earl E. Shelp and Ronald H. Sunderland. Pilgrim Press: New York, 1988: 30-67.

This article makes the case that Black theology was born when Black clergy seriously addressed essentially pastoral questions rising from the Black revolution of the 1960s, and in that respect has world-wide ecumenical implications. The author discusses the debate between disillusioned young Black activists and the church during the Black Power movement and argues for a "pragmatic spirituality" that has deeply personal as well as political significance.

Wilmore, Gayraud S. "Historical Mandate for African American Theological Education." *The A.M.E. Church Review* 105 (April-June 1990): 60-71.

In this article, first presented as a lecture at Payne Theological Seminary, Wilmore emphasizes the pedagogical implications of Black theology for American theological education, particularly in predominantly Black seminaries. The history of theological education among African-American students during the decades of the 1970s and '80s is reviewed. The conclusion is drawn that norms and goals more consistent with theological developments in the Black Church and academy need to be utilized. Seven specific propositions are suggested pursuant to that end.

Books Published

Baldwin, Lewis V. *To Make The Wounded Whole: The Cultural Legacy of Martin Luther King, Jr.* Minneapolis, Minn.: Fortress Press, 1992.

The significance of this book for the study of Black theology lies in the author's thorough examination of King's legacy for contemporary Black theology and ethics. The second chapter of the book provides a discussion of how major Black theologians and ethicists (e.g., James Cone, Albert Cleage, J. Deotis Roberts, Preston Williams, Peter Paris, and Katie Cannon) have treated King in their works. This book is a companion volume to the author's first book on King, *There Is A Balm in Gilead: The Cultural Roots of Martin Luther King, Jr.* (Fortress, 1991).

Boesak, Allan A. *Black and Reformed: Apartheid, Liberation, and the Calvinist Tradition.* Edited by Leonard Sweetman. Maryknoll, N.Y.: Orbis Books, 1984.

In this collection of sermons and addresses the author discusses the tasks of Black South Africans in the Reformed church in relation to the Black liberation struggle. The author argues that the Reformation movement associated with John Calvin is a tradition that is useful in the critique of the White Afrikaner Reformed churches in South Africa. This book provides important background on the liberation struggle in South Africa and its impact on the development of Black theology in that country.

Cannon, Katie G. *Black Womanist Ethics.* Atlanta: Scholars Press, 1988.

This book (originally the author's Ph.D. dissertation at Union Theological Seminary in New York) is an analysis of the ethical and moral wisdom of African-American women. The author first examines the moral situation of Black women from 1619 to the present, and then discusses the Black woman's literary tradition as a source for womanist ethics. The author argues that whereas Black male writers focus on the confrontation between Whites and Blacks, Black women writers focus more concretely on the daily issues of life within the Black community. After a thorough analysis of the life and work of Zora Neale Hurston, the author examines the theological ethics of Howard Thurman and Martin Luther King, Jr. This readable book makes an invaluable contribution to the development of womanist theology in particular and African-American religious thought in general.

Cone, James H. *My Soul Looks Back*. Nashville: Abingdon Press, 1982; Maryknoll, N.Y.: Orbis Books, 1986.

This book provides an autobiographical account of the author's theological career. The author discusses his formative years in Arkansas; his graduate education; the impact of Black power on his theological consciousness; and his involvement as a theologian of the AME Church. The author also discusses the impact of feminism, Marxism, and Third-World theologies on his thought. This book serves as an excellent introduction to the study of Black theology.

Cone, James H. *For My People: Black Theology and the Black Church*. Maryknoll, N.Y.: Orbis Books, 1984.

This book provides a thorough analysis of the origins and development of the Black theology movement in the United States and its relationship to the African-American church. The author examines the strengths and weaknesses of Black theology, and emphasizes the need for theologians and church leaders to enter into constructive dialogue on important issues such as: the role of women in the church and society; the theological views of the oppressed in the Third World, as well as other minorities within the United States; and the need to incorporate the Marxist analysis into the social vision of the Black Church. This book is the most thorough analysis of Black theology by one of its leading exponents.

Cone, James H. *Martin & Malcolm & America: A Dream or a Nightmare*. Maryknoll, N.Y.: Orbis Books, 1991.

This book examines the theological and political views of Martin Luther King, Jr., and Malcolm X. The author discusses the social and religious contexts that shaped each leader's views on America, and discusses their ideas in relation to the political ideologies of integration and nationalism. The author's central claim is that toward the end of their lives Martin and Malcolm began to incorporate some of each other's views on the problem of racism in America into their thinking, and were not as far apart as the media generally portrayed them. This book makes an important contribution to the study of these prophetic leaders and serves as a valuable introduction to the social, political, and religious contexts that gave rise to Black theology.

Evans, James H., Jr. *Black Theology: A Critical Assessment and Annotated Bibliography*. Conn.: Greenwood Press, 1987.

This book provides annotations for over 450 articles and books on Black theology through 1986. The compiler groups the data into three separate categories: Origin and Development of Black Theology; Liberation, Feminism, and Marxism; and Cultural and Global Discourse. This book is an invaluable resource for the study of Black theology.

Felder, Cain H. *Troubling Biblical Waters: Race, Class, and Family*. Maryknoll, N.Y.: Orbis Books, 1989.

This important first book by the author is the culmination of years of study, teaching, and writing on the Bible in relation to the African-American community. The author examines the African presence in the Bible, and discusses the themes of race, class, and family from a Black theological perspective. The author not only critiques Eurocentric biblical scholarship; he also issues a prophetic challenge to the Black Church on issues ranging from social justice to the ordination of women. This long-awaited book makes an important contribution to Black theology, African-American biblical scholarship, and the Black Church. It will no doubt remain a classic for many years to come.

Felder, Cain H., ed. *Stony the Road We Trod: African American Biblical Interpretation.* Minneapolis, Minn.: Fortress Press, 1991.

In this important collaborative work, eleven African-American biblical scholars offer essays that are grouped under four major headings: the relevance of biblical scholarship and the authority of the Bible; African-American sources for enhancing biblical interpretation; race and ancient Black Africa in the Bible; and reinterpreting biblical texts. The significance of this volume lies in its examination of the important role the Bible has played in shaping the religious experience of African Americans, and the exegetical treatment of issues relating to race, class, and gender in the biblical texts. This work is an excellent example of the Black theological enterprise from the perspective of biblical scholars, and will remain a classic for many years to come.

Grant, Jacquelyn. *White Women's Christ and Black Women's Jesus: Feminist Christology and Womanist Response.* Atlanta: Scholars Press, 1989.

In this work (originally the author's Ph.D. dissertation at Union Theological Seminary in New York) the author provides a thorough analysis of the variety of christological perspectives articulated by White feminist theologians. The author's major claim is that White feminist Christologies do not reflect the understanding of Jesus in the religious experience of Black women. The author discusses Black women's understanding of Jesus from slavery to the present, and lays the foundation for a womanist Christology that takes seriously the tridimensional reality of Black women's oppression (race, class, gender). This book makes an important contribution to Black theology in general and the emerging discipline of womanist theology in particular.

Harris, James H. *Pastoral Theology: A Black Church Perspective.* Minneapolis, Minn.: Fortress Press, 1991.

In this book the author helps to bridge the gap between Black liberation theology as an academic discipline and pastoral theology. The author argues that the Black Church must move beyond a mere imitation of White evangelicalism that supports the status quo, and reaffirm its historic commitment to liberation and social transformation. The author also discusses the role of the Black Church in the urban community, and emphasizes the need for Black theology and a practical theology to "be two sides of the same coin." In the second part of the book the author applies the principles of Black liberation theology to the practice of ministry in the Black Church. This work by a pastor and scholar makes an important contribution to ongoing efforts to construct a Black theology that is more relevant to the needs of pastors in local congregations.

Hopkins, Dwight N., and George Cummings, eds. *Cut Loose Your Stammering*

Tongue: Black Theology in the Slave Narratives. Maryknoll, N.Y.: Orbis Books, 1991.

This work is a collection of essays by an emerging group of younger African-American scholars who are seeking to ground contemporary Black theology in the rich cultural sources present in the historic Black community. This book examines the slave narratives as a source for Black liberation theology. Dwight Hopkins discusses slave theology and highlights the slaves' understanding of God, Jesus, and humanity. George Cummings examines the slaves' understanding of the Holy Spirit and eschatology, while Will Coleman discusses both the slaves' non-Christian and Christian experience of the Spirit and other spirits (ghosts, haunts, etc.). Sherrell Sanders examines the impact of the conversion experience on the diversity of ethical responses ex-slaves made to the problem of slavery. This book signals an important direction for future work in Black theology by emphasizing a collaborative approach to theological work that takes seriously the reflections of the Black poor as interpreters of the faith.

Hopkins, Dwight N. *Black Theology U.S.A. and South Africa: Politics, Culture, and Liberation*. Maryknoll, N.Y.: Orbis Books, 1989.

In this his first book (originally a Ph.D. dissertation at Union Theological Seminary in N.Y.) the author examines the similarities between Black theology in the United States and South Africa. Hopkins argues that both theologies view political and cultural liberation as the central message of the gospel for Black victims of White supremacy in North America and in South Africa. After describing the historical context that shaped the emergence of Black theology in the United States and South Africa, the author examines the political and cultural trends as they are found in leading theologians from each country. The first book to analyze both theologies in relation to each other, this work makes an invaluable contribution to African-American religious thought in particular and Third-World liberation theology in general.

Jones, Major J. *The Color of God: The Concept of God in Afro-American Thought*. Macon, Ga.: Mercer University Press, 1987.

Written as the author's response to the call for more publications on Black theology in the 1980s, this work traces the historical development of the concept of God in African-American religious thought from African traditional beliefs, through slavery, to contemporary Black theology. The author demonstrates the uniqueness of the African-American concept of God, and shows how it emerged from the Black struggle against slavery and oppression. At the same time, the author argues that Black theology is an expression of orthodox Christian theology, and discusses the African-American concept of God in trinitarian outline – God, Christ, and Holy Spirit. This work serves as a valuable commentary on the main issues of Black theology as it emerged in the 1960s and 1970s, especially the question of theodicy raised by William R. Jones.

Long, Charles H. *Significations: Signs, Symbols, and Images in the Interpretation of Religion*. Philadelphia: Fortress Press, 1986.

This book is a collection of essays written by the author over a period of twenty years. All of the essays are hermeneutical attempts to interpret the phenomenon of religion on a general level and of the problematic meaning of religion in the United States in particular. The author uses the term "signification" to point to the oppressive language and stereotypes that Western culture has used in reference to people of African descent, and seeks to interpret Black people's religious response to that oppression. This book provides an important introduction to the issues that have been at the center of the author's career as an historian of religions.

Mitchell, Henry H. and Nicholas C. Cooper-Lewter, *Soul Theology: The Heart of American Black Culture*. San Francisco: Harper & Row, 1986.

This book examines the core religious beliefs in African-American culture. The authors assert that core beliefs about the providence of God, justice, the goodness of creation, and the equality and uniqueness of persons constitute a folk or "soul" theology that has therapeutic value for Blacks as well as other ethnic groups. The authors utilize a case-study approach that shares the insights from the private practice of psychotherapist Cooper-Lewter (also a Baptist minister), and seek to illuminate the nourishing spirituality of African-American folk beliefs. The authors understand their work as an expression of Black folk theology as distinguished from the more political focus of Black liberation theology.

Mosala, Itumeleng J. and Buti Tlhagale, eds. *The Unquestionable Right to be Free: Black Theology from South Africa*. Maryknoll, N.Y.: Orbis Books, 1986.

This text is the second book of essays on Black theology published in South Africa (the first book of essays was banned by the government in 1972). This book represents the attempt of South African Black theologians to move beyond the polemical stage of Black theology to a constructive phase of theological reflection that utilizes the insights of Marxist analysis. These essays were originally papers presented at conferences sponsored by the Institute for Contextual Theology in 1983 and 1984.

Mosala, Itumeleng J. *Biblical Hermeneutics and Black Theology in South Africa*. Grand Rapids, Mich.: William B. Eerdmans Pub. Co., 1989.

In this book the author seeks to develop a biblical hermeneutics of liberation that can be used as an effective weapon in the Black freedom struggle in South Africa. The author critiques the class bias inherent in the traditional biblical hermeneutics of Allan Boesak and Desmond Tutu. The author then utilizes a historical-materialist method of analysis to develop a biblical hermeneutics of liberation that takes the historical and cultural struggles of the oppressed working class as its point of departure. The author concludes with a discussion of the implications of a materialist reading of Micah and Luke 1–2 for South African Black theology.

Roberts, J. Deotis. *Black Theology Today*. New York: Edwin Mellen Press, 1983.

This volume is a collection of the author's writings on the subject of Black theology from its beginnings in the Black Power movement through its dialogue with Third-World theology, to its relationship to the Black Church and Black family. These essays are important for understanding the development of Black theology, and shed valuable light on the similarities and differences among Black theologians.

Roberts, J. Deotis. *Black Theology in Dialogue*. Philadelphia: Westminster Press, 1987.

This work discusses Black theology in dialogue with other liberation theologies, including African theology, Korean Minjung theology, Latin American theology, and Jewish theology. The author argues that the methodological approach of contemporary liberation theology must be interdisciplinary, ecumenical, contextual, and political. After discussing the traditional theological themes of Christology, ecclesiology, and the Holy Spirit from a liberationist perspective, the author discusses theological ethics by treating the issues of love, justice, and power. The author concludes the work by making concrete suggestions about the future agenda of Black theology, emphasizing the need for Black theology to be grounded in the ministry of the church as it seeks to address the social, political, and economic realities facing the African-American community.

Rooks, Charles Shelby. *Revolution in Zion: Reshaping African-American Ministry, 1960–1974.* New York: Pilgrim Press, 1990.

This book provides an account of the author's efforts to recruit Black students for the ministry as pastors and theologians while executive director of the Fund for Theological Education. The author discusses the obstacles that had to be overcome in recruiting Black students for the ministry, and gives a detailed account of efforts to include the African-American religious experience in the curriculum at theological seminaries across the nation. The author examines the emergence of an African-American theological community in the late 1960s and the role of the Society for the Study of Black Religion (SSBR) in the early 1970s. This book by one of the leading figures in theological education in the United States provides important information on the context and issues that shaped the emergence and development of Black theology.

Shannon, David T. and Gayraud S. Wilmore. *Black Witness to the Apostolic Faith.* Grand Rapids, Mich.: William B. Eerdmans Pub. Co., 1988.

The articles and documents in this volume (sponsored by the Commission on Faith and Order of the National Council of Churches, U.S.A.) represent the response of African-American religious leaders to the World Council of Churches' call for Christians around the globe to reflect on the meaning of the Apostolic Faith as a means of fostering church unity. Most of the essays included in the volume were originally papers presented at the Black Churches Consultation held at Virginia Union University on December 14–15, 1984. Included are essays by Gayraud Wilmore, Jacquelyn Grant, Thomas Hoyt, Jr., Leonard Lovett, and J. Deotis Roberts. Among the documents is the 1984 Pastoral on Evangelization by the Black Bishops in the Roman Catholic Church.

Spencer, Jon Michael. *Protest and Praise: Sacred Music of Black Religion.* Minneapolis, Minn.: Fortress Press, 1990.

In this book, the author examines the vital role music has played in the African-American struggle for survival and liberation. In Part I of the book (Protest Song) the author examines the spirituals as the archetype of protest songs that later influenced White antislavery, White social gospel, and Black civil rights hymnody. Students of Black theology will especially want to note the author's treatment of the nonviolent emphasis of civil rights songs, and the repudiation of this theme by Black Power militants. The author concludes Part I with a discussion of the blues as an expression of Black theology. In Part II (Praise Song) the author discusses the impact of African religiosity on Black music, the development of music in the Black Holiness-Pentecostal tradition, and the theme of anticulturalism in the theology of gospel music. The author concludes the work with a discussion of the role of musicality in Black preaching.

Stewart, Carlyle Fielding, III. *God, Being, and Liberation: A Comparative Analysis of the Theologies and Ethics of James H. Cone and Howard Thurman*. New York: University Press of America, 1989.

This work (originally the author's Ph.D. dissertation at Northwestern University) is the first book-length analysis comparing the thought of James Cone and Howard Thurman, and thus it makes an important contribution to African-American religious thought. The author's main thesis is that both Thurman and Cone view ontology as the basis for Black liberation. However, by thorough analysis of the writings of each thinker, the author demonstrates that while Cone's theological ontology is focused on communal liberation from external elements, namely, racism, poverty, and institutional oppression, Howard Thurman's theological ontology is focused on internal elements of the individual self that cause one to acquiesce to oppression. The author argues that Black theology must consider the views of both Thurman and Cone and hold political and spiritual liberation in dialectical tension.

Walker, Theodore, Jr. *Empower the People: Social Ethics for the African-American Church*. Maryknoll, N.Y.: Orbis Books, 1991.

This book is a socioethical analysis of the urgent social problems facing the African-American community. The author advocates a "church elite perspective of Black theology" that addresses social issues such as: the high rate of Black male incarceration, teenage pregnancy, the demise of the Black family, drugs, crime, poverty, and homelessness. The author appropriates the philosophy of Black Power and discusses it in relationship to liberal coalition efforts to create public policies that will improve the quality of life for the Black oppressed.

West, Cornel. *Prophesy Deliverance! An Afro-American Revolutionary Christianity*. Philadelphia: Westminster Press, 1982.

In this book, the author proposes an alliance between prophetic African-American Christian thought and progressive Marxism. The author examines the similarities between Black theology and Marxist thought. The author's major claim is that Black theology and Marxist thought have something to offer each other: Marxist thought can provide Black theology with a theoretical framework for understanding how capitalism is a root cause of Black oppression, and Marxist thinkers can learn from Black theologians more about the liberating aspects of popular culture and religion in the struggle for social change. This book is the most important analysis of the relationship between Black theology and Marxist thought published to date.

Wilmore, Gayraud S. *Black and Presbyterian: The Heritage and the Hope*. Philadelphia: Geneva Press, 1983.

Commissioned by the Black Caucus of the United Presbyterian Church in the U.S.A., this book is a discussion of the identity of African Americans in the Presbyterian Church. The author discusses the uniqueness of Black Christianity, and outlines the history of Black involvement in the Presbyterian Church. The author concludes that African Americans in the Presbyterian Church can overcome their identity crisis (being a Black middle-class church, neither totally accepted by their own White denomination nor appreciative of their own religio-cultural heritage) by developing a new style of Black Presbyterianism that emphasizes Christian discipleship, social responsibility, and cultural awareness.

Wilmore, Gayraud S. *Last Things First*. Philadelphia: Westminster Press, 1982.

The first part of this book contains an analysis of the history of eschatology, the doctrine of "last things," to set the stage for the author's contention that African Americans are "another eschatological people." In the second part he examines Christian eschatology from the perspective of Black theology, comparing it critically with John S. Mbiti's description of eschatological thinking among the Akamba and other African peoples, and demonstrating similar orientations in the Black Church, from the Spirituals of the slave community to the "I Have A Dream" speech of Martin Luther King, Jr. The book is appended with questions for study and discussion for use by lay study groups in both Black and interracial congregations.

Witvliet, Theo. *The Way of the Black Messiah.* Oak Park, Ill.: Meyer-Stone Books, 1987.

Written by a Dutch theologian, this book is a critical interpretation of the contemporary Black theology movement. The author examines the hermeneutical challenge posed by liberation theology in general, and then analyzes the historical context that gave rise to Black liberation theology in particular. After thorough historical analysis, the author discusses the major issues debated among Black theologians, and concludes the work with a discussion of Black theology's dialogue with Third-World liberation theology and White European-American theology. This book is perhaps the most thorough critical analysis of Black theology published to date.

Young, Henry J. *Hope in Process: A Theology of Social Pluralism.* Minneapolis: Fortress Press, 1990.

In this book the author addresses issues related to doing theology in a multicultural context. The author applauds the rising ethnic consciousness of oppressed peoples in the United States, and suggests a theological paradigm that preserves the distinctiveness of minority groups while at the same time affirming their unity in the Christian faith. The author encourages those of the prominent social group to become acquainted with the history and theology of ethnic minorities, and advocates the full inclusion of diverse cultural expressions in the doing of theology. The author believes that authentic cultural pluralism must take seriously the contributions of all ethnic groups, and advocates the principle of "unity in diversity rather than unity in conformity."

Young, Josiah Ulysses, III. *Black and African Theologies: Siblings or Distant Cousins?* Maryknoll, N.Y.: Orbis Books, 1986.

A revision of the author's doctoral dissertation at Union Theological Seminary in New York, this work analyzes the similarities and differences between North American Black theology and African theology. After discussing the historical background that shaped the development of Black and African theologies, the author examines Black theologies of liberation and African theologies of indigenization. The author concludes that although there are sharp differences in both theologies due to different historical, social, and political contexts, there is sufficient common ground for the development of a Pan-African theology that would incorporate the insights from each perspective, and help to unite African peoples around the world. This book makes an important contribution to the development of Third-World liberation theology in general and to African-American religious thought in particular.

Young, Josiah Ulysses, III. *A Pan-African Theology: Providence and the Legacies of the Ancestors*. Trenton, N.J.: Africa World Press, 1992.

This book examines the theme of Pan-Africanism in African and African-American religious thought. The author outlines the elements of a Pan-African theology and discusses the theme in the thought of nineteenth-century figures Alexander Crummell and Edward Blyden. The author utilizes social and religio-cultural analyses to formulate a Pan-African theological perspective for the liberation of the Black poor of Africa and the diaspora.

INDEX

ALSO OF INTEREST

Delores S. Williams
SISTERS IN THE WILDERNESS
The Challenge of Womanist God-Talk
Combining social history, political theology, and literary criticism, Delores Williams'
exploration of the story of Hagar demonstrates the interplay of oppressions experienced by African-American women on account of their race, sex, and class.
225pp. index. ISBN 0-88344-772-X clothbound

Dwight N. Hopkins
SHOES THAT FIT OUR FEET
Sources for a Constructive Black Theology
Original and far-reaching, this book shows the resources for Black theology within
the rich and living tradition of African-American religion and culture.
230pp. index. ISBN 0-88344-848-3 paperback

New in the Bishop Henry McNeal Turner/Sojournor Truth Studies

Emilie M. Townes, editor
A TROUBLING IN MY SOUL
Womanist Reflections on Evil and Suffering
Brings together contributions by more than a dozen of the best-known womanist
theologians who address a central theological theme: the problem of evil and suf-
fering. Contributors include Delores Williams, M. Shawn Copeland, Katie Cannon,
Kelly Brown-Douglas.
300pp. index. ISBN 0-88344-783-5 paperback

George Cummings
A COMMON JOURNEY
Black Theology and Latin American Liberation Theology
Explores the distinctions and commonalities between these two strands of theology,
demonstrating how together they pose the terms for a wholistic theology of liberation.
225pp. index. ISBN 0-88344-825-4 clothbound

James H. Cone
MARTIN & MALCOLM & AMERICA
A Dream or a Nightmare?
Examines the lives and thought of the two most influential African-American leaders of this century.

"A major contribution to the discussion of race and ethnicity in modern America."
— *The New York Review of Books*
368pp. notes, biblio., index. ISBN 0-88344-824-6 paperback

Vincent Harding
HOPE & HISTORY
Why We Must Share the Story of the Movement
Senior advisor to *Eyes on the Prize* emphasizes the importance for those who educate — in whatever setting — of remembering and keeping alive the history of the African-American-led civil rights movement.

"A head-clearing blast from Gabriel's trumpet."
— *New York Times Book Review*
200pp. notes, biblio. ISBN 0-88344-664-2 paperback

Gayraud S. Wilmore
BLACK RELIGION & BLACK RADICALISM
An Interpretation of the Religious History
of the African-American People
Explores the religious history of the Black church in America, from its African roots to the 20th century.

"Critical for understanding the moods, nuances, and movements within the religious community of black America."
— C. Eric Lincoln
320pp. notes, index. ISBN 0-88344-032-6 paperback

Dwight N. Hopkins and George Cummings
CUT LOOSE YOUR STAMMERING TONGUE
Black Theology in the Slave Narratives
In the narratives of ex-slaves, the authors find resources for Black theology's approach to God, Jesus, human destiny, the spirit, and women's religious experience.
150pp. ISBN 0-88344-774-6 paperback

Also in the Turner/Truth Studies

Theodore Walker
EMPOWER THE PEOPLE
Social Ethics for the African-American Church
This penetrating work of analysis calls for adding the philosophy of black power to
the strengths of the black church to fashion a social ethics of survival and resistance
for the 90s and beyond.

"Calls for a common struggle for comprehensive social empowerment."
—Philip E. Devenish, University of Chicago
225pp. notes, biblio. ISBN 0-88344-771-1 paperback

Cain Hope Felder
TROUBLING BIBLICAL WATERS
Race, Class, and Family
Challenging exploration of the significance of the Bible for blacks, as well as the
importance of blacks *in* the Bible.

"Lucidly written."
—*Black Issues in Higher Education*

200pp. notes. ISBN 0-88344-535-2 paperback